MAJOR FACTORS AFFECTING EMPLOYEES' JOB PERFORMANCE AND PRODUCTIVITY

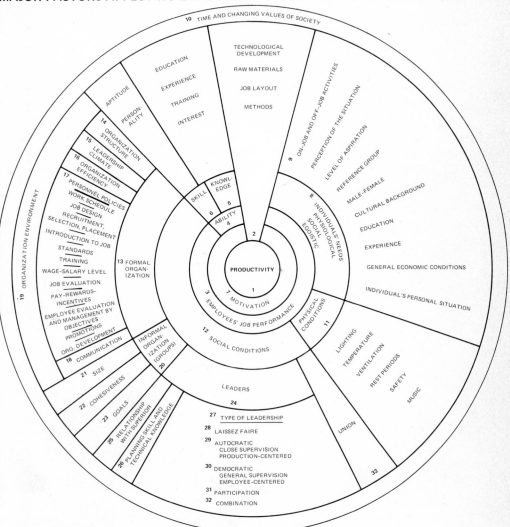

1. The size of each segment has no relationship to its relative importance, which would vary with different organizations, different departments, and even different individuals with their own distinct needs.

2. The factors in each segment affect factors in the corresponding segment of the next smaller circle; they may also affect and be affected by other segments in the same circle or other circles.

3. The numbers in the various sections of the diagram correspond to figures in parentheses throughout Chapters 1 to 18.

PEOPLE
AND
PRODUCTIVITY

McGRAW-HILL SERIES IN MANAGEMENT
Keith Davis, Consulting Editor

Allen   Management and Organization
Allen   The Management Profession
Argyris   Management and Organizational Development: The Path from XA to YB
Beckett   Management Dynamics: The New Synthesis
Benton   Supervision and Management
Bergen and Haney   Organizational Relations and Management Action
Blough   International Business: Environment and Adaptation
Bowman   Management: Organization and Planning
Brown   Judgment in Administration
Campbell, Dunnette, Lawler, and Weick   Managerial Behavior, Performance, and Effectiveness
Cleland and King   Management: A Systems Approach
Cleland and King   Systems Analysis and Project Management
Cleland and King   Systems, Organizations, Analysis, Management: A Book of Readings
Dale   Management: Theory and Practice
Dale   Readings in Management: Landmarks and New Frontiers
Davis   Human Behavior at Work: Human Relations and Organizational Behavior
Davis   Organizational Behavior: A Book of Readings
Davis and Blomstrom   Business and Society: Environment and Responsibility
DeGreene   Systems Psychology
Dunn and Rachel   Wage and Salary Administration: Total Compensation Systems
Dunn and Stephens   Management of Personnel: Manpower Management and Organizational Behavior
Edmunds and Letey   Environmental Administration
Fiedler   A Theory of Leadership Effectiveness
Finch, Jones, and Litterer   Managing for Organizational Effectiveness: An Experiential Approach
Flippo   Principles of Personnel Management
Glueck   Business Policy: Strategy Formation and Management Action
Golembiewski   Men, Management, and Morality
Hicks and Gullett   The Management of Organizations
Hicks and Gullett   Modern Business Management: A Systems and Environmental Approach
Hicks and Gullett   Organizations: Theory and Behavior

PEOPLE
AND
PRODUCTIVITY

ROBERT A. SUTERMEISTER
Graduate School of Business Administration
University of Washington

THIRD EDITION

McGRAW-HILL BOOK COMPANY
New York   St. Louis   San Francisco   Auckland   Düsseldorf   Johannesburg
Kuala Lumpur   London   Mexico   Montreal   New Delhi   Panama
Paris   São Paulo   Singapore   Sydney   Tokyo   Toronto

Library of Congress Cataloging in Publication Data

Sutermeister, Robert A   ed.
   People and productivity.

   (McGraw-Hill series in management)
   1.   Labor productivity—Addresses, essays, lectures.   2.   Psychology, Industrial—Addresses, essays, lectures.   3.   Industrial sociology—Addresses,
essays, lectures.   I.   Title.
HD57.S9   1976   658.31′4   75-17769
ISBN 0-07-062367-8
ISBN 0-07-062371-6 pbk.

PEOPLE AND PRODUCTIVITY

123456789 DODO 798765

This book was set in Times Roman by University Graphics, Inc.
The editors were William J. Kane and Joseph F. Murphy;
the cover was designed by Rafael Hernandez;
the production supervisor was Leroy A. Young.
New drawings were done by Vantage Art, Inc.
R. R. Donnelley & Sons Company was printer and binder.

Contents

Preface

This book is written for the layperson, the business man and woman, and the student.

Its unique contribution in the first and second editions was the conceptual scheme or diagram entitled "Major Factors Affecting Employees' Job Performance and Productivity." The diagram has been revised for this edition and appears on the first page of the book.

Another unique contribution, appearing for the first time in this edition, is a conceptual scheme or diagram entitled "Life Satisfaction Model" (page 39). This diagram is part of a section entitled "The Goals of People in Organizations: Job Satisfaction," which consists of six chapters, four of them entirely new.

Much new material appears in Section III, and Section V is entirely new. Numerous new readings have been added, but the total number of readings has been reduced. Readings have been selected which (1) discuss a factor or factors with important bearing on organizational productivity or employee job satisfaction, (2) are readily understandable, and (3) represent, in many instances, results of empirical research.

The following numbers on the productivity diagram are dealt with in the chapters indicated:

Diagram Number	Chapter
1	1
2	2
3–7	3
8	4
9	5
10	6
11	11
12–19	12
20–23	13
24–32	14
33	15

Readers may choose to read all chapters first to get an integrated explanation of the diagram, or they may choose to read one chapter at a time, followed by any readings related to that chapter.

My appreciation goes to the readers of the first two editions who have shared their ideas and suggestions with me. William F. Bernthal and Robert A. Zawacki deserve special mention.

I also appreciate the support of Borje Saxberg, my departmental chairman, and the typing provided by Sandra Goodman and Louise Uptmor.

Robert A. Sutermeister

PEOPLE
AND
PRODUCTIVITY

A Primary Goal of Organizations: Productivity

Chapter 1

Productivity

In this book increased productivity is considered a primary goal of business. Without a satisfactory level of productivity, a profit-oriented organization cannot survive; and most if not all nonprofit organizations are interested in doing more work (greater output) without a proportionate increase in money, equipment, and employee-hours (inputs).

Of course, most organizations have more than one goal. Changing values of society, discussed in Chapter 6, have forced most organizations to pay more attention to ecology, pollution control, consumerism, and civil rights of women and minority groups. Changing aspirations and expectations of employees have caused most organizations to pay more attention to their human assets. Some writers maintain that we must judge the efficiency of firms in terms of human costs of happiness and health. For example, Likert emphasizes the importance, in measuring organization performance, of including measurements of human assets.

Decentralization and delegation are powerful concepts based on sound theory. But there is evidence that, as now utilized, they have a serious vulnerability which can be costly. This vulnerability arises from the measurements being used to evaluate and reward the performance of those given authority over decentralized operations.

This situation is becoming worse. While companies have during the past decade made greater use of work measurements and measurements of end results in evaluating managers, and also greater use of incentive pay in rewarding them, only a few managements have regularly used measurements that deal directly with the human assets of the organization—for example, measurements of loyalty, motivation, confidence, and trust. As a consequence, many companies today are encouraging managers of departments and divisions to dissipate valuable human assets of the organization. In fact, they are rewarding these managers well for doing so![1]

Basil Georgopoulos and Robert Tannenbaum feel that "organizational effectiveness" is based on the "extent to which an organization, as a social system, fulfills its objectives without incapacitating its means and resources and without placing undue strain on its members." As criteria of effectiveness, they use not only organizational productivity but also organizational flexibility and absence of intraorganizational strain or tension.

Some write of higher profits, earnings per share, or return on investment as goals of business. These are normal financial goals of business, and productivity has a major impact on them. Other factors, however—prices or market conditions—also affect profit. A firm in a monopoly or unusually favorable market position could increase profits without increasing productivity or even while productivity is decreasing, but this would be unusual. Most firms are vitally interested in increasing productivity to increase profits or reduce losses.

With the economic competition from the European Common Market, from Japan, and from other countries, many firms in the United States are forced to place greater emphasis on productivity. And when inflation reaches a double-digit rate, firms have even more pressure for increased productivity.

Five years of inflation, recession, and uncertain recovery have forced the men who manage U.S. business and the men who make U.S. economic policy to a painful conclusion: Somehow the nation must make a quantum jump in efficiency. It must get more output from its men and machines. It must offset rising wage costs with higher production per worker. It must expand its income not just by increasing the inputs of labor and capital but also by increasing the effectiveness of these inputs.[2]

Service-Producing Organizations

In recent years there has been a dramatic increase in employment in service-producing organizations. "Shortly after the turn of this century, only 3 in every 10 workers were in service industries. By 1950, the weight had shifted to just over 5 in every 10 in service industries; by 1968 the proportion had inched to 6 in every 10. In 1980, close to 7 in every 10 workers—or 68 million—are projected to be in service industries."[3]

---

[1]"Measuring Organizational Performance," *Harvard Business Review,* vol. 36, no. 2, March–April 1958, pp. 41–50. Quoted by permission of *Harvard Business Review.*

[2]"Productivity: Our Biggest Undeveloped Resource," *Business Week,* Sept. 9, 1972, p. 80.

[3]"The U.S. Economy in 1980," *Monthly Labor Review,* vol. 93, no. 4, April 1970, p. 15.

It is appropriate, therefore, that increased attention is being given to productivity in service industries. The McDonald hamburger chain is an example of firms which are using manufacturing approaches to solve people-intensive service problems.[4] The Office of Management and Budget is attempting to measure the productivity of 70 percent of federal civilian employees.[5] Methods of increasing productivity are being devised for other service areas such as education and medicine.[6] Articles on productivity appear frequently in business and academic journals.[7]

Some Skepticism regarding Productivity Emphasis

Workers and union officials frequently are skeptical of emphasis on increased productivity. They fear that to increase productivity will mean that some workers will lose their jobs and/or will have to work harder. This can be true but is not necessarily so. Even executives appear to have some reticence about stressing increased productivity. A Harris poll showed that nearly one-half of executives agree with a majority of union members that productivity gains benefit companies at the expense of their companies workers.[8]

Clearly much remains to be done to convince American workers and business executives that increased productivity can not only help both organization and employees but is a vital necessity in the fight to control inflation and meet foreign competition.

Simplified Explanation of Productivity

Note that the diagram on the first page of this book shows Productivity as the bull's-eye of the "target." The bull's-eye might more accurately be labeled "increased productivity." ["Productivity" is defined for our purposes as "output per employee-hour, quality considered."[9]]The following paragraph serves to illustrate.

When twenty units were produced by one person in one hour last month and 22 identical units are produced by one person in one hour today, productivity has risen 10 percent. If 20 units were produced last month and 20 units of higher quality are produced today, productivity has also risen, although the measurement of it is more difficult.

The output per employee per hour results not from peoples' efforts alone but

---

[4]Theodore Levitt, "Production Line Approach to Service," *Harvard Business Review,* September–October 1972, p. 41.

[5]*Measuring and Enhancing Productivity in the Federal Government, Phase III: Summary Report,* Office of Management and Budget and other agencies, June 1973.

[6]John F. Rockart, "An Approach to Productivity in Two Knowledge-based Industries," *Sloan Management Review,* Fall 1973, p. 23.

[7]For example, "Productivity: Our Biggest Undeveloped Resource," *Business Week* (A *Business Week* Special Issue), Sept. 9, 1972, pp. 79ff.

[8]*Business Week,* Jan. 6, 1973, p. 28.

[9]Later on this will be referred to as short-run productivity. Long-run productivity will include output per employee-hour and also consider the effects of excessive absenteeism, turnover, theft, sabotage, etc.

jointly from all the factors of production used: labor, management, money, machines, raw materials, etc. When productivity is expressed as output per person per hour, it is done so only for convenience; productivity might also be expressed in terms of output per $100 invested, or output per 100 pounds of raw material, or output compared with any other input factor.[10]

The productivity diagram indicates that greater productivity depends upon or is determined by technical factors (Technological Development, Raw Materials, Job Layout, and Methods) and human factors (Employees' Job Performance). These are considered in the following two chapters.

---

[10]For a more extensive discussion of a definition of productivity, see chap. 2 in William A. Ruch and James C. Hershauer, *Factors Affecting Worker Productivity,* Arizona State University, College of Business Administration, Bureau of Business and Economic Research, Tempe, 1974.

Chapter 2

Technical Contributions
to Productivity

Productivity is not determined solely by how hard and how well people work. The technical factors play a role, sometimes an overwhelmingly important one,[1] sometimes a minor one.

The technical factors are all those other than employee performance which can affect output per hour. They include such factors as technological development (the machinery and equipment employees have to work with), the quality of raw materials, the layout of the work, and methods and techniques.[2] In industrial plants, technological development will often be the most important factor influencing productivity, as illustrated in Figure 1. For example, Goodman in *Man and Automation*[3] cites the use of a tape to operate a machine tool which

---

[1]The introduction of improved methods of working has shown increases in productivity ranging from 20 to 200 per cent, while the effect of supervision and group organization may be expected to lead to differences in productivity of 7 to 15 percent. These results are reported in Michael Argyle, Godfrey Gardner, and Frank Cioffi, "Supervisory Methods Related to Productivity, Absenteeism, and Labor Turnover," *Human Relations,* vol. 11, no. 1, February 1958, p. 24.

[2]Joan Woodward pointed out that different types of technologies (unit or small-batch, large-batch or mass-production, continuous-process) have different effects on organization structure, communication, and leadership. *Industrial Organization: Theory and Practice,* Oxford University Press, London, 1965.

[3]Penguin Books, Inc., Baltimore, 1957, p. 52.

manufactures an aircraft spar. "The time taken by the conventional method was ten hours. By the computer method, ninety-two minutes were taken in planning time, and the actual tape-controlled machining time was fourteen minutes." In a department store, on the other hand, the degree of technology would have relatively little effect on productivity, except, perhaps, in the office. The segments in the diagram for a department store might be similar to those shown in Figure 2.

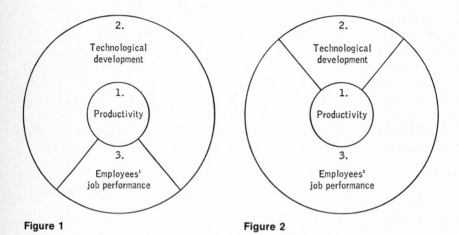

Figure 1   Figure 2

Other technical factors which have a bearing on productivity include ones such as:

The Plant: Its size, its capacity, the percentage of capacity utilized—all related to the ability to sell and distribute the product.

The Product: Its design, its quality (which may improve from year to year). This is related to research and development expenditures.

The Product Mix: If some items are produced more efficiently than others, the proportion in which they are combined will affect the overall productivity of the plant, without any change in the productivity of any individual item.

Plant and Job Layout: Work flow and methods.

Design of Machines and Equipment: To best match the limitations and capacities of people.

Degree of Integration of Production Processes: A plant which buys its raw materials partly processed will have a higher output of finished product per employee-hour than the plant which starts from scratch. Moreover, a single highly integrated plant should have fewer employee-hours spent for handling, sorting, shipping, etc., than two separate plants which are performing the same steps.

Utilization of Power: Output per employee-hour is usually increased with increased use of power.

Raw Materials: Quality of raw materials used and the continuity of their supply.

Percentage of Indirect Workers Employed: The firm with staffs of planners, quality control experts, industrial engineers, etc., should be able to devise methods which would result in greater output per employee per hour.

Scientific Management: With its emphasis on better planning and coordination, simplified methods, standardization, time and motion study, reduced waste and spoilage, contributes notably to increased productivity; although in some cases, the employees' attitudes and performance prevent the attainment of the full potential for increased productivity which scientific management provides.

For convenience, all these technical factors are included in segment 2, labeled "Technological Development—Raw Materials—Job Layout—Methods," of the productivity diagram on the first page of the book. There are some interrelations between this segment and segments 3 (Employees' Job Performance) and 7 (Motivation). If employees have good materials, equipment, and tools to work with, they are likely to be encouraged to work harder than if they have inferior tools and materials. And, of course, in the last analysis the technical factors themselves are determined by the performance of people, inside and outside the firm.

Chapter 3

Human Contributions
to Productivity

So much for the technical side. Let's turn to the human side, or to Employees'
Job Performance (3) and its effect on productivity or output per employee-hour.
"Employees" includes executives and managers, supervisors, professional staff
such as engineers and scientists, other white-collar workers, and blue-collar
workers.[1] Even if a plant has but one employee, that person's satisfactory
performance is vital to the proper functioning of the machinery and equipment;
and of course, in a company with many employees and little automation,
productivity is likely to be determined largely by what the employees, rather than
the machines, do.

The importance of human contributions to productivity has been stated by
one writer as follows:

Direct incentives will increase production 20–50% but "the ingredient I find in the
excellent companies has a potential that overshadows the productivity increase
achievable through industrial engineering techniques. When we learn to manage

[1]For a report on executive productivity, see American Management Association, *Executive
Productivity,* An AMA Survey Report, 1974.

10

people, the increased productivity will be likened to the relationship of the water wheel to nuclear energy."[2]

Sometimes an improvement in technology is more than offset by changes for the worse on the human side of productivity, so that productivity when expected to go up actually remains the same, or increases less than predicted, or even goes down. An excellent example of this is the longwall method of coal mining in England, where the psychological consequences of the changed method offset the great technical improvement from mechanization.[3]

In the diagram, the human contributions to productivity, or Employees' Job Performance (3), are considered to result from Ability (4) and Motivation (7), or more accurately, Ability *times* Motivation. Thus, if a person had no motivation, he or she could be the most capable individual in the world, but there would be no connection between ability and performance. Or, if a person had no ability, there could be terrific motivation, but there would be no connection between the motivation and the performance. Both ability and motivation are essential ingredients to good employee performance.

Ability (4)

Ability is deemed to result from Knowledge (5) and Skill (6). Knowledge, in turn, is affected by education, experience, training, and interest. Skill is affected by aptitude and personality, as well as by education, experience, training, and interest.

Motivation (7)

Motivation is here considered to result from the interacting forces in Physical Conditions of the job (11), Social Conditions of the job (12), and Individuals' Needs (8).

As we shall see, some of the forces are positive and contribute to motivation, improved employee performance, and increased productivity. They operate centripetally, working inward toward the bull's-eye on the diagram. Other forces are negative, reducing motivation, performance, and productivity. They operate centrifugally, or away from the target of increased productivity. What actually happens to employees' performance, (and through performance to productivity unless offset by changes in the technical factors), depends on the relative strength of the multitudinous centripetal and centrifugal forces.

One might jump to the conclusion that individuals whose needs are being fairly well met will be motivated to improve their performance and contribute to

---

[2]John Patton, president of John Patton Engineering firm, as quoted in Alfred G. Larke, "Human Relations Research: Academic Wool-Gathering or Guide to Increased Productivity?", *Dun's Review and Modern Industry,* vol. 68, no. 1, July 1956, pp. 42–44.

[3]E. L. Trist and K. W. Bamforth, "Some Social and Psychological Consequences of the Longwall Method of Coal-Getting," *Human Relations,* vol. 4, no. 1, 1951, pp. 3–38.

greater productivity. This is an unwarranted assumption.[4] It may be true generally, but it is possible, as we shall see, for individuals' needs to be pretty well met, for them to be fairly well satisfied with job and firm, and for them to have a fairly high level of morale[5] but to willfully restrict their output, not perform at their best, and in effect work against the company goal of increased productivity. The relation between need satisfaction, morale, employees' job performance, and productivity is much too complex for us to assume that satisfaction of individuals' needs will automatically lead to better job performance and increased productivity.[6] The relationship between satisfaction and productivity is considered at greater length in Section III, pages 43 to 52.

Before we continue our discussion of motivation and factors which affect it (in Section IV), we turn now to consider the goals of people in organizations (in Section II).

---

[4]For more detailed discussion of the relationship between individuals' needs and motivation, performance, and productivity, see Chap. 10.

[5]"Morale" and "attitude" are not single dimensions. The author chooses to explain motivation not as resulting from morale or attitude but rather as the result of the interacting forces involved in Physical Conditions, Social Conditions, and Individuals' Needs. For an excellent article on various definitions of "morale," see Robert M. Guion, "Some Definitions of Morale," in "Industrial Morale (A Symposium): 1. The Problem of Terminology," *Personnel Psychology,* vol. 11, no. 1, Spring 1958, pp. 59–61. Reprinted in E. Fleishman, *Studies in Personnel and Industrial Psychology,* The Dorsey Press, Homewood, Ill., 1961, pp. 301–304.

[6]In fact, even the measurement of job performance is fraught with difficulties. S. E. Seashore, B. Indik, and B. S. Georgopoulos in "Relationships among Criteria of Job Performance," *Applied Psychology,* vol. 44, no. 3, June 1960, p. 202, undertook a study of job performance in a delivery service firm. They selected five variables but did not propose that these five represented all aspects of performance: overall effectiveness, productivity, errors, accidents, and absences. They found that the first three criteria were internally consistent but that the last two were inconsistent with the first three and unrelated to each other. They concluded that "the relationships among certain different aspects of job performance are generally small, and that the size and direction of relationships are to a large degree unique to each population and situation, and somewhat different for organizations as contrasted to individuals. . . . These data are interpreted as contradicting the validity of 'overall job performance' as a unidimensional construct, and as a basis for combining job performance variables into a single measure having general validity."

Section II

The Goals of People in Organizations: Job Satisfaction

Chapter 4

Employees' Needs

Although employees themselves may not be aware of different kinds and levels of needs, their needs may be considered of three major types: physiological, social, and egoistic. A. H. Maslow presents a theory in "A Theory of Human Motivation," page 117, which places needs in five categories: physiological, safety, love, esteem, and self-actualization. For our purposes, we shall consider physiological and safety needs combined under physiological; love as a social need; and esteem and self-actualization included under egoistic needs.[1]

Physiological needs involve essentials such as air, water, food, housing, and clothing. These necessities must be at least partially fulfilled before a person gives much thought to other needs. They are met mainly through money and security on the job. As a person gets enough to eat, adequate clothing, and a

---

[1]No attempt is made here to discuss a variety of theories about motivation. David McClelland's work is mentioned on pages 16 and 66. Victor Vroom has postulated a valence and expectancy theory in his *Work and Motivation,* John Wiley & Sons, Inc., New York, 1964. Leon Festinger has proposed a cognitive dissonance theory in *A Theory of Cognitive Dissonance,* Row, Peterson & Company, Evanston, Ill., 1957. Lyman Porter and Edward Lawler have developed a model of motivation reproduced on page 192 of this book. Another approach to motivation is a management-by-objectives program, mentioned on page 64 of this volume. Frederick Herzberg's motivation-hygiene theories are presented on pages 136 to 140 of this volume.

decent place to live, he or she is inclined to place increasing emphasis on social and egoistic needs.

In our society, for people who have jobs, physiological needs are likely to be pretty well satisfied. A satisfied need is not a motivator of behavior.[2] Therefore, we cannot assume that more pay or more security will automatically lead to improved job performance. These traditional rewards of management provide little motivation because the struggle to satisfy subsistence needs has been won.[3]

On the other hand, we cannot assume that more pay or more security won't lead to improved performance. A higher salary to the employee may fulfill an egoistic need for recognition and status. The point is, where pay and security are adequate to satisfy physiological needs, we must turn our attention more to the social and egoistic needs of individuals if we are to motivate them to better performance.

Social needs can be satisfied only by contacts with others, such as fellow employees, the supervisor, or friends off the job. Social needs include such group needs as friendship, identification with the group, teamwork, and helping others and being helped.[4]

In our society, a great many employees probably have very satisfying relations with other people on or off the job and thus fulfill their social needs pretty well. To the extent that social needs are satisfied, they do not motivate. If an individual's social needs are already satisfied, the establishment of congenial and satisfying work groups through such means as sociometry will not necessarily lead to better employee job performance and higher productivity.

Egoistic needs are those that individuals have for a high evaluation of themselves and include such needs as knowledge, achievement,[5] competence, independence, self-respect, respect of others, status, power[6] and recognition. To maintain a high estimate of ourselves, most of us never stop needing reassurance that we are held in esteem by others. Thus, if we satisfy our egoistic needs today, we continue to seek such satisfaction tomorrow and the day after. This differentiates egoistic needs from physiological and social needs which, when satisfied, cease to motivate. It can be argued that both the physiological and social needs are largely satisfied in our society for those who have jobs. The continuing

---

[2]Douglas McGregor, *The Human Side of Enterprise,* McGraw-Hill Book Company, New York, 1960, p. 36.

[3]A. Zaleznik, C. R. Christenson, and F. Roethlisberger, *Motivation, Productivity, and Satisfaction of Workers,* Harvard Business School, Division of Research, Boston, 1958, p. 354.

[4]George Strauss and Leonard Sayles, *Personnel: The Human Problems of Management,* Prentice-Hall, Inc., Englewood Cliffs, N.J., 1960, p. 8.

[5]Much has been written about the "need for achievement" felt by many individuals in our society. See especially David C. McClelland, *The Achievement Motive,* Appleton-Century-Crofts, Inc., New York, 1953. The tendency or motivation to achieve success is a function of the need for achievement, the strength of expectancy or probability of achieving, and the incentive value of success. See John Atkinson, *A Theory of Achievement Motivation,* John Wiley & Sons, Inc., New York, 1966; also Bernard Indik, "Measuring Motivation to Work," *Personnel Administration,* November–December 1966, pp. 39–44.

[6]Robert N. McMurry, "Power and The Ambitious Executive," *Harvard Business Review,* November–December 1973, p. 140.

satisfaction of egoistic needs, then, would seem to offer the best opportunity to motivate employees to better job performance.

It should be noted that some needs, of course, fall into more than one of the types mentioned. For example, money will purchase food and clothing and thereby fill a physiological need; at the same time, in our society, it can fill a need for status and recognition. A modest home can fill our physiological need for shelter; an elaborate home in a high-class neighborhood can fill an egoistic need for status and recognition. A college graduate receiving his or her first paycheck fills some physiological needs with it but probably also some egoistic needs of achievement, independence, and status.

Let us concentrate on egoistic needs. Chris Argyris points out that as we mature as individuals, we seek self-fulfillment more and more—an egoistic need.[7] Frederick Herzberg and others in "Motivation versus Hygiene," page 136, differentiate between motivation and hygiene and contend that some factors operate as satisfiers and some as dissatisfiers. If the dissatisfiers are eliminated, good hygiene results and conditions are produced under which the satisfiers, if present, can motivate. The satisfiers fulfill the individuals's egoistic needs for self-actualization. The mere absence of dissatisfiers, however, does not result in motivation. Rensis Likert also emphasizes the importance of egoistic needs when he refers to the principle of supportive relationships which high-producing managers seem to be using.

> This provides the basis for stating the general principle which the high-producing managers seem to be using and which will be referred to as the *principle of supportive relationships*. This principle, which provides an invaluable guide in any attempt to apply the newer theory of management in a specific plant or organization, can be briefly stated: *The leadership and other processes of the organization must be such as to ensure a maximum probability that in all interactions and all relationships with the organization each member will, in the light of his background, values, and expectations, view the experience as supportive and one which builds and maintains his sense of personal worth and importance.*[8]

The area of egoistic needs assumes greater importance when we recognize that the educational level of employees in this nation is rising rapidly and that the number of white-collar and professional people is greater than the number of blue-collar employees.[9]

At the higher level of egoistic needs appear those for self-actualization or self-fulfillment. Such needs are often felt more strongly by professionals such as artists, doctors, and professors. Some writers feel that self-fulfillment needs are rarely activated for the average workers and that professors, for whom such

[7]Chris Argyris, *Personality and Organization,* Harper & Row, Publishers, Incorporated, New York, 1957, pp. 49–53.

[8]Rensis Likert, *New Patterns of Management,* McGraw-Hill Book Company, New York, 1961, chap. 8, "An Integrating Principle and an Overview." This chapter is reprinted in this book on pages 391 to 399.

[9]See Ch. 5, pages 23 and 24, for further discussion on this point.

needs may be quite active, are inclined to overstress their importance for all other workers.[10]

It seems clear that individual employees have different need patterns and thus seek different things from their jobs. This is discussed in more detail in Chapter 9.

---

[10]See, for example, Edward Gross, *Industry and Social Life,* Wm. C. Brown Company Publishers, Dubuque, Iowa, 1965, p. 143; and George Strauss, "Some Notes on Power Equalization," *The Social Science of Organizations,* Prentice-Hall, Inc., Englewood Cliffs, N.J., 1963, pp. 47–48.

Chapter 5

Factors Affecting Employees' Needs

It is important to recognize the wide diversity of factors which can influence the needs of a single individual. Some of them are discussed in the following pages.

On-Job and Off-Job Activities

Needs can be satisfied off-the-job, on-the-job, or by a combination of off- and on-job activities. This will be discussed in more detail in Chapters 7, 8, and 9.

Perception of the Situation

Basic to an understanding of motivation is the recognition that a person or group responds to other people, situations, or issues as they are perceived, not as they actually are.

Ross Stagner summarizes an excellent chapter on perception in the following way:

Behavior is governed, not by "objective" facts, but by facts as perceived by individuals. In some respects it is true that each of us lives in his own private universe—each of us sees the world in a manner slightly different from anyone else. These differences give rise to the unique individual personality.

Social psychology, however, is interested in the behavior of groups. This depends upon uniformities in perception: members of one group see the facts in one way, members of an opposing group see them differently. The data show that executives and workers differ sharply as to the "facts" regarding many industrial situations and issues. Executives and union officers likewise differ; and it may be that in some instances there will be differences between workers and union officers.

Uniformities in perception arise from a variety of influences common to members of a group. These may include a common objective situation (tasks, problems, tools) with which the individual must come to terms; common education and communications, company and union newspapers, stories handed down by word of mouth, and the like; and common personal environments, in the form of other persons who accept a certain view of the facts and punish members of the group who do not accept this common frame of reference. In addition, unique personal experiences and personal motives may cause an individual to adopt a certain view of industry, even though he is not a member of the group concerned.

As we have progressed with this analysis, it has become clear that motivation is inextricably linked with perception. A variety of motives are involved in group membership, for example, as well as in the unique personal experiences mentioned. It is therefore important that we turn now to a consideration of the psychology of motivation, and find what light it throws upon these problems of group conflict.[1]

And perception plays a major role in the path-goal approach to productivity.

If a worker sees high (or low) productivity as a path to the attainment of one or more of his personal goals in the work situation, he will tend to be a high (or low) producer, assuming that his need is sufficiently high, or his goal is relatively salient, and that he is free from barriers to follow the desired path (high or low productivity).[2]

A person's perception of and reaction to the product on which he or she is working may affect the person's attitudes and feeling of satisfaction on the job.

In both the cognitive and behavioristic approaches (to motivation), however, little if any emphasis is bestowed upon the *output itself*—the commodity or service produced. The tacit assumption seems to be that *what* one is producing has little to do with job attitudes and that the residual elements of job content and context are where the real sources of dissatisfaction reside. Perhaps this is a major omission. Can we be so numbed by modern life that the characteristics and dimensions of the means employed hold full dominion over the end sought?

Let us compare, for example, the construction of a fine piece of furniture and a mass-produced item such as an automobile or toothpaste. Aesthetic considerations aside, the furniture maker is conscious of the fact that he is fashioning a commodity that will, with appropriate care, last for generations. But the automobile worker,

---

[1]Ross Stagner, "Perception—Applied Aspects," *The Psychology of Industrial Conflict*, John Wiley & Sons, Inc., New York, 1956, pp. 53–88. Also see Robert Dubin. et al., "Implications of Differential Job Perceptions," *Industrial Relations*, October 1974, p. 265.

[2]B. S. Georgopoulos, G. M. Mahoney, and N. W. Jones, Jr., "A Path-Goal Approach to Productivity," *Journal of Applied Psychology*, vol. 41, no. 6, 1957, p. 353.

assuming he considers the matter at all, must be acutely aware that the result of his labor will last for only a few years, ultimately resting as a jarring eyesore in a roadside junkyard.

Although the tendency is to think of such considerations as applying only to workers in an organization's technical core, it seems equally plausible that a sensitive manager also can entertain these thoughts and be disturbed by his role in the production and sale of transitory commodities.[3]

Level of Aspiration

The level of aspiration refers to the goals individuals set for themselves and attempt to achieve. If they set their goals relatively low, their needs may be more easily satisfied. Individuals feel themselves successful if they meet or exceed their own goals. Stagner in his article "Level of Aspiration," page 141, points out that success in achieving one's goal usually leads a person to even higher aspiration.[4]

Reference Group

Related to the level of aspiration is the concept of reference group. "Reference groups are those groups with which an individual identifies or aspires to identify himself."[5] Thus, a new employee starting out on an assembly line in a factory may think in terms of eventually becoming a supervisor or executive (supervisors and executives are the employee's main reference group) and refuse to be governed by the standards and goals of the working group to which he or she currently belongs.

Male-Female

Up to 1940 women represented less than 25 percent of all workers. Today the figure is about 40 percent, and women are receiving greatly increased attention in organizations. Drastic changes in their positions have occurred since passage of the Civil Rights Act in 1964 and its amendments. New powers have been given to the Equal Employment Opportunity Commission to eliminate discrimination in employment practices against women and minorities, and courts in recent months have levied large fines on organizations which have been found in violation of the Civil Rights Act.

[3]Robert J. Waller, "Job Satisfaction: The 'Throwaway' Society," *Business Horizons,* October 1973, pp. 61–62.
[4]See also Robert A. Ullrich, "Levels of Aspiration," in *A Theoretical Model of Human Behavior in Organizations,* General Learning Press, Morristown, N.J., 1972, pp. 18–32.
[5]For further discussion of reference groups, see Muzafer Sherif and Carolyn W. Sherif, *An Outline of Social Psychology,* Harper & Row, Publishers, Incorporated, New York, 1956, pp. 175–178.
For reports of a study "demonstrating that attitude change over time is related to the group identification of the person—both his membership group identification and his reference group identification," see Alberta E. Siegel and Sidney Siegel, "Reference Groups, Membership Groups, and Attitude Change," *Journal of Abnormal and Social Psychology,* vol. 55, 1957, pp. 360–364, reprinted in D. Cartwright and A. Zander (eds.), *Group Dynamics,* 2d ed., Harper & Row, Publishers, Incorporated, New York, 1960, pp. 232–240.

Some ideas about women, widely accepted in the past, have undergone major revision. For example, a study from the University of Michigan proved *untrue* the following ideas:

1 That women work only for "pin money"
2 That women are more satisfied than men with intellectually undemanding jobs
3 That women are less concerned than men that a job help them realize their full potential

The study did show, however, that women attached more importance than men to good hours, pleasant physical surroundings, and convenient travel to and from work.[6]

Organizations are being cautioned not to assume how women perceive events but to ask them, and thus avoid making personnel decisions about women based on sex stereotyping so often used in the past.[7]

Stereotyping of women and its consequences are treated at length in Jane Torrey's "A Psychologist's Look at Women," page 145 of this volume.

Cultural Background

The standards of the society, the community, and the family in which an employee lives will greatly influence his or her perception of personal needs.

> If you focus on the social conduct of the person in a social position in an organization or even a small group, you are forced to take account of the cultural norms and groups to which he is sensitive. Whether you speak of job satisfaction, morale, the relative importance of economic and noneconomic incentives to work, types of leadership that make for high productivity, or what, you must go beyond the work group, beyond the organization, and into the community and society.[8]

> Groups have motivating value. But the outside world (class, religion) gives workers their values. There is little chance that managers will improve performance by persuading workers of their own (managers') values.[9]

Whether a person is from an urban or rural area may affect the degree to which he or she conforms to group norms or deviates from them (23). For

[6]Joan E. Crowley, Teresa E. Levitin, and Robert P. Quinn, *Facts and Fictions about the American Working Woman,* University of Michigan, Institute of Social Research, Ann Arbor. Reported in the *IRS Newsletter,* Autumn 1972.

[7]Benson Rosen and Thomas H. Jerdee, "Sex Stereotyping in the Executive Suite," *Harvard Business Review,* March–April 1974, p. 45.

[8]Harold L. Wilensky, "Human Relations in the Workplace," in C. M. Arensberg et al., *Research in Industrial Human Relations,* Harper & Row, Publishers, Incorporated, New York, 1957, p. 45. Quoted by permission of the publisher.

See also Mason Haire et al., *Managerial Thinking: An International Study,* John Wiley & Sons, Inc., New York, 1967 (section on cultural background); and Lawrence Williams et al., "Do Cultural Differences Affect Workers' Attitudes?", *Industrial Relations,* vol. 5, no. 3, May 1966, pp. 105–117.

[9]M. Komarovsky (ed.), *Common Frontiers of the Social Sciences,* The Free Press of Glencoe, Inc., New York, 1957, p. 331.

example, a person brought up on a farm, having worked hard and long hours, may be more inclined in a first factory job to accept management's production goals than the goals of the work group. However, a person who has spent much time in factories might be more inclined to conform to the goals of the group than to the goals of management. A study by John A. Fossum presents some evidence that employees from rural areas tend to be more satisfied with pay and with repetitive tasks than urban-socialized subjects.[10]

Although traditions in Germany, Japan, and other countries are now undergoing extensive changes, they have influenced employees' need patterns. In Germany, it was long a cultural tradition that when a company accepted a person as an apprentice, that person had a job for life, developed a paternalistic relationship with the master journeyman, was quality-oriented, and took great pride in the workmanship attained.

In Japan, companies traditionally assured employees of lifetime employment. The employees reciprocated with a feeling of tremendous obligation to the firm. A major difference between the American culture and the Japanese culture is dramatized by an incident of striking Japanese workers who continued to work as hard as ever but put on red headbands and sang before work to tell of their unhappiness with management.[11]

The culture in some countries is such that employees prefer directive management and supervision and view a nondirective approach as a sign of management weakness (31).[12]

David Sirota and J. Michael Greenwood, in "Understand Your Overseas Work Force," pages 157 to 167, set forth the different rankings of goals of employees in various countries and point out that "successful multinational management hinges on an objective, informed assessment of what foreign employees really want from their jobs."

Education

Other cultural factors influence employees' needs. The educational level of our citizens is constantly rising.

In March 1972, two-thirds of the people 16 years old and over in the civilian labor force had completed at least four years of high school, and nearly one worker in seven had completed at least four years of college. According to the latest projection, over three out of four persons in the civilian labor force will be high school graduates

[10]"Urban-Rural Differences in Job Satisfaction," *Industrial and Labor Relations Review*, April 1974, pp. 405–409. Also see George Strauss, "Job Satisfaction, Motivation and Job Redesign," *Organizational Behavior*, University of Wisconsin, Industrial Relations Research Association, Madison, 1974, pp. 27–28.

[11]Art Buchwald, "Management Sees Red but Strikers Work in Japan," *Seattle Times*, Oct. 12, 1973. For other Japanese cultural differences, see Peter F. Drucker, "What We Can Learn from Japanese Management," *Harvard Business Review*, March-April 1971, pp. 110.

[12]Bernard M. Bass and Gerald V. Barrett, *Man, Work and Organizations*, Allyn and Bacon, Inc., Boston, 1972, p. 157. For an excellent discussion of cultural differences, also read chap. 18, "The Multi-national Organization: A Behavioral Perspective," pp. 545–563.

by 1985 (73 percent by 1980, and 77 percent by 1985). At that time nearly one worker in five will have completed four years of college or more.[13]

Moreover, it is expected that the employment of professional and technical personnel will increase about 50 percent from 1972 to 1985, more rapidly than that for any other group.

> Employment growth in these occupations (professional, technical and kindred) has outdistanced that in all other major occupational groups in recent decades. From less than a million in 1890, the number of these workers has grown to 10.3 million in 1968.[14]

> And requirements for these occupations will continue to lead other categories between 1968 and 1980, increasing half again in size, which is twice the employment increase among all occupations combined.[15]

For many individuals in these groups, higher educational levels mean increased strength of egoistic and status needs, along with higher levels of aspiration.

Peter F. Drucker's article "Managing the Educated," page 167, explores some of the implications for motivation of higher educational levels and the rapidly increasing numbers in management, technical, and professional groups.

Experience

Individual experience in blue-collar, white-collar, professional, or executive jobs has an influence on the needs a person feels. A study made by the Survey Research Center of the University of Michigan reported that

> Comparatively few of the blue-collar workers were dissatisfied with their jobs on the grounds that they afforded them no sense of personal fulfillment, whereas this was the major source of dissatisfaction for the professional and managerial groups. It would appear, the researchers conclude, that blue-collar workers either start out with minimal expectations of finding fulfillment in their jobs, or eventually become adjusted to the lack of it. Either way, they do not seem to be particularly frustrated about their situation. . . . Easily the most dissatisfied and frustrated of all the groups questioned were men engaged in clerical and white-collar occupations, well over half of whom said they would rather be doing some other kind of work—a clear indication that they expected to obtain some ego-satisfactions from working but were not finding them in their present jobs. . . . With more and more of the work force now

---

[13]Denis F. Johnston, "The United States Economy in 1985: Population and Labor Force Projections," *Monthly Labor Review*, vol. 96, no. 12, December 1973, pp. 12–13.

[14]"The U.S. Economy in 1980: A Preview of BLS Projections," *Monthly Labor Review*, vol. 93, no. 4, April 1970, p.21.

[15]Edwin Harris, "Tomorrow's Jobs," *Manpower*, September 1974, p. 22.

moving into clerical occupations, the frustrations of the white-collar job may well become management's main area of future concern.[16]

Engineers, scientists, or professors might attach more importance to their status and reputation among their fellows in other organizations than among those in the organization to which they are presently attached. Thus they might be devoting their major efforts not centripetally toward the organization's goal of productivity but centrifugally to achieve status among their counterparts in other organizations.[17]

A modern professionally oriented manager will try to maximize his own lifetime income (in monetary and nonmonetary terms), and this goal will often coincide with the firm's goals of increased productivity, but not inevitably.[18]

General Economic Conditions

Needs of employees can vary with general economic conditions and changes in the business cycle. In times of depression, having a job and fulfilling their physiological needs may be the most important concerns of employees. Under these conditions poor morale and unsatisfied employee needs can go hand in hand with high productivity.[19] In times of rising living costs, getting higher wages to provide food and clothing for the family may be the predominant need—again a physiological one. In time of war, if survival is paramount, the physiological (safety) needs are likely to be of greatest importance. At other times, when one is reasonably well-assured of having and keeping a job which pays adequately to meet the physiological needs, the social and egoistic needs will probably be paramount.

Individual's Personal Situation

Furthermore, the needs of employees change with time in their individual lives. At one period in life, family illness or an additional child may force placement of greater emphasis on money to satisfy physiological needs. At other times, recognition or opportunity for self-expression (egoistic needs) may be most important.[20]

---

[16]Quoted by permission from *Personnel*, vol. 38, no. 2, March–April 1961, pp. 5–6, which reported from Gerald Gurin et al., *Americans View Their Mental Health*, Basic Books, Inc., Publishers, New York, 1960.

For a study concluding that if we accept status quo values we should emphasize the social content of the job for blue-collar workers and the task-centered opportunities for white-collar workers, see Frank Friedlander, "Comparative Work Value Systems," *Personnel Psychology*, vol. 18, no. 1, Spring 1965, pp. 1–28.

[17]For fuller discussion of "cosmopolitans" and "locals," see Alvin W. Gouldner, "Cosmopolitans and Locals," *Administrative Science Quarterly*, vol. 2, no. 3, December 1957, pp. 282–292.

[18]R. J. Monsen, B. O. Saxberg, and R. A. Sutermeister, "The Modern Manager: What Makes Him Run?", *Business Horizons*, vol. 9, no. 3, Fall 1966, pp. 23–24.

[19]For an example of such a situation, see W. J. Goode and Irving Fowler, "Incentive Factors in a Low Morale Plant," *American Sociological Review*, vol. 14, no. 5, October 1949, pp. 618–624.

[20]See Chap. 9 for further discussion of this point.

Chapter 6

Changing Values of Society, Organizations, and Individuals[1]

The past ten to fifteen years have witnessed tremendous changes in values—values in society, in organizations, and in individuals. Some of the words associated with Benjamin Franklin and the work ethic sound quaint today: honesty, punctuality, uprightness, integrity, sobriety, frugality, diligence, self-reliance, and hard work. Today we hear more about people "doing their own thing," the importance of "here and now," and history dismissed as irrelevant to life today. More and more groups are chiming in the chorus of charges of discrimination, that they are not getting their just desserts. Not only do minorities and women feel discriminated against, but Caucasians and males are increasingly charging "reverse discrimination." People who believe they are not getting their fair share of material goods sometimes "liberate" such goods from those who have more.

Other major changes in values are evident in more liberal standards for dress and for sexual behavior and in increasing emphasis on "consumerism."

In recent years we have seen a major switch in emphasis from "quantity" to

---

[1]This chapter is based on parts of articles by B. O. Saxberg and R. A. Sutermeister including "Human Motivation in the Smaller Enterprise," *Journal of Small Business Management*, July 1973, and "Today's Imperative: Humanizing the Organization," *Personnel Administration*, January 1974.

"quality." "Quality of life" has become a battle cry. This embraces many concepts such as more leisure time to enjoy life; population control to restrict the overcrowdedness of our cities; land use policies; environmental impact statements required for new highways, office buildings, and industrial developments; pollution control; and protection of parks, forests, and shorelines. There seems to be less emphasis on the materialistic aspects of living and greater emphasis on esthetic or spiritual aspects. Ian H. Wilson discusses "How Our Values are Changing" on page 179.

The changing values have had obvious impacts on organizations which have been forced to give more attention to their roles in our society, to social accounting, to long-range rather than short-range projects, and to considerations of ecology, environment, consumerism, and affirmative action.

Organizations, often under legal pressure, have been seeking out members of minority groups, employing them at all levels in the organization and at equal pay with the majority employees.

What effects have these changing values in society and organizations had on individuals? As society has placed greater emphasis on quality of life and enjoyment of leisure now possible in an affluent society, so individuals have made a reassessment of their values and goals in life.

In past, the "organization man" was satisfied to devote his entire life to one organization, with no thought of changing employers and with concern for family and problems of society decidedly secondary. Or the "professional man" devoted his life to his profession, even if this required frequent changes of organizations and great geographical mobility; he too often considered his family secondary and society's problems beyond his area of concern.

Today, more and more individuals view their work lives as one part of a broader life experience which involves not only job but family, community, social responsibilities, and concern for political and economic issues. As represented in Figure 1, more individuals strive to be total persons. Their organizations are one part of their lives, their professions another, their concern for society another, and their concern for family still another.

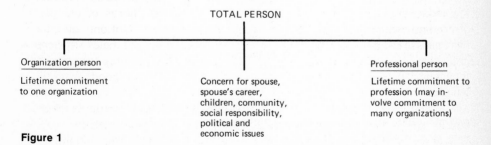

Figure 1

A person's commitment to an organization is increasingly influenced by spouse and family. The spouse may have a separate career which must be weighed before any move is made. Or the children's school location and the family's roots in the community may be important factors now in deciding whether to remain in the present location or transfer to a better job in another locality.

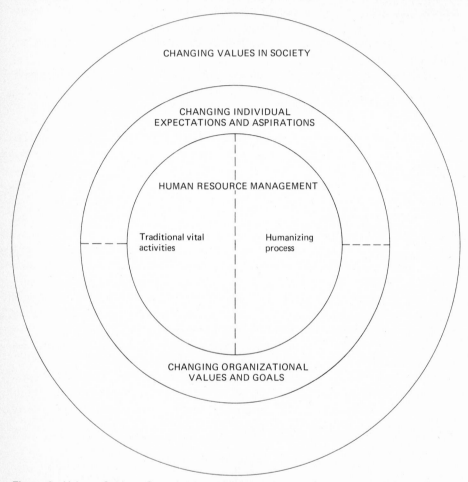

CHANGING VALUES IN SOCIETY

CHANGING INDIVIDUAL
EXPECTATIONS AND ASPIRATIONS

HUMAN RESOURCE MANAGEMENT

Traditional vital
activities

Humanizing
process

CHANGING ORGANIZATIONAL
VALUES AND GOALS

Figure 2   Values: Society, Organization, Individual. The broken lines indicate overlapping rather than discrete areas. (*From B. O. Saxberg and R. A. Sutermeister, "Human Motivation in the Smaller Enterprise,"* Journal of Small Business Management, *July 1973,* p. 8.)

Figure 2 illustrates the relationship among changing values in society, organizations, and individuals. The human resource management of an organization is affected by all these changes. Certain vital traditional activities of a personnel department continue, such as recruitment, selection, training, evaluating jobs, evaluating employee performance, collective bargaining, handling grievances, complying with laws and regulations, and the like. However, as will be pointed out later, the modern organization, in carrying out human resource mangement, must go beyond the traditional personnel activities and emphasize a humanizing process. This means paying greater attention to individual employees: their values today; how these differ from values in previous eras; and how they change over time.

Chapter 7

Employees' Search for Life Satisfaction

It can reasonably be assumed that every person strives for life satisfaction. In the words of our Constitution, all men are created equal and are endowed by their Creator with certain unalienable rights—among these are life, liberty, and the pursuit of happiness. The founding fathers rejected a different version of objectives—life, liberty, and property—because they realized that "property" was a means to an end rather than an end in itself. In today's language, they emphasized the "quality of life." Thus, "quality of life" or "life satisfaction" is an understandable, reasonable, and legitimate goal for every human being.

Life satisfaction means different things to different people. Every individual in the world has to make a personal search for life satisfaction and choose the path or paths he or she feels will most likely lead to that goal.

Some people doubtless find life satisfaction without working in the ordinary sense. They may be very wealthy and not have to work, yet obtain life satisfaction by various activities which contribute to society, the community, other individuals, or their own personal well-being. Others may live on welfare payments adequate to cover their needs. Still others may be working for themselves, as artists or members of a commune, and achieve a high degree of life satisfaction.

More and more individuals in today's society may attain life satisfaction by working on jobs but taking leave from them from time to time to make a contribution to society or to simply have a change of pace. Xerox Corporation now makes it possible for a limited number of its executives to use a sabbatical year in this manner. The United Steelworkers and the steel companies have for some time provided a sabbatical leave for certain employees.

In many cases, work does not occupy as important a position in employees' lives as it once did. With the increasing affluence of our society, with many different possible life-styles, with increasing appreciation of and opportunity for leisure time, work is less often the center of life's interest for employees. Shorter work hours, innovations such as the four-day week, assured paid retirement, and the increasing frequency of early retirement put more emphasis on off-work aspects of life.

As life expectancy between 1950 and 1968 increased and work life expectancy decreased, work came to account for a decreasing proportion of one's total life, as shown by the following figures for a 20-year-old (working) man:[1]

	1900	1950	1968
Life expectancy	42.2	48.9	49.2
Work life expectancy	39.4	43.1	41.5
Retirement expectancy	2.8	5.8	7.7
% of life in retirement	6.6	11.9	15.6

Increased leisure is a boon to many people searching for life satisfaction. For others, it may mean boredom, apathy, and an endless appointment with the television set. Perhaps in recent years we have focused too much on early retirement, assuming it would inevitably lead to life satisfaction; perhaps we should pay more attention to making work a satisfying experience.

For the majority of us who work on a job, life satisfaction is sought through a combination of on-job and off-job activities. We derive certain benefits and satisfactions from working, and other benefits and satisfactions from things we do away from work. Probably for most of us, the "quality of work" is a major component of "quality of life." We cannot attain life satisfaction if our work does not give us satisfaction.[2] Therefore, job satisfaction is a major goal for us. Figure 1 illustrates these relationships.

[1]From Dennis F. Johnston, "The Future of Work: Three Possible Alternatives," *Monthly Labor Review*, vol. 95, no. 5, May 1972, p. 4.

[2]Some raise the question whether it is worthwhile to strive for job satisfaction when leisure time keeps increasing and working time decreasing. Should we devote our efforts to making use of leisure time a satisfying experience and not attempt to achieve job satisfaction? Others come to the opposite conclusion that work is an increasingly important part of life satisfaction because opportunities for leisure activities which require use of gasoline or scarce resources may now be decreasing.

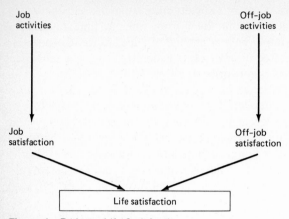

Figure 1   Paths to Life Satisfaction.

We now turn our attention to the area of job satisfaction.

Chapter 8

Employees' Search for Job Satisfaction

The Search for Job Satisfaction Is Universal

The search for job satisfaction seems to be going on at every level of organizations, by people in all types of jobs, by young and old, by men and women, and by minority and majority groups. The higher educational level of employees today and the increasing emphasis on "quality of life" have resulted in a rising level of expectations for "quality of work" and job satisfaction.

How Extensive Is Job Dissatisfaction?

We hear much about "blue-collar blues," especially of automobile assembly line workers said to be fed up with their jobs.[1] We hear of white-collar workers, such as keypunch operators working on a graveyard shift, who react much like blue-collar workers and are no less satisfied. We hear of "middle-management blues" and the increasing interest of this group in union organization. The author has a friend who is a professional engineer and another an owner-manager

---

[1] In contrast to this point of view, a survey of 1,000 automobile plant workers in Baltimore revealed that 95 percent reported they were satisfied with their jobs (I. Siassi, G. Crocetti, and H. Spiro, "Loneliness and Dissatisfaction in a Blue-Collar Population," *Archives of General Psychiatry,* vol. 30, February 1974, p. 261).

of a small retail store who report they hate to get up in the morning and face another day at their jobs. Even the president of General Motors was quoted as saying, "What's more boring than lugging home a big briefcase of papers to be read before going to bed every night?" And college professors may feel a certain monotony and disenchantment in grading a pile of 100 exam papers or term reports.

What evidence do we have that employees are dissatisfied? How widespread is such dissatisfaction? What is the degree of dissatisfaction? Which employees are dissatisfied—is there any pattern? Is job dissatisfaction increasing or decreasing?

The HEW-authorized study *Work in America* has chapters on "Sources of Dissatisfaction," "Blue-Collar Blues," "White-Collar Woes," and "Managerial Discontent" and concludes that there are a significant number of workers dissatisfied with the quality of their working lives.[2] Campbell and Converse examined ten major studies of dissatisfaction and found the proportion of dissatisfied workers varied from 10 to 21 percent; they conclude that most workers are pretty satisfied.[3]

Wool claims that the HEW study's conclusion is an overgeneralization. Citing trends in labor turnover, absenteeism, strikes, and productivity, he concludes that most workers are pretty satisfied and that there is little evidence of a rising wave of discontent.[4]

George Strauss has recently made a careful review of studies of job satisfaction and, speaking mainly of blue-collar workers, concludes that "there is no evidence of rising dissatisfaction," although there may be some latent dissatisfaction which has not yet appeared on quantitative measures.[5] He sees, at most, "some slight upward shift in preferences for more challenging work."

H. Roy Kaplan also concludes that the majority of workers appear satisfied.[6]

A 1974 Department of Labor study examined the results of seven national surveys spanning the years 1958–1974 and eight Gallup polls spanning the years 1963–1973; these showed that 81 to 91 percent of workers were satisfied.[7] Their conclusion is that "there has not been any significant decrease in overall levels of job satisfaction over the last decade."

Are there different degrees of dissatisfaction for people in different occupations? If we can accept the premise that people who would choose the same

[2]*Work in America: Report of a Special Task Force to the Secretary of Health, Education, and Welfare,* prepared under the auspices of the W. E. Upjohn Institute for Employment Research, The M.I.T. Press, Cambridge, Mass., 1973.

[3]Angus Campbell and Philip E. Converse (ed.), *The Human Meaning of Social Change,* Russell Sage Foundation, New York, 1972, pp. 172–173.

[4]Harold Wool, "What's Wrong with Work In America?: A Review Essay," *Monthly Labor Review,* March 1973, pp. 38–44, included in this book on pages 412 to 422.

[5]"Job Satisfaction, Motivation and Job Redesign," *Organizational Behavior: Research and Issues,* University of Wisconsin, Industrial Relations Research Association, Madison, 1974, pp. 20, 23, 49.

[6]"How Do Workers View Their Work in America?", *Monthly Labor Review,* June 1973, p. 46.

[7]*Job Satisfaction: Is There a Trend?,* U.S. Department of Labor, Manpower Administration, Manpower Research Monograph No. 30, 1974, pp. 4–5.

Table 1   Percentages in Occupational Groups Who Would Choose Similar Work Again

Professional and lower white-collar occupations	%	Working-class occupations	%
Urban university professors	93	Skilled printers	52
Mathematicians	91	Paper workers	42
Physicists	89	Skilled autoworkers	41
Biologists	89	Skilled steelworkers	41
Chemists	86	Textile workers	31
Firm lawyers	85	*Blue-collar workers, cross section*	*24*
Lawyers	83	Unskilled steelworkers	21
Journalists (Washington correspondents)	82	Unskilled autoworkers	16
Church university professors	77		
Solo lawyers	75		
White-collar workers, cross section	*43*		

Source: Reprinted by permission of The M.I.T. Press from *Work in America*, 1973, p. 16.

occupation again are satisfied, Table 1 shows wide variation in satisfaction for people in various occupations.

Survey results vary of course with the questions asked. In order to determine level of satisfaction, does one ask:

1 "Are you satisfied on your job?"
2 "Are you satisfied or dissatisfied with various aspects of your job such as pay, supervision, working conditions, job interest, chances for advancement, etc.?"
3 "Would you like to change jobs for something better?"
4 "Would you recommend your job to a good friend?"
5 "What type of work would you try to get into if you started over?"
6 "If you had enough money to live comfortably the rest of your life, would you retire or continue to work?"
7 "What would you do with the extra two hours if you had a twenty-six hour day?"

Even if employees are dissatisfied, will they feel it is a reflection on themselves to say so? Will they feel they had better reply that they are satisfied because this is a more socially desirable way of responding?

Aggregate Statistics on Job Satisfaction Are of Little Help to an Organization

There is great difficulty in getting accurate data on job satisfaction. Data which are obtained may not be adequate to answer the questions raised. My personal bias is that further studies of levels of job satisfaction for different occupational groups will not be fruitful. Saying 80 percent of employees in a group are satisfied tells us nothing about their reasons for feeling satisfied, or the reasons of the other 20 percent for feeling dissatisfied. The reasons can vary from personal characteristics of the employee, individual needs he or she is trying to satisfy by working, pay, supervisor, opportunities for advancement, the nature of the job, security, work conditions, rewards in comparison with expected rewards, relations with fellow employees, and a myriad of other considerations.

Organizations may devote their time much more effectively to working with individual employees and trying to remove dissatisfaction where it is found to exist. These ideas are dealt with at greater length in Section V.

Chapter 9

Various Paths
to Job Satisfaction

Hours of Work and Scheduling

In examining various employee paths to job satisfaction, let's consider the schedules of work desired by employees in order to meet their needs, or by the same employee at different times in his or her life span.

    1 *Full-time permanent job:* Perhaps most of the breadwinners of families need this type of job.

    2 *Full-time but temporary job:* This type of job frequently attracts women who wish to work when they finish school, drop out during child rearing, and return later to earn money for special purposes. Or they may become full-time permanent employees.

    3 *Part-time permanent job:* The needs of some people can be met best if they have permanent jobs which require only part of a day or part of a week. Employers have often been very successful in having two employees wishing part-time work fill one job, even letting the employees decide between them who will work when, with the employer's major concern being that the job is staffed by someone at all times.

    4 *Part-time temporary job:* Same as (2) except on part-time basis.

    5 *Job with sliding hours:* Some employees, such as working mothers, may be unable to get to work easily at 8 in the morning, but could come at 9 or 10 after the children have been fed and sent off to school. They might be able to work until 6 or 7 in the evening. Perhaps it makes no difference to the employer what particular hours are worked, so long as the employee is able to contribute eight hours a day. Other employees might find it better for their needs to come in at 7 and go home at 4, etc. This concept of "sliding hours" has been employed widely in Europe and is getting increased attention in the United States.[1]

6 *Job with flexible hours and/or days:* Some jobs might require the accomplishment of a certain amount of work, but the work can be performed at any time. In effect, the employee may be allowed to set his or her own hours and days of work, the only restriction being that the work be accomplished in adequate time, or that a specified total number of hours be worked each week.

7 *Voluntary overtime:* Many employees like to work overtime and earn extra pay. Others do not. Some like a moderate amount of overtime but quickly tire of too much. The United Automobile Workers in their 1973 contract specified certain limits on the amount of overtime which could be required by the employer. Their objective is eventually to have overtime on a purely voluntary basis. Sometimes an employer's insistence on overtime conflicts violently with the employee's plans for off-job activities and can cause extreme job dissatisfaction.

Selection and Placement

The likelihood of an employee achieving job satisfaction will be greater if the employment decision is a bilateral one. When the job is fully explained to the applicant; when the applicant is allowed to see it being performed and perhaps some other possible jobs as well; when the applicant is even allowed to try out several jobs before a selection and placement decision is finally made, the chances that he or she will be satisfied with the job are increased. The Department of Labor has had success in its "work samples" program whereby a disadvantaged person may "sample" several types of work before deciding with the employer which type is most suitable.[2]

Promotional Opportunities

With increasing pressure on employers to have women and minorities represented at all levels in the organization, many firms which have never before done so are beginning to "post" openings of jobs above the entry level and give any employee a chance to indicate that he or she would like to be considered for any opening. The procedure can contribute greatly to job satisfaction of employees by calling their attention to the frequency of promotional opportunities and giving them assurance that they will not be overlooked when better jobs open up.

Paths to Job Satisfaction

With the changing values of society and of individuals, many employees are searching for job satisfaction along paths different from traditional ones, often

---

[1]A. O. Elbing, et al., "Flexible Working Hours: It's About Time," *Harvard Business Review,* January–February 1974, p. 18.

[2]For a discussion of "self-selection," see Marvin Dunnette, et al., "Work and Nonwork: Merging Human and Societal Needs," in Marvin D. Dunnette, *Work and Nonwork in the Year 2001,* Wadsworth Publishing Company, Inc., Belmont, Calif., 1973, p. 109.

along several paths simultaneously, and more and more frequently along different routes at different time periods in their lives.

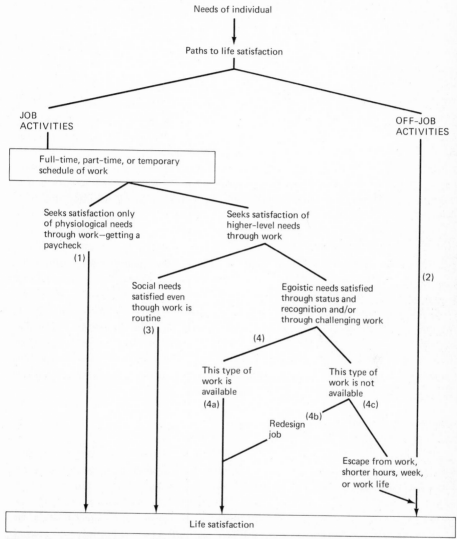

Figure 1 Life Satisfaction Model. (*An earlier version of this diagram appeared in B. O. Saxberg and R. A. Sutermeister, "Today's Imperative—Humanizing the Organization," The Personnel Administrator, January–February 1974, p. 53.*)

Figure 1 shows the various paths by which employees strive to attain life satisfaction. In this diagram we are again relying on Maslow's theory of hierarchy of needs and have condensed his five categories into three: physiological, social and egoistic.

Employees on the job may seek satisfaction of physiological needs only, paying a penalty of time in return for a paycheck and expecting their other needs to be fulfilled in off-job activities. They seek job satisfaction by traveling path 1 and, usually, life satisfaction by traveling paths 1 and 2. They may feel no aspiration to get ahead. They may feel no need for major improvement in job, income, or living conditions. Not everyone is seeking self-actualization at work.[3]

Not content with satisfying merely physiological needs, another employee may also seek to satisfy social needs: of belonging to a group; being accepted; and having a good relationship with fellow employees and/or boss. Social needs can be satisfied off the job in neighborhood, church, community, or union activities or on the job in relations with fellow employees and supervisors. Some can satisfy social needs on the job even though the work they perform is routine and unchallenging. These individuals, then, will be following two paths simultaneously on the job, 1 and 3. Unless the jobs represent their whole lives, they will also be following path 2 in their search for life satisfaction.

For still other individuals, egoistic needs will be activated in addition to physiological and social needs. Such egoistic needs can be fulfilled for some through status and recognition and for others through self-fulfillment which derives from meaningful, challenging, and stimulating work. If management can place an individual requiring status and recognition on a job which provides status and recognition, that person will be following a path to job satisfaction.

If management can place an individual requiring meaningful, challenging work on a job which provides meaningful, challenging work, that individual will be following a path to job satisfaction. This path is 4a on the diagram. However, sometimes the types of jobs required by individuals with activated egoistic needs may not be available. The possibilities then seem to be for management to redesign the job so it does provide status and recognition or does become challenging (path 4b) or to expect the individual to "escape from work" through absenteeism, a sabbatical, taking a job with another firm, shorter workweek, or early retirement, etc. (path 4c). Thus, individuals with activated egoistic needs who achieve job satisfaction will be following paths 1, 3, and either 4a or 4b and at the same time path 2 for life satisfaction. More attention will be devoted to job design and redesign in Chapter 12.

In summary, changing values of society have had an impact on the values of employees. In their search for life satisfaction, they place less emphasis than before on work and the organization and more emphasis on leisure time, family, community, and other off-job activities. For time spent on the job, job satisfaction or quality of job is increasingly important. Different individuals search for job satisfaction by different routes, different combinations of routes, and routes which are likely to change over a person's working life.

---

[3]Some individuals in this category may never have had higher-level needs activitated. Others may have sought fulfillment of higher-level needs at one time but became frustrated, so the higher-level needs have become inactive or dead. These individuals may have withdrawn psychologically from the job and lowered their expectations.

Organizations may welcome some employees who seek fulfillment only of physiological needs on the job. Some jobs require only an adequate level of performance; increased productivity on these jobs may not be an organization goal.

Organizations have so far only scratched the surface in changing methods to respond more adequately to the needs of employees. Organizations must increasingly recognize employees' needs and support employees in their search for job satisfaction and life satisfaction, along whatever paths the employees choose to travel. Work experience should add to rather than subtract from an individual's life satisfaction.

Section III

Organizational Productivity and Employee Job Satisfaction: Both Essential Goals in Today's Society

Chapter 10

A Shift of Focus Away from the Satisfaction-Productivity Relationship

Relationship between Satisfaction and Motivation

There is much discussion in the literature of the relationship between need satisfaction and motivation, employee performance, and productivity. Our analysis and the productivity diagram have recognized that *productivity* depends on both employee performance and technology. We have recognized that *employee performance* depends on both motivation and ability of the employee. Thus, even though an individual is highly motivated, this motivation alone does not automatically lead to increased productivity. This much seems clear and can be illustrated as Figure 1. But the relationship between need satisfaction and motivation is not so clear. If the physical and social conditions of the job are such

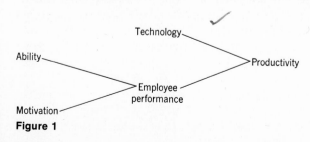

Figure 1

that employees satisfy their physiological, social, and egoistic needs,[1] will employees be motivated to improve performance? This important question can be illustrated as shown in Figure 2.

Figure 2

One is tempted to hypothesize that a high level of need satisfaction would invariably produce a high level of motivation and that a low level of need satisfaction would invariably produce a low level of motivation. Such a neat hypothesis has been exploded by studies which indicate that the opposite situation can exist: high need satisfaction associated with low motivation, or low need satisfaction associated with high motivation. Depending upon the many different variables or factors present in a specific situation, then, any of the associations shown in Figure 3 is possible.

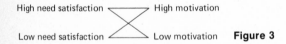

Figure 3

Let's consider in detail the various combinations.

High Need Satisfaction–High Motivation

Assume individuals whose needs are well satisfied. If only their physiological and social needs have been activated, they are satisfied with their pay and their relations with others including the supervisor and are highly motivated to perform well. If their egoistic needs have been activated, they have a continuing feeling of worthwhileness, status, recognition, and perhaps self-fulfillment about the job that motivates them to perform well.

Low Need Satisfaction–Low Motivation

Assume individuals whose needs are not satisfied. If only their physiological and social needs have been activated, they are not satisfied with their pay or their relations with others and may do just enough to get by yet still keep the job. If their egoistic needs have been activated, they have not been satisfied. They feel their efforts are not recognized or appreciated, their capabilities are not being utilized, and they are discouraged from giving their best efforts.

In connection with the preceding two combinations of factors, we might

---

[1]Or at least the individuals perceive themselves to be on the way to satisfying them.

remind ourselves of the importance of the employee's perception by repeating the conclusion reached by Basil Georgopoulos and others quoted previously on page 20:

> If a worker sees high (or low) productivity as a path to the attainment of one or more of his personal goals in the work situation, he will tend to be a high (or low) producer, assuming that his need is sufficiently high, or his goal is relatively salient, and that he is free from barriers to follow the desired path (high or low productivity).

High Need Satisfaction–Low Motivation

Assume individuals whose needs have been activated at all levels (physiological, social, and egoistic) and are well satisfied. Under what circumstances might this be associated with low motivation rather than high?

Arthur Brayfield and Walter Crockett in their article "Employee Attitudes and Employee Performance," page 183, emphasize that there is no necessary relationship between employees' attitudes and productivity, although employees whose needs are not reasonably well met may avoid the job situation entirely by having accidents, absenting themselves, or resigning.[2]

Many studies have demonstrated that a high level of need satisfaction and high morale do not necessarily assure high productivity. Robert Kahn points this fact out effectively in a review of the research of the Survey Research Center at the University of Michigan and shows why the center abandoned the use of satisfaction or morale indexes as variables intervening between supervisory and organizational characteristics on the one hand and productivity on the other.[3]

One possibility explaining high need satisfaction and low motivation is that an individual's social and egoistic needs are satisfied largely off the job. He or she is a member of the school board, or a bowling expert, etc., and derives social and egoistic need satisfactions from these activites. There may be no motivation to perform on the job any better than necessary to avoid discharge.

A second possibility is that an individual may attain satisfaction of social and egoistic needs by being an important and esteemed member of an informed, cohesive group whose goal is to restrict production. Thus the individual's needs are well satisfied through group membership, but his or her efforts are directed to working against the company goal of increased productivity. Arnold Tannenbaum in *Social Psychology of the Work Organization*[4] points out that an individual may be satisfied but this indicates little about motivation to work— particularly when satisfaction does not depend on the amount of effort put into the work.

---

[2]For a discussion of the point that people quit their jobs because the jobs do not satisfy their needs and also because the jobs keep the people from receiving satisfactions from other sources, see Ian C. Ross and Alvin F. Zander, "Need Satisfactions and Employee Turnover," *Personnel Psychology*, vol. 10, Autumn 1957, pp. 327–338. Reprinted in E. Fleishman, *Studies in Personnel and Industrial Psychology*, The Dorsey Press, Homewood, Ill., 1961, pp. 259–267.

[3]Robert L. Kahn, "Productivity and Job Satisfaction," *Personnel Psychology*, Autumn 1960, pp. 275–287.

[4]Wadsworth Publishing Company, Inc., Belmont, Calif., 1966, pp. 36–37.

A third possibility explaining high need satisfaction and low motivation is that an individual may have worked hard at first and made a favorable impression on the boss and now is coasting—doing just enough to get by. He or she is quite satisfied but has low motivation.[5] Behavior, of course, will be influenced by level of aspiration.[6]

Low Need Satisfaction–High Motivation

Assume an individual, a male worker, whose needs are not currently satisfied. His pay is low, he dislikes his job, perhaps dislikes his associates; but unemployment is high and he doesn't know where he could get another job. He works his hardest to keep from being fired. At least his physiological needs are being met through the weekly paycheck, and in times of widespread unemployment, social and egoistic needs become relatively unimportant for many people.[7]

A second combination of circumstances which may provide low need satisfaction for an individual but high motivation occurs when the person—let us say, a female worker—hopes to satisfy her needs in the future. She is starting out as a beginner, perhaps, but has supervisors as a reference group. She may ignore restrictive goals of her present membership group, thus foregoing satisfaction of social needs now, and be guided more by the goals of her supervisor, hoping herself one day to become a supervisor and at that time to satisfy her needs. As pointed out by James March and Herbert Simon, present satisfactions are often less important in influencing behavior than perceived relations between present alternatives and future states.[8] Donald Pelz and Frank Andrews write that effective scientists reported good opportunities for growth and higher status but were not necessarily satisfied,[9] and that "a certain amount of dissatisfaction, stemming from eager impatience, is perhaps inevitable in a healthy research atmosphere (though satisfaction generally characterizes high performance)."[10]

A third combination of circumstances where low need satisfaction is associated with high motivation could occur when the individual's egoistic needs are not satisfied but he or she belongs to a cohesive group. If production goals are high, the individual is under constant pressure to conform to peer expectations and does so to satisfy lower-level social needs.

The reward which individuals receive as a result of improved performance and increased productivity affects their satisfaction with the job. If there is no recognition, monetary or nonmonetary, of the improved performance, their need satisfaction could diminish. If there is appropriate reward for their behavior,

[5]Chris Argyris points out that human growth and productivity are not necessarily correlated with pleasure and happiness at all. See "Employee Apathy and Non-involvement: The House That Management Built," *Personnel*, vol. 38, no. 4, July–August 1961, p. 12.

[6]See pages 141 to 145 in this volume.

[7]See footnote 19, page 25.

[8]*Organizations*, John Wiley & Sons, Inc., New York, 1958, chap. 3.

[9]Donald Pelz and Frank Andrews, *Scientists in Organizations: Productive Climates for Research and Development*, John Wiley & Sons, Inc., New York, 1966, chap. 1.

[10]Ibid., p. 139.

need satisfaction could increase and contribute to even better performance. George Homans, furthermore, points out that the relationship between satisfaction and productivity depends on the *frequency* with which the activity is rewarded.[11] And March and Simon emphasize the *expected value of the rewards* as determining the individuals' satisfaction (as well as probably raising their level of aspiration, which in turn may make them less satisfied). The relationship as March and Simon see it is illustrated in Figure 4.[12]

Figure 4   *(Reproduced by permission of the publisher from James G. March and Herbert A. Simon,* Organizations, *John Wiley & Sons, Inc., New York, 1958, p. 49.)*

Circular Relationship between Satisfaction and Performance

A major question, which has probably not yet been answered conclusively, concerns the causal relationship between satisfaction and performance. Does high need satisfaction lead to high motivation and tend to improve employee performance? Or does improved performance result in higher need satisfaction?

Edwin A. Locke states:

There is no necessary relationship between overall job satisfaction and subsequent production. First, the fact that an individual likes his job says nothing about why he likes it. He may like it because he has set easy goals for himself and attained them or because the work interests him (despite his lack of ability), or because he likes his co-workers. In other words, high satisfaction may be caused by factors other than high production.[13]

The author agrees with Mason Haire that

[11]George C. Homans, *Social Behavior: Its Elementary Forms,* Harcourt, Brace & World, Inc., New York, 1961, p. 282. See also Edward E. Lawler III, "Antecedent Attitudes of Effective Managerial Performance," *Organization Behavior and Human Performance,* vol. 2, no. 2, May 1967, p. 125.

[12]Also see Lyman W. Porter and Edward E. Lawler III, "What Job Attitudes Tell about Motivation," *Harvard Business Review,* January–February 1968, pp. 118–126; and Kae H. Chung, "Developing a Comprehensive Model of Motivation and Performance," *Academy of Management Journal,* vol. 11, no. 1, March 1968, pp. 63–73.

[13]"Job Satisfaction and Job Performance: A Theoretical Analysis," *Organization Behavior and Human Performance,* vol. 5, no. 5, September 1970, p. 495.

The argument that more satisfied employees would become more effective employees led to a morass. It led to the investigation of the relation between morale and productivity—a miasmic welter of confused data whose upshot seemed to be that there was no consistent association between the two.[14]

Lyman Porter and Edward Lawler have developed a model, reproduced on page 192 of this book, which predicts that good performance is more likely to result in satisfaction than is satisfaction to result in good performance. In my article "Employee Performance and Employee Need Satisfaction: Which Comes First?", page 191, I adopt the view that performance and satisfaction are interacting, with a circular relationship existing between them.[15]

Increased Emphasis on Egoistic Needs

Another question concerns the importance of egoistic needs in the need hierarchy. With an ever-increasing part of our working population consisting of college-educated, technical, scientific, or professional people, egoistic needs such as desire for challenge, accomplishment, recognition, and self-fulfillment are becoming increasingly activated and important. Perhaps more individuals in the future will wish to follow the "challenging job" path as one of their paths to job satisfaction (refer to the diagram on page 39).

Time for a Change of Focus

In my opinion, it is time to change our focus away from the satisfaction-performance relationship. It is time to change our focus away from the study of satisfaction and dissatisfaction of groups of employees, such as blue-collar, white-collar, middle-management, executive, and professional. It is time to change our focus away from the percentages of employees in each group who are satisfied or dissatisfied and the aggregate reasons for their feelings.

I believe it will be much more fruitful if we focus on each individual employee and his or her own feelings of satisfaction or dissatisfaction. Section V explores this approach, which is referred to as "humanizing the organization."

Regardless of the Relationship between Satisfaction and Performance, Both Satisfaction and Productivity Are Essential Goals of the Organization

In light of the changing values of organizations and individuals today (as discussed in Chapter 6), my own value judgment is that employee satisfaction and increased productivity for the organization are both essential goals, even when it cannot be proved that employee satisfaction contributes to productivity.[16]

---

[14]Mason Haire, "Coming of Age in the Social Sciences," *Industrial Management Review* (now the *Sloan Management Review*), vol. 8, no. 2, Spring 1967, p. 111.

[15]See also Charles N. Greene, "The Satisfaction-Performance Controversy," *Business Horizons,* October 1972, pp. 31–41; and Donald P. Schwab and Larry L. Cummings, "Theories of Performance and Satisfaction: A Review," *Industrial Relations,* October 1970, p. 408–430.

[16]This argument assumes, necessarily, that the productivity level is high enough to sustain the organization. This value judgment is in agreement with Lawler, who declares; "Job satisfaction is one

Most studies show that high employee satisfaction does contribute to long-run productivity by reducing turnover, absenteeism, sabotage, theft, and worker alienation.[17] The evidence on short-run productivity, or output per employee-hour, is not so clear. Sometimes high employee satisfaction leads to higher short-run productivity, but there is no assurance that this is always true.

These relationships between job satisfaction, short-run productivity, and long-run productivity are represented in Figure 5.

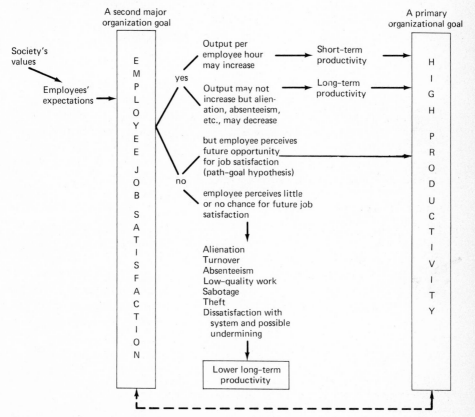

Figure 5 Relationship between Job Satisfaction and Productivity in the Short and Long Run.

measure of the quality of life in organizations and is worth understanding and increasing even if it doesn't relate to performance" (Edward E. Lawler III, *Motivation in Work Organizations,* Brooks/Cole Publishing Company, Monterey, Calif., 1973, p. 62).

[17]See Thomas A. Jeswald, "The Cost of Absenteeism and Turnover in a Large Organization," in W. Clay Hamner and Frank L. Schmidt, *Contemporary Problems in Personnel,* St. Clair Press, Chicago, 1974, p. 352; Lyman Porter and Richard M. Steers, "Organizational, Work and Personal Factors in Employee Turnover and Absenteeism," in Hamner and Schmidt, op. cit. p. 338; and *Job Satisfaction: Is There a Trend?*, U.S. Department of Labor, Manpower Administration, Manpower Research Monograph No. 30, 1974, pp. 23–27.

George Strauss, Raymond Miles, and Charles Snow raise some interesting value questions by asking: What if increased participation (meaning job enrichment, general supervision, organic organization structures, use of OD techniques to introduce change, etc.) increases satisfaction but reduces performance? To what extent will employees be willing to trade pay for participation? To what extent does society want its work organizations to contribute toward human growth?[18]

[18]George Strauss, Raymond E. Miles, and Charles E. Snow (eds.), "Implications for Industrial Relations," *Organizational Behavior: Research and Issues,* University of Wisconsin, Industrial Relations Research Association, Madison, 1974, p. 217.

Factors Affecting Employee Motivation

Section I considered productivity as a primary goal of organizations and discussed the technical and human factors contributing to productivity.

Section II dealt with the goals of people in organizations, their needs, and the various paths along which they can search for job satisfaction.

Section III pointed out that in today's society, productivity for the organization and job satisfaction for employees are both essential goals.

Section IV now returns to the productivity diagram to discuss major factors affecting employee Motivation (7). The reader will recall that Section I considered motivation as resulting from the interactions of employees' needs with the physical and social conditions of the job. If an organization goal of increased productivity is to be attained, either physical improvements (Technological Development, Raw Materials, Job Layout, Methods) must be made (2) and/or Employees' Job Performance (3) must be improved. Assuming that employees possess the necessary level of ability, they must have the Motivation (7) to improve their performance.

Chapter 11

Physical Working Conditions Relatively Unimportant in Motivation

Industrial psychologists and human engineers have often stressed the importance of Physical Conditions on the job (11) to employee performance. Noise, lighting, music, rest periods, ventilation, temperature, humidity—all these and others have been seen as factors which could improve or impair employees' performance.[1] The Hawthorne plant studies originally focused on this area but were unable to demonstrate any relation between physical conditions and output; the studies were redirected toward the areas of social conditions, group attitudes, and individual reactions. George Homans in his article on "The Western Electric Researches," page 199, describes in some detail the Hawthorne studies, the continuous increase in productivity irrespective of changing physical conditions of work, and the switch in direction by the researchers from physical conditions to attitudes of groups and individuals.

The subjective feelings of the employees and the way they view the physical changes, rather than the changes themselves, seem to influence motivation. Working conditions can, of course, affect the employees' comfort at work, but

[1]Refer to Elton Mayo, "The First Inquiry," chap. 3 of *The Social Problems of an Industrial Civilization,* Harvard University Press, Cambridge, Mass., 1945, for an example of an increase in productivity when rest periods were introduced for people working a fifty-hour week in a textile mill.

many are the examples of employees working under bad working conditions who have a high level of morale and, likewise, of employees working under the best physical working conditions who have low morale.[2]

This does not mean that management should ignore physical working conditions and make no effort to have them pleasant and comfortable. It does mean that if employees recognize that a job is unavoidably dirty or messy or hot and that management has done all it can to improve conditions, the poor conditions will not necessarily cause low morale of the employees. There may be some who will resign and seek jobs with more pleasant conditions. But others will stay and be satisfied in the knowledge that management has done what it can to ameliorate the poor conditions.

Safety conditions do, usually, have a direct impact on employees' attitudes and feelings. The needs that all of us have for safety and security can hardly be met in an unnecessarily hazardous plant or office. The Federal Occupational Safety and Health Act passed in 1971 has once again focused considerable public attention on the matter of safety.[3]

In most working places today the physical conditions are good: temperature and ventilation are adequate; rest periods and coffee breaks are provided; lighting is good, etc. Thus, the presence of good physical working conditions in most plants and offices today is taken for granted and has little, if any, motivating force.[4]

---

[2]See, for example, J. A. C. Brown, *The Social Psychology of Industry,* Penguin Books, Inc., Baltimore, 1954, pp. 192–194.

[3]See John J. Sheehan, "Safety Legislation—OSHA," in *Proceedings of the 26th Annual Winter Meeting, Industrial Relations Research Association,* University of Wisconsin, Madison, 1974, p. 57.

[4]For reports of studies of fatigue, monotony, rest pauses, shift work, noise reduction, illumination, and music and their effects on human functioning and proficiency, see E. Fleishman, *Studies in Personnel and Industrial Psychology,* The Dorsey Press, Homewood, Ill., 1967, sec. 7, "Fatigue, Monotony, and Working Conditions," and sec. 9, "Engineering Psychology."

Chapter 12

Social Conditions
of the Job:
Formal Organization

Since the Hawthorne experiments in the 1930s most research on employee motivation has concentrated on the area of social conditions in an organization and on their interactions with the needs of the employees. We have seen that Physical Conditions (11), while they can affect motivation and productivity, are usually of much less importance than Social Conditions. Although changes in an employee's performance can result from modification in Ability (4) or from forces outside the firm (10, 19), most changes probably can be attributed to alteration in social conditions and their effect upon need satisfactions. In this book, the major factors which establish the Social Conditions in an organization are considered to be Formal Organization (13), Informal Organization or Groups (20), Leaders or supervisors (24), and the Union (33).

The formal organization of a firm vitally influences the social conditions of the job, which in turn play an important part in motivating employees toward either improved or impaired job performance. What is meant by formal organization? "Formal organization is that existing on paper (the logical relationships prescribed by the rules and policy of the company). . . ."[1]

[1]J. A. C. Brown, *The Social Psychology of Industry,* Penguin Books, Inc., Baltimore, 1954, p. 94.

Some of the classical assumptions of organization theory are that each position on the organization chart is occupied by a person who has a known and unchanging task, that formal authority is the central indispensable means of managerial control, that an individual should have only one boss (unity of command), that tasks should be broken down into specialized units, that there should be a division between line and staff functions, that the span of control (number of individuals supervised by one person) should be fairly small, and that responsibility and authority are equated.[2] Classical organization theory views an organization member as a direct instrument to perform assigned tasks and as a "given" rather than a variable.[3]

How does formal organization affect the social conditions of the job?

> It follows that the overall structure of a firm, its organization, influences the behavior of the individuals and groups contained in it. Just as the individual's acts can only be understood in relation to the group in which he is functioning, so the behavior of a group can only be understood in the context of the larger group to which it belongs.[4]

> Management determines where men will work and what opportunities they will have to contact each other during the day. It also determines rates of pay, conditions of work, and the various symbols that are associated with each job. Given these basic elements, a sophisticated observer can predict the social relations that will exist within the organization long before the first employee enters the building.[5]

Recently organization theory has been defined to include the study of factors contributing to the effectiveness of the organization *and* of the individuals within the organization or group in terms of *both* productivity and satisfactions.

Robert Blake and Jane Mouton in constructing their managerial grid (Figure 1) point out the need for simultaneous concern for production and people by calling for 9,9 style of management: the manager who seeks high output through the medium of committed people, and commitment achieved through mutual trust, respect, and a realization of interdependence.[6] Rensis Likert makes a somewhat similar analysis in describing four different styles management may employ which will affect the production level of their departments.[7]

---

[2]Taken mostly from Douglas McGregor, *The Human Side of Enterprise,* McGraw-Hill Book Company, New York, 1960, pp. 15ff. See also chap. 2, "Classical Organization Theory," in J. G. March and H. A. Simon, *Organizations,* John Wiley & Sons, Inc., New York, 1958.

[3]March and Simon, ibid., p. 29.

[4]Brown, op. cit., p. 123. Quoted by permission.

[5]George Strauss and Leonard Sayles, *Personnel: The Human Problems of Management,* Prentice-Hall, Inc., Englewood Cliffs, N.J., © 1960, p. 61. Quoted by permission of the publisher.

[6]Robert R. Blake and Jane S. Mouton, *The Managerial Grid,* Gulf Publishing Company, Houston, 1964, p. 10.

For a study of line workers in an electronics plant showing that higher-level needs such as achievement, autonomy, and recognition could be satisfied even though the jobs were highly structured, see William P. Sexton, "Organizational and Individual Needs: A Conflict," *Personnel Journal,* vol. 46, no. 6, June 1967, pp. 337–343.

[7]"A Look at Management Systems," *The Human Organization,* McGraw-Hill Book Company, New York, 1967, p. 3.

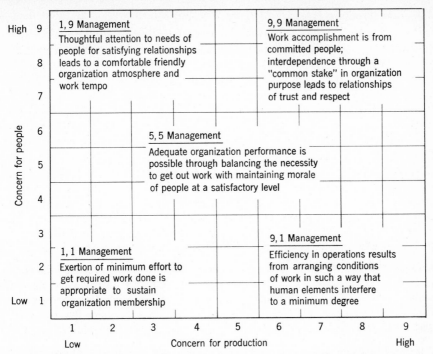

Figure 1 The Managerial Grid. (*Reprinted by permission of the publisher from Robert R. Blake and Jane S. Mouton,* The Managerial Grid, *Gulf Publishing Company, Houston, 1964, p. 10.*)

Chris Argyris in "A Basic Incongruency between the Needs of a Mature Personality and the Requirements of Formal Organization," page 207, points out the conflict between the goals of the formal organization (to make employees dependent, subordinate, and submissive) and the satisfaction of the individual's needs (particularly his egoistic needs for independence and self-esteem). Later in the same book he gives attention[8] to the ways in which management can decrease the degree of incongruency between the individual and the formal organization.

Douglas McGregor in his first selection, page 215, discusses "Theory X: The Traditional View of Direction and Control" and the assumptions it makes about motivation; in his second selection, page 222, he discusses "Theory Y: The Integration of Individual and Organization Goals."[9]

Some of the major factors affecting the Formal Organization are Organization Structure (14), Leadership Climate (15), Organization Efficiency (16), Personnel Policies (17), and Communication (18).

[8]Chris Argyris, *Personality and Organization,* Harper & Row, Publishers, Incorporated, New York, 1957, p. 237.

[9]For an excellent analysis of the ideas of Argyris and McGregor, as well as those of Robert N. McMurry, see Warren G. Bennis, "Revisionist Theory of Leadership," *Harvard Business Review,* vol. 39, no. 1, January–February 1961, p. 27.

Organization Structure (14)

Some writers have questioned the classical organization assumption about span of control that a supervisor should have relatively few subordinates. Organizations which follow this practice tend to have a "tall" organization structure, or many layers between president and employees, which allows for rather close supervision (Figure 2).

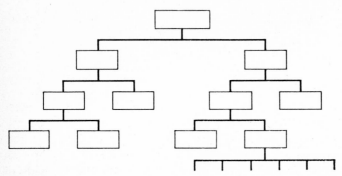

Figure 2

The question raised is whether a flat, decentralized organization structure (few layers between president and employees—see Figure 3) might not be preferable because it would give the subordinates more freedom to do the job in their own way, allow them to use more of their own initiative, permit them to become more self-reliant, and in general allow them to satisfy their egoistic needs. James Worthy has written of the advantages of the flat structure.[10] Lyman Porter and Edward Lawler agree that the flat structure has advantages but are less enthusiastic than Worthy regarding it.[11] A study by Edwin Ghiselli and Douglas Johnson partly supports Worthy's position in finding that satisfaction of

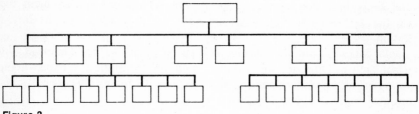

Figure 3

[10]James C. Worthy, "Organization Structure and Employee Morale," *American Sociological Review,* April 1950, pp. 169–179.

[11]Lyman W. Porter and Edward E. Lawler III, "The Effects of Tall vs. Flat Organization Structure on Managerial Job Satisfaction," *Personnel Psychology,* vol. 17, no. 2, Summer 1964, pp. 135–148.

needs for autonomy and self-actualization are more highly related to managerial success in flat organizations than in tall.[12]

In the article "People, Productivity, and Organizational Structure," page 230 of this volume, Joel Ross and Robert Murdick deal with the following types of organization structure and the extent of their use today:

Classical
Behavioral
Organic (temporary task forces)
Team (including project management, matrix management, and venture teams)
Contingency model

Leadership Climate (15)

The "tone" or the "climate" established for the organization by the president and top officials affects both the organization and the perception of the organization by informal groups, leaders, unions, and individual employees. The best policies may contribute to poor social conditions on the job if they are not administered fairly. The best training of leaders in democratic methods of supervision may go for naught if the climate of the organization is authoritarian. "Attempts to change attitudes at one level without modifying the attitudes held by those at higher levels may cause serious confusion within the management hierarchy."[13]

Edwin Fleishman's "Leadership and Supervision in Industry," on page 338 of this volume, points out that, to a considerable extent, specific training of foremen in human relations is wasted unless the environment in the plant, including leadership climate, is also strong in human relations and that the kind of supervisor a foreman has and the behavior of that supervisor influence the foreman's attitudes and behavior on the job more than the leadership training the foreman has received.

The degree of "participation" in any company depends upon the attitudes of top management or upon the leadership climate and whether "participation" is looked upon with favor or discouraged.

McGregor's two articles mentioned on page 59 spell out in detail two contrasting kinds of attitudes or climate that management might have: Theory X and Theory Y.

A study by George Litwin and Robert Stringer, "Motivation and Organizational Climate," page 238 of this book, discusses the measurement and control of

---

[12]Edwin E. Ghiselli and Douglas A. Johnson, "Need Satisfaction: Managerial Success and Organizational Structure," *Personnel Psychology*, vol. 23, 1970, pp. 569–576.

[13]Raymond E. Miles, "Attitudes toward Management Theory as a Factor in Managers' Relationships with Their Superiors," *Journal of the Academy of Management*, vol. 7, no. 4, December 1964, p. 313. See also A. J. M. Sykes, "The Effects of a Supervisory Training Course in Changing Supervisors' Perceptions and Expectations of the Role of Management," *Human Relations*, vol. 15, no. 3, August 1962, pp. 227–243.

human motives, organizational tasks, and climate and ways of changing an organization climate through changes in spatial arrangement, in job and goal specifications, in communication patterns, and/or in leadership styles.

Organization Efficiency (16)

If an organization is perceived by the supervisors and employees to be inefficiently run, it would be extremely difficult to motivate them to improve their job performance. One of the conclusions of Rice, in his study of an Indian textile plant, was that "irrespective of wages and working conditions, a work group will derive satisfaction from the efficient organization and performance of the task for which it has been organized, and an inefficient organization or performance will diminish the chances of satisfaction."[14]

Personnel Policies (17)

Work Schedules   As indicated in Chapter 9 of this book, employees will increasingly seek temporary or part-time jobs, or four-day-week jobs, or jobs with flexible hours, if they are to achieve job satisfaction and life satisfaction. One writer predicts that many firms will soon have 75 percent of their work force on a full-time permanent basis, 15 percent on a temporary basis, and 10 percent on a part-time basis.[15] Recently there have been numerous books and articles dealing with the advantages and problems of nonstandard scheduling.[16]

Job Design   The way jobs are designed can have a great impact on the motivation of those who perform them. Employees have often increased their job satisfaction through *job rotation:* instead of one person performing the same job all day long, he or she rotates with other employees on different jobs at approximately the same skill level. *Job enlargement* means giving the employee additional duties requiring the same skill level. *Job enrichment* means giving the employee some duties that require a higher level of skill and

[14]A. K. Rice, "Productivity and Social Organization in an Indian Weaving Shed," *Human Relations,* vol. 6, no. 4, 1953.
    Another author concludes that the workers' perception of the efficiency of management is closely associated with absenteeism. E. W. Holland in "Worker Attitudes and Industrial Absenteeism: A Statistical Appraisal," *American Sociological Review,* vol. 10, no. 4, August 1945, pp. 503–510, listed eight attitudinal areas ranked according to the closeness of their association with absenteeism. The second most important of these eight was the Workers' Opinion of the Efficiency of Management.
    [15]Elmer L. Winter, "Your Work Force: 1976 Style," *S.A.M. Advanced Management Journal,* vol. 37, no. 1, January 1972, p. 17.
    [16]Some examples are Kenneth E. Wheeler, et al., *The Four Day Week,* American Management Association Research Report, New York, 1972; Harvey Bolton, *Flexible Working Hours,* Anbar Publishers, London, 1971; "Will the Four-Day Forty-Hour Work Week Work?", *Personnel Administrator,* May–June 1973, pp. 27–29; "Temporary Duty," *Wall Street Journal,* Mar. 3, 1973, p. 1; "Scrapping the 9 to 5 Routine: What Some Firms Have Found," *U.S. News and World Report,* Aug. 20, 1973, pp. 64–66; Riva Poor, *4 Days 40 Hours,* New American Library, Inc., New York, 1973; "Flexible Working Hours," *Harvard Business Review,* January–February 1974, p. 18.

responsibility in order to make the job more interesting and challenging.[17] Job enrichment often involves more participation by the employee in decision making, and responsibility for planning and inspecting as well as doing.)

Numerous authors have proposed redesigning jobs to enrich their content and make them more satisfying to the holders.[18] *Work in America*[19] holds that work is central to the lives of most adults but that many workers are dissatisfied with the quality of work life. Work hasn't changed to match changes in attitudes, aspirations, and values. Therefore productivity, measured in terms of absenteeism, turnover, strikes, sabotage, and quality, is low. The authors state that job redesign is the keystone of their report: that workers need to have a voice in making decisions and also participate in the increased profits which may result from higher productivity. The appendix of *Work in America* contains a long listing of case studies in humanization of work, which includes many examples of job redesign in this country and abroad. Many other examples have received wide publicity.[20]

The labor disturbances in 1972 at the Lordstown plant of General Motors, where the Vega automobile was being manufactured, dramatized the dissatisfaction of automobile assembly line workers there, many of them with at least some college education.

In contrast to the American assembly line, some Swedish automobile firms, namely Volvo and Saab, are attempting to maintain productivity and increase employee satisfaction by breaking down the traditional automobile assembly line and arranging for at least part of their workers to operate in small groups and make some of the decisions as to how the work is to be done, who is to do what, etc. A report of this approach appears on page 251, "Job Redesign on the Assembly Line," by Louis Davis.

A report of this approach appears on page 251, "Job Redesign on the Assembly Line," by Louis Davis.

---

[17]Job enrichment is defined more broadly in Peter P. Schoderbeck and William E. Reif, *Job Enlargement: Key to Improved Performance,* University of Michigan, Graduate School of Business Administration, Ann Arbor, 1969.

[18]Some are Harold Rush, *Job Design for Motivation,* The Conference Board, New York, 1971; William J. Roche and Neil L. MacKinnon, "Motivating People with Meaningful Work," *Harvard Business Review,* May–June 1970, pp. 97–110; John J. Morse, "A Contingency Look at Job Design," *California Management Review,* Fall 1973, pp. 67–75; Robert Janson, "Job Enrichment: Challenge of the 70's," *Training and Development Journal,* vol. 24, no. 6, June 1970, pp. 7–9; Lyle Yorks, "Key Elements in Implementing Job Enrichment," *Personnel,* September–October 1973, pp. 45–52; Alan D. Greenblatt, "Maximizing Productivity through Job Enrichment," *Personnel,* March–April 1973, pp. 31–39; Fred Luthans and William E. Reif, "Job Enrichment: Long on Theory, Short on Practice," *Organizational Dynamics,* vol. 2, no. 3, Winter 1974, p. 30.

[19]*Work in America: Report of a Special Task Force to the Secretary of Health, Education, and Welfare,* prepared under the auspices of the W. E. Upjohn Institute for Employment Research, The M.I.T. Press, Cambridge, Mass., 1973.

[20]"The Drive to Make Dull Jobs Interesting," *U.S. News and World Report,* July 17, 1972, p. 50; "Wanted: Ways to Make the Job Less Dull," *Business Week,* May 12, 1973, p. 147; "GM Zeroes in on Employee Discontent," *Business Week,* May 12, 1973, p. 140; "Boredom Fighters Put Variety in Many Jobs, Find Productivity Rises," *Wall Street Journal* Aug. 21, 1972, p. 1; "Gene Cafiero Labors to Enhance the Quality of Assembly-Line Life," *Wall Street Journal,* Dec. 7, 1972, p. 1; "The Worth of Humanistic Management," *Business Horizons,* June 1973, pp. 41–50.

The author agrees with Harold Wool that the HEW report on *Work in America* overgeneralizes regarding the potential of work redesign.[21] As pointed out in Chapter 9 of this book, much depends upon the individual workers and what they are seeking in their jobs—their paths to life satisfaction. William Reif and Fred Luthans in "Does Job Enrichment Really Pay Off?", page 267, critically analyze job enrichment, indicating some advantages and some "neglected" points that need emphasis.

William W. Winpisinger of the Machinists Union, in "Job Enrichment: Another Part of the Forest," page 278, expresses the view that "if you want to enrich the job, one of the most important steps is to enrich the pay check."

Nat Goldfinger scoffs at the academics' argument that management responsibilities might relieve worker boredom: "All this talk of worker alienation is pop sociology, an upper-middle-class, college campus vogue."[22]

Furthermore, Sar A. Levitan and William B. Johnston, Center for Manpower Policy Studies, George Washington University, in *Work Is Here to Stay, Alas,* agree with Winpisinger that the most important factor in job satisfaction is not working conditions but take-home pay and that job redesign has little new to offer.[23]

The job design, or job redesign, can contribute to motivation and productivity under certain circumstances but is by no means a panacea. We must not lose sight of the numerous other factors in the productivity diagram which can also influence motivation and productivity, for better or worse.

Recruitment, Selection, and Placement   With the present laws and rulings outlawing discrimination on the basis of race, creed, color, national origin, age, sex, marital status, dress, education, invalid tests, arrest record, or mental or physical handicap—as long as the applicant is capable of doing the required job—one author has suggested that the day may come when an employer is required to hire anyone deemed trainable for the open position.[24] The National Alliance of Businessmen with its JOBS program (Job Opportunities Business Sector) has applied this approach successfully with disadvantaged workers.

Organizations are under increasing pressure from the Equal Employment Opportunity Commission, the Department of Health, Education, and Welfare, the Justice Department, the Office of Federal Contract Compliance, Federal Civil Service Commission, and other federal, state and local agencies to prepare and adhere to affirmative action plans for employing and promoting members of minority groups, including women. Under Title VII of the Civil Rights Act of 1964 and its 1972 amendments, an increasing number of firms are receiving large fines for violations of nondiscrimination laws. It behooves every organization, therefore, to actively seek out members of minority groups rather than to sit back

[21]"What's Wrong with Work in America?", *Monthly Labor Review*, March 1973, pp. 38–44. Reprinted on page 412 of this volume.

[22]*Wall Street Journal,* Nov. 15, 1973, p. 16.

[23]Olympus Publishing Company, Salt Lake City, 1973.

[24]Leon C. Megginson, *Personnel,* Richard D. Irwin, Inc., Homewood, Ill., 1972, p. 728.

and wait for these individuals to apply to the organization. At the same time, organizations must obtain people who either have the required abilities or can be trained in the skills required for the jobs they are to perform.

(Organizations will have to give more thought in the future to placing present and new employees on jobs where they can meet their needs for job satisfaction, whatever those needs may be.)

Introduction to Job   Most employees when they first report for work to a new company are highly motivated and want to do the best possible job.[25] Numerous factors work toward retention or destruction of this positive motivation and thus for or against improved job performance. John Kotter discusses the joining-up process in "The Psychological Contract: Managing the Joining-Up Process" on page 282 of this book.

Standards   It must be clear to the employees what is expected of them on the job—what standards of performance they are expected to meet. Increasingly, such standards are being set by the employees themselves with the approval of the supervisor. More and more firms are embarking on a mangement-by-objectives program, wherein the employees are encouraged to set down their ideas of major objectives to be accomplished in the forthcoming period, usually a year, and how those objectives will be measured. These are then discussed with and approved by the supervisor. At the end of the period they and the supervisor again sit down and review whether or not the objectives have been attained and, if not, why not. This procedure enables the supervisor to play a role of "coach" to help the subordinates and to remove obstacles in their way, rather than the role of a "judge" who "evaluates" how well the employees have performed.

Training   (If an organization hires employees who do not have adequate training for the job assigned to them, it must provide a training program. Many organizations today also provide training for promotion, preparing employees for higher responsibilities, and training for supervisors, managers, and executives.)

Wage and Salary Level   (Most organizations take care to see that their wages and salaries are at least comparable with those paid for similar jobs in the area. When there are soaring rates of inflation, organizations have to recognize that employee dissatisfaction can quickly occur if wages and salaries do not keep pace with the cost of living.)

Job Evaluation   (Many organizations make use of job evaluation to make sure that the pay range or salary range for each job reflects the relative difficulty and

---

[25]R. A. Sutermeister, "The First Day Makes the Difference," *Supervisory Management,* January 1959, pp. 2–10.

responsibility of that job in comparison with other jobs. If this is not done, it is easy for a feeling of inequity to exist among employees.[26]

Pay-Rewards-Incentives The degree to which money is a motivator for an individual will depend upon (1) whether compensation is important to the person, (2) whether additional compensation depends upon performance, and (3) whether the employee is sure that more effort will result in higher performance. These points are based on the expectancy theory of Victor Vroom and of Lyman Porter and Edward Lawler and are illustrated in O. Gene Dalaba, "Misuses of Compensation as a Motivator," on page 294 of this book.[27]

One should be careful about placing too much reliance on money alone as a way of increasing productivity. As stated by David McClelland:

> Money is one tool among many for managing motivation. It is a treacherous tool because it is deceptively concrete, tempting many managers to neglect variables in the work situation and climate that really affect productivity.[28]

The diagram on the first page of this book should remind the reader of the complexities of motivation and the large number of factors which have a bearing on motivation and productivity.

Incentive plans can cover individuals or groups or be plantwide or organizationwide. "It is clear that successful incentive programs are characterized by careful attention to a wide range of organizational variables."[29] Some of the most important of these are psychological variables such as the degree of participation of employees or unions in developing the plans, the degree of trust and confidence existing between the firm and its employees and/or union, and the perception that employees and unions have of the plans introduced.

Employee Performance Evaluation and Management by Objectives Most large organizations have a formal program by which a supervisor evaluates the work of subordinates and completes a "performance rating" or "performance evaluation" for each subordinate at regular intervals. The supervisor then typically calls in the subordinate and explains how the subordinate has been rated and why. Sometimes this procedure calls for a discussion between supervisor and subordinate, giving the subordinate an opportunity to "react" to the rating received and perhaps clear up some misconceptions on the part of the supervisor or some misconceptions the subordinate may have had of his or her duties and responsibilities.

[26]Extensive studies of inequity have been made by Stacy Adams. See "Wage Inequities, Productivity and Work Quality," *Industrial Relations*, October 1963, pp. 9–16.

[27]See also Robert L. Opsahl and Marvin D. Dunnette, "The Role of Financial Compensation in Industrial Motivation," *Psychological Bulletin*, vol. 66, no. 2, 1966, pp. 94–118.

[28]David C. McClelland, "Money as a Motivator: Some Research Insights," *The McKinsey Quarterly*, Fall 1967, pp. 10–21.

[29]Wendell L. French, "Incentive Systems," *The Personnel Management Process*, 3d ed., Houghton Mifflin Company, Boston, 1974, p. 549.

The trend today is toward the use of the management-by-objectives approach,[30] especially for subordinates at higher levels in the organization, those with some higher-level needs activated, and those who have some degree of latitude over their own jobs. (See the discussion above under "Standards.")

Promotions Promotions have a significant impact on motivation. (See Chapter 9, page 38.)

Organization Development Much attention has been devoted in recent years to a total system effort to develop an organization's internal resources for planned change. Laboratory training or sensitivity training usually plays a part in such development. Wendell French in "Organization Development Objectives, Assumptions, and Strategies," page 300, describes this in detail.[31]

In conclusion, good employee policies embracing the areas above help set up a framework of social conditions within which employees are most likely to be able to satisfy whatever needs have been activated for them and to follow the paths of their choosing to job satisfaction and life satisfaction.

Communication (18)

The importance of communication in affecting employees' attitudes and motivating them to improved job performance has been well recognized; almost every text on personnel management or human relations has a chapter on this subject.

The purpose of communication is to achieve mutual understanding in the minds of the sender and receiver of the message. Within an organization such understanding helps to establish the social conditions which will motivate the employees.[32]

Whether or not the purpose—mutual understanding—is achieved depends upon many factors including the following:

1 The relations among those communicating. In the absence of a warm, personal relationship and mutual trust and respect, giving more and better information is unlikely to improve communication.[33]

2 What is communicated.

3 The direction of the communication. It can be one-way from superior to subordinate; two-way, in which the subordinate listens to the superior and the

---

[30]For a recent book on this subject, see Anthony P. Raia, *Managing by Objectives,* Scott, Foresman and Company, Glenview, Ill., 1974.

[31]Addison-Wesley has a series of books dealing with organizational development. For the experience of one change agent who worked with an organization to increase productivity, see Alton C. Bartlett, "Changing Behavior as a Means to Increased Efficiency," *Journal of Applied Behavioral Science,* vol. 3, no. 3, 1967, pp. 381–411.

[32]An interesting model of the communication process, showing some of the complexities involved, has been prepared by E. Bormann et al., *Interpersonal Communication in the Modern Organization,* Prentice-Hall, Inc., Englewood Cliffs, N.J., 1969.

[33]See T. M. Higham, "Basic Psychological Factors in Communication," *Occupational Psychology,* vol. 31, 1957, p. 1–10.

superior in turn listens to the subordinate to make sure mutual understanding has been achieved; or several-way, in which there may be group discussion and participation.

4 The network of communication used. The network affects the accuracy and speed of the communication as well as the morale of those communicating.[34]

5 The obstructions in the communication lines, such as unwillingness to listen and refusal to believe.[35]

Nonverbal communication can also have an effect on mutual understanding. According to George W. Porter, nonverbal communication can be divided into the following four main categories:[36]

> Physical: including such things as facial expressions, touch, smell, body motions, etc.
> Esthetic: including such areas as music, painting, sculpture, dancing, etc.
> Symbolic: including those involved in religion and maintaining status
> Signs: including both mechanical and physical

Special Environment of the Company or Plant (19)

The Organization Structure (14), Leadership Climate (15), Efficiency (16), Personnel Policies (17), and Communication (18) are, of course, all subject to change with changing times and changing environmental conditions, whether physical, economic, political, or cultural. Some of the changing conditions, the changes in values in society, organizations, and individuals, were touched on in Chapter 6. The importance of the economic environment of an organization has been treated thoroughly by Abraham J. Siegel.[37]

[34]Networks of communcations are discussed in Alex Bavelas and Dermot Barrett, "An Experimental Approach to Organizational Communication," *Personnel,* vol. 27, no. 5, March 1951, pp. 366–371.

[35]These as well as content and feedback are discussed in Harold Leavitt, "Communication: Getting Information from A into B," *Managerial Psychology,* The University of Chicago Press, Chicago, 1958, pp. 118–128.

[36]"Nonverbal Communications," *Training and Development Journal,* June 1969, pp. 3–8. Copyright 1969 by the American Society for Training and Development, Inc. Reproduced by special permission.

[37]"The Economic Environment in Human Relations Research" in C. M. Arensberg et al., *Research in Industrial Human Relations,* Harper & Row, Publishers, Incorporated, New York, 1957, chap. 6, pp. 86–99. Also see Raymond C. Miles et al., "Organization Environment: Concepts and Issues," *Industrial Relations,* October 1974, p. 244.

Chapter 13

Social Conditions
of the Job:
Informal Organization

Just as the Formal Organization (13) vitally influences the social conditions of the job, so does the Informal Organization (20) or the informal groups of workers. Work is a social experience, and most workers can fulfill their social needs through membership in a small work group. The Informal Organization has its effect on the Formal Organization, on the Leader or supervisor, and on the individual employees constituting the group, and, in turn, the Informal Organization is influenced by all of these.

An individual employee can belong to several informal groups.[1] One is a group which has a common supervisor; another is a group engaged in a common task or function; another is a friendship clique, composed of employees who have a liking for each other;[2] another is an interest group of employees who

---

[1] The following two paragraphs are taken from Leonard R. Sayles, "Work Group Behavior and the Larger Organization," in C. M. Arensberg et al., *Research in Industrial Human Relations,* Harper & Row, Publishers, Incorporated, New York, 1957, pp. 132, 144–145. Quoted by permission of the publisher.

[2] This type of group cohesiveness can be promoted by the use of sociometry, finding out workers' likes and dislikes toward other workers and placing them in cogenial work groups. Other types of group cohesiveness may have little to do with friendship or likes and dislikes (see Harold L. Wilensky, "Human Relations in the Workplace: An Appraisal of Some Recent Research," in Arensberg, ibid., p. 48).

"share a common economic interest and seek to gain some objective relating to the larger organization."

> Clusterings of workers-on-the-job all have these characteristics: they stem from the uniqueness of individual personality, which refuses to combine into larger "wholes" without changing those entities. The sum of a group of individuals is something more than the total of the constituents; it is a new organization, because most of the members (there are significant exceptions as we have noted) obtain satisfaction in gaining acceptance as a part of the group, and the group itself wields an influence over its members. . . .
>
> This observance of group-sanctioned behavior and attitudes "fills out" the rationally conceived organization. What is on paper an organization becomes a "living, breathing" social organism, with all the intricacies, emotions, and contradictions we associate with human relations. While no organization would long persist which did not provide its members with this opportunity for spontaneous "human relations," a major problem of the larger organization becomes one of successfully incorporating the small group.

J. A. C. Brown stresses the informal working group as the main source of social control in an organization.[3]

Three aspects of informal work groups will be considered briefly: Size (21), Cohesiveness (22), and Goals (23).

Size of the Work Group (21)

> It is an ancient sociological generalization . . . that size of immediate work group is negatively correlated with productivity, or job satisfaction, or regular attendance, or industrial peace—other factors being equal. This is due in part to the greater likelihood that primary relations (relations that are intimate, personal, inclusive, and experienced as spontaneous) are more likely to develop in small groups than in large groups. It is due in part also to the fact that the worker in the smaller group is likely to have more knowledge of the relations between effort and earnings, and this seems to increase his incentive to work.[4]

Although the small work group may have greater potential for improved employee performance and increased productivity, whether or not the potential is realized depends in large measure on the Cohesiveness and the Goals of the group.

---

[3]J. A. C. Brown, "The Informal Organization of Industry," *The Social Psychology of Industry,* Penguin Books, Inc., Baltimore, 1954. For a point of view that "informal groups are not common among workers," especially at the lower organizational ranks, see Amitai Etzioni, *Modern Organizations,* Prentice-Hall, Inc., Englewood Cliffs, N.J., 1965, pp. 46–47. For a good discussion of "Group and Intergroup Relations," see Edgar H. Schein, *Organizational Psychology,* Prentice-Hall, Inc., Englewood Cliffs, N.J., 1970.

[4]Wilensky, op. cit., p. 28. Quoted by permission of Harper & Row, Publishers, Incorporated, New York.

Cohesiveness of the Work Group (22)

A cohesive work group is one whose members will stick closely to group norms, whatever they are.[5] A cohesive group is likely to exhibit greater teamwork, gain greater social satisfaction from working together, and have higher morale and less turnover and absenteeism than a group which lacks cohesion.[6] A cohesive work group has great potential, then, for motivating employees to better performance or to poorer performance, depending upon the group's Goals (23). Stanley Seashore has discussed the relations between productivity, degree of cohesiveness, and employees' confidence in management and points out that there is less variation in productivity within high-cohesive groups than within low-cohesive groups and that high-cohesive groups differ (up or down) from the plant norm of productivity more frequently and in greater degree than low-cohesive groups do.[7]

That the cohesive work group can exert tremendous pressure on individuals in the group to conform to the group norms is effectively demonstrated by Solomon Asch.[8]

The cohesive group can ostracize individuals who refuse to conform to group norms. It can reward those who do with acceptance, friendship, and approval.

The good and bad effects of groups on individual members are discussed by Dorwin Cartwright and Ronald Lippitt in "Group Dynamics and the Individual," page 319.

The Hawthorne studies showed that "the values and the customs of the group were more important to the individuals composing it than any cash benefits."[9]

In another study, A. Zaleznik, C. R. Christensen, and F. Roethlisberger concluded that group membership or reward by the group was a major determinant of worker productivity and satisfaction, while reward by management had no noticeable motivation effect.[10]

Raymond Van Zelst writes of a cohesive work group which motivated its members to better performance because the work teams were sociometrically selected. Production increased 5 percent among workers on a housing construc-

[5]George Strauss and Leonard Sayles, *Personnel: The Human Problems of Management*, Prentice-Hall, Inc., Englewood Cliffs, N.Y., 1960, p. 177.

[6]Loc. cit.

[7]Stanley E. Seashore, *Group Cohesiveness in the Industrial Work Group*, The University of Michigan Press, Ann Arbor, 1954, pp. 97–102.

[8]Solomon E. Asch, "Opinions and Social Pressure," *Scientific American*, November 1955, pp. 31–35.

[9]J. A. C. Brown, *The Social Psychology of Industry*, Penguin Books, Inc., Baltimore, 1954, p. 81.

[10]A. Zaleznik, C. R. Christensen, and F. Roethlisberger, *Motivation, Productivity, and Satisfaction of Workers*, Harvard Business School, Division of Research, Boston, 1958, p. 352.

tion project when they had an opportunity to indicate their preferences for co-workers, and work teams were set up on that basis.[11]

It must be remembered, however, that even if a group is highly cohesive, there may be some member(s) who does not accept the group goal because he has a different reference group or aspiration level, or a different cultural background, or for some other reason. For example, a "rate buster" may take pride in *not* being part of the work group.

Goals of the Work Group (23)

The potential in a small, cohesive work group can be used to support management's goals or to sabotage them.

> A work group may be cohesive in maintaining low production standards, resisting change, hostility toward supervision and/or other groups, denying membership to newcomers, and demanding strict conformity of its membership. On the other hand, a cohesive work group may have high work standards, accept technological change, be friendly to other groups, cooperate with supervision, and have minimum unwritten codes on conformity for membership.[12]

The Goals of the work group will be influenced by the reaction of the members to their Leader or supervisor (24) and to the whole Formal Organization (13). The goals can be strongly influenced by the Union (33).[13] In fact, almost all the segments indicated on the diagram will have an influence on the goals which an informal group will adopt for its members. For example, there can be overwhelming pressure from outside the group itself toward conformity: threat of unemployment, recognized danger to survival (war, pending bankruptcy of the firm), etc.[14]

Where there exist informal organizations or groups with effective control over their members, the problem for management is clear. If it wishes to change human behavior, its attack must be made through the group.[15] As Seashore indicates in the work already cited,

> To assure a positive benefit to the organization from group cohesiveness the administrator might well take steps first to provide the basic conditions of equity and supportiveness which warrant employee confidence in management.

---

[11]Raymond H. Van Zelst, "Sociometrically Selected Work Teams Increase Production," *Personnel Psychology,* vol. 5, no. 3, Autumn 1952, pp. 175–185.

[12]William H. Knowles, "Human Relations in Industry: Research and Concepts," *California Management Review,* vol. 1, no. 1, Fall 1958, p. 92. Quoted by permission.

[13]Groups may purposely restrict output and reduce their goals as a union tool for bargaining with the employer. See Mason Haire, "Psychology and the Study of Business: Joint Behavioral Sciences," in Robert Dahl et al., *Social Science Research on Business: Product and Potential,* Columbia University Press, New York, 1959, p. 76.

[14]Wilensky, op. cit., p. 35.

[15]Brown, op. cit., p. 126.

Thus, it is not enough for management to establish conditions (of Formal Organization, Leadership, relations with Union) in which employees can fulfill their physiological, social, and egoistic needs. Management must attempt to get the individual and the informal groups to work toward the organization's goal, or toward the target of increased productivity. Perhaps "the essential task of management is to arrange organizational conditions and methods of operation so that people can achieve their own goals *best* by directing *their own* efforts toward organizational objectives."[16]

[16] Douglas McGregor, "Adventure in Thought and Action," *Proceedings of the Fifth Anniversary Convocation of the School of Industrial Management,* Massachusetts Institute of Technology, Cambridge, Mass., Apr. 9, 1957, pp. 23–30. Reprinted as "The Human Side of Enterprise" in Paul Pigors et al. (eds.), *Management of Human Resources,* McGraw-Hill Book Company, New York, 1973, p. 5.

Chapter 14

Social Conditions of the Job: Leaders

Leadership[1] has been defined as the process of influencing the activities of the organized group in its effort toward goal setting and goal achievement. The idea that there are certain character traits or attributes, such as integrity, ambition, drive, loyalty, and judgment, which make an individual a leader has been seriously questioned:

> Examination of this literature reveals an imposing number of supposedly essential characteristics of the successful leader—over a hundred, in fact, even after elimination of obvious duplication and overlap of terms. The search still continues in some quarters. Every few months a new list appears based on the latest analysis. And each new list differs in some respects from the earlier ones.
>
> However, social science research in this field since the 1930s has taken new directions. Some social scientists have become interested in studying the behavior as well as the personal characteristics of leaders. As a result, some quite different ideas about the nature of leadership have emerged.[2]

[1] I. L. Heckmann and S. G. Huneryager, *Human Relations in Management,* South-Western Publishing Company, Cincinnati, 1960, p. 54.

[2] Douglas McGregor, *The Human Side of Enterprise,* McGraw-Hill Book Company, New York, 1960, p. 180. Quoted by permission of McGraw-Hill Book Company.

The small group theorists have also markedly changed the interpretation of leadership. Particularly in the industrial setting, the traditional view of the leader in the past was of a charismatic individual possessing the trait of leadership. A great deal of research went, without much success, into attempts to identify these qualities of leadership in the interest of selection. . . . We now speak of the "emergent" leader, we distinguish between "headship" and "leadership," and we use "buddy ratings" to identify leaders. The pendulum has swung a long ways to one side, and the reverse trend is already discernible in the assessment field, in a return to the search for the qualities of leadership within the individual instead of the group. However, even as the pendulum swings back, it is more group-oriented, and the variables tend to deal with relations with others rather than decisiveness, forcefulness, and determination.[3]

Many now believe the leader's influence on the activities of the organized group depends upon the leader, the followers, and the particular situation. In terms of the diagram, a supervisor's influence with the group would operate within the limitations imposed by the Technology, the Formal Organization, the Informal Organization, the Union, and the Needs of the Individuals comprising the group.

It cannot be said that the "trait" approach to leadership has been completely abandoned. Mason Haire in the quotation cited mentions that the pendulum may be swinging back toward traits, but toward traits that are group-oriented. Alex Bavelas argues that

The broad similarities which hold for a great number of organizations make it possible to say useful things about the kind of person who is likely to become a leader in any of these organizations. On various tests, persons who are leaders tend to be brighter, to be better adjusted psychologically, and to display better judgment. They tend to give more information, and to take the lead in summing up or interpreting a situation.[4]

Recently B. F. Skinner's ideas on behavior modification (operant conditioning) have been receiving great attention. The basic idea is that supervisors or leaders can induce their subordinates to do what the supervisor wants them to do by positive reinforcement or reward for their successful efforts. Fred Luthans and David Lyman explore this method in "Training Supervisors to Use Organizational Behavior Modification," page 333 of this book.

Major factors which seem to affect the leader's impact on the Group and on the Social Conditions of the job are the leader's Relationship with Superior (25), Planning Skill and Technical Knowledge (26), and Type of Leadership (27).

---

[3]Mason Haire, "Psychology and the Study of Business," quoted by permission of Columbia University Press from R. A. Dahl, M. Haire, P. F. Lazarsfeld, *Social Science Research on Business: Product and Potential,* Columbia University Press, New York, 1959, p. 77.

[4]Alex Bavelas, "Leadership: Man and Function," *Administrative Science Quarterly,* vol. 4, no. 4, March 1960. The first sentence is quoted from p. 494. The others are condensed from sentences on p. 492.

Relationship with Superior (25)

If supervisors are to succeed in influencing the activities of the group, they must have a good relationship and carry some weight with their own superior. They may wish to assist employees in satisfying their needs, and they may wish to use democratic or participative methods of supervision, but if their recommendations to their superior on behalf of their subordinates are frequently or consistently turned down, they are likely to have little influence with their group. Donald Pelz studied supervisors at Detroit Edison Company and set forth the implications of his findings for administrators as follows:

> According to these findings, if an influential supervisor attempts to help employees achieve their goals, his efforts will tend to succeed. Concrete results will be achieved, and therefore employee satisfaction will rise. But—according to the data—if a noninfluential supervisor tries to get the same results, his efforts may often fail. Employee expectations will be frustrated, and consequently their satisfactions will not rise and may even fall.
>
> Such findings have several implications:
>
> 1 It may not be possible to give supervisors a universal set of rules on how to behave so as to maximize their employees' satisfaction. What each man should do or should not try to do will depend, among other things, on how much weight he carries within the organization. In general, the supervisor should probably not attempt to do more for his employees than he can reasonably hope to accomplish.
>
> 2 The same principle applies to the current emphasis on the training of first-line supervisors. If the supervisors lack the authority or the influence to put the training into practice, in a way that produces concrete changes, then perhaps we may question whether the training should be given at all. Training courses should urge the supervisors to introduce changes only in matters where he has considerable authority or where he has the real support of supervision at higher levels. Otherwise the result may only be frustration for himself and his group.
>
> 3 Even further, it may in some cases be necessary to *increase* the amount of influence given to first-level supervisors—by increasing their voice in higher decisions, by delegating more autonomy to them. These are substantial changes, not to be suggested lightly. But it may be that many training courses cannot improve the effectiveness of supervisory leadership unless management is willing to give a larger share of influence to this supervisory level.
>
> 4 At the same time, it becomes essential to examine the effects of giving supervisors a larger voice, as many writers on administration are advising. How is this increased power to be used? It is a potential source of threat to employees as well as a benefit. Perhaps it should not be undertaken unless steps are taken simultaneously to make sure the increased power is used in helpful ways rather than in restraining and hindering ways.
>
> 5 And, finally, from the long-range standpoint of the science of management, it becomes clearer that "group leadership" and "organization" are not distinct concepts but are inseparably intertwined. The organization "conditions" the effects of leadership, and probably the reverse is true. An organization cannot be understood simply by breaking it up into small groups and studying them in isolation. Nor

can we understand the way a leader relates to his group unless we also study how they both relate to the rest of the organization.[5]

Planning Skill and Technical Knowledge (26)

In a study of human relations in a railroad, it was concluded that supervisors of high-producing units more often assume management functions of supervising and planning and clearly differentiate their roles from the roles of the workers.[6] Supervisors who can plan their work well, who have good technical knowledge, and who can install better production methods can raise productivity without necessarily increasing group satisfaction.[7]

Supervisors require administrative competence, human relations competence, and technical competence; the particular mixture of these skills which will be most effective varies with the level in the organization as well as with the type of organization and the point in time. These ideas are illustrated in Figure 1.

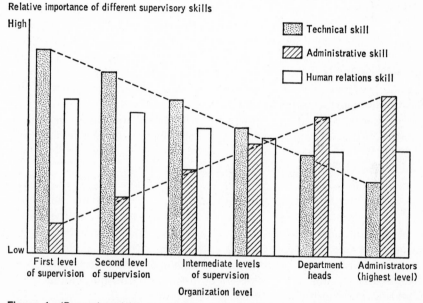

Figure 1 (*Reproduced by permission of the publisher from Basil S. Georgopoulos and Floyd C. Mann, "Supervisory and Administrative Behavior," The Community General Hospital, The Macmillan Company, New York, 1962, p. 431.*)

[5]Donald C. Pelz, "Influence: A Key to Effective Leadership in the First-Line Supervisor," *Personnel*, vol. 29, 1952, pp. 209–217. Reprinted by permission of the American Management Association.

[6]Daniel Katz et al., *Productivity, Supervision and Morale among Railroad Workers,* University of Michigan, Institute for Social Research, Survey Research Center, Ann Arbor, 1951, p. xi.

[7]Richard E. Andrews, *Leadership and Supervision,* U.S. Civil Service Commission, Personnel Management Series No. 9, 1955, p. 17.

Type of Leadership (27)

A leader may influence "the activities of an organized group in its efforts toward goal setting and goal achievement" by using an approach to subordinates which is Laissez Faire or free-rein (28), Autocratic (29), or Democratic (30), or by a Combination (32), using one approach at one time in one situation and other approaches at other times in other situations.

Laissez Faire or Free-Rein Leadership (28)

The laissez faire leader is likely to give the group information, provide materials, and let the individuals or the group make their own decisions with little control and few limitations by the leader. This type of leadership is little used because "the net result is frequently disorganization or chaos, principally because this type of leadership permits different individuals to proceed in different directions."[8] However, as Auren Uris has pointed out, under certain conditions (such as with a group of scientists in an experimental laboratory) it will produce more successful results than either of the other two kinds of leadership. Under the right conditions, laissez faire leadership could offer the greatest opportunities for subordinates to satisfy their egoistic needs.

Autocratic Leadership (29)

An autocratic leader is likely to determine the policy for the group, make the decisions, and assume full responsibility, asking the members only to be obedient in following orders. This leader is more likely to use close supervision (involving detailed instruction and frequent checking by the leader) and production-centered supervision (involving an emphasis on techniques and processes) rather than general supervision or employee-centered supervision.

Edwin Fleishman in his "Leadership and Supervision in Industry," page 338, reports on Ohio State University studies[9] which differentiate "initiating structure" from "consideration." "Initiating structure" means that the leader organizes and defines the relation between the leader and the members of the group, defines the role the leader expects each member to assume, and tries to establish well-defined patterns of organization, channels of communication, and ways of getting the job done. "Consideration" involves friendship, mutual trust, respect, and warmth between the leader and the group.

Autocratic leadership often involves close or restrictive supervision and production-oriented supervision. Does it also involve "initiating structure"? The Ohio research group found a low correlation between "consideration" and "initiating structure" and states that it is theoretically possible for a foreman to earn a high score in both.

---

[8]Heckmann and Huneryager, op. cit., p. 49.

[9]These studies are also discussed briefly by Floyd Mann in "Studying and Creating Change: A Means to Understanding Social Organization," *Research in Industrial Human Relations,* Harper & Row, Publishers, Incorporated, New York, 1957, chap. 10.

It would probably be difficult for an employee with a high level of egoistic needs to satisfy them under autocratic leadership.

Democratic Leadership (30)

A democratic leader is likely to encourage his or her followers to take part in setting goals and methods and to contribute ideas and suggestions. "General" supervision means that the leader tries primarily to maintain good human relations and a smoothly running organization. The leader does not give detailed instructions or check frequently on the followers but relies on their initiative and judgment; they have much freedom in planning their work.[10]

"Person-centered" or "employee-centered" supervision means that leaders indicate a personal interest in their followers and by their actions convey the impression that they are fair, will keep their promises, and take the individuals' needs into account.[11] Generally, high-producing groups are to be found under leaders who employ general supervision and who are employee-centered but who by no means overlook production.

Certainly the democratic type of leadership seems to offer subordinates the best opportunity to satisfy their egoistic needs.

Democratic leaders will carry out all aspects of the job in such a way as to indicate that they consider their subordinates important individual human beings, like themselves, with ideas of their own and an eagerness to put their brains as well as their brawn to work when given a chance. Thus, democratic leaders will exercise great care in the everyday activities discussed in the following paragraphs.

Introduction of new employee to the job: to make sure the employee feels at home, understands the function to be performed and its relation to the overall function of the department or firm, and knows the obligations and benefits of an employee.

Job instruction: to make sure the new employee thoroughly understands what the job is, what is expected of an employee, and that the employee is taught how to do the job in such a way that he grasps it fully and has confidence in his ability to perform it adequately.

Directions: so that the employee is motivated to the greatest extent to carry out the assignment. Sometimes the democratic supervisor may merely suggest that something ought to be done; at other times the supervisor may state a problem and request the employee to solve it; at all times the supervisor will be open to suggestions from the employee and encourage the employee who does not fully understand the assignment to ask questions.

Recognition or appreciation: to make sure the employee knows his or her good work has not gone unnoticed.

[10]Rensis Likert and Samuel Hayes, Jr., *Some Applications of Behavioral Research,* UNESCO, Basle, Switzerland, 1957, p. 63.
[11]Ibid., p. 57.

Correcting mistakes: to strive to see that the employee accepts the correction willingly and is motivated to do better in the future. This involves a democratic approach of stating what the difficulty seems to be, giving the employee an opportunity to tell his or her side of the story, and oftentimes asking for the employee's own suggestions for avoiding the trouble in the future. In this way, a mistake is considered a mutual problem which supervisor and employee, working together, can discuss and solve.

Hearing suggestions: to make sure the employee realizes his or her ideas are wanted, to help the employee see any "bugs," and to give the employee recognition when an idea is practical and is put to use.

Handling complaints: to make sure that the employee gets a complete and fair hearing, that mythical grievances are nipped in the bud, and that real grievances are rectified promptly and without bitterness.

In the democratic type of supervision, the leader often consults with his or her followers and actively seeks their Participation (31) in decisions confronting the group.

Some of the advantages of the democratic type of leadership are: It seems better suited to the American people, who have a democratic heritage and enjoy a rather high level of education; and it gives greater freedom to the group yet retains control in the supervisor.

Possible disadvantages of democratic leadership are that it requires better coordination and communication and demands that the leader be of a higher quality in order to deal with the intangibles and variables of group interaction.[12]

Participation (31)

Keith Davis defines participation as the "mental and emotional involvement of a person in a group situation which encourages him to contribute to group goals and share responsibility in them."[13]

Participation is widely used by democratic leaders, but it means different things to different people. Does participation mean that a supervisor lets subordinates' votes determine the action to be taken? This might occur at one extreme in a continuum of leadership behavior. Often, however, participation means something different. It could mean that the leader, instead of just telling subordinates what a decision is, explains it to them and tries to get them to accept it as being

[12]Keith Davis, *Human Relations in Business,* McGraw-Hill Book Company, New York, 1957, p. 170. The type of participation under discussion in this book is participation on the job, at all levels where decisions are being made. This does not include participation in the power circles at the highest level of management. The latter type of participation includes work councils and representation of employees on the board of directors. Recent works dealing with this type of participation include John M. Roach, *Worker Participation: New Voices in Management,* The Conference Board, New York, 1973; and David Jenkins, *Job Power,* Penguin Books Inc., Baltimore, 1974. Also see "What Foreign Firms Are Doing to Fight 'Blue-Collar Blues,'" *U.S. News and World Report,* July 23, 1973, pp. 76–78; "A Symposium: Workers Participation in Management: An International Comparison," *Industrial Relations,* February 1970; and "Systems of Formal Participation," *Organizational Behavior: Research and Issues,* University of Wisconsin, Industrial Relations Research Association, Madison, 1974, pp. 77–105.

[13]Davis, ibid., p. 288.

correct and reasonable. Many times participation will mean the leader discusses a problem with the subordinates, gets their ideas and suggestions as to possible solutions with the pros and cons of each possibility, and then, after a full discussion, decides what action to take.[14] Robert Tannenbaum and Warren Schmidt in "How to Chose a Leadership Pattern," page 352, demonstrate that the degree of participation may come at any point along a continuum between "boss-centered" leadership and "subordinate-centered" leadership.

Alfred J. Marrow tells of the effectivenss of participation in a pajama factory in an excerpt from "The Effect of Participation on Performance," page 363 of this volume.

From an examination of the productivity diagram, it can readily be seen that participation does not necessarily and automatically lead to greater productivity. Participation, on the contrary, may have either a positive or negative effect on employee motivation, performance, and productivity. Does the employee whose participation is desired have an authoritarian or equalitarian background (9)?[15] How does the employee perceive the situation in which his or her participation is invited (9)? Does the employee have confidence in the leader (9)? Does the employee believe the leader carries influence up the hierarchy with *the leader's superior* (25)? What is the attitude of the employee's group toward this participation (20)? Is the group working toward or against company goals (23)? How much time is available before a decision must be made (10)? What attitude does the Union have toward participation by employees in decisions they will be asked to carry out (33)?

Tannenbaum and Fred Massarik in "Participation by Subordinates in the Managerial Decision-making Process," page 365, have outlined conditions which they feel should exist if a leader is to have effective participation by his or her followers.[16]

There *can* be many advantages to the use of participation by a leader. The followers may accept the final decision more readily, feel more responsibility for carrying it out, exhibit less resistance to change, set higher production quotas than management would, and have an opportunity to fulfill their egoistic needs— to become more mature and responsible with greater dignity and status.

Some possible disadvantages to participation are that it requires a high degree of skill on the part of the leader and that, once started, participation which

---

[14]For a study showing how the individual satisfactions of employees increased significantly when changes were introduced into a firm under an autonomy program designed to increase the role of rank-and-file employees in the decision-making process, see Nancy C. Morse and Everett Reimer, "The Experimental Change of a Major Organizational Variable," *The Journal of Abnormal and Social Psychology,* vol. 52, no. 1, January 1956, pp. 120–129.

[15]Victor H. Vroom in *Some Personality Determinants of the Effects of Participation,* Prentice-Hall, Inc., Englewood Cliffs, N.J., 1960, concludes that "authoritarians and persons with weak independence needs are apparently unaffected by opportunity to participate in making decisions" while "equalitarians . . . develop more positive attitudes toward their job and greater motivation for effective performance through participation" (p. 60).

[16]Another listing of "critical elements in participation" appears in Harold J. Leavitt (ed.), *The Social Science of Organizations,* Prentice-Hall, Inc., Englewood Cliffs, N.J., 1963, p. 61.

gives the followers a greater feeling of responsibility and status could be discontinued only at the risk of damaging employee attitudes and production.

Another danger is that we become so enthusiastic about the benefits of participation that we view it as a cure-all and ignore or undervalue contributions made to the organization through industrial engineering and information and communication sciences.[17]

Participation raises some interesting questions. Is it possible to arrive at a group decision which is inferior to a decision the leader would have made on his or her own?[18] As automation increases, will the area in which it is possible for employees to participate steadily diminish? Will a leader who is now getting good results from using participation get better results by using more participation?

Participation, properly used under the right conditions, can be an effective means of allowing employees to fulfill their egoistic needs and of motivating employees to improve their job performance and increase productivity.[19]

Combination of Types of Leadership (32)

Many writers today agree that the knack of being a good leader is to analyze each situation and the people involved in it to decide which type of leadership (laissez faire, autocratic, or democratic) is appropriate to the situation. "Leadership" is not exercised in a vacuum but by a given leader with a given subordinate or group of subordinates, in a particular leadership climate, with particular organizational limitations, with a particular informal group structure, etc.

An administrator in charge of a group of highly trained and competent scientists may well secure best results by using laissez faire leadership much of the time. A foreman in charge of unskilled workers long used to autocratic leadership may discover that democratic methods don't produce the best results for that group. A supervisor of skilled workers or white-collar personnel may find

---

[17]Harold J. Leavitt, "Unhuman Organizations," *Harvard Business Review,* vol. 40, no. 4, July–August 1962, pp. 90–98.

[18]This question is discussed in Norman R. F. Maier, *Principles of Human Relations,* John Wiley & Sons, Inc., New York, 1952, chap. 10, "The Quality of Group Decisions as Influenced by the Discussion Leader."

[19]For an excellent discussion of participation, its critical elements, theories as to how it might increase motivation, and four possible dysfunctional aspects, see George Strauss, "Some Notes on Power Equalization," *The Social Science of Organizations,* Prentice-Hall, Inc., Englewood Cliffs, N.J., 1963, pp. 60–70.

It is not inevitable that use of participation will lead to improved performance.

One study of three executives with similar suborganizations where the performance of employees was approximately equal revealed that one executive was autocratic, one was recessive, and one permissive (James H. Mullen, *Personality and Productivity in Management,* Columbia University Press, New York, 1966).

In another study, involving government employees, it could not be demonstrated that greater participation led to increased productivity (Reed M. Powell and John L. Schlacter, "Participative Management: A Panacea?", *Academy of Management Journal,* June 1971, pp. 165–173).

Moreover, participation may have different results in other cultures. In a Norwegian factory, no significant differences in productivity were found under participative and nonparticipative supervision (J. R. P. French et al., "An Experiment on Participation in a Norwegian Factory," *Human Relations,* vol. 13, February 1960, pp. 3–19).

that most of the time democratic methods bring the best results, but sometimes it is necessary for the supervisor to be autocratic. Thus, as Tannenbaum and Schmidt point out, "the successful manager of men . . . is one who maintains a high batting average in accurately assessing the forces that determine what his most appropriate behavior at any given time should be and in actually being able to behave accordingly."

With reference to the productivity diagram, Chris Argyris' words seem most fitting:

> Effective leadership depends upon a multitude of conditions. There is no one predetermined, correct way to behave as a leader. The choice of leadership pattern should be based upon an accurate diagnosis of the reality of the situation in which the leader is imbedded. If one must have a title for effective leadership, it might be called *reality-centered leadership*. Reality-centered leadership is not a predetermined set of "best ways to influence people." The only predisposition that is prescribed is that the leader ought to first diagnose what *is* reality and then to use the appropriate leadership pattern. In making his diagnosis, he must keep in mind that all individuals see reality through their own set of colored glasses. The reality he sees may not be the reality seen by others in their own private world. Reality diagnosis, therefore, requires self-awareness and the awareness of others. This leads us back again to the properties of personality. A reality-oriented leader must also keep in mind the worth of the organization. No one can make a realistic appraisal if for some reason he weighs one factor in the situation as always being of minimal importance.[20]

And Basil Georgopoulos and Floyd Mann, on the basis of their hospital study, add their voices in agreement:

> In summary, the preceding review of representative research concerning supervision and organizational effectivenss suggests that: (*a*) the behavior of those in leadership and supervisory positions in organizations can typically be related to various measures of organizational effectiveness, but the relationships that can be expected may vary depending on what aspects of supervision are involved and what criteria of effectiveness are used; (*b*) depending upon the nature and requirements of the organizational situation, and upon the needs, goals, and expectations of organizational members, a particular style of supervision, or a particular supervisory skill or characteristic, may have different consequences for organizational effectiveness and for different aspects of effectiveness; and (*c*) the combination of the technical, administrative, and human relations skills and practices of supervisory personnel that is most effective from the standpoint of organizational effectiveness will probably be different for different types of organizations, and even for different levels within the same organization.[21]

---

[20]Chris Argyris, *Personality and Organization*, Harper & Row, Publishers, Incorporated, New York, 1957, p. 207. Quoted by permission of the author and of the publisher.
[21]From Basil S. Georgopoulos and Floyd C. Mann, *The Community General Hospital*, The Macmillan Company, New York, 1962, p. 447. Reprinted by permission.

One of the leading researchers in the field of leadership is Fred Fiedler. Over many years he has developed the contingency approach to leadership. His theory holds that:

> The effectiveness of a task group or of an organization depends on two main factors: the personality of the leader and the degree to which the situation gives the leader power, control, and influence over the situation or, conversely, the degree to which the situation confronts the leader with uncertainty.[22]

A brief explanation of his leadership theory is included under the title "The Contingency Model: New Directions for Leadership Utilization," on page 376 of this volume. Victor Vroom expresses reservations about the contingency theory in "The Search for a Theory of Leadership," page 386 of this volume.

Even if there were irrefutable evidence that a type of supervision appropriate to the leader, the followers, and the situation would increase productivity, we would want to know to what extent. One study, dealing mainly with first-line supervisors, concluded that productivity would be increased thus no more than 15 percent.[23] Other estimates range from zero to 30 percent and average from 10 to 20 percent.

Before we could attempt to predict the effect of the supervisor's style of leadership on the motivation of the employee, we would have to know a great deal about the employee (perception, background, needs, even expectation regarding supervisory behavior[24]); about the leadership climate of the formal organization; about the role of the informal group to which the individual belongs; and about the Union's influence on employees.

---

[22]Fred Fiedler, "The Contingency Model: New Directions for Leadership Utilization," *Journal of Contemporary Business,* Autumn 1974, p. 65.

[23]Michael Argyle et al., "Supervisory Methods Related to Production, Absenteeism, and Labor Turnover," *Human Relations,* vol. 11, no. 1, February 1958, pp. 23–40. For a brief discussion of the possible significance of the 15 percent figure, see George C. Homans, "Effort, Supervision and Productivity," in Robert Dubin et al., *Leadership and Productivity,* Chandler Publishing Company, San Francisco, 1965, pp. 57–58.

[24]U. G. Foa, who studied the relation of workers' expectations of supervisory behavior to satisfaction, concluded that satisfaction depends on whether the supervisor's attitude conforms with the workers' expectations. See "Relation of Workers' Expectations to Satisfaction with Supervisor," *Personnel Psychology,* vol. 10, Summer 1957, pp. 161–168.

Chapter 15

Social Conditions of the Job: Union

In an organization which has a very strong union, the diagram on the first page of the book might look like Figure 1. In an organization which has a rather ineffective union, the diagram might look like Figure 2. And, of course, if an organization has no union, that part of the diagram would be a sliver, reminding us simply that the possibility of a union obtaining jurisdiction in an organization is almost always present.

A strong Union (33) can wield a tremendous influence on employee performance and on productivity. It can affect the individual's perception of needs by telling satisfied employees that they are not being paid enough or are being cheated by the employer; or by telling them the employer is fair and honest and that the employees are getting a "good deal." The union can affect the technology in the firm by accepting new modern equipment and readily agreeing on the number of operators and their wages or by refusing to allow a modern machine to start operation until union demands have been met. The union can affect the formal organization, its structure, climate, efficiency, and its communication effectiveness with employees. It can approve company policies on job content, selection and placement, job evaluation, performance ratings, training, etc., or oppose them. The union can affect the informal organization and its goals—whether it will work toward company goals or against them. It can affect the

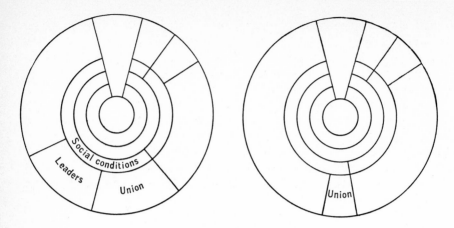

Figure 1   **Figure 2**

leaders, in extreme cases causing disliked supervisors to lose their jobs. The union can cause a work shutdown as strategy to force the employer to meet its demands in negotiations. The union can favor participation by employees or oppose it.

Some of the restrictions unions can place on management and productivity have been listed by Harold Wilensky:

> Economists have frequently criticized unions because union non-wage policies reduce incentives, limit productivity, or hamper technological change. The general lines of criticism can be summarized as follows: (1) By emphasizing and guaranteeing security through such devices as seniority, pensions, and grievance procedures, unions reduce the worker's incentive to work hard, and to strive for personal advancement. Unions also limit management's attempts to provide incentives through promotion on merit or incentive wage payment plans. (2) Unions often directly limit the amount of work performed on the job by means of working rules or informal pressures to restrict output. (3) Union rules (musicians, railroads) may require more men on a job than are needed to perform the work. (4) Unions may block the introduction of technological changes, or adopt policies designed to make such changes more expensive. (5) By interfering with management's "freedom to manage," unions may reduce the efficiency of an enterprise.[1]

The Union can exert a favorable influence on employee morale and cooperate with management in increasing production, or throw its forces on the side of restricting production. It can work with or against the organization in matters of work schedule, job redesign, incentives and rewards, and numerous other areas on the productivity diagram. Certainly no attempt to explain factors affecting productivity and employee job performance in a unionized firm would be com-

[1]Harold Wilensky, *Syllabus of Industrial Relations,* The University of Chicago Press, Chicago, pp. 116–117. Copyright 1954 by the University of Chicago. Quoted by permission.

plete without an examination of the union and its influence throughout the organization.

Developments in recent years indicate that unions will continue to play a strong role in representing blue-collar employees and will play an increasingly strong role in representing white-collar employees.

President Kennedy's Executive Order 10988, issued in January 1962, and subsequent orders encouraged federal employees to engage in union activity. On the state and local level, the American Federation of State, County, and Municipal Employees has increased its membership significantly and is the most rapidly growing of white-collar unions. Unions of engineers, nurses, and teachers are making new gains in their membership and are becoming increasingly militant. Some organizations which formerly were largely professional groups, such as the National Education Association and the American Nurses Association, have now embraced collective bargaining as a way of meeting their members' demands.

Blue-collar unions seem destined to continue as vital forces influencing employees' attitudes, need fulfillment, motivation, and productivity and white-collar unions seem destined to become increasingly vital forces in these areas.

Chapter 16

Complexity
of Interrelations:
A Summary

The productivity diagram includes the most important factors affecting employees' job performance and productivity. There are a large number of such factors. Most of them affect other factors in the diagram and are themselves affected by others. Thus there is an interdependency among them which is extremely complex. We cannot assume that a change in a factor in the outer circle will directly cause a change in employee job performance. More likely, a change in one factor in the outer circle would be accompanied by changes in other factors, so that any change in employees' job performance and ultimately in productivity would be the net result of all changes operating throughout the diagram.

There are, of course, other ways to show diagrammatically the complexity of the interrelations of various factors. James V. Clark demonstrates some relation between conditions in the work group's environment, motivation, satisfaction, productivity, and turnover-absenteeism and speaks of factors which both release and constrain different motivations.[1]

---

[1] "Motivation in Work Groups: A Tentative View," *Human Organization*, Winter 1960–1961, pp. 199–208.

William Ruch and James Hershauer have recently devised a "conceptual scheme model of factors affecting worker productivity."[2]

Floyd Mann and others have shown graphically how a large number of measures relative to supervisory practices and characteristics, worker perception and satisfaction, and work group effectiveness are interrelated at one point in time.[3]

In terms of the diagram used in this book, it is interesting to note that Rensis Likert in his "An Integrating Principle and an Overview," page 391, cites as significant to the *high-producing manager* such factors as technical resources (including time and motion study); supervisors with technical and planning skill; use of informal groups; use of participation; use of motives (such as ego, security, curiosity and creativity, and economic)—all in a cumulative and reinforcing manner; and attention to the needs and perceptions of all members of the organization.

Recognizing that the attainment of increased productivity is a complex phenomenon, we can readily see the superficiality of statements which attribute productivity changes to a change in one factor. In the left-hand column below are examples of the kinds of statements one sometimes hears. In the right-hand column are some of the assumptions which seem to be implied in the statements.

Statements	Apparent assumptions
If I want greater output per employee hour, I get it only through improved machinery and equipment.	The performance of employees is insignificant in importance.
Give me a worker with ability, and productivity will take care of itself.	Motivation is unimportant.
If our supervisors learn how to motivate, any workers are bound to turn in a good performance.	Workers' ability is unimportant.
Everybody knows that adopting a rest period will increase productivity.	Productivity is a function of physical working conditions.
The answer to all our problems is money. If we pay more in wages, we'll get greater productivity.	More money leads to greater satisfaction of physiological needs, which in turn leads to greater motivation. Social and egoistic needs do not have to be considered.
The answer to all our problems is participation. If we can train our supervisors to use participation, better employee performance is bound to result.	Organization structure, leadership climate, attitudes of the informal group, the leader's relation with his or her superior, union attitude, individual employee's preference for autocratic or democratic supervision have no bearing on the success of participation.

[2]William Ruch and James Hershauer, *Factors Affecting Worker Productivity,* Arizona State University, College of Business Administration, Bureau of Business and Economic Research, Tempe, 1974, pp. 28–29.

[3]F. Mann, Bernard P. Indik, and V. H. Vroom, *Productivity in Work Groups,* University of Michigan, Institute for Social Research, Survey Research Center, Ann Arbor, 1963, pp. 16–17.

All we need is another depression, with jobless people standing outside our plant, and worker performance will be maximized.	Union, groups, leaders make no difference then.
If our supervisors are fair with employees and we know they are fair, the employee's perception of the situation is unimportant.	The important thing is the way matters actually are, not the way employees think they are.
An individual employee of honesty and integrity will never work against the company goals but will inevitably accept the company production standards as fair and reasonable.	All honest employees are automatically interested in the company goals and will not yield to pressure from fellow employees to restrict output.
If we train our first-line supervisors to use democratic methods when appropriate, we can count on their doing so.	It makes no difference that our higher executives use autocratic methods most of the time.
Our company believes in good pay and in establishing congenial work groups. This should be enough to call forth the best effort from any employees.	Egoistic needs of employees are unrelated to employees' performance.
We have the best group of personnel policies in this part of the country: selection, job evaluation, performance ratings, training. Our employees should appreciate these and do their best possible work.	The way policies are perceived by the employees; the way they are administered; the pressures of the leader, the informal group, and the union; the individual needs of employees do not affect employee performance.

If management or supervisors have sometimes taken steps which they thought would improve employees' performance but didn't, the diagram should help them trace possible reasons for the failure.

Summary

Having recognized the superficiality of many statements about productivity which we have heard, let us now try to express verbally rather than digrammatically the complexities of productivity.

Productivity depends not just on employee performance; it also depends on the state of technological development and the raw materials used.

(Employee job performance depends not just on the ability of the employees; it depends also on their motivation)

Motivation of employees generally depends very little on physical work conditions, given a satisfactory minimum level of such conditions; it depends on social conditions in interaction with employees' needs.

A satisfied need is no motivator of behavior.

Physical job conditions in general in this country are good and have satisfied employees' needs for comfort and safety; as long as they remain satisfactory or good, they will have little or no motivating influence on employees. (The Hawthorne studies were unable to demonstrate any relation between physical conditions and output.)

Other physiological needs (met principally by money and security) are largely satisfied today in our country. Social needs are frequently satisfied. To the extent that physiological and social needs are satisfied, they do not motivate.

The largest remaining unsatisfied needs are the egoistic ones. Even if the egoistic needs are satisfied today, they demand continuing satisfaction and therefore never lose their motivating potential. Thus it is to the continuing satisfaction of these egoistic needs that management should devote major attention for a rapidly increasing number of employees.

Some employees may now be satisfying their egoistic (and even social) needs off the job. For them, social conditons which permit satisfaction of egoistic needs on the job are unlikely to motivate. Management would first have to arouse the employees' interest in their jobs so that their egoistic needs are activated at work.

But even when employees seek satisfaction of some social and egoistic needs on the job, there are further complications. The employees may be members of a group which is small, cohesive, and has high morale; they may have an excellent attitude toward the group and find satisfaction of egoistic needs through the group. But satisfaction of the employees' egoistic needs is not enough. The group can have goals in opposition to management's goals. Thus, satisfaction of egoistic needs does not necessarily lead to improved employee performance from the company standpoint. High employee morale may accompany good employee job performance or poor performance. The problem then becomes one of management's getting the group to work toward management's goals for better employee job performance and increased productivity.

How can management get the group to work toward management's goals? Recent and current research give us some clues as this book has pointed out. It would seem that attention should be concentrated on Egoistic Needs and on the entire area of Social Conditions. The many facets of the Formal Organization, the Informal Organization or group, the Leader or supervisor, and the Union all play their important parts. Democratic leadership will often be effective, sometimes with a type of participation in which a group adopts for itself goals equal to or higher than those management would have set.

There are still two major problems. One is that we cannot assume that a positive correlation between need satisfaction and job performance always exists. It is possible for an individual's needs to be well satisfied and his or her performance poor, or for needs to be unsatisfied and performance good. Some of these complex relationships between satisfaction and short-run and long-run productivity were dealt with in Chapter 10.

The other major problem is that of individual differences. If management succeeds in setting up social conditions which encourage the group to work with and not against the company, most employees in the group will usually conform to the group standards. However, there will often be one or more individuals whose perception of the situation or whose level of aspiration or whose reference group or whose cultural or experience background will not permit acceptance of the goals of the present work group and whose egoistic needs must be satisfied in some other manner if there is to be motivation toward improved job performance.

Moreover, each employee is a distinct individual with specific personal needs. These are likely to change over time. Each employee is consciously, or unwittingly, trying to follow his or her own path to job satisfaction and life satisfaction. Dual objectives of organizational productivity and employee job satisfaction are essential under the value conditions existing today.

In the next chapter we turn to ways of humanizing the organization and helping employees achieve job satisfaction while at the same time maintaining or increasing organizational productivity.

Today's Imperative: Humanizing the Organization

Chapter 17

Organization's Response to Employees' Needs

This chapter will stress six main points, the first two of which have been discussed in previous chapters.

1 Organizations Have Dual Goals of Increasing Productivity and Increasing Job Satisfaction Probably no organization will dispute the appropriateness of increased productivity as a major goal.

Increased job satisfaction will probably increase productivity over the long run. Increased job satisfaction may increase productivity over the short run (that is, output per employee-hour) but does not necessarily do so. Even if increased job satisfaction does not increase productivity over the short run, it is nevertheless an essential goal of organizations in light of today's values of society and of individuals. (See Chapters 6 and 10.)

2 Organizations Should Support Employees in Their Search for Job Satisfaction along Paths the Employees, Not the Organization, Choose One writer has proposed the "supportive theory of management":

> Early theories emphasized democratic leadership and participative management. More recent writers have contributed to a more comprehensive and more promising

theory called supportive management. This supportive theory of management identifies the manager's role as one of providing an organization environment which supports the individual's efforts toward the fulfillment of his personal needs—particularly his psychological growth needs.[1]

We have pointed out previously that psychological needs may remain unactivated or unimportant for some individuals and yet be extremely important to others. Surveys of satisfaction and dissatisfaction of groups of employees will be of little help to organizations wishing to support employees in their search for job satisfaction. Employees seek to follow too many different and often-changing paths to satisfaction, and each employee thus requires separate attention from the organization.

3 Organizations Must *Listen* to Individual Employees Much has been written about what different categories of employees—blue-collar workers, white-collar workers, middle managers, upper management—want. Mitchell Fein hit the nail on the head, in my opinion, in stating: "Let's not be so ready to decide for workers what they want. They express themselves quite clearly, if only we will listen."[2] Generally employees are so happy to find someone who is interested in them and the jobs they hold that they will open up quite readily and speak their minds. The recent book by Studs Terkel not only demonstrates how readily people will talk about themselves and their work but dramatizes the wide variety of reactions different people have to their jobs. An organization or supervisor cannot possibly know how particular individuals feel about their jobs, their paths to life satisfaction, etc., without getting input from the individuals themselves.[3]

One way to get employees to express their feelings is simply to ask them. How do they like their jobs? How are they getting along? What parts of their jobs do they like and dislike? How do they view their future in the organization? What would they like that future to be? And many other questions. Sometimes an organization can get the answers without asking the questions, but this is likely to occur when the employee has gotten completely fed up with the job and its frustrations and tells in an angry outburst just what he or she thinks of the job and the company.

It may be appropriate here to recall the experience of Thor Heyerdahl in unravelling a mystery of Easter Island:

[1]Sherman Tingey, "Management Today," *Hospital Administration,* vol. 14, no. 2, Spring 1969, pp. 32–41.

[2]Mitchell Fein, "The Real Needs and Goals of Blue-Collar Workers," *The Conference Board Record,* February 1973, p. 33.

[3]Such inputs provide the material for Studs Terkel, *Working: People Talk about What They Do All Day and How They Feel about What They Do,* Pantheon Books, a division of Random House, Inc., New York, 1974.

From our correspondent

Panama, July 31

Hr. Thor Heyerdahl, the Norwegian scientist of Kon Tiki fame, declared here last night that the mystery of the great stone statues of Easter Island is a mystery no longer. Hr. Heyerdahl has just led another archaeological expedition into the South Pacific, including several weeks on Easter Island.

Easter Islanders engaged by Hr. Heyerdahl and his party transported and erected one of the giant statues in what Hr. Heyerdahl is convinced is the same manner in which their forebears did. The team of 180 Easter islanders had no difficulty in towing the statue over level grass from the quarry where it lay. On the selected site it was raised by levering up one side an inch or so, blocking the space thus made with rocks, then levering the other side similarly. When the base of the statue reached the height of the plinth the levering and wedging process was applied only to the upper portion of the statue, which was thus raised gradually to a position from which it could be hauled vertical by ropes.

With 12 hired islanders Hr. Heyerdahl raised the 30-ton statue to the vertical in 18 days by this ancient method. This statue now ornaments the island skyline as the only one of the great monoliths standing as in ancient days.

Hr. Heyerdahl considers the statue plainly Polynesian though the expedition unearthed one which, instead of having the traditional Polynesian posture of hands folded across the stomach, was kneeling with hands on thighs.

Hr. Heyerdahl and his fellow archaeologists have a modest explanation of their discovery of the system by which ancient monuments were raised without mechanical aids. Previous expeditions to Easter Island have returned without the answer. Hr. Heyerdahl sought the opinion of the island's mayor on the methods used by ancient islanders to erect their statues, and the answer was immediately forthcoming. "Why did you not tell this to previous expeditions?" asked Hr. Heyerdahl. " They never asked me," vouchsafed the phlegmatic old mayor.[4]

So, the quickest and easiest way to find out how employees feel about their jobs and careers will often be simply to ask them.

Not all employees, however, will open up readily when asked. For some individuals, their supervisors will have to be alert to any clues given off regarding the employee's state of job satisfaction. Comments may be heard such as: "This job is getting me down," "I wonder if I ought to take a course at the university or a training course here in the organization," "I love what I'm doing and hope the company never takes me off this job," "I'd quit if I were ever promoted to the responsibility of a supervisor." A supervisor who is *alerted* to watch for clues regarding attitudes can pick up a tremendous amount of information without even asking questions. Of course, to place the proper interpretation on such information may require further probing or confirmation, and casual statements of employees cannot always be taken at face value. Yet, a supervisor who thinks of his or her subordinates as all striving for life satisfaction but along different and

[4]"An Easter Island Mystery Solved," *The Times* (London), Aug. 1, 1956. Reprinted by permission.

frequently changing paths can get many clues from them just by being tuned in to the possible importance of what they're saying.

The HEW report on *Work in America* stressed the need for redesigning jobs to make them more challenging to employees. William Gomberg in "Job Satisfaction: Sorting Out the Nonsense," page 401, argues that "trade unionists have done more to eliminate sub-human work by raising wages than all of the elaborate schemes of the scholars laid end to end." Harold Wool in "What's Wrong with Work in America?: A Review Essay," page 412, feels emphasis should be placed not on job enrichment but on high employment levels as a means to improving or eliminating undesirable jobs. A labor leader quoted earlier has said, "If you want to enrich the job, enrich the pay check." Each of these approaches may be justified, but for different employees. Not all employees want challenging jobs; not all employees seek self-fulfillment on the job; not all employees, at least in noninflationary times, are primarily interested in more pay; not all employees want to retire early.

The job of management is to find out what individual employees want. What are they seeking from their jobs and what are they seeking from off-job activities? This inquiry can be time-consuming and expensive. But how else can we hope to make it possible for employees to increase satisfaction on the job? Can't work be a satisfying experience? Does it necessarily have to be a place to escape from? Probably many people are happy to escape from work and are successful in achieving life satisfaction entirely through off-job activities. On the other hand, there are probably many people who have retired from the job, or escaped from work, who find themselves without much to do, endlessly bored, and far from achieving life satisfaction. How much better it might be to make it possible for these people to attain life satisfaction through job satisfaction.

Richard E. Walton of Harvard University, in an article entitled "Quality of Working Life: What Is It?", stresses the diversity of human preferences:

> Regardless of how one approaches the issue of the quality of working life, one must acknowledge the diversity of human preferences—diversity in culture, social class, family rearing, education, and personality. Society is becoming more conscious of the quality of work life at a time when there is a growing heterogeneity in life styles in America. Differences in subcultures and life styles are accompanied by different definitions of what constitutes a high quality of working life. The young person with a college degree who elects to work as an auto mechanic, a taxi driver, or a mail carrier is saying something significant about his or her preferred pattern of working life. Of two employees equally skilled in performing basic elements of their work, one may prefer autonomy and the other detailed instruction. Similarly one may prefer to be closely integrated into a work team and the other relatively unencumbered by work relations.
>
> How can these differing preferences be accommodated? Diversity within a single work unit may be realized by tailoring individual work assignments to fit individual preferences. Within an organization, diversity can be achieved by organizing work differently from one work unit to the next and allowing employees to select the pattern of work life they prefer. Finally diversity among organizations can be

attained if each organization develops a unique and internally consistent pattern of work life while providing persons on the job market with information for choosing an organization that is suitable for them. Employees are thus encouraged to exercise a free and informed choice that takes into account some of the more subtle aspects of the quality of working life.[5]

Job Satisfaction: Is There a Trend? likewise stresses the importance of individual differences:

If the cause of the problem has been attributed either in whole or in part to characteristics of workers themselves, a program of change must confront the additional question of the extent to which differences among workers, especially in terms of their motivation, demands, and skills, will be taken into account. At one extreme there is the assumption that each worker is a unique individual and should be treated as such. However philosophically appealing it may be, this assumption is not a very useful one, except perhaps when it comes to counseling, skill training, or programmed learning. When management plans to introduce a new machine or procedure, certain motivational assumptions must be made about the workers affected by the change.

At the other end of the spectrum is the assumption that all workers are pretty much alike, at least in terms of what they want from their jobs. Under this rubric of homogeneity are a number of stereotypes, including the "economic man," and the "self-actualizing man," described earlier, both of which can be faulted for their oversimplication in light of available data.

Between the two polar assumptions of "every worker is unique" and "all workers are basically alike," there are intermediate positions that make motivational assumptions only about workers in limited segments of the labor force or in a particular company where a program of change is about to be instituted.[6]

And Neal Herrick states:

A major source of disagreement, among union and government officials, employers and academics when they get together to discuss the problem of worker discontent is the question: "What's bugging them anyhow?" In general, union and government people seem to believe that it's a matter of money, while employers and academics feel that workers are angry because they expect—but do not get—fulfillment from their work.

Of course, when we talk of the "worker" we are talking about a nonexistent person. Some workers are no doubt motivated solely by money and look at the world of work as a marketplace where they can exchange their time for money. Just as certainly, there are other workers who wish to be active in their jobs and express themselves through the medium of work.[7]

---

[5]*Sloan Management Review,* Fall 1973, p. 20.

[6]U.S. Department of Labor, Manpower Administration, Manpower Research Monograph No. 30, 1974, p. 31.

[7]"Who's Unhappy at Work and Why?", *Manpower,* January 1972, p. 5.

Mitchell Fein, in refining data from the University of Michigan's *Survey of Working Conditions*[8] into occupation categories reports:

> The new data by occupations clearly show there are differences in needs and goals of people across the spectrum from managers to low-skilled workers. The data do not show that workers want pay and no interesting work; nor that managers and professionals want the reverse. On the contrary, all skill levels want both, but to differing degrees. . . .
>
> We might better now, I would urge, first reappraise our understanding of workers' needs. What's needed is further careful study of those needs, derived from data on workers, not contaminated by supervisors, technicians and others in highly skilled factory jobs.[9]

Additional aggregate data of this sort will be helpful, but it will not answer the question of what individual workers seek from their employment.

How can supervisors be trained to be alert for clues from individual workers? As mentioned before, this can be a time-consuming and costly process. Supervisors are under pressure for many things and may not take such a responsibility seriously unless they are rewarded for doing it. There are many ways this can be done. Organizations which use "employee performance evaluations" can evaluate their supervisors in part on their knowledge of career paths desired by their subordinates and on subordinate turnover, absenteeism, and other negative outcomes associated with dissatisfaction. Organizations with management-by-objectives programs can indicate knowledge of employees' career paths as an overall company objective and see if supervisors won't agree that this is a proper item to be included in objectives for their own jobs. Perhaps behavioral modification methods can be used with supervisors to reward them when they carry out this responsibility.

4   Organizations Have the Major Responsibility for the Proper Fit Between Employees and Their Jobs, Enabling Employees to Attain Job Satisfaction
Employees of course have some responsibility for their own careers, for obtaining the training and education necessary for them to achieve their career goals, and for communicating their aspirations to management, through words or performance.

The government has taken many steps to increase job satisfaction for employees through legislation. Herrick explains some of these in "Government Approaches to the Humanization of Work," page 422.[10]

But organizations themselves have the major responsibility to place employees in jobs where they are most likely to be able to follow their paths to job

---

[8]*Survey of Working Conditions,* University of Michigan, Institute for Social Research, Survey Research Center, Ann Arbor, November 1970.

[9]Mitchell Fein in op. cit., p. 32.

[10]See also William A. Steiger, "Can We Legislate the Humanization of Work?", in W. Clay Hamner and Frank L. Schmidt, *Contemporary Problems in Personnel,* St. Clair Press, Chicago, 1974, p. 499.

satisfaction. Edward Lawler argues effectively that "For a More Effective Organization: Match the Job to the Man," on page 427 of this volume. Industrial firms, under some technological constraints to be sure, still have to make some decisions on the relative importance of human beings and production facilities. Must the plant be set up on the most efficient technological basis and employees fitted into the slots created by the machines? Or can plants be constructed with a consideration of human needs and job satisfaction as with Volvo, Saab, and General Foods, Topeka? It is the organization which must decide what type of applicant to hire, where to place the new person in the organization, and how that job should be designed; the last two decisions are made in collaboration with the employee, with employee groups, or with the union. It is the organization which must find out what path the employee is trying to follow to achieve job satisfaction.

5 Organizations Need Imagination and Flexibility As organizations become increasingly aware of the tremendous changes in the values of society and of individuals, they will see the need for altering their own values. Traditional organizational policies and values will have to come under careful scrutiny to see whether and to what extent they can be altered to conform with the new demands of employees.

What changes in hiring procedure should be made? Should applicants be allowed to see the job or several jobs and even to try them out before accepting employment: should the selection process thus be more of a two-way street instead of a unilateral decision by management? What changes should be made in promotion policy? What changes in the scheduling of work and work hours should be made in adapting to peoples' needs? What changes in the design of jobs, organization structure, plant layout, (and many of the other items on the productivity diagram) need to be made?

6 Humanization of Work Is Urgently Needed Dale Tarnowieski in *The Changing Success Ethic* asserts that organizations that do not serve first the interests of people may experience increased difficulty in finding qualified people to serve them.[11] And it is not only academics who are calling for humanization of work. Louis Lundborg, chairman of the Bank of America in 1970 when its Isla Vista branch was burned by rioting students, declares:

> We have been passing through an era in which business and economic goals have been so dominant in our lives that we had begun to act as if *people* should be serving *businesses'* needs. We are now emerging into another era in which the corporate person and the animate person should be working together to fill a new order and a higher level of human needs.[12]

[11]Dale Tarnowieski, *The Changing Success Ethic,* An AMA Survey Report, Amacom, New York, 1973, p. 4.
[12]Louis B. Lundborg, *Future Without Shock,* W. W. Norton & Company, Inc., New York, 1974, p. 78.

Similarly, Howard C. Harder, former chairman and chief executive officer of CPC International, Inc., has said:

> The various movements, protests, and unrest of our society today are, in essence, the expression of a yearning for responsiveness from our institutions to individual needs and wants—a desire for a more humane community.

If the enactment and enforcement of civil rights legislation has saved us from internal destruction, is it too much to say that humanizing the organization—treating employees as individuals, humanizing the workplace—may save us from internal collapse?

Section VI

The Future

Chapter 18

Possible Changes to Come

The educational level of employees is constantly rising. The number of white-collar employees has for a long time exceeded the number of blue-collar employees. The number of white-collar employees is increasing much more rapidly than the number of blue-collar employees. The number of professional and technical employees is expected to increase much more rapidly than any other group. It appears that nonmanual workers will play an increasingly greater role in our economy. Drucker stated as early as 1956 that "from now on, our increases in productivity in this country will depend above all on our ability to increase the productivity of the nonmanual worker."[1] Probably the vast majority of these increasing numbers of highly educated, nonmanual employees will seek satisfaction of such egoistic needs as achievement, status, recognition, and self-fulfillment.

Following are some features of jobs which make it likely an incumbent can fulfill egoistic needs and achieve job satisfaction:

[1]Peter F. Drucker, "Managing the Educated," in Daniel H. Fenn (ed.), *Management's Mission in a New Society,* McGraw-Hill Book Company, New York, 1956, p. 168. Reprinted in this book on pages 167 to 178.

Control over own work: operate at own speed, not having to adjust to speed of an assembly line; receive work in batches rather than in a continuous stream

Participate in establishing goals for own job and ways to measure the accomplishment of those goals

Variety of duties

Job enrichment to offer the worker the desired challenge; may include some planning and inspection as well as "doing"

Autonomy: performance depends on own efforts

Feedback so the worker knows the results achieved as the work proceeds

If employees are to be motivated to perform at their best level, they must have the opportunities to satisfy their needs or to travel along the paths of their own choosing in an effort to find life satisfaction.

One cannot predict what paths to life satisfaction employees will be pursuing in the future. It seems likely that some will continue to work mainly for the paycheck, others will work for the paycheck and satisfaction of social needs, and others will seek work which will enable them to satisfy their egoistic needs for responsibility, challenge, and self-fulfillment. Employees will continue to change paths or combinations of paths over time. The future could see considerable changes in the distribution of employees along the various paths. What are some of the possibilities the future might bring?

As we know, in a major recession or depression, with an accompanying job shortage, having a job and getting a paycheck will assume relatively greater importance to employees. If over the decades the hours of work shorten considerably, a larger proportion of employees may look to off-job activities for their major satisfaction and what happens on the job may become of lesser importance. On the other hand, if opportunities for travel, for such activities as fishing, hunting, or mountain climbing, or for attending sports events and other entertainment are reduced, some employees may place greater emphasis on work activities for their satisfaction of needs. If future generations place less emphasis on college education, if craftsmen receive increased recognition from society for their skills and their contributions to society's good, perhaps employees' expectations and aspirations for challenging organizational responsibilities will be lowered.

Carl Rogers in an excerpt from "Interpersonal Relationships: USA 2000," page 437, stresses the importance of interpersonal relationships and open communication for organizations in the future.

Warren Bennis in his article "Organizations of the Future," page 438, writes of the conditions that will determine organizational life in the next several decades. He discusses the environment, population characteristics, work values, tasks and goals, organization structure, and motivation. Harold J. Leavitt in an excerpt from "The Yesterday, Today, and Tomorrow of Organizations," page 454, expresses the idea that organizations in the future will be run like universities by university-type people.

Several "prophets" predict that the concept of human asset accounting will someday be widely used. Rensis Likert in "Human Asset Accounting,"[2] page 456, recommends that all financial reports of a firm include estimates of the current value of the human organization; this will end "the present practice of treating, with great precision, a fraction of the firm's assets and completely ignoring assets of roughly the same or greater magnitude." Any liquidation of human assets to achieve temporarily higher earnings would thus be detected readily.

What can we build upon to maximize the potential of our human resources in the future? What methods are already being used by management which are designed to support employees in their search for life satisfaction? What additional methods have been proposed for use in the future?

The following numbers refer to segments in the productivity diagram on the first page of the book.

1 Discussion with employees (participation) about the need for *increased productivity.*

2 Discussion with the union and employees (participation) about the *technological* changes, and opportunities for union and employees to make suggestions regarding them.

3 Discussion with the employee of his or her own *job performance,* and help to improve it.

4 Selection of employees whose *abilities* can be fully utilized in this organization and whose needs can potentially be met under the social conditions existing in the firm.

8 Attempt by the organization to discover what the *needs* of its employees really are and what paths they are trying to follow in their search for job satisfaction. This requires listening on the part of supervisors—being "tuned in" to what employees are saying. It requires the organization to reward supervisors for accomplishing this part of their jobs.

10 Recognition that employees' needs may change over *time.*

11 Normal, decent *physical working conditions.*

14 A flat *organization structure,* under which considerable responsibility is placed on employees and they are given the leeway to use the initiative and ingenuity which they possess.

15 A company *climate* in which employee development and fulfillment of employee needs are looked upon as essentials which normally will contribute to increased productivity.

16 Overall *efficiency* of the organization so all employees can be proud of their association with it.

17a Flexible schedules of work, to accommodate as far as possible the off-job demands of employees.

17b Careful attention to the *content* of jobs. Use of job rotation, enlargement, and enrichment to increase interest and satisfaction of employees. Having work arranged in meaningful units.

---

[2]For a more extensive treatment, see Eric Flamholtz, *Human Resource Accounting,* Dickenson Publishing Company, Inc., Encino, Calif., 1974.

17c Proper *placement,* or matching individuals with their particular needs to jobs in which those needs are most likely to be met.

17d *Training* of employees, supervisors, and executives which takes into consideration the leadership climate of the firm and all the social conditions within which the trained person must function after his or her training is completed.

17e *Wage and salary level* no lower than average for the community.

17f Use of financial *incentives* such as wage incentives, bonus plans, profit sharing, or Scanlon plan only after consideration of union, informal organization, and employees' needs so that there is reasonable assurance that the use of incentives will help in motivating employees toward better job performance.

17g *Performance evaluation* carried out not as an act of judgment by the supervisor but perhaps as an act of self-appraisal by the employee, with counseling and coaching by the supervisor or in a collaborative management by objectives program.

18 *Communication,* establishing a relationship of confidence, using proper channels and providing for feedback.

21 Informal groups small enough in *size* to be supportive of their members.

22 *Cohesiveness* promoted, where appropriate, by sociometric selection of group members.

23 *Goals* of group determined through discussion and participation by group members with their supervisors.

26 Selection of leaders with necessary *technical skill and knowledge.*

27 Recognition of the various *types of leadership* and the appropriateness of each type for various situations and various employees.

31 Knowledge of benefits and limitations of *participation* and its use, when appropriate, to create situations in which the employees can satisfy their egoistic needs.

33 Communication with the *union* and management's frequent use of participation by the union in an attempt to get union support for the management goal of increased productivity.

Which of these methods, and what other methods yet to be revealed through continuing research in the behavioral sciences and continuing experimentation by management, can be utilized in the future to achieve increased productivity? Which of these methods, and what other methods, will be appropriate in the various parts of a particular organization, at a given time, with a particular informal group, composed of particular individuals, under a particular leader, and with a specific union situation?

This is the challenge of management!

Bibliography

Aaron, Benjamin, and Paul Seth Meyer et al: *A Review of Industrial Relations Research,* Vol. 2, University of Wisconsin, Industrial Relations Research Association, Madison, 1971.

Arensberg, Conrad M. et al: *Research in Industrial Human Relations,* Harper & Row, Publishers, Incorporated, New York, 1957.

Argyris, Chris: *The Human Organization,* McGraw-Hill Book Company, New York, 1967.

———: *Personality and Organization,* Harper & Row, Publishers, Incorporated, New York, 1957.

Athos, Anthony G., and Robert E. Coffey: *Behavior in Organizations: A Multidimensional View,* Prentice-Hall, Inc., Englewood Cliffs, N.J., 1968.

Bass, Bernard M., and Gerald V. Barrett: *Man, Work, and Organizations,* Allyn and Bacon, Inc., Boston, 1972.

———, and Samuel D. Deep: *Current Perspectives for Managing Organizations,* Prentice-Hall, Inc., Englewood Cliffs, N.J., 1970.

Beach, Dale S.: *Managing People at Work,* The Macmillan Company, New York, 1971.

Bolton, Harvey: *Flexible Working Hours,* Anbar Publishers, London, 1971.

Brown, J. A. C.: *The Social Psychology of Industry,* Penguin Books, Inc., Baltimore, 1954.

Campbell, Angus, and Philip E. Converse (eds.): *The Human Meaning of Social Change,* Russell Sage Foundation, New York, 1972.

Carroll, Bonnie: *Job Satisfaction: A Review of the Literature,* Cornell University, School of Industrial and Labor Relations, Ithaca, N.Y., 1969.

Davis, Keith: *Human Behavior at Work,* McGraw-Hill Book Company, New York, 1972.

Davis, Louis E., and James C. Taylor: *Design of Jobs,* Penguin Books, Inc., Baltimore, 1972.

DeMaria, Alfred T.: *Manager Unions,* American Management Association, New York, 1972.

Dowling, William F., Jr., and Leonard R. Sayles: *How Managers Motivate: The Imperatives of Supervision,* McGraw-Hill Book Company, New York, 1971.

Dubin, Robert: *Human Relations in Administration,* Prentice-Hall, Inc., Englewood Cliffs, N.J., 1974.

————et al.: *Leadership and Productivity,* Chandler Publishing Company, San Francisco, 1965.

Dunn, J.D., and Elvis C. Stephens: *Management of Personnel: Manpower Management and Organizational Behavior,* McGraw-Hill Book Company, New York, 1972.

Dunnette, Marvin: *Work and Nonwork in the Year 2001,* Wadsworth Publishing Company, Inc., Belmont, Calif., 1973.

Etzioni, Amitai: *Modern Organizations,* Prentice-Hall, Inc., Englewood Cliffs, N.J., 1965.

Fenn, Daniel H. (ed.): *Management's Mission in a New Society,* McGraw-Hill Book Company, New York, 1956.

Festinger, Leon: *A Theory of Cognitive Dissonance,* Row Peterson & Company, Evanston, Ill., 1957.

Fiedler, Fred E., and Martin M. Chemers: *Leadership and Effective Management,* Scott, Foresman and Company, Glenview, Ill., 1974.

Flamholtz, Eric: *Human Resources Accounting,* Dickenson Publishing Company, Encino, Calif., 1974.

Fleishman, Edwin: *Studies in Personnel and Industrial Psychology,* The Dorsey Press, Homewood, Ill., 1967.

Ford, Robert N.: *Motivation through the Work Itself,* American Management Association, New York, 1969.

Foulkes, Fred K.: *Creating More Meaningful Work,* American Management Association, New York, 1969.

French, Wendell: *The Personnel Management Process,* Houghton Mifflin Company, Boston, 1974.

Georgopoulos, Basil S., and Floyd C. Mann: *The Community General Hospital,* The Macmillan Company, New York, 1962.

Gibson, James L., John M. Ivancevich, and James H. Donnelly Jr.: *Organizations,* Business Publications, Inc., Dallas, 1973.

Ginsburg, Woodrow L. et al.: *A Review of Industrial Relations Research,* vol. 1, University of Wisconsin, Industrial Relations Research Association, Madison, 1970.

Hamner, W. Clay, and Frank L. Schmidt: *Contemporary Problems in Personnel,* St. Clair Press, Chicago, 1974.

Hampton, David R., Charles E. Summer, and Ross A. Webber: *Organizational Behavior and the Practice of Management,* Scott, Foresman and Company, Glenview, Ill., 1973.

Herzberg, Frederick: *Work and the Nature of Man,* The World Publishing Company, Cleveland, 1966.

Herzberg, Frederick et al.: *Job Attitudes: Review of Research and Opinions,* Psychological Service of Pittsburgh, Pittsburgh, 1957.

———et al.: *The Motivation to Work,* John Wiley & Sons, Inc., New York, 1959.

Huneryager, S. G., and I. L. Heckmann: *Human Relations in Management,* South-Western Publishing Company, Incorporated, Cincinnati, 1967.

Huse, Edgar F., and James L. Bowditch: *Behavior in Organizations: A Systems Approach to Managing,* Addison-Wesley Publishing Company, Inc., Reading, Mass., 1973.

Jacobs, Herman S.: *Executive Productivity,* Amacom, New York, 1974.

Jenkins, David: *Job Power,* Penguin Books, Inc., Baltimore, 1974.

Job Satisfaction: Is There a Trend?, U.S. Department of Labor, Manpower Administration, Manpower Research Monograph No. 30, 1974.

Lawler, Edward E.: *Motivation in Work Organizations,* Brooks/Cole Publishing Company, Monterey, Calif., 1973.

Leavitt, Harold J.: *Managerial Psychology,* The University of Chicago Press, Chicago, 1972.

———(ed.): *The Social Science of Organizations,* Prentice-Hall, Inc., Englewood Cliffs, N.J., 1963.

Levitan, Sar A., and William B. Johnston: *Work Is Here to Stay, Alas,* Olympus Publishing Company, Salt Lake City, 1973.

Likert, Rensis: *The Human Organization: Its Management and Value,* McGraw-Hill Book Company, New York, 1967.

———: *New Patterns of Management,* McGraw-Hill Book Company, New York, 1961.

———, and Samuel P. Hayes, Jr. (eds.): *Some Applications of Behavioral Research,* UNESCO, Paris, 1957.

Litwin, George H.: *Motivation and Organizational Climate,* Harvard University Press, Cambridge, Mass., 1968.

A Look at Business in 1990, A Summary of the White House Conference on the Industrial World Ahead, Feb. 7–9, 1972, U.S. Government Printing Office, 1972.

Lorsch, Jay W.: *Organizations and Their Members: A Contingency Approach,* Harper & Row Publishers, Incorporated, New York, 1974.

Lundborg, Louis B.: *Future Without Shock,* W. W. Norton & Company, Inc., New York, 1974.

Luthans, Fred: *Organizational Behavior,* McGraw-Hill Book Company, New York, 1973.

McGregor, Douglas L.: *The Human Side of Enterprise,* McGraw-Hill Book Company, New York, 1960.

———: *Leadership and Motivation,* The M.I.T. Press, Cambridge, 1966.

———: *The Professional Manager,* McGraw-Hill Book Company, New York, 1967.

Mann, Floyd C. et al.: *Productivity in Work Groups,* University of Michigan, Institute for Social Research, Survey Research Center, Ann Arbor, 1963.

Marrow, Alfred J.: *The Failure of Success,* Amacom, New York, 1972.

Maslow, A. H.: *Motivation and Personality,* Harper & Row, Publishers, Incorporated, New York, 1954.

Matteson, Michael T., Roger N. Blakeney, and Donald R. Domm: *Contemporary Personnel Management,* Harper & Row, Publishers, Incorporated, New York, 1972.

Megginson, Leon C.: *Personnel,* Richard D. Irwin, Inc., Homewood, Ill., 1972.

Mullen, James H.: *Personality and Productivity in Management,* Columbia University Press, New York, 1966.

O'Toole, James O.: *Work and the Quality of Life,* The M.I.T. Press, Cambridge, Mass., 1974.

Penzer, William N.: *Productivity and Motivation through Job Engineering,* Amacom, New York, 1973.

Pigors, Paul, and Charles A. Myers: *Personnel Administration,* McGraw-Hill Book Company, New York, 1973.

——, Charles A. Myers, and F. T. Malm: *Management of Human Resources,* McGraw-Hill Book Company, New York, 1973.

Poor, Riva: *Four Days Forty Hours,* New American Library, Inc., New York, 1973.

The Quality of Working Life: An Annotated Bibliography 1957–1972, University of California, Center for Organizational Studies, Los Angeles, 1973.

Raia, Anthony P.: *Managing by Objectives,* Scott, Foresman and Company, Glenview, Ill., 1974.

Roach, John M.: *Worker Participation: New Voices in Management,* The Conference Board, New York, 1973.

Rosow, Jerome: *The Worker and the Job,* Prentice-Hall, Inc., Englewood Cliffs, N.J., 1974.

Ruch, William A., and James C. Hershauer: *Factors Affecting Worker Productivity,* Arizona State University, Bureau of Business and Economic Research, Occasional Paper No. 10, Tempe, 1974.

Rush, Harold M. F.: *Job Design for Motivation,* The Conference Board, New York, 1971.

Schein, Edgar H.: *Organizational Psychology,* Prentice-Hall, Inc., Englewood Cliffs, N.J., 1970.

Schoderbek, Peter P., and William E. Reif: Job Enlargement, University of Michigan, Bureau of Industrial Relations, Ann Arbor, 1969.

Scott, W. E., and L. L. Cummings: *Readings in Organizational Behavior and Human Performance,* Richard D. Irwin, Inc., Homewood, Ill., 1973.

Somers, Gerald G. (ed.): *The Next Twenty-five Years of Industrial Relations,* University of Wisconsin, Industrial Relations Research Association, Madison, 1973.

Stagner, Ross: *The Psychology of Industrial Conflict,* John Wiley & Sons, Inc., New York, 1956.

Strauss, George, and Leonard Sayles: *Personnel: The Human Problems of Management,* Prentice-Hall, Inc., Englewood Cliffs, N.J., 1972.

——, Raymond E. Miles, and Charles E. Snow (eds.): *Organizational Behavior: Research and Issues,* University of Wisconsin, Industrial Relations Research Association, Madison, 1974.

Tarnowieski, Dale: *The Changing Success Ethic,* American Management Association, New York, 1973.

Terkel, Studs: *Working: People Talk about What They Do All Day and How They Feel about What They Do,* Pantheon Books, a division of Random House, Inc., New York, 1974.

Tosi, Henry L., and W. Clay Hamner: *Organizational Behavior and Management: A Contingency Approach,* St. Clair Press, Chicago, 1974.

Ullrich, Robert A.: *A Theoretical Model of Human Behavior in Organizations: An Eclectic Approach,* General Learning Press, Morristown, N.J., 1972.

Vroom, Victor: *Management and Motivation,* Penguin Books, Inc., Harmondsworth, England, 1970.

——: *Motivation in Management,* American Foundation for Management Research, New York, 1965.

Vroom, Victor: *Work and Motivation,* John Wiley & Sons, Inc., New York, 1964.

———(ed.): *Some Personality Determinants of the Effects of Participation,* Prentice-Hall, Inc., Englewood Cliffs, N.J., 1960.

Wilensky, Harold: *Syllabus of Industrial Relations,* The University of Chicago Press, Chicago, 1954.

Work in America: Report of a Special Task Force to the Secretary of Health, Education, and Welfare, prepared under the auspices of the W. E. Upjohn Institute for Employment Research, The M.I.T. Press, Cambridge, Mass., 1973.

Section VII

Readings

Readings Related to Chapter 4

A Theory of Human Motivation

A. H. Maslow

I Introduction

In a previous paper (13) various propositions were presented which would have to be included in any theory of human motivation that could lay claim to being definitive. These conclusions may be briefly summarized as follows:

1 The integrated wholeness of the organism must be one of the foundation stones of motivation theory.

2 The hunger drive (or any other physiological drive) was rejected as a centering point or model for a definitive theory of motivation. Any drive that is somatically based and localizable was shown to be atypical rather than typical in human motivation.

3 Such a theory should stress and center itself upon ultimate or basic goals rather than partial or superficial ones, upon ends rather than means to these ends. Such a stress would imply a more central place for unconscious than for conscious motivations.

4 There are usually available various cultural paths to the same goal. Therefore conscious, specific, local-cultural desires are not as fundamental in motivation theory as the more basic, unconscious goals.

5 Any motivated behavior, either preparatory or consummatory, must be understood to be a channel through which many basic needs may be simultaneously expressed or satisfied. Typically an act has *more* than one motivation.

6 Practically all organismic states are to be understood as motivated and as motivating.

7 Human needs arrange themselves in hierarchies of prepotency. That is to say, the appearance of one need usually rests on the prior satisfaction of another, more prepotent need. Man is a perpetually wanting animal. Also no need or drive can be treated as if it were isolated or discrete; every drive is related to the state of satisfaction or dissatisfaction of other drives.

From *Psychological Review*, vol. 50, 1943, pp. 370–396. Reprinted by permission of the American Psychological Association.

8 *Lists* of drives will get us nowhere for various theoretical and practical reasons. Furthermore any classification of motivations must deal with the problem of levels of specificity or generalization of the motives to be classified.

9 Classifications of motivations must be based upon goals rather than upon instigating drives or motivated behavior.

10 Motivation theory should be human-centered rather than animal-centered.

11 The situation or the field in which the organism reacts must be taken into account but the field alone can rarely serve as an exclusive explanation for behavior. Furthermore the field itself must be interpreted in terms of the organism. Field theory cannot be a substitute for motivation theory.

12 Not only the integration of the organism must be taken into account, but also the possibility of isolated, specific, partial or segmental reactions.

It has since become necessary to add to these another affirmation.

13 Motivation theory is not synonymous with behavior theory. The motivations are only one class of determinants of behavior. While behavior is almost always motivated, it is also almost always biologically, culturally and situationally determined as well.

The present paper is an attempt to formulate a positive theory of motivation which will satisfy these theoretical demands and at the same time conform to the known facts, clinical and observational as well as experimental. It derives most directly, however, from clinical experience. This theory is, I think, in the functionalist tradition of James and Dewey, and is fused with the holism of Wertheimer (19), Goldstein (6), and Gestalt Psychology, and with the dynamicism of Freud (4) and Adler (1). This fusion or synthesis may arbitrarily be called a "general-dynamic" theory.

It is far easier to perceive and to criticize the aspects in motivation theory than to remedy them. Mostly this is because of the very serious lack of sound data in this area. I conceive this lack of sound facts to be due primarily to the absence of a valid theory of motivation. The present theory then must be considered to be a suggested program or framework for future research and must stand or fall, not so much on facts available or evidence presented, as upon researches yet to be done, researches suggested perhaps by the questions raised in this paper.

II The Basic Needs

The "Physiological" Needs The needs that are usually taken as the starting point for motivation theory are the so-called physiological drives. Two recent lines of research make it necessary to revise our customary notions about these needs, first, the development of the concept of homeostasis, and second, the finding that appetites (preferential choices among foods) are a fairly efficient indication of actual needs or lacks in the body.

Homeostasis refers to the body's automatic efforts to maintain a constant, normal state of the blood stream. Cannon (2) has described this process for (1) the water content of the blood, (2) salt content, (3) sugar content, (4) protein content, (5) fat content, (6) calcium content, (7) oxygen content, (8) constant hydrogen-ion level (acid-base balance) and (9) constant temperature of the blood. Obviously this list can be extended to include other minerals, the hormones, vitamins, etc.

Young in a recent article (21) has summarized the work on appetite in its relation to body needs. If the body lacks some chemical, the individual will tend to develop a specific appetite or partial hunger for that food element.

Thus it seems impossible as well as useless to make any list of fundamental physiological needs for they can come to almost any number one might wish, depending on the degree of specificity of description. We can not identify all physiological needs as homeostatic. That sexual desire, sleepiness, sheer activity and maternal behavior in animals, are homeostatic, has not yet been demonstrated. Furthermore, this list would not include the various sensory pleasures (tastes, smells, tickling, stroking) which are probably physiological and which may become the goals of motivated behavior.

In a previous paper (13) it has been pointed out that these physiological drives or needs are to be considered unusual rather than typical because they are isolable, and because they are localizable somatically. That is to say, they are relatively independent of each other, of other motivations and of the organism as a whole, and secondly, in many cases, it is possible to demonstrate a localized, underlying somatic base for the drive. This is true less generally than has been thought (exceptions are fatigue, sleepiness, maternal responses) but it is still true in the classic instances of hunger, sex, and thirst.

It should be pointed out again that any of the physiological needs and the consummatory behavior involved with them serve as channels for all sorts of other needs as well. That is to say, the person who thinks he is hungry may actually be seeking more for comfort, or dependence, than for vitamins or proteins. Conversely, it is possible to satisfy the hunger need in part by other activities such as drinking water or smoking cigarettes. In other words, relatively isolable as these physiological needs are, they are not completely so.

Undoubtedly these physiological needs are the most prepotent of all needs. What this means specifically is, that in the human being who is missing everything in life in an extreme fashion, it is most likely that the major motivation would be the physiological needs rather than any others. A person who is lacking food, safety, love, and esteem would most probably hunger for food more strongly than for anything else.

If all the needs are unsatisfied, and the organism is then dominated by the physiological needs, all other needs may become simply non-existent or be pushed into the background. It is then fair to characterize the whole organism by saying simply that it is hungry, for consciousness is almost completely preempted by hunger. All capacities are put into the service of hunger-satisfaction, and the organization of these capacities is almost entirely determined by the one purpose of satisfying hunger. The receptors and effectors, the intelligence, memory, habits, all may now be defined simply as hunger-gratifying tools. Capacities that are not useful for this purpose lie dormant, or are pushed into the background. The urge to write poetry, the desire to acquire an automobile, the interest in American history, the desire for a new pair of shoes are, in the extreme case, forgotten or become of secondary importance. For the man who is extremely and dangerously hungry, no other interests exist but food. He dreams food, he remembers food, he thinks about food, he emotes only about food, he perceives only food and he wants only food. The more subtle determinants that ordinarily fuse with the physiological drives in organizing even feeding, drinking or sexual behavior, may now be so completely overwhelmed as to allow us to speak at this time (but *only* at this time) of pure hunger drive and behavior, with the one unqualified aim of relief.

Another peculiar characteristic of the human organism when it is dominated by a certain need is that the whole philosophy of the future tends also to change. For our chronically and extremely hungry man, Utopia can be defined very simply as a place where there is plenty of food. He tends to think that, if only he is guaranteed food for the rest of his life, he will be perfectly happy and will never want anything more. Life itself tends to be defined in terms of eating. Anything else will be defined as unimportant. Freedom, love, community feeling, respect, philosophy, may all be waved aside as fripperies which are useless since they fail to fill the stomach. Such a man may fairly be said to live by bread alone.

It cannot possibly be denied that such things are true but their *generality* can be denied. Emergency conditions are, almost by definition, rare in the normally functioning peaceful society. That this truism can be forgotten is due mainly to two reasons. First, rats have few motivations other than physiological ones, and since so much of the research upon motivation has been made with these animals, it is easy to carry the rat-picture over to the human being. Secondly, it is too often not realized that culture itself is an adaptive tool, one of whose main functions is to make the physiological emergencies come less and less often. In most of the known societies, chronic extreme hunger of the emergency type is rare, rather than common. In any case, this is still true in the United States. The average American citizen is experiencing appetite rather than hunger when he says "I am hungry." He is apt to experience sheer life-and-death hunger only by accident and then only a few times through his entire life.

Obviously a good way to obscure the "higher" motivations, and to get a lopsided view of human capacities and human nature, is to make the organism extremely and chronically hungry or thirsty. Anyone who attempts to make an emergency picture into a typical one, and who will measure all of man's goals and desires by his behavior during extreme physiological deprivation is certainly being blind to many things. It is quite true that man lives by bread alone—when there is no bread. But what happens to man's desires when there *is* plenty of bread and when his belly is chronically filled?

At once other (and "higher") needs emerge and these, rather than physiological hungers, dominate the organism. And when these in turn are satisfied, again new (and still "higher") needs emerge and so on. This is what we mean by saying that the basic human needs are organized into a hierarchy of relative prepotency.

One main implication of this phrasing is that gratification becomes as important a concept as deprivation in motivation theory, for it releases the organism from the domination of a relatively more physiological need, permitting thereby the emergence of other more social goals. The physiological needs, along with their partial goals, when chronically gratified cease to exist as active determinants or organizers of behavior. They now exist only in a potential fashion in the sense that they may emerge again to dominate the organism if they are thwarted. But a want that is satisfied is no longer a want. The organism is dominated and its behavior organized only by unsatisfied needs. If hunger is satisfied, it becomes unimportant in the current dynamics of the individual.

This statement is somewhat qualified by a hypothesis to be discussed more fully later, namely that it is precisely those individuals in whom a certain need has always been satisfied who are best equipped to tolerate deprivation of that need in the future, and that furthermore, those who have been deprived in the past will react differently to current satisfactions than the one who has never been deprived.

The Safety Needs   If the physiological needs are relatively well gratified, there then emerges a new set of needs, which we may categorize roughly as the safety needs. All that has been said of the physiological needs is equally true, although in lesser degree, of these desires. The organism may equally well be wholly dominated by them. They may serve as the almost exclusive organizers of behavior, recruiting all the capacities of the organism in their service, and we may then fairly describe the whole organism as a safety-seeking mechanism. Again we may say of the receptors, the effectors, of the intellect and the other capacities that they are primarily safety-seeking tools. Again, as in the hungry man, we find that the dominating goal is a strong determinant not only of his current world-outlook and philosophy but also of his philosophy of the future. Practically everything looks less important than safety (even sometimes the physiological needs which, being satisfied, are now underestimated). A man, in this state, if it is extreme enough and chronic enough, may be characterized as living almost for safety alone.

Although in this paper we are interested primarily in the needs of the adult, we can approach an understanding of his safety needs perhaps more efficiently by observation of infants and children, in whom these needs are much more simple and obvious. One reason for the clearer appearance of the threat or danger reaction in infants is that they do not inhibit this reaction at all, whereas adults in our society have been taught to inhibit it at all costs. Thus even when adults do feel their safety to be threatened we may not be able to see this on the surface. Infants will react in a total fashion and as if they were endangered, if they are disturbed or dropped suddenly, startled by loud noises, flashing light, or other unusual sensory stimulation, by rough handling, by general loss of support in the mother's arms, or by inadequate support.[1]

In infants we can also see a much more direct reaction to bodily illnesses of various kinds. Sometimes these illnesses seem to be immediately and *per se* threatening and seem to make the child feel unsafe. For instance, vomiting, colic or other sharp pains seem to make the child look at the whole world in a different way. At such a moment of pain, it may be postulated that, for the child, the appearance of the whole world suddenly changes from sunniness to darkness, so to speak, and becomes a place in which anything at all might happen, in which previously stable things have suddenly become unstable. Thus a child who because of some bad food is taken ill may, for a day or two, develop fear, nightmares, and a need for protection and reassurance never seen in him before his illness.

Another indication of the child's need for safety is his preference for some kind of undisrupted routine or rhythm. He seems to want a predictable, orderly world. For instance, injustice, unfairness, or inconsistency in the parents seems to make a child feel anxious and unsafe. This attitude may be not so much because of the injustice *per se* or any particular pains involved, but rather because this treatment threatens to make the world look unreliable, or unsafe, or unpredictable. Young children seem to thrive better under a system which has at least a skeletal outline of rigidity, in which there is a schedule of a kind, some sort of routine, something that can be counted upon, not only for the present but also far into the future. Perhaps one could express this more accurately by saying that the child needs an organized world rather than an unorganized or unstructured one.

The central role of the parents and the normal family setup are indisputable. Quarreling, physical assault, separation, divorce or death within the family may be particularly terrifying. Also parental outbursts of rage or threats of punishment directed to the child, calling him names, speaking to him harshly, shaking him, handling him roughly, or actual physical punishment sometimes elicit such total panic and terror in the child that we must assume more is involved than the physical pain alone. While it is true that in some children this terror may represent also a fear of loss of parental love, it can also occur in completely rejected children, who seem to cling to the hating parents more for sheer safety and protection than because of hope of love.

Confronting the average child with new, unfamiliar, strange, unmanageable stimuli or situations will too frequently elicit the danger or terror reaction, as for example, getting lost or even being separated from the parents for a short time, being confronted with new faces, new situations or new tasks, the sight of strange, unfamiliar or uncontrollable objects, illness or death. Particularly at such times, the child's frantic clinging to his parents is eloquent testimony to

[1]As the child grows up, sheer knowledge and familiarity as well as better motor development make these "dangers" less and less dangerous and more and more manageable. Throughout life it may be said that one of the main conative functions of education is this neutralizing of apparent dangers through knowledge, *e.g.*, I am not afraid of thunder because I know something about it.

their role as protectors (quite apart from their roles as food-givers and love-givers).

From these and similar observations, we may generalize and say that the average child in our society generally prefers a safe, orderly, predictable, organized world, which he can count on, and in which unexpected, unmanageable or other dangerous things do not happen, and in which, in any case, he has all-powerful parents who protect and shield him from harm.

That these reactions may so easily be observed in children is in a way a proof of the fact that children in our society feel too unsafe (or, in a word', are badly brought up). Children who are reared in an unthreatening, loving family do *not* ordinarily react as we have described above (17). In such children the danger reactions are apt to come mostly to objects or situations that adults too would consider dangerous.[2]

The healthy, normal, fortunate adult in our culture is largely satisfied in his safety needs. The peaceful, smoothly running, "good" society ordinarily makes its members feel safe enough from wild animals, extremes of temperature, criminals, assault and murder, tyranny, etc. Therefore, in a very real sense, he no longer has any safety needs as active motivators. Just as a sated man no longer feels hungry, a safe man no longer feels endangered. If we wish to see these needs directly and clearly we must turn to neurotic or near-neurotic individuals, and to the economic and social underdogs. In between these extremes, we can perceive the expressions of safety needs only in such phenomena as, for instance, the common preference for a job with tenure and protection, the desire for a savings account, and for insurance of various kinds (medical, dental, unemployment, disability, old age).

Other broader aspects of the attempt to seek safety and stability in the world are seen in the very common preference for familiar rather than unfamiliar things, or for the known rather than the unknown. The tendency to have some religion or world-philosophy that organizes the universe and the men in it into some sort of satisfactorily coherent, meaningful whole is also in part motivated by safety-seeking. Here too we may list science and philosophy in general as partially motivated by the safety needs (we shall see later that there are also other motivations to scientific, philosophical or religious endeavor).

Otherwise the need for safety is seen as an active and dominant mobilizer of the organism's resources only in emergencies, *e.g.,* war, disease, natural catastrophes, crime waves, societal disorganization, neurosis, brain injury, chronically bad situation.

Some neurotic adults in our society are, in many ways, like the unsafe child in their desire for safety, although in the former it takes on a somewhat special

---

[2]A "test battery" for safety might be confronting the child with a small exploding firecracker, or with a bewhiskered face, having the mother leave the room, putting him upon a high ladder, a hypodermic injection, having a mouse crawl up to him, etc. Of course I cannot seriously recommend the deliberate use of such "tests" for they might very well harm the child being tested. But these and similar situations come up by the score in the child's ordinary day-to-day living and may be observed. There is no reason why these stimuli should not be used with, for example, young chimpanzees.

appearance. Their reaction is often to unknown, psychological dangers in a world that is perceived to be hostile, overwhelming and threatening. Such a person behaves as if a great catastrophe were almost always impending, *i.e.*, he is usually responding as if to an emergency. His safety needs often find specific expression in a search for a protector, or a stronger person on whom he may depend, or perhaps, a Fuehrer.

The neurotic individual may be described in a slightly different way with some usefulness as a grown-up person who retains his childish attitudes toward the world. That is to say, a neurotic adult may be said to behave "as if" he were actually afraid of a spanking, or of his mother's disapproval, or of being abandoned by his parents, or having his food taken away from him. It is as if his childish attitudes of fear and threat reaction to a dangerous world had gone underground, and untouched by the growing up and learning processes, were now ready to be called out by any stimulus that would make a child feel endangered and threatened. [3]

The neurosis in which the search for safety takes its clearest form is in the compulsive-obsessive neurosis. Compulsive-obsessives try frantically to order and stabilize the world so that no unmanageable, unexpected or unfamiliar dangers will ever appear (14). They hedge themselves about with all sorts of ceremonials, rules and formulas so that every possible contingency may be provided for and so that no new contingencies may appear. They are much like the brain injured cases, described by Goldstein (6), who manage to maintain their equilibrium by avoiding everything unfamiliar and strange and by ordering their restricted world in such a neat, disciplined, orderly fashion that everything in the world can be counted upon. They try to arrange the world so that anything unexpected (dangers) cannot possibly occur. If, through no fault of their own, something unexpected does occur, they go into a panic reaction as if this unexpected occurrence constituted a grave danger. What we can see only as a none-too-strong preference in the healthy person, *e.g.*, preference for the familiar, becomes a life-and-death necessity in abnormal cases.

The Love Needs   If both the physiological and the safety needs are fairly well gratified, then there will emerge the love and affection and belongingness needs, and the whole cycle already described will repeat itself with this new center. Now the person will feel keenly, as never before, the absence of friends, or a sweetheart, or a wife, or children. He will hunger for affectionate relations with people in general, namely, for a place in his group, and he will strive with great intensity to achieve this goal. He will want to attain such a place more than anything else in the world and may even forget that once, when he was hungry, he sneered at love.

In our society the thwarting of these needs is the most commonly found core in cases of maladjustment and more severe psychopathology. Love and affec-

---

[3]Not all neurotic individuals feel unsafe. Neurosis may have at its core a thwarting of the affection and esteem needs in a person who is generally safe.

tion, as well as their possible expression in sexuality, are generally looked upon with ambivalence and are customarily hedged about with many restrictions and inhibitions. Practically all theorists of psychopathology have stressed thwarting of the love needs as basic in the picture of maladjustment. Many clinical studies have therefore been made of this need and we know more about it perhaps than any of the other needs except the physiological ones (14).

One thing that must be stressed at this point is that love is not synonymous with sex. Sex may be studied as a purely physiological need. Ordinarily sexual behavior is multi-determined, that is to say, determined not only by sexual but also by other needs, chief among which are the love and affection needs. Also not to be overlooked is the fact that the love needs involve both giving *and* receiving love.[4]

The Esteem Needs   All people in our society (with a few pathological exceptions) have a need or desire for a stable, firmly based, (usually) high evaluation of themselves, for self-respect, or self-esteem, and for the esteem of others. By firmly based self-esteem, we mean that which is soundly based upon real capacity, achievement and respect from others. These needs may be classified into two subsidiary sets. These are, first, the desire for strength, for achievement, for adequacy, for confidence in the face of the world, and for independence and freedom.[5] Secondly, we have what we may call the desire for reputation or prestige (defining it as respect or esteem from other people), recognition, attention, importance or appreciation.[6] These needs have been relatively stressed by Alfred Adler and his followers, and have been relatively neglected by Freud and the psychoanalysts. More and more today however there is appearing widespread appreciation of their central importance.

Satisfaction of the self-esteem need leads to feelings of self-confidence, worth, strength, capability and adequacy of being useful and necessary in the world. But thwarting of these needs produces feelings of inferiority, of weakness and of helplessness. These feelings in turn give rise to either basic discouragement or else compensatory or neurotic trends. An appreciation of the necessity of basic self-confidence and an understanding of how helpless people are without it, can be easily gained from a study of severe traumatic neurosis (8).[7]

[4]For further details see (12) and (16, Chap. 5).

[5]Whether or not this particular desire is universal we do not know. The crucial question, especially important today, is "Will men who are enslaved and dominated, inevitably feel dissatisfied and rebellious?" We may assume on the basis of commonly known clinical data that a man who has known true freedom (not paid for by giving up safety and security but rather built on the basis of adequate safety and security) will not willingly or easily allow his freedom to be taken away from him. But we do not know that this is true for the person born into slavery. The events of the next decade should give us our answer. See discussion of this problem in (5).

[6]Perhaps the desire for prestige and respect from others is subsidiary to the desire for self-esteem or confidence in oneself. Observation of children seems to indicate that this is so, but clinical data give no clear support for such a conclusion.

[7]For more extensive discussion of normal self-esteem, as well as for reports of various researches, see (11).

The Need for Self-Actualization   Even if all these needs are satisfied, we may still often (if not always) expect that a new discontent and restlessness will soon develop, unless the individual is doing what he is fitted for. A musician must make music, an artist must paint, a poet must write, if he is to be ultimately happy. What a man *can* be, he *must* be. This need we may call self-actualization.

This term, first coined by Kurt Goldstein, is being used in this paper in a much more specific and limited fashion. It refers to the desire for self-fulfillment, namely, to the tendency for him to become actualized in what he is potentially. This tendency might be phrased as the desire to become more and more what one is, to become everything that one is capable of becoming.

The specific form that these needs will take will of course vary greatly from person to person. In one individual it may take the form of the desire to be an ideal mother, in another it may be expressed athletically, and in still another it may be expressed in painting pictures or in inventions. It is not necessarily a creative urge although in people who have any capacities for creation it will take this form.

The clear emergence of these needs rests upon prior satisfaction of the physiological, safety, love and esteem needs. We shall call people who are satisfied in these needs, basically satisfied people, and it is from these that we may expect the fullest (and healthiest) creativeness.[8] Since, in our society, basically satisfied people are the exception, we do know much about self-actualization, either experimentally or clinically. It remains a challenging problem for research.

The Preconditions for the Basic Need Satisfactions   There are certain conditions which are immediate prerequisites for the basic need satisfactions. Danger to these is reacted to almost as if it were a direct danger to the basic needs themselves. Such conditions as freedom to speak, freedom to do what one wishes so long as no harm is done to others, freedom to express one's self, freedom to investigate and seek for information, freedom to defend one's self, justice, fairness, honesty, orderliness in the group are examples of such preconditions for basic need satisfactions. Thwarting in these freedoms will be reacted to with a threat or emergency response. These conditions are not ends in themselves but they are *almost* so since they are so closely related to the basic needs, which are apparently the only ends in themselves. These conditions are defended because without them the basic satisfactions are quite impossible, or at least, very severely endangered.

---

[8]Clearly creative behavior, like painting, is like any other behavior in having multiple determinants. It may be seen in "innately creative" people whether they are satisfied or not, happy or unhappy, hungry or sated. Also it is clear that creative activity may be compensatory, ameliorative or purely economic. It is my impression (as yet unconfirmed) that it is possible to distinguish the artistic and intellectual products of basically satisfied people from those of basically unsatisfied people by inspection alone. In any case, here too we must distinguish, in a dynamic fashion, the overt behavior itself from its various motivations or purposes.

If we remember that the cognitive capacities (perceptual, intellectual, learning) are a set of adjustive tools, which have, among other functions, that of satisfaction of our basic needs, then it is clear that any danger to them, any deprivation or blocking of their free use, must also be indirectly threatening to the basic needs themselves. Such a statement is a partial solution of the general problems of curiosity, the search for knowledge, truth and wisdom, and the ever-persistent urge to solve the cosmic mysteries.

We must therefore introduce another hypothesis and speak of degrees of closeness to the basic needs, for we have already pointed out that *any* conscious desires (partial goals) are more or less important as they are more or less close to the basic needs. The same statement may be made for various behavior acts. An act is psychologically important if it contributes directly to satisfaction of basic needs. The less directly it so contributes, or the weaker this contribution is, the less important this act must be conceived to be from the point of view of dynamic psychology. A similar statement may be made for the various defense or coping mechanisms. Some are very directly related to the protection or attainment of the basic needs, others are only weakly and distantly related. Indeed if we wished, we could speak of more basic and less basic defense mechanisms, and then affirm that danger to the more basic defenses is more threatening than danger to less basic defenses (always remembering that this is so only because of their relationship to the basic needs).

The Desires to Know and to Understand   So far, we have mentioned the cognitive needs only in passing. Acquiring knowledge and systematizing the universe have been considered as, in part, techniques for the achievement of basic safety in the world, or, for the intelligent man, expressions of self-actualization. Also freedom of inquiry and expression have been discussed as preconditions of satisfactions of the basic needs. True though these formulations may be, they do not constitute definitive answers to the question as to the motivation role of curiosity, learning, philosophizing, experimenting, etc. They are, at best, no more than partial answers.

This question is especially difficult because we know so little about the facts. Curiosity, exploration, desire for the facts, desire to know may certainly be observed easily enough. The fact that they often are pursued even at great cost to the individual's safety is an earnest of the partial character of our previous discussion. In addition, the writer must admit that, though he has sufficient clinical evidence to postulate the desire to know as a very stong drive in intelligent people, no data are available for unintelligent people. It may then be largely a function of relatively high intelligence. Rather tentatively, then, and largely in the hope of stimulating discussion and research, we shall postulate a basic desire to know, to be aware of reality, to get the facts, to satisfy curiosity, or as Wertheimer phrases it, to see rather than to be blind.

This postulation, however, is not enough. Even after we know, we are impelled to know more and more minutely and microscopically on the one hand, and on the other, more and more extensively in the direction of a world philosophy, religion, etc. The facts that we acquire, if they are isolated or atomistic, inevitably get theorized about, and either analyzed or organized or both. This process has been phrased by some as the search for "meaning." We shall then postulate a desire to understand, to systematize, to organize, to analyze, to look for relations and meanings.

Once these desires are accepted for discussion, we see that they too form themselves into a small hierarchy in which the desire to know is prepotent over the desire to understand. All the characteristics of a hierarchy of prepotency that we have described above seem to hold for this one as well.

We must guard ourselves against the too easy tendency to separate these desires from the basic needs we have discussed above, *i.e.,* to make a sharp dichotomy between "cognitive" and "conative" needs. The desire to know and to understand are themselves conative, *i.e.,* have a striving character, and are as much personality needs as the "basic needs" we have already discussed (19).

III Further Characteristics of the Basic Needs

The Degree of Fixity of the Hierarchy of Basic Needs   We have spoken so far as if this hierarchy were a fixed order but actually it is not nearly as rigid as we may have implied. It is true that most of the people with whom we have worked have seemed to have these basic needs in about the order that has been indicated. However, there have been a number of exceptions.

1   There are some people in whom, for instance, self-esteem seems to be more important than love. This most common reversal in the hierarchy is usually due to the development of the notion that the person who is most likely to be loved is a strong or powerful person, one who inspires respect or fear, and who is self confident or aggressive. Therefore such people who lack love and seek it, may try hard to put on a front of aggressive, confident behavior. But essentially they seek high self-esteem and its behavior expressions more as a means-to-an-end than for its own sake; they seek self-assertion for the sake of love rather than for self-esteem itself.

2   There are other, apparently innately creative people in whom the drive to creativeness seems to be more important than any other counter-determinant. Their creativeness might appear not as self-actualization released by basic satisfaction, but in spite of lack of basic satisfaction.

3   In certain people the level of aspiration may be permanently deadened or lowered. That is to say, the less prepotent goals may simply be lost, and may disappear forever, so that the person who has experienced life at a very low level, *i.e.,* chronic unemployment, may continue to be satisfied for the rest of his life if only he can get enough food.

4   The so-called "psychopathic personality" is another example of permanent loss of the love needs. These are people who, according to the best data available (9), have been starved for love in the earliest months of their lives and have simply lost forever the desire and the ability to give and to receive affection (as animals lose sucking or pecking reflexes that are not exercised soon enough after birth).

5   Another cause of reversal of the hierarchy is that when a need has been

satisfied for a long time, this need may be underevaluated. People who have never experienced chronic hunger are apt to underestimate its effects and to look upon food as a rather unimportant thing. If they are dominated by a higher need, this higher need will seem to be the most important of all. It then becomes possible, and indeed does actually happen, that they may, for the sake of this higher need, put themselves into the position of being deprived in a more basic need. We may expect that after a long-time deprivation of the more basic need there will be a tendency to reevaluate both needs so that the more prepotent need will actually become consciously prepotent for the individual who may have given it up very lightly. Thus, a man who has given up his job rather than lose his self-respect, and who then starves for six months or so, may be willing to take his job back even at the price of losing his self-respect.

6   Another partial explanation of *apparent* reversals is seen in the fact that we have been talking about the hierarchy of prepotency in terms of consciously felt wants or desires rather than of behavior. Looking at behavior itself may give us the wrong impression. What we have claimed is that the person will *want* the more basic of two needs when deprived in both. There is no necessary implication here that he will act upon his desires. Let us say again that there are many determinants of behavior other than the needs and desires.

7   Perhaps more important than all these exceptions are the ones that involve ideals, high social standards, high values and the like. With such values people become martyrs; they will give up everything for the sake of a particular ideal, or value. These people may be understood, at least in part, by reference to one basic concept (or hypothesis) which may be called "increased frustration-tolerance through early gratification." People who have been satisfied in their basic needs throughout their lives, particularly in their earlier years, seem to develop exceptional power to withstand present or future thwarting of these needs simply because they have strong, healthy character structure as a result of basic satisfaction. They are the "strong" people who can easily weather disagreement or opposition, who can swim against the stream of public opinion and who can stand up for the truth at great personal cost. It is just the ones who have loved and been well loved, and who have had many deep friendships who can hold out against hatred, rejection or persecution.

I say all this in spite of the fact that there is a certain amount of sheer habituation which is also involved in any full discussion of frustration tolerance. For instance, it is likely that those persons who have been accustomed to relative starvation for a long time are partially enabled thereby to withstand food deprivation. What sort of balance must be made between these two tendencies, of habituation on the one hand, and of past satisfaction breeding present frustration tolerance on the other hand, remains to be worked out by further research. Meanwhile we may assume that they are both operative, side by side, since they do not contradict each other. In respect to this phenomenon of increased frustration tolerance, it seems probable that the most important gratifications come in the first two years of life. That is to say, people who have been made secure and strong in the earliest years, tend to remain secure and strong thereafter in the face of whatever threatens.

Degrees of Relative Satisfaction   So far, our theoretical discussion may have given the impression that these five sets of needs are somehow in a step-wise, all-or-none relationship to each other. We have spoken in such terms as the following: "If one need is satisfied, then another emerges." This statement might give the false impression that a need must be satisfied 100 per cent before the next need emerges. In actual fact, most members of our society who are normal, are partially satisfied in all their basic needs and partially unsatisfied in all their basic needs at the same time. A more realistic description of the hierarchy would be in terms of decreasing percentages of satisfaction as we go up the hierarchy of prepotency. For instance, if I may assign arbitrary figures for the sake of illustration, it is as if the average citizen is satisfied perhaps 85 per cent in his physiological needs, 70 percent in his safety needs, 50 per cent in his love needs, 40 per cent in his self-esteem needs, and 10 per cent in his self-actualization needs.

As for the concept of emergence of a new need after satisfaction of the prepotent need, this emergence is not a sudden, saltatory phenomenon but rather a gradual emergence by slow degrees from nothingness. For instance, if prepotent need A is satisfied only 10 per cent then need B may not be visible at all. However, as this need A becomes satisfied 25 per cent, need B may emerge 5 per cent, as need A becomes satisfied 75 per cent, need B may emerge 90 per cent, and so on.

Unconscious Character of Needs   These needs are neither necessarily conscious nor unconscious. On the whole, however, in the average person, they are more often unconscious rather than conscious. It is not necessary at this point to overhaul the tremendous mass of evidence which indicates the crucial importance of unconscious motivation. It would by now be expected, on a priori grounds alone, that unconscious motivations would on the whole be rather more important than the conscious motivations. What we have called the basic needs are very often largely unconscious although they may, with suitable techniques, and with sophisticated people become conscious.

Cultural Specificity and Generality of Needs   This classification of basic needs makes some attempt to take account of the relative unity behind the superficial differences in specific desires from one culture to another. Certainly in any particular culture an individual's conscious motivational content will usually be extremely different from the conscious motivational content of an individual in another society. However, it is the common experience of anthropologists that people, even in different societies, are much more alike than we would think from our first contact with them, and that as we know them better we seem to find more and more of this commonness. We then recognize the most startling differences to be superficial rather than basic, *e.g.,* differences in style of hairdress, clothes, tastes in food, etc. Our classification of basic needs is in part an attempt to account for this unity behind the apparent diversity from culture to culture. No claim is made that it is ultimate or universal for all cultures. The claim is made only that it is relatively *more* ultimate, more universal, more basic, than the superficial conscious desires from culture to culture, and makes a somewhat closer approach to common-human characteristics. Basic needs are *more* common-human than superficial desires or behaviors.

Multiple Motivations of Behavior   These needs must be understood *not* to be *exclusive* or single determiners of certain kinds of behavior. An example may be found in any behavior that seems to be physiologically motivated, such as eating, or sexual play or the like. The clinical psychologists have long since found that any behavior may be a channel through which flow various determinants. Or to say it in another way, most behavior is multi-motivated. Within the sphere of motivational determinants any behavior tends to be determined by several or *all* of the basic needs simultaneously rather than by only one of them. The latter would be more an exception than the former. Eating may be partially for the sake of filling the stomach, and partially for the sake of comfort and amelioration of other needs. One may make love not only for pure sexual release, but also to convince one's self of one's masculinity, or to make a conquest, to feel powerful, or to win more basic affection. As an illustration, I may point out that it would be possible (theoretically if not practically) to analyze a single act of an individual and see in it the expression of his physiological needs, his safety needs, his love needs, his esteem needs and self-actualization. This contrasts sharply with the more naive brand of trait psychology in which one trait or one motive accounts for a certain kind of act, *i.e.,* an aggressive act is traced solely to a trait of aggressiveness.

Multiple Determinants of Behavior   Not all behavior is determined by the basic needs. We might even say that not all behavior is motivated. There are many determinants of behavior other than motives.[9] For instance, one other important class of determinants is the so-called "field" determinants. Theoretically, at least, behavior may be determined completely by the field, or even by specific isolated external stimuli, as in association of ideas, or certain conditioned reflexes. If in response to the stimulus word "table," I immediately perceive a memory image of a table, this response certainly has nothing to do with my basic needs.

Secondly, we may call attention again to the concept of "degree of closeness to the basic needs" or "degree of motivation." Some behavior is highly motivated, other behavior is only weakly motivated. Some is not motivated at all (but all behavior is determined).

Another important point[10] is that there is a basic difference between expressive behavior and coping behavior (functional striving, purposive goal seeking). An expressive behavior does not try to do anything; it is simply a reflection of the

---

[9] I am aware that many psychologists and psychoanalysts use the term "motivated" and "determined" synonymously, *e.g.,* Freud. But I consider this an obfuscating usage. Sharp distinctions are necessary for clarity of thought, and precision in experimentation.

[10] To be discussed fully in a subsequent publication.

personality. A stupid man behaves stupidly, not because he wants to, or tries to, or is motivated to, but simply because he is what he is. The same is true when I speak in a bass voice rather than tenor or soprano. The random movements of a healthy child, the smile on the face of a happy man even when he is alone, the springiness of the healthy man's walk, and the erectness of his carriage are other examples of expressive, non-functional behavior. Also the *style* in which a man carries out almost all his behavior, motivated as well as unmotivated, is often expressive.

We may then ask, is *all* behavior expressive or reflective of the character structure? The answer is "No." Rote, habitual, automatized, or conventional behavior may or may not be expressive. The same is true for most "stimulus-bound" behaviors.

It is finally necessary to stress that expressiveness of behavior and goal-directedness of behavior are not mutually exclusive categories. Average behavior is usually both.

Goals as Centering Principle in Motivation Theory   It will be observed that the basic principle in our classification has been neither the instigation nor the motivated behavior but rather the functions, effects, purposes, or goals of the behavior. It has been proven sufficiently by various people that this is the most suitable point for centering in any motivation theory.[11]

Animal- and Human-Centering   This theory starts with the human being rather than any lower and presumably "simpler" animal. Too many of the findings that have been made in animals have been proven to be true for animals but not for the human being. There is no reason whatsoever why we should start with animals in order to study human motivation. The logic or rather illogic behind this general fallacy of "pseudo-simplicity" has been exposed often enough by philosophers and logicians as well as by scientists in each of the various fields. It is no more necessary to study animals before one can study man than it is to study mathematics before one can study geology or psychology or biology.

We may also reject the old, naive, behaviorism which assumed that it was somehow necessary, or at least more "scientific" to judge human beings by animal standards. One consequence of this belief was that the whole notion of purpose and goal was excluded from motivational psychology simply because one could not ask a white rat about his purposes. Tolman (18) has long since proven in animal studies themselves that this exclusion was not necessary.

Motivation and the Theory of Psychopathogenesis   The conscious motivational content of eveyday life has, according to the foregoing, been conceived to be relatively important or unimportant accordingly as it is more or less closely related to the basic goals. A desire for an ice cream cone might actually be an

---

[11]The interested reader is referred to the very excellent discussion of this point in Murray's *Explorations in Personality* (15).

indirect expression of a desire for love. If it is, then this desire for the ice cream cone becomes extremely important motivation. If however the ice cream is simply something to cool the mouth with, or a casual appetitive reaction, then the desire is relatively unimportant. Everyday conscious desires are to be regarded as symptoms, as *surface indicators of more basic needs*. If we were to take these superficial desires at their face value we would find ourselves in a state of complete confusion which could never be resolved, since we would be dealing seriously with symptoms rather than with what lay behind the symptoms.

Thwarting of unimportant desires produces no psychopathological results; thwarting of a basically important need does produce such results. Any theory of psychopathogenesis must then be based on a sound theory of motivation. A conflict or a frustration is not necessarily pathogenic. It becomes so only when it threatens or thwarts the basic needs, or partial needs that are closely related to the basic needs (10).

The Role of Gratified Needs   It has been pointed out above several times that our needs usually emerge only when more prepotent needs have been gratified. Thus gratification has an important role in motivation theory. Apart from this, however, needs cease to play an active determining or organizing role as soon as they are gratified.

What this means is that, *e.g.,* a basically satisfied person no longer has the needs for esteem, love, safety, etc. The only sense in which he might be said to have them is in the almost metaphysical sense that a sated man has hunger, or a filled bottle has emptiness. If we are interested in what *actually* motivates us, and not in what has, will, or might motivate us, then a satisfied need is not a motivator. It must be considered for all practical purposes simply not to exist, to have disappeared. This point should be emphasized because it has been either overlooked or contradicted in every theory of motivation I know.[12] The perfectly healthy, normal, fortunate man has no sex needs or hunger needs, or needs for safety, or for love, or for prestige, or self-esteem, except in stray moments of quickly passing threat. If we were to say otherwise, we should also have to aver that every man had all the pathological reflexes, *e.g.,* Babinski, etc., because if his nervous system were damaged, these would appear.

It is such considerations as these that suggest the bold postulation that a man who is thwarted in any of his basic needs may fairly be envisaged simply as a sick man. This is a fair parallel to our designation as "sick" of the man who lacks vitamins or minerals. Who is to say that a lack of love is less important than a lack of vitamins? Since we know the pathogenic effects of love starvation, who is to say that we are invoking value-questions in an unscientific or illegitimate way, any more than the physician does who diagnoses and treats pellagra or scurvy? If I were permitted this usage, I should then say simply that a healthy man is primarily motivated by his needs to develop and actualize his fullest potentialities

---

[12]Note that acceptance of this theory necessitates basic revision of the Freudian theory.

and capacities. If a man has any other basic needs in any active, chronic sense, then he is simply an unhealthy man. He is as surely sick as if he had suddenly developed a strong salt-hunger or calcium hunger.[13]

If this statement seems unusual or paradoxical the reader may be assured that this is only one among many such paradoxes that will appear as we revise our ways of looking at man's deeper motivations. When we ask what man wants of life, we deal with his very essence.

IV Summary

1 There are at least five sets of goals, which we may call basic needs. These are briefly physiological, safety, love, esteem, and self-actualization. In addition, we are motivated by the desire to achieve or maintain the various conditions upon which these basic satisfactions rest and by certain more intellectual desires.

2 These basic goals are related to each other, being arranged in a hierarchy of prepotency. This means that the most prepotent goal will monopolize consciousness and will tend of itself to organize the recruitment of the various capacities of the organism. The less prepotent needs are minimized, even forgotten or denied. But when a need is fairly well satisfied, the next prepotent ("higher") need emerges, in turn to dominate the conscious life and to serve as the center of organization of behavior, since gratified needs are not active motivators.

Thus man is a perpetually wanting animal. Ordinarily the satisfaction of these wants is not altogether mutually exclusive, but only tends to be. The average member of our society is most often partially satisfied and partially unsatisfied in all of his wants. The hierarchy principle is usually empirically observed in terms of increasing percentages of non-satisfaction as we go up the hierarchy. Reversals of the average order of the hierarchy are sometimes observed. Also it has been observed that an individual may permanently lose the higher wants in the hierarchy under special conditions. There are not only ordinarily multiple motivations for usual behavior, but in addition many determinants other than motives.

3 Any thwarting or possibility of thwarting of these basic human goals, or danger to the defenses which protect them, or to the conditions upon which they rest, is considered to be a psychological threat. With a few exceptions, all psychopathology may be partially traced to such threats. A basically thwarted man may actually be defined as a "sick" man, if we wish.

4 It is such basic threats which bring about the general emergency reactions.

---

[13]If we were to use the word "sick" in this way, we should then also have to face squarely the relations of man to his society. One clear implication of our definition would be that (1) since a man is to be called sick who is basically thwarted, and (2) since such basic thwarting is made possible ultimately only by forces outside the individual, then (3) sickness in the individual must come ultimately from a sickness in the society. The "good" or healthy society would then be defined as one that permitted man's highest purposes to emerge by satisfying all his prepotent basic needs.

5 Certain other basic problems have not been dealt with because of limitations of space. Among these are (a) the problem of values in any definitive motivation theory, (b) the relation between appetites, desires, needs and what is "good" for the organism, (c) the etiology of the basic needs and their possible derivation in early childhood, (d) redefinition of motivational concepts, *i.e.,* drive, desire, wish, need, goal, (e) implication of our theory for hedonistic theory, (f) the nature of the uncompleted act, of success and failure, and of aspiration-level, (g) the role of association, habit and conditioning, (h) relation to the theory of inter-personal relations, (i) implications for psychotherapy, (j) implication for theory of society, (k) the theory of selfishness, (l) the relation between needs and cultural patterns, (m) the relation between this theory and Allport's theory of functional autonomy. These as well as certain other less important questions must be considered as motivation theory attempts to become definitive.

References

1 Adler, A.: *Social interest*. London: Faber & Faber, 1938.
2 Cannon, W. B.: *Wisdom of the body*. New York: Norton, 1932.
3 Freud, A.: *The ego and the mechanisms of defense*. London: Hagarth, 1937.
4 Freud, S.: *New introductory lectures on psychoanalysis*. New York: Norton, 1933.
5 Fromm, E.: *Escape from freedom*. New York: Farrar and Rinehart, 1941.
6 Goldstein, K.: *The organism*. New York: American Book Co., 1939.
7 Horney, K.: *The neurotic personality of our time*. New York: Norton, 1937.
8 Kardiner, A.: *The traumatic neuroses of war*. New York: Hoeber, 1941.
9 Levy, D. M.: *Primary affect hunger*. Amer. J. Psychiat., 1937, **94**, 643-652.
10 Maslow, A. H.: Conflict, frustration, and the theory of threat. *J. abnorm. (soc.) Psychol.*, 1943, **38**, 81-86.
11 ——: Dominance, personality and social behavior in women. *J. soc. Psychol.*, 1939, **10**, 3-39.
12 ——: The dynamics of psychological security-insecurity. *Character & Pers.*, 1942, **10**, 331-344.
13 ——: A preface to motivation theory. *Psychosomatic Med.*, 1943, **5**, 85-92.
14 ——, & Mittelmann, B.: *Principle of abnormal psychology*. New York: Harper & Bros., 1941.
15 Murray, H.A., *et al.: Explorations in personality*. New York: Oxford University Press, 1938.
16 Plant, J.: *Personality and the cultural pattern*. New York: Commonwealth Fund, 1937.
17 Shirley, M.: Children's adjustments to a strange situation. *J. abnorm. (soc.) Psychol.*, 1942, **37**, 201-217.
18 Tolman, E.C.: *Purposive behavior in animals and men*. New York: Century, 1932.
19 Wertheimer, M.: Unpublished lectures at the New School for Social Research.
20 Young, P. T.: *Motivation of behavior*. New York: John Wiley & Sons, 1936.
21 ——: The experimental analysis of appetite. *Psychol. Bull.*, 1941, **38**, 129-164.

Motivation versus Hygiene

Frederick Herzberg
Bernard Mausner
Barbara Bloch Synderman

Let us summarize briefly our answer to the question, "What do people want from their jobs?" When our respondents reported feeling happy with their jobs, they most frequently described factors related to their tasks, to events that indicated to them that they were successful in the performance of their work, and to the possibility of professional growth. Conversely, when feelings of unhappiness were reported, they were not associated with the job itself but with conditions that *surround* the doing of the job. These events suggest to the individual that the context in which he performs his work is unfair or disorganized and as such represents to him an unhealthy psychological work environment. Factors involved in these situations we call factors of *hygiene,* for they act in a manner analogous to the principles of medical hygiene. Hygiene operates to remove health hazards from the environment of man. It is not a curative; it is, rather, a preventive. Modern garbage disposal, water purification, and air-pollution control do not cure diseases, but without them we should have many more diseases. Similarly, when there are deleterious factors in the context of the job, they serve to bring about poor job attitudes. Improvement in these factors of hygiene will serve to remove the impediments to positive job attitudes. Among the factors of hygiene we have included supervision, interpersonal relations, physical working condition, salary, company policies and administrative practices, benefits, and job security. When these factors deteriorate to a level below that which the employee considers acceptable, then job dissatisfaction ensues. However, the reverse does not hold true. When the job context can be characterized as optimal, we will not get dissatisfaction, but neither will we get much in the way of positive attitudes.

The factors that lead to positive job attitudes do so because they satisfy the individual's need for self-actualization in his work. The concept of self-actualization, or self-realization, as a man's ultimate goal has been focal to the thought of many personality theorists. For such men as Jung, Adler, Sullivan, Rogers, and Goldstein the supreme goal of man is to fulfill himself as a creative, unique individual according to his own innate potentialities and within the limits of reality. When he is deflected from this goal he becomes, as Jung says, "a crippled animal."

Man tends to actualize himself in every area of his life, and his job is one of the most important areas. The conditions that surround the doing of the job cannot give him this basic satisfaction; they do not have this potentiality. It is only from the performance of a task that the individual can get the rewards that

From *The Motivation to Work,* John Wiley & Sons, Inc., New York, 1959, chap. 12, pp. 113–119. Reprinted by permission of the publisher.

will reinforce his aspirations. It is clear that although the factors relating to the doing of the job and the factors defining the job context serve as goals for the employee, the nature of the motivating qualities of the two kinds of factors is essentially different. Factors in the job context meet the needs of the individual for avoiding unpleasant situations. In contrast to this motivation by meeting avoidance needs, the job factors reward the needs of the individual to reach his aspirations. These effects on the individual can be conceptualized as actuating approach rather than avoidance behavior. Since it is in the approach sense that the term motivation is most commonly used, we designate the job factors as the "motivators," as opposed to the extra-job factors, which we have labeled the factors of hygiene. It should be understood that both kinds of factors meet the needs of the employee; but it is primarily the "motivators" that serve to bring about the kind of job satisfaction and, as we saw in the section dealing with the effects of job attitudes, the kind of improvement in performance that industry is seeking from its work force.

We can now say something systematic about what people want from their jobs. For the kind of population that we sampled, and probably for many other populations as well, the wants of employees divide into two groups. One group revolves around the need to develop in one's occupation as a source of personal growth. The second group operates as an essential base to the first and is associated with fair treatment in compensation, supervision, working conditions, and administrative practices. The fulfillment of the needs of the second group does not motivate the individual to high levels of job satisfaction and . . . to extra performance on the job. All we can expect from satisfying the needs for hygiene is the prevention of dissatisfaction and poor job performance.

In the light of this distinction, we can account for much of the lack of success that industry has had in its attempts to motivate employees. Let us examine two of the more ubiquitous avenues through which industry has hoped to gain highly motivated employees: human-relations training for supervisors and wage-incentive systems.

As part of this era of human relations, supervisory training directed toward improving the interpersonal relationships between superior and subordinate has been widely incorporated into industrial-relations programs. These programs have been initiated with expectations of bringing about positive job attitudes and, hopefully, increased performance on the job. When we examine the results of our study, we find interpersonal relationships appearing in an exceedingly small number of the high sequences; in only 15 per cent of the low sequences are poor interpersonal relationships with the superior reported. The negligible role which interpersonal relationships play in our data tallies poorly with the assumption basic to most human-relations training programs that the way in which a supervisor gets along with his people is the single most important determinant of morale. Supervisory training in human relations is probably essential to the maintenance of good hygiene at work. This is particularly true for the many jobs, both at rank-and-file and managerial levels, in which modern industry offers little chance for the operation of the motivators. These jobs are atomized, cut and dried, monotonous. They offer little chance for responsibility and achievement and thus little opportunity for self-actualization. It is here that hygiene is exceptionally important. The fewer the opportunities for the "motivators" to appear, the greater must be the hygiene offered in order to make the work tolerable. A man who finds his job challenging, exciting, and satisfying will perhaps tolerate a difficult supervisor. But to expect such programs to pay dividends beyond the effects that hygiene provides is going contrary to the nature of job motivation. In terms of the approach-avoidance concept, the advocates of human relations have suggested that by rewarding the avoidance needs of the individual you will achieve the desired approach behavior. But a more creative design will not emerge from an engineer as a result of fair supervisory treatment. To achieve the more creative design, one or more of the motivators must be present, a task that is interesting to the engineer, a task in which he can exercise responsiblity and independence, a task that allows for some concrete achievement. The motivators fit the need for creativity, the hygiene factors satisfy the need for fair treatment, and it is thus that the appropriate incentive must be present to achieve the desired job attitude and job performance.

The failure to get positive returns in both job attitudes and job performance from rewarding the avoidance needs of the individual is most clearly seen in the use of monetary incentives. We have listed salary among the factors of hygiene, and as such it meets two kinds of avoidance needs of the employee. First is the avoidance of the economic deprivation that is felt when actual income is insufficient. Second, and generally of more significance in the times and for the kind of people covered by our study, is the need to avoid feelings of being treated unfairly. Salary and wages are very frequently at the top of the list of factors describing answers to the question, "What don't you like about your job?" in morale surveys. They are at the middle of the list of answers to the question, "What do you want from your job?" We have explained this difference in emphasis by our distinction between factors that lead to job satisfaction and the factors that contribute to job dissatisfaction. Asking people what is important to them in their jobs will bring responses that we have classified as "motivators." The atmosphere of the usual morale survey encourages people to emphasize sources of dissatisfaction.

Where morale surveys have differentiated between dissatisfaction with amount of salary as opposed to the equity of salary, the latter looms as the more important source of dissatisfaction. In two consecutive morale surveys by the senior author, in which the employees were requested to illustrate their dissatisfaction or satisfaction with the various items on the morale questionnaire with critical incidents, the comments on the equity of salary greatly outnumbered the comments on the absolute amount of salary. All 1382 employees surveyed were at the supervisory level (21).

How then can we explain the success of the many employee motivational schemes that seem to rely directly on the use of wage incentives and bonuses? Reports on the Lincoln Electric Company of Cleveland, Ohio (37), and the George A. Hormel meat-packing plant at Austin, Minnesota (7), suggest good examples of the efficacy of money incentives for increasing production, job satisfaction, and company loyalty. But let us examine for a moment the nature of these programs and the nature of their success in the light of the findings presented here.

First, there are many other ingredients to these plans which are generally given less attention than they merit, ingredients that combine a large proportion of the factors that we have found to be motivators. The formation of Lincoln's Advisory Board and Hormel's Business Improvement Committee both resulted from attempts to increase job content and job responsibility by giving workers knowledge of, and responsibility for, operations and improvements. Both operate on the theory that the "boss" cannot know everything about all the work processes, that the workers are experts in their fields, and that their knowledge is of great value. Lincoln Electric, which is not unionized, has the additional advantage of being able to advance workers on the basis of merit, not seniority. James E. Lincoln, president of the company, says that "money is of relatively small importance. Beyond enough for our real needs, money itself is valued less for what it will buy than as an evidence of successful skill in achievement (37)." Money thus earned as a direct reward for outstanding individual performance is a reinforcement of the motivators of *recognition* and *achievement*. It is not hygiene as is the money given in across-the-board wage increases.

The Scanlon plan is a system for involving employees of a company in the improvement of production by the distribution of savings in labor costs to all of the personnel of a participating company. This aspect of participation and of increased responsibility is the real secret of whatever success the Scanlon plan and its imitators have achieved. Lincoln Electric is implementing man's natural striving for self-realization. No man wants to be just a cog in a wheel. Lincoln says, "The most insistent incentive is the development of self-respect and the respect of others. Earnings that are the reward for outstanding performance, progress, and responsibility are signs that he is a man among men. The worker must feel that he is part of a worthwhile project and that the project succeeded because his ability was needed in it. Money alone will not do the job."

When incentive systems do not permit any of the motivators to operate, then any increase in performance or in apparent job satisfaction is misleading. For in these instances the removal of a decrement in performance by the elimination of job dissatisfaction is often mistakenly referred to as a positive gain in performance. That voluntary restriction of output is practiced on an enormous scale is common knowledge in industry (26, 27, 58). The existence of a standard of "a fair day's work" has been well documented in systematic studies by industrial psychologists and sociologists as well as industrial engineers. It is likely that poor hygiene will depress performance below the level of "the fair day's work." Correction of this poor hygiene, or the application of monetary incentives not related to motivators, may return performance to the norm. The improvement produced under these circumstances is actually far less than one could obtain were motivators to be introduced.

Are good job attitudes and company loyalty engendered by these incentive plans? The surface answer often seems to be yes. Employees in such companies will report that they like working for their companies, but the "liking" seems to be little more than the absence of disliking, their satisfaction little more than the absence of dissatisfaction. Blum reports on the Hormel packinghouse workers in this regard:

> If I had to summarize workers' feelings about the company in one sentence, I would repeat the words of a worker: "If a man is going to work for anybody else, it's hard to beat Hormel." It is the single most often heard expression in any conversation about the company. I have never heard a worker express an unconditional acceptance of the company as an organization to work for (7).

Are they really saying they like their work? Or are they merely saying that they have found a place to work in which life is not unbearable?

What is the evidence? According to Blum's report, shop talk is deafening by its absence when the work day is over. There seems to be a deliberate effort on the part of the employees to repress any mention of their jobs away from the plant. Contrast this with the unceasing shop talk reported by Walker in his study of steel workers at the National Tube Company of Ellwood City, Pennsylvania (56). His description of their jobs emphasizes the large number of motivators present. They are not running away from their work at the shift bell. They continue to live their jobs at home. The employees of Hormel seem to be psychologically running away from their jobs. Their extra effort, while it increases production, albeit probably not to the level of which they are capable, is not indicative of positive job attitudes. Rather it provides the means for escape from a job toward which their attitudes are little better than neutral. The sooner they finish the job, the sooner they can get away from it; the more money they can earn, the more effective their escape in pleasant living off the job. It is doubtful that the true production potential of these workers is being tapped; it is undeniable that the incentive system, along with other hygienic factors, serves to make their jobs tolerable.

The definition of *hygiene* and *motivation* and the relationship of these complexes of factors to the behavior of men at work has many implications for industrial practice. In the next section we try to explore these implications after setting the findings of our study in an historical background.

References
7   Blum, F. A.: *Toward a Democratic Work Process.* New York: Harper, 1953.
21 Herzberg, F.: "An Analysis of Morale Survey Comments." *Personnel Psychol.,* 1954, 7 (2), pp. 267-275.
26 Horsfall, A. B., and C. M. Arensberg: "Teamwork and Productivity in a Shoe Factory." *Hum. Organization,* 1949, 8, pp. 13-25.
27 Hughes, E.C.: "The Knitting of Racial Groups in Industry." *American Sociol. Review,* 1946, 11, pp. 512-519.
37 Lincoln, J. F.: *Lincoln's Incentive System.* New York: McGraw-Hill, 1946.
56 Walker, C. R.: *Steeltown.* New York: Harper, 1950.
58 Whyte, W. F.: *Money and Motivation.* New York: Harper, 1955.

Readings Related to Chapter 5

Level of Aspiration

Ross Stagner

Since we are concerned with behavior of man in western culture, and specifically in industry in the United States, we must accept competitive impulses toward prestige and power as major considerations. We live in a society in which approximately 85 per cent of fathers say that they expect their sons to outdo their own achievements. The so-called "American dream" is that of the poor boy who rises to be a big business man, a famous inventor, or a great political leader. Children are urged to set goals above their present performance, and then work energetically to reach these goals. Such a projected or hoped-for future performance is known as the individual's *level of aspiration*.

The importance of aspirations is to be found chiefly in relation to social goals such as prestige and power. However, we can observe somewhat analogous phenomena at the simple biogenic level. Adolph (1941), for example, demonstrated that dogs when thirsty have a kind of quantitative notion of just how much water is needed to restore this particular equilibrium. Dogs were prepared with an esophageal fistula, so that water drunk fell out into a container and did not reach the stomach. (Needed water was later supplied through this same fistula.) The animals were then kept without water for specified numbers of hours, and the amount drunk was measured. Each animal took in almost exactly the amount required to restore his water balance, even though the liquid was not reaching his stomach and he therefore could not have any sensory feedback to inform him that he "had enough."

This kind of very simple, quantitative estimate of "how much I want" is quickly replaced by a socially determined craving for "something better" or higher in the scale of social values. Any house which provides shelter, warmth, and privacy might be said to satisfy biogenic needs. But people want houses which are attractive, in the right neighborhoods, and so on. We have already noted . . . that housing type is a fairly good predictor of attitude toward labor

From chap. 4, "Motivation: Principles," *The Psychology of Industrial Conflict*, John Wiley & Sons, Inc. New York, 1956, pp. 105–109. Reprinted by permission of the publisher.

unions. The significant determinant, of course, is income; as people get more money, they acquire more expensive housing, and also take on more conservative views on economic affairs.

Goal setting in an industrial society characteristically takes the form of an orientation toward a certain status or position just a short distance "up" from the individual's present achievement. Just as the private must become a corporal before he can become a sergeant, so there is a ladder to success in the business world. Even in terms of income, the typical American sets his sights just a short distance from his present earnings (cf. Table 1) rather than "hitching his wagon to a star."

We can take this process into the laboratory and study it experimentally. The basic technique is to have the subject attempt some task (dart throwing, card sorting, solving anagrams, etc.). After he is given his score on the first trial, he is asked to estimate "how well you will do next time." It is assumed that the person setting a goal is revealing a generalized characteristic of his personality; that he gives some indication of how he sets goals in everyday life.

The results of a large number of investigations (cf. Gould, 1939) indicate that the typical American youth's response to the instructions given is to set a goal just a little in advance of his performance on the first trial. This is considered to indicate a realistic kind of motivation, in that the goal is reasonably probable of achievement. However, in any group there will be some who will set absurdly high aspirations—perhaps indicative of motivation so strong that it overpowers

Table 1   Economic Level of Aspiration as a Function of Current Status*

Present income level	Occupation	Average estimate†
Negroes	Farm labor	$1,000–1,499
Poor	Miscellaneous labor	1,500–1,999
	Unemployed	
Lower middle	Factory labor	2,000–2,499
	Retired	
	Farm owners	
	White collar	2,500–2,999
	Housekeepers	
	Students	
	Miscellaneous	
	Proprietors	3,000–3,499
		3,500–4,499
Upper middle		4,500–4,999
	Professional	5,000–5,499
	Executives	
		5,500–5,999
Prosperous		10,000–14,999

*Fortune, February, 1940. Reprinted by permission of the publisher. See also Centers and Cantril (1946).

†The lowest income that would satisfy a majority of persons in each group named.

perception, distorting the situation so that it seems possible to attain so distant a goal. Conversely, there will generally be some youngsters who will actually estimate performance on the next trial *below* past performance; this is thought to reflect a need to avoid failure as being more powerful than the need to increase status (see, e.g., Gruen, 1945).

Effect of Success and Failure   One of the main reasons for taking a problem like this into the laboratory is to make possible manipulations of determining factors which cannot be controlled in everyday life. It was hypothesized that a series of successes would build up an expectancy of continued success, leading to higher aspirations; whereas a series of failures would lead to expectancy of failure, and hence to lowered aspiration. This has been confirmed by many investigators (cf. Gebhard, 1948). Since it is easy to manipulate scores on the performance task, the subject can be given successes and failures in any predetermined manner.

The results are in high agreement for almost all such studies. Success, with very few exceptions, leads to a rise in the reported aspiration. Failure, by contrast, leads to lowered aspirations, although these rarely become negative (predicting poorer performance than last time) except with maladjusted personalities. Failing individuals reduce their effort and attempt to get away from the experimental situation.

Group Norms   The level of aspiration experiment provides an excellent opportunity for studying the role of perception in the process of energy mobilization. Suppose we introduce a reference group into the above design by telling our subject that he has just made a score higher than the average college senior. If the subject looks up to and respects college seniors, he gets a vigorous boost from such a report, and his level of aspiration increases. On the other hand, if the group is one upon which the subject looks with contempt, he does not perceive surpassing their record as anything important, and his level of aspiration does not change. By contrast, the report that he is below the norm of some "inferior" group usually releases a burst of energy and higher aspiration.

Another interesting problem arises where a dominance-submission relationship exists between the reference group utilized and the person being tested. Preston and Bayton (1941) presented Negro college students with an experiment of the type described. As a reference group, they introduced alleged Negro college norms, and found their subjects trying harder in order to surpass these figures. But when they introduced alleged White college norms, the effect was much less. They interpreted this as reluctance to set up, even in fantasy, a situation involving direct competition with the dominant White group. This may have some connection with the reluctance of workers to admit that they have any desire for managerial status. To be "aiming at" the boss's job might make him hostile, and he might retaliate in some unpleasant way. It may seem much safer to set only a low level of aspiration and say nothing of higher ambitions. Public opinion polls repeatedly indicate that about 20 per cent of manual workers think they have a chance to become a foreman. When the question is put in terms of wish to achieve this status, the percentage goes up to about 30, whereas, if the American competitive pattern were effective, the per cent aspiring to foreman's jobs ought to be at least 50, if not more. (However, Lipset and Bendix (1952) report that about 67 per cent of manual workers express a desire for a small business of their own. In this case, aspiring to the boss's job is not involved.)

Income Aspirations Because the dollar provides a convenient unit, comparisons of present income with aspiration level are fairly easy to make. However, if a person were asked, ''how large an income would you like to have?'' he might be tempted to use the sky as the limit. If asked how much he expects next year, he will be cramped by immediate realistic possibilities. A *Fortune* poll in 1940 seems to have struck a happy compromise between these two unsatisfactory approaches by asking, ''What do you really think would be a perfectly satisfactory income for you?'' Under these circumstances people gave an aspiration level which apparently reflected both motivation and present achievement. As Table 1 shows, aspiration rises steadily with present economic status—almost everyone tested felt that he could be content with ''just a little more.'' The discrepancy between present status and aspiration ranges from a few hundred dollars at the bottom of the economic scale to a few thousand at the top. One might readily suspect that this is the familiar Weber law in perception, that the amount of increase in a stimulus which will be necessary for it to ''look bigger'' is a constant fraction of the starting stimulus.

Importance The implications of these studies on aspiration level, as regards industrial motivation, are no doubt obvious. Let us note just a few. First of all, children and adolescents who have had an accumulation of ''success'' experiences have higher aspirations than those who have more ''failure'' experiences. Thus, children from upper class families, with advantages in home background, intelligence, education, etc., characteristically have higher aspirations than those from poorer homes. Even during school years some youngsters learn ''not to hope for too much,'' whereas others are encouraged to try for higher accomplishments.

Stubbins (1950) has shown that a similar relationship holds for returning veterans. Those with higher vocational aspirations were more intelligent and better-educated. They had reached higher pay levels in the service, held postwar jobs of higher status, and had better jobs than their brothers. In other words, their higher aspirations could be considered as reflecting the successes that they have already experienced.

If we keep these observations in mind, we shall not be surprised at some of the dynamic differences observed in everyday industrial situations. The executive, with higher present attainment and a history of successes, will set his sights higher and strive for increasingly more income, power, and status. The worker, with a low income and probably some failures to look back upon, tends to hold his aspirations down and to strive for only fairly short-run, reasonably attainable goals. Such differences play an important part in producing the lack of mutual understanding between these groups, especially, the inability of many executives to understand the cautious, security-seeking behavior of the typical worker or union group.

References

Adolph, E. F.: 1941. The internal environment and behavior: water content. *Amer. J. Psychiat.* **97**, 1365–1373.

Centers, Richard, and Hadley Cantril: 1946. Income satisfaction and income aspiration. *J. abnorm. soc. Psychol.*, **41**, 64–69.

Gebhard, Mildred E.: 1948. Effect of success and failure upon the attractiveness of activities as function of experience, expectation and need. *J. exp. Psychol.*, **38**, 371–388.

Gould, Rosalind: 1939. An experimental analysis of "level of aspiration." *Genet. Psychol. Monogr.*, **21**, 3–115.

Gruen, E. W.: 1945. Level of aspiration in relation to personality factors in adolescents. *Child Developm.*, **16**, 181–188.

Lipset, Seymour M., and Reinhard Bendix: 1952. Social mobility and occupational career patterns. *Amer. J. Sociol.*, **57**, 366–374, 494–504.

Preston, M. G., and J. A. Bayton: 1941. Differential effect of a social variable upon three levels of aspiration. *J. exp. Psychol.*, **29**, 351–369.

Stubbins, Joseph: 1950. Relationship between level of vocational aspiration and certain personal data. *Genet. Psychol. Monogr.*, **41**, 327–408.

A Psychologist's Look at Women

Jane W. Torrey

Women are different from men. Biological differences are the most obvious, and they make some difference in the reactions of the two sexes. Nevertheless, the human being, whether man or woman, is primarily a social animal. The roles prescribed by the society and the personalities ascribed to go with the roles create differences that go far beyond biology. Neither the psychology of women nor the psychology of attitudes toward women can be understood outside the social context—the system of training, expectation and rewards—that molds people to fit their respective places. It is true of women in business as of all human beings that the way they are treated by others affects their capacities, motives and personalities as well as vice versa. For that reason we must begin by examining the economic position of women and the image of women in the eyes of those who make decisions before we can understand the psychology of women themselves.

Reprinted by permission of the publisher from *Journal of Contemporary Business*, Summer 1973, pp. 25–40.

The most important thing to know about the status of women is that they are the objects of prejudice. Like members of several ethnic minority groups, they have the status of a special kind of people, not "regular" individuals, but "one of those others." A prejudice is an attitude toward a whole group of people as a group. A member of the group is not judged individually on visible evidence of his or her own merits, but much more on the basis of an image of the group as a whole. This is quite different from the procedure used for evaluating a "regular" person, a white male. A potential employer, customer or creditor makes his decisions about a woman mainly on the mere fact that she is a woman, with relatively little regard for her own training, experience, credit record or personality. For example, a college graduate is asked if she can type, and a wife gets only the use of her husband's credit. This fact severly limits a woman's range of opportunities as well as her power to influence them because there is nothing she herself can do to affect the outcome. The special treatment usually results in a disadvantage for a woman as it does for minority people, but to understand the characteristic reactions of women, we must look first at the particular kind of stereotype imposed upon them.

Stereotypes of Women

A woman finds that society has certain preconceived notions about her personality. So-called "feminine" traits are expected in her regardless of what she is really like, and her job is assigned on the basis, partly, of an imaginary person, not her real self. She is supposed to be *submissive, passive* and *dependent* in contrast to men who are *assertive, independently responsible* and *full of initiative*. Women are reputed to be *diligent*, especially at *routines*, rather than *imaginative* like men. They are *selfless* and *devoted*, rather than *ambitious* like men. They are *sensitive* to the *feelings* of others rather than coolly *objective*, like men, and their own feelings are also more sensitive than those of *rational, thinking* men. These "sex differences" in personality are often perceived regardless of actual behavior. A woman who works hard is content with dull repetitive work; a diligent man is working his way to the top. A woman who accepts reproof is submissive; a man who does the same is "biding his time." A woman who is upset by reproof is being emotional; a man who does the same is refusing to be pushed around. In those cases in which a woman's behavior clearly doesn't fit the feminine pattern, she is often perceived as abnormal, as competitive and as threatening to men. She is undesirable because she is "unfeminine"; whereas, a man with the same traits is approved. Competition from other men is all right because they are expected to be unfeminine.

The reason for reviewing these beliefs about women is not to discuss whether on the average they are realistic or not. The question of what traits are more characteristic of women as a whole is hard to determine because any research would have to be based upon the judgments of people who are already prejudiced. The important point here, as with all prejudice, is that judgments are made of individuals, not on the basis of their own behavior but because of traits rightly or wrongly attributed to the group in which they belong. Even when stereotypes represent real average differences, they are seldom valid bases for judging one individual, and their use forces all members of the group into the same tight mold.

In business, the supposed personality differences between the sexes may be less important than the expectations which people have about the life-pattern of any woman. It commonly is assumed that every woman will marry before or shortly after finishing her education; that she may be employed for a few years, but that she will give birth within a few years and at that time will quit any job she may have to become a housewife and be dependent upon the income of her husband; that some years later she may return to a marginal, probably part-time job, but that her principal income will still be her husband's; that she will never be the sole supporter of dependents and that her income will always be pin money to buy extra luxuries. Like other elements of prejudice, this pattern is attributed to every woman regardless of her individual situation and regardless of the fact that increasing numbers of women do not follow this pattern. If a woman is, in reality, single, it is still assumed that she will marry and quit. If childless, she is expected to become a mother and quit. If she is already a mother, it is decided for her that she will soon leave employment to become a housewife. Her salary and her credit standing are decided on this basis, even if her husband is unemployable and she is the sole support of her family. Women are expected to quit their paid jobs because of some irresistible, instinctual lure of motherhood, even though statistics show that the better the job (the higher the status and pay), the less likely it is that a young mother will quit to become a housewife. If a valued male employee quits, his employer asks himself what could have been done to keep him. If a valued woman quits, it is assumed that nothing could have been done, that she is merely following the typical life-pattern of women. It is assumed that her commitment to the work was low because she was a woman, never because it was a low-pay, low-status, no-future job. What the average woman would do with her life if she had the same job status as a similarly qualified man cannot be known. What we do know is that stereotyped expectations can become self-fulfilling prophecies.

Consequences of the Stereotypes

As every victim of prejudice knows, the ideas which people have about his or her group have serious economic consequences—and women are no exception. The kinds of jobs that are considered appropriate for them are those that fit the stereotypes. Most of these turn out to be low-level, subordinate jobs with little or no future. Employers do not want to make an investment in the training of someone who they assume is sure to quit after a few years. The lure of a good salary and a promising future is used to keep a good man, but women are not supposed to be influenced by such things. Their personalities also suggest subordinate jobs. They are dependent, submissive and diligent—the ideal secretary or research assistant.

At the professional level, women find themselves most acceptable in the helping professions, e.g., social work, teaching and nursing. Unselfishness and emotional sensitivity are important qualities in these professions. (Unselfishness is especially important because these professions are very poorly paid despite their fairly high training requirements.) The imagined life role of women also fits well with these professions. The housewife and mother job is a helping profession par excellence. Not only is there a minimum of role-conflict, but also it is often possible, especially with nursing, to work part-time while maintaining a house.

On the other hand, higher status, supervisory and leadership positions require a set of traits defined as unfeminine and, therefore, not seen as belonging to women. Even in teaching and social work, the supervisors and principals are usually men. Ambition and initiative are qualities needed in most higher positions, so people like women, who are defined as not having these traits, are less likely to be considered for them. Among the professions, those requiring high intellectual ability are seen as more appropriate for the thinking rather than the feeling person. Despite the fact that school and test performances show women to be equal or better than men in the key intellectual abilities, the image of women as emotional rather than rational has a powerful deterring effect on their admission to schools of medicine, law and engineering, which, not incidentally, happens to result in high incomes. The prestige of these professions also seems inconsistent with woman's subordinate destiny. Even within the professions, specialties with the most status and compensation, such as surgery, are reserved for men almost exclusively, despite the fact that women are thought to be especially skilled at fine hand work. Another trait often demanded by the higher level positions is imagination and creativity. The stereotype that associates these traits with men tends to prevent such abilities from being seen in women.

It is probably important to assert once again that we need not argue here that women on the average equal men in all these capacities in order to assert that individual women could be considered for their personal qualifications in the same way that men are. There is large variation within both sexes in all the traits mentioned, so that even if women did average lower in one of them than men, there still would be many women who were as well qualified as most men. However, the fact of prejudice means that individuals often are not even considered because of a group stereotype; whereas, an unbiased consideration often would show them to be eminently well-suited as individuals.

The expected life-pattern of women is probably even more of a barrier than ascribed personality in the higher-level professions and jobs. Most of these require long education or experience, an investment that legitimately may be questioned for people who are almost certain to leave the profession early in life. To understand how prejudice enters this picture, it is necessary to examine the statistics which show that, in fact, women who are highly trained usually do not quit their profession or the business world to become housewives. Over 80 percent of married women physicians are practicing medicine. Those who regard the PhD degree as primarily preparation for college teaching often are not aware of the fact that more women PhDs than men PhDs teach college. Yet women very often are denied these opportunities because someone sees them only in terms of his own stereotype of a woman's life.

Another aspect of the imagined life-pattern of women that works against their employment in responsible positions is the expectation that married women, especially mothers, always will be more devoted to their personal lives than to the job. Whereas husbands and fathers are expected to put their position in the economy first, women's commitment outside the home is generally perceived as secondary. The pattern of family life fosters this belief in that housework and child care are generally done by the wife and mother, so that she really does spend a much larger portion of her time doing those things than does the father. However, again, employers commonly do not examine the individual case but assume that it will *always* be the mother who stays home when children are sick and that only fathers can be counted on for overtime or sudden travel.

Even the single woman suffers because of these expected life patterns of women. If she is young, the pattern of motherhood is projected for her into her future, and she is treated like any other mother regardless of her intentions. If she is not young, her very singleness makes her appear abnormal and, thus, possibly maladjusted.

Still another aspect of the life-pattern expectation for women is the fact that a housewife is conceived as a dependent whose position is subordinate to her husband. This means that she is often refused credit on her own no matter how much she earns or how promptly she pays bills. The role of the housewife is that of helpmeet, of follower rather than leader, taker rather than giver of orders, with public status clearly below that of the husband. Therefore, there is a threat of an anomaly if the wife's job should be higher in pay or status than her husband's. There is also a perceived role conflict for a woman whenever her job is a leading or supervising one because of the presumed need to shift gears and act quite differently in private life.

One of the most damaging aspects of the life-pattern image for a woman's employment is its implications for pay. By lumping together all women as dependent housewives, regardless of their status, employers tend to think of them as "not needing" a living wage. If every woman's "real" living comes from her husband, all women's earnings can be regarded as extra income, not as family support. This supposed sex-difference in obligations frequently is cited as both cause and justification for the very large pay differential between the sexes. (The difference is even greater than the difference between whites and blacks.[1]) The role of prejudice in this argument is shown by the fact that a woman's or a man's actual family responsibilities seldom are used as the basis of pay decisions. Men who are unmarried are paid as though they were. Women who are the sole supporters of parents, children, husband or others are paid as though they were dependents supplementing another income. The result is that almost a third of all families that depend upon women for support live in poverty, and poverty is even more closely associated with sex than it is with race in this country.[2] Even when a woman holds a relatively superior position, she is frequently paid less than her male subordinates without regard to her importance or value to the employer. Women who are employed full-time, year round in this country earn 58 percent of what men get, although they average more years of education. Furthermore, this percentage has been decreasing in recent years despite equal pay and equal opportunity legislation. It applies to all levels of employment without major variation.[3]

Reactions of the Traditional Woman

Up to this point, "the psychologist" has been looking not at women themselves, but at their image in the minds of employers and businessmen and at the effects of this image on woman's place in the economy. The emphasis has been upon the obviously unjust discrimination that results from other people's prejudice. If we now turn to women themselves and their attitudes toward this situation, we may be surprised to find that resentment of injustice and angry determination to fight for their rights are by no means the universal responses of women, even though they are largely aware of the business practices described. Almost half of a national sample of women described themselves as unsympathetic to "women's liberation," and more than a third said they "opposed efforts to strengthen or change women's status in society."[4] Why should so many women oppose measures to overcome discrimination against themselves? The psychology of the nonfeminist, this diminishing but still sizeable minority of American women, has to be understood against a background of the beliefs we have just described, which are shared by women as well as men in our society. Women also commonly accept these images of the personality and life-pattern of women and, furthermore, regard these images as natural and inevitable, so that all else must accommodate to the stereotype as a given fact. In this context, a number of attitudes and motives will dispose women to be indifferent or even hostile to equal rights or "women's liberation."

One psychological factor is general conservatism about changes that would appear to affect fundamental institutions like the family. Feminists assert that the role prescriptions of husbands and wives should be changed. People whose lives and identities are built around the traditional family roles do not want these changed. For example, a woman whose husband depends on her subservience to maintain his confidence in his masculinity, will not want to "castrate" the man she loves by earning as much as he. If religion prescribes a family role, then change is sacrilegious.

Another psychological barrier to feminism is the reluctance to perceive oneself as victim. People like to think they have done as well as possible in life: nobody enjoys being told that she might have been happier, richer or more successful if it weren't for some injustice. The unavoidable disadvantage is easier to tolerate than the barrier that might have been conquered. The woman who toils daily at dull and illpaid or unpaid work and who sees no means of changing it has a strong motive to think that it is inevitable or only fair or even virtuous. A stupid boss is a joke as long as you do not contemplate how much better you could have done his job, but, if you had dared to aspire to his position and salary yourself, he would be salt in the wound. Similarly, the woman who has made the choice now often dictated by society between marriage and a career has an interest in believing that the choice was a necessary one. The housewife and mother prefers to think that she really wanted this full-time job to fulfill her highest destiny. The belief makes her feel important and creates less anxiety about her position. It is easier in the mind to attribute her frustrations to personal inadequacies than it is to contemplate the difficulties involved in moving toward an equal status marriage. The same may be true for a woman who has chosen a career. It raises great anxiety for her to suggest that she has been *unjustly* deprived of the joys of motherhood, that she should have been able to have them along with her career as do the men around her on the job. A glimpse of the feminist vision makes her feel like a helpless victim of circumstances beyond her control. Thus, the belief that it is woman's destiny to have to choose between the slavery of marriage and the loneliness of a career may be a comfort to one who has had to make the choice.

Another damper on feminist militancy is the fact that many women enjoy what success they have at a price of playing a traditional feminine role. Married, they are dependent on their husbands for everything they want; employed, their bosses are men also. Any signs of discontent or protest are, realistically, likely to bring punishment. Women who are active in the feminist movement very frequently find that they are simply fired from jobs after they have taken some slight action in their own behalf. Promotions from employers or hand-outs from husbands are made less likely by any attempt to rock the boat. This is true even at high levels. Caroline Bird,[5] attempting to interview the nation's top business and professional women for a book on women's status, found a number of very successful women who were afraid, literally, for their jobs if they were quoted publicly on women's rights. A woman who has her relatively good niche in the world may realize that her position depends upon the good will of men who would be hostile to feminism. The "Uncle Tom" stance is often as useful in a woman's position as in a slave's, and it is always more comfortable to really believe what you profess.

In at least one respect, women may be deterred from seeking change by a genuine advantage in the traditional woman's role. Women are allowed to be satisfied with much less demanding work than men are. Because society does not expect women to succeed or to wield power, it absolves them of any pressure to do so. A man who continues in a routine job often feels that he has not fulfilled his destiny, whereas, even a very able housewife is under no pressure for higher achievement. If women had more opportunities, they would have to work harder to reach greater heights or feel guilty for not having tried. The fear of failure so oppressive to many men is absent for their wives and female co-workers, and the men rightly envy this freedom.

Another basis for a relatively unfriendly attitude toward the women's movement exists for the woman who has succeeded in the man's world without anyone's help. Very few women have reached top ranks in business and the professions, and, among the few who have, there are some women who profess never to have experienced discrimination. More frequently, the successful woman is well aware of the obstacles facing women but is indifferent to them because they have not succeeded in thwarting her as an individual. There are capable women who have been lucky enough to be in positions where their worth could not be ignored. Even the most ingrained prejudices are frequently vulnerable to "the exception." Mediocre women must sit far back in the bus while mediocre men do the driving, but there is much truth in the dictum that a woman can succeed if she is superior enough. The experience of successful women suggests to them that the barriers to women are not as high as they seem to others. These women have taken the obstacles into account shrewdly and found their own ways around them. Especially when their devices have involved some of the traditional feminine ways, such as careful attention to looks and careful avoidance of direct challenges to men, they are often disposed to advise other women to do it their way instead of rocking the boat. Instead of comparing themselves with more successful men, they withdraw from that competition and compare themselves with less successful women. It is much more flattering to the ego, but it blinds them to the issue of sex discrimination.

No matter what their own beliefs are, women often are inhibited from asserting themselves or demanding equal rights by ingrained patterns of behavior, especially in relation to men. Habits of speech, posture and dress that support the traditional girlish image are difficult to overcome, even though they often invite a kind of treatment that the woman resents. Even more serious for the woman who seeks equal treatment with men are the personality traits she acquired in preparation for a dependent and relatively powerless status in life. Many women find that no matter how angry or resentful they feel toward some men, they cannot bring themselves to do anything that might offend a man or say anything that they think men might not want to hear. It is very hard for some women to compete with men or to assert their ambition in any way. Women who know they are underpaid often feel that it is beneath their dignity to go and ask for a raise. They ask themselves fearfully whether they really deserve it, whereas, many men feel no such qualms. Women have been taught not to feel at home defending their own interests, even though they are ready to be quite assertive on behalf of someone else. Furthermore, some women who have learned well the role of the powerless have become quite skillful at getting their way in small matters through the devious means known as "feminine wiles." More direct assertion of power often would make it impossible for them to go on getting these little favors in the old way, and they are reluctant to give them up unless they are first convinced that direct action is potentially more successful. The fear of losing femininity is difficult to exaggerate. To divest oneself of the feminine image is to risk being thought "abnormal." What's sauce for the gander may be something else again for the goose. A woman has to tread a thin line between too little assertion to get what she wants and more assertion than can be tolerated in a woman. These are the reasons why it is often said that, "Women are their own worst enemies." "Worst" is going too far, for women are not the source of the trouble, but their own psychological reactions often reinforce rather than overcome the obstacles that exist.

Reactions of the Feminist Woman

So far we have been trying to understand the women who share the traditional expectations and stereotypes of women and who, therefore, seem to side with their oppressors. Traditionalists are not necessarily women who profit the most from the status quo; in fact, this category includes some of the most downtrodden. Whether a woman willingly suffers the slings and arrows of her outrageous fortune or takes arms against them depends not so much upon her particular degree of oppression as upon the extent to which she regards the whole situation as inevitable. Revolutions are the products of rising expectations, more than simply of discrimination, exploitation or suffering. Nobody goes on a crusade that she thinks is hopeless, no matter how much its success might benefit her. The difference between a feminist and a traditional woman lies in her degree of optimism about ending this sea of troubles. A feminist has to be a person who has a vision of a better future and is convinced that it is possible.

"The psychology of the feminist" has two different meanings: first, it means the psychology of women as understood by the feminist psychologist, her concept of what women are and how they got that way; second, it means the psychology of the feminist herself, what she wants and why she wants it. It is not possible to understand the second without the first.

The feminist psychology of women is a social psychology. It does not, of course, deny biological differences, but it examines those differences critically to see what aspects of social sex role really stem from biology and finds that very few of them are related to anatomical or physiological sex differences. It further finds that society provides a rigorous early training in sex roles and continues to pressure men and women throughout life to conform to those roles. Such pressures hardly would be necessary if the sex roles were part of biological nature. It follows that if the training were changed and the economic and social factors revised, sex roles could be very different from what they are. The feminist has a vision of a new world in which women would no longer be forced as a group into a subordinate mold and then be told that they must submit because it is in their nature. She sees what changes would be necessary in the training, the social pressure and the economy to provide for equality between the sexes. She also sees the means by which these changes could be made without destroying society or its basic value system and a timetable that would enable the young women of today to enjoy its benefits.

The civil rights movement has made women aware of such means as antidiscrimination legislation, legal suits based on constitutional rights and the power of advertising and education to change public images of social groups. Proponents of black rights have introduced a new black image into textbooks, commercials and other public media and discouraged many practices that had the effect of training black children for self-hatred and subordinate roles. Most feminists are people who see the possibility of using similar techniques effectively to change both the public image and the self-image of women.

An understanding of the causes that shape the psychology of women, together with the political means by which those factors can be changed, combine to make the feminist vision seem like a feasible program. "Freedom Now," the slogan of blacks and women alike, expresses both determination and the optimism needed to maintain it. In the light of these beliefs, then, we can begin to examine the program of the feminists in order to see the motives behind each proposal—why each is considered necessary.

Changes in business practice are among the first goals. As long as employers and creditors can discriminate at will in hiring and granting credit, women and minorities have to suffer the full brunt of society's prejudices. Legislation requiring equal opportunity and equal pay or a constitutional amendment requiring equal rights gives hope of by-passing the discouraging task of persuasion. Many people, including nonfeminists, support such laws and expect them to work. However, the roots of discrimination against women go much deeper than the prejudices of personnel and credit managers. Feminists see changes needed both in people and in the society at large before equality of opportunity can become a reality.

Some of these changes would be encouraged directly by equal employment opportunity. The submissiveness of women is now at least partly due to the kinds of jobs they have. A person in a subordinate position, especially if she knows she is unlikely to get any other kind of work, will adopt a submissive stance because it is the way to succeed in the job. The same individual might have quite a different personality in a supervisory position. Initiative and ambition are much more likely to show up in someone who knows she has a chance for promotion. (Feminists feel that some "feminine" characteristics should not be changed. Unselfishness, diligence or sensitivity to feelings are desirable in people of either sex, especially because there is no good reason to think that they are incompatible with objectivity, imagination and rational thinking.)

However, the biggest disadvantage to women in the economy stems not from business practices alone, but from the family pattern that lies behind them. It is a pattern which defines housework and child care as, first, outside the economic system, so that it need not be paid for normally but is exacted from each family on a volunteer basis; and, second, further defines it as women's work, so that a husband and father, though he lives in the house and is as closely related to the children biologically as the mother, is absolved from most of the labor. This sex role difference in the family is consistent with the notion that the father takes the entire burden of economic support, but, in fact, it applies regardless of whether the wife and mother is also contributing, and, many times, even when she alone brings home the bacon. Thus, women who hold jobs must either forgo family life entirely or shoulder two simultaneous, demanding full-time jobs. No such dilemma is imposed upon their husbands. Naturally, then, employers will tend to prefer the parties who do not feel obliged to commit themselves personally to so many outside responsibilities.

In order to foresee possible changes in this family pattern, it is necessary to envision ways in which the society and economy realistically can encompass housekeeping and child care within the system of paid productive work instead of demanding that women alone contribute it for free. The feminist program is devoted largely to such changes, and they are radical changes in that they alter the most intimate aspects of personal life. Yet, because this family pattern is a key obstacle to sex equality, the feminist vision requires it to change. Feminists are inclined to think that it is possible within the larger framework of the economy to provide for housework and child care without overburdening wives more than husbands. The production of household machinery and ready-made clothes and meals has been a step in this process, but the comfortable household still requires much repetitive labor. In this context, the emphasis in the women's movement on sharing of housework by husbands can be understood, not husband helping wife with *her* work, but both regarding the responsibility as a joint one. Child care is an even more demanding task, and the women's movement has no more important (or radical) doctrine than that the care of children is as much the right and responsibility of the father as of the mother. Although biology prevents much sharing in the 9 months of gestation, as soon as birth is accomplished, the father is as well equipped by nature to see to all a baby's needs, with the exception of a few minutes a day of (optional) breast feeding. However, child care is a round-the-clock job, and whoever does it or even shares it equally has less than full time in a day for another job. For this reason, there is much emphasis among feminists upon the idea that young parents should be able to launch their careers on a part-time basis without having to accept the marginal status, low pay and lack of promotions that part-time work now usually carries with it.

The motivation behind the feminist's interest in child care outside the home also must be understood in this same context, but its purposes are more complex. It is argued strongly that child care outside the home would make that important work part of the economy and establish the principle that it is a skilled professional job. Unless and until the economy provides for professional level compensation for this work, it will continue to be thought of as nonwork (cf. "nonworking mother"), work suitable for teenagers, retardates and relatively uneducated people. Attempts to romanticize child care presently are contradicted by an economic system in which the hand that rocks the cradle is paid little or nothing, and years spent at the task are given no status whatever as work experience when the mother later wishes to change to a paid job. It is argued also that child care outside the home would be better for the child than exclusive upbringing by one person. The basis of that belief cannot be detailed here. The point is raised only in order to underscore that the women's movement is not motivated to neglect children; rather, it is motivated to see to it that the work of caring for them is upgraded and compensated within the economic system. Feminists are sometimes accused of not liking children or of wanting to get away from them. Actually, they are not showing any less concern about their children than the traditional father who leaves his children all day to work.

The scope of the feminist vision is that with these relatively minor changes in the job market (equal opportunity), in public services (child care) and in family roles (equal sharing of housework), women would be freed of most of the objective reasons why they are now treated as a special kind of person. The economy could take each woman as an individual and thus give her as wide a choice of life-patterns as a man now has. All the disadvantages that now accrue to women in the job market because of the special life-pattern expected for them would disappear if the pattern were no longer made so necessary for so many women. Probably some women and also some men would choose full-time housekeeping and child care for part of their young lives, but there would be no excuse, as there is now, to attribute this pattern to all women and only to women and, thus, force every woman to live as though it were her destiny. Women would then become as promising as men for on-the-job training, for promotion and for employment generally. There would no longer be implicit excuse not to pay women competitively with men on the basis of merit, because most wives would be no more dependent upon husbands than vice versa. It would also remove the excuses now used to deny women their own credit and business confidence.

It is important to notice that while these changes in life patterns "revolution-ize" family life, they are still perfectly compatible with monogamous marriage and sexual fulfillment. In fact, many feminists anticipate that marriages will be more stable and sex more fun when men and women can relate to one another more equally.

Summary

This psychologist's view often may seem to be more that of a sociologist, economist or politician. (Certainly it is that of a feminist.) The reason is, as stated at the outset, that human beings are so largely conditioned and controlled by the society in which they live. It follows that changes in society and economy will be followed by changes of attitude in both men and women rather than having to wait upon them. Thus, social movements for equal treatment, whether because of sex or other factors, need not be seen as battles against impossible odds of ingrained prejudice. Equality is not an impossible dream; however, much persis-tence and effort may still be required to effect it. As more and more women become aware of the possibilities, their goals and ambitions will change, and people who deal with women will find that fewer of them accept the status quo. Once the real possibility of equal opportunity is understood, the issue turns into one of justice. The burden of proof is no longer on those who ask for change to show why it should be done. It shifts to those who resist to show why it shouldn't.

Notes

1 *1969 Handbook on Women Workers: Women's Bureau Bulletin 294* (Washington, D.C.: U.S. Government Printing Office, 1969).
2 *Ibid.*
3 *Ibid.*
4 *The 1972 Virginia Slims American Women's Opinion Poll,* A Study Conducted by Louis Harris and Associates.
5 Caroline Bird, *Born Female, The High Cost of Keeping Women Down* (New York: Pocket Books, 1969).

Understand Your Overseas Work Force

David Sirota
J. Michael Greenwood

One of the major problems facing multinational corporations is the need to tailor management practices and styles to the business conditions and cultural milieus of those countries in which they employ nationals. Inability or unwillingness to do so is frequently cited as a primary cause of U.S. business difficulties abroad.

Successful approaches to the problem depend, of course, on access to reliable information about these nations. In addition to what can be observed and easily identified, concerned companies must inquire into what lies behind the observable: the norms, values, aspirations—in a word, the culture—of the countries in which they operate.

Scholarly and popular publications are replete with characterizations of other nationalities, and there are numerous experts on culture; but what, really, do they tell us? We have been told, for example, that—

- Frenchmen are the most individualistic people on the earth;
- Germans are docile under government;
- Mexicans are passionate, aggressive, and warlike;
- Japanese minimize the importance of accumulation of wealth;
- Americans, more than any other people, view money as the universal standard of value.

While these observations are interesting, and perhaps enlightening, they are generalizations based almost entirely on the subjective, impressionistic experiences of the observers. Acceptance of these conclusions must therefore depend largely on faith—faith both in the observer's objectivity and in the representativeness of the anecdotal evidence he usually presents as proof of his case.

The history of cross-cultural observation—colored as it is by power and economic disparities, nationalism, and feelings of ethnic superiority and inferiority—encourages us to place much faith in faith as the basis for adapting management practices to the particular needs of foreign employees. Futhermore, many of the conclusions are contradictory and obviously transient. Consider, for example, how World War II affected our views of Germans, Japanese, and Russians and how postwar events succeeded remarkably in altering these concepts.

It is clear that the results of our largely impressionistic efforts to understand other nationalities need to be tested and supplemented by an increased use of

Reprinted by permission from the *Harvard Business Review*, January–February 1971, pp. 53–60. © 1971 by the President and Fellows of Harvard College; all rights reserved.

scientific methods. This field has an overabundance of "wisdom"; what it requires now is the kind of evidence that lends itself to objective verification.[1]

This article presents the results of a research project undertaken to determine the differences and similarities in work goals of thousands of industrial workers employed in 25 countries by a large international corporation. We elicited opinions on 14 work goals from three different occupational sectors: sales, technical, and service (see the ruled insert on this page). The evidence provided by this study offers objective, verifiable information to those executives seeking to adapt management practices to the cultural environment of overseas operations, and it contradicts some common stereotypes that often dictate attempts to motivate employees of differing national origins. The main findings:

- The most important goals of these workers are all concerned with opportunity for individual achievement.
- Occupational and national comparisons reveal remarkable similarity in the goals of workers around the world.
- Although differences among nations are relatively small, it is possible to identify country "clusters" within which goals are nearly identical.

What Do They Want?

Before considering occupational and national comparisons, we shall discuss the importance attached to each goal by the overall group of surveyed workers.

Each respondent was asked to rate the importance of 14 various work-related objectives on a five-point scale ranging from "of utmost importance" to "of no importance at all." *Exhibit I* shows the rank order of work goals, according to average importance scores (starting with the goal assigned the highest average importance). The data allow us to make a set of rough generalizations about the goal-importance pattern of these employees:

- The five most important goals concern achievement—in particular, individual achievement. This includes both getting ahead (i.e., advancement and earnings) and job-related accomplishment (i.e., training, challenge, and autonomy).
- As the list progresses downward, concern shifts from individual achievement and opportunity to what the organization *gives* its employees. Most of these less important goals pertain to: (a) the employee's immediate environment (efficiency and friendliness of his department), (b) the general features of the organization (its success), and (c) the basic contract of employment (working hours, physical working conditions, and benefits).

This interpretation of the goal hierarchy of employees in different countries and cultures conforms generally with much of behavioral science theory and research

---

[1]While cross-cultural observation and research have traditionally been impressionistic in method, the following studies are notable for employing a more objective approach: Mason Haire, Edwin E. Ghiselli, and Lyman W. Porter, *Managerial Thinking: An International Study* (New York, John Wiley & Sons, Inc., 1966); Bernard M. Bass et al, *Technical Reports* (Rochester, Management Center, University of Rochester, 1967, 1968, 1969); and David C. McClelland, *The Achieving Society* (Princeton, D. Van Nostrand Company, 1961).

Exhibit I   Goal Ranking for the Total Population

Rank	Goal	Questionnaire wording
1	Training	Have training opportunities (to improve your present skills or learn new skills)
2	Challenge	Have a challenging work to do—work that gives you a personal sense of accomplishment
3	Autonomy	Have considerable freedom to adopt your own approach to the job
4	Earnings	Have an opportunity for high earnings
5	Advancement	Have an opportunity for advancement to higher level jobs
6	Recognition	Get the recognition you deserve for doing a good job
7	Security	Have job security (steady work)
8	Friendly department	Work in a department where the people are congenial and friendly to one another
9	Personal time	Have a job which leaves you sufficient time for your personal and/or family life
10	Company contribution	Have a job which allows you to make a real contribution to your company's success
11	Efficient department	Work in a department which is run efficiently
12	Benefits	Have good fringe benefits
13	Physical conditions	Have good physical working conditions (good ventilation and lighting, adequate work space, etc.)
14	Successful company	Work for a company which is regarded in your country as successful

currently being applied in U.S. industry. It indicates that asking the perennial question, "How do we motivate employees?" is as inane internationally as it is in the United States. These employees do not have to be *motivated*. They are eager and ambitious, interested both in having their skills utilized on present jobs and in moving ahead to more responsible and better paying jobs. The task of management—in the United States as well as multinationally—is to create organizational and job conditions that harness, rather than stifle, the considerable energy employees bring to their work.

Some Qualifications   Before discussing occupational and national comparisons, there are two qualifications of our findings which should be mentioned.

First, none of the 14 goals are really unimportant to these employees. Even the lowest ranked goal—successful company—still had an average score close to the middle of the scale (i.e., near moderate importance). Therefore, all the goals are of at least some importance, and the distinctions among them are relative in nature—more important versus less important.

Second, it could be argued that employees in this study responded to the questions not as they really felt but, rather, as the company's values (and perhaps their own) dictated they *should* feel. It is certainly possible that "social desirability" did affect the results to some extent, but other research conducted in this corporation tends to support the basic validity of our current findings. For example, we found that the best predictors, by far, of whether employees in these occupations leave or stay with the company are job-related satisfaction (challenge, utilization of skills, and so on) and perceived advancement opportunities. Satisfaction with benefits, physical working conditions, and the like showed no relationship whatsoever to attrition.

Occupational Influences   The goals of employees in each of the three occupations studied are similar to each other and generally conform to the pattern described earlier for the total population (see *Exhibit II*). As the data show, the highest ranked goals in all three groups still tend to be those relating to individual achievement. But within this pattern of overall similarity, certain deviations do occur. Two of the larger differences concern job security and job autonomy:

• Job security is ranked 2.5 by service personnel but only 10 and 11 by salesmen and technical personnel, respectively. This difference no doubt reflects the way goals are influenced by environment—in this case, by labor market conditions. Opportunities for employment outside the company are smaller for those in service positions than for those in the other two occupations. This difference is reflected in the voluntary attrition rates of the three groups; in almost all countries, the attrition rate of service employees is much less than that of sales and technical employees. Clearly, as outside job opportunities increase, loss of present employment becomes less of a threat.

• Job autonomy is ranked 3 by salesmen, 3 by technical personnel, but 7 by service personnel. In our view, this variation also reflects differences in environmental conditions. Service personnel—workers with responsibility for equipment maintenance—do, in fact, have less autonomy than the salesmen or technical employees. One might postulate, therefore, that the less autonomy required for effective job performance, the less will be the desire of workers for autonomy. Employees working on routine factory jobs, for example, would probably show even less desire for autonomy than would service employees.

The occupational goal rankings appear, then, to be products of two major influences. On the one hand, the considerable similarity of goal importance for workers in all three occupations indicates a general motivational pattern in which

Exhibit II Goal Ranking by Occupation

Goal	Average rank		
	Salesmen	Technical personnel	Service personnel
Training	2	1	1
Challenge	1	2	2.5
Autonomy	3	3	7
Earnings	4	4.5	4
Advancement	5	6	5
Recognition	6	4.5	9
Security	10	11	2.5
Friendly department	9	8	8
Personal time	11	7	6
Company contribution	7.5	9.5	10
Efficient department	7.5	9.5	11
Benefits	13	13	12
Physical conditions	14	12	13
Successful company	12	14	14

individual achievement needs predominate. On the other hand, certain deviations do appear, which we interpret as reflecting environmental differences.

Of course, even the general pattern may be affected by environment—namely, the internal environment of this company. For example, the great importance placed on the training goal may be a consequence of the company's rapidly changing and advanced technology.

Since we have no comparable data from other organizations, we cannot at this time comment on possible differences between companies. But we do have data on another form of variation, that of nation, and it is to this subject that we now turn.

The National Level

Exhibit III presents rankings of the 14 goals for each of the 25 countries surveyed. In all three of the occupational sections of *Exhibit III*, the five most important goals in each country have been printed in boldface and the five least important in italic. (Thus, if the most important and least important goals were identical around the world, the top and bottom portions of the charts would be solid blocks of boldface and italic.)

While it is obvious that perfect identity does not exist in any of the three occupations, the country rankings are still remarkably similar to each other; boldface ranks dominate upper portions of the charts and italic ranks dominate the lower portions. Note that each goal is ranked 75 separate times (25 countries times 3 occupations). Consider the two goals that, overall, were thought to be most important (training and challenge) and the two that were ranked the least important (successful company and physical conditions). Of the 75 ranks received:

Exhibit III Goal Ranking by Country

A Salesmen

	Argentina	Australia	Austria	Belgium	Brazil	Canada	Chile	Colombia	Denmark	Finland	France
Challenge	7	**2.5**	**4**	**3**	**4**	**1**	**4**	**3.5**	**2.5**	**1**	**2**
Training	**1**	5	**2**	6	**2**	**3**	**1**	**1.5**	**2.5**	**2**	**1**
Autonomy	**2**	5	**1**	**4**	7	**4**	6	**1.5**	**1**	**3**	**3**
Earnings	5	**1**	5	**2**	**1**	5	6	5	**4**	6.5	5.5
Advancement	5	**2.5**	**3**	**1**	5	**2**	11.5	**3.5**	6	6.5	**4**
Recognition	9.5	7	6	**5**	10	6	14	9	8	11	7
Company contribution	5	9.5	7	9.5	**3**	9	6	7.5	11.5	10	8
Efficient department	8	8	8	7	8.5	8	9	11	**5**	**4.5**	5.5
Friendly department	11	9.5	9	11	6	10	9	6	7	**4.5**	9
Security	**3**	11	10	9.5	12	13	**2**	7.5	11.5	9	10
Personal time	9.5	5	13	8	11	7	**3**	11	10	8	11
Successful company	12	11	11	14	14	11	13	13.5	13	13	13
Benefits	14	14	14	13	13	14	11.5	11	14	12	14
Physical conditions	11	13	12	12	8.5	12	9	13.5	9	14	13

B Technical personnel

	Argentina	Australia	Austria	Belgium	Brazil	Canada	Chile	Colombia	Denmark	Finland	France
Training	**1**	**3**	**2**	**2**	**1**	**2**	**1**	**1**	**1**	**3**	**1**
Challenge	**3**	**1**	**1**	**1**	**3**	**1**	7	**2**	**4**	**2**	**2**
Autonomy	**2**	**2**	**3**	4.5	9	**3**	12.5	5.5	**2**	**1**	**3**
Earnings	6	7	5	4.5	9	6	10.5	5.5	5.5	7	6
Recognition	**4**	8	6	**3**	6	5	12.5	7	8	11.5	**4**
Advancement	9	5	**4**	6	**4**	**4**	**2**	**3**	7	5.5	8
Personal time	6	**4**	10	7	**2**	7	7	9.5	9.5	5.5	5
Friendly department	10	11	11	9	8	10	**3.5**	11.5	**3**	**4**	7
Company contribution	11	9	7	11	5	8	7	**4**	12	10	11
Efficient department	8	6	9	10	10	9	7	9.5	5.5	8	9
Security	6	10	8	8	11	11	**3.5**	8	9.5	9	10
Physical conditions	13	12	13	13	12	12.5	7	14	11	11.5	12
Benefits	12	14	12	12	13	14	10.5	11.5	13	13	13
Successful company	14	13	14	14	14	12.5	14	13	14	14	14

C Service personnel

	Argentina	Australia	Austria	Belgium	Brazil	Canada	Chile	Colombia	Denmark	Finland	France
Training	**1**	**2**	**2**	3.5	**1**	2.5	**1**	**1**	**1**	**1**	**3**
Challenge	**4**	**1**	**1**	3.5	**3**	**1**	7	**2**	**4**	**2.5**	6
Security	**2**	**3**	6	**1**	12	6	**2**	**3**	**2**	**4**	**1**
Earnings	9.5	6	**4**	**2**	9	5	6	8	9	6	8
Advancement	6.5	**4**	**3**	8.5	8	**2.5**	9.5	**4**	10	5	**4**
Personal time	8	5	10	6	6.5	**4**	8	14	5	**2.5**	**2**
Autonomy	5	7	5	5	11	9	11	6	**3**	8	7
Friendly department	**3**	10	9	8.5	**2**	10	5	10.5	7	9	5
Recognition	6.5	9	7	7	10	8	**3**	5	12	13	10
Company contribution	12	11	8	10.5	4.5	11	13	7	11	12	11
Efficient department	9.5	8	11	11.5	6.5	7	12	10.5	6	10	9
Benefits	11	13	12	12	13	13	**4**	9	8	14	12
Physical conditions	13	12	13	14	4.5	12	9.5	12	13	11	13
Successful company	14	14	14	13	14	14	14	13	14	7	14

Key: Goals of high importance in boldface; goals of low importance in italic.

- *Training* is listed among the five most important goals 69 times.
- *Challenge* is among the five most important goals 70 times.
- *Successful company* is listed among the five least important goals 71 times.
- *Physical conditions* is among the five least important goals 70 times.

Just as we were able to refer to a general pattern of goals across occupations, so can we speak of a general pattern of goals across nations—in all countries, individual achievement is the main concern of this company's employees.

Germany	India	Israel	Japan	Mexico	New Zealand	Norway	Peru	South Africa	Sweden	Switzerland	United Kingdom	Venezuela	United States
5	1	1	3	4	1	2.5	5	1	1	1	2	3	1
1	6.5	8	9	1	6	1	1	3	2	4	5	1	8
2	3.5	4.5	5	6	4	2.5	7.5	8	7.5	2	4	3	4
4	6.5	7	1	5	3	6.5	5	2	6	8	1	12	3
3	3.5	2.5	2	2	2	6.5	9.5	4.5	3.5	3	3	7	2
8	5	10	4	10	8.5	10	12	6.5	11	9	7	11	5
7	2	4.5	11.5	7	7	8	2	4.5	3.5	5	8	3	6
11	13.5	6	6	8	5	4	9.5	6.5	7.5	10	6	9.5	10
9	11	9	7	9	10.5	12	7.5	11	5	6.5	11	8	9
6	9	2.5	8	3	12	11	5	13	10	13	10	5	12
12	8	14	13	13	10.5	5	14	10	13	6.5	9	13	7
13	12	12	10	11	8.5	14	13	12	9	14	12	9.5	11
10	10	11	14	12	14	9	3	9	12	11	14	6	13
14	13.5	13	11.5	14	13	13	11	14	14	12	13	14	14
1	2.5	1	4	1	2.5	1.5	1	3	2	2	4	1	3
3	2.5	3	1	2	1	1.5	2	1	1	1	1	2	1
2	6.5	2	5	4.5	2.5	3	3	7	6	3	5	3	5
5	6.5	10	3	7	8.5	4	10.5	5	5	9	7	11.5	6
6	1	5	6	10	6	8	10.5	5	10	7	2	9.5	7
4	4.5	7.5	2	3	4	5	7	2	8	4	3	5.5	2
10	9.5	9	10.5	11	8.5	6	12	10	10	5	6	11.5	4
9	11.5	4	9	9	12	9	7	12	4	6	10	9.5	8
8	8	6	12	7	6	10	5	5	3	8	9	8	10
12	13	7.5	8	4.5	6	7	4	8	10	10	8	5.5	11
7	4.5	13	7	7	13	11	7	9	7	12	11	4	9
13	11.5	12	10.5	14	10	12	14	14	14	13	12	13	14
11	9.5	14	14	12	14	13	9	11	13	11	14	7	12
14	14	11	13	13	11	14	13	13	12	14	13	14	13
2	1	1	3	1	4	1	1	2	2	2	3	1	5
3.5	3	5	4	5	1	2	2	1	3	1	1	8	1
1	5.5	8	7	2	6	3	8	4	1	11	7	2	3
3.5	9	11	2	8	7.5	8	6	7	7	7	5	6	4
5	2	6	1	6	2	7	3.5	5	9	3	2	7	2
9	11.5	2.5	13	13	3	5	9	6	5	5	6	10.5	6.5
6	8	7	9	9	5	9	5	9	11	4	4	9	10
10	7	9.5	6	7	10	6	10	10	4	6	11	3	12
8	4	2.5	5	11.5	7.5	10	11	11	13	9	8.5	10.5	8
11	5.5	9.5	10	3	11	12	3.5	8	6	10	10	12	6.5
12	11.5	4	8	4	9	4	7	3	8	12	8.5	5	11
7	14	13	14	10	14	11	14	13	10	8	13	4	9
13	10	12	11	11.5	12	13	12	12	12	13	12	13	13
14	13	14	12	14	13	14	13	14	14	14	14	14	14

Overcoming Stereotypes The overall similarity in country goal patterns came as a surprise to many managers of the company studied. Managers, too, are human beings, and thus not completely immune to stereotyped thinking about other nations and people. Stereotypes simplify the world and simplify one's job. They provide automatic and simple explanations for complex problems. If, for example, there is difficulty in a Latin American country, the ready response might be, "Well, you know those Latins."

Our research indicates that "those Latins" (at least those Latins studied) may not be so different in their aspirations from "those Americans." However, if people *want* to see a particular group in a certain way, that is the way they will see it. They seek to confirm their preconceptions and tend to ignore contradictory evidence (perhaps even the evidence from this study). Furthermore, managers often act in ways likely to elicit employee behavior that justifies the stereotype. For example:

● Country X employees are believed to have little potential for higher level management positions and are therefore denied the experience and training necessary for developing this potential. Their subsequent very limited advancement provides all the proof management needs that its initial, pessimistic assessment of employees' abilities was correct.

● Country Y employees are seen as "lazy," and, consequently, are subject to stringent controls. They rebel against these controls, often by acting lazy. The appropriateness of management's assumptions and behavior is thus confirmed and reinforced by the negative employee reactions.

Cultural Aggregates   As can be seen in *Exhibit III,* no two countries are entirely identical in their goal hierarchies. While goals are similar overall, it is obvious that individual differences do exist. It is impractical to discuss the individual goal orderings of 25 countries, but it is possible to look for general patterns—that is, for clusters of countries which can be distinguished on the basis of extremely high goal similarity. We have been able to identify five such groupings (see *Exhibit IV*). These are:

1 Anglo.
2 French.
3 Northern Europe.
4 Southern Latin America.
5 Northern Latin America.

In addition to the foregoing clusters, six countries stand alone and are labeled "Independents." The goal orderings of these six are not closely and consistently related to that of any other country.

The analysis method we used ("Q" version of factor analysis) grouped countries so as to minimize differences within clusters and maximize differences between them. It should be emphasized, however, that the clusters are still quite similar to each other in their goal orderings, and, despite the differences between clusters, the general goal hierarchical pattern is not markedly upset in any of them. For example, while training is less important for the Anglos than for any other group, it is nevertheless one of the most important goals within the Anglo hierarchy. Similarly, while the Japanese rate successful company higher in importance than do the other clusters and nations, this goal is still among the least important to them.

The major differences may be summarized as follows:

Exhibit IV   Country Clusters

1 Anglo	4 Southern Latin
Australia	America
Austria	Argentina
Canada	Chile
India	5 Northern Latin
New Zealand	America
South Africa	Columbia
Switzerland	Mexico
U.K.	Peru
U.S.A.	6 Independents
2 French	Brazil
Belgium	Germany
France	Israel
3 Northern Europe	Japan
Denmark	Sweden
Finland	Venezuela
Norway	

● The Anglo cluster is higher than other clusters on goals pertaining to individual achievement and low on the desire for security.

● The French cluster is quite similar to the Anglos, except that the French give greater importance to security and somewhat less importance to challenging work.

● The countries in the Northern Europe cluster seem to be less oriented than the others to the getting-ahead and recognition kinds of goals and more oriented to job accomplishment. Here, people exhibit more concern with the immediate environment (friendly and efficient department) and less with the organization as a whole (working for a successful company and contributing to the company). They place considerable emphasis on their jobs not interfering with their personal lives.

● The individual achievement goals tend to be somewhat less important in both Latin clusters than in the other groupings. This relative de-emphasis of individual achievement is especially pronounced in the Southern Latin countries. The Southern Latins are also highest of all in their desire for security, and both Latin clusters place considerable emphasis on fringe benefits.

● Germany exhibits a pattern similar in many respects to the countries of the Latin clusters. It too is high on the desire for security and fringe benefits. A difference appears on the getting-ahead goals (advancement and earnings), where the Germans are among the highest.

● Japan shows a rather unique pattern in that many of the goals which ordinarily relate to one another do not seem to do so in this case. For example, while the Japanese are higher than others in their desire for earnings opportunities, their desire for advancement is relatively low. They are second highest on challenge, but are lowest on autonomy. The one internally consistent pattern for this nation relates to the immediate department environment; the Japanese place relatively strong emphasis on working in a friendly and efficient department and on having good physical working conditions.

Conclusion

The implications of our study may be considered at a number of different levels.

First—at the most general level—our research reinforces the need to put assumptions about people to the empirical test. Organizational policies cannot be more effective than the validity of the assumptions on which they are based. This need to test assumptions is particularly important in international organizations where accurate information is so difficult to obtain and where judgments are so heavily influenced by the preconceptions different nationalities have about each other.

Second, the research data do tend to support the current models of human motivation developed by industrial social psychologists. However, some of these findings suggest that existing models need to be modified. The importance of certain goals—most strikingly, job autonomy and job security—is markedly affected by what we interpret to be environmental conditions. The job autonomy data deserve emphasis because of the key position this variable occupies in so much of modern management theory.

Job autonomy appears in the literature under a number of labels—e.g., "participative management," "consultative management," "democratic management"—and is assumed to be a major goal of most employees. But this emphasis on autonomy may be little more than a projection of the theorists' own goals that stem from their own professional environments. Our data suggest that in some work environments—especially those with tasks that are routinized and predictable—high degrees of autonomy may be neither desired nor appropriate.

Third, and perhaps most relevant to the managers of international organizations, is the considerable similarity we have found in the goals of employees around the world. This finding has an extremely important policy implication: since the goals of employees are similar internationally, corporate policy decisions, to *the extent that they are based on assumptions about employee goals,* can also be international in scope.

It is not only Americans who want money, or Frenchmen who want autonomy, or Germans who want their work skills utilized and improved. A management whose policies and practices reflect these stereotypes (for example, providing few advancement opportunities in some countries or using certain countries as dumping grounds for routine, unchallenging work) should be prepared to suffer the consequences of managing a frustrated and uncommitted work force whose apathy and anxieties it helped nurture.

In this respect, it would be interesting to determine how much of the difficulty experienced in managing employees in other countries is due not to cultural differences at all but, rather, to the automatic and psychologically self-serving assumption of differences that, in reality, may be minor or even nonexistent.

The Research Method

The company studied in our survey is a large manufacturer of electrical equipment. During 1967 and 1968, an opinion questionnaire was administered to about

13,000 of this company's employees working in 46 countries. Three different occupations were represented; and, for comparative purposes, the company's U.S. workers in similar occupations were also sampled.

The questionnaire consisted of about 200 multiple-choice items and was administered in group sessions, on site, and on company time. Respondent anonymity was guaranteed. The original version of the questionnaire was written in English and then translated into the 12 other required languages. The translation process was checked both by independent retranslations into English and by exhaustive pretesting. Only that section of the questionnaire dealing with employee work goals is reported in this article.

While 46 countries were included in the study, the results presented here are limited to the 25 countries which had at least 40 employees in all three of the surveyed occupations. (Some such size cutoff was necessary to help ensure the reliability of data.) The following countries were included in our analysis:

Argentina	Israel
Australia	Japan
Austria	Mexico
Belgium	New Zealand
Brazil	Norway
Canada	Peru
Chile	South Africa
Colombia	Sweden
Denmark	Switzerland
Finland	United Kingdom
France	United States
Germany	Venezuela
India	

Managing the Educated

Peter F. Drucker

For the first time in our history—or indeed in the history of any country—managerial, professional, and technical employees have become the largest group in our work force. They not only outnumber all other white-collar groups, but they have even overtaken manual working groups, especially the machine workers.

Equally significant, for the first time in our history, and again for the first

From Dan H. Fenn (ed.), *Management's Mission in a New Society,* McGraw-Hill Book Company, Inc., New York, 1956, pp. 163–178. Reprinted by permission of the publisher.
Editor's note: Mr. Drucker is a consultant on business policy and management organization. He is also Professor of Management at the Graduate School of Business, New York University, and author of many well-known books and articles on American society and business management.

time in the history of any country, people with a high degree of education—that is, people who have finished high school—constitute more than half of our total labor force, including those employed in agriculture.

This trend is certain to accelerate sharply. The number of managerial, professional, and technical employees is growing at the rate of 10% each year—three times as fast as the total population. The number of machine workers, on the other hand, has not grown at all since the end of World War II and is indeed beginning to shrink not only in its proportionate importance but even in absolute numbers. Today managerial, professional, and technical people are one fifth of the American population at work. Fifteen or twenty years hence they are likely to constitute two fifths, perhaps even one half. This would mean that every other American gainfully employed would work as a manager, professional, or technician.

The development of an "educated society" is going to come even faster, for the people who do not have a high school education are to be found predominantly among the older population. Among those under 50, high school graduates already account for something like three quarters of the total. College-educated people, who 30 years ago were still so insignificant in number as almost to escape statistical notice, are a full third of all the newcomers to the labor force, so that 20 years hence 1 out of every 3 people gainfully employed in this country is likely to have attended college, if not graduated.

Here is a basic change in the structure of this country and of our economy. In times of economic swings and of international crisis little attention has been paid to it, for other events seize the headlines. Yet it is so important in the long run, and perhaps even in the short run, that it may prove to be more significant than any other single change. Surely its impact on us in business and management will be both profound and long-lasting. It challenges basic axioms of business management and business economics. It creates new opportunities and new problems for management. And it will force us into basic new thinking about organizational structure, authority and responsibility, and the relation of people working together in an organization.

A good many managers today are familiar with the management of highly educated people in special organizations like research laboratories or design-engineering departments. All of us know that these groups pose a good many new problems. Indeed, our meetings and our magazines are full of discussions on how one manages research people, how one makes a human being out of a Ph.D. in mathematics, and how one goes about managing the professional in an organization.

Yet very little of this, I am afraid, is really relevant to the basic problems we face, or is really concerned with them. For the essence of the big change—and we are well past the mid-point in it—is not that we have to learn how to organize highly educated people for special work outside or next to the traditional business organization. The essential point is that tomorrow, if not today, more and more of the people in the normal traditional organization, in the day-to-day operations of a business, are going to be people with very high education; people who work with their minds rather than their hands; people who do everyday "line" work rather than special "long-hair" work and yet who are different in their background, their expectations, and the way they work from the people who did these line jobs yesterday.

Specifically, we face major new situations in three areas: (1) the economics of business enterprise, (2) the personnel management and the personnel behavior of the great bulk of our employees, and (3) basic organization. I shall try to outline some of the directions we can already see in each of these three areas.

New Economic Outlook　　Economists will undoubtedly be busy for many years trying to analyze the causes, lessons, and characteristics of the recession of 1957–1958. One of the most important lessons we can already define:

> In the industries that were hard-hit—especially the manufacturers of durable consumer goods and their main supplier, the steel industry—production dropped faster between the summer of 1957 and the spring of 1958 than it ever has in any major industry during a comparable period in our history (faster even than during the 1937–1938 slump). In some companies it dropped 50% or so. Yet employment fell only 20%. Actually, while we headlined the unemployment news, the real story should have been the tremendous crisis resistance of our employment. And, much more important, personnel costs hardly fell at all. They too showed almost complete recession resistance, which, of course, explains why profits in these industries tended to disappear altogether. This is simply a manifestation of the great structural change in our labor force, the structural change which has made the "production worker," that is, the machine operator, increasingly secondary, and those employees more important whom the accountants call "nonproduction workers," that is, the white-collar employees and especially the managerial, professional, and technical employees.
>
> The industries that were particularly hard-hit by the recession are among the ones that have changed the least in their employment structure during the last ten years. They are essentially old-fashioned in the composition of their labor force, compared, for instance, with the chemical industry, the petroleum industry, or the paper industry. Yet even their manufacturing employment dropped much more slowly than production, and total employment fell even more slowly—as evidenced by the personnel costs. Also, employment fell the most in respect to low-income labor; it barely moved in respect to high-income labor. In other words, even in these industries labor costs have ceased to be elastic; they have become more or less fixed.
>
> It is important to stress that this happened in industries which in their production concepts are industries of yesterday rather than industries of tomorrow. They also rank with those firms that have the highest average age in the work force. Thus, they are still much closer to yesterday's labor structure, both in respect to job and educational background, than the growth industries in our economy like electronics, chemistry, and so on. Yet even in these industries, which could have been expected to behave pretty much in the traditional pattern—could have been expected to decrease employment at least as fast as production and labor costs at the same rate as production—employment proved highly inelastic and total personnel costs even more so.

I submit that this is the "normal" in an economy in which managerial, professional, and technical employees are the largest single group. If you add to this group the foremen, craftsmen, and highly skilled workers, you have 22 million employed people, out of a total of 64 or 65 million, whose employment is of necessity highly stable. Or to put it more accurately: the need for these people does not fluctuate directly with the volume of production, and to a very large extent their employment is tied more to the expectation of future production than to current orders. These are, in other words, people who are employed not according to the number of pieces or the number of hours worked but rather according to the expected capacity. And in the majority of cases they have to be on the payroll regardless of the present volume of business—partly because they are needed as long as the business operates at all, partly because they represent too much of an investment, too much of a "capital resource," to be discharged.

This is in sharp, indeed irreconcilable, contrast to the axioms of the economists. Every economist still assumes that business adjusts to short-term fluctuations in the economy by laying off or hiring people. They disagree whether this adjustment is the way out of a recession or whether it is the cause of recessions and depressions, but they all still believe in the phenomenon itself. It is quite clear, however, that this is no longer true. Though this would have been clear even without the lesson of the recession, since it follows from the structure of our labor force, the economic dip served to dramatize the change. So the economists—and let me add the accountants too—would be well advised to assume that business cannot adjust at all by varying labor costs; that labor costs, for any short-term period, can be considered fixed, determined by future expectations rather than by present volume of business. In many industries—a conspicuous example would be retailing—this is indeed already an established fact. Yet we lack economic theory for such a situation. As a result, we do not really understand it.

We also lack business policy for it. It is obvious that what I have just said spells out great fluctuation of profit, since it is the only factor left that can give. This is one of the functions of profit in a free enterprise economy. If we cannot adjust easily to short-term fluctuation by adjusting labor costs, the leverage on profits must become conspicuously greater, as indeed it proved to be during the recent recession. We need, therefore, a financial policy which starts out with the assumption of high year-to-year fluctuations in actual profits, and which therefore focuses on a rate of return over a cyclical period—over a wide range of fluctuations—rather than on annual profits. We need instruments of financial analysis and control for such a new situation. And we need to think through our capital investments with much greater sophistication, instead of simply basing them on the idea that today's expected rate of return will actually be realized in any one year during the life of the new investment.

But there is another and perhaps even more important implication in this new economic situation. The rise of our economy was based on the steady increase in the productivity of the direct, manual producer, the farmer, and the machine operator. Incidentally, most of us in business are not sufficiently aware of the tremendous contribution the increase in farm productivity has made to our economic growth. During the last 30 years the annual step-up in productivity on the farm was at least of the order of 6% per year—twice that of manufacturing industry. In very large measure our economic growth and our capacity to produce can be credited to this progress.

There is reason to believe that the main increase in agricultural productivity is over. There is still a very substantial number of farmers with sub-standard productivity, farmers who are indeed marginal in every sense of the word. They may account for almost one third of our farm population. But even if all of them left farming—and over the next 20 years most of them will—it would not materially decrease our farm production or farm productivity, since these marginal farmers contribute almost nothing to the supply of foods and industrial raw materials for our economy. All the flight from the farm will contribute is additional workers for industry, and workers who unfortunately are precisely the kind we need the least: unskilled and very largely uneducated people.

We can expect, by contrast, very sharp productivity increases in the manufacturing industries, simply as a result of increased mechanization and automation. But these increases may be largely an illusion. We will indeed have dramatic upswings in output per man-hour of production workers. But the very fact that our managerial, professional, and technical groups have been growing so much faster than the total economy indicates that we can obtain these productivity increases of the machine operator only by adding nonmanual workers. In other words, I would submit that all evidence today, both that derived from an analysis of the over-all figures and that derived from any study of an individual company's shift to automation, indicates that increased automation only shifts the demand for labor from the machine operator and his manual work to the highly educated man and his mind work, but does not result in actual increase in the over-all productivity of the business or of the economy.

What I am saying is simply that from now on our increases in productivity in this country will depend above all on our ability to increase the productivity of the nonmanual worker. Two thirds of our total labor force in 1956 were not working with their hands—the managerial, professional, and technical workers; the clerical and sales people; the workers in service work; and finally the supervisors. Yet no one even knows how one measures the productivity of people in this kind of work. All we can measure today is the productivity of people who work with their hands to produce a physical output. No one, I am afraid, would claim that the productivity of these mind workers has gone up appreciably. Certainly such data as we have do not indicate that there has been a great increase. Since their numbers have gone up at least as fast as total production of goods and services, one must deduce that the productivity has at best remained the same.

This I submit is the primary challenge to American management. First, here is our major inflationary factor. The wages of these people go up, or are pushed up by the union contracts of industries in Detroit and Schenectady. You may or may not agree that the manufacturing worker should have received the full benefit of higher productivity; but whatever you would like to believe, over a long period of time manufacturing productivity has risen roughly parallel to manufacturing wages. The major inflationary factor is the nonmanufacturing workers' income, which goes up along with manufacturing workers' incomes but without any noticeable increase in productivity. Because of its impact, this is a bigger responsibility than the cost control of a business, for we are talking here about the cost control of the American economy.

The productivity of these people can, to a substantial extent, be increased in the way that we have increased the productivity of the manual worker: by the investment of capital in machinery. This is certainly true in clerical and other office work, where automation will undoubtedly have a major impact and where it may be more important and have greater results than in the factory. This may also be true for the very substantial number of people who are engaged in selling—where automation may not mean so much in terms of use of machinery but certainly will bring great changes because of the planning and systematizing of work that it demands.

But for the managerial, professional, and technical people, and they are the real core of the problem and the real opportunity, capital investment in machinery—in physical tools—is not going to mean much. Their work is not physical; it is work of the mind. The only way to increase their productivity is to increase the output and the effectiveness of the mind. This can be accomplished only if we succeed both in making each of these men more productive in his own right and then in making his contribution more effective throughout the entire company.

Future Personnel Problems This leads me to my second major topic: the management of highly educated people at work. Let me say again that I am not talking about the management of highly educated people in special programs such as research. I am talking about highly educated people in the ordinary, everyday, line organization.

Our concepts of personnel management were largely formed around World War I or shortly thereafter. They grew essentially out of experience in working with machine operators of very limited education. The famous Hawthorne experiments, for instance, were conducted with people who had on the average, barely finished grade school. I think there is serious reason to doubt that tomorrow's employee will conform to the image upon which our current personnel management practices depend.

What are the expectations of people who have sat on school benches for at least 12, if not for 16 years, and, however little they may have learned otherwise, have learned to expect to work with their minds and to apply thinking, concept, system, and theories to their jobs? What are the expectations of people who have, as a matter of course, been given an education which only a short generation ago was reserved for a very small, essentially upper-class group? What work, opportunities, and treatment do they expect?

Is "scientific management," as the term is commonly understood, at all applicable to them, let alone "scientific" for them? Is it right to try to make the job as simple, repetitive, or highly organized as we possibly can? I doubt it.

Let me say that we have evidence that people who now come out of school expect something different from what we offer them. I do not want to attempt to define "automation." I do not want to argue whether we mean by this the substitution of machine for manual labor or a new concept of the organization of work by system and process. It is already fairly clear that the major driving force in the development is neither machines nor concepts but the changed educational structure of our work population.

People who have spent 12 or 16 years in formal education are not attracted to the job of a preautomated factory, least of all to the assembly line, which socially, if not technologically, is already obsolete. They are looking for jobs in which they can exercise what they have learned—that is, jobs in which they can work by using their minds—and they are looking for jobs in which they have the opportunities of educated people for better pay, advancement, and chances to make a contribution. The assembly line as we have known it cannot survive in this country—there is plenty of evidence that the young people in Detroit, Flint, or Schenectady simply do not want assembly-line jobs and will take them only as a last resort and with a deep consciousness of frustration and defeat.

Another new problem turns around the mobility of this kind of worker. To the old laborer, who at best had a manual skill but no education, mobility was a threat. Even in this, the most mobile country in the world, he was much more afraid of losing a job than he was attracted by better opportunities elsewhere. Stability of employment and job security ranked highest in his priorities.

Is this still likely to be true of today's and tomorrow's worker with his high degree of education and his conceptual training and skill? I doubt this very much. We see today in the electronics industry, for instance, a revival of the itinerant specialist in the tradition of the exceedingly highly skilled trades of old, like the printing business of 50 or 100 years ago. We see young men with a specialty who simply look on a job as an opportunity to ply their craft, who could not care less for job security, and who are almost unbelievably mobile. This is very much more characteristic of tomorrow's most important employees than fear of job loss, attachment to a job, and the resulting very low mobility of today's or yesterday's worker. This poses a very real problem for us in management, and it is a problem which we are not attacking by trying to keep down turnover rates. We have to think through how we can best make use of such workers, who are inherently mobile, who know a good deal of the world and are at home every-where, and whose contribution to us very largely consists of their mobile and easily transported knowledge and skill.

The real problem of managing people at work, however, is not to satisfy their expectations. It is to think through the demands on them. What should we expect from people who are highly educated and who work as managers, professionals, and technicians? We have, during the last 30 or 50 years, increasingly tended to talk about "average jobs." "Scientific management" is focused on finding the "standard job," or the amount of work that can reasonably be expected of everyone. This, I am afraid, is the wrong way to make demands on tomorrow's workers. There we shall have to make demands for extraordinary performance, for performance that contributes not the minimum but the optimum, for performance that steadily pushes the limitations outward and reaches for new contributions and new excellence. Otherwise we can never expect to obtain the benefit of the great, almost revolutionary, change in the structure of our work force and of our work. And this in turn quite obviously means very real changes in the way we structure and define jobs.

Above all, however, we must recognize that this new worker cannot be supervised and that his performance cannot be easily measured. He can only be motivated. He must reach for excellence. He must want to contribute. He must try to develop himself, his capacity, and his contribution. All we can do is pay him. The supervision that we could give to the manual worker simply cannot be applied effectively to people who have to contribute their knowledge, conceptual skill, imagination, and judgment.

While we have been talking a great deal about motivation these last 20 or 30 years, we know very little about it—and I do not believe that many of us would claim that we even apply the little we know. The comments made in Mr. Zaleznik's chapter [in *Management's Mission in a New Society*] are most interesting in this regard.

The New Organization   The greatest challenges, however, may well come to our concept of organization. Let me give you an illustration—intentionally taken from the armed forces rather than from business. If you look at a modern air base, you will find on it, in addition to a fairly small number of flying personnel, a very large complement of highly trained professional and technical people who exercise judgment. In rank they may be quite low. The crew chief in charge of the maintenance of a group of planes, for instance, is a master sergeant—and will never be more than that. Yet who "commands" the crew chief? Who can give him orders? The commanding general of the base can remove the crew chief, demote him in rank, or overrule him. But he cannot "command" him. The crew chief decides whether a plane is airworthy, what has to be done to put it in shape, and how long it will take. In other words, he exercises judgment, and he has a high degree of final authority within his field.

Or take the meteorologist. Again there is a ceiling on his rank—he is rarely more than a captain or a major, and will not rise higher. Yet while he works within a highly specialized area, his sphere of concern is the entire base rather than a part of it. He is a "specialist" with a "general" sphere of authority and responsibility. Again, who can "command" him? It is his professional judgment and knowledge to which he is really responsible rather than a superior officer. He can be removed, and he can be overrruled, but he cannot be commanded.

You could go through the entire base and pick out one technical or professional function after the other and say exactly the same thing about it. Yet the commanding general has a final decision and a final responsibility. He does "command"—and the difference in performance between a mediocre and an outstanding commanding general is still the most important and the one truly decisive "variable" in the performance of the whole base. The general is not just a "coordinator," nor does he just listen to his functional people and synthesize their judgment and advice. He has real, final authority. And yet, except in a merely formal sense, he can hardly be said to be over all these people. He has a *different* job to do rather than a higher job.

On the chart, of course, none of this is shown. The chart shows the line of command from the general on down as it has always existed. And, in polite fiction, every one of these men exercises delegated authority—though the Air Force, smarter in this than most businesses, realizes that these people do not do part of the general's work but do their own work. The reality of organization we can muddle through, though no one is very happy with the way we do it. But we do not really understand what we are doing, nor do we really understand how to organize such a system.

This is the new organization, in which highly educated people contribute theoretical and conceptual knowledge, through responsible judgment, for a joint effort. This is the organization of an educated society, the organization in which the bulk of the people are managerial, professional, or technical. And this organization does not answer to our traditional organization concept and indeed cannot be organized on this basis.

Our organization concepts, no matter how refined, are all really variations on the traditional organization of a fighting force as it first emerged well over 3,000 years ago—in China, in Egypt, and then, shortly after the Trojan War, in Greece. It was an organization which succeeded in bringing together fairly large numbers of people for unskilled, repetitive, drilled work. When we began to build large-scale business organizations some 75 years or so ago, we simply took the prevailing concepts of military organization and adapted them. The principle of such an organization was authority, and the basic problem was to make responsibility commensurate with authority. To this day, the relationship of authority to responsibility is central to our concept of organization.

For the new organization of highly educated people, authority and responsibility may well be the wrong principles of organization. It may well be that we will have to learn to organize not a system of authority and responsibility—a system of command—but an information and decision system—a system of judgment, knowledge, and expectations.

Let me say that this does not involve a greater emphasis on human relations. In fact, we cannot solve the organizational problems we face by an emphasis on relations between people. We cannot, for instance, solve them by emphasizing the informal organization as against a formal one. We need a formal organization that is focused on the new reality. This will have to be an objective focus on the work to be done, the risks to be taken, the decisions to be made, and the actions to follow therefrom, rather than a focus on the relations between people.

We have some tools for this—but only the beginning. Even the little we have indicates that we may well face very radical changes—changes aimed not at making the central decision-making authority less effective but at making it more effective and, at the same time, at building the organization according to the need for information, judgment, decision, and execution rather than according to the hierarchical concept of command and response. This is anything but easy or painless. We may have to learn to consider authority, responsibility, rank, and reward as four separate and distinct variables to be merged in a configuration, rather than as synonyms for the same thing. We may even have to learn to look at an organization as a process (and as one that corresponds to organic biological processes) rather than as merely a mechanism; in other words, as something in which there is no "higher" or "lower," but only a "different."

Other Problems I could discuss a good many other things. For instance, what impact will this change in the basic structure of our work force and of our work have on the labor union? Here is a major institution of American life, a major power center, and a major element in our society and our economy. Historically, it has been able to embrace only yesterday's worker, the manual machine operator. Will it succeed in reaching tomorrow's worker? Or will it become essentially stagnant and sterile? It is perhaps not irrelevant that, in sharp contrast to 25 years ago, the age structure of the labor union is today a good deal older than that of the work population in general. In other words, labor is becoming an institution of the old rather than the cause of the young.

Another area for discussion is the way in which we direct our personnel efforts. What emphasis, for instance, do we still give to the first-line supervisor and to labor relations in our management thinking, even though these are the tasks and priorities of the past rather than of tomorrow? It is possible that tomorrow we will have two employee groups, distinguished primarily by sex. It may be that the women will provide the bulk of our unskilled labor force, both of machine tenders and unskilled service workers, whereas the men will do the new work, the managerial, professional, and technical work. Here is a change for which we are totally unprepared and which would introduce some very serious tensions and problems into American life and business.

There is also the question whether this shift in the basic structure of the American population is likely to result in basic changes in demand; whether there will be a move, for instance, from more durable consumer goods, which have a high-status importance for the low-income groups, to more community satisfactions, such as education, which have a high-status importance for the managerial, professional, and technical group. But I think I have said enough to indicate that we face very real problems, enough to substantiate my own conviction that the shift in the structure of American Society and in the jobs in American business is, in retrospect, the really fundamental event of these last years, rather than the recession on which so much of our attention has been focused. And I think I have also said enough to show why I do not believe that I am writing about something in the future; the challenges and the opportunities are already here, and they demand thinking, understanding, and action from business and management.

Questions and Answers[1]

From the Floor: In England we have found the typical organizational structure breaking down under conditions of very rapid change, whether in growth or in rapid technological advance. A recent study of about eight or ten electronics firms in England has shown that under conditions of rapid change the old hierarchy breaks down. Then either the firm becomes chaotic and gives up working in this sphere, or people relax and say "Well, we have got to get the job done, so the heck with the formalities."

Once the organization relaxes this way, you release a sudden and terrific enthusiasm and you are off. When you get over the stage where the line hierarchy feels uncertain, unstable, and by-passed, you begin to move. And when things clear up, the line men find that they don't have to worry about their jobs; they still are needed in the organization!

One other point on this matter of autocratic command: we have been looking into this, and we have decided that to get the job done when you have educated people in your work force, you have to give people a chance to use their brains and training. We have come around to saying that we don't command, but are aiming at a catalytic organization.

Mr. Drucker: Since I am so unsympathetic to this point of view, I hesitate to comment! First, I don't think I was talking of autocratic management. Very few of us in this room would believe in it. Let us forget how many practice it; we don't believe in it. Still, we do have an authority structure because of the responsibility involved—an authority not just of position but of knowledge, which is not unimportant and has its own responsibility—so this is not, I think, the problem.

The issue is not only one of methods; it is one of basic organizational structure, too. Good methods may release a tremendous enthusiasm, but they only release *real* enthusiasm if the mess was unspeakable before! What you do need is a new kind of organization to cope with rapid growth and change. This implies a very considerable degree of conceptual rigidity, though not of organizational rigidity. You cannot create it by sitting down and being nice to everyone or discussing it together. You can create it only by analyzing a very difficult society and building the machinery for that society.

It is quite conceivable that a wave of enthusiasm will carry you a considerable way. All our electronics people have been through what you are discussing, but every one of them has run out of enthusiasm within three years and been up against the hard fact of the need for organized management if they are to have a solid operation in which people can work independently and yet together. But what do they have to know to do this? What do they have to tell? Whom do they have to tell? Who makes these decisions? These are not riddles that you can solve by being enthusiastic. I love enthusiasm, but it burns out.

---

[1]Businessmen present at the panel session on which this chapter is based raised certain questions which brought about the interplay of ideas reported more or less verbatim in this section.

From the Floor: Do you think this new group, in establishing its status symbols, will bring a change in the direction of production output, and thereby meet some of the shortcomings Mr. Canham pointed out?

Mr. Drucker: Leaving aside any discussion of values and looking at the economy as an economist, I think you can anticipate some changes in detail. If you ask me what is going to be the main growth industry in the next ten years, I would say, "Obviously education is."

If you ask which industry in our country has shown the greatest growth in the last ten years, I may surprise you. It happens to be paper-book publishing, not aircraft or television. On a percentage basis, that has been our most rapidly growing industry, and the record industry is second. I am not saying that these two will replace the washing machine, but I am saying that it is very likely that we are seeing a shift of priority in demand preferences.

From the Floor: If the major problem in management in the years to come will be managing the educated, do you think it is possible that we could get some help on how to proceed from institutions like universities which already manage the educated?

Mr. Drucker: I think we have to learn to look for lessons wherever we can find them. The institution which has the most experience and can teach us the most things not to do is the hospital! We can learn a lot from such groups as the engineering department of a defense contractor. But a university would not teach us very much, because essentially its structure is so different. Basically, most universities consist of individual scholars working in one house but not actually working together.

From the Floor: What do we do with the large group of people in the next ten years who have been forced to grow beyond their capacity, and are now being pushed by this group of experts for their jobs?

Mr. Drucker: I think this is going to be a very real problem. We have it in our first-line supervision in many places. Our first-line supervision in many industries today is the oldest age group, and the least educated. They have dead-end jobs. It isn't polite to say it, but it is true. And what about the hordes of narrow specialists who have suddenly seen their jobs expand beyond their abilities? These people are perfectly adequate to do the job of yesterday and perhaps even of today. Can we give them an understanding of the new knowledge that is hammering in on them? Obviously management development programs would not be flourishing if the problem were not acute. You can't fire them, and you can't retire them yet, not for 20 more years. We have to make them effective, somehow, or live it out. The real question is now to make their successors tomorrow, who *may* well have the education, much better.

Reading Related to Chapter 6

How Our Values Are Changing

Ian H. Wilson

*   *   *

All organizations will be operated less and less by the dictates of administrative convenience, more and more to meet the wants and aspirations of their membership.

So long as organizations were concerned principally with a relatively stable environment and the maintenance of internal order, they could rely on the routine administration of detailed procedures (the great strength of bureaucratic systems). Dealing with the uncertainty of change reduces the value of set procedures, and increases the value of individual initiative.

This fact, coupled with increasing affluence and education, will greatly strengthen the individual in his relationships with organizations. By the same token, the power of the administrator will be weakened, or at least made considerably more difficult. Managers (of *any* organization) must expect that considerations of individual motivation, group relationships and personnel costs (including the "hidden" costs of poor performance, withheld cooperation, high turnover and extra recruiting and training) will weigh much more heavily in their decision-making in the future.

*   *   *

. . . *Attitudes toward job-requirements, and the character of work, will change more in the coming decade than will attitudes toward work as such.*

We are not going to see the emergence of a leisure-oriented society overnight, or even over the next decade.

However,

• There will be a growing, but still tiny, minority drawn from the upper end of the affluence scale who either "drop out" from a sense of alienation or choose the life of the "perpetual student."

Excerpts reprinted from *The Futurist,* February 1970, pp. 5–9. Published by the World Future Society, P.O. Box 30369 (Bethesda), Washington, D.C. 20014, by permission of the publisher.

- The structure of work will be changing, as work/student programs become more common, sabbaticals are more widely adopted, and part-time work accounts for a greater percentage of total hours worked (perhaps leading to the introduction of modular work-scheduling to enable employees to select the number of modules they want to work). Already one tenth of hours worked in the U.S. economy come from part-time work.

* * *

Organization → Individual

In all types of organizations, the rights and position of the individual, due process and participative forms of management will become the dominant mode. It is not too much to say that, for many key employees, an organization will be accepted or rejected according to whether it assists or hinders them in their plans for self-actualization.

* * *

Materialism → Quality of Life

As increasing affluence brings possession of material goods more easily within reach, and education induces a greater regard for self-development, materialism progressively loses much of its appeal as a prime motivating force. For those affected most by these twin factors, the search for a new sense of meaning and purpose in life will become a matter of real importance. Although it may be expected that the current student emphasis on the "quality of life" will be somewhat muted by more material concerns as they move into the world of work, the trend to a new concern for quality and the human dimension in a technological world is most likely to continue. . . .

* * *

Authority → Participation

The democratizing effect of technology and the rising level of education combine to change the nature of authority and to limit its arbitrary exercise. The scope and impact of authority may well be increased, but increasingly it will be the authority of knowledge rather than the authority of position alone. And since those in authority will be dependent for much of this knowledge on the expertise of specialist professionals, the processes of decision-making will necessarily tend toward a more participative mode.

* * *

Economic Efficiency → "Social Justice"

Economic efficiency is a prime value in a society that is primarily concerned with the production and distribution of material goods. Although individuals benefit from the resulting material wealth, efficiency is rated as an organizational value. As more and more individuals progress beyond the material concerns of Maslow's hierarchy, and as organizational values are diminished in favor of individual values, the ranking of efficiency in the scale of values will tend to be reduced—to nearer a parity with social values such as justice, equality, individual dignity.

On the other hand, "social action" programs such as education, man power development programs and the War on Poverty will be expected to meet higher standards of efficiency. . . .

Readings Related to Chapter 10

Employee Attitudes and
Employee Performance

Arthur H. Brayfield
Walter H. Crockett

Theoretical Considerations

Morale as an Explanatory Concept in Industrial Psychology   One principal generalization suffices to set up an expectation that morale should be related to absenteeism and turnover, namely, that organisms tend to avoid those situations which are punishing and to seek out situations that are rewarding. To the extent that worker dissatisfaction indicates that the individual is in a punishing situation, we should expect dissatisfied workers to be absent more often and to quit the job at a higher rate than individuals who are satisfied with their work. Since the general proposition about the effects of reward has received a great amount of verification in psychology, it is not strange that it has been carried to the analysis of absenteeism and turnover.

A plausible connection between satisfaction and performance on the job is less obvious. Let us consider specifically the possible relationship between satisfaction and productivity. Under conditions of marked dissatisfaction it is likely that low productivity may serve as a form of aggression which reflects worker hostility toward management. But the hypothesis that production should increase monotonically with increases in satisfaction apparently rests on the assumption that the worker will demonstrate his gratitude by increased output, or that the increased satisfaction frees certain creative energies in the worker, or that the satisfied employee accepts management's goals, which include high production.

In any event, it is commonly hypothesized that, whatever the causes, increased satisfaction makes workers more motivated to produce. Given this condition, it should follow that increased productivity can be attained by increas-

From *Psychological Bulletin*, vol. 52, no. 5, 1955, pp. 415–422. Reprinted by permission of the American Psychological Association.

ing worker satisfaction. We are going to advance the proposition that the motivational structure of industrial workers is not so simple as is implied in this formula. We feel that research workers have erred by overlooking individual differences in motivations and perceptions because of their concern with discovering important and applicable generalizations. Most of what follows is an effort to point out areas in which differences between workmen may make a difference in their adjustment to the situation.

At the outset let us make it clear that we expect the relation between satisfaction and job performance to be one of concomitant variation rather than cause and effect. It makes sense to us to assume that individuals are motivated to achieve certain environmental goals and that the achievement of these goals results in satisfaction. Productivity is seldom a goal in itself but is more commonly a means to goal attainment. Therefore, as G. M. Mahoney has suggested,[1] we might expect high satisfaction and high productivity to occur together when productivity is perceived as a path to certain important goals and when these goals are achieved. Under other conditions, satisfaction and productivity might be unrelated or even negatively related. In the light of this consideration, we shall center our discussion on an analysis of industrial motivation as it relates specifically to employee satisfaction and to productivity.

For the sake of convenience we may distinguish between threats and rewards as incentives to productivity. Goode and Fowler (21) have described a factory in which morale and productivity were negatively related but productivity was kept high by the continuance of threats to workers. Here the essential workers—people with considerable skill—were marginal to the labor force because of their sex or because of physical handicaps. Since the plant was not unionized, it was possible for management to demand high productivity from these workers on threat of discharge. This meant that the workers, although most dissatisfied with their jobs, produced at a very high rate because of the difficulty they would face in finding another position should they be discharged.

There is little doubt that threat was widely used as a motivating device in our own society in the past and is presently used in more authoritarian societies. However, it is doubtful if any great amount of at least explicit threat is currently used by industries in this country in efforts to increase productivity or reduce absenteeism. First of all, considerable change has occurred in management philosophy over the past fifty years, and such tactics are repugnant to many industrial concerns. Secondly, the growth of unions has virtually outlawed such tendencies except in small, semi-marginal industries which are not unionized.

Threats of discharge, then, probably do not operate as incentives unless the worker falls considerably below the mean in quantity and/or quality of output. For a number of reasons management has settled upon rewards for motivating workers to produce, including such tangible incentives as increased pay and promotion, as well as verbal and other symbolic recognition. Let us examine whether this system of rewards actually provides motivation for increased productivity by the worker.

---

[1] G. M. Mahoney. Personal communication. March, 1953.

It is a commonplace observation that motivation is not a simple concept. It is a problem which may be attacked at a number of different levels and from many theoretical points of view. Whatever their theoretical predilection, however, psychologists generally are agreed that human motivation is seldom directed only toward goals of physical well-being. Once a certain minimum level of living has been achieved, human behavior is directed largely toward some social goal or goals. Thus, in our own society, goals such as achievement, acceptance by others, dominance over others, and so on, probably are of as great concern to the average workman as the goals of finding sufficient food and shelter to keep body and psyche together.

We assume that social motives are of considerable importance in industry. We assume, further, that the goals an individual pursues will vary, depending upon the social systems within which he is behaving from time to time. Most industrial workers probably operate in a number of social systems. Katz and Kahn (33) suggest four such systems: first, the system of relations outside the plant; and, within the plant, the systems of relationship with fellow workers on the job, with members of the union, and with others in the company structure. We may ask whether job performance, and particularly productivity, is a path to goal achievement within these various sets of social relations.

Outside the Plant   It is often argued that any worker who is motivated to increase his status in the outside community should be motivated toward higher productivity within the plant. Productivity frequently leads directly to more money on the job, or involves movement to jobs with higher prestige or with authority over others. If productivity does result in such in-plant mobility, increased output may enable the individual to achieve a higher level of living, to increase his general status in the community, and to attempt such social mobility as he may desire. In this way productivity may serve as a path to the achievement of goals outside the plant.

The operation of this chain of relationships, however, depends not only upon the rewards given the high producer, but also upon the original motivation of the workman to increase his status position in the outside community. The amount of status motivation among production-line employees is open to question. Certainly the findings of Warner (57), Davis and Gardner (12), and others (6, 11, 13), indicate that there are systematic differences in the goals which are pursued in the different segments of our society. It is not impossible that a very large proportion of America's work force is only minimally motivated toward individual social achievement. The assumption that such a motivation does exist may reflect in considerable part a projection of certain middle-class aspirations onto working-class employees.

Furthermore, it is not unlikely that the reference group against which an individual workman evaluates his success may be only a segment of the community, rather than the community as a whole. An individual whose accomplishments are modest at best when compared with the range of possible accomplishments in the community may have a feeling of great accomplishment when he compares his achievements with those of others in his environment. If this is true, and if he desires to continue to operate within this segment of society, any further increase in rewards within the plant might lead to his exclusion from personally important groups outside the plant rather than to increased prestige in such groups.

Finally, there are many goals outside the industrial plant which may be socially rewarding to the individual and which require only minimal financial and occupational rewards inside the plant. Active participation in veterans' organizations, in churches, in recreational programs and similar activities may be and frequently are carried out by individuals at all positions in the industrial hierarchy. As a matter of fact, to the extent that the individual receives extensive social rewards from such activities he may have only slight interest in his work on the job, and he may continue to remain in industry only to maintain some minimum economic position while carrying out his outside functions. For such an individual, high productivity may lead to *no* important goals.

Relations with Other Workers in the Plant   The studies by Elton Mayo and his associates (43, 50, 51) introduced the work group into the analysis of industry, and a wealth of subsequent investigations have confirmed the importance of on-the-job groups. Throughout these studies has run the observation that members of the work group develop group standards of productivity and attempt to force these standards upon those workmen who deviate. Thus, in the Bank Wiring Room (51) it was the socially maladjusted individual, the deviant from the work group, who maintained a level of production above that of the group even though his native ability was considerably below that of many of the others.

Mathewson's (42) classic study of restriction of output among unorganized workers was an early demonstration of the operation of group norms.

Schachter and associates (52) have conducted an experiment which indicates that in cohesive groups an individual's productivity may be either raised or lowered, depending upon the kind of communications directed toward him by congenial co-workers. In an actual factory setting, Coch and French (8) presented existent groups with evidence that a change in job methods and in productivity was necessary if the factory was to remain in a favorable position relative to other, competing factories. These groups, through group discussion, arrived at a decision as to the proper job set up, and modified the group judgment of "fair" output markedly upward.

There is evidence, then, that the level of performance on the job frequently depends upon a group norm, and that performance level may be changed by changing the group norm in a direction desired by management. This change in the norm probably results from a conviction among the workers that higher production is in their own interest as well as management's, i.e., that their interests and management's interests coincide. This raises the perplexing question of whether, with regard to productivity, the interests of management and labor do, in fact, coincide.

Management, presumably, is interested in higher production as a way of reducing the ratio of cost to output, and thereby bettering management's financial and competitive position. In an expanding market, the argument goes, this makes possible the expansion of the company, increased wages, a larger labor force, and general prosperity not only for the corporation but for the employees as well.

The case may not be so attractive to the workers, especially when the market is not expanding and demand for the product is constant, nearly constant, or declining. In this event, higher productivity per worker means that fewer people are required for the same level of output, or that fewer hours are worked by the same number of workers. In either case, many workers may lose, rather than gain, by the increase in productivity. It may be argued that in normal times such individuals usually find fairly rapid employment in some other segment of the economy. However true this may be, from the viewpoint of the individual workman this involves a considerable disruption in working habits and in his social life in general, and is to be avoided wherever possible. Viewed in this light the interests of management and labor are inimical.

As psychologists we steer clear of such arguments. But we should be sensitive to the fact that the question is a debatable one, that a final decision will probably rest upon values rather than data, that each side is capable of convincing arguments, and that the perception of a certain inevitable conflict of interests between the two groups is honestly and intelligently held by many people. We should also recognize that any reduction in work force after a joint labor-management effort to increase productivity will likely be interpreted as resulting from the increased productivity, and may lead to a future avoidance not only of high productivity levels but also of labor-management cooperation.

At any rate, we often find that individual workers interpret higher productivity as counter to the interests of the employees. To the extent that this perception constitutes a group norm, such motives as are rewarded through the individual's social relationships with other workmen may be blocked by increased productivity. In such cases, productivity may serve as a path to certain goals, but as a block to social acceptance.

The Union Structure   One system of relationships of considerable importance in many industrial concerns is the union. In many companies much of what was said in the preceding section may be extended to refer also to the relations of the worker in the system of social relations within the union.

In some plants high productivity is not a deterrent to active union participation. Nevertheless, it probably is true that productivity is seldom a prerequisite for advancement within the union hierarchy. If the individual is oriented toward the union structure, it is unlikely that high productivity will serve as a path to such goals, whatever its effects on other goals he may pursue.

The Company Structure   We have indicated above that many of the worker's social motives outside the plant, as well as his desires for in-plant associations with fellow workmen and within the union, may be only slightly affected by increases in productivity and sometimes may be blocked by increased productivity. The apparent range of goals that a worker may have is so wide that productivity may be a path to only a few of them.

However, workers are often motivated toward goals within the plant such as turning out a quality product, higher wages, and promotion. Let us examine the relationship between satisfaction and productivity for workers who are motivated toward these in-plant goals.

At the start it is evident that productivity and quality are sometimes mutually exclusive. If the individual must concentrate on maintaining high quality work, speed of production probably plays a secondary role. Conversely, if he must emphasize speed, quality often must be reduced to some degree. The speed-quality dilemma is sometimes resolved by making the individual work units so routine and concerned with such minute changes in the material that increased speed will not affect the quality of the product. However, if a worker is more highly motivated when he is performing some meaningful job, the above procedure may be resolving one dilemma by raising another. At any rate, the artisan, motivated toward the goal of quality, may be highly satisfied with his job while turning out a very limited number of finished pieces per unit of time. If he is forced to increase productivity and lower in some measure the quality, we might expect his satisfaction to decrease. For such a person satisfaction and productivity would be negatively related.

Consider now the individual who is motivated toward higher wages and promotion. While these rewards may not be exclusively dependent upon job performance, at the same time productivity and other aspects of performance often are weighted heavily at promotion time in most companies. In other words, productivity and other aspects of job performance constitute a path to the goal of promotion and wage increases.

Now it is likely that people with aspirations to change position in the company structure will often be quite dissatisfied with their present position in the company. Aspiration to move within a system implies not only a desire for some different position in the future, but some degree of dissatisfaction with the position one is presently occupying. The amount of dissatisfaction probably depends upon the length of time the individual has occupied this position. Thus, although productivity may be a path to the goal, failure to achieve the goal to date may result in dissatisfaction and the high producer may be less satisfied than the low producer.

Evidence sustaining this point of view is to be found in Katz and associates' (34) report of a large insurance company in which the best, most productive workers were also considerably more critical of company policy than were less productive workers. S. Lieberman reports a similar finding in a large appliance factory.[2] A year after all workers in the factory had filled out a questionnaire, Lieberman compared the earlier responses of those who had been promoted to foreman with a matched group of workers who were not promoted. Those promoted had been significantly less satisfied with company practices at the earlier time than had the control group.

Once again the question arises as to what is meant by satisfaction. It may be that extremely high satisfaction is indicative of a certain amount of complacency, a satisfaction with the job as it is, which may be only slightly related to job performance, if it is related at all. On the other hand, individuals who are highly

[2]S. Lieberman. Personal communication. July 15, 1954.

motivated may perceive productivity as a path to their goals, but may also be more realistically critical of whatever deficiencies exist within the organization. They may feel, in addition, that their output is not being rewarded as rapidly as it deserves.

Implications for Future Research   We have arrived at two conclusions: first, that satisfaction with one's position in a network of relationships need not imply strong motivation to outstanding performance within that system, and, second, that productivity may be only peripherally related to many of the goals toward which the industrial worker is striving. We do not mean to imply that researchers should have known all along that their results would be positive only infrequently and in particular circumstances. We have been operating on the basis of hindsight and have attempted to spell out some of the factors which may have accounted for the failure of industrial investigators to find positive relationships in their data.

However, certain implications seem logical from the foregoing sections of this report. Foremost among these implications is the conclusion that it is time to question the strategic and ethical merits of selling to industrial concerns an assumed relationship between employee attitudes and employee performance. In the absence of more convincing evidence than is now at hand with regard to the beneficial effects on job performance of high morale, we are led to the conclusion that we might better forego publicizing these alleged effects.

The emphasis on predicting job performance, and particularly productivity, rests upon the acceptance of certain values. That is, the many studies that have used productivity as the criterion to be predicted have been performed because productivity has direct economic value to industry, and, presumably, to society at large. But the fact that it has economic value does not mean that job performance is the only, or even the most important, aspect of organizational behavior. From the viewpoint of studying, analyzing, and understanding the industrial setting and individual reactions thereto, productivity and other aspects of job performance may be only one of several important factors. It would seem worthwhile to study the causes, correlates, and consequence of satisfaction, per se. It seems possible, for example, that conditions conducive to job satisfaction will have an effect on the quality of the workman drawn into the industry, the quality of job performance, and the harmony of labor-management relations. Such potential correlates, among others, merit exploration.

Another potentially fruitful approach involves studying the differential effect of particular kinds of management practices upon the attitudes and performances of workers with different motives, aspirations, and expectations. The appropriate questions may concern how, for particular workers, productivity comes to be perceived as instrumental to the achievement of some goals but not others, while for other workers a different perception develops.

The experimental approach has largely been neglected in this area of industrial research, yet the control of variables that it provides seems essential to the development and refinement of our knowledge in the area. Certainly, where experimentation has been used, as by Schachter and associates (52) and by Coch and French (8), the results have been both enlightening for the understanding of present problems and encouraging for its future application. As our concepts become increasingly precise, we may expect an increased use of experimentation both within the industrial setting and in the laboratory.

Perhaps the most significant conclusion to be drawn from this survey of the literature is that the industrial situation is a complex one. We have suggested that an analysis of the situation involves analysis not only of the individual's relation to the social system of the factory, the work group, and the union, but the community at large as well. It is important to know what motives exist among industrial workers, how they are reflected in the behavior of the workers, and how the motives develop and are modified within the framework of patterned social relationships in the plant and in the larger community.

We seem to have arrived at the position where the social scientist in the industrial setting must concern himself with a full-scale analysis of that situation. Pursuit of this goal should provide us with considerable intrinsic job satisfaction.

References

6 Centers, R.: *The psychology of social classes.* Princeton: Princeton Univer. Press, 1949.

8 Coch, L., & French, J. R., Jr.: Overcoming resistance to change. *Hum. Relat.,* 1948, **1**, 512–532.

11 Davis, A.: *Social class influences upon learning.* Cambridge: Harvard Univer. Press, 1948.

12 Davis, A., Gardner, B. B., & Gardner, Mary R.: *Deep south: A social and anthropological study of caste and class.* Chicago: Univer. of Chicago Press, 1941.

13 Ericson, Martha C.: Social status and child rearing practices. In T. M. Newcomb & E. L. Hartley (Eds.), *Readings in social psychology.* New York: Holt, 1947. Pp. 494–501.

21 Goode, W. J., & Fowler, I.: Incentive factors in a low morale plant. *Amer. sociol. Rev.,* 1949, **14**, 618–624.

33 Katz, D., & Kahn, R. L.: Some recent findings in human relations research in industry. In G. E. Swanson, T. M. Newcomb & E. L. Hartley (Eds.), *Readings in social psychology.* New York: Holt, 1952, Pp. 650–665.

34 Katz, D., Maccoby, N., & Morse, Nancy: *Productivity, supervision and morale in an office situation.* Univer. of Michigan: Survey Research Center, 1950.

✓ **42** Mathewson, S. B.: *Restriction of output among unorganized workers.* New York: Viking Press, 1931.

43 Mayo, E.: *The social problems of an industrial civilization.* Cambridge: Graduate School of Business Administration, Harvard Univer., 1945.

50 Roethlisberger, F. J.: *Management and morale.* Cambridge: Harvard Univer. Press, 1943.

51 Roethlisberger, F. J., & Dickson, W. J.: *Management and the worker.* Cambridge: Harvard Univer. Press, 1939.

✓ **52** Schachter, S., Ellertson, N., McBride, D., & Gregory, D.: An experimental study of cohesiveness and productivity. *Hum. Relat.,* 1951, **4**, 229–238.

57 Warner, W. L., & Lunt, P. S.: *The social life of a modern community.* New Haven: Yale Univ. Press, 1941.

Employee Performance and Employee Need Satisfaction: Which Comes First?

Robert A. Sutermeister

Assuming Maslow's hierarchy of needs theory is correct,[1]

- What is the cause and effect relationship between employee performance and need satisfaction?
- Does high performance result in satisfaction of needs?
- Does satisfaction of needs result in improved performance?
- Or is there a circular relationship, each contributing to the other and each being affected by the other?

These are difficult questions. Brayfield and Crockett established in 1955 that "satisfaction with one's position in a network of relationships need not imply strong motivation to outstanding performance within that system."[2] Roberts *et al.* conclude there is no present technique for determining cause and effect of performance and satisfaction.[3] Porter and Lawler state that the greatest future research need is for data to provide evidence on the direction of causality in their model relating performance and satisfaction (see Figure 1).[4]

A number of authors state or imply that satisfaction contributes to improved performance and productivity. Herzberg *et al.* examined studies in which the effect of job attitudes on productivity was measured. They found "that in 54 percent of the reported surveys high morale was associated with high productivity" although the correlations in many of these studies were low; they concluded there was "frequent evidence for the often suggested opinion that positive job attitudes are favorable to increased productivity."[5] Sorcher and Meyer in a study of factory employees found that giving more meaning to routine jobs, making them more satisfying, and meeting some of the human needs of workers resulted in greater productive motivation and higher quality workmanship.[6] Pigors and Myers state a working hypothesis that job satisfaction of a certain kind and at a given level may have a positive relationship to individual productivity.[7] And Sutermeister proposes a generalization for individuals who have strong egoistic needs: that the chances of motivating good employee performance are greater if the egoistic needs are fairly well satisfied on a continuing basis or if the employees feel that their present activities will lead to such satisfaction in the future.[8] The suggestion is that satisfaction (now or anticipated) of needs (especially egoistic) leads to improved performance.

Other authors state or imply a different point of view: that outstanding performance leads to greater satisfaction of needs. Miles, Porter, and Craft state

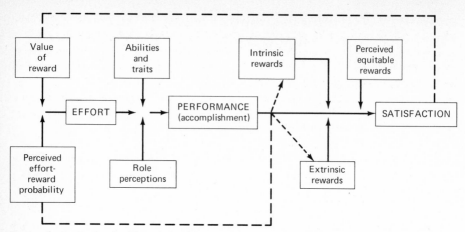

Figure 1   Porter-Lawler Theoretical Model. (*Reprinted by permission of the publisher from Lyman W. Porter and Edward E. Lawler,* Managerial Attitudes and Performance, *Richard D. Irwin, Inc., Homewood, Ill., 1968, p. 165.*)

that work satisfaction may improve as a by-product of subordinates' making full use of their resources: that satisfaction is intrinsic in the work; that subordinates get a major portion of their rewards merely from their own feelings of accomplishment and doing the job well.[9]

The Porter and Lawler Model

Porter and Lawler devised perhaps the most complete model of a satisfaction-performance relationship in their study of managerial attitudes and performance. Their model *predicts* that satisfaction results from performance itself, the rewards for performance, and the perceived equitability of those rewards.[10] (Ideally rewards come as a result of performance, but actually people can and often do receive rewards unrelated to performance.) However, they are careful to point out that the direction of causality the model predicts remains to be validated in future research.

In the Porter and Lawler model, if an individual is attracted by the value of the reward he envisions for a higher level of performance, and if he perceives as highly probable that increased effort will lead to that reward, he will increase his effort. And, if he has the required abilities and accurate role perceptions, his performance or accomplishment will improve. If the intrinsic and extrinsic rewards he receives from improved performance are perceived as equitable, then satisfaction will result, satisfaction being the difference between perceived equitable and actual rewards. In short, the model predicts that performance leads to satisfaction rather than satisfaction to improved performance.

The Cycle Concept

It may be useful to think of the performance-satisfaction relationship in terms of a series of cycles. The Porter-Lawler study did not collect data to predict how "changes in level of need satisfaction affect the future values of certain rewards." This is a major area well worth further study and research.

Since psychologists seem agreed that a satisfied need is no motivator, one could hypothesize that if an individual's needs are met and satisfaction has been achieved, he would not be motivated to improve his performance. Such an hypothesis overlooks the possibility that higher level needs may become activated, and the individual may now be motivated to satisfy them. It may be helpful to view satisfaction in the Porter and Lawler model as the end of one cycle and as the beginning of another.

It is difficult, of course, to pinpoint the end of one cycle and the start of another. In general it might be said one cycle ends when the individual receives his rewards, whether intrinsic, extrinsic, or both. Some people whose satisfaction depends mostly on pay (as an extrinsic reward) receive their rewards annually at pay increase time. Other people whose satisfaction depends mostly on intrinsic rewards may receive their rewards in the form of recognition and accomplishment at annual performance review time (which may be different from pay increase time). For others, who view their most important rewards as meeting challenges and self-fulfillment through utilization of their highest capacities, the rewards may be self-bestowed and come at any time. Thus various individuals are likely to have different times for ending one performance-reward cycle and starting the next.

Life Cycle and Aspiration Level

In addition to considering a performance-satisfaction cycle, it is convenient to consider a "life cycle" through which each person passes.

The young man getting out of school and embarking on his career is likely to be eager and enthusiastic and his aspiration level high. The role which he plays during these early years in his career may be quite different from the roles he plays later on. Money may be an important incentive as he tries to carve out his niche among his peers. On the other hand, some individuals are more interested in the opportunities a job offers than in its immediate financial reward. If they feel the job is "leading to something," represents a path to a goal they have set for themselves, the money may be of secondary importance.

A man's turning point often comes in the middle of his career. Here he may find a definite fork in the road. If he has accumulated a string of successes in achieving his goals, he may follow one fork and set his cap for a higher goal; or if he has become thwarted in achieving his goals, he may follow the other fork and resign himself to something less than he had started out to achieve. This is a critical period in which the "climber" may change into the "conserver," when reality may replace idealism and one may compromise or settle for less than earlier goals.[11] The level of aspiration a person now adopts will depend on whether he has achieved his previously set levels of aspiration or whether he has failed to reach them and now therefore lowers his aspirations.

In his late career a man is even more likely to become a conserver and hold on to what he has. He may feel that insufficient years remain for him to achieve the high-level goals sought in his youth, so he may be tempted to ride out his career until retirement at 65.

This description of a life cycle represents, of course, a general pattern. Specific individuals vary widely from the described scheme. Many men are going strong at 65 and have distinguished careers into their 80's and 90's. Others become conservers and "retire" at 30. The important point is not that there is a single pattern the same for everyone, but rather that the position one occupies in his life cycle is likely to have a great bearing on his level of aspirations.

Level of Needs   At the end of a cycle, and referring only to needs activated on the job, have the individual's needs been fully met or are they unfulfilled? Has the fulfillment of certain egoistic needs been followed by activation of higher-level needs? For some individuals higher-level needs are never completely satisfied. Fulfillment of one need simply activates a higher-level need in a never-ending striving for complete self-fulfillment.

Alternatives for the Unsatisfied

Let's assume for the moment that at the end of a cycle the individual's needs are not satisfied (see Figure 2). Whether he begins a search for a way to satisfy them depends upon his level of aspiration, which in turn is affected by his position in his life cycle.

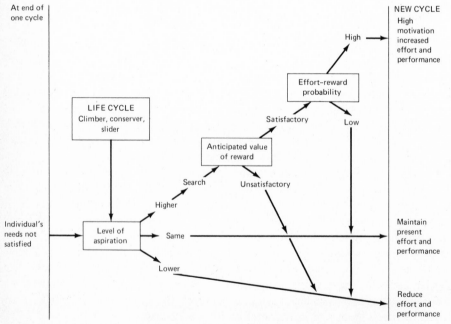

Figure 2 Alternatives for the Individual Whose Needs Are Not Satisfied at End of a Performance-Satisfaction Cycle.

- A person late in his life cycle may have become a conserver or a backslider and have lowered his level of aspiration; or,
- Even if he is a climber in his life cycle, his failure to satisfy his needs in the previous cycle could lower his level of aspiration in the new cycle; or,
- He may have a high level of aspiration and intensify his need-satisfaction search.

He may do this by seeking a different job in the same firm or in a new firm. He may do this by exerting greater effort on his present job, provided, in accordance with the Porter-Lawler model, the value of the reward he anticipates in the next cycle is high enough, and the effort-reward probability strong enough.

If he becomes convinced that his chances of satisfying his needs are not good or are not worth the effort, he may give up his search. Thus his actual behavior will be strongly influenced by his level of aspiration, which in turn is affected by what happened in the previous performance-satisfaction cycle and by his place in his life cycle.

Alternatives for the Satisfied

Now let's assume that when the individual receives his reward he perceives it as equitable and is satisfied (see Figure 3). He now has to plan his behavior for the next cycle.

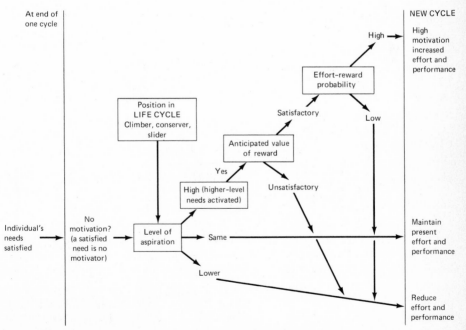

Figure 3 Diagram Representing Individual Whose Needs are Satisfied at End of a Performance-Satisfaction Cycle.

- Will his effort drop to a lower level?
- Will he maintain it at the present level?
- Will he try to improve it?

If a satisfied need is no motivator, his initial reaction may be to reduce his effort. His decision again will depend on a number of factors.

- What is the individual's level of aspiration as influenced by his position in his life cycle?
- Have higher-level needs been activated?
- If so, is the anticipated value of the reward in the next cycle satisfactory?
- And, is the effort-reward probability perceived as satisfactory?

For some individuals higher-level needs may become activated. They may be in a climbing period in their life cycles, or for other reasons have high aspiration levels; and if the value of reward and perceived effort-reward probability are satisfactory, they may be motivated to greater effort and improved performance. (A unionized worker may find his higher level needs activated. But if his rewards come from higher pay, and pay is determined through union negotiations and not through personal effort, there is low probability of effort leading to reward. In the new cycle, then, his effort and performance are not likely to be high.)[12]

A second group of individuals may decide that they would like only to continue enjoying their present satisfaction. They may be in the middle of their life cycles, and have become conservers, wishing merely to retain their present level of power, prestige, and income. Their needs are satisfied, but this does not mean that they have no motivation. Rather they are motivated to continue their efforts at a level which will retain the rewards they now enjoy, provided, of course, the value of the reward and the perceived effort-reward probability remain the same.

A third group of individuals may decide to lower their levels of aspiration. Perhaps they are far along in their life cycles and desire to ease up on their efforts and be satisfied with a lower reward. In this case the value of the reward and the perceived effort-reward probability, even if high, are of little concern.

Conclusion

The degree of satisfaction at the end of one performance-satisfaction cycle and the individual's position in his life cycle will affect his level of aspiration in the new performance-satisfaction cycle. If his level of aspiration is raised, and if the value of the reward and the perceived effort-reward probability appear satisfactory to him, he will be motivated to improve his effort and performance in the new cycle. If his level of aspiration remains the same, and value of reward and perceived effort-reward probability remain the same, he will be motivated to continue his previous level of effort in the new cycle. And if his level of aspiration is lowered, he will reduce his effort in the new cycle regardless of the value of reward and perceived effort-reward probability.

Figure 4   Satisfaction-Productivity Relationship.

We may theorize, then, that effort and performance affect satisfaction, and that satisfaction by its influence on level of aspiration affects subsequent effort and performance. Thus it would seem as if the satisfaction-productivity relationship is circular, as the final figure [Figure 4] shows.

References

1   A. H. Maslow, "A Theory of Human Motivation," *Psychological Review,* 50 (1943), 370–396.
2   Arthur H. Brayfield and Walter H. Crockett, "Employee Attitudes and Employee Performance," *Psychological Bulletin,* 52:5 (1955), 415–422.
3   Karlene Roberts, Raymond E. Miles, and L. Vaughn Blankenship, "Organizational Leadership Satisfaction and Productivity: A Comparative Analysis," *Academy of Management Journal,* 11:4 (December 1968), 401–414.
4   Lyman Porter and Edward E. Lawler, *Managerial Attitudes and Performance* (Homewood, Ill.: Irwin, 1968), p. 167.
5   F. Herzberg *et al., Job Attitudes: Review of Research and Opinion* (Pittsburgh: Psychological Service of Pittsburgh, 1957), p. 103.
6   Melvin Sorcher and Herbert H. Meyer, "Motivating Factory Employees," *Personnel* (Jan.–Feb. 1968), 22–28.
7   Paul Pigors and Charles Myers, *Personnel Administration,* 6th ed., (New York: McGraw-Hill, 1969), pp. 160–161.
8   Robert A. Sutermeister, *People and Productivity,* 2d ed. (New York: McGraw-Hill, 1969), pp. 54–55.
9   Raymond E. Miles, Lyman Porter, and Joseph A. Craft, "Three Models of Leadership Attitudes," in Paul Pigors, Charles Myers, and F. T. Malm, *Management of Human Resources* (New York: McGraw-Hill, 1961), pp. 48–49.
10 Porter and Lawler, p. 165.
11 The terms "climber" and "conserver" are from Anthony Downs, *Inside Bureaucracy* (Boston: Little Brown, 1967), pp. 92 and 96.
12 See Porter and Lawler, "What Job Attitudes Tell About Motivation," *Harvard Business Review* (Jan.–Feb. 1968), 121.

Reading Related to Chapter 11

The Western Electric Researches

George C. Homans

Perhaps the most important program of research studied by the Committee on Work in Industry of the National Research Council is that which has been carried on at the Hawthorne (Chicago) Works of the Western Electric Company. This program was described by H. A. Wright and M. L. Putnam of the Western Electric Company and by F. J. Roethlisberger, now Professor of Human Relations, Graduate School of Business Administration, Harvard University, particularly at a meeting of the Committee held on March 9, 1938. These men, together with Elton Mayo and G. A. Pennock, both members of the Committee, had been intimately associated with the research.[1]

A word about the Western Electric Company is a necessary introduction to what follows. This company is engaged in manufacturing equipment for the telephone industry. Besides doing this part of its work, it has always shown concern for the welfare of its employees. In the matter of wages and hours, it has maintained a high standard. It has provided good physical conditions for its employees; and it has tried to make use of every established method of vocational guidance in the effort to suit the worker to his work. The efforts of the company have been rewarded in good industrial relations: there has been no strike or other severe symptom of discontent for over twenty years. In short there is no reason to doubt that while these researches were being carried out, the morale of the company was high and that the employees, as a body, had confidence in the abilities and motives of the company management. These facts had an important bearing on the results achieved.

The program of research which will be described grew out of a study conducted at Hawthorne by the Western Electric Company in collaboration with

From *Fatigue of Workers,* Reinhold Publishing Corporation, New York, 1941, pp. 56–65. Reprinted by permission.

[1]This research has been described in detail in a number of papers and in at least three books. The books are: Elton Mayo, *The Human Problems of an Industrial Civilization* (New York: The Macmillan Company, 1933); T. N. Whitehead, *The Industrial Worker,* 2 vols. (Cambridge: Harvard University Press, 1938); F. J. Roethlisberger and W. J. Dickson, *Management and the Worker* (Cambridge: Harvard University Press, 1939).

the National Research Council, the aim of which was to determine the relation between intensity of illumination and efficiency of workers, measured in output. One of the experiments made was the following: Two groups of employees doing similar work under similar conditions were chosen, and records of output were kept for each group. The intensity of the light under which one group worked was varied, while that under which the other group worked was held constant. By this method the investigators hoped to isolate from the effect of other variables the effect of changes in the intensity of illumination on the rate of output.

In this hope they were disappointed. The experiment failed to show any simple relation between experimental changes in the intensity of illumination and observed changes in the rate of output. The investigators concluded that this result was obtained, not because such a relation did not exist, but because it was in fact impossible to isolate it from the other variables entering into any determination of productive efficiency. This kind of difficulty, of course, has been encountered in experimental work in many fields. Furthermore, the investigators were in agreement as to the character of some of these other variables. They were convinced that one of the major factors which prevented their securing a satisfactory result was psychological. The employees being tested were reacting to changes in light intensity in the way in which they assumed that they were expected to react. That is, when light intensity was increased they were expected to produce more; when it was decreased they were expected to produce less. A further experiment was devised to demonstrate this point. The light bulbs were changed, as they had been changed before, and the workers were allowed to assume that as a result there would be more light. They commented favorably on the increased illumination. As a matter of fact, the bulbs had been replaced with others of just the same power. Other experiments of the sort were made, and in each case the results could be explained as a "psychological" reaction rather than as a "physiological" one.

This discovery seemed to be important. It suggested that the relations between other physical conditions and the efficiency of workers might be obscured by similar psychological reactions. Nevertheless, the investigators were determined to continue in their course. They recognized the existence of the psychological factors, but they thought of them only as disturbing influences. They were not yet ready to turn their attention to the psychological factors themselves. Instead, they were concerned with devising a better way of eliminating them from the experiments, and the experiments they wanted to try by no means ended with illumination. For instance, there was the question of what was called "fatigue." Little information existed about the effect on efficiency of changes in the hours of work and the introduction of rest pauses. The investigators finally came to the conclusion that if a small group of workers were isolated in a separate room and asked to cooperate, the psychological reaction would in time disappear, and they would work exactly as they felt. That is, changes in their rate of output would be the direct result of changes in their physical conditions of work and nothing else.

The decision to organize such a group was in fact taken. A small number of workers was to be selected and placed in a separate room, where experiments were to be made with different kinds of working conditions in order to see if more exact information could be secured. Six questions were asked by those setting up the experiment. They were the following:

1   Do employees actually get tired out?
2   Are rest pauses desirable?
3   Is a shorter working day desirable?
4   What is the attitude of employees toward their work and toward the company?
5   What is the effect of changing the type of working equipment?
6   Why does production fall off in the afternoon?

It is obvious that several of these questions could be answered only indirectly by the proposed experiment, and several of them touched upon the "psychological" rather than the "physiological" factors involved. Nevertheless, all of them arose out of the bewilderment of men of experience faced with the problem of dealing with fellow human beings in a large industrial organization. In fact, one of the executives of the company saw the purpose of the experiment in even simpler and more general terms. He said that the experiment grew out of a desire on the part of the management to "know more about our workers." In this way began the experiment which is referred to as the Relay Assembly Test Room. With this experiment and the others that followed, members of the Department of Industrial Research of the Graduate School of Business Administration, Harvard University, came to be closely associated.

In April, 1927, six girls were selected from a large shop department of the Hawthorne Works. They were chosen as average workers, neither inexperienced nor expert, and their work consisted of the assembling of telephone relays. A coil, armature, contact springs, and insulators were put together on a fixture and secured in position by means of four machine screws. The operation at that time was being completed at the rate of about five relays in six minutes. This particular operation was chosen for the experiment because the relays were being assembled often enough so that even slight changes in output rate would show themselves at once on the output record. Five of the girls were to do the actual assembly work; the duty of the sixth was to keep the others supplied with parts.

The test room itself was an area divided from the main department by a wooden partition eight feet high. The girls sat in a row on one side of a long workbench. Their bench and assembly equipment was identical with that used in the regular department, except in one respect. At the right of each girl's place was a hole in the bench, and into this hole she dropped completed relays. It was the entrance to a chute, in which there was a flapper gate opened by the relay in its passage downward. The opening of the gate closed an electrical circuit which controlled a perforating device, and this in turn recorded the completion of the relay by punching a hole in a tape. The tape moved at the rate of one-quarter of an inch a minute and had space for a separate row of holes for each operator. When punched, it thus constituted a complete output record for each girl for each instant of the day. Such records were kept for five years.

In this experiment then, as in the earlier illumination experiments, great emphasis was laid on the rate of output. A word of caution is needed here. The Western Electric Company was not immediately interested in increasing output. The experiments were not designed for that purpose. On the other hand, output is easily measured, i.e., it yields precise quantitative data, and experience suggested that it was sensitive to at least some of the conditions under which the employees worked. Output was treated as an index. In short, the nature of the experimental conditions made the emphasis on output inevitable.

From their experience in the illumination experiments, the investigators were well aware that factors other than those experimentally varied might affect the output rate. Therefore arrangements were made that a number of other records should be kept. Unsuitable parts supplied by the firm were noted down, as were assemblies rejected for any reason upon inspection. In this way the type of defect could be known and related to the time of day at which it occurred. Records were kept of weather conditions in general and of temperature and humidity in the test room. Every six weeks each operator was given a medical examination by the company doctor. Every day she was asked to tell how many hours she had spent in bed the night before and, during a part of the experiment, what food she had eaten. Besides all these records, which concerned the physical condition of the operators, a log was kept in which were recorded the principal events in the test room hour by hour, including among the entries snatches of conversation between the workers. At first these entries related largely to the physical condition of the operators: how they felt as they worked. Later the ground they covered somewhat widened, and the log ultimately became one of the most important of the test room records. Finally, when the so-called Interviewing Program was instituted at Hawthorne, each of the operators was interviewed several times by an experienced interviewer.

The girls had no supervisor in the ordinary sense, such as they would have had in a regular shop department, but a "test room observer" was placed in the room, whose duty it was to maintain the records, arrange the work, and secure a cooperative spirit on the part of the girls. Later, when the complexity of his work increased, several assistants were assigned to help him.

When the arrangements had been made for the test room, the operators who had been chosen to take part were called in for an interview in the office of the superintendent of the Inspection Branch, who was in general charge of the experiment and of the researches which grew out of it. The superintendent described this interview as follows:

> The nature of the test was carefully explained to these girls and they readily consented to take part in it, although they were very shy at the first conference. An invitation to six shop girls to come up to a superintendent's office was naturally rather startling. They were assured that the object of the test was to determine the

effect of certain changes in working conditions, such as rest periods, midmorning lunches, and shorter working hours. They were expressly cautioned to work at a comfortable pace, and under no circumstances to try to make a race out of the test.

This conference was only the first of many. Whenever any experimental change was planned, the girls were called in, the purpose of the change was explained to them, and their comments were requested. Certain suggested changes which did not meet with their approval were abandoned. They were repeatedly asked, as they were asked in the first interview, not to strain but to work "as they felt."

The experiment was now ready to begin. Put in its simplest terms, the idea of those directing the experiment was that if an output curve was studied for a long enough time under various changes in working conditions, it would be possible to determine which conditions were the most satisfactory. Accordingly, a number of so-called "experimental periods" were arranged. For two weeks before the operators were placed in the test room, a record was kept of the production of each one without her knowledge. In this way the investigators secured a measure of her productive ability while working in the regular department under the usual conditions. This constituted the first experimental period. And for five weeks after the girls entered the test room no change was made in working conditions. Hours remained what they had been before. The investigators felt that this period would be long enough to reveal any changes in output incidental merely to the transfer. This constituted the second experimental period.

The third period involved a change in the method of payment. In the regular department, the girls had been paid according to a scheme of group piecework, the group consisting of a hundred or more employees. Under these circumstances, variations in an individual's total output would not be immediately reflected in her pay, since such variations tended to cancel one another in a large group. In the test room, the six operators were made a group by themselves. In this way each girl received an amount more nearly in proportion to her individual effort, and her interests became more closely centered on the experiment. Eight weeks later, the directly experimental changes began. An outline will reveal their general character: Period IV: two rest pauses, each five minutes in length, were established, one occurring in midmorning and the other in the early afternoon. Period V: these rest pauses were lengthened to ten minutes each. Period VI: six five-minute rests were established. Period VII: the company provided each member of the group with a light lunch in the midmorning and another in the midafternoon accompanied by rest pauses. This arrangement became standard for subsequent Periods VIII through XI. Period VIII: work stopped a half-hour earlier every day—at 4:30 P.M. Period IX: work stopped at 4 P.M. Period X: conditions returned to what they were in Period VII. Period XI: a five-day work week was established. Each of these experimental periods lasted several weeks.

Period XI ran through the summer of 1928, a year after the beginning of the experiment. Already the results were not what had been expected. The output curve, which had risen on the whole slowly and steadily throughout the year, was obviously reflecting something other than the responses of the group to the imposed experimental conditions. Even when the total weekly output had fallen off, as it could hardly fail to do in such a period as Period XI, when the group was working only five days a week, daily output continued to rise. Therefore, in accordance with a sound experimental procedure, as a control on what had been done, it was agreed with the consent of the operators that in experimental Period XII a return should be made to the original conditions of work, with no rest pauses, no special lunches, and a full-length working week. This period lasted for twelve weeks. Both daily and weekly output rose to a higher point than ever before: the working day and the working week were both longer. The hourly output rate declined somewhat but it did not approach the level of Period III, when similar conditions were in effect.

The conclusions reached after Period XII may be expressed in terms of another observation. Identical conditions of work were repeated in three different experimental periods: Periods VII, X, and XII. If the assumptions on which the study was based had been correct, that is to say, if the output rate were directly related to the physical conditions of work, the expectation would be that in these three experimental periods there would be some similarity in output. Such was not the case. The only apparent uniformity was that in each experimental period output was higher than in the preceding one. In the Relay Assembly Test Room, as in the previous illumination experiments, something was happening which could not be explained by the experimentally controlled conditions of work.

There is no need here to go into the later history of the test room experiment, which came to an end in 1933. It is enough to say that the output of the group continued to rise until it established itself on a high plateau from which there was no descent until the time of discouragement and deepening economic depression which preceded the end of the test. The rough conclusions reached at the end of experimental Period XII were confirmed and sharpened by later research. T. N. Whitehead, Associate Professor of Business in the Graduate School of Business Administration, Harvard University, has made a careful statistical analysis of the output records. He shows that the changes which took place in the output of the group have no simple correlation with the experimental changes in working conditions. Nor can they be correlated with changes in other physical conditions of which records were kept, such as temperature, humidity, hours of rest, and changes of relay type. Even when the girls themselves complained of mugginess or heat, these conditions were not apparently affecting their output. This statement, of course, does not mean that there is never any relation between output rate and these physical conditions. There is such a thing as heat prostration. It means only that, within the limits in which these conditions were varying in the test room, they apparently did not affect the rate of work.

The question remains: with what facts, if any, can the changes in the output rate of the operators in the test room be correlated? Here the statements of the girls themselves are of first importance. Each girl knew that she was producing more in the test room than she ever had in the regular department, and each said that the increase had come about without any conscious effort on her part. It seemed easier to produce at the faster rate in the test room than at the slower rate in the regular department. When questioned further, each girl stated her reasons in slightly different words, but there was uniformity in the answers in two respects. First, the girls liked to work in the test room; "it was fun." Secondly, the new supervisory relation or, as they put it, the absence of the old supervisory control, made it possible for them to work freely without anxiety.

For instance, there was the matter of conversation. In the regular department, conversation was in principle not allowed. In practice it was tolerated if it was carried on in a low tone and did not interfere with work. In the test room an effort was made in the beginning to discourage conversation, though it was soon abandoned. The observer in charge of the experiment was afraid of losing the cooperation of the girls if he insisted too strongly on this point. Talk became common and was often loud and general. Indeed the conversation of the operators came to occupy an important place in the log. T. N. Whitehead has pointed out that the girls in the test room were far more thoroughly supervised than they ever had been in the regular department. They were watched by an observer of their own, an interested management, and outside experts. The point is that the character and purpose of the supervision were different and were felt to be so.

The operators knew that they were taking part in what was considered an important and interesting experiment. They knew that their work was expected to produce results—they were not sure what results—which would lead to the improvement of the working conditions of their fellow employees. They knew that the eyes of the company were upon them. Whitehead has further pointed out that, although the experimental changes might turn out to have no physical significance, their social significance was always favorable. They showed that the management of the company was still interested, that the girls were still part of a valuable piece of research. In the regular department, the girls, like the other employees, were in the position of responding to changes the source and purpose of which were beyond their knowledge. In the test room, they had frequent interviews with the superintendent, a high officer of the company. The reasons for the contemplated experimental changes were explained to them. Their views were consulted and in some instances they were allowed to veto what had been proposed. Professor Mayo has argued that it is idle to speak of an experimental period like Period XII as being in any sense what it purported to be—a return to the original conditions of work. In the meantime, the entire industrial situation of the girls had been reconstructed.

Another factor in what occurred can only be spoken of as the social development of the group itself. When the girls went for the first time to be given a physical examination by the company doctor, someone suggested as a joke that ice cream and cake ought to be served. The company provided them at the next examination, and the custom was kept up for the duration of the experiment. When one of the girls had a birthday, each of the others would bring her a present, and she would respond by offering the group a box of chocolates. Often one of the girls would have some good reason for feeling tired. Then the others would "carry" her. That is, they would agree to work especially fast to make up for the low output expected from her. It is doubtful whether this "carrying" did have any effect, but the important point is the existence of the practice, not its effectiveness. The girls made friends in the test room and went together socially after hours. One of the interesting facts which has appeared from Whitehead's analysis of the output records is that there were times when variations in the output rates of two friends were correlated to a high degree. Their rates varied simultaneously and in the same direction—something, of course, which the girls were not aware of and could not have planned. Also, these correlations were destroyed by such apparently trivial events as a change in the order in which the girls sat at the workbench.

Finally, the group developed leadership and a common purpose. The leader, self-appointed, was an ambitious young Italian girl who entered the test room as a replacement after two of the original members had left. She saw in the experiment a chance for personal distinction and advancement. The common purpose was an increase in the output rate. The girls had been told in the beginning and repeatedly thereafter that they were to work without straining, without trying to make a race of the test, and all the evidence shows that they kept this rule. In fact, they felt that they were working under less pressure than in the regular department. Nevertheless, they knew that the output record was considered the most important of the records of the experiment and was always closely scrutinized. Before long they had committed themselves to a continuous increase in production. In the long run, of course, this ideal was an impossible one, and when the girls found out that it was, the realization was an important element of the change of tone which was noticeable in the second half of the experiment. But for a time they felt that they could achieve the impossible. In brief, the increase in the output rate of the girls in the Relay Assembly Test Room could not be related to any changes in their physical conditions of work, whether experimentally induced or not. It could, however, be related to what can only be spoken of as the development of an organized social group in a peculiar and effective relation with its supervisors.

Many of these conclusions were not worked out in detail until long after the investigators at Hawthorne had lost interest in the Relay Assembly Test Room, but the general meaning of the experiment was clear at least as early as Period XII. A continuous increase in productivity had taken place irrespective of changing physical conditions of work. In the words of a company report made in January, 1931, on all the research which had been done up to that date:

> Upon analysis, only one thing seemed to show a continuous relationship with this improved output. This was the mental attitude of the operators. From their conversations with each other and their comments to the test observers, it was not only clear that their attitudes were improving but it was evident that this area of employee reactions and feelings was a fruitful field for industrial research.

Readings Related to Chapter 12

A Basic Incongruency between the Needs of a Mature Personality and the Requirements of Formal Organization

Chris Argyris

Bringing together the evidence regarding the impact of the formal organizational principles upon the individual, it is concluded that there are some basic incongruencies between the growth trends of a healthy personality and the requirements of the formal organization. If the principles of formal organization are used as ideally defined, employees will tend to work in an environment where (1) they are provided minimal control over their workaday world, (2) they are expected to be passive, dependent, and subordinate, (3) they are expected to have a short time perspective, (4) they are induced to perfect and value the frequent use of a few skin-surface shallow abilities and, (5) they are expected to produce under conditions leading to psychological failure.

All these characteristics are incongruent to the ones *healthy* human beings are postulated to desire. . . . They are much more congruent with the needs of infants in our culture. In effect, therefore, organizations are willing to pay high wages and provide adequate seniority if mature adults will, for eight hours a day, behave in a less than mature manner! *If the analysis is correct, this inevitable incongruency increases as* (1) *the employees are of increasing maturity,* (2) *as the formal structure* (based upon the above principles) *is made more clear-cut and logically tight for maximum formal organizational effectiveness,* (3) *as one goes down the line of command, and* (4) *as the jobs become more and more mechanized* (i.e., take on assembly line characteristics).

As in the case of the personality developmental trends, this picture of formal organization is also a model. Clearly, no company actually uses the formal principles of organization exactly as stated by their creators. There is ample evidence to suggest that they are being modified constantly in actual situations.

From "The Formal Organization," *Personality and Organization,* Harper & Row, Publishers, Incorporated, New York, 1957, chap. 3, pp. 66–75. Reprinted by permission of the author and the publisher.

However, those who expound these principles would probably be willing to defend their position that this is the reason that human relations problems exist; the principles are not followed as they should be.

In the proposed models of the personality and the formal organization, we are assuming the extreme of each in order that the analysis and its results can be highlighted. Speaking in terms of extremes helps us to make the position sharper. In doing this, no assumption is made that all situations in real life are extreme (i.e., that the individuals will always want to be more mature and that the formal organization will always tend to make people more dependent and passive all the time). In fact, much evidence is presented in subsequent chapters to support contrary tendencies.

The model ought to be useful, however, to plot the degree to which each component tends toward extremes and then to predict the problems that will arise. . . .

It is not difficult to see why some students of organization suggest that immature and even mentally retarded individuals would probably make excellent employees. There is little documented experience to support such a hypothesis. One reason for this lack of information is probably the "touchiness" of the subject. Examples of what might be obtained if a systematic study is made may be found in the work by Brennan.[1] He cites the Utica Knitting Mill, which made arrangements during 1917 with the Rome Institution for Mentally Defective Girls to employ 24 girls whose mental ages ranged from six to ten years. The girls were such excellent workers that their employment continued after the war emergency ended. In fact the company added forty additional mentally defective girls in another of their plants. The managers praised the subnormal girls highly.

> In several important reports, they said that "when business conditions required a reduction of the working staff," the hostel girls were never "laid off" in dispropor-tion to the normal girls; that they were more punctual, more regular in their habits, and did not indulge in as much "gossip and levity." They received the same rate of pay, and they had been employed successfully at almost every process carried out in the workshops.

In another experiment, the Works Manager of the Radio Corporation Ltd. reported that of five young morons:

> The three girls compared very favourably with the normal class of employee in that age group. The boy employed in the store performed his work with satisfaction. . . . Although there was some doubt about the fifth child, it was felt that getting the most out of him was just a matter of right placement.

In each of the five cases, the morons were quiet, respectful, well-behaved, and obedient. The Works Manager was especially impressed by their truthful-ness, and lack of deceit or suppression of the facts. A year later, the same Works Manager was still able to advise that,

In every case, the girls proved to be exceptionally well-behaved, particularly obedient, and strictly honest and trustworthy. They carried out work required of them to such a degree of efficiency that *we were surprised they were classed as subnormals for their age.*[2] Their attendance was good, and their behavior was, if anything, certainly better than any other employee of the same age.

Let us now turn to the literature to see if there are illustrations of the points made regarding the dependence and subordination created by the nature of formal organization and its impact upon the individuals. Unfortunately, there are not many available studies that focus on the impact of the formal organization on the individuals (holding the leadership variable "constant").

Probably the best available evidence of the impact of formal organization based upon unity of command and task specialization is the experimental work on communication by Bavelas[3] and Leavitt,[4] which is confirmed by Heise and Miller[5] and Shaw and Rothchild.[6] They focus on the question—can the structure of certain patterns of communication result in significantly better performance than others? Their results clearly imply that in a structure where one individual has a "central" position in the communications network and thereby is able to control communications, as would an executive in a plant, he will probably be chosen the leader and have the best morale in the group. The individuals who depend upon him (e.g., supervisors) will tend to have lower morale, feel more frustrated, confused, and irritated at others along the network. Guetzkow and Simon confirm these results, and through the use of more refined experimental procedure they show strong evidence to support the hypothesis that of all communications structures tried, the "wheel"[7] created initially the *least* organizational problem for the group, thereby permitting the group to organize itself most quickly in order to solve a particular problem.[8]

Further indirect evidence is provided by Arensberg,[9] who "revisited" the famous Hawthorne Studies. He noted that many of the results reported about the relay assembly experiments occurred *after* the girls were placed in a work situation where they were (1) made "subjects" of an "important" experiment, (2) encouraged to participate in decisions affecting their work, (3) given veto power over their supervisors to the point where, as the girls testify, "we have no boss." Clearly these conditions constitute a sweeping shift in the basic relationship of modern industrial work where the employee is subordinate to people above him.

Bakke's study of the unemployed worker[10] includes much evidence that the workers are clearly aware of the differences in the degree of authority and control manifested by themselves and their boss. His evidence suggests that independently of the personality of the boss, the workers perceived their boss as someone with power to achieve his goals; a power which they did not believe they had. For example, one worker defines the boss as someone who, "When he decides to do something, he can carry it through." Another states, "Some birds have got enough (authority) and stand high enough so that what they say goes

. . . and anybody who can do that won't be found very often to be what you might call a worker.''[11]

Blau,[12] in a study of the departmental structure in a federal enforcement agency, reports that even when deliberate attempts were made to minimize the social distance between leaders and subordinates and where leaders tried to use a "democratic" approach, the supervisors frequently but inadvertently lapsed into behavior more appropriate to the formal authoritarian relationships with the subordinates. Thus, the impact of the formal structure influences leadership behavior toward being more "autocratic" even when there exist informal norms emphasizing a more egalitarian climate and when the leaders consciously try to be more "democratic."

Not only do the supervisors "slip" into more directive leadership, but the subordinates "slip" into dependent, submissive roles even if the supervisor requests their increased participation. As one subordinate states, "Lots of times, I've differed with the supervisor, but I didn't say anything. I just said, 'Yes,' with a smile, *because he gives the efficiency rating.*" Blau continues:

> Bureaucratic authority is *not* based on personal devotion to the supervisor or on respect for him as a person but on an adaptation necessitated by his rating power. The *advancement chances of officials and even their chances to keep their civil service jobs depend on the rating they periodically receive from their superior.* . . . The group's insistence that the supervisor discharge his duty of issuing directives— "That's what he gets paid for"—serves to emphasize that their obedience to them does *not* constitute submission to his will but *adherence, on his part as well as theirs, to abstract principles* which they have socially accepted.[13]

In comprehensive reviews of the literature Gibb,[14] Blau[15] and Bierstedt[16] conclude that it is important to differentiate between formal leadership (headship or authority) based upon formal organization and informal leadership (leadership). For example, Gibb states:

> . . . leadership is to be distinguished, by definition, from domination or headship. The principal differentia are these: (i) Domination or headship is maintained through an organized system and not by the spontaneous recognition, by fellow group members, of the individual's contribution to group goals. (ii) The group goal is chosen by the head man in line with his interests and is not internally determined by the group itself. (iii) In the domination or headship relation there is little or no sense of shared feeling or joint action in the pursuit of the given goal. (iv) There is in the dominance relation a wide social gap between the group members and the head, who strives to maintain this social distance as an aid to his coercion of the group. (v) Most basically, these two forms of influence differ with respect to the *source* of the authority which is exercised. The leader's authority is spontaneously accorded him by his fellow group members, the followers. *The authority of the head derives from some extra-group power which he has over the members of the group, who cannot meaningfully be called his followers. They accept his domination on pain of punishment, rather than follow. The business executive is an excellent example of a head*

exercising authority derived from his position in an organization through member-
ship in which the workers, his subordinates, satisfy many strong needs. They obey his
commands and accept his domination because this is part of their duty as organiza-
tion members and to reject him would be to discontinue membership, with all the
punishments that would involve. [14]

Carter, [17] in some recent controlled field experiments, points up the importance of the power and status inherent in the formal organizational structure by
an interesting study of the behavior of "emergent" vs. "appointed" leaders. He
concludes that appointed leaders tend to support their own purposes, defend
their proposals from attack, express their own opinions, and argue—all *less* than
emergent leaders. Apparently, the data suggests, because the appointed leader
feels that he has power and status, he feels less need to defend his position than
does an emergent leader.

Fleishman's [18] descriptions of leadership training also point up the degree of
dependence and leader-centeredness of a subordinate upon his boss. He reports
that subordinates tend to use the same leadership style that their boss tends to
use regardless of the training they receive.

Probably no review of the literature would be complete without mentioning
the classic work of Max Weber on the study of bureaucracy.[19],[20] It is important
to keep in mind that Weber conceived of bureaucracy (formal organization) as
"the most efficient form of social organization ever developed." [21] He maintained
that bureaucracy was one of the characteristic forms of organization of all
modern society, finding wide expression in industry, science, and religion, as
well as government. [22] In fact, it may be said that he saw no difference between
socialism and capitalism, since the fundamental characteristic of both was (a
particular kind of) formal organization. "If Marx said that the workers of the
world had nothing to lose but their chains by revolting, Weber contended that
they really had nothing to gain." [23] It remained for Merton to try to balance the
"rosy" picture that Weber painted about bureaucracy. At the outset of this
work, Merton, in clear and concise terms, describes some of the essential
conditions of formal organization. Again we note the emphasis made here on the
inherent authoritarian power structure of the formal organization which is independent of the leadership pattern of the person holding the power position.

Authority, the power of control which derives from an acknowledged status, inheres
in the office and not in the particular person who performs the official role. Official
action ordinarily occurs within the framework of preexisting rules of the organization. The system of prescribed relations between the various offices involves a
considerable degree of formality and clearly defined social distance between the
occupants of these positions. Formality is manifested by means of a more or less
complicated social ritual which symbolizes and supports the "pecking order" of the
various offices. Such formality, which is integrated with the distribution of authority
within the system, serves to minimize friction by largely restricting (official) contact
to modes which are previously defined by the rules of the organization...[24]

Charles Walker, Robert Guest, and Arthur Turner have been studying the impact of the assembly line (an example of a highly specialized aspect of organizational structure) and of the management upon the workers. Their find-ings show the degree and kind of impact of the mass production type of organizational structure upon the employee, independent of the personality of the management. Walker and Guest report that about 90 per cent (of 180) workers dislike their actual job because of its mechanical pacing, repetitiveness, minimum skill requirements, minute subdivision of work, and surface mental attention. Their results show that the degree of dislike for the job increased in proportion to the degree to which the job embodies mass production characteris-tics[25] and to the degree to which the employees are dependent upon manage-ment. These results have been confirmed in another study by the same team. [26]

Turner, in an article based upon the second study mentioned above, expands on the impact of the assembly line. The employees especially dislike the mechanical pacing of the assembly line which (1) decreases their control over their own activities, (2) makes them dependent, subordinate, and passive to a machine process, and (3) leads them to forget quality production and aspire to an acceptable minimum quantity output. Turner[27] points out that the men dislike the necessity to work at a job that requires only a minimum skill, and forces them, through repetitiveness, to continue using only a minimum skill. These findings are understandable since these requirements run counter to the needs of rela-tively mature human beings. Finally, the characteristics of impersonality and anonymity also inveigh against the needs of "ego integrity" and feelings of self worth.

Indirect evidence comes from two studies of organization reported by the writer. In both organizations the employees' degree of morale with the company increased as the degree of directive leadership decreased. Passive leadership (i.e., leadership that seldom contacts the employees) minimized the pressure from above and permitted the employees to feel more "self-responsible" (i.e., they could be their own boss). Over 91 per cent of the respondents (total group sampled about 300) reported that passive leadership (i.e., "we hardly ever talk with the boss") permits them to be their own boss and thereby reduces the potential pressure from above. However, the same number of employees also reported they still feel pressure from the very way the work and the companies are organized. For example, a bank teller states,

> I don't know what I would do if Mr. B. supervised us closely. The pressure would be terrific. As it is, I hardly see him. He leaves me alone and that's fine with me. But don't get me wrong. It isn't that I don't feel I haven't got a boss. I have one. *I know I will always have one, if it's Mr. B. or Mr. X.*[28]

Some trade union leaders are aware that the formal organization places the workers in dependent and dissatisfying situations. Many report that the process of management (independent of the personality of the leader) carries with it certain "inevitable" dislikes by the workers, because the workers view management (who represent the formal organization) as the ones who place them in dissatisfying work situations. This may be one reason that many trade union leaders do not aspire to gain political control over the management.

Mr. Green, for example, said, "The line of distinction between the exercise of the rights of labor and of management must be scrupulously observed. The philosophy which some have advanced that labor should join with management in the actual management of the property could not and cannot be accepted."[29] Mr. Murray agrees when he states, "To relieve the boss or the management of proper responsibility for making a success of the enterprise is about the last thing any group of employees would consider workable or even desirable."[30]

The fears implied by these two labor leaders exist as facts in countries like Norway, England, and Holland. The trade union leaders in these countries are partially or indirectly responsible for the economic health of the country (because the party identified with labor has strong political power). It is not uncommon to see trade union leaders "selling" work study, scientific management, and increased productivity to the workers.[31] Many workers feel that their national leaders are closer in outlook with management than with their own members.[32] In short, the American trade union leaders may realize that because of the impact of the nature of formal organization, even if they were perfect administrators, they still would have human problems with the employees.

Summary

On the basis of a logical analysis, it is concluded that the formal organizational principles make demands of relatively healthy individuals that are incongruent with their needs. Frustration, conflict, failure, and short time perspective are predicted as resultants of this basic incongruency.

Empirical evidence is presented to illustrate the rational character of the formal organization and to support the proposition that the basic impact of the formal organizational structure is to make the employees feel dependent, submissive, and passive, and to require them to utilize only a few of their less important abilities.

In the next chapter [of *Personality and Organization*], empirical evidence is amassed to illustrate the existence in the employee of the predicted frustration, conflict, failure, and short time perspective and to show some of the resultants of these factors.

References

1 Brennan, Mal: *The Making of a Moron* (New York: Sheed and Ward, 1953), pp. 13–18.
2 Mr. Brennan's emphasis.
3 Bavelas, Alex: "Communication Patterns in Task-Oriented Groups." Chapter X in *The Policy Sciences* (ed.) by D. Lerner and H. L. Lasswell (Palo Alto: Stanford University Press, 1951), pp. 193-202. ———, "A Mathematical Model for Group Structures," *Applied Anthropology, Vol. VII,* 1948, pp. 16–30.
4 Leavitt, H. J.: "Some Effects of Certain Communication Patterns on Group Performance," *Journal of Abnormal Social Psychology,* Vol. 46, 1951, pp. 38–50.

✓ 5 Heise, G. C., and Miller, G. A.: "Problem-Solving by Small Groups Using Various Communications Nets," *Journal of Abnormal Social Psychology,* Vol. 46, 1951, pp. 327–335.

6 Shaw, Marvin E., and Rothchild, Gerard H.: "Some Effects of Prolonged Experience in Communication Nets," *Journal of Applied Psychology,* Vol. 40, No. 5, October, 1956, pp. 281–286.

7 A "wheel" structure is similar to the structure that is created by the use of the principles of chain of command and space of control. One individual becomes the "boss" of the structure.

✓ 8 However, they also point out that once the other structures "got going," they were as efficient (in terms of time required to achieve the task) as the wheel. Guetzkow, Harold, and Simon, Herbert A.: "The Impact of Certain Communication Nets upon Organization and Performance in Task-Oriented Groups," *Management Science,* Vol. 1, April–July, 1955, pp. 233–250.

9 Arensberg, Conrad M.: "Behavior and Organization: Industrial Studies," (eds.) John H. Rohrer and Musafer Sherif, *Social Psychology at the Crossroads* (New York: Harper, 1951), p. 340.

10 Bakke, E. Wight: *Citizens Without Work, op. cit.,* p. 90.

11 *Ibid.,* p. 91.

12 Blau, Peter M.: *The Dynamics of Bureaucracy* (Chicago: University of Chicago Press, 1955), pp. 167 ff.

13 *Ibid.,* pp. 172–173.

14 Gibb, Cecil A.: "Leadership," in *Handbook of Social Psychology* (ed.), Gardner Lindzey (Reading, Mass.: Addison-Wesley, 1954), pp. 887–920. (Italics mine.)

15 Blau, Peter M.: *Bureaucracy in Modern Society* (New York: Random House, 1956).

16 Bierstedt, Robert: "The Problem of Authority," in Morroe Berger, Theodore Abel, and Charles H. Page (eds.), *Freedom and Control in Modern Society* (New York: Van Nostrand, 1954), pp. 67–81.

17 Carter, Launor: "Leadership and Small Group Behavior," in M. Sherif and M. O. Wilson (eds.); *Group Relations at the Crossroads* (New York: Harper, 1953), p. 279.

18 Fleishman, Edwin A.: "The Description of Supervisory Behavior," *Journal of Applied Psychology,* Vol. 37, No. 1. Although I was unable to obtain it, E. F. Harris' thesis is also reported to include valuable data. It is entitled, "Measuring Industrial Leadership and Its Implications for Training Supervisors," Ph.D. thesis, Ohio State, 1952. It should be pointed out that Fleishman's study was not limited to the impact of the formal structure. It includes leadership patterns.

19 Weber, Max: *The Theory of Social and Economic Organization,* A. M. Henderson (tr.) and Talcott Parsons (ed.) (New York: Oxford, 1947).

20 For an interesting discussion of Weber's and others' work, see Merton, Robert K., Gray, Ailsa P., Hackey, Barbara, and Selvin, Hanan C.: *Reader in Bureaucracy* (Glencoe, Illinois: The Free Press, 1952).

21 Gouldner, Alvin (ed.): *Studies in Leadership* (New York: Harper, 1950), p. 75.

22 *Ibid.,* p. 57

23 *Ibid.,* p. 58.

24 Merton, Robert K.: "Bureaucratic Structure and Personality," *Social Forces,* 1940, printed also in *Studies in Leadership, op. cit.,* pp. 67–68.

25 Walker, Charles R., and Guest, Robert H.: *The Man on the Assembly Line* (Cambridge: Harvard University Press, 1952).

26 Personal communication. Publication in progress.

27 Turner, Arthur N.: "Management and the Assembly Line," *Harvard Business Review*, September–October, 1955, pp. 40–48.

28 Argyris, Chris: *Organization of a Bank, op. cit.,* and *Human Relations in a Hospital, op. cit.*

29 *New York Sun,* December, 1954.

30 Lewisohn, Sam: *Human Leadership in Industry* (New York: Harper, 1945).

31 Ruttenberg (one of the originators of the idea of the Guaranteed Annual Wage, while an economist for the CIO Steel Workers and now a plant president) insists that if "pay by the year" becomes effective the employees must take on management responsibilities. *Harper's,* December, 1955, pp. 29–33.

32 Argyris, Chris: *An Analysis of the Human Relations Policies and Practices in England, Norway, Holland, France, Greece, and Germany,* OEEC, Dept. of Management Reports, Paris, France, 1955.

Theory X: The Traditional View of Direction and Control

Douglas McGregor

Behind every managerial decision or action are assumptions about human nature and human behavior. A few of these are remarkably pervasive. They are implicit in most of the literature of organization and in much current managerial policy and practice:

1 *The average human being has an inherent dislike of work and will avoid it if he can.* This assumption has deep roots. The punishment of Adam and Eve for eating the fruit of the Tree of Knowledge was to be banished from Eden into a world where they had to work for a living. The stress that management places on productivity, on the concept of "a fair day's work," on the evils of featherbedding and restriction of output, on rewards for performance—while it has a logic in terms of the objectives of enterprise—reflects an underlying belief that management must counteract an inherent human tendency to avoid work. The evidence for the correctness of this assumption would seem to most managers to be incontrovertible.

2 *Because of this human characteristic of dislike of work, most people must be coerced, controlled, directed, threatened with punishment to get them to put forth adequate effort toward the achievement of organizational objectives.* The dislike of work is so strong that even the promise of rewards is not generally enough to overcome it. People will accept the rewards and demand continually

From *The Human Side of Enterprise,* McGraw-Hill Book Company, Inc., New York, 1960, chap. 3, pp. 33–44, Reprinted by permission of the publisher.

higher ones, but these alone will not produce the necessary effort. Only the
threat of punishment will do the trick.

The current wave of criticism of "human relations," the derogatory comments about "permissiveness" and "democracy" in industry, the trends in some
companies toward recentralization after the postwar wave of decentralization—
all these are assertions of the underlying assumption that people will only work
under external coercion and control. The recession of 1957–1958 ended a decade
of experimentation with the "soft" managerial approach, and this assumption
(which never really was abandoned) is being openly espoused once more.

3   *The average human being prefers to be directed, wishes to avoid responsibility, has relatively little ambition, wants security above all.* This assumption
of the "mediocrity of the masses" is rarely expressed so bluntly. In fact, a good
deal of lip service is given to the ideal of the worth of the average human being.
Our political and social values demand such public expressions. Nevertheless, a
great many managers will give private support to this assumption, and it is easy
to see it reflected in policy and practice. Paternalism has become a nasty word,
but it is by no means a defunct managerial philosophy.

I have suggested elsewhere the name Theory X for this set of assumptions. . . . Theory X is not a straw man for purposes of demolition, but is in fact a
theory which materially influences managerial strategy in a wide sector of
American industry today. Moreover, the principles of organization which com-
prise the bulk of the literature of management *could only have been derived from
assumptions such as those of Theory X.* Other beliefs about human nature would
have led inevitably to quite different organizational principles.

Theory X provides an explanation of some human behavior in industry.
These assumptions would not have persisted if there were not a considerable
body of evidence to support them. Nevertheless, there are many readily observable phenomena in industry and elsewhere which are not consistent with this view
of human nature.

Such a state of affairs is not uncommon. The history of science provides
many examples of theoretical explanations which persist over long periods
despite the fact that they are only partially adequate. Newton's laws of motion
are a case in point. It was not until the development of the theory of relativity
during the present century that important inconsistencies and inadequacies in
Newtonian theory could be understood and corrected.

The growth of knowledge in the social sciences during the past quarter
century has made it possible to reformulate some assumptions about human
nature and human behavior in the organizational setting which resolve certain of
the inconsistencies inherent in Theory X. While this reformulation is, of course,
tentative, it provides an improved basis for prediction and control of human
behavior in industry.

Some Assumptions about Motivation

At the core of any theory of the management of human resources are assumptions about human motivation. This has been a confusing subject because there

have been so many conflicting points of view even among social scientists. In recent years, however, there has been a convergence of research findings and a growing acceptance of a few rather basic ideas about motivation. These ideas appear to have considerable power. They help to explain the inadequacies of Theory X as well as the limited sense in which it is correct. In addition, they provide the basis for an entirely different theory of management.

The following generalizations about motivation are somewhat oversimplified. If all of the qualifications which would be required by a truly adequate treatment were introduced, the gross essentials which are particularly significant for management would be obscured. These generalizations do not misrepresent the facts, but they do ignore some complexities of human behavior which are relatively unimportant for our purposes.

Man is a wanting animal—as soon as one of his needs is satisfied, another appears in its place. This process is unending. It continues from birth to death. Man continuously puts forth effort—works, if you please—to satisfy his needs.

Human needs are organized in a series of levels—a hierarchy of importance.* At the lowest level, but preeminent in importance when they are thwarted, are the physiological needs. Man lives by bread alone, when there is no bread. Unless the circumstances are unusual, his needs for love, for status, for recognition are inoperative when his stomach has been empty for a while. But when he eats regularly and adequately, hunger ceases to be an important need. The sated man has hunger only in the sense that a full bottle has emptiness. The same is true of the other physiological needs of man—for rest, exercise, shelter, protection from the elements.

A satisfied need is not a motivator of behavior! This is a fact of profound significance. It is a fact which is unrecognized in Theory X and is, therefore, ignored in the conventional approach to the management of people. I shall return to it later. For the moment, an example will make the point. Consider your own need for air. Except as you are deprived of it, it has no appreciable motivating effect upon your behavior.

When the physiological needs are reasonably satisfied, needs at the next higher level begin to dominate man's behavior—to motivate him. These are the safety needs, for protection against danger, threat, deprivation. Some people mistakenly refer to these as needs for security. However, unless man is in a dependent relationship where he fears arbitrary deprivation, he does not demand security. The need is for the "fairest possible break." When he is confident of this, he is more than willing to take risks. But when he feels threatened or dependent, his greatest need is for protection, for security.

The fact needs little emphasis that since every industrial employee is in at least a partially dependent relationship, safety needs may assume considerable importance. Arbitrary management actions, behavior which arouses uncertainty with respect to continued employment or which reflects favoritism or discrimina-

Editor's note: For a more detailed explanation of the hierarchy of needs, see A. H. Maslow, "A Theory of Human Motivation," reprinted in this volume, pages 117–135.

tion, unpredictable administration of policy—these can be powerful motivators of the safety needs in the employment relationship at every level from worker to vice president. In addition, the safety needs of managers are often aroused by their dependence downward or laterally. This is a major reason for emphasis on management prerogatives and clear assignments of authority.

When man's physiological needs are satisfied and he is no longer fearful about his physical welfare, his social needs become important motivators of his behavior. These are such needs as those for belonging, for association, for acceptance by one's fellows, for giving and receiving friendship and love.

Management knows today of the existence of these needs, but it is often assumed quite wrongly that they represent a threat to the organization. Many studies have demonstrated that the tightly knit, cohesive work group may, under proper conditions, be far more effective than an equal number of separate individuals in achieving organizational goals. Yet management, fearing group hostility to its own objectives, often goes to considerable lengths to control and direct human efforts in ways that are inimical to the natural "groupiness" of human beings. When man's social needs—and perhaps his safety needs, too—are thus thwarted, he behaves in ways which tend to defeat organizational objectives. He becomes resistant, antagonistic, uncooperative. But this behavior is a consequence, not a cause.

Above the social needs—in the sense that they do not usually become motivators until lower needs are reasonably satisfied—are the needs of greatest significance to management and to man himself. They are the egoistic needs, and they are of two kinds:

1   Those that relate to one's self-esteem: needs for self-respect and self-confidence, for autonomy, for achievement, for competence, for knowledge
2   Those that relate to one's reputation: needs for status, for recognition, for appreciation, for the deserved respect of one's fellows

Unlike the lower needs, these are rarely satisfied; man seeks indefinitely for more satisfaction of these needs once they have become important to him. However, they do not usually appear in any significant way until physiological, safety, and social needs are reasonably satisfied. Exceptions to this generalization are to be observed, particularly under circumstances where, in addition to severe deprivation of physiological needs, human dignity is trampled upon. Political revolutions often grow out of thwarted social and ego, as well as physiological, needs.

The typical industrial organization offers only limited opportunities for the satisfaction of egoistic needs to people at lower levels in the hierarchy. The conventional methods of organizing work, particularly in mass production industries, give little heed to these aspects of human motivation. If the practices of "scientific management" were deliberately calculated to thwart these needs—which, of course, they are not—they could hardly accomplish this purpose better than they do.

Finally—a capstone, as it were, on the hierarchy—there are the needs for self-fulfillment. These are the needs for realizing one's own potentialities, for continued self-development, for being creative in the broadest sense of that term.

The conditions of modern industrial life give only limited opportunity for these relatively dormant human needs to find expression. The deprivation most people experience with respect to other lower-level needs diverts their energies into the struggle to satisfy *those* needs, and the needs for self-fulfillment remain below the level of consciousness.

Now, briefly, a few general comments about motivation:

We recognize readily enough that a man suffering from a severe dietary deficiency is sick. The deprivation of physiological needs has behavioral consequences. The same is true, although less well recognized, of the deprivation of higher-level needs. The man whose needs for safety, association, independence, or status are thwarted is sick, just as surely as is he who has rickets. And his sickness will have behavioral consequences. We will be mistaken if we attribute his resultant passivity, or his hostility, or his refusal to accept responsibility to his inherent "human nature." These forms of behavior are *symptoms* of illness—of deprivation of his social and egoistic needs.

The man whose lower-level needs are satisfied is not motivated to satisfy *those* needs. For practical purposes they exist no longer. (Remember my point about your need for air.) Management often asks, "Why aren't people more productive? We pay good wages, provide good working conditions, have excellent fringe benefits and steady employment. Yet people do not seem to be willing to put forth more than minimum effort." It is unnecessary to look far for the reasons.

Consideration of the rewards typically provided the worker for satisfying his needs through his employment leads to the interesting conclusion that most of these rewards can be used for satisfying his needs *only when he leaves the job.* Wages, for example, cannot be spent at work. The only contribution they can make to his satisfaction on the job is in terms of status differences resulting from wage differentials. (This, incidentally, is one of the reasons why small and apparently unimportant differences in wage rates can be the subject of so much heated dispute. The issue is not the pennies involved, but the fact that the status differences which they reflect are one of the few ways in which wages can result in need satisfaction in the job situation itself.)

Most fringe benefits—overtime pay, shift differentials, vacations, health and medical benefits, annuities, and the proceeds from stock purchase plans or profit-sharing plans—yield needed satisfaction only when the individual leaves the job. Yet these, along with wages, are among the major rewards provided by management for effort. It is not surprising, therefore, that for many wage earners *work is perceived as a form of punishment* which is the price to be paid for various kinds of satisfaction away from the job. To the extent that this is their perception, we would hardly expect them to undergo more of this punishment than is necessary.

Under today's conditions management has provided relatively well for the satisfaction of physiological and safety needs. The standard of living in our country is high; people do not suffer major deprivation of their physiological needs except during periods of severe unemployment. Even then, social legislation developed since the thirties cushions the shock.

But the fact that management has provided for these physiological and safety needs has shifted the motivational emphasis to the social and the egoistic needs. Unless there are opportunities *at work* to satisfy these higher-level needs, people will be deprived; and their behavior will reflect this deprivation. Under such conditions, if management continues to focus its attention on physiological needs, the mere provision of rewards is bound to be ineffective, and reliance on the threat of punishment will be inevitable. Thus one of the assumptions of Theory X will appear to be validated, but only because we have mistaken effects for causes.

People *will* make insistent demands for more money under these conditions. It becomes more important than ever to buy the material goods and services which can provide limited satisfaction of the thwarted needs. Although money has only limited value in satisfying many higher-level needs, it can become the focus of interest if it is the only means available.

The "carrot and stick" theory of motivation which goes along with Theory X works reasonably well under certain circumstances. The *means* for satisfying man's physiological and (within limits) safety needs can be provided or withheld by management. Employment itself is such a means, and so are wages, working conditions, and benefits. By these means the individual can be controlled so long as he is struggling for subsistence. Man tends to live for bread alone when there is little bread.

But the "carrot and stick" theory does not work at all once man has reached an adequate subsistence level and is motivated primarily by higher needs. Management cannot provide a man with self-respect, or with the respect of his fellows, or with the satisfaction of needs for self-fulfillment. We can create conditions such that he is encouraged and enabled to seek such satisfactions for himself, or we can thwart him by failing to create those conditions.

But this creation of conditions is not "control" in the usual sense; it does not seem to be a particularly good device for directing behavior. And so management finds itself in an odd position. The high standard of living created by our modern technological know-how provides quite adequately for the satisfaction of physiological and safety needs. The only significant exception is where management practices have not created confidence in a "fair break"—and thus where safety needs are thwarted. But by making possible the satisfaction of lower-level needs, management has deprived itself of the ability to use the control devices on which the conventional assumptions of Theory X has taught it to rely: rewards, promises, incentives, or threats and other coercive devices.

The philosophy of management by direction and control—*regardless of whether it is hard or soft*—is inadequate to motivate because the human needs on which this approach relies are relatively unimportant motivators of behavior in our society today. Direction and control are of limited value in motivating people whose important needs are social and egoistic.

People, deprived of opportunities to satisfy at work the needs which are now important to them, behave exactly as we might predict—with indolence, passivity, unwillingness to accept responsibility, resistance to change, willingness to follow the demagogue, unreasonable demands for economic benefits. It would seem that we may be caught in a web of our own weaving.

Theory X explains the *consequences* of a particular managerial strategy; it neither explains nor describes human nature although it purports to. Because its assumptions are so unnecessarily limiting, it prevents our seeing the possibilities inherent in other managerial strategies. What sometimes appear to be new strategies—decentralization, management by objectives, consultative supervision, "democratic" leadership—are usually but old wine in new bottles because the procedures developed to implement them are derived from the same inadequate assumptions about human nature. Management is constantly becoming disillusioned with widely touted and expertly merchandised "new approaches" to the human side of enterprise. The real difficulty is that these new approaches are no more than different tactics—programs, procedures, gadgets—within an unchanged strategy based on Theory X.

In child rearing, it is recognized that parental strategies of control must be progressively modified to adapt to the changed capabilities and characteristics of the human individual as he develops from infancy to adulthood. To some extent industrial management recognizes that the human *adult* possesses capabilities for continued learning and growth. Witness the many current activities in the fields of training and management development. In its *basic* conceptions of managing human resources, however, managment appears to have concluded that the average human being is permanently arrested in his development in early adolescence. Theory X is built on the least common human denominator: the factory "hand" of the past. As Chris Argyris has shown dramatically in his *Personality and Organization,* conventional managerial strategies for the organization, direction, and control of the human resources of enterprise are admirably suited to the capacities and characteristics of the child rather than the adult.

In one limited area—that of research administration—there has been some recent recognition of the need for selective adaptation in managerial strategy. This, however, has been perceived as a unique problem, and its broader implications have not been recognized. As pointed out in this and the previous chapter [of *The Human Side of Enterprise*], changes in the population at large—in educational level, attitudes and values, motivation, degree of dependence—have created both the opportunity and the need for other forms of selective adaptation. However, so long as the assumptions of Theory X continue to influence managerial strategy, we will fail to discover, let alone utilize, the potentialities of the average human being.

References

Allen, Louis A.: *Management and Organization.* New York: McGraw-Hill Book Company, Inc., 1958.

Bendix, Reinhard: *Work and Authority in Industry.* New York: John Wiley & Sons, Inc., 1956.

Brown, Alvin: *Organization of Industry*. Englewood Cliffs, N.J.: Prentice-Hall, Inc., 1947.

Fayol, H.: *Industrial and General Administration*. London: Sir Isaac Pitman & Sons, Ltd., 1930.

Gouldner, Alvin W.: *Patterns of Industrial Bureaucracy*. Glencoe, Ill.: Free Press, 1954.

Koontz, Harold, and Cyril O'Donnell: *Principles of Management*. New York: McGraw-Hill Book Company, Inc., 1955.

Maslow, Abraham: *Motivation and Personality*. New York: Harper & Brothers, 1954.

Urwick, Lyndall: *The Elements of Administration*. New York: Harper & Brothers, 1944.

Walker, Charles R.: *Toward the Automatic Factory*. New Haven, Conn.: Yale University Press, 1957.

Whyte, William F.: *Money and Motivation*. New York: Harper & Brothers, 1955.

Zaleznick, A., C. F. Christensen, and F. J. Roethlisberger: *Motivation, Productivity, and Satisfaction of Workers*. Cambridge, Mass.: Harvard University Press, 1958.

Theory Y: The Integration of Individual and Organizational Goals

Douglas McGregor

To some, the preceding analysis will appear unduly harsh. Have we not made major modifications in the management of the human resources of industry during the past quarter century? Have we not recognized the importance of people and made vitally significant changes in managerial strategy as a consequence? Do the developments since the twenties in personnel administration and labor relations add up to nothing?

There is no question that important progress has been made in the past two or three decades. During this period the human side of enterprise has become a major preoccupation of management. A tremendous number of policies, programs, and practices which were virtually unknown thirty years ago have become commonplace. The lot of the industrial employee—be he worker, professional, or executive—has improved to a degree which could hardly have been imagined by his counterpart of the nineteen twenties. Management has adopted generally a far more humanitarian set of values; it has successfully striven to give more equitable and more generous treatment to its employees. It has significantly reduced economic hardships, eliminated the more extreme forms of industrial warfare, provided a generally safe and pleasant working environment, *but it has done all these things without changing its fundamental theory of management*. There are exceptions here and there, and they are important; nevertheless, the assumptions of Theory X remain predominant throughout our economy.

Management was subjected to severe pressures during the Great Depression

From *The Human Side of Enterprise*, McGraw-Hill Book Company, Inc., New York, 1960, chap. 4, pp. 45–57. Reprinted by permission of the publisher.

of the thirties. The wave of public antagonism, the open warfare accompanying the unionization of the mass production industries, the general reaction against authoritarianism, the legislation of the New Deal produced a wide "pendulum swing." However, the changes in policy and practice which took place during that and the next decade were primarily adjustments to the increased power of organized labor and to the pressures of public opinion.

Some of the movement was away from "hard" and toward "soft" management, but it was short-lived, and for good reasons. It has become clear that many of the initial strategic interpretations accompanying the "human relations approach" were as naïve as those which characterized the early stages of progressive education. We have now discovered that there is no answer in the simple removal of control—that abdication is not a workable alternative to authoritarianism. We have learned that there is no direct correlation between employee satisfaction and productivity. We recognize today that "industrial democracy" cannot consist in permitting everyone to decide everything, that industrial health does not flow automatically from the elimination of dissatisfaction, disagreement, or even open conflict. Peace is not synonymous with organizational health; socially responsible management is not coextensive with permissive management.

Now that management has regained its earlier prestige and power, it has become obvious that the trend toward "soft" management was a temporary and relatively superficial reaction rather than a general modification of fundamental assumptions or basic strategy. Moreover, while the progress we have made in the past quarter century is substantial, it has reached the point of diminishing returns. The tactical possibilities within conventional managerial strategies have been pretty completely exploited, and significant new developments will be unlikely without major modifications in theory.

The Assumptions of Theory Y

There have been few dramatic break-throughs in social science theory like those which have occurred in the physical sciences during the past half century. Nevertheless, the accumulation of knowledge about human behavior in many specialized fields has made possible the formulation of a number of generalizations which provide a modest beginning for new theory with respect to the management of human resources. Some of these assumptions were outlined in the discussion of motivation [on page 216]. Some others, which will hereafter be referred to as Theory Y, are as follows:

1   *The expenditure of physical and mental effort in work is as natural as play or rest.* The average human being does not inherently dislike work. Depending upon controllable conditions, work may be a source of satisfaction (and will be voluntarily performed) or a source of punishment (and will be avoided if possible).

2   *External control and the threat of punishment are not the only means for bringing about effort toward organizational objectives. Man will exercise self-direction and self-control in the service of objectives to which he is committed.*

3 *Commitment to objectives is a function of the rewards associated with their achievement.* The most significant of such rewards, e.g., the satisfaction of ego and self-actualization needs, can be direct products of effort directed toward organizational objectives.

4 *The average human being learns, under proper conditions, not only to accept but to seek responsibility.* Avoidance of responsibility, lack of ambition, and emphasis on security are generally consequences of experience, not inherent human characteristics.

5 *The capacity to exercise a relatively high degree of imagination, ingenuity, and creativity in the solution of organizational problems is widely, not narrowly, distributed in the population.*

6 *Under the conditions of modern industrial life, the intellectual potentialities of the average human being are only partially utilized.*

These assumptions involve sharply different implications for managerial strategy than do those of Theory X. They are dynamic rather than static: They indicate the possibility of human growth and development; they stress the necessity for selective adaptation rather than for a single absolute form of control. They are not framed in terms of the least common denominator of the factory hand, but in terms of a resource which has substantial potentialities.

Above all, the assumptions of Theory Y point up the fact that the limits on human collaboration in the organizational setting are not limits of human nature but of management's ingenuity in discovering how to realize the potential represented by its human resources. Theory X offers management an easy rationalization for ineffective organizational performance: It is due to the nature of the human resources with which we must work. Theory Y, on the other hand, places the problems squarely in the lap of management. If employees are lazy, indifferent, unwilling to take responsibility, intransigent, uncreative, uncooperative, Theory Y implies that the causes lie in management's methods of organization and control.

The assumptions of Theory Y are not finally validated. Nevertheless, they are far more consistent with existing knowledge in the social sciences than are the assumptions of Theory X. They will undoubtedly be refined, elaborated, modified as further research accumulates, but they are unlikely to be completely contradicted.

On the surface, these assumptions may not seem particularly difficult to accept. Carrying their implications into practice, however, is not easy. They challenge a number of deeply ingrained managerial habits of thought and action.

The Principle of Integration

The central principle of organization which derives from Theory X is that of direction and control through the exercise of authority—what has been called "the scalar principle." The central principle which derives from Theory Y is that of integration: the creation of conditions such that the members of the organization can achieve their own goals *best* by directing their efforts toward the success of the enterprise. These two principles have profoundly different implications with respect to the task of managing human resources, but the scalar principle is so firmly built into managerial attitudes that the implications of the principle of integration are not easy to perceive.

Someone once said that fish discover water last. The "psychological environment" of industrial management—like water for fish—is so much a part of organizational life that we are unaware of it. Certain characteristics of our society, and of organizational life within it, are so completely established, so pervasive, that we cannot conceive of their being otherwise. As a result, a great many policies and practices and decisions and relationships could only be—it seems—what they are.

Among these pervasive characteristics of organizational life in the United States today is a managerial attitude (stemming from Theory X) toward membership in the industrial organization. It is assumed almost without question that organizational requirements take precedence over the needs of individual members. Basically, the employment agreement is that in return for the rewards which are offered, the individual will accept external direction and control. The very idea of integration and self-control is foreign to our way of thinking about the employment relationship. The tendency, therefore, is either to reject it out of hand (as socialistic, or anarchistic, or inconsistent with human nature) or to twist it unconsciously until it fits existing conceptions.

The concept of integration and self-control carries the implication that the organization will be more effective in achieving its economic objectives if adjustments are made, in significant ways, to the needs and goals of its members.

A district manager in a large, geographically decentralized company is notified that he is being promoted to a policy level position at headquarters. It is a big promotion with a large salary increase. His role in the organization will be a much more powerful one, and he will be associated with the major executives of the firm.

The headquarters group who selected him for this position have carefully considered a number of possible candidates. This man stands out among them in a way which makes him the natural choice. His performance has been under observation for some time, and there is little question that he possesses the necessary qualifications not only for this opening but for an even higher position. There is genuine satisfaction that such an outstanding candidate is available.

The man is appalled. He doesn't want the job. His goal, as he expresses it, is to be the "best damned district manager in the company." He enjoys his direct associations with operating people in the field, and he doesn't want a policy level job. He and his wife enjoy the kind of life they have created in a small city, and they dislike actively both the living conditions and the social obligations of the headquarters city.

He expresses his feelings as strongly as he can, but his objections are brushed aside. The organization's needs are such that his refusal to accept the promotion would be unthinkable. His superiors say to themselves that of course when he has settled in to the new job, he will recognize that it was the right thing. And so he makes the move.

Two years later he is in an even higher position in the company's headquarters organization, and there is talk that he will probably be the executive vice-president before long. Privately he expresses considerable unhappiness and dissatisfaction. He (and his wife) would "give anything" to be back in the situation he left two years ago.

Within the context of the pervasive assumptions of Theory X, promotions and transfers in large numbers are made by unilateral decision. The requirements of the organization are given priority automatically and almost without question. If the individual's personal goals are considered at all, it is assumed that the rewards of salary and position will satisfy him. Should an individual actually refuse such a move without a compelling reason, such as health or a severe family crisis, he would be considered to have jeopardized his future because of this "selfish" attitude. It is rare indeed for management to give the individual the opportunity to be a genuine and active partner in such a decision, even though it may affect his most important personal goals. Yet the implications following from Theory Y are that the organization is likely to suffer if it ignores these personal needs and goals. In making unilateral decisions with respect to promotion, management is failing to utilize its human resources in the most effective way.

The principle of integration demands that both the organization's and the individual's needs be recognized. Of course, when there is a sincere joint effort to find it, an integrative solution which meets the needs of the individual *and* the organization is a frequent outcome. But not always—and this is the point at which Theory Y begins to appear unrealistic. It collides head on with pervasive attitudes associated with management by direction and control.

The assumptions of Theory Y imply that unless integration is achieved *the organization will suffer*. The objectives of the organization are *not* achieved best by the unilateral administration of promotions, because this form of management by direction and control will not create the commitment which would make available the full resources of those affected. The lesser motivation, the lesser resulting degree of self-direction and self-control are costs which, when added up for many instances over time, will more than offset the gains obtained by unilateral decisions "for the good of the organization."

One other example will perhaps clarify further the sharply different implications of Theory X and Theory Y.

It could be argued that management is already giving a great deal of attention to the principle of integration through its efforts in the field of economic education. Many millions of dollars and much ingenuity have been expended in attempts to persuade employees that their welfare is intimately connected with the success of the free enterprise system and of their own companies. The idea that they can achieve their own goals best by directing their effort toward the objectives of the organization has been explored and developed and communicated in every possible way. Is this not evidence that management is already committed to the principle of integration?

The answer is a definite no. These managerial efforts, with rare exceptions, reflect clearly the influence of the assumptions of Theory X. The central message is an exhortation to the industrial employee to work hard and follow orders in order to protect his job and his standard of living. Much has been achieved, it says, by our established way of running industry, and much more could be achieved if employees would adapt themselves *to management's definition* of what is required. Behind these exhortations lies the expectation that of course the requirements of the organization and its economic success must have priority over the needs of the individual.

Naturally, integration means working together for the success of the enterprise so we all may share in the resulting rewards. But management's implicit assumption is that working together means adjusting to the requirements of the organization *as management perceives them*. In terms of existing views, it seems inconceivable that individuals, seeking their own goals, would further the ends of the enterprise. On the contrary, this would lead to anarchy, chaos, irreconcilable conflicts of self-interest, lack of responsibility, inability to make decisions, and failure to carry out those that were made.

All these consequences, and other worse ones, *would* be inevitable unless conditions could be created such that the members of the organization perceived that they could achieve their own goals *best* by directing their efforts toward the success of the enterprise. If the assumptions of Theory Y are valid, the practical question is whether, and to what extent, such conditions can be created. To that question the balance of this volume is addressed.

The Application of Theory Y

In the physical sciences there are many theoretical phenomena which cannot be achieved in practice. Absolute zero and a perfect vacuum are examples. Others, such as nuclear power, jet aircraft, and human space flight, are recognized theoretically to be possible long before they become feasible. This fact does not make theory less useful. If it were not for our theoretical convictions, we would not even be attempting to develop the means for human flight into space today. In fact, were it not for the development of physical science theory during the past century and a half, we would still be depending upon the horse and buggy and the sailing vessel for transportation. Virtually all significant technological developments wait on the formulation of relevant theory.

Similarly, in the management of the human resources of industry, the assumptions and theories about human nature at any given time limit innovation. Possibilities are not recognized, innovating efforts are not undertaken, until theoretical conceptions lay a groundwork for them. Assumptions like those of Theory X permit us to conceive of certain possible ways of organizing and directing human effort, *but not others*. Assumptions like those of Theory Y open up a range of possibilities for new managerial policies and practices. As in the case of the development of new physical science theory, some of these possibilities are not immediately feasible, and others may forever remain unattainable. They may be too costly, or it may be that we simply cannot discover how to create the necessary "hardware."

There is substantial evidence for the statement that the potentialities of the average human being are far above those which we typically realize in industry today. If our assumptions are like those of Theory X, we will not even recognize the existence of these potentialities and there will be no reason to devote time, effort, or money to discovering how to realize them. If, however, we accept assumptions like those of Theory Y, we will be challenged to innovate, to discover new ways of organizing and directing human effort, even though we recognize that the perfect organization, like the perfect vacuum, is practically out of reach.

We need not be overwhelmed by the dimensions of the managerial task implied by Theory Y. To be sure, a large mass production operation in which the workers have been organized by a militant and hostile union faces management with problems which appear at present to be insurmountable with respect to the application of the principle of integration. It may be decades before sufficient knowledge will have accumulated to make such an application feasible. Applications of Theory Y will have to be tested initially in more limited ways and under more favorable circumstances! However, a number of applications of Theory Y *in managing managers and professional people* are possible today. Within the managerial hierarchy, the assumptions can be tested and refined, techniques can be invented and skill acquired in their use. As knowledge accumulates, some of the problems of application at the worker level in large organizations may appear less baffling than they do at present.

Perfect integration of organizational requirements and individual goals and needs is, of course, not a realistic objective. In adopting this principle, we seek that degree of integration in which the individual can achieve his goals *best* by directing his efforts toward the success of the organization. "Best" means that this alternative will be more attractive than the many others available to him: indifference, irresponsibility, minimal compliance, hostility, sabotage. It means that he will continuously be encouraged to develop and utilize voluntarily his capacities, his knowledge, his skill, his ingenuity in ways which contribute to the success of the enterprise.[1]

Acceptance of Theory Y does not imply abdication, or "soft" management, or "permissiveness." As was indicated above, such notions stem from the acceptance of authority as the *single* means of managerial control, and from attempts to minimize its negative consequences. Theory Y assumes that people will exercise self-direction and self-control in the achievement of organizational objectives *to the degree that they are committed to those objectives*. If that commitment is small, only a slight degree of self-direction and self-control will be likely, and a substantial amount of external influence will be necessary. If it is large, many conventional external controls will be relatively superfluous, and to some extent self-defeating. Managerial policies and practices materially affect this degree of commitment.

Authority is an inappropriate means for obtaining commitment to objectives. Other forms of influence—help in achieving integration, for example—are

---

[1]A recent, highly significant study of the sources of job satisfaction and dissatisfaction among managerial and professional people suggests that these opportunities for "self-actualization" are the essential requirements of both job satisfaction and high performance. The researchers find that "the wants of employees divide into two groups. One group revolves around the need to develop in one's occupation as a source of personal growth. The second group operates as an essential base to the first and is associated with fair treatment in compensation, supervision, working conditions, and administrative practices. *The fulfillment of the needs of the second group does not motivate the individual to high levels of job satisfaction and . . . to extra performance on the job*. All we can expect from satisfying [this second group of needs] is the prevention of dissatisfaction and poor job performance." Frederick Herzberg, Bernard Mausner, and Barbara Bloch Snyderman, *The Motivation to Work*. New York: John Wiley & Sons, Inc., 1959, pp. 114–115. (Italics mine.)

required for this purpose. Theory Y points to the possibility of lessening the emphasis on external forms of control to the degree that commitment to organizational objectives can be achieved. Its underlying assumptions emphasize the capacity of human beings for self-control, and the consequent possibility of greater managerial reliance on other means of influence. Nevertheless, it is clear that authority *is* an appropriate means for control under certain circumstances— particularly where genuine commitment to objectives cannot be achieved. The assumptions of Theory Y do not deny the appropriateness of authority, but they do deny that it is appropriate for all purposes and under all circumstances.

Many statements have been made to the effect that we have acquired today the know-how to cope with virtually any technological problems which may arise, and that the major industrial advances of the next half century will occur on the human side of enterprise. Such advances, however, are improbable so long as management continues to organize and direct and control its human resources on the basis of assumptions—tacit or explicit—like those of Theory X. Genuine innovation, in contrast to a refurbishing and patching of present managerial strategies, requires first the acceptance of less limiting assumptions about the nature of the human resources we seek to control, and second the readiness to adapt selectively to the implications contained in those new assumptions. Theory Y is an invitation to innovation.

References

Brown, J. A. C.: *The Social Psychology of Industry*. Baltimore: Penguin Books, Inc., 1954.

Cordiner, Ralph J.: *New Frontiers for Professional Managers*. New York: McGraw-Hill Book Company, Inc., 1956.

Dubin, Robert: *The World of Work: Industrial Society and Human Relations*. Englewood Cliffs, N.J.: Prentice-Hall, Inc., 1958.

Friedmann, Georges: *Industrial Society: The Emergence of the Human Problems of Automation*. Glencoe, Ill.: Free Press, 1955.

Herzberg, Frederick, Bernard Mausner, and Barbara Bloch Snyderman: *The Motivation to Work*. New York: John Wiley & Sons, Inc., 1959.

Krech, David, and Richard S. Crutchfield: *Theory and Problems of Social Psychology*. New York: McGraw-Hill Book Company, Inc., 1948.

Leavitt, Harold J.: *Managerial Psychology*. Chicago: University of Chicago Press, 1958.

McMurry, Robert N.: "The Case for Benevolent Autocracy," *Harvard Business Review*, vol. 36, no. 1 (January–February), 1958.

Rice, A. K.: *Productivity and Social Organizations: The Ahmedabad Experiment*. London: Tavistock Publications, Ltd., 1958.

Stagner, Ross: *The Psychology of Industrial Conflict*. New York: John Wiley & Sons, Inc., 1956.

People, Productivity, and Organizational Structure

Joel E. Ross
Robert G. Murdick

Of all the current concerns of business and government, the most far-reaching is productivity, chiefly because it is so linked to foreign competition, and, related to that, because the declining rate of increase in productivity is a primary cause of monetary problems and inflation. If improved work output from both professional and production workers is the answer, threats certainly won't get it, and neither will exhortations. But organizational and management restructure might.

To quote chairman Gerstenberg of General Motors, "Better productivity results from better management." Another automotive executive, Chrysler's Eugene Cafiero, puts it more forcefully: "We've got to stop bossing and start managing." The 3M chief executive, Harry Heltzer, adds, "You can't press the button any harder and make the automated equipment run any faster. In a rising cost spiral you've just got to find ways of pressing it more intelligently." Among those more intelligent ways of pressing the button are innovative forms of organization and methods of managing.

By and large, managers have overlooked or underemphasized two major sources of increased productivity. The first is the salaried side of the company, that broad area known as white collar and middle management. One company that examined it was Hercules Incorporated, the chemical giant. It reached the conclusion that those groups are over-compensated in relation to their attributable productivity gains to a greater extent than hourly workers. Other companies and studies have found that in general those groups are growing relative to direct labor; they exceed 60 percent in many cases. Moreover, few of them work to any standard of performance or under any productivity measurement system, and it is widely estimated that they seldom top 50 percent of their potential.

A possibility of immediate improvement here lies in stimulating and helping lower and middle managers to do a better job. They are often so bogged down in procedures, paperwork, red tape, and other trappings of organization structure that they have little time left for the more productive jobs of planning, organizing, and communicating. Their jobs are so narrowly defined and supervision is so close that motivation is killed.

The second source of increased productivity is the organization structure, the framework that facilitates organizational dynamics and guides company operations. Most managers are handling their physical and financial assets acceptably but are overlooking their human resources. A careful analysis of the costs of the human resources would very likely lead to better management and

Reprinted by permission of the publisher from *Personnel,* September–October 1973, pp. 8–18. © 1973 by AMACOM, a division of the American Management Association.

organization of these resources. In general, payrolls are running in the neighborhood of eight times earnings, so it is obvious that an increase of, say, 5 percent in productivity (through improved turnover, better organization, and so on) would have a really significant impact. Surely, such potential gains make trying new approaches to organization worthwhile. Let's see where our choices lie in this area.

The Classical Organization Structure

The classical or bureaucratic, hierarchical organization continues to be the most common corporate structure. It is easily understood; it is traditional; and it works reasonably well. This traditional structure provides the foundation on which modern adaptations are constructed. The basic tenets of the classical structure are specialization of work (departments), span of management (nobody supervises over six subordinates), unity of command (nobody reports to more than one boss), and chain of command (authority delegation). The manager determines work activities to get the job done, writes job descriptions, and organizes people into groups and assigns them to superiors. He then establishes objectives and deadlines and determines standards of performance. Operations are controlled through a reporting system. The whole structure takes on the shape of a pyramid.

How do we arrive at a bureaucratic, pyramidal structure? The answer lies in an understanding of how a company grows and develops. In the beginning communication is simple and effective because activities and communication channels are few in number, but as operations grow in size and communications become more complex, proper coordination and direction demand written directives and procedures. Communication is between offices, not people. More growth means more complexity, and that calls for more policies, procedures, and further formalization. In time the proliferation of systems, procedures, and regulations demands greater departmentation and more staff people to coordinate operations. But a characteristic of the pyramidal structure is the rather tight hold the man at the top has on the reins of authority.

Criticizing the systems, formality, and controls of the bureaucracy is getting to be a profitable vocation—witness *Parkinson's Law, The Peter Principle, and Up the Organization*. Some of the charges leveled at the classical structure are these:

- It is too mechanistic and ignores major facets of human nature.
- It is too structured to adapt to change.
- Its formal directives and procedures hinder communication.
- It inhibits innovation.
- It pays the job and not the man.
- It relies on coercion to maintain control.
- Its job-defensive behavior encourages make-work.
- Its goals are incompatible with those of its members.
- It is simply out of date with the needs of the Seventies.

Many of those criticisms have a basis in truth, but except in small organizations, the classical structure appears to be the easiest way to cope effectively with complexity. Bureaucracy, with all of its "evils," is an organizational requirement when we go beyond the face-to-face stage of communication. The major arguments in favor of the classical approach are these:

- It has overwhelming acceptance by practicing businessmen.
- It works.
- It is easily understood and applied.
- It isn't set in concrete—it can accommodate modifications such as the behavioral or organic ones when the need arises.

Recent business events point to the value of classical methods. In the late Sixties, LTV Corp., Litton Industries, Gulf & Western, and other conglomerates were having a field day with free-form management, which was characterized by loose controls and a high degree of decentralization of authority. For a while, it appeared that doing without some of the old standbys such as performance standards and controls was having some success, but now tight controls are back in favor. Two outstanding conglomerates, IT&T and TRW, never fell for the free-form management idea; both retained the fundamentals of planning and control, maintained strict reporting procedures that required substantial involvement on the part of division managers, and insisted on accurate projections, but they did establish an environment of reporting informality that made the best advice in the company accessible to everyone. In short, they used the old-time, proven methods with the necessary adaptation for human involvement to make them work.

Despite the criticisms frequently leveled at it, this structure will probably be around for a long time to come. Not long ago, a survey of the Fellows of the Academy of Management, a group of distinguished senior management professors, attempted to forecast the shape of the organization of the future. The result was a 75 percent probability prediction that the dominant organizational structure in 1985 will still be the classical pyramid.

The Behavioral Model of Organization

The most persistent criticism of the classical organization structure comes from the behavioral scientists. Their basic quarrel with this structure is that it is too mechanistic and therefore tends to overlook human nature and the needs of people. Some maintain that organizational trappings such as structure, procedures, and controls actually violate human wants and inhibit productivity; others contend that the pyramidal structure, although perhaps suitable for a stable environment, is unable to accommodate the change that is characteristic of modern organizations.

In the behavioral model an attempt is made to overcome some of the mechanistic-structural objections to the classical organization. The model assumes the objective of economic productivity output as given, but it adds a new dimension—employee satisfaction. This satisfaction, which presumably leads to greater productivity, is a function not so much of structure as of individual perception and personal value systems. Harlan Cleveland, who has had a distinguished career in business, government, and higher education, expresses the view of the behaviorists fairly well when he decrees, "The pyramid structure of less than a generation ago must be replaced by 'horizontal systems' in which control is loose, power diffused, and centers of decision widespread."

Essentially, the idea is that the pyramid should be modified to provide:

- A more democratic attitude on the part of managers.
- More participation in major decisions at lower levels.
- Decentralization of decision making as far as possible.
- Less emphasis on hierarchy and authority delegation.
- Less narrow specialization of work tasks.

Most managers react to the behavioral model in one of four ways—with skepticism, with a pretense of acceptance but an actual intention to manipulate people and decisions, with general agreement but confusion about how to implement the model, or with an enthusiastic desire to adopt the model as a modern way to motivate people in the company. Among those who seem to be genuinely committed is Chrysler's Cafiero; he has said, "Let responsibility extend down to its lowest practical level and give authority to go along with it. The lowest level in a lot of cases is the guy right on the line."

At Chrysler, assembly workers in selected plants are authorized to reject substandard parts, work sitting instead of standing, and paint their machines any color they wish. Other companies that have acted to involve workers and let them participate in decisions about their work and to reduce the specialized and monotonous nature of the job include AT&T, where selected typists can now research, compose, and sign their own letters without supervision. Another is Motorola, where female hourly workers who formerly performed very specialized tasks (for example, wiring or soldering) on a walkie-talkie assembly line now assemble the entire product and approve its final checkout.

There is a lot of talk and speculation about the behavioral approach to improving organizational productivity, but its application is still limited and experimental. Companies that have tried to modify their organizational approach in that way are few and most have done so on a trial basis, but its acceptance should accelerate because it makes good economic sense and because it looks as if the workforce, including lower and middle management, will demand it.

The Organic Model of Organization

Also behavioral in nature, the organic approach to organizational design goes one step further in that it addresses itself to the fundamentals of structure and specialization of tasks. Warren Bennis, its foremost proponent, argues that the traditional structure is too rigid to adapt to the frequent changes brought about by modern technology, and to accommodate those changes, organizations should be made up of temporary task forces.

He summarizes his proposal this way:

> First of all, the key word will be temporary. Organizations will become adaptive, rapidly changing temporary systems. Second, they will be organized around problems-to-be-solved. Third, these problems will be solved by groups of relative strangers who represent a diverse set of professional skills. Fourth, given the requirements of coordinating the various projects, articulating points or "linking pin" personnel will be necessary who can speak the diverse languages of research and who can relay and mediate between the various project groups. Fifth, the groups will be conducted on organic rather than on mechanical lines; they will emerge and adapt to the problems, and leadership and influence will fall to those who seem most able to solve the problems, rather than according to the programmed role expectations. People will be differentiated, not according to rank or roles, but according to skills and training. . . . Though no catchy phrase comes to mind, it might be called an organic-adaptive structure.

Generally speaking, the organic approach to organization and productivity has had only moderate acceptance, although its use is spreading. In many ways it overcomes the familiar objections to bureaucracy by allowing more freedom of action and less narrow specialization.

Emerging Concepts: The Team Approach

How can the essential characteristics of the organic model—described as temporary, flexible, and accommodating to change—be achieved within the traditional pyramidal structure? The answer is the team approach, which has several versions. The one called project management is widely used; matrix management and venture teams management are evolving.

The team, or plural, approach to problem solution and management is nothing new—committees and other coordinative devices have been with us for centuries. The modern team approach, however, was popularized by the Navy's Special Projects Office use of PERT in the Polaris program and is finding increased use in nondefense applications. Indeed, some form of team organization promises to be the major innovation in dealing with complexity and change during the coming decades.

Now let's turn to the various versions of the team approach.

Project Management   Assume that you have a plan that requires the coordination of two or more functional departments, such as accounting, marketing, finance, or engineering. The plan may involve the development and design of a new product, deeper market penetration of an existing product, cost reduction, acquisition of or merger with an outside company, management development, new financing, construction and location of a new plant, or even overhaul of the entire company. How do you organize to accomplish the job?

The first inclination is to form a task force or committee, the device that comes to mind when one department has difficulty in handling a problem alone and where the organization structure is admittedly unable to deal with change.

The drawback is that the committee is rarely given the power to make decisions and implement plans of action, and, in fact, that type of body, with its diffused power and lack of specific individual responsibility, is not appropriate for decision making.

Another solution might be to assign responsibilities for the various parts of the task to an operating manager of one of the functional departments, but here the problem is that serious top management involvement is necessary to resolve conflicts and to assure that all steps are coordinated and taken. Therefore, this tack is bound to be disruptive.

A third approach might be to establish a project manager with complete, undiluted authority for all aspects of the project. That is the organizational device being used more and more in aerospace as well as a variety of other industries, and we'll become better acquainted with it as we move away from process production systems into unit production and service output. The central idea is to assign one individual, the project manager, the responsibility for planning, work scheduling, budgeting, and controlling. His job is to ensure that the task or the project is completed within the established standards of time, cost and technical specifications.

Matrix Management   Matrix organization gets its name from the fact that a number of project managers exercise planning, scheduling, and cost control over people who have been assigned to their projects, while the functional managers exert line control, in terms of technical direction, training, compensation, and the like, over the same workers. Thus, there is shared responsibility for the worker, and he must please two bosses.

Two excellent examples of this kind of management in operation can be found at Honeywell and Texas Instruments. When General Electric decided to quit the computer business, Honeywell acquired the pieces. It set up 20 managerial task forces, made up of about 200 people from both its own staff and GE's to integrate manufacturing, marketing, engineering, field services, personnel, software, and the inventory of actual product lines. Honeywell's chairman called it a textbook exercise in how to merge painlessly.

In the case of Texas Instruments, matrix management is a way of life, and has been carried to a high degree of sophistication. Broad company objectives are broken down into a series of strategies and methods for achieving them, and those strategies, in turn, are translated into several hundred tactical action programs (TAPS). Each TAP has a project management system.

By contrast, it should be mentioned, in the line project management organization each employee has only one home—the project to which he is assigned or an auxiliary service group. Usually, a number of projects are active at the same time but in different stages of their life cycles. As new projects build up, people are transferred from the projects that are approaching their ends. The project manager has complete responsibility for resources of money and men and contracts for auxiliary services, such as centralized testing in an R&D organization.

Venture Teams   "The greatest challenge facing most corporations today is the development and marketing of new products or services that will produce a profit in the face of increased risks of failure," says a manager in a leading marketing research firm. The venture team is a recent organizational innovation designed to meet the demand for a breakthrough in product marketing.

The venture team is somewhat like the project matrix management team in that its personnel resources are obtained from the functional departments. Other similarities include organizational separation, the team of multidisciplinary personnel, and the goal-directed effort toward the achievement of a single result— here, product development and introduction. The venture team also may have a flexible life span, with a completion time loosely defined by broad time and financial goals. To be successful, members of venture teams have to be generally well accepted by others in the organization, because the interaction of the venture manager with those in other segments is considerable.

For companies that are committed to growth and for those whose success depends on the marketing of existing products and the development of new ones, the venture team approach offers a promising alternative to the operations traditionally found in marketing departments.

Emerging Concepts: The Contingency Model

Thus far we have examined the classical, pyramidal form of organization structure, modifications of it, and a number of related approaches, behavioral and organic. Unfortunately, however, even taken together all of these concepts fail to come up with a workable systems approach to organization. The contingency model, which attempts to do so, represents the latest thinking and research in this area. (Howard M. Carlisle, of the University of Utah, explains it in detail in *Situational Management: A Contingency Approach to Leadership,* to be published in October by AMACOM, a division of American Management Association.)

The contingency model seeks to answer the question of what factors, forces, or variables—contingencies—should be considered in deciding how to design an organization structure. The most important are these:

The Manager   Corporate personality, strategy, policies, and plans reflect the personal, social, and ideological goals of the top-management group, frequently of the top man himself. It follows that top management is the most important variable in shaping the company's organization structure. Organizations per se don't have objectives; people have them, and through them, they set organizational goals. Their value systems and their philosophy of management combine to act as the shaping force in organizational design. For example, how do the managers view individual freedom to make decisions, as opposed to normal authority channels within the company? What is their attitude about leadership? How do they see the interaction between the company and its external environment?

The Work   Since accomplishment of tasks to achieve organizational goals is the primary reason for organizing, a fundamental determinant of structure is the nature of the tasks. The work determines factors such as span of control, authority delegation, and the extent to which an organic, as opposed to a bureaucratic, structure is adopted. And a growing body of research evidence relates technology to organization design—different technologies seem to have different "management content." At the risk of oversimplification, we can probably conclude that in low-technology, stable, continuous-process industries, there is less need for adaptive organizations.

The Environment   The elements that set the climate of a company are social, political, economic, and technological, as well as those related to product and supply markets. The environment is therefore complex, and the more a company interacts with it, the greater its impact on the organization design.

     The greatest environmental interaction probably occurs in the context of hard-headed market considerations, such as the availability of resources and capital, the products or services the company sells, and the competition anticipated. Other market considerations are the changing demand for the company's output and the technological or other factors that may change both demand and production methods. It isn't difficult to see why a stable environment, such as that of the steel industry, would demand a different pattern of design and behavior than would an environment of uncertainty and flux, such as that of the computer industry.

The Individual Contributors   Because an organization structure is nothing without people to man it, the human element is an essential factor. We now have a growing and perhaps conclusive body of evidence that increased productivity and other desirable results can be achieved by adapting the structure to accommodate the needs of organizational members. That is not academic clap-trap, but practical business sense.

Building an Adaptive Organization

What does all this suggest and what practical use has it? It suggests that the right structure is a function of the interaction of the variables, each of which must be balanced against the effect of the others and against the desired output of the organization. In practice, no one style of organization design is universally appropriate; perhaps, however, there is a universal truth in the observation of Joseph C. Wilson, of Xerox, that the greatest strength of a company is the spirit of innovation and adaptation to change. To check the presence of that spirit and the "adaptability quotient," here are some questions:

- Do you blame most of your productivity problems on labor?
- Have you identified the output and costs of the nonhourly workforce, including white collar and lower and middle management? If so, are those groups working to a standard and can you identify changes in their productivity?

- Do you know what a 5 percent increase in productivity of each category of worker would do for profits?
- Do you have a program for identifying the value of your human resources and the costs associated with them in much the same way as other assets?
- Do you have a true management of human resources program, not just a personnel department that maintains records?
- Do your people cling to old ways of working after they have been confronted with new situations?
- Are the older managers living in the past and passing their thinking along to the younger men?
- Is your reputation one of safety, security, and "a nice place to work"?
- Has management developed a low criticism tolerance?
- Does company esprit depend upon one or more outdated "rites"?
- Does your entire operation depend on tight controls?
- As you see it, is line-staff conflict nonexistent and staff specialists are doing their job properly?
- Have you reviewed the company situation to see whether some form of team organization would work?
- Are you willing to delegate and let subordinates make mistakes?
- Have you reviewed the relationship between these determinants of organizational design—managers, work, environment, individual contributors— to see whether you have a mix that fits your structure?

The focus of all this probing of the organizational structure is, obviously, human resource management. Here we come full circle, back to the concern with productivity, because that is determined to a large extent by employees' reaction to the company's "socio-work" environment, and it, in turn, is determined to a large extent by company structure—the organization of work and people.

Motivation and Organizational Climate

George H. Litwin
Robert A. Stringer

Motivation in Perspective

In this monograph we have dealt with an area vital in the management process. Managers must control and direct the behavior of their subordinates, but such direction and control cannot be aimed only at *behavior*. Managers cannot afford to operate solely at the behavioral level. They must concern themselves with the determinants of behavior, that is, with *motivation*.

Reprinted by permission of Harvard University Press from *Motivation and Organizational Climate* by George H. Litwin and Robert A. Stringer, Jr., Harvard University, Graduate School of Business Administration, Division of Research, Boston. Copyright © 1968 by the President and Fellows of Harvard College.

We have shown that managers can and do influence the thoughts, feelings, and desires of workers. It is these thoughts, feelings, and desires that arouse motivation and direct behavior. If managers are to become more effective, they must learn to understand and control some of the critical psychological factors in the work environment. In other words, *managers must manage motivation.*

We have stated previously that there are managers who seem to be particularly sensitive to this aspect of the management function. These are "gifted" managers who know what influences make men work harder, who know what factors create high morale, and who know how to get the best out of each worker. It has been our experience that such managers are rare. For the vast majority, the job of managing motivation is a trial and error affair. Armed only with the logics of common sense and past experience, most managers must wait until late in their careers before they become experts in problems of motivating others. For most managers, a systematic framework for managing motivation is needed. This monograph has presented such a framework, and—once understood—it may provide the needed perspective for more effective handling of problems of managing human motivation.

The Key Elements of Managing Motivation

Our framework includes four of the critical variables that any manager must consider in managing motivation. These elements are not exclusive, nor are they independent. Each is—to a certain extent—beyond the control of the operating manager, but each represents a "leverage point" that the manager can use to influence the motivated performance of organization members. These four elements are:

1 The motives and needs the individuals bring to the situation;
2 The organizational tasks that must be performed;
3 The climate that characterizes the work situation; and
4 The personal strengths and limitations of the operating manager.

Personality differences account for much of the variation of individual behavior in organizations. We have defined these differences largely in terms of needs: for achievement, for power, and for affiliation. As outlined in Chapter 2, individuals come to the work situation with different kinds of needs, and a manager cannot afford to overlook these differences.

The second element that a manager must consider in his efforts to manage motivation is the basic nature of the tasks to be performed. Different tasks involve or require different kinds of individual behavior and different patterns of motivation. For example, many sales tasks require risk taking, the assumption of individual responsibility, and so on, and achievement motivation seems especially relevant. Very routine tasks do not require this kind of motivation. Assembly lines are often most efficient when they are set up to afford the workers opportunities for mutual interaction, and affiliation motivation seems to be relevant.

We have emphasized the importance of the third element in managing motivation, organizational climate. The climate that characterizes the work situation helps determine the kinds of worker motivation that are actually aroused. Climates tend to mediate between the task requirements and the needs of the individual. We have said that sales tasks often require achievement-related behaviors, and thus salesmen should have high levels of achievement motivation. But, if the sales office climate fails to emphasize risk taking, responsibility, and flexible structure, then the salesmen's achievement concerns will not be stimulated. The capacity to influence the organizational climate is perhaps the most powerful leverage point in the entire management system. Because climates can affect the motivation of organization members, changes in certain climate properties could have immediate and profound effects on the motivated performance of all employees.

If the job of managing motivation revolves around managing organizational climate, then the manager's personal strengths and limitations must be considered. For the *manager's leadership style is a critical determinant of organizational climate*. Many managers, once they have diagnosed their motivational problems as climate-based, may find that they have to develop new skills in order to *change* the climate in the desired direction. A manager wishing to build stronger feelings of mutual support and encouragement (in order to arouse affiliation motivation, or in order to reinforce achievement motivation), may find that he is too aloof and impersonal in his dealings with his subordinates. This manager may decide to take a warmer and more personal interest in his men, and this may require skills and attitudes he does not presently possess.

Improving Our Diagnostic Abilities: Specific Examples

In the introduction to this monograph, we presented several examples of motivation and motivated behavior that seemed to contradict the "conventional wisdom." Using the conceptual framework we have developed in this monograph, we are now prepared to analyze these examples systematically. At the same time, we will put ourselves into the position of the operating manager and decide which of the key elements are most important in each situation, and how he might develop an action plan to better manage the motivation of the workers in question.

1   The first example was elaborated in one of the field studies presented in Chapter 8. The young girls worked in an office where none of their dominant needs was being satisfied. They brought high n Achievement to the job, but this need was frustrated. The climate failed to emphasize flexible structure, individual responsibility, rewards, support, or group loyalty. The tasks that these workers performed were moderately challenging, but the elements of challenge were not emphasized by management. This led to below-average performance and high levels of dissatisfaction and resentment. Two major alternative approaches to dealing with this problem include: (a) changing the needs of the workers; that is, hiring girls who would respond better to the highly structured office climate (girls high in n Power); and (b) changing the climate so that it tapped the achievement concerns of the employees.

2   The second example is more complicated. It illustrates the fact that many salesmen *are* made, rather than born. Salesmen were "turned into" top performers by the office climate in which they worked. In other offices, they had been mediocre performers. We must conclude that their success is due to the fact that their needs are now being satisfied and stimulated, whereas before they were being frustrated. As shown in Chapter 5, the sales task is typically one that demands strong achievement motivation. Developing top-performing salesmen depends, then, on: (a) attracting men with high *n* Achievement; and (b) stimulating and satisfying this need once they are on board by creating an achieving climate in the sales office.

3   The final example involved the manager who had successfully innovated with "Theory Y" management principles. This success can be understood if we concentrate on the organizational climate that was created. (This example is also elaborated in Chapter 8.) The employees in this plant were not only performing well, but they were very enthusiastic about their work situation. There was a workable "match" between the task requirements, the needs of the workers, and the working climate. In addition, this particular manager seems to have evaluated and utilized his own strengths and weaknesses. As suggested in Chapter 8, he will probably find that future development of his organizational climate will depend on how well he is able to continue implementing his system without creating backlash in the larger corporation, with its more traditional philosophy.

These specific examples outline some of the potential applications of our motivation and climate framework. To facilitate diagnosis and action planning, a simpler means of measuring and evaluating the key elements is needed. In the next sections, we will present guidelines for managing motivation, based on the theoretical and empirical evidence presented in this volume.

Human Motives: Their Measurement and Control

If a manager knew what the dominant needs of a man were, he would be in a much better position to satisfy these needs. When a man likes people, when he needs friendship, when he has a strong *need for affiliation,* it is certainly unwise to make him work alone. It is equally bad to make him work in a hostile atmosphere which discourages friendship and affiliation. When there is a job to be done that requires risk taking and responsibility, it is foolish to place a man with low *need for achievement* in that position.

Managers can control the motive patterns of organization members by careful recruitment and placement of personnel. To do so efficiently and effectively, a manager must learn to assess the strength of important human motives. The most straightforward method of measuring needs for achievement, affiliation, and power is through thematic apperception tests. Standardized test instruments, scored by content analysts trained in the McClelland-Atkinson procedures, provide measures of *n* Achievement, *n* Affiliation, and *n* Power.[1] These

---

[1]The only professional scoring service we know of is operated by the Motivation Research Group, a division of the Behavioral Science Center, Suite 3750, Prudential Tower, Boston, Mass. This group also provides standardized test instruments and assessment packages. The scoring manuals are published in Atkinson, ed., *Motives in Fantasy, Action, and Society* (1958).

measures have been demonstrated to have reasonable reliability and considerable predictive validity (see Atkinson, 1958; McClelland, 1961).

Under some circumstances, the use of thematic apperception measures is not very practical. The alternative available to the operating manager involves his conducting a reasonably systematic assessment program. While this is time-consuming, it may also lead to real insights into the needs of organization members.

First, the manager may pay particular attention to the *thoughts and feelings* of individuals. How do they talk about their experiences? What seems to be on their minds when they are involved in a task? What do they seem to get the most satisfaction from? If the manager can train himself to "tune in" to these kinds of questions, he will soon find that he is able to judge the dominant motives of his men. He will be tuning in on the everyday imaginative material that people generate.

Let's take as an example a salesman who seems to be enthusiastic. He talks about his sales goals and seems to gain more satisfaction from reaching these goals than he does from receiving his commissions. He likes to call himself a planner, and he is proud of the detail that he goes into before he makes a sales call. Not only does he enjoy the competitive nature of his work, but he has commented to his boss several times that he appreciates the freedom and responsibility of his job. All these elements signify that this salesman is high in *need for achievement.* His co-worker talks mainly about the money he is earning (or not earning). He doesn't seem to enjoy the long hours he is forced to put in, and he talks about his job in terms of the people he has met and the friendliness of the other salesmen in the office. We might conclude from this small sample of thoughts and feelings that this man is motivated by a *need for affiliation,* rather than a *need for achievement.*

A second alternative involves paying close attention to the *behavior* of different workers under different circumstances. Since *behavior is a function of aroused motivation,* careful assessment of behavior should allow reasonable inferences about motivation patterns. The following list of key questions may help the manager identify different kinds of motivated behavior:

A   *High Achievement:*
When he starts a task, does he stick with it?
Does he try to find out how he is doing, and does he try to get as much feedback as possible?
Does he respond to difficult, challenging situations? Does he work better when there is a deadline or some other challenge involved?
Is he eager to accept responsibility? When he is given responsibility, does he set (and meet) measurable standards of high performance?

B   *High Power:*
Does he seem to enjoy a good argument?
Does he seek positions of authority where he can give orders, rather than take them? Does he try to take over?

Are status symbols especially important to him, and does he use them to gain influence over others?

Is he especially eager to be his own boss, even where he needs assistance, or where joint effort is required?

C   High Affiliation:

Does he seem to be uncomfortable when he is forced to work alone?

Does he interact with the other workers and go out of his way to make friends with new workers?

Is he always getting involved in group projects, and is he sensitive to other people (especially when they are "mad" at him)?

Is he an apple-polisher, and does he try hard to get personally involved with his superiors?

"Yes" answers to these questions mean that the motivation in question is strong.

Organizational Tasks: Their Measurement and Control

Even if a manager knew what the basic needs of his work force were, he would have to match these needs with the demands of each organizational task to get the most out of each person. It is a waste of human resources to hire a group of enthusiastic high school or college graduates to do relatively routine and repetitive tasks. It is poor management to promote a power-motivated individual into a position where *you know* he will have to take orders, rather than give them.

It is a fact of life that there are boring *and* exciting jobs to be done in business. For maximum long-run worker motivation and top performance, managers must *match* the needs of their subordinates with the various task demands. If it is impractical to shift personnel, then the attributes of the tasks might be altered somewhat. The problem is to measure the motivational demands of various jobs in the organization so that the manager knows *how* to change them and *where* to place different workers.

The following questions were designed to aid in the analysis of the motivational demands of tasks.[2]

TASK ANALYSIS

Is It an Achievement Task?

1   How much latitude does a worker have in setting his work pace and work methods?

2   How much choice does a worker have when it comes to getting help or direction from someone else?

3   To what degree does errorless and efficient performance contribute to increased sales or company profits?

---

[2]Parts of the following stem from the "Requisite Task Attributes" scheme developed by Arthur N. Turner and Paul R. Lawrence in *Industrial Jobs and the Worker* (1965).

4 To what extent does the task challenge the abilities and skills of the worker?

5 Does the task provide clear, unambiguous feedback about the quality of performance?

Is It a Power Task?

6 How much opportunity does a worker have to personally direct his co-workers?

7 How much time is available for personal interactions while working?

8 To what degree does the task require the worker to deal directly with his superior?

9 How much control does the worker have over his work pace and work methods?

10 How many times can the worker leave his work area without reprimand?

Is It an Affiliation Task?

11 How many people *must* the worker interact with every two hours?

12 How many people *can* the worker interact with in his working area?

13 How dependent is successful task accomplishment on the cooperation of co-workers?

14 How much time is available for personal nontask interactions while working?

15 To what extent does the task allow for the maintenance of stable working relationships?

Rules for using these questions for task analysis are as follows:

1 Each task measured is to be ranked high, moderate, or low in response to each of the 15 questions.

2 A ranking of high   = 3 points
A ranking of moderate = 2 points
A ranking of low   = 1 point

3 For each question, standards will have to be set as to what constitutes a high, moderate, or low score. For example, high for question #11 would be 8 to 10 people, moderate would be 3 to 8, and low less than 3.

4 Total scores mean little. It is the relative scores in each of the three groups that measure the motivational demands of the task.

Exhibit 1 outlines a completed task analysis. The particular task being described is that of an assembly line worker in an electronic tube manufacturing plant. We can see from Exhibit 1 that this assembly line task taps affiliation motivation. This means that, *in and of itself,* the task is one that seems to satisfy a person's *need for affiliation.* If the workers on this assembly line have strong affiliative needs, then there is an appropriate *fit* between tasks and motives. If the workers were motivated by *n* Achievement or *n* Power, there is a poor *fit,* and the manager might consider altering certain aspects of the job. A task analysis can help him decide which aspects need to be changed.

Exhibit 1   A Sample Task Analysis for an Assembly Line Worker

	High (3)	Moderate (2)	Low (1)
Is it an achievement task?			
1.			X
2.		X	
3.		X	
4.			X
5.			X
Total: 7			
Is it a power task?			
6.			X
7.		X	
8.		X	
9.			X
10.			X
Total: 7			
Is it an affiliation task?			
11.		X	
12.	X		
13.		X	
14.		X	
15.	X		
Total: 12			

    Thus, the measurement scheme presented above can be used by the manager as part of an action-planning program to manage the motivation of his subordinates. By matching task demands with motives, the potential for high motivation and high performance is dramatically increased. But, as stated in Chapter 2, *this potential may never be realized.* High levels of worker motivation depend on the strength of the motive, the basic nature of the task, *and the arousal effects of the entire work situation. The expectancies and incentives that surround the work determine the level of aroused motivation.* And motivation level, in turn, determines how hard a subordinate will work, how long he will work, and what quality of work he will turn out. The final, and most powerful, leverage point available to the operating manager is his influence on expectancies and incentives.

Controlling Expectancies and Incentives in Specific Situations

Under certain circumstances the manager can have a strong influence on the worker's expectancies and incentives. In performance review meetings a manager can explain to his subordinates exactly what the rewards for top flight performance are. He can influence, to some extent, the worker's feelings and anticipations about his job, thus directly arousing motivation. In such one-to-one situations an effective manager can strongly arouse motivation, at least temporarily.

For example, if a manager knew that his subordinate was motivated by a strong *need for affiliation,* he could go out of his way to tap this need by creating a warm relationship. He could appeal to this "special relationship" in urging the worker to improve his performance. He could hold out specific affiliative rewards (more opportunities for interaction with his co-workers, a closer relationship with himself, etc.).

While such one-to-one interactions are an important leverage point in arousing motivation, they have several shortcomings:

1 They are time consuming;
2 They demand that the manager himself be present to manipulate the arousal cues;
3 Even if the manager succeeded in *arousing* the desired worker motivation, once the interaction was terminated other external factors might "erase" or destroy the arousal effects.

In other words, controlling expectancies and incentives in specific situations *may not be* the most efficient way of arousing and maintaining high levels of worker motivation. If the manager has successfully matched his organization's tasks with the needs of his workers, the most practical and powerful approach to the management of motivation involves controlling expectancies and incentives in nonspecific situations. The entire *organizational climate* must become the focus of management actions.

Climate: Measurement and Control

Controlling climate involves five action phases.

Phase One   Deciding what kind of climate is most appropriate (given the nature of your workers and the jobs to be done).
Phase Two   Assessing the present climate.
Phase Three   Analyzing the "climate gap" and establishing a plan to reach the ideal climate.
Phase Four   Taking concrete steps to improve the climate.
Phase Five   Evaluating your effectiveness in terms of your action plan and (redirecting your climate control emphases).

Phase One   Deciding on the most appropriate or ideal climate involves an integration of the first two leverage points. If a work group is characterized by high *need for achievement,* and if there are achievement tasks to be performed, the ideal climate could be defined solely in terms of the achievement syndrome. Whenever there is a good task/motive fit, the ideal climate will emphasize those dimensions which arouse the motive in question.

However, when it is impossible to arrive at a good fit between a worker's dominant needs and the task demands, the ideal climate becomes more complicated. In such situations there are several alternative definitions of "ideal."

Further research and experience are needed to determine the "optimum" and most useful solution to this problem, but two kinds of ideal climates may be described here.

The first kind of ideal climate would arouse the worker's dominant motive and *direct it toward task accomplishment*—even though the task normally requires some other pattern of motivation. The second kind of ideal climate would seek to arouse task-appropriate motivation even though it is not the worker's dominant need. To understand the strengths and weaknesses of these two alternative definitions of ideal climate, a brief example is outlined below.

A sales manager finds himself "stuck" with affiliation-oriented workers. He had attempted to hire achievement-oriented replacements but as yet has been unsuccessful. His sales tasks demand risk taking, use of performance feedback, and the like. They were achievement tasks and could not be altered. The manager might define his ideal climate as one that aroused affiliation motivation (high levels of warmth, friendliness, approval, support, and group identity). *He would then have to make sure that the workers received affiliative rewards for performing in achievement-related ways.* He would have to pay his salesmen "in friendship" for taking risks, using feedback, and setting high standards.

On the other hand, the manager might attempt to arouse the weaker achievement needs of his affiliation-oriented salesmen. In this case, he would define his ideal climate as an achieving climate, utilizing as many achievement arousal cues as possible. The induced achievement motivation would trigger task-related behavior without any special reinforcement or reward program, but the intensity or "energy investment" of the induced motivation would be only moderate (since the basic need was weak).

The first alternative (the affiliative climate) works with the strongest latent needs of the salesmen and should lead to highly motivated behavior. However, this alternative requires more supervision and direction, and it does not provide for the effective introduction of salesmen with stronger achievement needs. The second alternative (the achieving climate) should lead to less highly motivated behavior initially, but would allow for the recruiting and introduction of achievement-oriented salesmen. The choice among these alternatives should be based on an analysis of short-term and long-term organizational requirements, and on the manager's capacity to create one or the other kind of climate (or an effective combination).

Phase Two   Once the manager has decided on the general dimensions of his ideal climate, he must assess the "here and now" climate. The measurement problems associated with assessing organizational climates are discussed in Chapter 5, and we need not review them here. The important point is that the manager understand and believe in his measurement instrument.

The exact form of the questionnaire will depend on the specific needs of the manager. The improved questionnaire (Form B) described in Chapter 5 and in Appendix B is a useful general-purpose instrument. However, a manager may want to develop a special questionnaire, tailored to his measurement objectives and to the specific organization.

A sample of such a tailored climate questionnaire is presented below. The manager involved was a college professor interested in the secretarial climate in his department, and he restricted himself to the assessment of two aspects or dimensions of the climate, involving work standards and identification with the teaching group.

Work Standards
   1   My boss sets explicit standards for me and my work in the office.
   2   It's generally understood around here that secretaries are expected to be expert typists.
   3   Around here there is considerable pressure to improve your secretarial skills.
   4   None of the girls takes much pride in the way she does her work.
   5   Most of the professors want an attractive and friendly secretary and don't care about the quality of the work.
   6   If you want to be known as a good secretary, it's more important to be well-liked than it is to do good work.

Group Identification
   7   As far as I can see, there is very little loyalty to this teaching group.
   8   Most of the girls are proud of working for this teaching group.
   9   I feel that my boss and I work together well.
   10   All the secretaries around here are out for themselves.

Phase Three   By comparing the ideal climate with the here and now situation, the nature and size of the *climate gap* can be determined. There will usually be discrepancies between the ideal and the actual climate, and a manager will be able to see where his motivation arousal problems lie. For example, the college professor referred to above found that the secretaries were quite loyal to the teaching group, but perceived very little emphasis on high performance. For this professor, climate development seemed to center around raising the performance standards, *and communicating these higher standards to the secretaries*. This specific climate gap became the focus for action planning, as described below.

Phase Four   The action alternatives available to managers to control their organizational climate may be divided into four broad categories:

   1   Spatial arrangement changes;
   2   Changes in job and goal specifications;
   3   Changes in communication/reporting patterns;
   4   Changes in leadership style.

Some of the major action alternatives within each of these categories are outlined in Exhibit 2, along with a brief statement of the behavioral and climate effects that might be anticipated as a result of each action.

Exhibit 2   Action Alternatives for Controlling Climate

Category	Action alternatives	Anticipated behavioral effects	Anticipated effects on climate*
Spatial arrangements	Put people close together	Interaction and cohesion	Increase in warmth, support, identity
	Put work partners close together	Task-related interaction	Increase in support, identity, responsibility
	Determined by status	Interaction within status levels	Increase in structure, responsibility
Job and goal specifications	Define job duties in detail	Constrained (stereotyped) behavior	Increase in structure
			Decrease in warmth, responsibility
	Delegate overall responsibility and allow individual job planning	Individuality of work activity	Increase in responsibility, risk
			Decrease in structure
	Set and review goals periodically	Mutual goal-oriented activity (of managers and subordinates)	Increase in responsibility, standards, reward, support
Communication reporting patterns	Establish formal channels and procedures	Constrained (stereotyped) behavior and decreased interaction	Increase in structure
			Decrease in warmth, support
	Maintain informal contact	Manager-subordinate interaction and information sharing	Increase in support, reward, identity
Leadership style	Recognize and reward excellent performance	Increase in quality of output	Increase in reward, standards
	Provide coaching	Manager-subordinate problem solving	Increase in support, standards, reward

*Climate effects are described as changes in the salience of dimensions discussed in Chapters 4 and 5 [of *Motivation and Organizational Climate*—Ed.].

Spatial arrangement changes include the allocation of space to activities (and people) and the placement of desks, workbenches, and workers. As suggested in Exhibit 2, members of the organization could be placed close together, increasing interaction and cohesion, and leading to an affiliation-oriented climate. Or work partners and those who have to interact could be placed together, increasing task-related interaction and leading to a more achieving climate.

Changes in job and goal specifications include the extent to which job duties are defined in detail, the emphasis placed on prescribed job activities vs. performance goals, and the way goal-setting is handled. As indicated in Exhibit 2, the action alternatives in this area allow the creation of highly structured climates (through detailed job definition) or climates high in responsibility (through delegation and mutual goal-setting). In Exhibit 2, a distinction is made between delegation of overall job responsibility and infrequent review, which leads to a climate very high in personal responsibility but not very supportive or team-oriented and periodic mutual goal-setting, which leads to a climate characterized by responsibility, support, and team spirit.

Changes in communication/reporting patterns involve the kind of management control and information systems that are utilized, particularly the channels of communication, required reports (if any), and the typical quantity and content of communication. The major differences we have observed among communication/reporting patterns center around the emphasis on formal reporting through channels vs. informal sharing of information. As Exhibit 2 suggests, formal communication/reporting systems will often lead to a highly structured climate and to a decrease in interaction and information flow. More informal systems, where the manager often uses himself as a channel, will be more likely to lead to increased warmth, support, and sense of reward, since the increased interaction allows more frequent personal recognition for goal performance.

Changes in leadership style involve the manager's behavior, his assumptions about people, his style of relating, and so on. In Exhibit 2 two aspects of leadership style which we have found to be important are described. The first of these involves the manager's ability to recognize and reward excellent performance. Throughout our studies, the emphasis placed on reward vs. punishment has been shown to be a critical determinant of achievement and affiliation motivation. Yet many managers fail to take advantage of opportunities to recognize and reward goal performance, often arguing that "money is the only reward people want." The second aspect of leadership style described in Exhibit 2 involves what we call *coaching* behavior. By coaching, we mean the extent to which a manager works *with* his people on the job (or in the field) to solve problems and encourage more effective goal-directed behavior. Coaching tends to lead to a climate characterized by very high support and team spirit.

Phase Five   Periodic assessment of changes in the organizational climate is the final phase of our action planning framework. This assessment allows the manager to "track" the development of certain climate characteristics and evaluate the effectiveness of attempts he has made to influence and change the climate. In a rapidly changing situation, it may be necessary to make fairly frequent assessments. Generally, we believe that a climate assessment should be conducted every six months. To avoid problems involved in too frequent administration of the questionnaire, it is desirable to create two or more reasonably representative groups of organization members, with each group completing no more than one questionnaire within a year.

The importance of periodic assessment cannot be overemphasized. A manager may *think* he is having the desired effect, but it is the *workers' perceptions* that count. In conversations and interviews, a manager may get positive (or negative) feedback on his actions, but this may or may not be confirmed by a systematic climate assessment. Without data that allow tracking changes in climate, a manager is unable to evaluate the impact of his actions or to establish revised goals for improving the climate. In business it is critical that a manager be aware of inventory, projected sales, cash flow, and available financial resources. Why is it any less important to be aware of the condition of the organizational climate, and the availability of motivational resources which climate represents?

Job Redesign on the Assembly Line: Farewell to Blue-Collar Blues?

Louis E. Davis

The authors of the much-quoted, much-praised, and much-criticized HEW report *Work in America* wound up their study with a rhetorical bang: "Albert Camus wrote that 'without work life goes rotten. But when work is soulless, life stifles and dies.' Our analysis of work in America leads to much the same conclusion: Because work is central to the lives of so many Americans, either the absence of work or employment in meaningless work is creating an increasingly intolerable situation."

Most who argue that the rhetoric in the report is exaggerated and the thesis overstated would exempt the assembly line, particularly the auto assembly line, from their dissent. The auto assembly line epitomizes the conditions that contribute to employee dissatisfaction: fractionation of work into meaningless activities, with each activity repeated several hundred times each workday, and with the employees having little or no control over work pace or any other aspect of working conditions.

Two generations of social scientists have documented the discontent of auto workers with their jobs. Yet the basic production process hasn't changed since Ford's first Highland Park assembly plant in 1913. We read a lot about the

Reprinted by permission of the publisher from *Organizational Dynamics*, Autumn 1973, pp. 51–67. © 1973 by AMACOM, a division of the American Management Association.

accelerating pace of technology: Here's a technology that's stood still for 60 years despite the discontent.

The social explanations are easy. The automakers—when they thought about the problem at all—dismissed it. The economic advantages of the assembly line seemingly outweighed any possible social costs—including the high wages, part of which might properly be considered discontentment pay. In short, the cash register rang more clearly than the gripes.

Recently, the situation has changed. The advent of an adversary youth culture in the United States, the rising educational levels, with a concomitant increase in employee expectations of the job, the expansion of job opportunities for all but the least skilled and the most disaffected, have raised the level of discontent. One of the big three automakers, for example, now has an annual turnover rate of close to 40 percent. G.M.'s famous Lordstown Vega plant, the latest triumph of production engineering—with the average time per job activity pared to 36 seconds and workers facing a new Vega component 800 times in each eight-hour shift—has been plagued with strikes, official and wildcat, slowdowns, and sabotage. At times, the line has shut down during the second half of the day to remedy the defects that emerged from the line during the first half.

Is Job Redesign the Answer?

Much has been written about the two automobile plants in Sweden, Volvo and Saab-Scania, that have practiced job redesign of the assembly line on a large scale. The results, variously reported, have appeared in the world press. Also receiving wide press coverage have been the efforts of Philips N.V. in The Netherlands to redesign jobs on the lines assembling black-and-white and color TV sets. So much for instant history!

We visited the three companies during a recent trip to Europe and shall attempt to evaluate and compare them. But first a caveat: We eschew chic terms, such as job enrichment, autonomy, job rotation, and employee participation, in favor of the drabber job redesign for several reasons. First, the other terms have taken on emotional connotations; they've become the rallying ground for true believers who view them as a partial answer or panacea to the problem of employee alienation in an industrial society. The term job redesign, by contrast, has no glamor and no followers. Second, most efforts at job redesign, certainly the three we're going to write about, include elements of job enrichment, autonomy, job rotation, and employee participation in varying degrees at different times, but none of the competing terms affords a sufficiently large umbrella to cover what's happened and what's planned in the three organizations. Last, true believers passionately define their faiths differently; using any of the other terms as central would involve us in tiresome and trivial questions of definition. Hence, our choice of job redesign. It's comprehensive, and noncontroversial.

"Job redesign—the answer to what?" might have been a more descriptive subhead than one implying that our sole concern would be the question of employee discontent and its converse, employee satisfaction. Ours is a wider net. We're going to ask and answer (the answers, of course, being partial and tentative) these questions:

1 What conditions on the assembly line are economically favorable to which forms of job redesign?

2 Do many employees resent and resist job redesign? Do they prefer monotonous, repetitious work?

3 Are the "best" results from job redesign obtained when it's at its most thorough (job rotation plus job enrichment plus autonomy plus employee participation)?

4 Is there any single element in job redesign that seems to account for the biggest increase in employee satisfaction?

5 What are the benefits of job redesign—both those we can measure and monetize and those that can only be described?

6 On balance, does management gain as much from job redesign as the employee whose job is redesigned?

7 Last, what's the impact of the overall culture and political system on job redesign? What's the evidence, pro or con, that the success of job redesign at Volvo, Saab-Scania, or Philips—or the lack of it—would be replicated on similar assembly lines in the United States?

A tall order, but remember that we promised only tentative and partial answers to the seven questions.

Job Redesign at Philips

First Generation, 1960–1965   We start with Philips because, of our three companies, Philips is the pioneer; its experience with job redesign goes back to 1960. We use the term first generation, second generation, and so on to mark the stages of the Philips program because this is Philips' terminology—obviously appropriated from computer lingo.

In the first experiment, concern was more with the deficiencies of long assembly lines than it was with improving job satisfaction. Breaking up the existing line of 104 workers into five shorter assembly lines, installing buffer stocks of components between groups, and placing inspectors at the end of each group instead of the whole assembly line reduced waiting times by 55 percent, improved feedback, and improved the balance of the system—various short chains being stronger than one long chain because the line can never travel faster than the worker with the longest average time per operation.

Almost incidentally, morale also improved: Only 29 percent of the workers on the assembly line responded positively to the survey question "I like doing my job," versus a 51 percent positive response from the test line. Furthermore, when the test line was restructured with half the number of workers, so that each one performed twice the original cycle and workplaces alternated with empty seats, production flowed more smoothly and quality improved. Dr. H. G. Van Beek, a psychologist on the original study team, drew a dual lesson from the experiment: "From the point of view of production, the long line is very vulnerable; from the point of view of morale—in the sense of job satisfaction—downright bad."

Subsequent experiments in several plants involved rotating workers between different jobs on the assembly line, enriching jobs by having employees set their own pace within overall production standards, and enlarging them by making employees responsible for inspecting their own work. Most of the gains from the experiments Philips entered under the heading of "social profit." In other words, morale and job satisfaction improved but bread-and-butter items such as productivity and scrap showed little improvement.

Second Generation, 1965–1968   The key feature of the second phase, a program that involved a few thousand employees scattered over 30 different locations, was the abolition of foremen. With supervisors' enlarged span of control, the men on the assembly line acquired autonomy and more control over their jobs. Even an authoritarian supervisor would find that he was spread too thin to exercise the same amount of control as the previous foreman had.

Once again, the bulk of the profits were social. The bill for waste and repairs dropped slightly, and, of course, Philips pocketed the money that had been paid to the foremen. Otherwise, the gains to Philips were nonmonetary.

Third Phase, 1968   This phase, one that is ongoing, has focused on giving various groups of seven or eight employees total responsibility for assembling either black-and-white TV sets or color selectors for color TV sets, a task equivalent in complexity to assembling a black-and-white set from scratch.

We want to emphasize the word *total:* The group responsible for assembling the black-and-white sets, for example, not only performs the entire assembling task but also deals directly with staff groups such as procurement, quality, and stores, with no supervisor or foreman to act as intermediary or expediter. If something is needed from another department or something goes wrong that requires the services of another department, it's the group's responsibility to deal with the department.

"This third phase has had its problems," concedes Den Hertog, staff psychologist. "Typically, it's taken about six months for the groups to shake down—adjust to the increased pressures and responsibilities." Establishing effective relationships with unfamiliar higher-status employees in staff departments has proved the biggest single problem. On the other hand, anyone in an experimental group can opt out at any time—an option that has yet to be taken up. Of course, it may be the satisfaction of being a member of a select group, even physically separated from other work groups by a wall of green shrubbery, that accounts for no employee's having made a switch. Hertog, however, believes that the increase in intrinsic job satisfactions has more than compensated for any pains of adjustments and accounts for the lack of turnover.

What about results? What's the measurable impact of the program? There have been additional costs, such as increased training costs; more important, small, autonomous groups require new and smaller machines to perform traditional assembly line tasks. On the other hand, there have been measurable benefits. Overall, production costs in manhours have dropped 10 percent, while waiting times have decreased and quality levels have increased by smaller but still significant amounts.

To restructure work and redesign jobs in ways that increase employee job satisfaction at no net cost to the company over the long run is all that Philips, as a matter of policy, requires of such programs. Short-term deficits caused by purchases of new equipment are something it's prepared to live with.

Where is Philips going from here? Obviously, the potential for effective job redesign is large. With 90,000 workers in 60 plants, Philips has barely scratched the surface. Part of the answer would seem to lie in the future strength of the movement for employee participation and power equalization that is particularly strong in Norway and Sweden and is gaining adherents in The Netherlands.

At Philips the primary response has been the establishment of worker consultation in some 20 different departments. Worker consultation is just what it sounds like: Employees meet with first- and second-level supervision to discuss problems of joint interest. Worker consultation exists at different levels in different departments, stresses Hertog, who attributes the difference to the level of maturity of the group itself: "In some groups we're still at the flower pot phase, talking about what should be done to improve meals in the cafeteria, while at other extremes we have departments where we have left the selection of a new supervisor for the group up to the workers."

It's significant that those groups who have considered the question of job redesign consistently have criticized Philips for not doing more of it. The expansion of job redesign, in part, would seem to depend on the expansion of work consultation and the pressures exerted by the workers themselves to get job redesign extended.

Job Redesign at Saab-Scania

To claim that Saab-Scania has abolished the auto assembly line would misrepresent the facts. Saab-Scania, or to speak more precisely, the Scania Division, has instituted small-group assembly of auto engines—not the whole car—in its new engine plant. Even so, this effort is limited to 50 employees in a plant with a workforce of approximately 300, most of whom monitor automatic transfer machines that perform various machining tasks. There's only one manual loading operation in the entire machining process.

More important, the humanization of the auto assembly line is the most dramatic single instance in a series starting in 1969 that Palle Berggen, the head of the industrial engineering department, characterized as "one phase in the development of enhanced industrial democracy."

We won't quarrel with his description, although we think he succumbed to the rhetoric of public relations. Scania, in its actions from 1969 on, has responded to some problems for which the best word is horrendous. Employee turnover was running around 45 percent annually, and in the auto assembly plant, 70 percent. Absenteeism was also extraordinary—close to 20 percent. Under such conditions, the maintenance of an even flow of production, something crucial in an integrated work system like Scania's, presented insuperable problems. Also, it was increasingly difficult to fill jobs on the shop floor at all. A survey taken in 1969 indicates what Scania was up against: Only four out of 100 students graduating from high school in Sweden indicated their willingness to take a rank-and-file factory job. In consequence, Scania became heavily dependent on foreign workers—58 percent of the current workforce are non-Swedes. This in turn created problems, both expected and otherwise—among the former, problems of training and communications, among the latter, an epidemic of wildcat strikes, previously unknown in Sweden, that largely resulted from the manipulation by extreme left elements of foreign workers ignorant of the tradition among Swedish employees of almost total reliance upon the strong trade union organization to protect their interests.

Any response to these conditions *had* to have as its number one objective the maintenance of productivity. To assert anything else is window dressing—unconvincing as well as unnecessary. No one can fault an industrial organization for undertaking a program whose primary goal is the maintenance of productivity.

This is not to deny that one byproduct of the program has been "enhanced industrial democracy." What happened is that the pursuit of productivity led to an examination of the conditions that created job satisfactions; these, in turn, suggested the series of actions "that enhance industrial democracy"—a term subject to almost as many definitions as there are interpreters.

Production Groups and Development Groups   Employee representation is nothing new at Scania. Like every company in Sweden with more than 50 employees, it's had an employee-elected Works Council since 1949. However, these bodies have no decision-making function; their role is limited to receiving and responding to information from top management, and their effectiveness depends on the willingness of top management to seriously consider suggestions from the Works Council. David Jenkins, in his recent book *Job Power,* tells of asking a company president if he had ever been influenced by worker suggestions. His reply: "Well, yes. We were going to build a new plant and we showed the workers the plans at one of the meetings. They objected very much to the fact that the plant would have no windows. So we changed the plans and had some windows put in. It doesn't cost much more and, actually, the building looks better. And the workers feel better."

The production and development groups initiated in the truck chassis assembly plant in 1969, by contrast, have real decision-making power. Production groups of five to 12 workers with related job duties decide among themselves how they will do their jobs, within the quality and production standards defined by higher management; they can rotate job assignments—do a smaller or larger part of the overall task. At the same time, the jobs of all members of the production group were enlarged by making them jointly responsible for simple service and maintenance activities, housekeeping, and quality control in their work area, duties formerly performed by staff personnel.

Development groups, a parallel innovation, consist of foremen, industrial engineers, and two representatives of one or more production groups whose function is to consider ideas for improving work methods and working conditions. Representatives of the production groups are rotated in a way that guarantees that every member of a production group will serve each year on a development group.

Employee reception of the production group has been mixed but largely positive. The results appear to be favorable, although Scania has done little or nothing to measure them quantitatively. However, impressions have been sufficiently favorable so that within four years production and development groups have expanded to include 2,200 out of the 3,600 employees in the main plant at Södertälje, and within the year they will be extended throughout the company.

Work Design in the Engine Plant   The four machine lines for the components in the engine factory—the cylinder block, the cylinder head, the connecting rod, and the crankshaft—mainly consist of transfer machines manned or monitored by individual operations. Group assembly is restricted to the seven final assembly stations, each of which contains a team of fitters that assemble an entire engine.

Team members divide the work among themselves; they may decide to do one-third of the assembly on each engine—a ten-minute chore—or follow the engine around the bay and assemble the entire engine—a 30-minute undertaking. In fact, only a minority prefer to do the total assembly job. (Using traditional assembly line methods, each operation would have taken 1.8 minutes.) The team also decides its own work pace, and the number and duration of work breaks within the overall requirement of assembling 470 engines in each ten-day period, a specification that allows them a good deal of flexibility in their pacing. Incidentally, over half the employees in the engine plant are women, while the assembly teams are over 80 percent female. We personally saw four assembly teams with only a single man in the lot.

Benefits and Costs   Kaj Holmelius, who is responsible for planning and coordination of the production engineering staff, ticked off the principal credits and debits, along with a few gray areas in which it would be premature to estimate results. On the plus side, he cited the following:

   1   Group assembly has increased the flexibility of the plant, making it easier to adjust to heavy absenteeism.
   2   The group assembly concept is responsible for a lower balancing loss due to a longer station time.
   3   Less money is invested in assembly tools. Even allowing for the fact that you have to buy six or seven times as many tools, the simpler tools make for a smaller overall cost.
   4   Quality has definitely improved, although by how much it's hard to estimate.
   5   Productivity is higher than it would have been with the conventional assembly line—although once more, there is no proof. Lower production speed per engine, because it's not economical to use some very expensive automatic tools, is outweighed by higher quality and reduced turnover.

6 Employee attitudes have improved, although there have been no elaborate surveys taken. To Holmelius the best indication of job satisfaction is that it's impossible to fill all the requests to transfer from other parts of the plant to the assembly teams.

On the negative side, in addition to the reduced production speed, group assembly takes up considerably more space than the conventional assembly line.

In the neutral corner is the impact on absenteeism and turnover. Absenteeism is actually higher in the engine plant—18 percent versus 15 percent for overall plant operations at Södertälje. However, Holmelius attributes the difference to the fact that the engine plant employs a heavier percentage of women. As for turnover, with the plant in operation for a little more than a year, it's too early to tell. Because of an economic slowdown, turnover generally is down from the 45 percent crisis level of 1969 to 20 percent, and it's Holmelius' belief that turnover in the assembly teams will prove significantly lower than average.

What's the Future of Group Assembly?   It's easier to point out the directions in which Scania does *not* plan to extend group assembly. An experiment with having employees assemble an entire truck diesel engine—a six-hour undertaking involving 1,500 parts—was abandoned at the employees' request; they couldn't keep track of all the parts. Similarly, group assembly wouldn't work with the body of the trucks—truck bodies are too complex, and group assembly would require twice the space currently needed. The moot question at the moment is car assembly. So far, group assembly has been applied only to assembling doors. We suspect that in any decision, economic calculations will predominate, including, of course, the inherently fuzzy calculation about the economic value of job satisfaction.

Job Redesign at Volvo

Job redesign at Volvo began, almost accidentally, in the upholstery shop of the car assembly plant during the mid-1960s, but a companywide effort had to wait until 1969, when Volvo faced the same problems that plagued Scania—wildcat strikes, absenteeism, and turnover that were getting out of hand and an increasing dependence on foreign workers. Turnover was over 40 percent annually; absenteeism was running 20 to 25 percent, and close to 45 percent of the employees of the car assembly plant were non-Swedes. One other event in 1971 made a difference: Volvo acquired a young, hard-driving new managing director, Pehr Gyllenhammar, who developed a keen interest in the new methods of work organization.

Ingvar Barrby, head of the upholstery department, started job redesign by persuading production management to experiment with job rotation along the lines he had read about in Norway. The overwhelmingly female workforce complained frequently about the inequity of the various jobs involved in assembling car seats; some jobs were easier than others, while still others were more comfortable and less strenuous, and so on. To equalize the tasks, Barrby divided the job into 13 different operations and rotated the employees among tasks that were relatively arduous and those that were relatively comfortable. Jealousy and bickering among employees disappeared: First, jobs were no longer inequitable; second, employees perceived that they had exaggerated the differences between jobs anyway—the grass-is-greener syndrome. More important, turnover that had been running 35 percent quickly fell to 15 percent, a gain that has been maintained over the years.

Job Alternation and "Multiple Balances"   Volvo uses these phrases instead of the more commonly used job rotation and job enrichment, but the concepts are the same. In job alternation or job rotation, the employee changes jobs once or several times daily, depending on the nature of the work in his group. Take Line IV A, for example, whose function is to do the external and internal sealing and insulation of car bodies. Because internal sealing is such uncomfortable work—employees work in cramped positions inside the car body—the work is alternated every other hour. The remaining jobs are rotated daily.

"Multiple balances" is our old friend, job enrichment, under another name. One example involves the overhead line where the group follows the same body for seven or eight stations along the line for a total period of 20 minutes—seven or eight times the length of the average job cycle.

Not all employees have had their jobs rotated or enriched—only 1,500 out of 7,000 in the car assembly at Torslanda are affected by the program. Because participation is strictly voluntary, the figures at first glance seem to indicate a massive show of disinterest on the part of Volvo employees. Not so. True, some employees prefer their jobs the way they are. The bigger problem is that Volvo has, to date, lacked the technical resources to closely scrutinize many jobs to determine whether and how they can be enlarged or enriched, or it has scrutinized them and determined that it isn't economically feasible to enlarge or enrich them. A company spokesman gave the job of coating under the car body to prevent rust as an example of a thoroughly unpleasant job that so far has defied redesign.

Production Teams at Volvo Lundbyverken   In the truck assembly plant at Lundbyverken, Volvo has carried job redesign several steps further, with production teams who, in form and function, roughly duplicate the production groups previously described at Scania. The production team, a group of five to 12 men with a common work assignment, elects its own chargehand, schedules its own output within the standards set by higher management, distributes work among its members, and is responsible for its own quality control. In these teams, group piecework replaces individual piecework and everyone earns the same amount, with the exception of the chargehand. Currently, there are 23 production teams involving 100 out of the plant's 1,200 employees. Plans call for the gradual extension of the production team approach to cover most, if not all, of the factory workforce.

The Box Score at Volvo   Have the various forms of job redesign, job rotation, job enrichment, and production teams paid off for Volvo? If so, what forms have the payoff taken? Anything we can measure or monetize? Or are we reduced to subjective impressions and interesting although iffy conjectures about the relationship between factors such as increased job satisfaction and reduced turnover?

The two plants deserve separate consideration: Absenteeism and turnover traditionally have been lower at the truck assembly plant than at the car assembly plant. The jobs are inherently more complex and interesting—even before job enrichment, some individual jobs took up to half an hour. The workers, in turn, are more highly skilled and tend to regard themselves as apart from and above the rank-and-file auto worker. They see themselves more as junior engineers. Within this context, it's still true that the introduction of production teams has led to further improvement: less labor turnover, less absenteeism, an improvement in quality, and fewer final adjustments.

At the auto assembly plant the picture isn't clear. Turnover is down from 40 to 25 percent. However, an economic slowdown undoubtedly accounts for some of the decline, while other actions unrelated to job redesign may account for part of the remainder. When Volvo surveyed its employees to probe for the causes of turnover and absenteeism, most of the causes revealed were external—problems with housing, child care, long distances traveling to the plant, and so on. Volvo responded with a series of actions to alleviate these causes, such as extending the bus fleet, together with the community, to transport employees, loaning money to employees to purchase apartments at very favorable rates of interest, putting pressure on the community to expand day care centers, and so on. Such measures presumably contributed to the decline of turnover. Nevertheless, Gyllenhammar is convinced that "we can see a correlation between increased motivation, increased satisfaction on the job, and a decrease in the turnover of labor." Absenteeism is a sadly different picture: It's double what it was five years ago, a condition that Gyllenhammar attributes to legislation enabling workers to stay off the job at practically no cost to themselves.

As for output in that part of the auto assembly plant covered by job enrichment or job enlargement, there was no measurable improvement. Quality, on balance, has improved, and the feeling is that improved quality and decreased turnover had more than covered the costs of installing the program.

The Future of Job Redesign at Volvo   Despite the relatively ambiguous success of Volvo's job redesign efforts, whatever Volvo has done in the past is a pale prologue to its future plans. In about nine months, Volvo's new auto assembly plant at Kalmar will go on stream. And, for once, that overworked term "revolutionary" would seem justified.

Physically, the plant is remarkable. Gyllenhammar describes it as "shaped like a star and on each point of the star you have a work group finishing a big share of the whole automobile—for example, the electrical system or the safety system or the interior." Assembly work takes place along the outer walls, while component parts are stored in the center of the building. Architecturally, the building has been designed to preserve the atmosphere of a small workshop in a large factory, with each work team having its own entrance, dressing room, rest room, and so on. Each team is even physically shielded from a view of the other teams.

Each work team, of 15 to 25 men, will distribute the work among themselves and determine their own work rhythm, subject to the requirement of meeting production standards. If the team decides to drive hard in the morning and loaf in the afternoon, the decision is theirs to make. As with production teams in the truck assembly plant, the team will choose its own boss, and deselect him if he turns out poorly.

The new plant will cost about 10 percent more—some 10 million Swedish kroner—than a comparable conventional auto assembly plant. Time alone will tell whether the extra investment will be justified by the decreased turnover, improved quality, and even reduced absenteeism that its designers confidently expect at the new facility. In announcing the plan for the new factory, Gyllenhammar's economic objectives were modest enough, his social objectives more ambitious. "A way must be found to create a workplace that meets the needs of the modern working man for a sense of purpose and satisfaction in his daily work. A way must be found of attaining this goal without an adverse effect on productivity." With luck, he may achieve both.

What Does It Add Up to?

On the basis of what we learned at Philips, Saab-Scania, and Volvo, what answers—tentative and partial—do we have to the seven questions that we raised earlier in the article? Or are the results of the programs so ambiguous and inconclusive that, as long as we restrict ourselves to the context of these three companies, we must beg off attempting to answer some of the questions at all? That none of the companies answered all of the questions, and that many of the answers rely on subjective impressions haphazardly assembled, rather than on quantitative data systematically collected, of necessity, limit our answers, but they don't prevent us from presenting them—with the appropriate caveats.

1   *What conditions on the assembly line are economically favorable to which forms of job redesign?* The basic question here is under what conditions can a man-paced assembly line replace a machine-paced assembly line? Unless this is economically feasible, no form of job redesign is likely to be adopted. Even allowing for rhetoric, none of our three companies—and no other organization of which we are aware—has indicated a willingness to suffer economic losses in order to increase the satisfactions employees might feel if they switched over from machine-paced to man-paced assembly lines. Take the case of manufacturing a pair of man's pants in a garment factory. Give the job to one man and he will take half a day; divide the work among many people on a line with each one using advanced technical equipment, and it takes one man-hour to produce a pair of trousers. The future of job redesign is not bright in a pants factory.

The man-paced assembly line, however, has a couple of widely recognized advantages over the machine-paced line: First, it's much less sensitive to disruption; the whole line doesn't have to stop because of one breakdown—human or technical; second, extensive and costly rebalancing need not be undertaken every time production is increased or decreased. You simply add more people or groups. Of course, there are advantages to machine-paced production, the outstanding one being speed of production, which depends, in turn, on an even flow of production.

There's the rub—and there's the number one cause for job redesign, certainly at Volvo and Saab-Scania. Absenteeism and turnover had risen to the point where they canceled out the economic advantages of machine-paced production. At the same time, evidence had accumulated that job redesign organized around a man-paced assembly line might strike at the root causes of inordinate turnover and absenteeism.

If you look at the design of the new engine plant at Scania, it incorporates Drucker's insight that "the worker is put to use to use a poorly designed one-purpose machine tool, but repetition and uniformity are two qualities in which human beings are weakest. In everything but the ability to judge and coordinate, machines can perform better than man." In the new engine plant, everything that can be automated economically has been—probably 90 percent of the total task—with the final assembly paced by teams on the assumption that the relatively slight increases in production time will be more than compensated for by better balancing and decreased disruption—improvements inherent in the technical change—and improvements in quality, turnover, and absenteeism, the anticipated byproducts of job satisfaction.

The results, as you have seen, are sketchy. However, we can affirm that none of the three organizations, by their own testimony, has lost economically by the changeover from a machine-paced to a man-paced assembly line. How much they have gained is decidedly a more iffy question.

2 *Do many employees resent and resist job redesign? Do they prefer monotonous, repetitive work?* A flip answer might be "God only knows—and he isn't talking." Any answer, at best, is based largely on conjecture. Joseph E. Godfrey asserts that "workers may complain about monotony, but years spent in the factories lead me to believe that they like to do their jobs automatically. If you interject new things you spoil the rhythm of the job and work gets fouled up." As head of the General Motors Assembly Line Division he is qualified, but biased. But even Fred Herzberg, whose bias is obviously in the other direction, concedes that "individual reaction to job enrichment is as difficult to forecast in terms of attitudes as it is in terms of performance. Not all persons welcome having their job enriched." The Survey Research Center at The University of Michigan in a 1969 study concluded that factors such as having a "nutrient supervisor, receiving adequate help, having few labor standard problems all seem to relate at least as closely to job satisfaction as having a challenging job with 'enriching demands.'" One thing does seem clear: Assuming the job level is held constant, education is inversely related to satisfaction. And when Pehr Gyllenhammar foresaw a near future in which 90 percent of the Swedish popula-

tion would at least have graduated from high school, he was realistically antici-
pating a situation in which Volvo would become almost entirely dependent on
foreign employees unless it found ways of enriching the auto assembly jobs.

3 *Are the "best" results from job redesign obtained when it's at its most
thorough (job rotation plus job enrichment plus autonomy plus employee participation)? Work in America* flatly endorses the thesis that "it is imperative that
employers be made aware of the fact that thorough efforts to redesign work, not
simply 'job enrichment' or 'job rotation,' have resulted in increases of productivity from 5 to 40 percent. In no instance of which we have evidence has a major
effort to increase employee participation resulted in a long-term decline in
productivity." Obviously, in this context "best" results means increased productivity.

Before we can answer the question and respond to the claims asserted in
Work in America a few definitions are necessary. Most descriptions of the
elements that enter into a satisfying job concentrate on three: (1) variety, (2)
responsibility, and (3) autonomy. Variety defines itself. Responsibility is more
complex; it involves both working on a sufficiently large part of the total job to
feel that it is a meaningful experience, and also having a sufficient amount of
control over what you are doing to feel personally responsible.

Companies responding to this need for more responsibility may add set-up
and inspection to the employee's duties or ask him to assemble one-third of an
engine instead of a single component—both examples of horizontal job enrichment; and the employee may be permitted to control the pace at which he
works—an example of vertical job enrichment. Everything that is subsumed
under vertical job enrichment is included in autonomy but it also means something else and something more—giving to the employee himself some control
over how his job should be enlarged or enriched—a clear demarcation point
between almost all American approaches to job enrichment and some European.

We're describing a circular process; the worker in Sweden and The Netherlands places a higher value on autonomy than the worker in the United States.
Therefore, job redesign that incorporates increased autonomy for the employee
will be more appreciated and lead to more job satisfaction than comparable
efforts would in the United States. Here, Huey Long's concept of a satisfying
job, with allowances for the regional overtones, and the hyperbole, still makes
sense: "There shall be a real job, not a little old sowbelly black-eyed pea job, but
a real spending money beefsteak, and gray Chevrolet Ford in the garage, new
suit, Thomas Jefferson, Jesus Christ, red, white, and blue job for every man."
The employee did then and still does define, although to a progressively decreasing degree, a satisfying job in terms of how much it pays. For a measure of the
difference, take the definition of a dissatisfying job by Malin Lofgren, a 12-year-
old Swedish schoolboy: "A bad job is one where others make all the decisions,
and you have to do what others say."

Now that the tedious, although necessary, business of definition is out of the
way, how do we answer the question with reference to our three companies?
Inconclusively. If we define "best" results in terms of gains in productivity, the

only certifiable gain occurred with the Philips production groups that scored high on both horizontal and vertical job enrichment, and in which employees were consulted in advance about the ways in which their job should be enriched. In the body of the article, we didn't go into their institutional arrangements, but suffice it to say that both Saab-Scania and Volvo have comparable consultative institutions. Thus, the autonomy factor assumes less significance. The only significant differences would appear to be: (1) The increased status caused by making the production groups at Philips wholly responsible for liaison with other departments, (2) the Hawthorne, or, as the Philips personnel call it, the "Princess" effect—the groups having been visited and complimented by such dignitaries as Queen Juliana and Marshal Tito. On the other hand, the groups at Volvo that chose their own supervisors—certainly a measure of autonomy—have not increased their productivity. Quality, turnover, attendance had improved. But with productivity, there was no measurable impact.

4   *Is there any single element in job redesign that seems to account for the biggest increase in employee satisfaction?* In a word—no. But that requires an explanation. Our failure to respond principally reflects lack of evidence; none of the organizations concerned asked themselves the question. None tried on any systematic basis to relate what they were doing in redesigning jobs to what they were accomplishing in increased job satisfaction. Word-of-mouth testimony and more cheerful figures—as in the case of Volvo and Saab-Scania with turnover—seemed sufficient to confirm the efficacy of past efforts and sanction future ones, on similar although expanded lines.

5   *What are the benefits of job redesign—both those we can measure and monetize and those that can only be described?* We begin with a proposition shared by a generation of social scientists who have studied the problem and attempted to answer the question: Employee attitudes and job satisfaction are correlated much more clearly with factors such as absenteeism, turnover, and quality than they are with productivity.

The three companies reinforce this finding. Only one experiment at Philips establishes a positive correlation between job satisfaction and productivity, while several—Philips with productivity groups in Phase III, Saab-Scania in the engine plant and the truck assembly plant, and Volvo in its truck plant—all report improvements in quality, the problem in each case being the absence of quantifiable data. Turnover is another area in which the responses are positive, but suggestive rather than conclusive—"probably lower" in the Scania engine plant; lower in the truck assembly plant; down in both the truck assembly and auto assembly plant at Volvo—but there are no firm figures at the Volvo truck assembly line, while the decrease in turnover at the auto assembly plant is partly attributed to causes unrelated to job redesign. Philips proffers no comparisons of absenteeism or turnover before and after job redesign. All we know is that so far no one in the production groups has decided to quit. In short, the evidence—what there is of it—is positive, but fragmented and based more on impressions than on data.

6   *On balance, does management gain as much from job redesign as the employee whose job is redesigned?* A two-headed question that logically requires both extensive employee attitude surveys before and after job redesign, along with firm measurements that demonstrate the impact of job redesign on factors such as quality, output, absenteeism, and turnover. As we have seen, we have very little of either. The only attitude surveys were first, the one conducted at the Volvo auto assembly plant to determine the causes of excessive absenteeism and turnover—most of which had nothing to do with job satisfaction and where the subsequent substantial drop in turnover at best could only partially be ascribed to job redesign—and the survey at Philips, where the switchover from machine-paced to man-paced assembly line improved employees' satisfaction with their jobs.

On balance, as previously stated, management has achieved at least an economic draw from its efforts at job redesign, along with a measure of insurance against a fretful future in which employee expectations will become increasingly difficult to fulfill and the job redesign carried out or contemplated will, it is hoped, help to meet those expectations.

As for the satisfactions the employees have gained from the collective efforts at enlarging and enriching their jobs, we can only guess. We have a few pieces of anecdotal evidence, such as the flood of applications to work in the final assembly at Scania's engine plant, or the absence of turnover among the production groups at Philips. In short, we know too little to generalize.

7   *Last, what's the impact of the overall culture and political system on job redesign? What's the evidence, pro or con, that the success of job redesign at Volvo, Saab-Scania, or Philips—or lack of it—would be replicated in similar assembly lines in the United States?* Technologically, there are no convincing reasons why assembly lines in new automobile factories or television plants in the United States couldn't be redesigned along lines similar to what has been done at Philips, Saab-Scania, and Volvo. It might prove prohibitively expensive in existing plants—after all, job redesign at Volvo's auto assembly plant was largely restricted, on economic grounds, to job rotation. However, new plants in the United States should present no more inherent problems of job redesign than new plants in Sweden. Yet auto executives in the United States have gone on record as feeling that the situation is hopeless. A 1970 report of the Ford Foundation found that none of the corporation executives interviewed "really believe that assembly line tasks can be significantly restructured," and "no one really believes that much can be done to make the assembly jobs more attractive."

Not that all the features of job redesign at Philips, Saab-Scania, and Volvo are equally exportable. The three companies exist in a different political and social ethos, one in which both management and the workers have gone much further in accepting the idea of employee participation in decision making than all but a handful of managers and a small minority of workers in the United States. A survey of Swedish managers in 1970, for example, showed that 75 percent favored more employee decision making in all departments. Even the idea of replacing the decision of the supervisor with collective employee decisions elicited a favorable response from 11 percent of the managers. Given this different ethos, it is not surprising that all three companies have experimented with what would be in the United States the radical step of either dispensing with first-level supervision or leaving it up to the employees to choose their own supervisor. It is a form of autonomy that few managements in the United States would consider for an instant, and one in which few employees would take much interest.

But why not consider it, as long as management continues to set overall standards of production and quality and to hold the group responsible for meeting them? The experiment of having employees choose their own bosses with the experimental groups in the truck assembly plant at Volvo works so well that it has been incorporated as one of the basic design features in the new auto assembly plant. Employees demonstrated that, given the opportunity, they would choose as leaders men who could organize the work and maintain order and discipline.

Let's indulge in speculation. The single quality that most clearly distinguishes between the efforts at job enrichment here and in the three companies we visited is the emphasis abroad on letting the employees have a part—and sometimes a decisive part—in deciding how their jobs should be enriched. By contrast, most exponents of job enrichment in the United States take the "papa-knows-best" approach. Fred Herzberg, the best-known work psychologist, asserts that when people took part in deciding how to change their own jobs, "the results were disappointing." We suspect that Herzberg's real objection is not to the results themselves, but to the difficulty of selling most managements on the idea that employee participation should be an integral part of any process of job enrichment. The experiences at Volvo, Saab-Scania, and Philips suggest that the objection to the employee's participating in how his own job should be enriched or redesigned has its roots in symbolism, rather than substance, in the irrational preoccupation with management prerogatives, rather than in any real or potential threat to productivity or profits.

What about the future? Technologically, there seem to be no compelling reasons why Ford, G.M., and Chrysler cannot take a leaf from Volvo and Saab-Scania. Whether they will is another question. The combination of inertia, custom, and commitment is a formidable one. So far the automakers have chosen to move in the opposite direction: shorter work cycles, smaller jobs, more rapidly moving lines. We should recall that it took a crisis—nothing less than the probability that most people would refuse to work at all or only for uneconomic periods on the jobs the organization had to offer them—to "break the cake of custom" at Volvo and Saab-Scania. Even today, it is clear that there are limits to which auto assembly jobs can be enriched, a limitation obvious in Gyllenhammar's bitter observation that "'absenteeism with pay' is based on the very utopian hypothesis that people love to work, and no matter what happens they will strive to go to their job every morning." Still, the situation he is in is preferable to the situation he faced. And some of the difference is due to job redesign.

We suspect that it will take a crisis of similar magnitude, together with the belief that they have no choice, to unfreeze the attitudes of automakers in the United States and get them moving in the direction of man-paced assembly lines and the forms of job redesign they facilitate. That such a development, over the long run, is in the cards we strongly believe, but how long it will take for the cards to show up, we leave to the astrologers.

Does Job Enrichment Really Pay Off?

William E. Reif
Fred Luthans

During the last few years, behavior-oriented management scholars and practitioners have generally extolled the virtues of Frederick Herzberg's job enrichment approach to employee motivation. Much of the management literature, especially journals aimed at the practicing manager, propose that "Job Enrichment Pays Off."[1] Lately, it has become commonplace for behavioral scientists to criticize Herzberg's research methodology but then admit the overall motivational value of the technique of job enrichment.[2] Only in a few instances have scholars or, especially, practitioners, seriously questioned the motivating effect of job enrichment. It is widely felt to be an excellent way of motivating employees in today's organizations.

In the mad dash to modernize and get away from the Theory X (Douglas McGregor) or Systems I and II (Rensis Likert) or Immaturity (Chris Argyris) or 9,1 (Robert Blake and Jane Mouton) approaches to the management of people, both professors of management and practicing managers may be guilty of the same thing: blindly accepting and over-generalizing about the first seemingly logical, practical and viable alternative to old style management—Herzberg's job enrichment. It now seems time to take a step back, settle down, and take a hard look at the true value that job enrichment has for motivating employees. Does job enrichment really pay off or is it merely a convenient crutch used by professors and practitioners to be modern in their approach to the management of human resources? This article attempts to provide another point of view and play the devil's advocate in critically analyzing job enrichment.

Enrichment or Enlargement?

The logical starting point in the analysis would be to see how, if at all, job enrichment differs from the older job enlargement concept. Although Herzberg,

M. Scott Myers, Robert Ford and others portray job enrichment as one step beyond job enlargement, the real difference may lie more in the eyes of the definer than any actual differences in practice. The distinction between the terms becomes even cloudier when concepts such as job extension and job rotation enter the discussion. The differences between these various terms can perhaps best be depicted on a continuum of variety, responsibility, and personal growth on the job. Most job enrichment advocates carefully point out that enrichment, relative to rotation, extension, and enlargement, infers that there is greater variety, more responsibility, and increased opportunity for personal growth. Yet, for practical purposes, the differences, especially between enlargement and enrichment, may be more semantic than real. Researchers who have studied job enlargement define their term almost exactly the same way that Herzberg defines job enrichment.

Job Variety, Responsibility & Growth

Low   *High*

| Rotation | Extension | Enlargement | Enrichment |

Conclusions from Research

To develop a framework of analysis for job enrichment, conclusions from research must first be summarized. William Reif and Peter Schoderbek's 1965 study revealed that 81 percent of the firms which responded to a mailed questionnaire survey were not using job enlargement. Of the 19 percent (forty-one firms) who were using the concept, only four indicated their experience was "very successful."[3] A more recent National Industrial Conference Board study disclosed that even though 80 percent of the responding companies expressed interest in the behavioral sciences, that even though 90 percent replied that their executives read books and articles about the behavioral sciences, and that more than 75 percent sent their executives to outside courses and seminars dealing with behavioral science concepts, there were very few firms which indicated they had put such concepts into actual practice.[4] Although a number of companies stated they were engaged in some form of job design activity, the N.I.C.B. study revealed that few have made any *sustained* effort in redesigning jobs.

The two companies which are cited most often in discussions of job enrichment are Texas Instruments and American Telephone and Telegraph. The two are given as examples of the outstanding success that can be attained when applying the job enrichment concept. However, one may question what constitutes "success." For example, Mitchell Fein, a long-time industrial engineer, assessed the Texas Instruments' job enrichment program as follows:

> Texas Instruments' management was probably more dedicated to job enrichment than any other company in the world. They earnestly backed their managing philosophies with millions of dollars of efforts. After 15 years of unrelenting diligence,

management announced in its 1968 report to the stockholders its program for "increasing human effectiveness," with the objective: "Our goal is to have approximately 10,000 TI men and women involved in team improvement efforts by the end of 1968 or 1969." Since TI employed 60,000, the program envisioned involving only 16 percent of its work force. The total involved was actually closer to 10 percent.[5]

In another instance, Robert Ford, who has been primarily responsible for implementing job enrichment in AT&T, reports, "Of the nineteen studies, nine were rated 'outstandingly successful,' one was a complete 'flop,' and the remaining nine were 'moderately successful.'"[6] Even more noteworthy perhaps is the fact that although Ford does not hesitate to generalize from the nineteen studies, he appears at one point to question his own optimism over the applicability of and benefits derived from job enrichment. He states: "No claim is made that these 19 trials cover a representative sample of jobs and people within the Bell system. For example, there were no trials among the manufacturing or laboratory employees, nor were all operating companies involved. There are more than a thousand different jobs in the Bell system, not just the nine in these studies."[7]

In an early study (1958), James Kennedy and Harry O'Neill published findings on the effects job enlargement had had on the opinions and attitudes of workers in an automobile assembly plant. Attitude surveys were given to both assembly line workers whose jobs were highly routine, unskilled, and paced by the assembly line, and to utility men whose jobs were quite varied. The results showed no statistical difference between the two sets of scores. This finding led Kennedy and O'Neill to conclude:

If job content is a factor in determining how favorably workers view their supervisors and their work situation, the difference in content apparently must be along more fundamental dimensions than those observed in this study.[8]

In 1968, Charles Hulin and Milton Blood conducted an in-depth study of job enlargement. They concluded that, "The case for job enlargement has been drastically overstated and overgeneralized. . . . Specifically, the argument for larger jobs as a means of motivating workers, decreasing boredom and dissatisfaction, and increasing attendance and productivity is valid only when applied to certain segments of the work force—white-collar and supervisory workers and nonalienated blue-collar workers."[9]

Unfortunately, these studies are not widely cited in the management literature. Instead, a number of widely known and quoted management oriented behavioral scientists, among them Herzberg, McGregor, Likert, Argyris, and Blake and Mouton, are most often interpreted, sometimes wrongly, to advocate the opposite.[10] The popular position is that job enrichment is a key to successful motivation and productivity and many scholars, consultants, and practitioners actively campaign for its widespread use in modern organizations. McGregor summed up the feelings of job enrichment advocates when he said, "Unless there is opportunity *at work* to satisfy these high level needs (esteem and self-actualization), people will be deprived, and their behavior will reflect this deprivation."[11] In other words, the predominant conclusion is that people have a need to find fulfillment in their work and job enrichment provides them with the opportunity.

Why the wide divergence on the conclusions about job enrichment? Why the differences of opinion not only among scholars but also among practitioners, and between scholars and practitioners, about the efficacy of job enrichment? These are questions that the article tries to answer. The approach taken is to critically analyze the three most important concepts in job enrichment: (1) worker motivation, (2) job design, and (3) resistance to change.

Worker Motivation: One More Time

The stated purpose of early job enlargement programs was to provide job satisfaction for unskilled blue-collar and low level white-collar (clerical) workers whose jobs were highly standardized and repetitive, operated on a short time cycle, required little knowledge and skill, and utilized only a few low-order abilities. Only a cursory review of management literature reveals that the majority of job enlargement programs in existence today are concerned with enriching the jobs of highly skilled workers, technicians, professionals, supervisors and managers, not unskilled blue- and white-collar employees. For example, in the William Paul, Keith Robertson, and Frederick Herzberg article on job enrichment in British companies, *none* of the employees in the studies could be classified as blue-collar workers.[12] Fein reports, "My experience in numerous plants has been that the lower the skills level, the lower the degree to which job enlargement can be established to be meaningful to the employees and management."[13]

The Reif and Schoderbek study discovered that of the firms using job enlargement, 73 percent used it at the supervisory level, 51 percent used it to enlarge clerical jobs, and 49 percent used it in the production area. Of the firms practicing job enlargement in the plant, 35 percent replied that the employees were primarily skilled, while only 15 percent classified the employees on enlarged jobs as unskilled.[14] In follow-up interviews three major reasons clearly emerged why it was more difficult to get unskilled workers to accept job enlargement than skilled or semi-skilled workers: (1) the unskilled prefer the status quo, (2) the unskilled seem to prefer highly specialized work, and (3) the unskilled show a lack of interest in improvements in job design which require learning new skills or assuming greater responsibility. A representative comment was: "Most unskilled workers prefer the routine nature of their jobs, and it has been my experience that they are not eager to accept responsibility or learn new skills."

In a parallel manner, the most frequent response to another question, "What are the major considerations taken into account in determining the particular job(s) to be enlarged?" was "The potential skills of employees." The survey respondents noted that in their experience, the higher the skill level of employees, the greater the probability of success with the enlarged job. Another question was, "What do you consider to be the major disadvantages of job enlargement?" The second most frequent response was that some workers were just not capable of growing with the enlarged job that was designed for them. Follow-up interviews indicated that the workers referred to by the respondents were primarily unskilled and semi-skilled blue-collar workers. Of particular interest was the response from a number of company spokesmen that in their experience many workers seemed capable of growing with the job but simply were not willing to do so. This observation was confirmed in interviews with a number of workers who had declined the opportunity to work on enlarged jobs.

The above results seem to directly contradict the commonly held motivational assumptions made by well-known behavioralists. It has become widely accepted that:

1 *Man seeks and needs meaningful work.*—Many behaviorists would contend that man's psychological well-being is dependent upon his ability to find expression and challenge in his work.

2 *Motivation is a function of job satisfaction and personal freedom.*—As was noted in a comprehensive N.I.C.B. study on job design: "Satisfaction with job content and the freedom to work on a self-sufficient independent basis are viewed as the crucial variables in the motivation to work."[15]

3 *Job content is related to job satisfaction.*—This major assumption is primarily derived from Herzberg's two-factor theory of motivation which provides the foundation for job enrichment. Herzberg implies that people are capable and desirous of greater responsibility and can be positively motivated by work which provides "meaning" to them.

These motivational assumptions do not account for why some workers show little or no interest in job enlargement. Beside the overall social and cultural impact on the values toward work, there are other specific but less widely held assumptions about worker motivation. One possible alternative assumption is that some people actually prefer highly routine, repetitive jobs. Numerous studies have pointed out that repetitive work can have positively motivating characteristics for some workers.[16] For example, Maurice Kilbridge found that assembly line workers in a television factory did not necessarily regard repetitive tasks as dissatisfying or frustrating. Also, the mechanical pacing of the conveyors was not necessarily distasteful to most workers. The Reif and Schoderbek study found that some workers preferred routine tasks because there was little thinking involved, and as a result, they were free to socialize and daydream without impairment to their productivity.[17]

Do these results suggest that workers' attitudes toward work and their ideas of what constitute satisfactory working conditions have gradually conformed to the technical requirements of our modern, industrialized society? For decades scholars and practitioners have been concerned with changing the design of work in order for it to be compatible with the psychological make-up of today's workers. In the meantime, is it possible that scholars and managers alike have failed to observe adaptation of the worker to his environment or, even more important, fundamental changes in the psychological need structure of the individual? Is there any tangible evidence which would give positive support to these intriguing possibilities?

Although not widely known to students of management, there is a small but significant literature which contradicts and is in opposition to the widely held assumptions made by job enrichment advocates. The study by Hulin and Blood is a good example. After closely analyzing practically all relevant research, they conclude that the effects of job enrichment on job satisfaction and worker motivation are generally overstated and in some cases unfounded.[18] Their study raises a number of interesting questions about the popular assumptions of worker motivation and the relationship between job enrichment, job satisfaction, and motivation. They argue that many blue-collar workers are not alienated from the work environment but are alienated from the work norms and values of the middle class. The middle class norms include: (a) positive effect for occupational achievement, (b) a belief in the intrinsic value of hard work, (c) a striving for the attainment of responsible positions, and (d) a belief in the work-related aspects of the Protestant ethic. On the other hand, these blue-collar workers do follow the norms of their own subculture. The implications are that workers who are alienated from middle class values do not actively seek meaning in their work and therefore are not strongly motivated by the job enlargement concept.

Fein's study of blue-collar and white-collar worker motivation came up with essentially the same conclusion. He states:

> Workers do not look upon their work as fulfilling their existence. Their reaction to their work is the opposite of what the behavioralists predict. It is only because *workers choose not to find fulfillment in their work* that they are able to function as healthy human beings. By rejecting involvement in their work which simply cannot be fulfilling, workers save their sanity.[19]

Fein goes on to say:

> . . . the concepts of McGregor and Herzberg regarding workers' needs to find fulfillment through their work are sound *only for those workers who choose to find fulfillment through their work*. In my opinion, this includes about 15–20% of the blue-collar work force. These behavioralists' concepts have little meaning for the others. Contrary to their postulates, the majority of workers seek fulfillment outside their work.[20]

Whether one agrees or disagrees with the above observation, it does raise an interesting point. One could speculate that Fein's 15 to 20 percent is about the proportion of the worker population that David McClelland and David Winter would regard as high achievers.[21] Assuming this percentage were accurate, it would be vitally important to the analysis of job enrichment. It would follow that high achievers are essentially self-motivated and would not require the external stimulus of job enrichment to perform well. By the same token, the low-achievers would not respond to job enrichment because work holds too little meaning for them to be motivated by it. They find satisfaction outside the work place.

Another interesting parallel is provided by Hulin and Blood's analysis of

William F. Whyte's study of rate busters.[22] They contend that Whyte's rate busters rejected the norms of their peer group and accepted the norms of management whereas the "quota restricters" retained their peer group norms. One might safely speculate that Whyte's quota restricters belong to the group known as the "alienated from the work norms of the middle class" workers or McClelland's low-achievers or Fein's 80 to 85 percent. Thus, a plausible answer to the question, "Why isn't job enrichment used more extensively on jobs of blue-collar and low-level white-collar workers?" is that a majority of these workers may not be positively motivated by an enriched job content with the accompanying motivators. Instead, they may be willing to exchange their minimum efforts on the job so that they can live satisfactorily outside the job.

A Re-examination of Job Design

Louis Davis defines job design as the "specification of the contents, methods, and relationships of jobs in order to satisfy technological and organizational requirements as well as the social and personal requirements of the job holder."[23] Traditionally, the technological requirements of work were given primary consideration in designing a job. For example, Frederick W. Taylor's work improvement efforts were directed at the task. Adjustments between technology and human needs were made in terms of the individual's adjustment to the system rather than designing the system to meet human needs. Because of the recent influence of the behavioralists, more emphasis has been devoted to the human aspects of job design. Today, the commonly expressed purpose of job design is to create more meaningful and satisfying work with the assumption being that productivity can be increased not so much by improving the technology as by improving the motivational climate.

Job enrichment is very compatible with "work is a human as well as a technical process" approach to job design. The conceptual similarity between job enrichment and the human approach to job design is very evident in the two factor motivation theory of Frederick Herzberg.[24] According to Herzberg, motivation is intrinsic to the job and the true rewards (achievement, recognition, work itself, responsibility, advancement, growth) come from doing the work, from performing effectively on the job. Many other behaviorally oriented theorists are in agreement with Herzberg's emphasis on job content, notably Argyris and McGregor who both express the desire to redesign jobs so they are capable of fulfilling esteem and self-actualization needs.

If Herzberg is correct, why hasn't job enrichment been more readily implemented into modern organizations? Possibly one of the major reasons is the failure to fully understand the significance of that part of job design which is concerned with meeting the social and personal requirements of the job holder. Everyone agrees that work is a social activity and probably most would agree that the framework for social interaction is largely an outgrowth of technology, the specific task, and the authority relationships prescribed by the formal organization. As a result, the social system or informal organization is usually structured along the lines of plant layout, machine processes, job specifications, the physical proximity of workers to each other, and operating policies and procedures. Finally, most would agree that the social system is an important means of fulfilling workers' needs for companionship, affection, reputation, prestige, respect, and status; of providing for interpersonal communication; and of helping protect the integrity and self-concept of the individual. This conclusion is brought out in a classic statement by Chester Barnard:

> The essential need of the individual is association, and that requires local activity or immediate interaction between individuals. Without it the man is lost. The willingness of men to endure onerous routine and dangerous tasks which they could avoid is explained by this necessity for action at all costs in order to maintain the sense of social integration, whether the latter arises from "instinct," or from social conditioning, or from physiological necessity, or all three.[25]

It is entirely possible that for many blue-collar workers, the affiliation motive is much stronger than the Herzberg "motivators" to which job enrichment is aimed. Enriched job designs that reduce the opportunities for social interaction may have a negative rather than positive impact on worker satisfaction and productivity. The Reif and Schoderbek study found a number of workers dissatisfied with the job enrichment program for this reason. A typical response was: "I don't see my old friends anymore except during coffee breaks and at lunch. On the line a bunch of us used to talk and tell jokes all the time."[26] For these workers the only satisfaction they had experienced at work was their interaction and identification with other members of their primary group. It should not be surprising that they expressed an unwillingness to give up their group membership for the promise of more meaningful work through job enrichment. To them, a newly enriched job which threatened to destroy the established social pattern was unacceptable.

Resistance to Change: The Dilemma of Job Enrichment

In the Reif and Schoderbek study, the most frequent reply (almost half of firms using job enlargement) to the inquiry "What are the major problems encountered in applying job enlargement?" was "overcoming resistance to change." By far the most frequent response to another question, "What are the major problems experienced by the workers in adjusting to job enlargement?" was "adjustment to increased duties."[27] It became clear during follow-up interviews that the two answers were related. This led to a specific investigation of why workers would resist the opportunity to work on enlarged jobs. Four basic reasons emerged as to why workers resisted job enlargement:

- First, there was anxiety expressed by some workers who felt they would not be able to learn the new and modified skills required by the job enlargement design. Was this lack of confidence in one's ability to perform efficiently on the new job justified? The answer appeared to be yes. Most of the routine jobs did not require a great amount of skill and initiative. The very routine nature of a job reduced the possibility that an employee could ever develop the necessary knowledge and skills required by the enlarged or enriched job design.

- Closely related to the feeling of inadequacy was the fear of failure. Many workers spend years developing the skills which make them highly proficient at their present jobs. Why change now? Why give up a job which affords a relatively high degree of security for one which requires learning new skills, adjusting to unfamiliar methods and operating procedures, and establishing new working relationships? Furthermore, it should be recognized that over time most workers become highly competent in performing specialized, routine tasks. Despite the seemingly unchallenging nature of a job, the worker develops a sense of pride in knowing he can execute his job better than anyone else. This feeling of accomplishment, however limited it may appear to academicians and managers, may give the employee cause to decline an offer, or react negatively, to an enriched job.
- Third, employees' attitudes toward change can be influenced by their relationship with superiors. As workers become highly proficient in their jobs, they require less direct supervision and, as a result, achieve a high degree of freedom and independence. This feeling can be quite satisfying to the worker. Initially, the move to an enriched job would require closer and more frequent supervision, especially if the worker has to rely on his supervisor for the training necessary to master new and often more difficult job skills. Going from a state of independence to even a temporary state of dependence may not be welcomed by the worker.
- A fourth reason for resisting job enrichment is characteristic of any change, at work or otherwise, and is commonly known as psychological habit.

Originally Chester Barnard, and since, many others, believed that psychological habit is a major cause of resisting change. Barnard noted that "Another incentive . . . is that of customary working conditions and conformity to habitual practices and attitudes. . . . It is taken for granted that men will not or cannot do well by strange methods or under strange conditions. What is not so obvious is that men will frequently not attempt to cooperate if they recognize that such methods or conditions are to be accepted."[28] Barnard's argument seems to directly apply to the modern job enrichment technique.

Conclusions

The preceding discussion of worker motivation, job design, and resistance to change was geared toward answering the question of whether job enrichment really pays off. Obviously, there is no simple answer. On the other hand, the preceding analysis of job enrichment has raised some very significant but badly neglected points that need emphasis. These include the following:

1 There seems to be a substantial number of workers who are not necessarily alienated from work but are alienated from the middle class values expressed by the job enrichment concept. For these workers, job content is not automatically related to job satisfaction, and motivation is not necessarily a function of job satisfaction. These alienated workers are capable of finding need satisfaction outside the work environment. If they do experience satisfaction at work, it is not strictly the result of job content or formal job design but instead is largely influenced by social interactions with other primary group members. Job enrichment may not motivate this type of worker.

2   For some workers, improved job design by job enrichment is not seen as an even trade for the reduced opportunity for social interaction. The present job may be considered unpleasant and boring, but breaking up existing patterns or social isolation is completely unbearable.

3   The introduction of a job enrichment program may have a negative impact on some workers and result in feelings of inadequacy, fear of failure, and a concern for dependency. For these employees, low level competency, security, and relative independence are more important than the opportunity for greater responsibility and personal growth in enriched jobs.

These three points do not negate nor are they intended to be a total indictment of the job enrichment concept. On the other hand, they are intended to emphasize that job enrichment is not a cure-all for all the human problems presently facing modern management. This word of caution seems very appropriate at the present time. Many management professors and practitioners have jumped on the job enrichment bandwagon without carefully considering the research and analysis that is reported in this article. If nothing else, both professors and practitioners should take another hard look at their position on job enrichment as a method of motivating workers.

Like all sound management programs, job enrichment must be used *selectively* and with due consideration to situational variables such as the characteristics of the job, the organizational level, and the personal characteristics of the employees. Finally, job enrichment probably works best in organizations which have a supportive climate for innovation and change and a management which is genuinely interested in achieving greater job satisfaction for *its own sake*. Under these conditions, job enrichment can be practiced successfully and can offer great potential for the future, not only in terms of enriching the work experience for countless organizational participants, but also for increased productivity and organizational goal accomplishment.

References

1   See William J. Paul, Jr., Keith B. Robertson, and Frederick Herzberg, "Job Enrichment Pays Off," *Harvard Business Review,* (March-April, 1969), pp. 61–78.

2   See Valerie M. Bockman, "The Herzberg Controversy," *Personnel Psychology* (Vol. 24, No. 2, 1971), pp. 155–189.

3   See Peter P. Schoderbek and William E. Reif, *Job Enlargement* (Ann Arbor, Michigan: Bureau of Industrial Relations, Graduate School of Business Administration, The University of Michigan, 1969).

4   Harold M. F. Rush, "Behavioral Science—Concepts and Management Application," *Studies in Personnel Policy, No. 216* (New York: National Industrial Conference Board, 1969).

5   Mitchell Fein, *Approaches to Motivation* (Hillsdale, N.J.: 1970), p. 20.

6   Robert N. Ford, *Motivation Through the Work Itself* (New York: American Management Association, Inc., 1969), p. 188.

7   *Ibid.,* p. 189.

8   James E. Kennedy and Harry E. O'Neill, "Job Content and Workers' Opinions," *Journal of Applied Psychology* (Vol. 42, No. 6, 1958), p. 375.

9 Charles L. Hulin and Milton R. Blood, "Job Enlargement, Individual Differences, and Worker Responses," *Psychological Bulletin* (Vol. 69, No. 1, 1968), p. 50.

10 See Frederick Herzberg, *Work and the Nature of Man* (Cleveland: The World Publishing Company, 1966); also, Douglas McGregor, *Leadership and Motivation* (The MIT Press, 1966); also Rensis Likert, *The Human Organization* (New York: McGraw-Hill Book Company, 1967); also Chris Argyris, *Personality and Organization* (New York: Harper & Row, Publishers, 1957); also Chris Argyris, *Integrating the Individual and the Organization* (New York: John Wiley & Sons, Inc., 1964); and Robert Blake and Jane Mouton, *Corporate Excellence Through Grid Organizational Development* (Houston: Gulf Publishing Company, 1968).

11 Douglas McGregor, *op. cit.,* p. 40.

12 Paul, Robertson, and Herzberg, *op. cit.*

13 Mitchell Fein, *op. cit.,* p. 15.

14 Peter P. Schoderbek and William E. Reif, *op. cit.,* pp. 41–72.

15 Harold M. F. Rush, *Job Design for Motivation, Conference Board Report, No. 515* (New York: The Conference Board, Inc., 1971), p. 10.

16 Patricia C. Smith, "The Prediction of Individual Differences in Susceptibility to Industrial Monotony," *Journal of Applied Psychology* (Vol. 39, No. 5, 1955), pp. 322–329; also Patricia C. Smith and Charles Lem, "Positive Aspects of Motivation in Repetitive Work: Effects of Lot Size Upon Spacing of Voluntary Work Stoppages," *Journal of Applied Psychology* (Vol. 39, No. 5, 1955), pp. 330–333; also Maurice D. Kilbridge, "Do Workers Prefer Larger Jobs?" *Personnel* (Sept.–Oct., 1960), pp. 45–48; also Wilhelm Baldamus, *Efficiency and Effort: An Analysis of Industrial Administration* (London: Tavistock Publications, 1967); also Victor H. Vroom, *Some Personality Determinants of the Effects of Participation* (Englewood Cliffs: Prentice-Hall, Inc., 1960); also Arthur N. Turner and Amelia L. Miclette, "Sources of Satisfaction in Repetitive Work," *Occupational Psychology* (Vol. 36, No. 4, 1962), pp. 215–231; and Arthur W. Kornhauser, *Mental Health of the Industrial Worker: a Detroit Study* (New York: John Wiley & Sons, Inc., 1965).

17 William E. Reif and Peter P. Schoderbek, "Job Enlargement: Antidote to Apathy," *Management of Personnel Quarterly* (Spring, 1966), pp. 16–23.

18 Hulin and Blood, *op. cit.*

19 Mitchell Fein, *op. cit.,* p. 31.

20 *Ibid.,* p. 37.

21 David C. McClelland and David J. Winter, *Motivating Economic Achievement* (New York: The Free Press, 1969).

22 Hulin and Blood, *op. cit.,* p. 49.

23 Louis E. Davis, "The Design of Jobs," *Industrial Relations* (October, 1966), pp. 21–45.

24 Herzberg, *op. cit.*

25 Chester I. Barnard, *The Functions of the Executive* (Cambridge, Mass.: Harvard University Press, 1938), p. 119.

26 Reif and Schoderbek, *op. cit.,* pp. 16–23.

27 *Ibid.,* pp. 64–70.

28 Chester I. Barnard, *op. cit.,* p. 77.

Job Enrichment:
Another Part of the Forest

William W. Winpisinger

After some years of seeking legislative alternatives to collective bargaining, plus even more years of academic discussion and debate on the pros and cons of union responsibilities in relation to public rights it now appears that labor's good friends in government, intellectual and academic circles have discovered an interesting new malady. They've already provided it with a name, a diagnosis and even a cure.

The name is the "Blue Collar Blues." The diagnosis is that because younger workers are brighter and better educated than their fathers they refuse to accept working conditions that past generations took for granted. The cure consists of a shot of psychic penicillin known as job enrichment.

There can be little doubt as to the existence of a rising tide of dissatisfaction, or alienation, among those who are increasingly and even sneeringly referred to as the Archie Bunkers of America.

Employers feel it in more absenteeism, more turnover and more strikes over working conditions. Politicians feel it in the perceptible shift of blue collar workers from the principles of the New Deal to the philosophy by George Wallace. Unions feel it in the rising level of contract rejections and the growing number of defeats suffered by long established business representatives and officers in union elections.

Just a couple of months ago *Time Magazine,* in an essay on the work ethic noted that according to a Gallup poll taken in 1971, 19% of all workers expressed dissatisfaction with their jobs. This was viewed with some pessimism by the learned editors of *Time*. If they had chosen to be optimistic they could have just as validly noted that 81% of all workers seem to be satisfied with their jobs.

There is, of course, no way to prove it but I feel reasonably certain that at no time in the entire history of man would Mr. Gallup have found 100% happiness and job satisfaction in the labor force. I doubt if 100% of the ancient Egyptians who built the pyramids, or 100% of the medieval craftsmen who constructed the great cathedrals, or 100% of the 19th century Irishmen who laid the tracks for American railroads were so filled with job satisfaction that they consistently whistled while they worked.

The right to bitch about the job, or the boss, or the system, or even the union, is one of the inalienable rights of a free work force. Whether workers today are generally happier than those in the so-called good old days is not provable one way or the other. There are those who claim that the increasing atomization of work processes and the mind-deadening monotony of the modern assembly line cannot help but lead to anything *except* increasing alienation in the

From the Industrial Relations Research Association *25th Anniversary Proceedings,* 1972, pp. 154–159. Reprinted by permission.

work force. And yet, the assembly line has been with us for a long time. The concept of the robotized worker, endlessly repeating one function, tightening the same bolt over and over, was already well established long before Charlie Chaplin satirized it in the movie "Modern Times" more than 40 years ago.

Strangely enough, Mr. Gallup's polls on worker dissatisfaction, which were started in 1949, consistently registered slow but steady increases in the level of worker satisfaction right up to 1969. And I think that is very significant. Though workers throughout the 1950's and 1960's were never really affluent, in the Galbraithian sense, they *were* making progress. On the whole, jobs were plentiful and the gap between what the average production worker earned and what the Bureau of Labor Statistics said he needed for a "modest but adequate" standard of living was narrowing. But then between 1969 and 1971 the overall rate of job satisfaction, according to Mr. Gallup, fell 6%. If this decrease were due to some substantial change in the nature of the jobs that people did I would have to agree with those who prescribe job enrichment as the answer to worker dissatisfaction. And don't get me wrong. I am not opposed to efforts by management or industrial psychologists to make assembly line jobs less monotonous and more fulfilling.

But one of the points I intend to make here today may not be too palatable to some of my friends and associates in management or government or academic circles, because the point is that just as job dissatisfaction in the work place yielded to trade union solutions in the past, such dissatisfaction can be decreased to the extent that trade union solutions are applied today.

One of the reasons that worker satisfaction declined in the late 1960's and early 1970's is that worker income, in relation to inflation and taxation and the purchasing power of the dollar that was earned by labor, also declined.

The fact is that because of government policies leading to rising unemployment, establishing one-sided controls on wages and permitting multi-national corporations to export thousands of American jobs to Hong Kong and Taiwan and other low-wage areas, the gap between what the average worker earns and what his family needs for a decent standard of living has been growing. So it should come as no surprise to anyone that worker dissatisfaction is also growing.

The recent rash of strikes and other labor problems at the General Motors plant in Lordstown, Ohio, has been seized upon by those who write articles for learned journals as proof that even if the nature of the assembly line hasn't changed, the work force has. As every student of industrial relations knows, the overwhelming majority of the work force at Lordstown is young. On the basis of management's unhappy experiences with these kids, the experts have solemnly proclaimed the discovery of a new kind of work force. They inform us that here is a generation that has never known a depression and thus has no interest in security. Here is a generation that grew up in a time of crass materialism and thus rejects the work ethic. Here is a generation that has been infected by the rebellion of youth and thus has no respect for authority. I have seen one scholarly analysis, in fact, that compares the "rebellion" at Lordstown in the early 1970's with the free speech movement at Berkeley in the early 1960's. And the conclusion was drawn that the nation's factories, like her colleges, would never be the same again.

Quite frankly, I submit that that kind of analysis overlooks one salient fact. The young workers at Lordstown were reacting against the same kind of grievances, in the same kind of way, as did generations of workers before them. They were rebelling against an obvious speed up. They were protesting safety violations. They were reacting against working conditions that had been unilaterally imposed by a management that was determined to get tough in the name of efficiency. Anyone who thinks that wild cats or slow downs or even sabotage started with a bunch of hippie-looking kids at Lordstown doesn't know very much about the history of the American labor movement.

An almost identical series of incidents took place over much the same issues at Norton, Ohio, at almost the same time but very few inferences were drawn about the changing nature of the work force because, in this case, it was older workers who were involved.

Many people, including President Nixon, are viewing the decline of the work ethic in the United States with alarm. On the basis of my experience, which includes many day to day contacts with rank and file members of the Machinists Union, I can assure you that the work ethic is alive and well and living in a lot of good work places.

But what the aerospace workers and auto mechanics and machinists and airline mechanics and production workers *we* represent want, in the way of job satisfaction, is a wage that is commensurate with their skill.

If you want to enrich the job, enrich the pay check. The better the wage, the greater the job satisfaction. There is no better cure for the "blue collar blues."

If you want to enrich the job, begin to decrease the number of hours a worker has to labor in order to earn a decent standard of living. Just as the increased productivity of mechanized assembly lines made it possible to decrease the work week from 60 to 40 hours a couple of generations ago, the time has come to translate the increased productivity of automated processes into the kind of enrichment that comes from shorter work weeks, longer vacations and earlier retirements.

If you want to enrich the job, do something about the nerveshattering noise, the heat and the fumes that are deafening, poisoning and destroying the health of American workers. Thousands of chemicals are being used in work places whose effects on humans have never been tested. Companies are willing to spend millions advertising quieter refrigerators or washing machines but are reluctant to spend one penny to provide a reasonably safe level of noise in their plants. And though we are now supposed to have a law that protects working people against some of the more obvious occupational hazards, industry is already fighting to undermine enforcement, and the Nixon Administration has gone along with them by cutting the funds that are needed to make it effective.

If you want to enrich the jobs of the men and women who manufacture the goods that are needed for the functioning of our industrialized society, the time has come to reevaluate the snobbery that makes it noble to possess a college degree and shameful to learn skills that involve a little bit of grease under the finger nails. The best way to undermine a worker's morale, and decrease his satisfaction with himself and his job is to make him feel that society looks down on him because he wears blue coveralls instead of a white collar. I think it is ironic that because of prevailing attitudes many kinds of skilled craftsmen are in short supply while thousands of college graduates are tripping over one another in search of jobs.

Some of the most dissatisfied people I know are those who got a college degree and then couldn't find a position that lived up to their expectations. And that's been especially true the last few years. There are a lot of college-trained people driving cabs today who would have had a lot more job satisfaction and made a lot more money if they had apprenticed as auto mechanics.

If you want to enrich the job, give working people a greater sense of control over their working conditions. That's what they, and their unions, were seeking in the early 1960's when management was automating and retooling on a large scale. That's why we asked for advance consultation when employers intended to make major job changes. That's why we negotiated for clauses providing retraining and transfer rights and a fair share of the increased productivity that resulted from automation.

What workers resent, and what really causes alienation, are management decisions that rearrange job assignments or upset existing work schedules without reference to the rights of the work force.

If you want to enrich the job, you must realize that no matter how dull or boring or dirty it may be an individual worker must feel that he has not reached the end of the line. If a worker is to be reasonably satisfied with the job he has today he must have hope for something better tomorrow.

You know this is true in universities, in government and in management. I submit that even on the assembly line there must be some chance of movement, even if it's only from a job that requires stooping down to one that involves standing erect. But here again, we are talking about a job problem for which unionism provides an answer. And the name of that answer is the negotiated seniority clause. Perhaps workers were not thinking in terms of job enrichment when they first negotiated the right to bid on better shifts, overtime or promotions on the basis of length of service. Perhaps they were only trying to restrict management's right to allocate jobs and shifts and overtime on the basis of favoritism. But even if they weren't thinking in terms of "job enrichment," in actual practice that's what they got.

It's true that many young workers in their 20's resent the fact that while they have to tighten the same old bolt in the same old spot a thousand times a day the guys in their 40's are walking up and down the line with inspection sheets or running around the factory on forklifts.

They may resent and bitch about it *now* but they also know that they are accumulating seniority which they can trade for a better job of their own some day.

Yes, there are many ways in which jobs can be enriched. But I don't think those I have mentioned are what management has in mind when it talks about job enrichment. On the basis of fairly extensive experience as a union representative, I find it hard to picture management enriching jobs at the expense of profits. In fact, I have a sneaking suspicion that "job enrichment" may be just another name for "time and motion" study. As Thomas Brooks said in a recent article in the AFL-CIO *Federationist* "Substituting the sociologist's questionnaire for the stop watch is likely to be no gain for the workers. While workers have a stake in productivity it is not always identical with that of management. Job enrichment programs have cut jobs just as effectively as automation and stop watches. And the rewards of productivity are not always equitably shared."

I also have a feeling that what some companies call job enrichment is really little more than the introduction of gimmicks, like doing away with time clocks or developing "work teams" or designing jobs to "maximize personal involvement"—whatever that means.

In conclusion let me say that I know there are those who worry about what the younger generation is coming to, and wonder whether the rebellious young workers of today will be willing to fill their father's shoes in the factory jobs of tomorrow. We can't generalize from isolated examples but I was very interested in an NBC television documentary recently that studied the dissatisfaction of young workers. The part that interested me the most was the transformation in an assembly line hippie who followed his electrician father's footsteps by becoming an apprentice and cutting his hair.

There is little doubt, and all the studies tend to prove, that worker dissatisfaction diminishes with age. And that's because older workers have accrued more of the kinds of job enrichment that unions have fought for—better wages, shorter hours, vested pensions, a right to have a say in their working conditions, the right to be promoted on the basis of seniority and all the rest. That's the kind of job enrichment that unions believe in. And I assure you that that's the kind of job enrichment that we will continue to fight for.

The Psychological Contract:
Managing the Joining-Up Process
John Paul Kotter

A growing number of organizations in recent years have been reporting problems that center around getting the new man, often a recent college graduate, "on board." These problems take on many forms:

- Some organizations have reported as much as a 50 percent turnover rate of new men after their first year of work.

© 1973 by The Regents of the University of California. Reprinted from *California Management Review*, vol. XV, no. 3, 1973, pp. 91–99, by permission of The Regents.

• Recently, some corporations have complained about a generation gap between new men and older managers which was putting a severe strain on their organization.

• Other companies complain about the loss of creativity, innovativeness and energy in their new employees during their first few years (often labeled a "stifling of creativity").

• Managers have often complained about the naiveté of new employees. ("They come in with unrealistic expectations and then get mad when they don't come true!")

• Organizations have reported that it takes some managerial and technical specialists two years or more to really get on board, while others have reported that it takes one-half or one-fourth that time.

This article is concerned with the process of assimilating new employees into an organization, which we call the "joining-up" process. All of the above incidents are symptomatic of problems in this process. It is the purpose of this article to present research that argues the following points:

1 Early experiences (the joining-up period) have a major effect on an individual's later career in an organization. Specifically, early experiences can significantly affect job satisfaction, employee attitude, productivity level, and turnover.

2 Efficient management of the joining-up process can save an organization a great deal of money by making employees more efficient faster, by increasing job satisfaction, morale and productivity, by decreasing turnover, by increasing the amount of creativity, by decreasing counterproductive conflict and tension, and by increasing the number of truly effective members within the organization.

For an organization that hires twenty-five college graduates with bachelor's degrees each year, the difference between a well-managed and a mismanaged joining-up process is $200,000 a year at a minimum.

3 Due to a complex set of forces most organizations do a poor job of managing the joining-up process. Often because of a problem of measurement, organizations either do not realize this problem exists or do not realize its magnitude.

This article will outline some recent research and present the results. To clarify the implications of the research, two case studies will be presented, followed by a summary and a set of conclusions.

The Research

Research was recently undertaken at MIT's Sloan School of Management to explore problems in the joining-up process and to try to understand how it can be better managed.[1] A simple model of the process was constructed and data was gathered with an eight-page questionnaire given to a randomly selected group of Sloan masters graduates and Sloan Fellows. These Sloan masters graduates had completed a two-year masters degree program in management somewhere between 1961 and 1969. Sloan Fellows are managers in their 30s and 40s who had just completed a one-year "masters" program. Ninety responses from middle managers ranging in age from twenty-three to forty-five were eventually used in the data analysis.[2]

At the heart of the model was the concept of the "psychological contract," which was first introduced a decade ago by Chris Argyris[3] and Harry Levenson.[4] As it was defined for this research, the psychological contract is an implicit contract between an individual and his organization which specifies what each expect to give and receive from each other in their relationship.

When an individual joins an organization, he has expectations of what he expects to receive (such as advancement opportunities, salary, status, office space and decor, amount of challenging vs. dull work, and so on) as well as expectations of what he expects to give (such as technical skills, time and energy commitment, communication ability, supervisory skills, loyalty, and so on). The organization also has expectations of what it expects to receive from the new employee, (examples of which are similar to what the employee expects to give) and expectations of what it expects to offer him in return (examples of which are similar to what the employee expects to receive).

These expectations can be the same, or they can be quite different. For example, a young chemical engineer from MIT may expect that he will be given his own office when he goes to work for a company. If the company also expects to give him an office of his own, then there is a "match." If they do not expect to give him his own office, there is a "mismatch." This mismatch can be small (they expect he will share an office with one other person) or large (they expect he won't be given an office, desk, or anything). These four sets of expectations and the matches and mismatches make up the "psychological contract."

This contract is very different from a legal or labor contract. It may have literally thousands of items in it (see Table 1 for an example of some categories used in the research) although the job seeker or new employee may consciously think of only a few. His expectations of the types of technical skills he will give may be very clear, while his expectation of how willing he is to take on company values may be very unclear. Likewise, the organization may have a clearer picture of some expectations than others. These expectations may be explicitly discussed during recruiting or with the first supervisor or they may not. The new recruit may have a deep, clear understanding of some, all or none of the company's expectations and vice versa. Finally, this contract changes as the individual's and the company's expectations alter.

Research Results

The research findings can be summarized in the following points:

1   The first finding confirmed the major research hypothesis that psychological contracts, which are made up primarily of matches in expectations, are related to greater job satisfaction, productivity, and reduced turnover than are other contracts which have more mismatches and less matches. In other words, those people who established a contract that was comprised of more matches in expectations, had a more satisfying and productive first year and remained longer with the company than those people whose contract had fewer matches.

Table 1   Types of Expectations*

(a)

The following list of thirteen items are examples of areas in which an individual has expectations of receiving and an organization has expectations of giving. That is, for each item in this list, the individual will have an expectation about what the organization will offer him or give him in that area. Likewise, the organization has an expectation about what it will offer or give the individual in that area.

1   A sense of meaning or purpose in the job.
2   Personal development opportunities.
3   The amount of interesting work (stimulates curiosity and induces excitement).
4   The challenge in the work.
5   The power and responsibility in the job.
6   Recognition and approval for good work.
7   The status and prestige in the job.
8   The friendliness of the people, the congeniality of the work group.
9   Salary.
10 The amount of structure in the environment (general practices, discipline, regimentation).
11 The amount of security in the job.
12 Advancement opportunities.
13 The amount and frequency of feedback and evaluation.

(b)

The following list of seventeen items are examples of areas in which an individual has expectations of giving and the organization has expectations of receiving. That is, for each item in this list, the individual will have an expectation about what he is willing or able to give or offer the organization in that area. Likewise, the organization has an expectation about what it will receive from the individual in that area.

1   The ability to perform nonsocial job related tasks requiring some degree of technical knowledge and skill.
2   The ability to learn the various aspects of a position while on the job.
3   The ability to discover new methods of performing tasks; the ability to solve novel problems.
4   The ability to present a point of view effectively and convincingly.
5   The ability to work productively with groups of people.
6   The ability to make well-organized, clear presentations both orally and written.
7   The ability to supervise and direct the work of others.
8   The ability to make responsible decisions well without assistance from others.
9   The ability to plan and organize work efforts for oneself or others.
10 The ability to utilize time and energy for the benefit of the company.
11 The ability to accept company demands which conflict with personal prerogatives.
12 Social relationships with other members of the company off the job.
13 Conforming to the folkways of the organization or work group on the job in areas not directly related to job performance.
14 Further education pursued off-company time.
15 Maintaining a good public image of the company.
16 Taking on company values and goals as one's own.
17 The ability to see what should or must be done, and to initiate appropriate activity.

---

*These thirty types of expectations were adapted from earlier research by Berlew and Hall.[5]

We have all observed personal examples of this phenomenon in its extreme. A number of the Sloan masters graduates reported that they took their first job with completely unrealistic expectations of how hard it would be to introduce new techniques into their companies. This expectation, although unrealistic, was an important one to each of them initially. They lasted in their first jobs on the average of one year.

The more subtle differences in job satisfaction or productivity resulting from a greater or lesser number of matches in the psychological contract are more difficult to observe. The pattern often looks like this: The contract formed during the joining-up period has mismatches, but neither the employee nor his boss really recognizes them or confronts them. After the first year the employee begins to "feel" those mismatches as disappointments, letdowns, and so on. Since he thinks the company has broken their contract, he reacts by slowly breaking his part of the bargain. He often "digs in" and becomes another moderately productive, uncreative, body.

2 The concept that showed a measurable relationship to productivity, satisfaction, and turnover was "matching," not getting more or less than was expected. Mismatches that gave more than one expected caused as many problems as those which gave less than one expected. In other words, organizations or individuals who approach the contract trying to get "the most," or "the best" instead of "a fit" or "a match" are missing the boat. Often we don't have strong preferences for something, but we still plan for the future based on what we expect. For example, Warren, a twenty-five year old bachelor working for a West Coast aeronautics firm, expected that he would be transferred East after one year of work. He really didn't care one way or the other, but based on his expectation he made elaborate plans for the move, which, when it didn't occur, left Warren very upset.

The sales department of a moderate sized industrial products firm put on a strong recruiting campaign a few years ago to get the "best men possible for the money." Their strong recruiting effort did succeed in getting a remarkably strong group of new men. Unfortunately, the job did not require the skills many of these young men had. The contracts formed had many large mismatches in them (but mismatches which the company thought were in its "favor"). Within two years the company lost 60 percent of these men and only 10 percent (two men) were doing very well.

3 It was found that the clearer an individual understood his own expectation on an item, the higher was the probability of a match. Likewise, the clearer an expectation was to the organization, the higher the probability of a match.

It is fairly obvious what is happening in this case. Many times people do not explicitly think of all the areas in which they have expectations. Often a new employee out of college isn't consciously aware of what he wants and needs, or what he is capable and prepared to give. Unfortunately organizations also are not clear as to what they expect (in detail) either. As a result they don't talk about many areas nor pay attention to them. Mismatches can occur by accident, out of neglect.

What is needed then is for the new man, the company, and his boss to carefully consider all areas of expectations in order to overcome the problem of clarity. One of the reasons this hasn't been done in the past is that people have not considered its importance.

4   If the new man explicitly discussed his expectations with a company representative, the two parties' mutual understanding of the other's expectations increased and so did the probability of matching.

There are a number of reasons why this doesn't happen more frequently. There often appear to be norms surrounding the interview and the initial work period which define some items as not legitimate to talk about. The fact that the new man often feels powerless limits his ability to initiate such a discussion. His supervisor may be overworked and not rewarded for helping the new man and as a result doesn't initiate what could be a complex deep discussion.

These first four points are summarized in model form in Figure 1.

5   It was further discovered that clarity (point 3), discussion (point 5), and even some give and take were not enough to resolve some mismatches, which we called basic. In this situation, an individual and his organization, having clarified and discussed their expectations, find themselves unwilling or unable to find a commonality of expectations in an area which is important to both of them. In

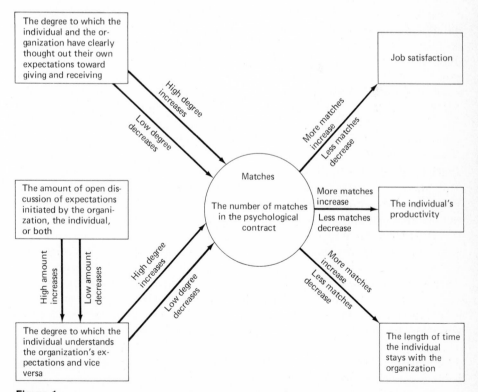

Figure 1

some cases, this may mean that the employee should resign, a reality that some people and some organizations don't like to face.

It was also discovered that there were small but statistically significant differences—mismatches—between the expectations of all individuals as a group and all organizations as a group on some items (see Table 2).

As the reader can see, the individuals had higher expectations with respect to the personal development opportunities they would be offered, the amount of interesting work they would be offered, and the amount of meaning or purpose in their work. On the other hand, the organizations had higher expectations toward the amount of security that they would offer the individual. The organizations also had higher expectations of the individual's ability to work with groups, his taking on of organizational values and goals, and his willingness to conform.

Schein, in an earlier article, suggested that basic differences in expectations seemed to be developing between recent college graduates and industry.[7] In particular he reported that college graduates seemed to have higher expectations of advancement opportunities, increased responsibility, and personal growth opportunities. He also reported very different expectations on how to sell ideas and get things done, how important and practical "theoretical" knowledge was, and how ready the new man was for use. These findings are consistent with the ones reported in Table 2.

It is important then for a particular organization to be sensitive to growing differences in expectations between it and its new men. Resolving these basic differences can be a much more difficult task than resolving the other types of differences. In an extreme case, resolving this problem could require an organization to find a new labor pool or to undergo major internal changes in order to survive on a long-run basis.

6 Finally, for the particular sample used in this study (Sloan School graduates and Sloan Fellows), the nature of the conflict in the process looked something like this: the individual was most interested in exchanging non-people related skills (technical knowledge, drive, writing ability, and so on) for exciting, challenging, meaningful work and development (and advancement) opportunities. The organization, however, expected to give the individual less of that which he expected most, and expected to receive in addition to skills, more on such items as conformity, loyalty, and so on.

In summary, there are a number of general points that result from this research which are not usually found in "conventional wisdom." First, the initial period *is* very important, and as such is worth carefully managing. Second, what you don't know *can* hurt you. A clear understanding of one's own expectations and the other party's will help form better contracts. Third, the key in contract formulation is achieving a match or a fit, *not* getting more, or the best, or whatever. Fourth, if an organization and an individual have one or more very central, basic mismatches, it may be in their best interests to shake hands and part. Finally, if an organization's expectations get too far out of line with its labor pool, it can get into deep trouble.

In order to obtain a better feel for the implications of this research, let us

Table 2 Basic Mismatches[6]

Expectation	Mean for individual*	Mean for organization*
1 Personal development opportunities	4.54 (individual expects to receive)	4.20 (organization expects to give)†
2 Security	2.30 (individual expects to receive)	2.94 (organization expects to give)†
3 Taking on values and goals	2.80 (individual expects to give)	3.30 (organization expects to receive)†
4 Ability to work with groups	3.75 (individual expects to give)	4.06 (organization expects to receive)†
5 Conforming	2.19 (individual expects to give)	2.53 (organization expects to receive)†
6 Interesting work	4.36 (individual expects to receive)	4.10 (organization expects to give)†
7 Sense of meaning or purpose	4.24 (individual expects to receive)	3.98 (organization expects to give)†

Note: All differences are statistically significant at .05. The expectations are listed in decreasing order of statistically significant differences (from .0003 to .048).

*As measured on a 1 to 5 scale, (1 = not expected, 5 = strongly expected.)

†As perceived by the respondent.

look at a few examples of organizations who have tried to improve the management of their joining-up process.

Applications: Case Study I   This first case involves a manufacturing plant of a large consumer product company, employing about 300 workers and forty managers. In June, the plant hired three new college engineering graduates as junior managers. For their first three months they participated in a combined program of work and training. A senior manager at the plant was concerned that the plant could do a better job of getting the new employees on board. In particular his concerns were:

● He wanted the new men to get up to speed, to become "socialized" and to learn the plant's norms faster (in general to learn more about the plant, the people, and so on).

● The new men (almost through with training) would be getting their "first boss" soon. He wanted them to explore their expectations and to be prepared for negotiating a psychological contract with their new boss.

● He wanted to receive feedback from the new men on their three month history with the company and to explore better methods for future training programs.

● In addition, he wanted some of the plant's top management to get a feel for what the new college graduates were like, and to explore management's implicit expectations of the new men.

● Finally he wanted to do some team building. He wanted to help the new men feel part of their management team.

To accomplish these goals, four senior managers, three supervisors, and the three trainees were invited to a twelve-hour session, led by an outside consultant, spread out over three days during their shut-down period. Prior to the session the three trainees and three supervisors (who had been with the organization only one to two years) filled out questionnaires on their specific expectations of giving and receiving, and answered how clear each expectation was to them (see Table 1 for such a list of expectations). The senior managers filled out questionnaires on what the company expected to give and receive to each of the new employees. This exercise was designed to help the participants explore explicitly their expectations before the session.

The session began with a "contract setting" exercise for the twelve-hour session. The participants were asked to state explicitly what they expected to give and to receive from this session and the consultant, as the workshop leader, did the same. A contract was then explicitly established among all the participants which included the goals of the session, the roles each person would assume, the schedule we would follow, and so on. This provided the group with a good start for the session and with some real-time experience concerning psychological contracts and contract setting.

The next input was a brief lecture on the joining-up process and the concept of the psychological contract. Following this, the group was divided into three homogeneous groups (new men, supervisors, senior managers) and given time to develop lists of "mismatches." The new men and young supervisors were told to identify mismatches from their own experiences, including the cause. The senior managers were told to develop a list of what mismatches they thought new men often have when they join the company.

It was interesting to note that all three lists were different. The mismatches the new men presently felt were different from those of the one to two year men. The senior managers' list reflected their own experiences and was also different. In a sense the three lists provided a chronological picture of the problems and concerns an employee faced as he grew up in this organization.

The three groups, one at a time, presented their lists, point by point, and the entire group discussed them. This discussion was one of information exchange, exploration and confrontation. Information was candidly exchanged on subjects that were not normally discussed but which were important (performance criteria, dress, hair length, career paths in the company, money, company policy, and so on). Many misunderstandings and misperceptions (on the part of all three groups) were aired and resolved. One of the new men started asking some questions about how to get something done that he had been suppressing for weeks out of a fear of looking stupid. A major conflict that one of the supervisors faced was confronted (he was seriously considering leaving) and, after the session, resolved (he was transferred).

The session ended with some group problem solving on the issue, "what can we do better concerning our joining-up process." They developed several recommendations including the use of similar sessions in the future. The participants' response to the session was enthusiastic and the senior manager who initiated it felt it had accomplished his five goals.

Case Study II   A much larger effort, which is in progress at this writing, involves an R&D division of a giant consumer products company. Some of the top management became concerned about the joining-up process in their division due to a number of factors, including a speech on socialization and joining-up by Ed Schein. They established a task force comprised of a diagonal slice of the organization, an internal organizational development specialist, and an external consultant.

The division contains about 400 people, twenty of whom had been with the company one and one-half years or less. The first task of the group was a diagnostic one, in which information was collected from various sources in and out of the organization. As a part of this effort, almost all of the new employees (two groups of eight) met for a one day session designed to help them examine and articulate their brief experiences with the company. Questionnaires were given to all new people, their bosses, and their boss's bosses. These inputs and others from other divisions, academia, and so on led to a diagnosis of critical variables that could be improved upon.

The most important factor turned out to be the skills of the new man's supervisor. The process was facilitated if the new man's supervisor had skills in the following areas: giving and receiving feedback, articulating expectations and performance criteria, explaining realistically decisions passed down from above, coaching and helping, communicating, understanding new people's problems, and so on. Other important factors included the selection of the first project, the selection of the first environment (including boss, peers, and section), formal and informal training, opportunities for quickly learning about the company and facilities, the clarity of key policies, the reward system, and so forth.

At this writing, the task force is planning and implementing changes in the organization based on their diagnosis and understanding of the joining-up process. The types of changes they have developed can help the reader to see what can be done to improve a joining-up process.

Creation of a Training Program for a New Man's Boss   This program is designed to help him better understand the new man and the joining-up process and to help him develop better skills as a coach.

Creation of a Criterion for Project Selection   A more careful selection of first projects can speed up a new man's learning.

New Formal Training Activities to Replace Old Ones   New formal training was created to replace the old based on new employee feedback of inefficiencies, usefulness, and so on.

Explicitly Stated Division Policies   Unclear policies in some key areas were causing false expectations in important areas. Top management is changing this.

Creation of a Joining-Up Workshop   This workshop is somewhat similar to the one described in the first case study, except that the new man's boss is present, and there is more emphasis on relationship building and contract setting.

Planning Aid for Supervisors Who Expect New Men   A number of devices have been created to help supervisors plan for their new man's arrival. These include help in setting training objectives, in meeting a wide range of new man needs, and so forth.

Creation of Performance Criteria   Vague performance criteria have caused unreal expectations. Supervisors are now creating more explicit, but not mechanistic ones.

This effort, which is still in progress, will take about one and one-half years in total.

Summary and Conclusions

Early experiences in an organization can have a great effect on a person's career. The joining-up process, which determines these experiences, must be carefully managed. The quality of the management of the joining-up process will effect two major outcomes: the cost of getting new people on board and keeping them in the firm, and the level of productivity, commitment, innovativeness, and so on of people when they get on board.

Unfortunately in many organizations this process is mismanaged, or not managed at all. The costs of mismanagement are very high.

The concept of the psychological contract has proven to be a useful one in examining the joining-up process. Recent research has shown that if a new person's expectations are out of line with the company's this will show up in low production, low creativity, dissatisfaction, and turnover.

While it is not really useful to propose "cookbook" solutions for better management of the joining-up process beyond the conclusions drawn from the research, the following are key variables in most organizations' joining-up process.

A   Recruiting Effort   Does your recruiting effort allow both the recruitee and your organization to exchange accurate expectations? Does the recruitee get a fairly realistic picture of the challenges and problems in your organization? Do you carefully explore his expectations and try to get the best fits or matches or do you look for "good people"?

B   The First Supervisor   Do the managers who supervise new employees have the skills and knowledge to help create sound psychological contracts? Are they good coaches and teachers? Do they know enough about the organization to help someone else learn? Are they effective members themselves? Do you carefully select and train first supervisors? In many organizations this man is the key variable in this process.

C   Reward and Control System   Do the supervisors of new men perceive that they are being rewarded for efficient and effective management of a new man's joining-up process or do they think they are rewarded only for doing the "real work"?

D First Job Environment Does the environment a new man is put into contribute or detract from his getting on board? Does it help reduce his initial anxieties and help make him a part of the group? Will his peers teach him what you want him to learn about his job and the organization? Careful selection of the first environment and activities outside of it (as in Case I) can prove useful.

E Performance Criteria and Training Objectives Do the supervisor and the new man know what the reward system is for the new man? Is the performance criteria clear to both? Are training objectives clear to both? In other words, how clear are your expectations of new men?

F Training Do the formal and informal training activities achieve the training objectives quickly and effectively or do they waste time, frustrate the new man, teach the wrong things and bore everyone? What assumptions do you make when you design the training activities? Do they come close to meeting the expectations of new men?

G First Assignment How is the first assignment or project chosen? Does it provide an opportunity for the new employee to learn, meet people, grow, and so on. Is it clear to the new man why he was given that assignment, what he can get out of it, and what is expected of him?

Obviously this isn't an exhaustive list, and the importance of these items will vary from organization to organization, but it should give the reader a feeling of what can be adjusted for better results.

In the final analysis, the payoff for a particular organization will depend upon its awareness of the importance of this process, and upon the creativity with which it systematically examines its unique situation and derives solutions for better management of this process.

References

Based on a Master's Thesis by the author completed at the Sloan School of Management at MIT under the direction of Professors Edgar Schein and Irwin Rubin.

1　See "The Psychological Contract: Expectations and the Joining-Up Process," an unpublished Master's thesis by the author (Sloan, 1970).
2　Data was collected during January and February, 1970.
3　Chris Argyris, *Understanding Organizational Behavior* (Homewood, Ill.: Dorsey Press, 1960).
4　Harry Levenson, *Men, Management & Mental Health,* (Cambridge, Mass.: Harvard University Press, 1962).
5　David E. Berlew, and Douglas T. Hall, "The Socialization of Managers: Effects of Expectations on Performance," *An Administrative Science Quarterly* (September, 1966), pp. 207–223.
6　"The Psychological Contract: Expectations and the Joining-Up Process," an unpublished Master's thesis by the author (Sloan, 1970).
7　Edgar H. Schein, "How to Break in the College Graduate," *Harvard Business Review* (November-December, 1964), pp. 68–76.

Misuses of Compensation as a Motivator

O. Gene Dalaba

Is money really a prime motivator of performance, or is it merely some kind of psychic salve to mitigate the discomforts an employee has to put up with in his work? No doubt, hypotheses will continue to proliferate to "prove" either side of the question, but motivation is a highly complex subject that defies either simplistic or unidimensional explanations. Probably for that reason, in recent years we have seen the development of more sophisticated approaches to the study of motivation in organizational settings, in both theory and design of research.

An example is the expectancy theory formulated by researchers such as Vroom, Porter, and Lawler. In simple terms, this theory states that an individual will be a motivated high performer only to the extent that he sees that his work effort actually results in high performance and that high performance results in the receipt of desired rewards. Within this context we can set the conditions necessary for predicting whether compensation will motivate high performance in an individual:

- Compensation must be important to the individual employee.
- The employee must feel that getting more compensation is directly dependent on his performance.
- The employee must know that if he expends appropriate effort it will result in higher performance.

Some interesting research was reported two years ago by Professor Donald P. Schwab, of the University of Wisconsin, in support of this model. By questionnaire, he asked about 300 male and female semiskilled and skilled piece-rate production workers at a particular plant to indicate (1) how closely they thought their efforts were linked to high performance, (2) how closely they felt making more money was dependent on high performance, and (3) the degree to which making more money was important to them. The findings demonstrated that each of these three components was positively related to productivity, as hypothesized by the theory. A conclusion of the study was that high-producing piece-rate employees, compared with low-producing ones, tended to (1) value money more, (2) perceive a stronger link between their performance and money, and (3) perceive a stronger link between their effort and performance.

A follow-up study showed that these piece-rate employees had continued to have the highest degree of performance-reward perceptions, whereas group incentive and hourly paid employees had lower degrees of such perceptions. Of the three groups, the piece-rate employees also had the highest effort-perfor-

Reprinted by permission of the publisher from *Personnel*, September–October 1973, pp. 30–37. © 1973 by AMACOM, a division of the American Management Association.

mance perceptions. Thus, piece-rate workers felt more strongly not only that their pay was dependent upon how well they performed, but also that their performance was definitely a function of their own efforts.

Although these particular studies were confined to the production employee level, they do have some relevance when it comes to establishing precise and measurable objectives for managerial and executive performance. For example, when asked to state the objectives of a compensation program, a typical executive is likely to answer, "To attract, retain, and motivate effective performers at all levels in the organization." This is normally the rationale when companies design competitive pay practices and highly complex incentive schemes, particularly for those who are most responsible for the success of the organization. The implementation of these programs, however, brings up a paradox: The more we pay those to whom pay is of primary importance, the more we may demotivate.

When Money Runs Out of Steam as a Motivator . . .

A primary weakness in much of the conceptualization about the relationship between pay and performance is the failure to distinguish among incentive, motivation, and reward. Ever since the first psychologist set the precedent for a few thousand doctoral dissertations by running a rat through a maze, it has been recognized that two conditions are necessary in order to achieve results: a need and a reduction or fulfillment of that need. Therefore, you start by making sure the rat is genuinely hungry or genuinely thirsty—or you explore other needs, such as the need to avoid a jolt of electricity, to avoid pain and reduce anxiety. Thus, Frederick Herzberg is quite right in arguing that money per se doesn't motivate. It is only the desire or need for money, coupled with some expectation of receiving it, that motivates.

Of course, from a motivational point of view, the distinction here would be only academic if we could safely assume that the need or desire for money is insatiable, a thirst that is never quenched. But, although this assumption seems to lie behind a lot of motivational conceptualizing and compensation planning, it is often fallacious. The following cases illustrate the point:

- A few years ago, I was asked to evaluate three key executives of a major electronics firm, whose president and founder, then worth many millions of dollars, was still a highly driven man who often worked 14 to 16 hours a day. Of his three colleagues he said, "I just don't understand these men. They started with me in a garage several years ago when we were just launching the company, and we all worked tremendously hard and tremendously long hours. Now they've changed. Most of the time you're lucky if one of them gets in here by 10 in the morning, and on a sunny day it's a good bet that they'll be out on the golf course by 2:30."

These three men had a number of things in common: They had come from fairly modest backgrounds, had worked hard to obtain engineering degrees, and had developed successful careers with the company. More important, all of them, through very generous stock options, were now worth more than $500,000. During the evaluation interviews, each stated in one way or another: "That is more money than I ever expected to earn in my life; why should I keep knocking myself out when I have it made? I just don't see any reason for killing myself to make more. After all, the reason for trying to earn it was to be able to enjoy it.''

• The other case involved a similar problem, but with different dimensions. Here, I was asked to evaluate four middle managers in a small cannery operation that had been acquired by a medium-size conglomerate. The problem was familiar: "These men just don't seem to be motivated to work very hard any more. They aren't putting in the time and effort." Our interviews revealed that through the sale of the company, the men had realized from their stock ownership capital gains that ranged from $50,000 to $100,000.

To a great many managers and executives, that certainly would not be a significant factor leading to reduced motivation, but as Einstein observed, everything is relative. All of these managers were born and grew up in small, rural environments, had very modest economic backgrounds, had at most a high school education, and had worked hard most of their lives. They drove low-priced cars, lived in very unpretentious homes, generally drank beer if they drank at all, and enjoyed the outdoor life, with hunting and fishing their primary avocations. They had no particular desire for bigger homes, more expensive cars, or higher standards of living. To each of these men, the capital gains received from their stock sales represented a high degree of financial reward and security, which carried a psychological and motivational impact just as great as significantly larger amounts did for the electronics firm executives.

These two cases are reminders of a truism that we all acknowledge and yet very easily forget: People are individuals, and as such, each has his own value system, level of aspiration, and trade-offs he is willing to make in terms of his own complex economic and motivational needs and desires. To take another example, in the salary war that erupted with the National Hockey League when the World Hockey League was formed, many players were lured away from NHL teams by very impressive money offers; now, however, a lot of WHL owners complain that some of these team members are not playing up to their potential, that they show little motivation because "they're fat and happy— they're earning too much money."

Of course, this is not to suggest that we should universally start reducing pay in order to maintain motivation. Still, there is no doubt that the mere desire for reward, plus the expectation that it will be tied to effort, can lead to a lot of productive performance—even if the reward sometimes is never received. This has been demonstrated by many an entrepreneur, and to the bitter disappointment but effective education of many a manager and executive (though it is hardly recommended as a deliberate course of action to build an organization with a continuing record of success).

The point, again, is that we should be more attentive to individual differences, desires, needs, and expectations of the people in the company if we want to find the motivational buttons that turn individual employees on. There are periods in a man's career when the desire for and expectation of obtaining more financial reward through his personal efforts may have very high priority, but as these needs become more and more satisfied, we may have to be much more attentive to the "higher order" needs described by Herzberg, Maslow, and others.

When Security Becomes Too Much of a Good Thing . . .

Indirect compensation in the form of benefits is becoming an increasingly important part of the total compensation package. That we all know, and no one questions that benefits are here to stay; if private employers don't provide them, the government will, with the company ending up paying for them anyway. We should recognize, however, that from a motivational standpoint, most of these indirect forms of pay tend to meet a set of individual needs different from those met by direct compensation. The needs met by benefits basically have to do with security—protection from the vicissitudes of fate, unemployment, or old age. Here, from a motivational standpoint, we come to a second paradox: The more security we provide those to whom security is of primary importance, the more we may demotivate.

Again, it is the need that is the motivator of performance, not the fulfillment of that need, a fact that has some interesting implications in terms not only of employee selection and retention, but also of various managerial styles and their effectiveness. Companies and organizations that emphasize highly attractive security packages should be aware that they are appealing primarily to employees who are likely to be very much security-oriented; consequently, their greatest turnover tends to take place among those to whom security, at least at that particular stage of their careers, is relatively less important. A comprehensive and generous security package may be quite a positive factor in staffing a great number of fairly routine and highly structured positions, but it may make it increasingly difficult to attract and hold the risk-taking, innovative decision makers who can provide the flexible, adaptive, and creative leadership necessary to success in a rapidly changing and increasingly competitive business world.

The dynamics of security needs also helps to explain the generation gap. Recently, a senior corporate recruiter remarked, "I just don't understand these kids any more. You don't interview them, they interview you, and they act as if they are doing you a favor to even consider working for you." We forget that our younger generation is not a product of anxiety-ridden depression days; our very economic success has brought about different values and in this sense is actually demotivating, because it has canceled out concern for pure "survival" jobs.

The new preoccupation with higher-order needs is a matter not of behavioristic jargon and idealism, but of pragmatic realism. The increasing demand for significant psychological rewards, such as recognition, meaningful work, sense of personal dignity, personal challenge, and social usefulness and meaning are not just youthful perversities. To younger employees, neither fear of hunger nor the work ethic so persuasive to many older persons is likely to be a strong performance motivator today or in the future.

When Everyone's Like Me, or Everyone's the Same . . .

To a considerable degree, the inadequacy and inappropriateness of current compensation and benefits planning and practices can be traced to common psychological phenomena—the mirror image and the composite image. Let's consider each of these in some detail.

The Tendency to Project One's Own Values as Others'   This is to assume that others share the feelings, needs, desires, and values that we have. Pay and benefits policies and practices are still determined primarily by senior management, and in many organizations, senior in title is closely correlated with senior in age. If this is so, compensation practices are likely to put a fairly high proportion of the total compensation dollar in areas such as retirement plans or other forms of deferred compensation, because an officer of 64 certainly has a much keener interest in this kind of reward than does the typical employee in his early twenties who is just starting his career. Properly designed and implemented, retirement plans can serve an important and useful organizational purpose by making it easier for older employees to retire, thereby opening new channels of promotion for younger ones, but if too large a proportion of the total compensation dollar goes into security packages, the organization may not be able to offer base salaries competitive enough to attract and hold competent younger people with quite different motivational patterns.

Even at the strictly managerial and professional level, this tendency to project one's own needs and values appears to play too large a part in determining compensation policies and practices. Some top executives are reluctant to pay competitive salaries to subordinates because, for a variety of personal reasons, they don't want to set their own salaries significantly higher. Other executives may be strongly motivated by income as an indicator of success or status, in spite of the fact that they are already quite wealthy, and so they believe that this is just about the only thing that will really spur others.

How many companies have ever thought of offering a key manager a choice of ways to achieve certain objectives, say a cash bonus or a year's sabbatical to do anything he wanted to do? (If a sabbatical were an alternative, one appropriate performance objective might be the development of a competent subordinate to take over while the boss was gone.)

More and more companies are coming to realize that their people really do want compensation alternatives, and we will undoubtedly see the further development of cafeteria, or market basket, compensation plans that give employees an opportunity—up to certain limits—to pick and choose the forms of compensation that best meet their individual needs at a given time in their working lives.

The Tendency to Generalize   Here, we are talking about the natural inclination to reduce the complexities of the world and of individual behaviors by grouping and by denying individuality. This "smoothing" is necessary, of course, for the development of any management science or behavioral theory, but every generalization is bound to blur the picture. Carried too far, this composite approach can do more to inhibit than to enhance compensation planning suited to a particular organization's situation.

For example, when a well-known electronics firm was quite young and small, it adopted a policy of distributing a profit sharing cash bonus to every employee at the end of each year. The policy was continued until the company had grown to several thousand employees, at which point a consultant suggested to the president a preferential way of handling this distribution, by putting these monies into an investment retirement trust. The president interviewed several of his senior and middle managers about the idea and found almost unanimous agreement that it was a good one. The result: About a month after the plan was announced to all employees, a representative of the machinists' union walked into the president's office and asked for union recognition, since he had 40 percent of the employees signed up. A hastily designed and conducted employee attitude survey affirmed a comment that was all over the place: "You know what those rats did to us? They took our cash bonus away!"

Obviously, something that was seen as desirable by those in the managerial ranks was perceived in a wholly different way by those at the production level, where the need for direct cash outweighed the need for long-term retirement security. This incident represented a combination of the generalizing tendency and the tendency to project one's own values to others.

In another case of generalizing, a leading West Coast paper products firm had a tradition of tying its salaried and exempt employees' benefits closely to negotiated ones. Among the benefits was a first-dollar medical insurance coverage with a fairly limited maximum. An attitude survey elicited many variations of this comment from the salaried and exempt employees: "The company doesn't do anything for us in the way of benefits; it's the union that gets us our benefits. Whatever the union people get, we get, and that is all—only we have to wait for it a little longer. I'm not nearly so concerned about a deductible as the union people are, but I'm much more concerned about the fact that if any of my family had a long-term serious illness, we would be wiped out. Our coverage doesn't begin to be adequate for that sort of thing."

By recognizing and responding to these perceived need differences, the company was able to provide a better-designed medical insurance plan for the exempt salaried employees at approximately the same cost per individual as for the organized employees. Moreover, it severed the invisible bonds that tied salaried and exempt employees to union negotiators.

Recognizing the diversity of human needs and values, any attempt to provide both appropriate rewards for past performance and effective incentives for continuing optimum performance on an individual basis would be an administrative nightmare. And it would also be so costly to implement and maintain that it would seriously reduce the amount of money available for providing a competitive level of total compensation. That does not mean, however, that we should be content to settle for what is traditional, simple, and desirable to those who carry the primary decision-making responsibilities. Obviously, compromises and trade-offs have to be made, but they can be more significant and more satisfactory all around if we are willing seriously to explore and study what various individuals and groups find most attractive and desirable. What we should *not* do is take it for granted that others share our own needs and values or—even worse—that "we know what's best for them."

Organization Development Objectives, Assumptions and Strategies

Wendell French

Organization development refers to a long-range effort to improve an organization's problem solving capabilities and its ability to cope with changes in its external environment with the help of external or internal behavioral-scientist consultants, or change agents, as they are sometimes called. Such efforts are relatively new but are becoming increasingly visible within the United States, England, Japan, Holland, Norway, Sweden, and perhaps in other countries. A few of the growing number of organizations which have embarked on organization development (OD) efforts to some degree are Union Carbide, Esso, TRW Systems, Humble Oil, Weyerhaeuser, and Imperial Chemical Industries Limited. Other kinds of institutions, including public school systems, churches, and hospitals, have also become involved.

Organization development activities appear to have originated about 1957 as an attempt to apply some of the values and insights of laboratory training to total organizations. The late Douglas McGregor, working with Union Carbide, is considered to have been one of the first behavioral scientists to talk systematically about and to implement an organization development program.[1] Other names associated with such early efforts are Herbert Shepard and Robert Blake who, in collaboration with the Employee Relations Department of the Esso Company, launched a program of laboratory training (sensitivity training) in the company's various refineries. This program emerged in 1957 after a headquarters human relations research division began to view itself as an internal consulting group offering services to field managers rather than as a research group developing reports for top management.[2]

Objectives of Typical OD Programs

Although the specific interpersonal and task objectives of organization development programs will vary according to each diagnosis of organizational problems, a number of objectives typically emerge. These objectives reflect problems which are very common in organizations:

1 To increase the level of trust and support among organizational members.

2 To increase the incidence of confrontation of organizational problems, both within groups and among groups, in contrast to "sweeping problems under the rug."

3 To create an environment in which authority of assigned role is augmented by authority based on knowledge and skill.

4 To increase the openness of communications laterally, vertically, and diagonally.

5 To increase the level of personal enthusiasm and satisfaction in the organization.

6 To find synergistic solutions[3] to problems with greater frequency. (Synergistic solutions are creative solutions in which 2 + 2 equals more than 4, and through which all parties gain more through cooperation than through conflict.)

7 To increase the level of self and group responsibility in planning and implementation.[4]

Difficulties in Categorizing

Before describing some of the basic assumptions and strategies of organization development, it would be well to point out that one of the difficulties in writing about such a "movement" is that a wide variety of activities can be and are subsumed under this label. These activities have varied all the way from inappropriate application of some "canned" management development program to highly responsive and skillful joint efforts between behavioral scientists and client systems.

Thus, while labels are useful, they may gloss over a wide range of phenomena. The "human relations movement," for example, has been widely written about as though it were all bad or all good. To illustrate, some of the critics of the movement have accused it of being "soft" and a "hand-maiden of the Establishment," of ignoring the technical and power systems of organizations, and of being too naively participative. Such criticisms were no doubt warranted in some circumstances, but in other situations may not have been at all appropriate. Paradoxically, some of the major insights of the human relations movement, e.g., that the organization can be viewed as a social system and that subordinates have substantial control over productivity have been assimilated by its critics.

In short, the problem is to distinguish between appropriate and inappropriate programs, between effectiveness and ineffectiveness, and between relevancy and irrelevancy. The discussion which follows will attempt to describe the "ideal" circumstances for organization development programs, as well as to point out some pitfalls and common mistakes in organization change efforts.

Relevancy to Different Technologies and Organization Subunits

Research by Joan Woodward[5] suggests that organization development efforts *might be more relevant to certain kinds of technologies and organizational levels, and perhaps to certain workforce characteristics, than to others.* For example, OD efforts may be more appropriate for an organization devoted to prototype manufacturing than for an automobile assembly plant. However, experiments in an organization like Texas Instruments suggest that some manufacturing efforts which appear to be inherently mechanistic may lend themselves to a more participative, open management style than is often assumed possible.[6]

However, assuming the constraints of a fairly narrow job structure at the rank-and-file level, organization development efforts may inherently be more productive and relevant at the managerial levels of the organization. Certainly OD efforts are most effective when they start at the top. Research and development units—particularly those involving a high degree of interdependency and joint creativity among group members—also appear to be appropriate for organization development activities, if group members are currently experiencing problems in communicating or interpersonal relationships.

Basic Assumptions

Some of the basic assumptions about people which underlie organization development programs are similar to "Theory Y" assumptions[7] and will be repeated only briefly here. However, some of the assumptions about groups and total systems will be treated more extensively. The following assumptions appear to underlie organization development efforts.[8]

About People

- Most individuals have drives toward personal growth and development, and these are most likely to be actualized in an environment which is both supportive and challenging.
- Most people desire to make, and are capable of making, a much higher level of contribution to the attainment of organization goals than most organizational environments will permit.

About People in Groups

- Most people wish to be accepted and to interact cooperatively with at least one small reference group, and usually with more than one group, e.g., the work group, the family group.
- One of the most psychologically relevant reference groups for most people is the work group, including peers and the superior.
- Most people are capable of greatly increasing their effectiveness in helping their reference groups solve problems and in working effectively together.
- For a group to optimize its effectiveness, the formal leader cannot perform all of the leadership functions in all circumstances at all times, and all group members must assist each other with effective leadership and member behavior.

About People in Organizational Systems

- Organizations tend to be characterized by overlapping, interdependent work groups, and the "linking pin" function of supervisors and others needs to be understood and facilitated.[9]
- What happens in the broader organization affects the small work group and vice versa.

- What happens to one subsystem (social, technological, or administrative) will affect and be influenced by other parts of the system.
- The culture in most organizations tends to suppress the expression of feelings which people have about each other and about where they and their organizations are heading.
- Suppressed feelings adversely affect problem solving, personal growth, and job satisfaction.
- The level of interpersonal trust, support, and cooperation is much lower in most organizations than is either necessary or desirable.
- "Win-lose" strategies between people and groups, while realistic and appropriate in some situations, are not optimal in the long run to the solution of most organizational problems.
- Synergistic solutions can be achieved with a much higher frequency than is actually the case in most organizations.
- Viewing feelings as data important to the organization tends to open up many avenues for improved goal setting, leadership, communications, problem solving, intergroup collaboration, and morale.
- Improved performance stemming from organization development efforts needs to be sustained by appropriate changes in the appraisal, compensation, training, staffing, and task-specialization subsystem—in short, in the total personnel system.

Value and Belief Systems
of Behavioral Scientist-Change Agents

While scientific inquiry, ideally, is value-free, the applications of science are not value-free. Applied behavioral scientist-organization development consultants tend to subscribe to a comparable set of values, although we should avoid the trap of assuming that they constitute a completely homogeneous group. They do not.

One value, to which many behavioral scientist-change agents tend to give high priority, is that the needs and aspirations of human beings are the reasons for organized effort in society. They tend, therefore, to be developmental in their outlook and concerned with the long-range opportunities for the personal growth of people in organizations.

A second value is that work and life can become richer and more meaningful, and organized effort more effective and enjoyable, if feelings and sentiments are permitted to be a more legitimate part of the culture. A third value is a commitment to an action role, along with a commitment to research, in an effort to improve the effectiveness of organizations.[10] A fourth value—or perhaps a belief—is that improved competency in interpersonal and intergroup relationship will result in more effective organizations.[11] A fifth value is that behavioral science research and an examination of behavioral science assumptions and values are relevant and important in considering organizational effectiveness. While many change agents are perhaps overly action-oriented in terms of the utilization of their time, nevertheless, as a group they are paying more and more attention to research and to the examination of ideas.[12]

The value placed on research and inquiry raises the question as to whether the assumptions stated earlier are values, theory, or "facts." In my judgment, a substantial body of knowledge, including research on leadership, suggests that there is considerable evidence for these assumptions. However, to conclude that these assumptions are facts, laws, or principles would be to contradict the value placed by behavioral scientists on continuous research and inquiry. Thus, I feel that they should be considered theoretical statements which are based on provisional data.

This also raises the paradox that the belief that people are important tends to result in their being important. The belief that people can grow and develop in terms of personal and organizational competency tends to produce this result. Thus, values and beliefs tend to be self-fulfilling, and the question becomes "What do you choose to want to believe?" While this position can become Pollyannaish in the sense of not seeing the real world, nevertheless, behavioral scientist-change agents, at least this one, tend to place a value on optimism. It is a kind of optimism that says people can do a better job of goal setting and facing up to and solving problems, not an optimism that says the number of problems is diminishing.

It should be added that it is important that the values and beliefs of each behavioral science-change agent be made visible both to himself and to the client. In the first place, neither can learn to adequately trust the other without such exposure—a hidden agenda handicaps both trust building and mutual learning. Second, and perhaps more pragmatically, organizational change efforts tend to fail if a prescription is applied unilaterally and without proper diagnosis.

Strategy in Organization Development:
An Action Research Model

A frequent strategy in organization development programs is based on what behavioral scientists refer to as an "action research model." This model involves extensive collaboration between the consultant (whether an external or an internal change agent) and the client group, data gathering, data discussion, and planning. While descriptions of this model vary in detail and terminology from author to author, the dynamics are essentially the same.[13]

Figure 1 summarizes some of the essential phases of the action research model, using an emerging organization development program as an example. The key aspects of the model are *diagnosis, data gathering, feedback to the client group, data discussion and work by the client group, action planning, and action*. The sequence tends to be cyclical, with the focus on new or advanced problems as the client group learns to work more effectively together. Action research should also be considered a process, since, as William Foote Whyte says, it involves " . . . a continuous gathering and analysis of human relations research data and the feeding of the findings into the organization in such a manner as to change behavior."[14] (Feedback we will define as nonjudgmental observations of behavior.)

Ideally, initial objectives and strategies of organization development efforts stem from a careful diagnosis of such matters as interpersonal and intergroup

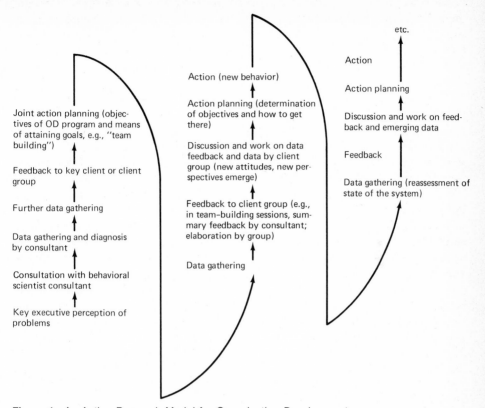

Figure 1   An Action Research Model for Organization Development.

problems, decision-making processes, and communication flow which are currently being experienced by the client organization. As a preliminary step, the
behavioral scientist and the key client (the president of a company, the vice
president in charge of a division, the works manager or superintendent of a plant,
a superintendent of schools, etc.), will make a joint initial assessment of the
critical problems which need working on. Subordinates may also be interviewed
in order to provide supplemental data. The diagnosis may very well indicate that
the central problem is technological or that the key client is not at all willing or
ready to examine the organization's problem-solving ability or his own managerial behavior.[15] Either could be a reason for postponing or moving slowly in the
direction of organization development activities, although the technological
problem may easily be related to deficiencies in interpersonal relationships or
decision making. The diagnosis might also indicate the desirability of one or more
additional specialists (in engineering, finance, or electronic data processing, for
example) to simultaneously work with the organization.

This initial diagnosis, which focuses on the expressed needs of the client, is
extremely critical. As discussed earlier, in the absence of a skilled diagnosis, the
behavioral scientist-change agent would be imposing a set of assumptions and a

set of objectives which may be hopelessly out of joint with either the current problems of the people in the organization or their willingness to learn new modes of behavior. In this regard, it is extremely important that the consultant *hear and understand* what the client is trying to tell him. This requires a high order of skill.[16]

Interviews are frequently used for *data gathering* in OD work for both initial diagnosis and subsequent planning sessions, since personal contact is important for building a cooperative relationship between the consultant and the client group. The interview is also important since the behavioral scientist-consultant is interested in spontaneity and in feelings that are expressed as well as cognitive matters. However, questionnaires are sometimes successfully used in the context of what is sometimes referred to as survey feedback, to supplement interview data.[17]

Data gathering typically goes through several phases. The first phase is related to diagnosing the state of the system and to making plans for organizational change. This phase may utilize a series of interviews between the consultant and the key client, or between a few key executives and the consultant. Subsequent phases focus on problems specific to the top executive team and to subordinate teams. (See Fig. 2.)

Typical questions in data gathering or "problem sensing" would include: What problems do you see in your group, including problems between people, that are interfering with getting the job done the way you would like to see it done?; and what problems do you see in the broader organization? Such open-ended questions provide wide latitude on the part of the respondents and encourage a reporting of problems *as the individual sees them.* Such interviewing is usually conducted privately, with a commitment on the part of the consultant that the information will be used in such a way as to avoid unduly

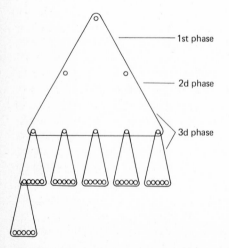

1st phase

1st phase. Data gathering, feedback, and diagnosis—consultant and top executive only

2d phase

2d phase. Data gathering, feedback, and revised diagnosis—consultant and two or more key staff or line people

3d phase

3d phase. Data gathering and feedback to total top executive team in "team-building" laboratory, with or without key subordinates from level below

4th and additional phases. Data gathering and team-building sessions with 2d or 3d level team
Subsequent phases. Data gathering, feedback, and interface problem-solving sessions across groups
Simultaneous phases. Several managers may attend "stranger" T-Groups; courses in the management development program may supplement this learning

Figure 2 Organization Development Phases in a Hypothetical Organization.

embarrassing anyone. The intent is to find out what common problems or themes emerge, with the data to be used constructively for both diagnostic and feedback purposes.

Two- or three-day offsite *team-building or group problem-solving sessions* typically become a major focal point in organization development programs. During these meetings the behavioral scientist frequently provides *feedback* to the group in terms of the themes which emerged in the problem-sensing interviews.[18] He may also encourage the group to determine which items or themes should have priority in terms of maximum utilization of time. These themes usually provide substantial and meaningful data for the group to begin work on. One-to-one interpersonal matters, both positive and negative, tend to emerge spontaneously as the participants gain confidence from the level of support sensed in the group.

Different consultants will vary in their mode of behavior in such sessions, but will typically serve as *"process" observers and as interpreters of the dynamics of the group interaction* to the degree that the group expresses a readiness for such intervention. They also typically encourage people to take risks, a step at a time, and to experiment with new behavior in the context of the level of support in the group. Thus, the trainer-consultant(s) serves as a stimulant to new behavior but also as a protector. The climate which I try to build, for example, is: "Let's not tear down any more than we can build back together."[19] Further, the trainer-consultant typically works with the group to assist team members in improving their skills in diagnosing and facilitating group progress.[20]

It should be noted, however, that different groups will have different needs along a task-process continuum. For example, some groups have a need for intensive work on clarifying objectives; others may have the greatest need in the area of personal relationships. Further, the consultant or the chief consultant in a team of consultants involved in an organization development program will play a much broader role than serving as a T-group or team-building trainer. He will also play an important role in periodic data gathering and diagnosis and in joint long-range planning of the change efforts.[21]

Laboratory Training and Organization Development

Since organization development programs have largely emerged from T-group experience, theory, and research, and since laboratory training in one form or another tends to be an integral part of most such programs, it is important to focus on laboratory training per se. As stated earlier, OD programs grew out of a perceived need to relate laboratory training to the problems of ongoing organizations and a recognition that optimum results could only occur if major parts of the total social system of an organization were involved.

Laboratory training essentially emerged around 1946, largely through a growing recognition by Leland Bradford, Ronald Lippitt, Kenneth Benne, and others, that human relations training which focused on the feelings and concerns of the participants was frequently a much more powerful and viable form of education than the lecture method. Some of the theoretical constructs and insights from which these laboratory training pioneers drew stemmed from earlier research by Lippitt, Kurt Lewin, and Ralph White. The term "T-Group" emerged by 1949 as a shortened label for "Basic Skill Training Group"; these terms were used to identify the programs which began to emerge in the newly formed National Training Laboratory in Group Development (now NTL Institute for Applied Behavioral Science).[22] "Sensitivity Training" is also a term frequently applied to such training.

Ordinarily, laboratory training sessions have certain objectives in common. The following list, by two internationally known behavioral scientists,[23] is probably highly consistent with the objectives of most programs:

Self Objectives
- Increased *awareness* of own feelings and reactions, and own impact on others.
- Increased *awareness* of feelings and reactions of others, and their impact on self.
- Increased *awareness* of dynamics of group action.
- *Changed attitudes* toward self, others, and groups, i.e., more respect for, tolerance for, and faith in self, others, and groups.
- Increased *interpersonal competence,* i.e., skill in handling interpersonal and group relationships toward more productive and satisfying relationships.

Role Objectives
- Increased *awareness* of own organizational role, organizational dynamics, dynamics of larger social systems, and dynamics of the change process in self, small groups, and organizations.
- *Changed attitudes* toward own role, role of others, and organizational relationships, i.e., more respect for and willingness to deal with others with whom one is interdependent, greater willingness to achieve collaborative relationships with others based on mutual trust.
- Increased *interpersonal competence* in handling organizational role relationships with superiors, peers, and subordinates.

Organizational Objectives
- Increased *awareness* of, *changed attitudes* toward, and increased *interpersonal competence* about specific organizational problems existing in groups or units which are interdependent.
- *Organizational improvement* through the training of relationships or groups rather than isolated individuals.

Over the years, experimentation with different laboratory designs has led to diverse criteria for the selection of laboratory participants. Probably a majority of NTL-IABS human relations laboratories are "stranger groups," i.e., involving participants who come from different organizations and who are not likely to have met earlier. However, as indicated by the organizational objectives above, the incidence of special labs designed to increase the effectiveness of persons already working together appears to be growing. Thus terms like "cousin labs," i.e., labs involving people from the same organization but not the same subunit, and "family labs" or "team-building" sessions, i.e., involving a manager and all of his subordinates, are becoming familiar. Participants in labs designed for organizational members not of the same unit may be selected from the same rank level ("horizontal slice") or selected so as to constitute a heterogeneous grouping by rank ("diagonal slice"). Further, NTL-IABS is now encouraging at least two members from the same organization to attend NTL Management Work Conferences and Key Executive Conferences in order to maximize the impact of the learning in the back-home situation.[24]

In general, experienced trainers recommend that persons with severe emotional illness should not participate in laboratory training, with the exception of programs designed specifically for group therapy. Designers of programs make the assumptions, as Argyris states them,[25] that T-Group participants should have:

1   A relatively strong ego that is not overwhelmed by internal conflicts.

2   Defenses which are sufficiently low to allow the individual to hear what others say to him.

3   The ability to communicate thought and feelings with minimal distortion.

As a result of such screening, the incidence of breakdown during laboratory training is substantially less than that reported for organizations in general.[26] However, since the borderline between "normalcy" and illness is very indistinct, most professionally trained staff members are equipped to diagnose severe problems and to make referrals to psychiatrists and clinical psychologists when appropriate. Further, most are equipped to give adequate support and protection to participants whose ability to assimilate and learn from feedback is low. In addition, group members in T-Group situations tend to be sensitive to the emotional needs of the members and to be supportive when they sense a person experiencing pain. Such support is explicitly fostered in laboratory training.

The duration of laboratory training programs varies widely. "Micro-Labs," designed to give people a brief experience with sensitivity training, may last only one hour. Some labs are designed for a long weekend. Typically, however, basic human relations labs are of two weeks duration, with participants expected to meet mornings, afternoons, and evenings, with some time off for recreation. While NTL Management Work Conferences for middle managers and Key Executive Conferences run for one week, team-building labs, from my experience, typically are about three days in length. However, the latter are usually only a part of a broader organization development program involving problem sensing and diagnosis, and the planning of action steps and subsequent sessions. In addition, attendance at stranger labs for key managers is frequently a part of the total organization development effort.

Sensitivity training sessions typically start with the trainer making a few comments about his role—that he is there to be of help, that the group will have control of the agenda, that he will deliberately avoid a leadership role, but that he might become involved as both a leader and a member from time to time, etc. The following is an example of what the trainer might say:

> This group will meet for many hours and will serve as a kind of laboratory where each individual can increase his understanding of the forces which influence individual behavior and the performance of groups and organizations. The data for learning will be our own behavior, feelings, and reactions. We begin with no definite structure or organization, no agreed-upon procedures, and no specific agenda. It will be up to us to fill the vacuum created by the lack of these familiar elements and to study our group as we evolve. My role will be to help the group to learn from its own experience, but not to act as a traditional chairman nor to suggest how we should organize, what our procedure should be, or exactly what our agenda will include. With these few comments, I think we are ready to begin in whatever way you feel will be most helpful.[27]

The trainer then lapses into silence. Group discomfort then precipitates a dialogue which, with skilled trainer assistance, is typically an intense but generally highly rewarding experience for group members. What goes on in the group becomes the data for the learning experience.

Interventions by the trainer will vary greatly depending upon the purpose of the lab and the state of learning on the part of the participants. A common intervention, however, is to encourage people to focus on and own up to their own feelings about what is going on in the group, rather than to make judgments about others. In this way, the participants begin to have more insight into their own feelings and to understand how their behavior affects the feelings of others.

While T-Group work tends to be the focal point in human relations laboratories, laboratory training typically includes theory sessions and frequently includes exercises such as role playing or management games.[28] Further, family labs of subunits of organizations will ordinarily devote more time to planning action steps for back on the job than will stranger labs.

Robert J. House has carefully reviewed the research literature on the impact of T-Group training and has concluded that the research shows mixed results. In particular, research on changes as reflected in personality inventories is seen as inconclusive. However, studies which examine the behavior of participants upon returning to the job are generally more positive.[29] House cites six studies, all of which utilized control groups, and concludes:

> All six studies revealed what appear to be important positive effects of T-Group training. Two of the studies report negative effects as well . . . all of the evidence is based on observations of the behavior of the participants in the actual job situations. No reliance is placed on participant response; rather, evidence is collected from those having frequent contact with the participant in his normal work activities.[30]

John P. Campbell and Marvin D. Dunnette,[31] on the other hand, while conceding that the research shows that T-Group training produces *changes in behavior,* point out that the usefulness of such training in terms of *job perfor-mance* has yet to be demonstrated. They urge research toward "forging the link between training-induced behavior changes and changes in job-performance effectiveness."[32] As a summary comment, they state:

> . . . the assumption that T-Group training has positive utility for organizations must necessarily rest on shaky ground. It has been neither confirmed nor disconfirmed. The authors wish to emphasize . . . that utility for the organization is not necessarily the same as utility for the individual.[33]

At least two major reasons may account for the inconclusiveness of research on the impact of T-Group training on job performance. One reason is simply that little research has been done. The other reason may center around a factor of cultural isolation. To oversimplify, a major part of what one learns in laboratory training, in my opinion, is how to work more effectively with others in group situations, *particularly with others who have developed comparable skills.* Unfortunately, most participants return from T-Group experiences to environments including colleagues and superiors who have not had the same affective (emotional, feeling) experiences, who are not familiar with the terminology and underlying theory, and who may have anxieties (usually unwarranted) about what might happen to them in a T-Group situation.

This cultural distance which laboratory training can produce is one of the reasons why many behavioral scientists are currently encouraging more than one person from the same organization to undergo T-Group training and, ideally, all of the members of a team and their superior to participate in some kind of laboratory training together. The latter assumes that a diagnosis of the organization indicates that the group is ready for such training and assumes such training is reasonably compatible with the broader culture of the total system.

Conditions and Techniques for Successful Organization Development Programs

Theory, research, and experience to date suggest to me that *successful* OD programs tend to evolve in the following way and that they have some of these characteristics (these statements should be considered highly tentative, however):

- There is strong pressure for improvement from both outside the organization and from within.[34]
- An outside behavioral scientist-consultant is brought in for consultation with the top executives and to diagnose organizational problems.
- A preliminary diagnosis suggests that organization development efforts, designed in response to the expressed needs of the key executives, are warranted.
- A collaborative decision is made between the key client group and the consultant to try to change the culture of the organization, at least at the top initially. The specific goals may be to improve communications, to secure more

effective participation from subordinates in problem solving, and to move in the direction of more openness, more feedback, and more support. In short, a decision is made to change the culture to help the company meet its organizational goals and to provide better avenues for initiative, creativity, and self-actualization on the part of organization members.

- Two or more top executives, including the chief executive, go to laboratory training sessions. (Frequently, attendance at labs is one of the facts which precipitates interest in bringing in the outside consultant.)

- Attendance in T-Group program is voluntary. While it is difficult to draw a line between persuasion and coercion, OD consultants and top management should be aware of the dysfunctional consequences of coercion (see the comments on authentic behavior below). While a major emphasis is on team-building laboratories, stranger labs are utilized both to supplement the training going on in the organization and to train managers new to the organization or those who are newly promoted.

- Team-building sessions are held with the top executive group (or at the highest point where the program is started). Ideally, the program is started at the top of the organization, but it can start at levels below the president as long as there is significant support from the chief executive, and preferably from other members of the top power structure as well.

- In a firm large enough to have a personnel executive, the personnel-industrial relations vice president becomes heavily involved at the outset.

- One of two organizational forms emerges to coordinate organization development efforts, either (a) a coordinator reporting to the personnel executive (the personnel executive himself may fill this role), or (b) a coordinator reporting to the chief executive. The management development director is frequently in an ideal position to coordinate OD activities with other management development activities.

- Ultimately, it is essential that the personnel-industrial relations group, including people in salary administration, be an integral part of the organization development program. Since OD groups have such potential for acting as catalysts in rapid organizational change, the temptation is great to see themselves as "good guys" and the other personnel people as "bad guys" or simply ineffective. Any conflicts between a separate organization development group and the personnel and industrial relations groups should be faced and resolved. Such tensions can be the "Achilles heel" for either program. In particular, however, the change agents in the organization development program need the support of the other people who are heavily involved in human resources administration and vice versa; what is done in the OD program needs to be compatible with what is done in selection, promotion, salary administration, appraisal, and vice versa. In terms of systems theory, it would seem imperative that one aspect of the human resources function such as any organization development program must be highly interdependent with the other human resources activities including selection, salary administration, etc. (TRW Systems is an example of an organization which involves top executives plus making the total personnel and industrial relations group an integral part of the OD program.[35])

- Team-building labs, at the request of the various respective executives, with laboratory designs based on careful data gathering and problem diagnosis, are conducted at successively lower levels of the organization with the help of outside consultants, plus the help of internal consultants whose expertise is gradually developed.

• Ideally, as the program matures, both members of the personnel staff and a few line executives are trained to do some organization development work in conjunction with the external and internal professionally trained behavioral scientists. In a sense, then, the external change agent tries to work himself out of a job by developing internal resources.

• The outside consultant(s) and the internal coordinator work very carefully together and periodically check on fears, threats, and anxieties which may be developing as the effort progresses. Issues need to be confronted as they emerge. Not only is the outside change agent needed for his skills, but the organization will need someone to act as a "governor"—to keep the program focused on real problems and to urge authenticity in contrast to gamesmanship. The danger always exists that the organization will begin to punish or reward involvement in T-Group kinds of activities per se, rather than focus on performance.

• The OD consultants constantly work on their own effectiveness in interpersonal relationships and their diagnostic skills so they are not in a position of "do as I say, but not as I do." Further, both consultant and client work together to optimize the consultant's knowledge of the organization's unique and evolving culture structure, and web of interpersonal relationships.

• There needs to be continuous audit of the results, both in terms of checking on the evolution of attitudes about what is going on and in terms of the extent to which problems which were identified at the outset by the key clients are being solved through the program.

• As implied above, the reward system and other personnel systems need to be readjusted to accommodate emerging changes in performance in the organization. Substantially improved performance on the part of individuals and groups is not likely to be sustained if financial and promotional rewards are not forthcoming. In short, management needs to have a "systems" point of view and to think through the interrelationships of the OD effort with the reward and staffing systems and the other aspects of the total human resources subsystem.

In the last analysis, the president and the "line" executives of the organization will evaluate the success of the OD effort in terms of the extent to which it assists the organization in meeting its human and economic objectives. For example, marked improvements on various indices from one plant, one division, one department, etc., will be important indicators of program success. While human resources administration indices are not yet perfected, some of the measuring devices being developed by Likert, Mann, and others show some promise.[36]

Summary Comments

Organization development efforts have emerged through attempts to apply laboratory training values and assumptions to total systems. Such efforts are organic in the sense that they emerge from and are guided by the problems being experienced by the people in the organization. The key to their viability (in contrast to becoming a passing fad) lies in an authentic focus on problems and concerns of the members of the organization and in their confrontation of issues and problems.

Organization development is based on assumptions and values similar to "Theory Y" assumptions and values but includes additional assumptions about total systems and the nature of the client-consultant relationship. Intervention strategies of the behavioral scientist-change agent tend to be based on an action-research model and tend to be focused more on helping the people in an organization learn to solve problems rather than on prescriptions of how things should be done differently.

Laboratory training (or "sensitivity training") or modifications of T-group seminars typically are a part of the organizational change efforts, but the extent and format of such training will depend upon the evolving needs of the organization. Team-building seminars involving a superior and subordinates are being utilized more and more as a way of changing social systems rapidly and avoiding the cultural-distance problems which frequently emerge when individuals return from stranger labs. However, stranger labs can play a key role in change efforts when they are used as part of a broader organization development effort.

Research has indicated that sensitivity training generally produces positive results in terms of changed behavior on the job, but has not demonstrated the link between behavior changes and improved performance. Maximum benefits are probably derived from laboratory training when the organizational culture supports and reinforces the use of new skills in ongoing team situations.

Successful organization development efforts require skillful behavioral scientist interventions, a systems view, and top management support and involvement. In addition, changes stemming from organization development must be linked to changes in the total personnel subsystem. The viability of organization development efforts lies in the degree to which they accurately reflect the aspirations and concerns of the participating members.

In conclusion, *successful organization development tends to be a total system effort; a process of planned change—not a program with a temporary quality; and aimed at developing the organization's internal resources for effective change in the future.*

References

This article is largely based on the forthcoming second edition of my *The Personnel Management Process: Human Resources Administration* (Boston: Houghton Mifflin Company, 1970), chap. 28.

1 Richard Beckhard, W. Warner Burke, and Fred I. Steele, "The Program for Specialists in Organization Training and Development," mimeographed, NTL Institute for Applied Behavioral Science, Dec. 1967, p. ii; and John Paul Jones, "What's Wrong With Work?" in *What's Wrong With Work?* (New York: National Association of Manufacturers, 1967), p. 8. For a history of NTL Institute for Applied Behavioral Sciences, with which Douglas McGregor was long associated in addition to his professorial appointment at M.I.T. and which has been a major

factor in the history of organization development, see Leland P. Bradford, "Biography of an Institution," *Journal of Applied Behavioral Science,* III:2 (1967), 127–143. While we will use the word "program" from time to time, ideally organization development is a "process," not just another new program of temporary quality.

2 Harry D. Kolb, Introduction to *An Action Research Program for Organization Improvement* (Ann Arbor: Foundation for Research in Human Behavior, 1960), p. i.

3 Cattell defines synergy as "the sum total of the energy which a group can command." Daniel Katz and Robert L. Kahn, *The Social Psychology of Organizations* (New York: John Wiley and Sons, 1966), p. 33.

4 For a similar statement of objectives, see "What is OD?" *NTL Institute: News and Reports from NTL Institute for Applied Behavioral Science,* II (June 1968), 1–2. Whether OD programs increase the overall level of authority in contrast to redistributing authority is a debatable point. My hypothesis is that both a redistribution and an overall increase occur.

5 Joan Woodward, *Industrial Organization: Theory and Practice* (London: Oxford University Press, 1965).

6 See M. Scott Myers, "Every Employee a Manager," *California Management Review,* X (Spring 1968), 9–20.

7 See Douglas McGregor, *The Human Side of Enterprise* (New York: McGraw-Hill Book Company, 1960), pp. 47–48.

8 In addition to influence from the writings of McGregor, Likert, Argyris, and others, this discussion has been influenced by "Some Assumptions About Change in Organizations," in notebook "Program for Specialists in Organization Training and Development," NTL Institute for Applied Behavioral Science, 1967; and by staff members who participated in that program.

9 For a discussion of the "linking pin" concept, see Rensis Likert, *New Patterns of Management* (New York: McGraw-Hill Book Company, 1961).

10 Warren G. Bennis sees three major approaches to planned organizational change, with the behavioral scientists associated with each all having "a deep concern with applying social science knowledge to create more viable social systems; a commitment to action, as well as to research . . . and a belief that improved interpersonal and group relationships will ultimately lead to better organizational performance." Bennis, "A New Role for the Behavioral Sciences: Effecting Organizational Change," *Administrative Science Quarterly,* VIII (Sept. 1963), 157–158; and Herbert A. Shepard, "An Action Research Model," in *An Action Research Program for Organization Improvement,* pp. 31–35.

11 Bennis, "A New Role for the Behavioral Sciences," 158.

12 For a discussion of some of the problems and dilemmas in behavioral science research, see Chris Argyris, "Creating Effective Relationships in Organizations," in Richard N. Adams and Jack J. Preiss, eds., *Human Organization Research* (Homewood, Ill.: The Dorsey Press, 1960), pp. 109–123; and Barbara A. Benedict, *et al.,* "The Clinical Experimental Approach to Assessing Organizational Change Efforts," *Journal of Applied Behavioral Science,* (Nov. 1967), 347–380.

13 For further discussion of action research, see Edgar H. Schein and Warren G. Bennis, *Personal and Organizational Change Through Group Methods* (New York: John Wiley and Sons, 1966), pp. 272–274.

14 William Foote Whyte and Edith Lentz Hamilton, *Action Research for Management* (Homewood, Ill.: Richard D. Irwin, 1964), p. 2.

15 Jeremiah J. O'Connell appropriately challenges the notion that there is "one best way" of organizational change and stresses that the consultant should choose his role and intervention strategies on the basis of "the conditions existing when he enters the client system" (*Managing Organizational Innovation* [Homewood, Ill.: Richard D. Irwin, 1968], pp. 10–11).

16 For further discussion of organization diagnosis, see Richard Beckhard, "An Organization Improvement Program in a Decentralised Organization," *Journal of Applied Behavioral Science,* II (Jan.-March 1966), 3–4, "OD as a Process," in *What's Wrong with Work?,* pp. 12–13.

17 For example, see Floyd C. Mann, "Studying and Creating Change," in Timothy W. Costello and Sheldon S. Zalkind, eds., *Psychology in Administration—A Research Orientation* (Englewood Cliffs: Prentice-Hall, 1963), pp. 321–324. See also Delbert C. Miller, "Using Behavioral Science to Solve Organization Problems," *Personnel Administration,* XXXI (Jan.-Feb. 1968), 21–29.

18 For a description of feedback procedures used by the Survey Research Center, Univ. of Michigan, see Mann and Likert, "The Need for Research on the Communication of Research Results," in *Human Organization Research,* pp. 57–66.

19 This phrase probably came from a management workshop sponsored by NTL Institute for Applied Behavioral Science.

20 For a description of what goes on in team-building sessions, see Beckhard, "An Organizational Improvement Program," 9–13; and Newton Margulies and Anthony P. Raia, "People in Organizations—A Case for Team Training," *Training and Development Journal,* XXII (August 1968), 2–11. For a description of problem-solving sessions involving the total management group (about 70) of a company, see Beckhard, "The Confrontation Meeting," *Harvard Business Review,* XLV (March–April 1967), 149–155.

21 For a description of actual organization development programs, see Paul C. Buchanan, "Innovative Organizations—A Study in Organization Development," in *Applying Behavioral Science Research in Industry* (New York: Industrial Relations Counselors, 1964), pp. 87–107; Sheldon A. Davis, "An Organic Problem-Solving Method of Organizational Change," *Journal of Applied Behavioral Science,* III:1 (1967), 3–21; Cyril Sofer, *The Organization from Within* (Chicago: Quadrangle Books, 1961); Alfred J. Marrow, David G. Bowers, and Stanley E. Seashore, *Management by Participation* (New York: Harper and Row, 1967); Robert R. Blake, Jane S. Mouton, Louis B. Barnes, and Larry E. Greiner, "Breakthrough in Organization Development," *Harvard Business Review,* XLII (Nov.-Dec. 1964), 133–155; Alton C. Bartlett, "Changing Behavior as a Means to Increased Efficiency," *Journal of Applied Behavioral Science,* III:3 (1967), 381–403; Larry E. Greiner, "Antecedents of Planned Organization Change," *ibid.,* III:1 (1967), 51–85; and Robert R. Blake and Jane Mouton, *Corporate Excellence Through Grid Organization Development* (Houston, Texas: Gulf Publishing Company, 1968).

22 From Bradford, "Biography of an Institution." See also Kenneth D. Benne, "History of the T Group in the Laboratory Setting," in Bradford, Jack R. Gibb, and Benne, eds., *T/Group Theory and Laboratory Method* (New York: John Wiley and Sons, 1964), pp. 80–135.

23 Schein and Bennis, p. 37.

24 For further discussion of group composition in laboratory training, see Schein and Bennis, pp. 63–69. NTL-IABS now include the Center for Organization Studies, the Center for the Development of Educational Leadership, the Center for Commu-

nity Affairs, and the Center for International Training to serve a wide range of client populations and groups.

25 Chris Argyris, "T-Groups for Organizational Effectiveness," *Harvard Business Review,* XLII (March-April 1964), 60–74.

26 Based on discussions with NTL staff members. One estimate is that the incidence of "serious stress and mental disturbance" during laboratory training is less than one percent of participants and in almost all cases occurs in persons with a history of prior disturbance (Charles Seashore, "What is Sensitivity Training," *NTL Institute News and Reports,* II [April 1968], 2).

27 *Ibid.,* 1.

28 For a description of what goes on in T-groups, see Schein and Bennis, pp. 10–27; Bradford, Gibb, and Benne, pp. 55–67; Dorothy S. Whitaker, "A Case Study of a T-Group," in Galvin Whitaker, ed., *T-Group Training: Group Dynamics in Management Education,* A.T.M. Occasional Papers, (Oxford: Basil Blackwell, 1965), pp. 14–22; Irving R. Weschler and Jerome Reisel, *Inside a Sensitivity Training Group* (Berkeley: University of California, Institute of Industrial Relations, 1959); and William F. Glueck, "Reflections on a T-Group Experience," *Personnel Journal,* XLVII (July 1968), 501–504. For use of cases or exercises based on research results ("instrumented training") see Robert R. Blake and Jane S. Mouton, "The Instrumented Training Laboratory," in Irving R. Weschler and Edgar H. Schein, eds., *Five Issues in Training* (Washington: National Training Laboratories, 1962), pp. 61–76; and W. Warner Burke and Harvey A. Hornstein, "Conceptual vs. Experimental Management Training," *Training and Development Journal,* XXI (Dec. 1967), 12–17.

29 Robert J. House, "T-Group Education and Leadership Effectiveness: A Review of the Empiric Literature and a Critical Evaluation," *Personnel Psychology,* XX (Spring 1967), 1–32. See also Dorothy Stock, "A Survey of Research on T-Groups," in Bradford, Gibb, and Benne, pp. 395–441.

30 House, *ibid.,* pp. 18–19.

31 John P. Campbell and Marvin D. Dunnette, "Effectiveness of T-Group Experiences in Managerial Training and Development," *Psychological Bulletin,* LXX (August 1968), 73–104.

32 *Ibid.,* 100.

33 *Ibid.,* 101. See also the essays by Dunnette and Campbell and Chris Argyris in *Industrial Relations,* VIII (Oct. 1968), 1–45.

34 On this point, see Larry E. Greiner, "Patterns of Organization Change," *Harvard Business Review,* XLV (May-June 1967), 119–130.

35 See Sheldon A. Davis, "An Organic Problem-Solving Method."

36 See Rensis Likert, *The Human Organization: Its Management and Value* (New York: McGraw-Hill Book Company, 1967).

Reading Related to Chapter 13

Group Dynamics and the Individual

Dorwin Cartwright
Ronald Lippitt

How should we think of the relation between individuals and groups? Few questions have stirred up so many issues of metaphysics, epistemology, and ethics. Do groups have the same reality as individuals? If so, what are the properties of groups? Can groups learn, have goals, be frustrated, develop, regress, begin and end? Or are these characteristics strictly attributable only to individuals? If groups exist, are they good or bad? How *should* an individual behave with respect to groups? How *should* groups treat their individual members? Such questions have puzzled man from the earliest days of recorded history.

In our present era of "behavioral science" we like to think that we can be "scientific" and proceed to study human behavior without having to take sides on these problems of speculative philosophy. Invariably, however, we are guided by certain assumptions, stated explicitly or not, about the reality or irreality of groups, about their observability, and about their good or bad value.

Usually these preconceptions are integral parts of one's personal and scientific philosophy, and it is often hard to tell how much they derive from emotionally toned personal experiences with other people and how much from coldly rational and "scientific" considerations. In view of the fervor with which they are usually defended, one might suspect that most have a small basis at least in personally significant experiences. These preconceptions, moreover, have a tendency to assume a homogeneous polarization—either positive or negative.

Consider first the completely negative view. It consists of two major assertions: first, groups don't really exist. They are a product of distorted thought processes (often called "abstractions"). In fact, social prejudice consists precisely in acting as if groups, rather than individuals, were real. Second, groups are bad. They demand blind loyalty, they make individuals regress, they reduce

Reprinted by permission from *International Journal of Group Psychotherapy,* vol. 7, no. 1, January 1957, pp. 86–102.

man to the lowest common denominator, and they produce what *Fortune* magazine has immortalized as "group-think."

In contrast to this completely negative conception of groups, there is the completely positive one. This syndrome, too, consists of two major assertions: first, groups really do exist. Their reality is demonstrated by the difference it makes to an individual whether he is accepted or rejected by a group and whether he is part of a healthy or sick group. Second, groups are good. They satisfy deep-seated needs of individuals for affiliation, affection, recognition, and self-esteem; they stimulate individuals to moral heights of altruism, loyalty, and self-sacrifice; they provide a means, through cooperative interaction, by which man can accomplish things unattainable through individual enterprise.

This completely positive preconception is the one attributed most commonly, it seems, to the so-called "group dynamics movement." Group dynamicists, it is said, have not only *reified* the group but also *idealized* it. They believe that everything should be done by and in groups—individual responsibility is bad, man-to-man supervision is bad, individual problem-solving is bad, and even individual therapy is bad. The only good things are committee meetings, group decisions, group problem-solving, and group therapy. "If you don't hold the group in such high affection," we were once asked, "why do you call your research organization the Research Center For Group Dynamics? And, if you are for groups and group dynamics, mustn't you therefore be *against* individuality, individual responsibility, and self-determination?"

Five Propositions about Groups

This assumption that individuals and groups must necessarily have incompatible interests is made so frequently in one guise or another that it requires closer examination. Toward this end we propose five related assertions about individuals, groups, and group dynamics, which are intended to challenge the belief that individuals and groups must necessarily have incompatible, or for that matter, compatible interests.

1   Groups do exist; they must be dealt with by any man of practical affairs, or indeed by any child, and they must enter into any adequate account of human behavior. Most infants are born into a specific group. Little Johnny may be a welcome or unwelcome addition to the group. His presence may produce profound changes in the structure of the group and consequently in the feelings, attitudes, and behavior of various group members. He may create a triangle where none existed before or he may break up one which has existed. His development and adjustment for years to come may be deeply influenced by the nature of the group he enters and by his particular position in it—whether, for example, he is a first or second child (a personal property which has no meaning apart from its reference to a specific group).

There is a wealth of research whose findings can be satisfactorily interpreted only by assuming the reality of groups. Recall the experiment of Lewin, Lippitt, and White in which the level of aggression of an individual was shown to depend upon the social atmosphere and structure of the group he is in and not merely upon such personal traits as aggressiveness.[1] By now there can be little question about the kinds of results reported from the Western Electric study which make it clear that groups develop norms for the behavior of their members with the result that "good" group members adopt these norms as their *personal* values.[2] Nor can one ignore the dramatic evidence of Lewin, Bavelas, and others which shows that group decisions may produce changes in individual behavior much larger than those customarily found to result from attempts to modify the behavior of individuals *as* isolated individuals.[3]

2   Groups are inevitable and ubiquitous. The biological nature of man, his capacity to use language, and the nature of his environment which has been built into its present form over thousands of years require that man exist in groups. This is not to say that groups must maintain the properties they now display, but we cannot conceive of a collection of human beings living in geographical proximity under conditions where it would be correct to assert that no groups exist and that there is no such thing as group membership.

3   Groups mobilize powerful forces which produce effects of the utmost importance to individuals. Consider two examples from rather different research settings. Seashore has recently published an analysis of data from 5,871 employees of a large manufacturing company.[4] An index of group cohesiveness, developed for each of 228 work groups, permitted a comparison of members working in high and in low cohesive groups. Here is one of his major findings: "Members of high cohesive groups exhibit less anxiety than members of low cohesive groups, using as measures of anxiety: (a) feeling 'jumpy' or 'nervous,' (b) feeling under pressure to achieve higher productivity (with actual productivity held constant), and (c) feeling a lack of support from the company."[5] Seashore suggests two reasons for the relation between group cohesiveness and individual anxiety: "(1) that the cohesive group provides effective support for the individual in his encounters with anxiety-provoking aspects of his environment, thus allaying anxiety, and (2) that group membership offers direct satisfaction, and this satisfaction in membership has a generalized effect of anxiety-reduction."[6]

Perhaps a more dramatic account of the powerful forces generated in groups can be derived from the publication by Stanton and Schwartz of their studies of a mental hospital.[7] They report, for example, how a patient may be thrown into an extreme state of excitement by disagreements between two staff members over the patient's care. Thus, two doctors may disagree about whether a female patient should be moved to another ward. As the disagreement progresses, the doctors may stop communicating relevant information to one another and start lining up allies in the medical and nursing staff. The patient, meanwhile, becomes increasingly restless until, at the height of the doctors' disagreement, she is in an acute state of excitement and must be secluded, put under sedation, and given special supervision. Presumably, successful efforts to improve the interpersonal relations and communications among members of the staff would improve the mental condition of such a patient.

In general, it is clear that events occurring in a group may have repercussions on members who are not directly involved in these events. A person's position in a group, moreover, may affect the way others behave toward him and such personal qualities as his levels of aspiration and self-esteem. Group membership itself may be a prized possession or an oppressive burden; tragedies of major proportions have resulted from the exclusion of individuals from groups, and equally profound consequences have stemmed from enforced membership in groups.

4 Groups may produce both good and bad consequences. The view that groups are completely good and the view that they are completely bad are both based on convincing evidence. *The only fault with either is its one-sidedness.* Research motivated by one or the other is likely to focus on different phenomena. As an antidote to such one-sidedness it is a good practice to ask research questions in pairs, one stressing positive aspects and one negative: What are the factors producing conformity? *and* what are the factors producing nonconformity? What brings about a breakdown in communication? *and* what stimulates or maintains effective communications? An exclusive focus on pathologies or upon positive criteria leads to a seriously incomplete picture.

5 A correct understanding of group dynamics permits the possibility that desirable consequences from groups can be deliberately enhanced. Through a knowledge of group dynamics, groups can be made to serve better ends, for knowledge gives power to modify human beings and human behavior. At the same time, recognition of this fact produces some of the deepest conflicts within the behavioral scientists, for it raises the whole problem of social manipulation. Society must not close its eyes to Orwell's horrible picture of life in 1984, but it cannot accept the alternative that in ignorance there is safety.

To recapitulate our argument: groups exist; they are inevitable and ubiquitous; they mobilize powerful forces having profound effects upon individuals; these effects may be good or bad; and through a knowledge of group dynamics there lies the possibility of maximizing their good value.

A Dilemma

Many thoughtful people today are alarmed over one feature of groups: the pressure toward conformity experienced by group members. Indeed, this single "bad" aspect is often taken as evidence that groups are bad in general. Let us examine the specific problem of conformity, then, in order to attain a better understanding of the general issue. Although contemporary concern is great, it is not new. More than one hundred years ago Alexis de Tocqueville wrote: "I know of no country in which there is so little independence of mind and real freedom of discussion as in America. . . . In America the majority raises formidable barriers around the liberty of opinion. . . . The master (majority) no longer says: 'You shall think as I do or you shall die': but he says: 'You are free to think differently from me and to retain your life, your property, and all that you possess, but they will be useless to you, for you will never be chosen by your fellow citizens if you solicit their votes; and they will affect to scorn you if you ask for their esteem. You will remain among men, but you will be deprived of the rights of mankind. Your fellow creatures will shun you like an impure being; and even those who believe in your innocence will abandon you, lest they should be shunned in their turn.'"[8]

Before too readily accepting such a view of groups as the whole story, let us invoke our dictum that research questions should be asked in pairs. Nearly everyone is convinced that individuals should not be blind conformers to group norms, that each group member should not be a carbon copy of every other member, but what is the other side of the coin? In considering why members of groups conform, perhaps we should also think of the consequences of the removal of individuals from group membership or the plight of the person who really does not belong to any group with clear-cut norms and values. The state of anomie, described by Durkheim, is also common today. It seems as if people who have no effective participation in groups with clear and strong value systems either crack up (as in alcoholism or suicide) or they seek out groups which will demand conformity. In discussing this process, Talcott Parsons writes: "In such a situation it is not surprising that large numbers of people should . . . be attracted to movements which can offer them membership in a group with a vigorous esprit de corps with submission to some strong authority and rigid system of belief, the individual thus finding a measure of escape from painful perplexities or from a situation of anomie."[9]

The British anthropologist, Adam Curle, has stressed the same problem when he suggested that in our society we need not four, but five freedoms, the fifth being freedom from that neurotic anxiety which springs from a man's isolation from his fellows, and which, in turn, isolates him still further from them.

We seem, then, to face a dilemma: the individual needs social support for his values and social beliefs; he needs to be accepted as a valued member of some group which *he* values; failure to maintain such group membership produces anxiety and personal disorganization. But, on the other hand, group membership and group participation tend to cost the individual his individuality. If he is to receive support from others and, in turn, give support to others, he and they must hold in common some values and beliefs. Deviation from these undermines any possibility of group support and acceptance.

Is there an avenue of escape from this dilemma? Certainly, the issue is not as simple as we have described it. The need for social support for some values does not require conformity with respect to all values, beliefs, and behavior. Any individual is a member of several groups, and he may be a successful deviate in one while conforming to another (think of the visitor in a foreign country or of the psychologist at a convention of psychiatrists). Nor should the time dimension be ignored; a person may sustain his deviancy through a conviction that his fate is only temporary. These refinements of the issue are important and should be examined in great detail, but before we turn our attention to them, we must assert that we do *not* believe that the basic dilemma can be escaped. To avoid complete personal disorganization man must conform to at least a minimal set of values required for participation in the groups to which he belongs.

Pressures to Uniformity

Some better light may be cast on this problem if we refer to the findings of research on conformity. What do we know about the way it operates?

Cognitive Processes Modern psychological research on conformity reflects the many different currents of contemporary psychology, but the major direction has been largely determined by the classic experiment of Sherif on the development of social norms in perceiving autokinetic movement[10] and by the more recent study of Asch of pressures to conformity in perceiving unambiguous visual stimuli.[11]

What does this line of investigation tell us about conformity? What has it revealed, for instance, about the conditions that set up pressures to conformity? Answers to this question have taken several forms, but nearly all point out that social interaction would be impossible if some beliefs and perceptions were not commonly shared by the participants. Speaking of the origin of such cognitive pressures to uniformity among group members, Asch says: "The individual comes to experience a world that he shares with others. He perceives that the surroundings include him, as well as others, and that he is in the same relation to the surroundings as others. He notes that he, as well as others, is converging upon the same object and responding to its identical properties. Joint action and mutual understanding require this relation of intelligibility and structural simplicity. In these terms the 'pull' toward the group becomes understandable."[12]

Consistent with this interpretation of the origin of pressures to uniformity in a perceptual or judgmental situation are the findings that the major variables influencing tendencies to uniformity are (a) the quality of the social evidence (particularly the degree of unanimity of announced perceptions and the subject's evaluation of the trustworthiness of the other's judgments), (b) the quality of the direct perceptual evidence (particularly the clarity or ambiguity of the stimuli), (c) the magnitude of the discrepancy between the social and the perceptual evidence, and (d) the individual's self-confidence in the situation (as indicated either by experimental manipulations designed to affect self-confidence or by personality measurements).

The research in this tradition has been productive, but it has emphasized the individual and his cognitive problems and has considered the individual apart from any concrete and meaningful group membership. Presumably any trustworthy people adequately equipped with eyes and ears could serve to generate pressures to conformity in the subject, regardless of his specific relations to them. The result of this emphasis has been to ignore certain essential aspects of the conformity problem. Let us document this assertion with two examples.

First, the origin of pressures to uniformity has been made to reside in the person whose conformity is being studied. Through eliminating experimentally any possibility that pressures might be exerted by others, it has been possible to study the conformity of people as if they existed in a world where they can see or hear others but not be reacted to by others. It is significant, indeed, that conformity does arise in the absence of direct attempts to bring it about. But this approach does not raise certain questions about the conditions which lead to *social* pressures to conformity. What makes some people try to get others to conform? What conditions lead to what forms of pressure on others to get them to conform? The concentration of attention on the conformer has diverted attention away from the others in the situation who may insist on conformity and make vigorous efforts to bring it about or who may not exert any pressure at all on deviates.

A second consequence of this emphasis has been to ignore the broader social meaning of conformity. Is the individual's personal need for a social validation of his beliefs the only reason for conforming? What does deviation do to a person's acceptance by others? What does it do to his ability to influence others? Or from the group's point of view, are there reasons to insist on certain common values, beliefs, and behavior? These questions are not asked nor answered by an approach which limits itself to the cognitive problems of the individual.

Group Processes The group dynamics orientation toward conformity emphasizes a broader range of determinants. Not denying the importance of the cognitive situation, we want to look more closely at the nature of the individual's relation to particular groups with particular properties. In formulating hypotheses about the origin of pressures to uniformity, two basic sources have been stressed. These have been stated most clearly by Festinger and his co-workers, who propose that when differences of opinion arise within a group, pressures to uniformity will arise (a) if the validity or "reality" of the opinion depends upon agreement with the group (essentially the same point as Asch's), or (b) if locomotion toward a group goal will be facilitated by uniformity within the group.[13]

This emphasis upon the group, rather than simply upon the individual, leads one to expect a broader set of consequences from pressures to uniformity. Pressures to uniformity are seen as establishing: (a) a tendency on the part of each group member to change his own opinion to conform to that of the other group members, (b) a tendency to try to change the opinions of others, and (c) a tendency to redefine the boundaries of the group so as to exclude those holding deviate opinions. The relative magnitudes of these tendencies will depend on other conditions which need to be specified.

This general conception of the nature of the processes that produce conformity emerged from two early field studies conducted at the Research Center for Group Dynamics. It was also influenced to a considerable extent by the previous work of Newcomb in which he studied the formation and change of social attitudes in a college community.[14] The first field study, reported by Festinger, Schachter, and Back, traced the formation of social groups in a new student housing project. As each group developed, it displayed its own standards for its members. The extent of conformity to the standards of a particular group was found to be related directly to the degree of cohesiveness of that group as measured by sociometric choices. Moreover, those individuals who deviated from their own group's norms received fewer sociometric choices than those who conformed. A process of rejection for nonconformity had apparently set in.[15] The second field study, reported by Coch and French, observed similar processes. This study was conducted in a textile factory and was concerned with conformity to production standards set by groups of workers. Here an individual worker's reaction to new work methods was found to depend upon the standards of his group and, here too, rejection for deviation was observed.[16]

The next phase of this research consisted of a series of experiments with groups created in the laboratory. It was hoped thereby to be able to disentangle the complexity of variables that might exist in any field setting in order to understand better the operation of each. These experiments have been reported in various publications by Festinger, Back, Gerard, Hymovitch, Kelley, Raven, Schachter, and Thibaut.[17,18,19,20,21,22] We shall not attempt to describe these studies in detail, but draw upon them and other research in an effort to summarize the major conclusions.

First, a great deal of evidence has been accumulated to support the hypothesis that pressures to uniformity will be greater the more members want to remain in the group. In more attractive or cohesive groups, members attempt more to influence others and are more willing to accept influence from others. Note that here pressures to conformity are high in the very conditions where satisfaction from group membership is also high.

Second, there is a close relation between attempts to change the deviate and tendencies to reject him. If persistent attempts to change the deviate fail to produce conformity, then communication appears to cease between the majority and the deviate, and rejection of the deviate sets in. These two processes, moreover, are more intense the more cohesive the group. One of the early studies which documented the process of rejection was conducted by Schachter on college students.[23] It has recently been replicated by Emerson on high school students who found essentially the same process at work, but he discovered that among his high school students efforts to influence others continued longer, there was a greater readiness on the part of the majority to change, and there was a lower level of rejection within a limited period of time.[24] Yet another study, conducted in Holland, Sweden, France, Norway, Belgium, Germany, and England, found the same tendency to reject deviates in all of these countries. This study, reported by Schachter, et al., is a landmark in cross-cultural research.[25]

Third, there is the question of what determines whether or not pressures to uniformity will arise with respect to any particular opinion, attitude, and behavior. In most groups there are no pressures to uniformity concerning the color of necktie worn by the members. Differences of opinion about the age of the earth probably would not lead to rejection in a poker club, but they might do so in certain fundamentalist church groups. The concept of *relevance* seems to be required to account for such variations in pressures to uniformity. And, if we ask, "relevance for what?" we are forced again to look at the group and especially at the goals of the group.

Schachter has demonstrated, for example, that deviation on a given issue will result much more readily in rejection when that issue is relevant to the group's goals than when it is irrelevant.[26] And the principle of relevance seems to be necessary to account for the findings of a field study reported by Ross.[27] Here attitudes of fraternity men toward restrictive admission policies were studied. Despite the fact that there was a consistent policy of exclusion in these fraternities, there was, surprisingly, little evidence for the existence of pressures toward uniformity of attitudes. When, however, a field experiment was conducted in which the distribution of actual opinions for each fraternity house was reported to a meeting of house members together with a discussion of the relevance of these opinions for fraternity policy, attitudes then tended to change to conform to the particular modal position of each house. Presumably the experimental treatment made uniformity of attitude instrumental to group locomotion where it had not been so before.

Sources of Heterogeneity

We have seen that pressures to uniformity are stronger the more cohesive the group. Shall we conclude from this that strong, need-satisfying, cohesive groups must always produce uniformity on matters that are important to the group? We believe not. We cannot, however, cite much convincing evidence since research has focused to date primarily upon the sources of pressures to uniformity and has ignored the conditions which produce heterogeneity. Without suggesting, then, that we can give final answers, let us indicate some of the possible sources of heterogeneity.

Group Standards about Uniformity It is important, first, to make a distinction between conformity and uniformity. A group might have a value that everyone should be as different from everyone else as possible. Conformity to this value, then, would result not in uniformity of behavior but in nonuniformity. Such a situation often arises in therapy groups or training groups where it is possible to establish norms which place a high value upon "being different" and upon tolerating deviant behavior. Conformity to this value is presumably greater the more cohesive the group and the more it is seen as relevant to the group's objectives. Unfortunately, very little is known about the origin and operation of group standards about conformity itself. We doubt that the pressure to uniformity which arises from the need for "social reality" and for group locomotion can simply be obliterated by invoking a group standard of tolerance, but a closer look at such processes as those of group decision-making will be required before a deep understanding of this problem can be achieved.

Freedom to Deviate A rather different source of heterogeneity has been suggested by Kelley and Shapiro.[28] They reason that the more an individual feels accepted by the other members of the group, the more ready he should be to deviate from the beliefs of the majority under conditions where objectively correct deviation would be in the group's best interest. They designed an experiment to test this hypothesis. The results, while not entirely clear because acceptance led to greater cohesiveness, tend to support this line of reasoning.

It has been suggested by some that those in positions of leadership are freer to deviate from group standards than are those of lesser status. Just the opposite conclusion has been drawn by others. Clearly, further research into group properties which generate freedom to deviate from majority pressures is needed.

Subgroup Formation   Festinger and Thibaut have shown that lower group-wide pressures to uniformity of opinion result when members of a group perceive that the group is composed of persons differing in interest and knowledge. Under these conditions subgroups may easily develop with a resulting heterogeneity within the group as a whole though with uniformity within each subgroup.[29] This conclusion is consistent with Asch's finding that the presence of a partner for a deviate greatly strengthens his tendency to be independent.[30] One might suspect that such processes, though achieving temporarily a greater heterogeneity, would result in a schismatic subgroup conflict.

Positions and Roles   A more integrative achievement of heterogeneity seems to arise through the process of role differentiation. Established groups are usually differentiated according to "positions" with special function attached to each. The occupant of the position has certain behaviors prescribed for him by the others in the group. These role prescriptions differ, moreover, from one position to another, with the result that conformity to them produces heterogeneity within the group. A group function, which might otherwise be suppressed by pressures to uniformity, may be preserved by the establishment of a position whose responsibility is to perform the function.

Hall has recently shown that social roles can be profitably conceived in the context of conformity to group pressures. He reasoned that pressures to uniformity of prescriptions concerning the behavior of the occupant of a position and pressures on the occupant to conform to these prescriptions should be greater the more cohesive the group.[31] A study of the role of aircraft commander in bomber crews lends strong support to this conception.

In summary, it should be noted that in all but one of these suggested sources of heterogeneity we have assumed the process of conformity—to the norms of a subgroup, to a role, or to a group standard favoring heterogeneity. Even if the price of membership in a strong group be conformity, it need not follow that strong groups will suppress differences.

More than One Group

Thus far our analysis has proceeded as though the individual were a member of only one group. Actually we recognize that he is, and has been, a member of many groups. In one of our current research projects we are finding that older adolescents can name from twenty to forty "important groups and persons that influence my opinions and behavior in decision situations." Indeed, some personality theorists hold that personality should be viewed as an "internal society" made up of representations of the diverse group relationships which the individual now has and has had. According to this view, each individual has a unique internal society and makes his own personal synthesis of the values and behavior preferences generated by these affiliations.

The various memberships of an individual may relate to one another in various ways and produce various consequences for the individual. A past group may exert internal pressures toward conformity which are in conflict with a present group. Two contemporaneous groups may have expectations for the person which are incompatible. Or an individual may hold a temporary membership (the situation of a foreign student, for example) and be faced with current conformity pressures which if accepted will make it difficult to readjust when returning to his more permanent memberships.

This constant source of influence from other memberships toward deviancy of every member of every group requires that each group take measures to preserve its integrity. It should be noted, however, that particular deviancy pressures associated with a given member may be creative or destructive when evaluated in terms of the integrity and productivity of the group, and conformity pressures from the group may be supportive or disruptive of the integrity of the individual.

Unfortunately there has been little systematic research on these aspects of multiple group membership. We can only indicate two sets of observations concerning (a) the intrapersonal processes resulting from multiple membership demands, and (b) the effects on group processes of the deviancy pressures which arise from the multiple membership status of individual members.

Marginal Membership   Lewin, in his discussion of adolescence and of minority group membership, has analyzed some of the psychological effects on the person of being "between two groups" without a firm anchorage in either one.[32] He says: "The transition from childhood to adulthood may be a rather sudden shift (for instance, in some of the primitive societies), or it may occur gradually in a setting where children and adults are not sharply separated groups. In the case of the so-called 'adolescent difficulties,' however, a third state of affairs is often prevalent: children and adults constitute two clearly defined groups; the adolescent does not wish any longer to belong to the children's group and, at the same time, knows that he is not really accepted in the adult group. He has a position similar to what is called in sociology the 'marginal man' . . . a person who stands on the boundary between two groups. He does not belong to either of them, or at least he is not sure of his belongingness in either of them."[33] Lewin goes on to point out that there are characteristic maladjustive behavior patterns resulting from this unstable membership situation: high tension, shifts between extremes of behavior, high sensitivity, and rejection of low status members of both groups. This situation, rather than fostering strong individuality, makes belonging to closely knit, loyalty-demanding groups very attractive. Dependency and acceptance are a welcome relief. Probably most therapy groups have a number of members who are seeking relief from marginality.

Overlapping Membership   There is quite a different type of situation where the person does have a firm anchorage in two or more groups but where the group standards are not fully compatible. Usually the actual conflict arises when the person is physically present in one group but realizes that he also belongs to other groups to which he will return in the near or distant future. In this sense, the child moves between his family group and his school group every day. The member of a therapy group has some sort of time perspective of "going back" to a variety of other groups between each meeting of the therapy group.

In their study of the adjustment of foreign students both in this country and after returning home, Watson and Lippitt observed four different ways in which individuals cope with this problem of overlapping membership.

1   Some students solved the problem by "living in the present" at all times. When they were in the American culture all of their energy and attention was directed to being an acceptable member of this group. They avoided conflict within themselves by minimizing thought about and contact with the other group "back home." When they returned to the other group they used the same type of solution, quickly shifting behavior and ideas to fit back into the new present group. Their behavior appeared quite inconsistent, but it was a consistent approach to solving their problem of multiple membership.

2   Other individuals chose to keep their other membership the dominant one while in this country. They were defensive and rejective every time the present group seemed to promote values and to expect behavior which they felt might not be acceptable to the other group "back home." The strain of maintaining this orientation was relieved by turning every situation into a "black and white" comparison and adopting a consistently rejective posture toward the present, inferior group. This way of adjusting required a considerable amount of distorting of present and past realities, but the return to the other group was relatively easy.

3   Others reacted in a sharply contrasting way by identifying wholeheartedly with the present group and by rejecting the standards of the other group as incorrect or inferior at the points of conflict. They were, of course accepted by the present group, but when they returned home they met rejection or felt alienated from the standards of the group (even when they felt accepted).

4   Some few individuals seemed to achieve a more difficult but also more creative solution. They attempted to regard membership in both groups as desirable. In order to succeed in this effort, they had to be more realistic about perceiving the inconsistencies between the group expectations and to struggle to make balanced judgments about the strong and weak points of each group. Besides taking this more objective approach to evaluation, these persons worked on problems of how the strengths of one group might be interpreted and utilized by the other group. They were taking roles of creative deviancy in both groups, but attempting to make their contributions in such a way as to be accepted as loyal and productive members. They found ways of using each group membership as a resource for contributing to the welfare of the other group. Some members of each group were of course threatened by this readiness and ability to question the present modal ways of doing things in the group. [34]

Thus it seems that the existence of multiple group memberships creates difficult problems both for the person and for the group. But there are also potentialities and supports for the development of creative individuality in this situation, and there are potentialities for group growth and achievement in the fact that the members of any group are also members of other groups with different standards.

Some Conclusions

Let us return now to the question raised at the beginning of this paper. How should we think of the relation between individuals and groups? If we accept the assumption that individuals and groups are both important social realities, we can then ask a pair of important questions. What kinds of effects do groups have on the emotional security and creative productivity of the individual? What kinds of effects do individuals have on the morale and creative productivity of the group? In answering these questions it is important to be alerted to both good and bad effects. Although the systematic evidence from research does not begin to provide full answers to these questions, we have found evidence which tends to support the following general statements.

Strong groups do exert strong influences on members toward conformity. These conformity pressures, however, may be directed toward uniformity of thinking and behavior, or they may foster heterogeneity.

Acceptance of these conformity pressures, toward uniformity or heterogeneity, may satisfy the emotional needs of some members and frustrate others. Similarly, it may support the potential creativity of some members and inhibit that of others.

From their experiences of multiple membership and their personal synthesis of these experiences, individuals do have opportunities to achieve significant bases of individuality.

Because each group is made up of members who are loyal members of other groups and who have unique individual interests, each group must continuously cope with deviancy tendencies of the members. These tendencies may represent a source of creative improvement in the life of the group or a source of destructive disruption.

The resolution of these conflicting interests does not seem to be the strengthening of individuals and the weakening of groups, or the strengthening of groups and the weakening of individuals, but rather a strengthening of both by qualitative improvements in the nature of interdependence between integrated individuals and cohesive groups.

References

1 K. Lewin, R. Lippitt, and R. White, "Patterns of Aggressive Behavior in Experimentally Created 'Social Climates,'" *Journal of Social Psychology,* 10 (1939), pp. 271–299.

2 F. J. Roethlisberger and W. J. Dickson, *Management and the Worker* (Cambridge: Harvard University Press, 1939).

3 K. Lewin, "Studies in Group Decision," in *Group Dynamics: Research and Theory,* D. Cartwright and A. Zander, ed. (Evanston: Harper & Row, Publishers, 1953).

4 S. E. Seashore, *Group Cohesiveness in the Industrial Group* (Ann Arbor: Institute for Social Research, 1954).

5 *Ibid.*, p. 98.

6 *Ibid.*, p. 13.

7 A. H. Stanton and M. S. Schwartz, *The Mental Hospital* (New York: Basic Books, Inc., Publishers, 1954).

8 A. Tocqueville, *Democracy in America,* Vol. 1 (New York: Alfred A. Knopf, Inc., 1945 (original publication, 1835), pp. 273–275.

9 T. Parsons, *Essays in Sociological Theory,* rev. ed. (New York: Free Press of Glencoe, Inc., 1954), pp. 128–129.

10 M. Sherif, *The Psychology of Social Norms* (New York: Harper & Row, Publishers, 1936).

11 S. E. Asch, *Social Psychology* (New York: Prentice-Hall, Inc., 1952).

12 *Ibid.*, p. 484.

13 L. Festinger, "Informal Social Communication," *Psychology Review,* 57 (1950), pp. 271–292.

14 T. M. Newcomb, *Personality and Social Change* (New York: Holt, Rinehart & Winston, Inc., 1943).

15 L. Festinger, S. Schachter, and K. Back, *Social Pressures in Informal Groups* (New York: Harper & Row, Publishers, 1950).

16 L. Coch and J. R. P. French, "Overcoming Resistance to Change," *Human Relations,* I (1948), pp. 512–532.

17 K. W. Back, "Influence Through Social Communication," *Journal of Abnormal and Social Psychology,* 46 (1951), pp. 9–23.

18 L. Festinger, H. B. Gerard, B. Hymovitch, H. H. Kelley, and B. Raven, "The Influence Process in the Presence of Extreme Deviates," *Human Relations,* 5 (1952), pp. 327–346.

19 L. Festinger and J. Thibaut, "Interpersonal Communication in Small Groups," *Journal of Abnormal and Social Psychology,* 46 (1951) pp. 92–99.

20 H. B. Gerard, "The Effect of Different Dimensions of Disagreement on the Communication Process in Small Groups," *Human Relations,* 6 (1953) pp. 249–271.

21 H. H. Kelley, "Communication in Experimentally Created Hierarchies," *Human Relations,* 4 (1951), pp. 39–56.

22 S. Schachter, "Deviation, Rejection, and Communication," *Journal of Abnormal and Social Psychology,* 46 (1951), pp. 190–207.

23 *Ibid.*

24 F. M. Emerson, "Deviation and Rejection: An Experimental Replication," *American Sociological Review,* 19 (1954), pp. 688–693.

25 S. Schachter, *et al.*, "Cross-cultural Experiments on Threat and Rejection," *Human Relations,* 7 (1954), pp. 403–439.

26 Schachter.

27 I. Ross, "Group Standards Concerning the Admission of Jews," *Social Problems,* 2 (1955), pp. 133–140.

28 H. H. Kelley and M. M. Shapiro, "An Experiment on Conformity to Group Norms Where Conformity Is Detrimental to Group Achievement," *American Sociological Review,* 19 (1954), pp. 667–677.

29 Festinger and Thibault.

30 Asch.

31 R. L. Hall, "Social Influence on the Aircraft Commander's Role," *American Sociological Review,* 20 (1955), pp. 292–299.

32 K. Lewin, *Field Theory in Social Science* (New York: Harper & Row, Publishers, 1951).

33 *Ibid.*, p. 143.

34 J. Watson and R. Lippitt, *Learning Across Cultures* (Ann Arbor: Institute for Social Research, 1955).

Readings Related to Chapter 14

Training Supervisors to Use Organizational Behavior Modification

Fred Luthans
David Lyman

The contingency theory of management as applied to leadership and organizational design has already been well validated, and in mental health and education, contingency-based behavior modification approaches are also being widely used. Largely overlooked, however, has been the potential of these concepts and principles in the overall management of human resources. This article points out how contingency management in general and behavior modification techniques in particular can be taught to and successfully employed by supervisors in managing workers in modern organizations.

The authors, along with Robert Ottemann, all of the University of Nebraska, recently completed a training program for a group of supervisors in a medium-size manufacturing plant. (There were ten foremen in the initial program; subsequently, 17 more first-line supervisors, five general foremen, and two plant managers went through it.) In ten weekly, 90-minute sessions, the trainers used a process, rather than a lecture, method to teach the supervisors how to use the principles of operant psychology/behavior modification in analyzing and solving human performance problems in their departments. This new contingency strategy for managing human resources is called organizational behavior modification, or O.B. Mod.

The O.B. Mod. Training Program

There are several identifiable steps in training supervisors to utilize O.B. Mod. effectively. Here we shall briefly summarize some of them and how they were actually implemented in the training program for the manufacturing plant.

Reprinted by permission of the publisher from *Personnel,* September–October 1973, pp. 38–44. © 1973 by AMACOM, a division of the American Management Association.

Identifying Behavioral Events   The early sessions in the program were spent teaching the foremen to pinpoint employee problems in terms of observable, measurable behavioral events. This meant taking constructs such as attitudes or values and defining them in a manner that would allow them to be observed and measured. Initially, this was no small task, because the men spoke only of problem employees as having "bad attitudes" or being "unmotivated."

Measuring Frequencies of Behavior   After the supervisors were able to identify an employee's problem behavior, they were taught to keep records of how often and/or when this behavior occurred. Since it was often impossible to keep track of every instance, time sampling methods were worked out. For example, one foreman observed a particular employee twice an hour on a random basis. By observing their subordinates at random intervals, the foremen were able to get an overall picture, or baseline measure, of the frequency and circumstance of the problem behavior.

Making Functional Analyses of Behavior   In addition to keeping records, the supervisors were shown how to observe the events immediately preceding a pinpointed behavior—its antecedents—and the events immediately following the behavior—its consequences. By observing these before-and-after circumstances, they were able to make a functional analysis of what cues, or stimuli, elicited the behavior and what kinds of things reinforced or maintained that behavior.

Developing Intervention Strategies   Once the foremen were able to analyze functionally, they were ready to devise strategies to encourage desirable behaviors and discourage undesirable behaviors. These intervention strategies took many forms, but the essential goal was to reinforce appropriate behaviors and extinguish inappropriate behaviors. Extinguishing meant ignoring or providing no gratifying consequence for an undesirable job behavior. To encourage desired behaviors, the foremen had to determine what sorts of events were reinforcing to their workers, often a trail-and-error process. When a reinforcer was found, the desired behavior often increased dramatically. Reinforcers that were found to be effective included social approval, additional responsibilities, rescheduling of breaks, job rotation, special housekeeping or safety duties, positive feedback, and more enjoyable tasks upon completion of less enjoyable tasks. All the reinforcers used in the program lay within the normal pattern of the organizational environment; no artificial or contrived reinforcers were necessary. (For cost-conscious management, this is one of the most persuasive aspects of the program.)

Converting to Positive Reinforcement   Adopting a positive, rather than punitive, reinforcement strategy at first was not easy for the foremen, because even though they all believed in reinforcement, punishment was a consequence they had traditionally resorted to in order to change behavior. The trainers stressed the point that punishment would, indeed, suppress unwanted behavior, but seldom permanently, and would often create counterproductive hostility and resentment toward the supervisor. Having adopted a positive reinforcement intervention strategy, the foremen implemented it on the job and recorded the results.

Understanding the Importance of Being Contingent   By keeping records the supervisors were able to compare the rate of behavior occurrence prior to the intervention strategy with the later rate. Not all of the foremen met with success in their first attempts, but by analyzing what happened in the training sessions and modifying their behavior or their strategies, all of them were eventually able to effect some change. This was a crucial learning step, for it dramatically showed the power of being contingent, the relationship between the worker's behavior and their own. The supervisors found that by setting up "if-then" contingencies with their people, they could effectively manage behaviors toward improved performance: *If* the worker evidenced certain desirable, productive behaviors, *then,* and only then, was he reinforced by the supervisor.

The Training Experience:
Practicing What Was Preached

Some familiar problems were encountered in the training program. At times, attendance was one of them, even though top management "highly recommended" the program. The noncompulsory attendance policy, plus daily "brush fires" to put out, worked against perfect attendance. And some of the supervisors didn't always complete their "homework" assignments (recording behaviors on the job), largely because of the minor crises and poor management of time. This problem lessened, however, when they learned better use of time sampling and were themselves reinforced when they began to see the results of record keeping. The trainers also helped alleviate this situation by paying attention to participants who had their data and, to a degree, ignoring those who had not carried out their assignments. Since the trainer was a source of social reinforcement, his ignoring those not prepared was a negative consequence and his attending to those who were was a positive consequence. In other words, the trainer himself was being contingent with the trainees. As a result, data collection improved.

Again, when the group discussion during a session was moving in a productive direction, the trainer would give his attention to those who were contributing; if they digressed, he would bring the verbal interaction back on track and ignore inappropriate comments. Thus, group participation was encouraged and reinforced during the sessions, while general conversation and banter were held to a minimum, so that each participant had a chance to make suggestions and provide alternatives or interpretations to the problem situations being discussed. Since those who made contributions experienced social reinforcement from the trainer, the foremen came to understand first-hand how O.B. Mod. might have an effect on their subordinates.

All in all, the training experience was very successful. Every supervisor in the program was able to improve the performance of at least one worker in his department, and most were able to effect change on the part of several workers. And these changes were reflected in the supervisors' effectiveness ratings, which were calculated daily. The foremen boosted their individual effectiveness ratings at least 5 percent, an increase that represented a considerable cost saving to the company. In general, the foremen reported that the training they received was very useful and that they would continue using the O.B. Mod. techniques learned in the program.

Evaluation of an O.B. Mod. Approach

A program to train supervisors to be contingency managers offers several advantages. It also has its problems, but let's consider the advantages first.

• This approach deals only with behaviors that can be tied to job performance. Unlike training programs that attempt to change vaguely defined internal states of employee attitudes and values, this program precisely measures whether or not an observable job behavior of an employee has been changed. The measures may take the form of units produced, tasks completed, orders filled, or even the number of words typed. When a daily performance record is kept, a change in the rate of behavior change becomes immediately apparent. This feedback is continuous and can be used as a learning device and source of reinforcement. Thus, performance feedback is one of the biggest pluses of O.B. Mod.

• A second advantage of O.B. Mod. supervisory training is the assumption that if an employee cannot currently perform a particular task, he can be taught to do it. Of course, this does not imply that employees can perform *all* jobs in the organization; it would be foolish to expect key punchers to solve engineering types of problems or personnel managers to take on maintenance of machines. On the other hand, through the process of shaping behaviors, where successive approximations of desired behaviors are selectively reinforced, new behaviors can be effectively learned and maintained and the job can be enlarged in scope, or the employee can be moved to a more demanding one.

• A third advantage is that O.B. Mod. is an effective means of altering organizational environments to prevent or solve employee behavioral problems. This entails altering some behaviors in the environment, including those of supervisors, to maintain others. It is unrealistic to assume that as a result of several traditional human relations training sessions supervisors are going to change their ways; changes in supervisory behavior will come about only when the actual job environment changes, and the O.B. Mod. approach is meant to do just that—alter environmental situations to allow and encourage people to perform in a more productive manner.

• Perhaps the most important advantage of the O.B. Mod. is that it is based on a rational, scientific methodology. It requires the collection and analysis of data, decision making on the basis of the data, implementation of the decisions on the job, and assessment of results. More sepcifically, this means pinpointing problem behavioral events, observing and recording the frequency of this behavior, carrying out a functional analysis by examining antecedents and consequences of the behavior, devising an intervention strategy utilizing positive reinforcers, implementing the strategy in practice by being contingent, and observing and measuring the results. These O.B. Mod. techniques for managing human resources lead in no haphazard way to improved performance and greater satisfaction.

Now we come to the problems and criticisms that an O.B. Mod. training program is likely to run into.

• Probably the most frequently encountered reason for reluctance to use the approach has to do with manipulation of people. Critics contend that changing behavior in this way is "using" people, making them do things against their will, or perhaps even exploiting them. What the critics overlook is not only that control of behavior is inevitable, but that it can be desirable. When a job requires a person to wear a suit and tie (formally or informally), the job is controlling certain behaviors. Schedules, time clocks, appointments, and even daily memos are only a few of the everyday controls found in all organizations. The O.B. Mod. approach is merely a systematic way of changing behaviors so that desirable, productive behaviors occur more often, as they are systematically reinforced. Indeed, the person whose behavior is being changed is "manipulating" the behavior of the modifier, too. One is reminded of the old cartoon about the rat in the Skinner box, with the caption reading, "I really have the experimenter conditioned. Every time I push the bar he gives me a reward." The accusation of manipulation can be countered by a clear explanation of the content and purpose of O.B. Mod.

• Another negative element is the complexity of the modern organizational environment. Unlike a research laboratory, mental hospital, or classroom where behavior modification has been successfully carried out with experimental subjects, patients, and children, a manufacturing plant or business office has many distractions that can disrupt the use of any technique. During a typical day in a business organization, there are phone calls, hastily called meetings, special orders, machinery breakdowns, to name but a few of the noncontrollable events that occur. An O.B. Mod. approach must be able to try to deal with these events so that the intervention strategy being employed is not damaged or misleading. To write off the business organization as being too complex an environment does not seem justified.

• A third obstacle to overcome is plain, old resistance to change. Managers—and training directors—are naturally hesitant about launching new techniques that they do not completely understand. In this case, they should spend as much time as is needed to find out what O.B. Mod. is based on, what it can and cannot do, how it can and cannot be used, and how long it would take to get it going in a supervisory training program of their own. This and subsequent articles should be useful in this respect and in breaking down resistance to change. The authors and their associates in the department of management at the University of Nebraska are actively involved in expanding the theory, research, and practice of O.B. Mod.

Implications of O.B. Mod. for the Future

As modern organizations become more automated and productivity-conscious, workers seem to become more dissatisfied, and some apparently, deliberately do not perform anywhere near their potential. The experience of the Vega Plant at Lordstown, Ohio is an extreme case in point, but every day newpapers, television specials, and formal and informal discussions focus on the management (or mismanagement) of human resources vis-à-vis the productivity concern. To turn the trend around, or even turn it in another direction, managers of all organizations must look to new approaches. One thing they can do immediately is provide a more reinforcing organizational climate for their employees.

There are many reinforcers readily available to any supervisor. The tried-and-true pat on the back for a job well done is one, but it soon gets to be old-hat to an employee, and other means of reinforcement must be found. Money is definitely a reinforcer, but it is unrealistic to propose that every time a worker does a good job he should get a monetary reward. It is necessary, then, for supervisors to make better use of the reinforcers that are already at hand on the job. Through O.B. Mod. supervisors can be taught how to be contingency managers. If they understand that behavior depends on its consequences and if, on this premise, they utilize the steps of O.B. Mod. to change behaviors, they should be able to manage their human resources more effectively, with lower cost to the company and greater satisfaction to its employees.

There is no reason that O.B. Mod. should not work just as well with personnel in other situations as it did with workers in the plant we have talked about. Actually, applications of O.B. Mod. seem limited only by the creativity and ingenuity of those who study it and recognize the capacity of contingency management to direct human effort toward, instead of away from, organizational objectives.

Leadership and Supervision in Industry

Edwin A. Fleishman
Edwin F. Harris
Harold E. Burtt

[*Leadership and Supervision in Industry*] describes a research study of the leadership of the first-line industrial supervisor. It notes how that leadership is influenced by a systematic training program for foremen and also by the leadership provided by the foreman's own boss. It determines the relationship of different foreman leadership patterns to the efficiency and morale of their work groups. The project was conducted under the supervision of the Personnel Research Board of the Ohio State University with the co-operation of the International Harvester Company.

Based on chap. 9, "Summary for Non-technical Readers," in Fleishman, Harris, and Burtt, *Leadership and Supervision in Industry*, Columbus, Ohio, Bureau of Educational Research, Ohio State University, 1955. Reprinted by permission of Ohio State University. Professor Fleishman re-edited the chapter in 1969 and included some more recent work.

There has been considerable interest during the last decade or so in "human relations" training for foremen. Reports have been published about projects in which foremen responded to some type of attitude questionnaire before and after training and did show progress in an understanding of human relations after such training. But these projects did not determine whether the effects were permanent, how they were influenced by the actual work situation in which a foreman operates, or the results such effects had on the over-all efficiency of the industrial enterprise. It was toward a study of these particular aspects that our project was directed.

Our research involved three principal phases. The first determined just what aspects of the foremen's leadership were important for our problem and then developed reliable instruments for measuring those aspects. The second phase used these instruments to determine what happened to the foremen's attitudes as a result of leadership training at a special school and, more important still, the nature of those attitudes and of his supervisory behavior when he returned to his plant. A further question was how his leadership attitudes and behavior were influenced by the type of leadership at the levels above him or what we call the "leadership climate." The third phase related the different types of leadership to certain criteria of departmental and managerial performance, such as work group absenteeism, grievances, turnover, and accidents, as well as worker attitudes and foreman proficiency ratings.

The major part of the research was done at a motor-truck manufacturing plant, having five thousand employees, which is the largest factory in a city of eighty thousand. Other research data were obtained at the Company's Central School for supervisors in Chicago. This school provides an intensive two-weeks program for foremen sent in from the Company's various plants on a quota basis. The curriculum stresses heavily principles of human relations, but also has courses in Planning and Organizing, Economics, Effective Speaking, etc. Instructional methods include role-playing, visual aids, and group discussion, as well as the conventional lecture and textbook approach.

Measuring Instruments

The first research phase, as indicated, was the development of devices for measuring leadership behavior and attitudes. The initial focus was on a form, Supervisory Behavior Description, which could be filled out by subordinates to describe their own foremen. It included items like, "He expresses appreciation when one of his men does a good job," or "He rules with an iron hand." For each item, the subordinate checked alternatives, such as *always, often, occasionally, seldom, never,* with reference to his foreman. These same items, with some slight changes in wording, could be used as a Foreman's Leadership Opinion Questionnaire in which the foreman himself indicated how he thought he *should* operate with his particular work group; for instance whether he should "rule with an iron hand" *always, often, occasionally, seldom,* or *never.*

Much research went into the development of these instruments. The first problem was what aspects or underlying factors of leadership we wanted to measure. We benefited here from the previous work of the Personnel Research Board. Originally there was a pool of 1,800 items about leader behavior but this was reduced to 150 on the basis of expert judgment of the staff. A group of three hundred Air Force crew members had answered the 150 items with reference to their commanders. These data then were analyzed to determine the underlying factors which were characteristic of leadership, as indicated by this question-naire.[1]

The usual method is to get the correlation of each item with every other item, for instance, the extent to which those who "rule with an iron hand" also "criticize poor work," or whether those who "express appreciation of good work" likewise "accept suggestions for changes." There may be "negative" correlations, too, as when those who always rule with an iron hand never accept suggestions. It is possible to compute a correlation co-efficient which may come out between $+1.00$ and -1.00 and tell the statistician just how close is the relation between any two items. Then a "factor analysis" of this array of intercorrelations is made. This technique assumes that the correlations between all the items may result from just a few underlying factors or dimensions of leadership. Although the analysis determines how many factors are necessary to explain these intercorrelations, we do not know what the factors are because they are just abstract. We do know, however, the "loading" of each item on each factor. For instance, the "iron hand" item might involve very little of the first factor, much of the second factor, and very little of the remaining factors. Then, if we look at the items that have high loadings on a given factor, we may be able to determine what that factor is and name it. In the present case it was necessary to use a modification of this method because of the prohibitively large number of items.

In the present instance, items with high positive loadings on the first factor involved behavior indicating a high degree of two-way communication, mutual trust, rapport and warmth between the leader and his group and more participa-tion in decisions by the group; on the other hand, negative loadings were found for items suggesting authoritarian and impersonal behavior. This factor was identified as "consideration." The second factor had high loadings for items dealing with assigning of tasks, emphasis on production goals, defining channels of communication, and ways of getting the job done. This factor was identified as "initiating structure." Two minor factors were found but need not concern us here.

The next step was to adapt the questionnaire to industrial use. A scoring key was developed for each dimension of leadership which attached most signifi-cance to an item with high loading on a given factor and low loadings on the other factors. The questionnaire was then given to 100 foremen attending the Central School, who described their own boss. Starting with the Air Force scoring keys, a completely separate correlational and factor analysis was carried out. Accord-

---

[1] The detailed statistical procedure in this project will not be presented here but merely a general description of the method.

ingly the instrument was further revised, item by item, selecting items that had the highest correlation with the dimension they were supposed to represent and that were independent of the other dimensions. Some items were discarded. In this process, the two minor factors disappeared. The final result was a reliable instrument and scoring keys to measure "consideration" and "initiating structure," and to measure them quite independently in the industrial context. The keys gave different weights (4, 3, 2, 1, or 0) to the alternative answers (such as *always, often, sometimes, seldom,* and *never*) to each item. Thus, an "always" response to "rule with an iron hand" added zero to a supervisor's consideration score, while "never" would add 4. Total scores on consideration and structure were simply the sums of these item scores within each factor key.

The foregoing analysis dealt mainly with the Supervisory Behavior Description by which a person evaluated his boss. With some revision and item analysis the parallel instrument was devised, the Leadership Opinion Questionnaire, which indicated a supervisor's own attitudes.[2]

The fact that consideration and initiating structure correlate low to zero with each other is an important finding in its own right. This means they are complementary dimensions of leadership and not opposite poles of a single continuum. Supervisors may be high on both, low on both, or high on one and low on the other.

Subsequent use of these questionnaires to measure consideration and initiating structure in other phases of the research tended to indicate the adequacy of the instruments. There was, for instance, good agreement among different persons describing the same supervisor and high stability of estimates of foremen made on two occasions eleven months apart. The analysis just described may seem like a great amount of work, but it is scientifically justified. For if there are defects in the instrument, then those defects will show up in the results obtained with it. For example, a carpenter who used a yardstick 37 inches long would do a weird construction job. We feel that we really did get the "bugs" out of our questionnaires, and thus our results can be accepted with more confidence.

Immediate Effects of Leadership Training

The next phase of the research used these instruments just described to determine how the leadership of the foreman is influenced by formal leadership training. The training in question was the Central School mentioned earlier. The Leadership Opinion Questionnaire was given to a group of foremen the day they entered the school and the day they finished the course two weeks later. It will be recalled that in this questionnaire the foreman indicated how frequently he *should* conform with whatever the item called for. The blanks were scored for consideration and initiating structure. The results were quite clear, with a general increase in consideration attitudes after training and a decrease in attitudes of initiating structure. . . .

---

[2] The items in these two forms appear in the original book. The "Leadership Opinion Questionnaire" by Edwin A. Fleishman is available through Science Research Associates, 259 Erie Street, Chicago.

Another way to show the trend would be to compare the average scores before and after training and to note the difference between the averages. In this connection, we must digress to make one statistical point. When we have a difference between two averages, there is a possibility that it might be just accidental and not represent a real difference between the things we are measuring. This is especially apt to be the case if the scores contributing to an average are scattered rather than bunched near the average, and if we do not have very many scores in the average to begin with. The statistician has formulas which take account of the number of scores and how well they are bunched, and which yield an index that tells whether the difference between the averages is "significant." For instance, we often read that a difference is "significant at the one per cent level of confidence." This means that such a difference could occur less than one per cent of the time by chance. Our results, of course, were interpreted from this standpoint, and appropriate indexes appear in the main discussion.

To return to the discussion of the results, there was an increase in the average consideration score after training which was "significant," and there was likewise a significant decrease in the average initiating structure score. The changes appeared to be due to the training course. The data were further broken down according to foremen who were initially high or low (above or below average) in each dimension. It developed that the general increase in consideration after training was due primarily to changes in those who were initially low in this dimension. However, for initiating structure, both those initially high and low showed a significant decrease after training. Another important finding was the significant increases in the spread of scores after training. The training did not make the group more alike, but more different from one another in these attitudes.

Permanent Effects of Leadership Training

The increase in consideration might have been expected because much of the program at the Central School was aimed at improved human relations. There was also less initiation of structure, which is surprising since "structure" subjects are also taught. But these results do not indicate what happens when the trained foreman gets back to his plant.

It was not possible to follow a group from school back to a plant because at any given Central School session there might be men from 17 different plants. It was possible, however, to get a comparable answer at the one factory available for our research by comparing foremen who had not been to Central School with foremen who had been there. Actually, we divided the latter into three carefully matched sub-samples, according to the time elapsed since their training—2 to 10 months, 11 to 19 months and 20 to 39 months. One possible source of error was checked at this point; namely, that those who were selected to attend the school might differ from the remainder in some other respect and even those selected early might differ from those selected later. However, no significant differences appeared among the groups in average age, education, years with the company, years as supervisor, or number of men supervised.

The members of these four groups, one untrained and three trained, were given the same Leadership Opinion Questionnaire as that used at Central School in order to measure their *attitudes* in the same two dimensions. It was also possible to get data on their leadership *behavior* by having several workers under each man fill out the form entitled Supervisory Behavior Description.

Gathering these data at the factory posed some administrative problems in the way of maintaining co-operation and safeguarding confidential information. The program was presented to plant officials as a project of Ohio State University parallel to some other leadership studies in progress. The research personnel spent some time around the plant, getting acquainted and being "seen." The foremen had an explanatory letter from the factory manager and were scheduled by the training director, who had good rapport with them. They were assured that no one in the company would see their individual answers. As to the workers, at least three under each foreman were selected at random. They did not write their names on their papers but merely wrote the name of the foreman they were rating, thus assuring anonymity. Several union stewards were included in the first session and co-operation appeared excellent.

We now had available for the four groups of foremen data on their own expressed leadership attitudes and on their leadership behavior as perceived by the workers under them. The next step was to compare the averages for the untrained and trained groups. This comparison showed little differences between the groups, except for a significant tendency for the most recently trained group to be *lower* in consideration behavior than the untrained group. There was a similar drop in consideration attitudes although it was not statistically significant. Moreover, there appeared to be some increases in initiating structure attitudes and behavior for some of the trained groups *versus* the untrained. The close correspondence between attitudes expressed by the foremen and the independent reports of their behavior made by their workers lent further support to the trends indicated.

The striking, and possibly disquieting, thing about all this is the discrepancy between the results of the questionnaire given the foremen at Chicago immediately after the two-weeks school and the results after the foremen's return to the plant. At the school, the men's attitudes change in the direction of more consideration, but the effect does not last. One explanation that occurs to us is that, while the course makes the foreman more concerned with human relations, the course also makes him more aware of his part as a member of management. He is singled out for this special training, and he participates without cost to himself in a program that is obviously expensive. Perhaps the human relations aspect persists long enough for the post-training questionnaire, but what the man takes back to his plant is a tendency to assume more of a leadership role. What is "right" and approved in training may be different from what is "right" in the plant. We shall see presently that the "climate" to which he returns is also a controlling factor.

The discrepancy between the results at Central School and at the plant indicate the danger of evaluating the outcome immediately after the training.

There have been quite a few foreman-training projects in which the evaluation has been made this soon. The acid test is the ultimate conduct and attitudes of the foreman back in the work situation.

An additional evaluation of leadership training was made in connection with a "refresher" course which some of the foremen took. This was organized locally, had considerable similarity to the Chicago course, and lasted one week. Two groups of foremen were selected, all of whom had attended the Central School, but one group (experimental) had the local refresher and the other (control) did not. The groups were matched in that they had about the same average scores for consideration and initiating structure before the refresher course was given. The groups were also matched for age, education, years as supervisor, seniority, number of men supervised, and months since attending Central School. Some three months after the experimental group took the refresher course, both groups were evaluated again by the Supervisory Behavior and Leadership Opinion instruments. The differences between the groups were slight, and none of them were statistically significant. The trend, if any, was toward slightly more initiation of structure in the experimental group. Certainly the refresher course did nothing to reinforce the human-relations aspect.

Leadership Climate

Up to this point, we have noted the discrepancy between the foreman's attitudes immediately after Central School and the attitudes and behavior back home. It is pertinent now to take a look at the home environment, or "climate" as we have called it. The situations to which the different foremen returned varied in leadership climate. Some foremen went back to a boss high in "consideration" and some to a boss low in consideration.

It was possible to measure climate by the instruments already developed, with slight modifications in some cases. Four types of data were used. The foreman's *boss* (General Foreman) filled out the usual Leadership Opinion Questionnaire regarding his own attitudes, telling essentially "How I should lead my foremen." He also filled out one as to "How I think my foremen should lead." Then the foreman filled out the schedule as to "How my supervisor actually leads," and again as to "What my boss expects of me." Each of these four schedules yielded scores on consideration and on initiating structure for the climate in which a foreman worked. However, it did not seem wise to average these four schedules into a single index of climate. They were used separately. On the basis of scores on a leadership-climate instrument, the foremen were divided into those with climates high (above average) in consideration and those low in consideration. This was done likewise for initiating structure. The same procedure was followed for the other three instruments. We then examined the leadership attitudes and behavior of the different foremen operating under these different "climates." The results showed that foremen who operated under leadership climates high in consideration scored significantly higher themselves in both consideration attitudes and behavior. In other words, a boss who was considerate tended to have foremen who believed and behaved that way. With reference to initiating structure, the trend was the same. In a climate high in initiating structure the foremen had higher initiating structure attitudes. Their behavior showed the same tendency although that trend was not statistically significant.

This was the general result of the analysis. But a further breakdown was made for the four matched groups mentioned earlier which differed in the length of time since they had attended Central School; one group had never attended. Curves were plotted for the high and low climates separately. At each point in time the results showed the day-to-day climate to be more important than whether or not the foreman had been to training. To a considerable extent, the specific training in human relations is wasted unless the environment in the plant is also strong in human relations.

We then became concerned in our analysis with what happens to a foreman emotionally, or otherwise, when he learns one point of view at school and then returns to a different "leadership climate" in the plant. We might expect that this experience would be frustrating. Accordingly, we developed a "conflict index" to investigate this point. The index was merely the discrepancy between the foreman's scores on the Leadership Opinion Questionnaire and on the Supervisory Behavior Description. If he felt one way but behaved otherwise, that presumably involved conflict. When we looked at these conflict indexes with reference to climate, it was apparent that there was more conflict on the part of the foremen who returned to a climate either low in consideration or high in initiation of structure. With the *untrained* foremen, however, the climate in which they operated made no difference as far as their own conflict index was concerned. Again we see the interaction of "climate" and training effects.

Another evaluation of the training was made in terms of an index of "leadership adequacy," the degree to which the foreman's behavior conformed with what his own men expected of him. The men had filled out a questionnaire with reference to "How you expect an ideal foreman to act," as well as a form describing the behavior of their own foreman. The difference between scores on these two instruments was the index of "leadership adequacy" used. A comparison of such indexes for trained and untrained foremen showed a tendency for the trained foremen to have higher leadership adequacy on the consideration dimension. No significant tendency was found on the initiation of structure dimension. Further analysis indicated that these results were due primarily to an increase in leadership adequacy for those who returned to climates high in consideration. This is just another indication of the importance of the supervisory climate on the training effects.

It was of passing interest to compare leadership attitudes at the different organizational levels quite apart from any of the other factors. Superintendents, general foremen, foremen, and workers had all filled out questionnaires which indicated their attitudes toward how work groups should be led. The workers were in favor of more consideration and less initiation of structure and differed significantly from the others in this respect. The foremen were intermediate between the workers and higher-level supervisors, but much closer to the latter. The higher up in the hierarchy the less consideration and more structure was expected of the foremen.

Leadership and Effectiveness

Up to this point, we have said nothing about what is a desirable leadership pattern. One way to find out is to compare foremen with different degrees of consideration and initiating structure on independent criteria of their effectiveness and that of their work groups. For this, we need some indexes of the performance of each foreman's department or work group which we can relate to his leadership attitudes and behavior as measured by our instruments.

After some elimination we developed four objective criteria and two others which depended on some type of judgment or rating. The objective criteria were: absenteeism excluding legitimate absences, accidents that involved a trip to the dispensary, grievances that were actually filed, and employee turnover. These indexes were computed for each foreman's work group during the previous eleven-month period. A further indication of the effectiveness of the foremen was obtained from proficiency ratings made by plant management. Finally, we obtained an index of how well workers in each foreman's group liked working for that foreman.

Before correlating foreman leadership patterns with these various independent criteria, it was desirable to see whether any other variables were cutting across the criteria and influencing the results. For instance, if there was more absenteeism in a certain department, it might happen that the men were older, more of them were married, or the job was unusually hazardous so that the absenteeism was not related to poor leadership at all. The statistician calls such things "contaminating" variables. It was possible to analyze our four objective criteria from this standpoint. The items suspected of contamination were age, education, marital status, skill, seniority, method of pay, hazards, and pleasantness of the job. The last two were obtained from estimates by supervisors at higher levels. The statistical analysis was somewhat involved and will not be discussed here except to indicate that we noted the correlations between the suspected variables and criteria and then determined whether they had some underlying factors in common. The technique of factor analysis mentioned earlier was used. The ultimate goal was to eliminate these underlying "contaminating" factors. There is a straightforward technique (partial correlation) for doing this, once the factors are identified. The four objective criteria, absenteeism, accidents, grievances, and turnover, were "decontaminated" in so far as was statistically possible. Such treatment of the other criteria was not feasible.

We turn first to the relation between the leadership patterns of foremen and the proficiency ratings given them by higher management in the plant. The proficiency estimates were obtained using the "paired comparison" technique in which each rater compared each foreman with every other foreman an equal number of times. Each foreman's proficiency score was the number of times he was rated as more proficient. We found a high degree of agreement among different members of top management on how these foremen were ranked. For each foreman, then, we had a proficiency estimate, a consideration score, and a structuring score. Correlations were then computed. The first analysis was made by divisions. There were five divisions concerned with some aspect of production, and there were three (stores, inspection, and maintenance) that were essentially non-production divisions. An interesting difference between results for production and nonproduction divisions turned up. In the production divisions there was a significant positive correlation between proficiency and initiating structure, and a significant negative correlation with consideration. In other words, the foremen who were regarded by their supervisors as most proficient turned out to be those higher in "structure" and lower in "consideration." In the non-production divisions the relations tended to be reversed. Two divisions did not follow this trend for reasons which became apparent. One was a production division which at the time the data were collected was in the midst of a vigorous campaign to reduce the grievance rate, which was causing some alarm. The supervisors who rated foremen in that division were presumably a bit more sensitive at the time to considerate behavior on the part of the foremen. The other exception was a non-production division which, nevertheless, was under considerable pressure from a time schedule. In this respect it was much like a production divison, and perhaps its foremen were rated accordingly. When this latter idea was followed up by having the divisions rated as to the "demandingness of time schedule," the non-production division just mentioned was under more pressure than some of the production divisons. It was simple to arrange all the divisions in the order of the demands of the time schedule and present the correlations between proficiency and leader behavior in that same order. The trend was rather obvious toward higher positive correlations between proficiency ratings and structure where there was more urgency. The correlations of proficiency with consideration went in the other direction; that is, in those divisions with more pressure the negative correlations between proficiency ratings and consideration became higher.

A further analysis was made by putting all the production divisions together and thus having a much larger number of foremen on which to figure correlations. The non-production divisions also were combined separately. With reference to the two exceptional divisions already mentioned, the one with the grievance campaign was dropped altogether and the other was placed with the production divisons, because, like them, it was operating under a demanding time schedule. When the correlations were computed as before, in the combined production divisons the trend was confirmed that the more proficient foremen (as rated by management) do more initiation of structure and are somewhat less considerate. In the combined non-production divisions the relations were not statistically significant, although the directions of the relations were just the opposite of what they were in the production divisions.

One other analysis related the urgency of a division's time schedule to the leadership behavior of its foremen. We had the eight divisions ranked in order as to this demandingness. We then averaged the consideration scores for all foremen in a division and likewise the structuring scores, so that we could rank the divisions with reference to considerate or structuring behavior of their foremen. When these ranks were compared or correlated, there was a clear-cut tendency for the divisions that were under the most pressure of time to have foremen who were most inclined toward initiating structure and *vice versa*. There was also a fairly marked tendency for the foremen in the most demanding divisions to operate with the least consideration.

Thus, the results of the various methods of analyzing the estimated efficiency of the foremen are clear in production divisions. The more efficient foremen, as rated by the boss, are inclined to show more initiation structure and less consideration. This trend is accentuated as the demandingness of the time schedule increases. In non-production divisions, this relation does not hold, and there is even a hint of rated efficiency going with consideration. But, if there is any underlying tendency of this sort, the pressure of deadlines certainly does not let it operate.

But what about the other criteria, the ones derived not from management's evaluation but from indexes derived from each foreman's work group? The index of how well workers liked working for a particular foreman used a laboriously developed "scaling technique" which we will not describe here. Suffice it to say that the relations between this index and foreman behavior were very clear. Foremen originally described high on consideration tended to be those for whom workers like to work. Workers tend not to like working for foremen high in structure, but this correlation was not nearly as high. It is clear that the kind of foreman liked by these workers is quite different from the kind rated "most proficient" by management.

The final evaluation of leadership behavior used the four objective criteria— absenteeism, accidents, grievances, and turnover. These are obviously related to industrial efficiency, although morale may be involved also. These criteria dealt, of course, with the behavior of work groups, but they may be a function of the conduct of the foremen in charge of those work groups. The analysis involved the correlation of consideration and initiating structure as obtained from the Supervisory Behavior Description with the four criteria. We can say that every one of these criteria showed some relationship to at least one of these leadership dimensions in either the production or non-production departments or both. Without dealing with each of the sixteen separate correlations involved (two leadership dimensions x four criteria x four kinds of departments), we can summarize as follows. In general: high structure and low consideration tended to go with more absenteeism, accidents, grievances and turnover. There were no reversals of this picture, although some of the individual correlations were not significant. The highest relationships were those showing more absenteeism among workers with foremen low in consideration (in both production and non-production departments) and high grievances where initiating structure was high. Accidents were most marked in non-production departments having low consideration foremen and turnover was especially high in non-production departments with foremen emphasizing high structure.

The reader should keep in mind that low consideration does not necessarily follow from high structure. These were shown to be independent and many foremen exhibit a high degree of both kinds of behavior. Since the original study

Fleishman and Harris[3] pursued this matter further using grievances and turnover as the primary criteria. These results clarify the earlier results. The main findings were that foremen with low consideration tend to have high turnover and grievances regardless of the amount of structuring done. However, high consideration foremen can increase structure without increasing turnover and grievances. It was also shown in this later study that some of these relations are "curvilinear." That is, decreased consideration and increased structure have little relation to turnover and grievances until some critical point is reached. Then there is a sharp rise in both turnover and grievances. In any case, it is clear that the group indexes produce a different picture of what is effective leader behavior than was derived from management rating.

One final result is worth noting before further discussion. We found one group of foremen who were nominally foremen on the organization chart, but who were not perceived as the foremen of workers supposedly working for them. Consequently, we compared the Supervisory Behavior Descriptions of these foremen with those of foremen not by-passed. According to an analysis of separate items, the most discriminating ones showed that the foreman who was not by-passed stood behind his men when they were in trouble, encouraged both quantity and quality of production, explained the reasons for what he did, and took account of ideas presented by members of his work group. In general, these functional foremen were higher on both consideration and structure than the by-passed foremen.

Conclusions

So where does that leave us in our effort to promote the best kind of leadership in industry, or anywhere else for that matter? For industrial, educational, and military leaders have a lot in common. It is probable that some of the psychological principles which we uncovered have implications outside the immediate situation in which we operated. Some of our findings may have a bearing on training in general, and on human-relations training in particular.

For one thing, after our experience with the school for foremen, we have some reservations about the conventional method of evaluating a training program. The immediate checkup at the end of the program is not the whole story. For instance, the final examination in an academic course is supposed to indicate whether the students have profited by the course, and, in a sense, they do profit by getting a mark on the registrar's record. But we are inclined to assume, further, that if they presently encounter some life situation where the material of that course will be useful, then the examination indicates how they will make out in that life situation. This looks to us like a mistaken assumption. While these foremen knew the answers immediately after their course at Central School, they did not carry out what they had learned when they got back to the plant. The immediate and the ultimate effects of training are not necessarily the same.

[3]Fleishman, E. A. and Harris, E. F., "Patterns of Leadership Behavior Related to Employee Grievances and Turnover," *Personnel Psychology,* 1962, **15,** 43–56.

Certainly we did not find it that way. If we are involved specifically in leadership training and rely entirely on an attitude questionnaire right after the training, we are certainly fooling ourselves.

With reference to training in human relations our study yields one clear implication. Such training conducted in isolation from the practical situation falls short of its objective. It does not take much to upset whatever the training seemed to have accomplished. It is necessary to involve the social situation in which a person is going to operate. Our foremen developed a point of view in school but lost it on their return to the plant if their supervisor had a different point of view. What is socially correct in the school, and hence rewarded, may not be the same in the plant. The foreman "learns" two sets of attitudes, one for each situation. All this suggests that to improve social relations almost anywhere, it is important to work on the whole social setting. It is not possible to pull people out of this setting, tell or teach them some ideas, and then return them to the setting and consider everything fixed. In fact, if we are concerned with a supervisory hierarchy, it looks as if we should really begin working on the leadership attitudes *at the top,* so that the favorable leadership climate will spread down to the first-line supervisors, because certainly it will not spread up the line in the usual industrial organization. The powerful influence of "leadership climate" may be our most important finding. Leadership behavior is not a thing apart but is imbedded in a social setting. Besides, the foreman is actually being "trained" every day by the rewards and example provided by his own boss. We are apt to lose sight of the fact that this everyday kind of learning is more potent than a "one shot" training course. In this plant it was very clear that the kind of leadership management rated most proficient was very different from the training department's concept.

One result, not stressed earlier, was that the training did affect different people differently. We need to have more research into the personal and situational factors that interact with such training.

The criterion phase of our study, like the training phase, results in some contradictions. Employees like to work under a foreman whose leadership is high in consideration and lower in structuring. They are also less inclined toward absenteeism, labor grievances, turnover, and accidents. On the other hand, in production divisions, at least, the foreman who is more proficient in the eyes of higher-level supervisors turns out to emphasize initiating structure and low consideration. It looks like a conflict between productive efficiency, as judged by the boss, and effectiveness inferred from the worker's behavior. It is barely possible that the supervisors who rated the proficiency of the foremen were wrong. They may have been thinking primarily of production and attendant profits and hence have given high ratings to foremen who were high in initiation of structure. It may be that they were responding to a "stereotype" of how they thought an effective foreman "should" act. It should be noted that these same kinds of foremen tended to have more absenteeism, grievances, turnover, and accidents which would work against production and profits. If the supervisors had taken account of factors such as these, they might have tempered their enthusiasm for the high structure—low consideration type of foreman. Another thing that might help would be to decrease the urgency of time schedules. In the non-production divisions which did not work against deadlines, there was no problem. The foreman could exercise the kind of leadership his employees liked and still be seen as proficient by management. While this may seem a naive suggestion in view of the difficulties in changing modern production tempo, our results show another consequence of a pressure atmosphere in which "emergencies" are the rule instead of the exception. Better production programming might resolve some of the conflicts revealed here. The finding of a low correlation between the two leadership dimensions shows that it is possible for supervisors to earn high scores in *both* consideration and initiating structure and many supervisors do. Some later research suggests that supervisors who are able to do this are more likely to "optimize" the various effectiveness criteria which may seem to be in conflict. The mechanism for this seems to be that consideration behavior, with its attendant rapport, keeps communication channels open and leads to an atmosphere of approval rather than threat. Subordinates are more apt to accept higher structure as supporting rather than threatening. However, more research is needed to clarify this.

We have drawn another disquieting generalization. The often stated proposal that good morale leads directly to increased efficiency needs to be qualified somewhat. Very often this is true, but it is advisable in the individual case to find out if it is that simple. To be sure, our concept of morale was limited to the techniques and indexes already described, and it was in production departments that we found the difficulties indicated. It would be interesting to explore the same problem using actual production units—this was not feasible in our assembly-line case—instead of estimated proficiency. And there might even be some "bugs," which we could not detect, in the estimates. But it did appear that the kind of leader the subordinates like best is not necessarily the one who is most proficient in getting results. Perhaps some of the things he does promote both morale and efficiency while other things help morale but hinder efficiency. It is well to watch both aspects simultaneously. Other concerns may find a situation similar to ours. It would thus be unwise to do a good job of building up morale and then relax on the assumption that a new day has dawned for the entire enterprise.

One final point with some possible generality deals with the actual role and responsibility of the applied scientist. He contributes, obviously, a lot of know-how, but his contribution may fall short of indicating what actually ought to be done. This is sometimes phrased to the effect that the scientist is concerned with means but some other agency must be concerned with ends. In our case, at least, we were able to determine some of the long-range effects of training, the importance of leadership climate, and the comparative effectiveness of the different leadership dimensions for different proficiency criteria. But, on the other hand, we were not close enough to the ultimate goals of the enterprise to determine what policy should be carried out with reference to first-line supervision. We had to return the problem to management. It may be like this in many other practical situations where the scientist discovers principles and how to predict the outcome of certain practices but is not in a position to decide long-range policy. To do this he would have to step out of character.

Nevertheless, such studies do raise questions about managerial values, policies, and goals. For example, the data show that in production departments, the leadership patterns of foremen rated proficient by plant management are also related to high turnover and grievances. What kind of leadership should we strive for in such departments? Such data may suggest a better definition of supervisory proficiency. They may also require an evaluation of managerial goals, short range as well as long range. Somebody will have to determine the relative importance of such goals for the industrial enterprise. Perhaps immediate efficiency may not be so important as a long-time balance between productivity and morale. That is the challenge.

How to Choose a Leadership Pattern
Robert Tannenbaum
Warren H. Schmidt

I put most problems into my group's hands and leave it to them to carry the ball from there. I serve merely as a catalyst, mirroring back the people's thoughts and feelings so that they can better understand them.

It's foolish to make decisions oneself on matters that affect people. I always talk things over with my subordinates, but I make it clear to them that I'm the one who has to have the final say.

Once I have decided on a course of action, I do my best to sell my ideas to my employees.

I'm being paid to lead. If I let a lot of other people make the decisions I should be making, then I'm not worth my salt.

I believe in getting things done. I can't waste time calling meetings. Someone has to call the shots around here, and I think it should be me.

Each of these statements represents a point of view about "good leadership." Considerable experience, factual data, and theoretical principles could be cited to support each statement, even though they seem to be inconsistent when placed together. Such contradictions point up the dilemma in which the modern manager frequently finds himself.

From *Harvard Business Review*, vol. 36, no. 2, March–April 1958, pp. 95–101. Reprinted by permission of the *Harvard Business Review*.

New Problem

The problem of how the modern manager can be "democratic" in his relations with subordinates and at the same time maintain the necessary authority and control in the organization for which he is responsible has come into focus increasingly in recent years.

Earlier in the century this problem was not so acutely felt. The successful executive was generally pictured as possessing intelligence, imagination, initiative, the capacity to make rapid (and generally wise) decisions, and the ability to inspire subordinates. People tended to think of the world as being divided into "leaders" and "followers."

New Focus   Gradually, however, from the social sciences emerged the concept of "group dynamics" with its focus on *members* of the group rather than solely on the leader. Research efforts of social scientists underscored the importance of employee involvement and participation in decision making. Evidence began to challenge the efficiency of highly directive leadership, and increasing attention was paid to problems of motivation and human relations.

Through training laboratories in group development that sprang up across the country, many of the newer notions of leadership began to exert an impact. These training laboratories were carefully designed to give people a first-hand experience in full participation and decision making. The designated "leaders" deliberately attempted to reduce their own power and to make group members as responsible as possible for setting their own goals and methods within the laboratory experience.

It was perhaps inevitable that some of the people who attended the training laboratories regarded this kind of leadership as being truly "democratic" and went home with the determination to build fully participative decision making into their own organizations. Whenever their bosses made a decision without convening a staff meeting, they tended to perceive this as authoritarian behavior. The true symbol of democratic leadership to some was the meeting—and the less directed from the top, the more democratic it was.

Some of the more enthusiastic alumni of these training laboratories began to get the habit of categorizing leader behavior as "democratic" *or* "authoritarian." The boss who made too many decisions himself was thought of as an authoritarian, and his directive behavior was often attributed solely to his personality.

New Need   The net result of the research findings and of the human relations training based upon them has been to call into question the stereotype of an effective leader. Consequently, the modern manager often finds himself in an uncomfortable state of mind.

Often he is not quite sure how to behave; there are times when he is torn between exerting "strong" leadership and "permissive" leadership. Sometimes new knowledge pushes him in one direction ("I should really get the group to help make this decision"), but at the same time his experience pushes him in another direction ("I really understand the problem better than the group and therefore I should make the decision"). He is not sure when a group decision is really appropriate or when holding a staff meeting serves merely as a device for avoiding his own decision-making responsibility.

The purpose of our article is to suggest a framework which managers may find useful in grappling with this dilemma. First we shall look at the different patterns of leadership behavior that the manager can choose from in relating himself to his subordinates. Then we shall turn to some of the questions suggested by this range of patterns. For instance, how important is it for a manager's subordinates to know what type of leadership he is using in a situation? What factors should he consider in deciding on a leadership pattern? What difference do his long-run objectives make as compared to his immediate objectives?

Range of Behavior

Figure 1 presents the continuum or range of possible leadership behavior available to a manager. Each type of action is related to the degree of authority used by the boss and to the amount of freedom available to his subordinates in reaching decisions. The actions seen on the extreme left characterize the manager who maintains a high degree of control while those seen on the extreme right characterize the manager who releases a high degree of control. Neither extreme is absolute; authority and freedom are never without their limitations.

Now let us look more closely at each of the behavior points occurring along this continuum:

The Manager Makes the Decision and Announces It   In this case the boss identifies a problem, considers alternative solutions, chooses one of them, and then reports this decision to his subordinates for implementation. He may or may not give consideration to what he believes his subordinates will think or feel about his decision; in any case, he provides no opportunity for them to partici-

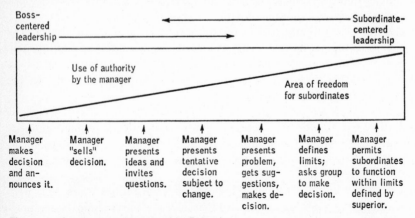

Figure 1   Continuum of Leadership Behavior.

pate directly in the decision-making process. Coercion may or may not be used or implied.

The Manager "Sells" His Decision   Here the manager, as before, takes responsibility for identifying the problem and arriving at a decision. However, rather than simply announcing it, he takes the additional step of persuading his subordinates to accept it. In doing so, he recognizes the possibility of some resistance among those who will be faced with the decision, and seeks to reduce this resistance by indicating, for example, what the employees have to gain from his decision.

The Manager Presents His Ideas, Invites Questions   Here the boss who has arrived at a decision and who seeks acceptance of his ideas provides an opportunity for his subordinates to get a fuller explanation of his thinking and his intentions. After presenting the ideas, he invites questions so that his associates can better understand what he is trying to accomplish. This "give and take" also enables the manager and the subordinates to explore more fully the implications of the decision.

The Manager Presents a Tentative Decision Subject to Change   This kind of behavior permits the subordinates to exert some influence on the decision. The initiative for identifying and diagnosing the problem remains with the boss. Before meeting with his staff, he has thought the problem through and arrived at a decision—but only a tentative one. Before finalizing it, he presents his proposed solution for the reaction of those who will be affected by it. He says in effect, "I'd like to hear what you have to say about this plan that I have developed. I'll appreciate your frank reactions, but will reserve for myself the final decision."

The Manager Presents the Problem, Gets Suggestions, and Then Makes His Decision   Up to this point the boss has come before the group with a solution of his own. Not so in this case. The subordinates now get the first chance to suggest solutions. The manager's initial role involves identifying the problem. He might, for example, say something of this sort: "We are faced with a number of complaints from newspapers and the general public on our service policy. What is wrong here? What ideas do you have for coming to grips with this problem?"

The function of the group becomes one of increasing the manager's repertory of possible solutions to the problem. The purpose is to capitalize on the knowledge and experience of those who are on the "firing line." From the expanded list of alternatives developed by the manager and his subordinates, the manager then selects the solution that he regards as most promising.[1]

The Manager Defines the Limits and Requests the Group to Make a Decision   At this point the manager passes to the group (possibly including himself as a member) the right to make decisions. Before doing so, however, he defines the problem to be solved and the boundaries within which the decision must be made.

---

[1]For a fuller explanation of this approach, see Leo Moore, "Too Much Management, Too Little Change," HBR January–February 1956, p. 41.

An example might be the handling of a parking problem at a plant. The boss decides that this is something that should be worked on by the people involved, so he calls them together and points up the existence of the problem. Then he tells them:

> There is the open field just north of the main plant which has been designated for additional employee parking. We can build underground or surface multilevel facilities as long as the cost does not exceed $100,000. Within these limits we are free to work out whatever solution makes sense to us. After we decide on a specific plan, the company will spend the available money in whatever way we indicate.

The Manager Permits the Group to Make Decisions within Prescribed Limits This represents an extreme degree of group freedom only occasionally encountered in formal organizations, as for instance, in many research groups. Here the team of managers or engineers undertakes the identification and diagnosis of the problem, develops alternative procedures for solving it, and decides on one or more of these alternative solutions. The only limits directly imposed on the group by the organization are those specified by the superior of the team's boss. If the boss participates in the decision-making process, he attempts to do so with no more authority than any other member of the group. He commits himself in advance to assist in implementing whatever decision the group makes.

Key Questions

As the continuum in Figure 1 demonstrates, there are a number of alternative ways in which a manager can relate himself to the group or individuals he is supervising. At the extreme left of the range, the emphasis is on the manager— on what *he* is interested in, how *he* sees things, how *he* feels about them. As we move toward the subordinate-centered end of the continuum, however, the focus is increasingly on the subordinates—on what *they* are interested in, how *they* look at things, how *they* feel about them.

When business leadership is regarded in this way, a number of questions arise. Let us take four of especial importance:

Can a Boss Ever Relinquish His Responsibility by Delegating It to Someone Else? Our view is that the manager must expect to be held responsible by his superior for the quality of the decisions made, even though operationally these decisions may have been made on a group basis. He should, therefore, be ready to accept whatever risk is involved whenever he delegates decision-making power to his subordinates. Delegation is not a way of "passing the buck." Also, it should be emphasized that the amount of freedom the boss gives to his subordinates cannot be greater than the freedom which he himself has been given by his own superior.

Should the Manager Participate with His Subordinates Once He Has Delegated Responsibility to Them? The manager should carefully think over this question and decide on his role prior to involving the subordinate group. He should ask if his presence will inhibit or facilitate the problem-solving process. There may be some instances when he should leave the group to let it solve the problem for itself. Typically, however, the boss has useful ideas to contribute, and should function as an additional member of the group. In the latter instance, it is important that he indicate clearly to the group that he sees himself in a *member* role rather than in an authority role.

How Important Is It for the Group to Recognize What Kind of Leadership Behavior the Boss Is Using?   It makes a great deal of difference. Many relationship problems between boss and subordinate occur because the boss fails to make clear how he plans to use his authority. If, for example, he actually intends to make a certain decision himself, but the subordinate group get the impression that he has delegated this authority, considerable confusion and resentment are likely to follow. Problems may also occur when the boss uses a "democratic" facade to conceal the fact that he has already made a decision which he hopes the group will accept as its own. The attempt to "make them think it was their idea in the first place" is a risky one. We believe that it is highly important for the manager to be honest and clear in describing what authority he is keeping and what role he is asking his subordinates to assume in solving a particular problem.

Can You Tell How "Democratic" a Manager Is by the Number of Decisions His Subordinates Make?   The sheer *number* of decisions is not an accurate index of the amount of freedom that a subordinate group enjoys. More important is the *significance* of the decisions which the boss entrusts to his subordinates. Obviously a decision on how to arrange desks is of an entirely different order from a decision involving the introduction of new electronic data-processing equipment. Even though the widest possible limits are given in dealing with the first issue, the group will sense no particular degree of responsibility. For a boss to permit the group to decide equipment policy, even within rather narrow limits, would reflect a greater degree of confidence in them on his part.

Deciding How to Lead

Now let us turn from the types of leadership that are possible in a company situation to the question of what types are *practical* and *desirable*. What factors or forces should a manager consider in deciding how to manage? Three are of particular importance:

> Forces in the manager.
> Forces in the subordinates.
> Forces in the situation.

We should like briefly to describe these elements and indicate how they might influence a manager's action in a decision-making situation.[2] The strength of each of them will, of course, vary from instance to instance, but the manager who is sensitive to them can better assess the problems which face him and determine which mode of leadership behavior is most appropriate for him.

[2]See also Robert Tannenbaum and Fred Massarik, "Participation by Subordinates in the Managerial Decision-making Process," *Canadian Journal of Economics and Political Science,* August 1950, pp. 413–418. [Reprinted in this volume, pages 365–374.—Ed.]

Forces in the Manager   The manager's behavior in any given instance will be influenced greatly by the many forces operating within his own personality. He will, of course, perceive his leadership problems in a unique way on the basis of his background, knowledge, and experience. Among the important internal forces affecting him will be the following:

1 His Value System   How strongly does he feel that individuals should have a share in making the decisions which affect them? Or, how convinced is he that the official who is paid to assume responsibility should personally carry the burden of decision making? The strength of his convictions on questions like these will tend to move the manager to one end or the other of the continuum shown in Figure 1. His behavior will also be influenced by the relative importance that he attaches to organizational efficiency, personal growth of subordinates, and company profits.[3]

2 His Confidence in His Subordinates   Managers differ greatly in the amount of trust they have in other people generally, and this carries over to the particular employees they supervise at a given time. In viewing his particular group of subordinates, the manager is likely to consider their knowledge and competence with respect to the problem. A central question he might ask himself is: "Who is best qualified to deal with this problem?" Often he may, justifiably or not, have more confidence in his own capabilities than in those of his subordinates.

3 His Own Leadership Inclinations   There are some managers who seem to function more comfortably and naturally as highly directive leaders. Resolving problems and issuing orders come easily to them. Other managers seem to operate more comfortably in a team role, where they are continually sharing many of their functions with their subordinates.

4 His Feelings of Security in an Uncertain Situation   The manager who releases control over the decision-making process thereby reduces the predictability of the outcome. Some managers have a greater need than others for predictability and stability in their environment. This "tolerance for ambiguity" is being viewed increasingly by psychologists as a key variable in a person's manner of dealing with problems.

The manager brings these and other highly personal variables to each situation he faces. If he can see them as forces which, consciously or unconsciously, influence his behavior, he can better understand what makes him prefer to act in a given way. And understanding this, he can often make himself more effective.

Forces in the Subordinate   Before deciding how to lead a certain group, the manager will also want to consider a number of forces affecting his subordinates' behavior. He will want to remember that each employee, like himself, is influenced by many personality variables. In addition, each subordinate has a

---

[3]See Chris Argyris, "Top Management Dilemma: Company Needs vs. Individual Development," *Personnel,* September 1955, pp. 123–134.

set of expectations about how the boss should act in relation to him (the phrase "expected behavior" is one we hear more and more often these days at discussions of leadership and teaching). The better the manager understands these factors, the more accurately he can determine what kind of behavior on his part will enable his subordinates to act most effectively.

Generally speaking, the manager can permit his subordinates greater freedom if the following essential conditions exist:

If the subordinates have relatively high needs for independence. (As we all know, people differ greatly in the amount of direction that they desire.)

If the subordinates have a readiness to assume responsibility for decision making. (Some see additional responsibility as a tribute to their ability; others see it as "passing the buck.")

If they have a relatively high tolerance for ambiguity. (Some employees prefer to have clear-cut directives given to them; others prefer a wider area of freedom.)

If they are interested in the problem and feel that it is important.

If they understand and identify with the goals of the organization.

If they have the necessary knowledge and experience to deal with the problem.

If they have learned to expect to share in decision making. (Persons who have come to expect strong leadership and are then suddenly confronted with the request to share more fully in decision making are often upset by this new experience. On the other hand, persons who have enjoyed a considerable amount of freedom resent the boss who begins to make all the decisions himself.)

The manager will probably tend to make fuller use of his own authority if the above conditions do *not* exist; at times there may be no realistic alternative to running a "one-man show."

The restrictive effect of many of the forces will, of course, be greatly modified by the general feeling of confidence which subordinates have in the boss. Where they have learned to respect and trust him, he is free to vary his behavior. He will feel certain that he will not be perceived as an authoritarian boss on those occasions when he makes decisions by himself. Similarly, he will not be seen as using staff meetings to avoid his decision-making responsibility. In a climate of mutual confidence and respect, people tend to feel less threatened by deviations from normal practice, which in turn makes possible a higher degree of flexibility in the whole relationship.

Forces in the Situation   In addition to the forces which exist in the manager himself and in his subordinates, certain characteristics of the general situation will also affect the manager's behavior. Among the more critical environmental pressures that surround him are those which stem from the organization, the work group, the nature of the problem, and the pressures of time. Let us look briefly at each of these:

Type of Organization   Like individuals, organizations have values and traditions which inevitably influence the behavior of the people who work in them. The manager who is a newcomer to a company quickly discovers that certain kinds of behavior are approved while others are not. He also discovers that to deviate radically from what is generally accepted is likely to create problems for him.

These values and traditions are communicated in many ways—through job descriptions, policy pronouncements, and public statements by top executives. Some organizations, for example, hold to the notion that the desirable executive is one who is dynamic, imaginative, decisive, and persuasive. Other organizations put more emphasis upon the importance of the executive's ability to work effectively with people—his human relations skills. The fact that his superiors have a defined concept of what the good executive should be will very likely push the manager toward one end or the other of the behavioral range.

In addition to the above, the amount of employee participation is influenced by such variables as the size of the working units, their geographical distribution, and the degree of inter- and intra-organizational security required to attain company goals. For example, the wide geographical dispersion of an organization may preclude a practical system of participative decision making, even though this would otherwise be desirable. Similarly, the size of the working units or the need for keeping plans confidential may make it necessary for the boss to exercise more control than would otherwise be the case. Factors like these may limit considerably the manager's ability to function flexibly on the continuum.

Group Effectiveness   Before turning decision-making responsibility over to a subordinate group, the boss should consider how effectively its members work together as a unit.

One of the relevant factors here is the experience the group has had in working together. It can generally be expected that a group which has functioned for some time will have developed habits of cooperation and thus be able to tackle a problem more effectively than a new group. It can also be expected that a group of people with similar backgrounds and interests will work more quickly and easily than people with dissimilar backgrounds, because the communication problems are likely to be less complex.

The degree of confidence that the members have in their ability to solve problems as a group is also a key consideration. Finally, such group variables as cohesiveness, permissiveness, mutual acceptance, and commonality of purpose will exert subtle but powerful influence on the group's functioning.

The Problem Itself   The nature of the problem may determine what degree of authority should be delegated by the manager to his subordinates. Obviously he will ask himself whether they have the kind of knowledge which is needed. It is possible to do them a real disservice by assigning a problem that their experience does not equip them to handle.

Since the problems faced in large or growing industries increasingly require knowledge of specialists from many different fields, it might be inferred that the more complex a problem, the more anxious a manager will be to get some assistance in solving it. However, this is not always the case. There will be times when the very complexity of the problem calls for one person to work it out. For example, if the manager has most of the background and factual data relevant to a given issue, it may be easier for him to think it through himself than to take the time to fill in his staff on all the pertinent background information.

The key question to ask, of course, is: "Have I heard the ideas of everyone who has the necessary knowledge to make a significant contribution to the solution of this problem?"

The Pressure of Time   This is perhaps the most clearly felt pressure on the manager (in spite of the fact that it may sometimes be imagined). The more that he feels the need for an immediate decision, the more difficult it is to involve other people. In organizations which are in a constant state of "crisis" and "crash programming" one is likely to find managers personally using a high degree of authority with relatively little delegation to subordinates. When the time pressure is less intense, however, it becomes much more possible to bring subordinates in on the decision-making process.

These, then, are the principal forces that impinge on the manager in any given instance and that tend to determine his tactical behavior in relation to his subordinates. In each case his behavior ideally will be that which makes possible the most effective attainment of his immediate goal within the limits facing him.

Long-Run Strategy

As the manager works with his organization on the problems that come up day by day, his choice of a leadership pattern is usually limited. He must take account of the forces just described and, within the restrictions they impose on him, do the best that he can. But as he looks ahead months or even years, he can shift his thinking from tactics to large-scale strategy. No longer need he be fettered by all of the forces mentioned, for he can view many of them as variables over which he has some control. He can, for example, gain new insights or skills for himself, supply training for individual subordinates, and provide participative experiences for his employee group.

In trying to bring about a change in these variables, however, he is faced with a challenging question: At which point along the continuum *should* he act?

Attaining Objectives   The answer depends largely on what he wants to accomplish. Let us suppose that he is interested in the same objectives that most modern managers seek to attain when they can shift their attention from the pressure of immediate assignments:

1   To raise the level of employee motivation.
2   To increase the readiness of subordinates to accept change.
3   To improve the quality of all managerial decisions.
4   To develop teamwork and morale.
5   To further the individual development of employees.

In recent years the manager has been deluged with a flow of advice on how best to achieve these longer-run objectives. It is little wonder that he is often both bewildered and annoyed. However, there are some guidelines which he can usefully follow in making a decision.

Most research and much of the experience of recent years give a strong factual basis to the theory that a fairly high degree of subordinate-centered behavior is associated with the accomplishment of the five purposes mentioned.[4] This does not mean that a manager should always leave all decisions to his assistants. To provide the individual or the group with greater freedom than they are ready for at any given time may very well tend to generate anxieties and therefore inhibit rather than facilitate the attainment of desired objectives. But this should not keep the manager from making a continuing effort to confront his subordinates with the challenge of freedom.

Conclusion

In summary, there are two implications in the basic thesis that we have been developing. The first is that the successful leader is one who is keenly aware of those forces which are most relevant to his behavior at any given time. He accurately understands himself, the individuals and group he is dealing with, and the company and broader social environment in which he operates. And certainly he is able to assess the present readiness for growth of his subordinates.

But this sensitivity or understanding is not enough, which brings us to the second implication. The successful leader is one who is able to behave appropriately in the light of these perceptions. If direction is in order, he is able to direct; if considerable participative freedom is called for, he is able to provide such freedom.

Thus, the successful manager of men can be primarily characterized neither as a strong leader nor as a permissive one. Rather, he is one who maintains a high batting average in accurately assessing the forces that determine what his most appropriate behavior at any given time should be and in actually being able to behave accordingly. Being both insightful and flexible, he is less likely to see the problems of leadership as a dilemma.

[4]For example, see Warren H. Schmidt and Paul C. Buchanan, *Techniques that Produce Teamwork* (New London, Arthur C. Croft Publications, 1954); and Morris S. Viteles, *Motivation and Morale in Industry* (New York, W. W. Norton & Company, Inc., 1953).

The Effect of Participation on Performance

Alfred J. Marrow

*   *   *

One of the most serious managerial problems at the plant during the years of Lewin's association with us was the resistance of production workers to changes in methods and job tasks even though these were required by competitive conditions, new engineering methods, and change in consumer demands. When it came time to change product styles—something that happened several times a year—workers complained bitterly about being transferred from old jobs they knew well to new jobs that required unlearning and relearning. Interviews showed that the morale of transferred groups dropped very low; many individuals were despondent to the point of tears. There was evidence of frustration, of loss of hope of ever regaining the former level of production, of feelings of failure and a very low level of ambition. All of this, it seemed, could be attributed to "loss of face" resulting from the sharp contrast between their previous elevated status in terms of production and their present reduced status of having to learn everything all over again.

A number of earlier investigations suggested that the strong resistance to transfers, and the slow relearning process, were primarily problems of motivation. An experiment was planned to test whether or not participation would help overcome the resistance to change.

Three groups were formed, but for the purposes of a brief summary, we will refer to only two. The first, which was the control group, would not participate in the transfer process any more than usual. They were merely told that changes were being made and the production manager explained, as usual, the new mode of work, the new job assignments, and new piecework rates.

The second group—the participative group—was asked to meet with the management and was given a complete explanation of why the change was mandatory. The employees were told frankly that business had fallen off. They were told that unless new orders could be attracted by less expensive models there might well be layoffs. They were shown the simplified and less costly model that was being proposed. They were asked to discuss cost reduction and job methods as a joint problem of the management and the workers. It was stated this way: "We don't want to sacrifice quality, and we don't want you to lose income. What ideas do you have about this?"

The workers responded with a good many practical and useful suggestions

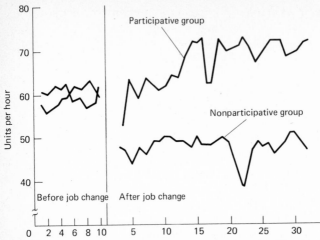

Figure 1 Output by Two Groups of Workers after Job Change.

on both counts. Along with the management they discussed new models, new ways of working, and new production rates. They also asked for another meeting for further discussion. Management and all the operators sat together until all the issues were agreed upon. Decisions were reached by consensus; there was no formal vote.

The results were extremely pleasing to those of us who had felt that joint problem solving would work well. Production by Group I, the nonparticipative group, dropped by 35 percent after the changeover and did not improve for a month afterwards. The employees were markedly hostile to the company and restricted output accordingly. We learned later that they had made an explicit agreement to "get even" with management. Within two weeks after the change, 9 percent of the operators had quit. Others filed grievances about the pay rates, although the rates, in fact, were a little too high. Morale was expectedly bad. At the end of six weeks the group was dissolved and its members assigned to other work stations.

The participative group, on the other hand, learned the new mode of work remarkably fast. By the second day they were back to their former level of production, and after three weeks they had raised their production level 14 percent higher than ever before. Their relationship with their supervisor was friendly and cooperative. Not one operator quit and no grievances were filed with the union.

Two and a half months later it was possible to confirm even more dramatically the value of the participative method. The members of the earlier nonparticipative group, which had been broken up, were brought together when another new order had to be filled. This time, however, the management followed the procedures that had been used for the participative group. The result was that now the same people who before had conspired to "get even" with the company and hold down production did the reverse. Their productivity recovered rapidly after the changeover. They attained a new and much higher level of output. There was no manifestation of hostility and there were no quits. It was clear that the lowered resistance to change was proportional to the amount of participation, and that the rate of turnover and aggression was inversely proportional to the amount of participation. Figure 1 contrasts the two groups graphically.

*   *   *

Participation by Subordinates in the Managerial Decision-making Process

Robert Tannenbaum
Fred Massarik

I Introduction

The role of "participation" by individuals or groups in American culture in general and in industrial organizations specifically has been treated by many writers. Its implications for political theory as well as for a theory of human relations in formal organizations are numerous. However, in spite of this academic and extra-academic interest, a clear-cut, operational definition of the concept, or a precise set of hypotheses regarding its dynamics, has not been developed. While to do so will be the object of this paper, the treatment will not be completely operational. The development of appropriate methods of measurement is conceived as a next step that should follow the preliminary one of conceptual clarification undertaken in this paper.

A review of the literature indicates that three major approaches have been taken in dealing with "participation":

1 The Experiential Approach This approach is exemplified by writers who in the course of their experience in enterprise work have obtained a "feel" for the role of participation in the decision-making process and have put down their experiences in article or book form.[1] Writings such as these provide a set of insights and hunches whose verification in any systematic fashion has not been

From *Canadian Journal of Economics and Political Science*, 1950, pp. 408–418. Reprinted by permission of the authors and the Canadian Journal of Economics and Political Science.

[1]For example: H. H. Carey, "Consultative Supervision and Management" (*Personnel*, Mar., 1942); Alexander R. Heron, *Why Men Work* (Palo Alto, 1948); Eric A. Nicol, "Management through Consultative Supervision" (*Personnel Journal*, Nov., 1948); James C. Worthy, "Changing Concepts of the Personnel Function" (*Personnel*, Nov., 1948).

attempted. The actual referents from which these formulations are derived often are single sets of observations in a single or in a few enterprises—observations generally made in an uncontrolled fashion.

The experiential approach, operating outside the bounds of scientific method, nonetheless adds to scientific knowledge indirectly by providing the raw material from which hypotheses may be moulded. The precise structure of these hypotheses is not stated neatly by the experiential writers, but rather remains to be formulated.

2 The Conceptual, Non-experimental Approach This approach characterizes the writings of authors who are, essentially, academicians with strong theoretical backgrounds. It is typified by writings that deal with "conditions," "functions," and other abstractions, generally of a socio-psychological nature, that attempt to explain the dynamics of participation.[2] The conceptual, non-experimental approach at its best is the process of theory or hypothesis formulation. Ideally it lays the groundwork for actual testing and experimental work, but much of this type of technical literature so far published on participation lacks the clarity of conceptual definition necessary to make it useful as a basis for experimental work.

3 The Experimental Approach This approach is found in the writings of authors who have seen fit to apply experimental techniques either to especially constructed social situations involving participation, or else in natural settings in which participational activities prevail.[3] With adequate controls and with a meaningful theoretical structure within which individual findings may be placed, this approach is doubtless the most fruitful. Ideally it indicates what will happen under specified sets of conditions and with what degree of probability. Unfortunately, up to now experimental work on the dynamics of participation in the decision-making process has been sporadic.[4]

The present paper is of the conceptual, non-experimental type. Participation in the decision-making process is conceived here as an instrument that may be used by the formal leadership of an enterprise in the pursuit of its goals. No attempt will be made to examine it from an ethical standpoint or in terms of its consistency within the frame of a democratic society, although it is by no means assumed that such considerations are less important than the ones set forward here.

[2]For example: Douglas McGregor, "Conditions for Effective Leadership in the Industrial Situation" (*Journal of Consulting Psychology,* vol. VIII, Mar.–Apr., 1944); Gordon W. Allport, "The Psychology of Participation" (*Psychological Review,* May, 1945).

[3]For the concept of the "natural experiment," see F. Stuart Chapin, *Experimental Designs in Sociological Research* (New York, 1947), and Ernest Greenwood, *Experimental Sociology* (New York, 1945).

[4]For a good summary of relevant experimental work, see Ronald Lippitt, "A Program of Experimentation on Group Functioning and Productivity" (in *Current Trends in Social Psychology,* Pittsburgh, 1948).

II Definition of Participation

It is essential, in dealing with participation, to make clear the meaning which is to be attached to the concept. One must specify both who the participators are and in what they are participating. Too frequently in the available literature on the subject the reader must determine these matters for himself since no explicit statements bearing on them are made by the writers.

As already indicated, this paper is primarily concerned with participation as a managerial device. Attention is therefore focused on the subordinates of managers in enterprises as the participators. It is important to note that these subordinates may be either non-managers or managers.[5] If they are managers, they are subordinates of superior managers in the formal organization of the enterprise in addition to having subordinates who are responsible to them.

Because of space limitations, consideration of the participation of individuals as union members in specific activities of an enterprise is excluded from the scope of this paper. Suffice it to say here that in those cases where the participation of union members is direct and personal, the benefits to be derived by the enterprise are similar to those derived from participation within the superior-subordinate relationship. However, in those cases (which are the greatest in number) where the participation of the union member is indirect and impersonal, it is doubtful if such is the result. It is our conclusion that most of the statements which follow are relevant to the former cases.[6]

What then is the meaning of participation, and with what type of participation by subordinates are we here concerned? An individual participates in something when he takes a part or share in that thing. Since taking a part or sharing is always involved, participation takes place in a social context. Managerial subordinates in formal enterprises are responsible to their superiors for the performance of designated tasks. In such performance, they are participating in the production of the good or service of the enterprise. They also participate (share), through the receipt of wages or salaries, in the distribution of the total revenue received by the enterprise. These types of participation are common to all enterprises. But there is another type of participation which is much less frequently encountered, although its use as a managerial device has, of recent years, grown rapidly in importance. This type involves participation by subordinates with their superiors in the managerial decision-making process.

Decisions are made by managers in order to organize, direct, or control responsible subordinates to the end that all service contributions be coordinated in the attainment of an enterprise purpose.[7] Since managers are those who

---

[5]For definitions of these terms as used here, see Robert Tannenbaum, "The Manager Concept: A Rational Synthesis" (*Journal of Business,* Oct., 1949).

[6]In connexion with this discussion, it should be noted that when participation takes place within the superior-subordinate relationship, managers have primary control over the nature of the activity; when it takes place as part of the manager-union relationship, they may or may not, depending upon the relative power of the two parties.

[7]See Tannenbaum, "The Manager Concept: A Rational Synthesis."

accomplish results through subordinates, the latter are always directly and intimately affected by managerial decisions and therefore may have a considerable interest in them. Because of this possible interest, subordinates may have a strong desire, particularly in a nation with deeply ingrained democratic traditions, to participate in the determination of matters affecting them. It is of importance, therefore, to consider the form which such participation might assume.

Decision-making involves a conscious choice or selection of one behaviour alternative from among a group of two or more behaviour alternatives.[8] Three steps are involved in the decision-making process. First, an individual must become aware of as many as possible of those behaviour alternatives which are relevant to the decision to be made. Secondly, he must define each of these alternatives, a definition which involves a determination of as many as possible of the consequences related to each alternative under consideration. Thirdly, the individual must exercise a choice between the alternatives, that is, make a decision.

In enterprises, managerial subordinates, as subordinates, can participate in the first two steps of the managerial decision-making process. They cannot participate in the third step. The actual choice between relevant alternatives must be made or accepted by the manager who is responsible to his superior for the decision.[9] However, subordinates can provide and discuss with their manager information with respect both to relevant alternatives and to the consequences attendant upon specific alternatives. In so doing they are participating in the managerial decision-making process.[10]

[8]This discussion of the decision-making process is based upon Robert Tannenbaum, "Managerial Decision-Making" (*Journal of Business,* Jan., 1950).

[9]In a democratic group, the choice can be made through a vote participated in by the rank and file. But, in such a case, the leader is organizationally responsible to the rank and file, and the members of the rank and file are not properly, in so far as the decision is concerned, subordinates of the leader.

Members of a democratic group, making the final choice in matters directly affecting them, may be more highly motivated as a result thereof than managerial subordinates who are granted the right to participate only in the first two steps of the managerial decision-making process. For evidence of the motivational effects of group decision, see Kurt Lewin, "Group Decision and Social Change" (in T. M. Newcomb and E. L. Hartley (eds.), *Readings in Social Psychology,* New York, 1947.

[10]It is this type of participation that most writers, who deal with human relations in enterprises, have in mind when they use the concept. The following examples illustrate this contention: "One of the most important conditions of the subordinate's growth and development centers around his opportunities to express his ideas and to contribute his suggestions before his superiors take action on matters which involve him. Through participation of this kind he becomes more and more aware of his superiors' problems, and he obtains genuine satisfaction in knowing that his opinions and ideas are given consideration in the search for solutions" (D. McGregor, "Conditions for Effective Leadership in the Industrial Situation," p. 60); "I am not suggesting that we take over intact the apparatus of the democratic state. Business cannot be run by the ballot box. . . . We must develop other inventions, adapted to the special circumstances of business, which will give employees at all levels of our organizations a greater sense of personal participation and 'belonging'" (J. Worthy, "Changing Concepts of the Personnel Function," p. 175); "Action initiated by the responsible head to bring his subordinates into the picture on matters of mutual concern is not a sharing of prerogatives of authority. Rather, it is an extension of the opportunity of participation in the development of points of view and the assembly of facts upon which decisions are made" (H. Carey, "Consultative Supervision and Management," p. 288).

The participation with which we are here concerned may take place in two different ways. First, it may involve interaction solely between a subordinate and his manager.[11] This would be the case where a worker originates a suggestion which he transmits to his boss. Secondly, it may involve interaction between a group of subordinates and their manager. This would be the case where a manager calls his subordinates together to discuss a common problem or to formulate a recommendation.[12]

III Possible Advantages of Participation as a Managerial Device

It becomes useful to inquire why managers might find it advantageous to use this device. In other words, what are the possible benefits which might accrue to an enterprise whose managers made it possible for subordinates to participate in the decision-making process? In providing an answer to this question, it is first necessary to indicate the criterion which would guide the managerial choice relating to the use of participation.

A manager of an enterprise (profit or nonprofit) who behaves rationally will attempt to make a selection from among alternatives related to any problem which will maximize results (the degree of attainment of a given end) at a given cost or which will attain given results at the lowest cost.[13] This is the criterion of rationality. Guided by this criterion, rational managers will find it advantageous to use participation whenever such use will lead to increased results at a given cost or to the attainment of given results at a lower cost.

There are many advantages which *may* stem from the use of participation as a managerial device. The following are the principal ones:

1 A higher rate of output and increased quality of product (including reduced spoilage and wastage) as a result of greater personal effort and attention on the part of subordinates.[14]

2 A reduction in turnover, absenteeism, and tardiness.

[11]The concept of interaction as used here is not restricted to direct person-to-person, two-way communication (as in the process of superior-subordinate discussion), but encompasses more indirect forms (such as, for example, written communication) as well.

[12]It may be observed that participation in the latter way, where there is communication between participators and where the act of participation is carried out through the medium of the group (as in cases of "group decision"), may often yield the more useful results. The level of derivable benefits may be higher than if participation had proceeded through channels in which there had been no interparticipator communication. Some factors important in this context are the following: (a) the feeling of "group belongingness" obtained by means of "action together" and (b) the role of norms, set as a result of group discussion, toward which behaviour will tend to gravitate.

[13]The term *cost* is here used in its highly precise form to refer to whatever must be given or sacrificed to attain an end. See "Price," *Webster's Dictionary of Synonyms*. The term *end* is broadly conceived to embrace whatever factors (monetary or nonmonetary) the managers themselves define as the formal ends of the enterprise.

[14]For examples, see Lippitt, "A Program of Experimentation on Group Functioning and Productivity"; John R. P. French, Jr., Arthur Kornhauser, and Alfred Marrow, "Conflict and Co-operation in Industry" *(Journal of Social Issues,* Feb., 1946); *Productivity, Supervision and Morale* (Survey Research Center Study no. 6, Ann Arbor, 1948).

3 A reduction in the number of grievances and more peaceful manager-subordinate and manager-union relations.

4 A greater readiness to accept change.[15] When changes are arbitrarily introduced from above without explanation, subordinates tend to feel insecure and to take countermeasures aimed at a sabotage of the innovations. But when they have participated in the process leading to the decision, they have had an opportunity to be heard. They know what to expect and why, and they may desire the change. Blind resistance tends to become intelligent adaptation as insecurity is replaced by security.

5 Greater ease in the management of subordinates.[16] Fewer managers may be necessary, the need for close supervision may be reduced, and less disciplinary action may be called for. Subordinates who have participated in the process leading toward a determination of matters directly affecting them may have a greater sense of responsibility with respect to the performance of their assigned tasks and may be more willing to accept the authority of their superiors. All managers possess a given amount of formal authority delegated to them by their superiors. But formal authority is not necessarily the equivalent of effective authority. The real source of the authority possessed by an individual lies in the acceptance of its exercise by those who are subject to it. It is the subordinates of an individual who determine the authority which he may wield. Formal authority is, in effect, nominal authority. It becomes real only when it is accepted. Thus, to be effective, formal authority must coincide with authority determined by its acceptance. The latter defines the useful limits of the former.[17] The use of participation as a managerial device may result in a widening of these limits, reducing the amount of resistance to the exercise of formal authority and increasing the positive responses of subordinates to managerial directives.

6 The improved quality of managerial decisions. It is seldom if ever possible for managers to have knowledge of *all* alternatives and *all* consequences related to the decisions which they must make. Because of the existence of barriers to the upward flow of information in most enterprises, much valuable information possessed by subordinates never reaches their managers. Participation tends to break down the barriers, making the information available to managers. To the extent that such information alters the decisions which managers make, the quality of their decisions may thereby be improved.

These, then, are the principal advantages which *may* stem from the use of participation as a managerial device.[18] The conditions under which it *will* accomplish them—under which participation will lead to motivation—is the concern of the section which follows.

[15]See, for example, Alex Bavelas, "Some Problems of Organizational Change" (*Journal of Social Issues,* Summer, 1948); Elliott Jacques, "Interpretive Group Discussion as a Method of Facilitating Social Change" (*Human Relations,* Aug., 1948); Lewin, "Group Decision and Social Change."

[16]See, for example, L. P. Bradford and R. Lippit, "Building a Democratic Work Group" (*Personnel,* Nov., 1945); O. H. Mowrer, "Authoritarianism vs. 'Self-Government' in the Management of Children's Aggressive (Anti-Social) Reactions as a Preparation for Citizenship in a Democracy" (*Journal of Social Psychology,* Feb., 1939, pp. 121–126).

[17]This concept of effective authority is expanded upon in Tannenbaum, "Managerial Decision-Making."

[18]These advantages will henceforth be referred to as enterprise advantages.

IV   The Psychological Conditions
of Effective Participation

All managers of an enterprise are faced with the problem of eliciting service contributions from their subordinates at a high level of quality and intensity. These service contributions are essential if the formal goals of the enterprise are to be attained. What induces subordinates to contribute their services? What motivates them?

A motivated individual is one who is striving to achieve a goal; his activity is goal-oriented.[19] But it should be stressed that motivation is only *potential* motion towards a goal. Whether or not the goal is reached depends not only upon the strength of the force in the direction of the goal, but also upon all other forces (both driving and restraining) in the given situation.[20] To illustrate, a person may be motivated to produce 200 units of an item per day, but the restraining force in the form of machine failure or a quarrel with the foreman may lead him to attain an output of only 150 units.

In enterprises, the goals towards which individuals strive may be of two kinds. They may be the formal goals of the enterprise, or they may be other goals which are complementary to the formal goals. The latter is the typical case. Individuals may strive for monetary reward, prestige, power, security, and the like; or they may strive for certain psychological gratifications through the very act of doing the job (that is, they work because they like their work). The primary reason why they contribute their services is to attain these latter goals. In attaining these desired goals, they make possible the attainment of the formal goals of the enterprise which to them are simply means to their own ends. In this sense, the desired goals and the formal goals are complementary.

In the former case, the goals desired by the individual and the formal goals are the same. The individual contributes his services primarily because such contribution makes possible the attainment of the formal goals of the enterprise which coincide with his own personal goals. To the extent that this coincidence of goals exists, the necessity for managers to provide complementary goals for subordinates is thereby lessened, and related costs are reduced. It is suggested that participation tends to bring about a coincidence of formal and personal goals.[21] It may be that through participation, the subordinate who formerly was

---

[19]A goal is defined as a result which, when achieved, has the power to reduce the tension of the organism that has caused the organism to seek it.

[20]Thus, motion in the direction of goals may be achieved not only by adding forces in the goal-direction, but also by reducing forces impeding such motion. See K. Lewin, "Frontiers in Group Dynamics" (*Human Relations,* vol. I, no. 1, 1947, pp. 26–27).

[21]It must be noted that participation as used in this context is only one device which may lead to additional motivation by bringing about a coincidence of formal and personal goals. For example, some other devices that under certain conditions may result in motivational increases and their derivative benefits to the enterprise are permitting personal discretion to the person to be motivated and stimulation of a sense of pride of workmanship. In the former context, managers in all enterprises must always decide the amount of discretion to permit to subordinates. Many considerations naturally underlie this decision. For present purposes, it is important to emphasize that in many circumstances, the granting of considerable discretion may lead to substantial increases in motivation. Several devices may be used concurrently, and the dynamics of the devices themselves are interrelated. For example, use of discretion may bring about an enhanced pride-of-workmanship feeling.

moved to contribute his services only because he sought, for example, security and financial rewards, now comes to be moved additionally because he recognizes that the success of the enterprise in turn will enhance his own ability to satisfy his needs.[22]

Whether one conceives of participation as involving separate subordinates with their superiors or subordinates-in-groups with their superiors, in the final analysis one must not lose sight of the fact that the subordinate is a unique human being with a given personality. This implies that whether or not participation will bring forth the restructuring of his goal pattern (incorporating the formal goals within the scope of the personal goals) will depend upon a set of dynamic psychological conditions, the primary ones of which are outlined below:

1 The subordinate must be capable of becoming psychologically involved in the participational activities. He must be free from "blockages" which may prevent him from re-arranging his particular goal pattern in the light of new experience. He must possess some minimum amount of intelligence so that he may grasp the meaning and implications of the thing being considered. He must be in touch with reality. If he responds to a dream world, any "real" developments, such as opportunities to take part in certain decision-making processes, may not penetrate without gross distortion and as a result miss their point.

2 The subordinate must favour participational activity. In other words, the person who believes that "the boss knows best" and that the decision-making process is none of his business is not likely to become strongly motivated if given an opportunity to participate. It is apparent that for personality types shaped intensely by an authoritarian system, opportunities for participation may be regarded as signs of weakness and leadership incompetence and on that basis may be rejected unequivocally.[23]

3 The subordinate must see the relevance to his personal life pattern of the thing being considered. When he realizes that through participation he may affect the course of his future in such a fashion as to increase its positive goal elements and to diminish the negative ones, he will become motivated. For example, a person who can see the relationship between "putting his two bits" into a discussion of a new way of using a stitching machine and the fact that this may mean greater job security and increased pay for himself may be motivated.

4 The subordinate must be able to express himself to his own satisfaction with respect to the thing being considered. He must be psychologically able to communicate; and, further, he must feel that he is making some sort of contribution. Of course, if he cannot communicate (owing to mental blocks, fear of being conspicuous, etc.), by definition he is not participating. If he does not feel that he is contributing, he may, instead of becoming motivated, come to feel inadequate and frustrated. This presupposes that not only is he articulate, but that he has a certain fund of knowledge on which to draw. Participation may fail if it involves

---

[22]It must be recognized that typically goal configurations, rather than single goals, act as motivating agents.

[23]For example, see A. H. Maslow, "The Authoritarian Character Structure" (in P. L. Harriman (ed.), *Twentieth Century Psychology*, New York, 1946). For more detailed treatments see the major works of Erich Fromm and Abram Kardiner.

considering matters that are quite outside the scope of experience of the participators.

All of the above conditions must be satisfied to some minimum extent. Beyond this requirement, however, the conditions may be mutually compensating, and a relatively low degree of one (although necessarily above the minimum) may be offset somewhat by an extremely high degree of another. For example, if a subordinate is unusually anxious to take part in participational activity (perhaps for reasons of prestige desires), he may come to be quite involved in the process of restructuring his goal pattern so that it will include some of the formal goals, even though he is not always certain as to whether or not he is really contributing anything worthwhile. Further, the relationships specified by the conditions are essentially dynamic. Opportunities for participation, reluctantly used at first, ultimately may lead to a change of mind and to their enthusiastic acceptance.[24]

It is apparent that individual differences are highly important in considering the effectiveness of participation as a motivational device; however, the "amount of participation opportunities" made possible by the managers is also a variable quantity. Thus, it is necessary to enquire what the limits to opportunities to participate are in terms of maximum results.

Common sense experience indicates that when some subordinates are given too many opportunities for participation, or too much leeway in participating, they may tend to flounder; they may find themselves unable to assimilate effectively the range of "thinking opportunities" with which they are faced.[25] On the other hand, if they are given little or no opportunity to take part in the decision-making process, by definition they will not come to be motivated by participational activity. For each individual, an amount of participation opportunities lying somewhere between these two extremes will result in a maximum amount of motivation. A hypothesis stemming from this formulation is that for effective operation of participation as a motivational device in a group situation, the members of the group must respond similarly to given amounts of participation, for wide divergences of response may bring forth social tensions and lack of team work within the group.

Of course, many factors act together to motivate an individual. Therefore, the usefulness of the conceptualization advanced depends upon the possibility of breaking down the total of motivational forces into those owing to participation and those owing to other factors. Experimental control methods, matching of cases, and similar devices may have to be utilized to make such an analysis possible. Whether or not the increment of motivation owing to participation is

[24]It should be stressed that "life spaces" of individuals (that is, their conceptions of themselves in relation to the totality of a physical and psychological environment) and their readiness for action in the light of these conceptions are never static. Constant change and "restructuring" take place, making for an essentially dynamic patterning of behaviour. For alternative definitions of the concept "life space" see Robert W. Leeper, *Lewin's Topological and Vector Psychology* (Eugene, 1943), p. 210.

[25]For the belief that "thinking" as a solution for the industrial problem of motivation is usable more effectively on the supervisory level, but less applicable on the "lower levels" of the organizational hierarchy, see Willard Tomlison; "Review of A. R. Heron, *Why Men Work*" (*Personnel Journal,* July–Aug., 1948, p. 122).

worthwhile depends to an important extent upon the level of intensity of motivation that prevailed previous to introduction of the device of participation. No doubt, there are upper limits to intensity of motivation, and, if motivation has been strong all along, the effect of participation may not be very great.

V Extra-participational Conditions for Effective Participation

Beyond the factors governing the relationship between participation and possible resultant motivation, certain conditions "outside" the individual must be considered by the managers in deciding whether or not this particular device is applicable.[26] It would be possible to distinguish a great number of such outside conditions that may determine whether or not the use of participation is feasible in a given situation. Those here indicated are suggestive rather than fully definitive. All are viewed with this question in mind: "Granting that participation may have certain beneficial effects, is it useful in a given instance if the ends of the enterprise are to be achieved?"

To answer this question affirmatively, the following conditions must be met:

1 Time Availability The final decision must not be of a too urgent nature.[27] If it is necessary to arrive at some sort of emergency decision rapidly, it is obvious that even though participation in the decision-making process may have a beneficial effect in some areas, slowness of decision may result in thwarting other goals of the enterprise or even may threaten the existence of the enterprise. Military decisions frequently are of this type.

2 Rational Economics The cost of participation in the decision-making process must not be so high that it will outweigh any positive values directly brought about by it. If it should require outlays which could be used more fruitfully in alternative activities (for example, buying more productive though expensive equipment), then investment in it would be ill-advised.

3 Intra-plant Strategy

a Subordinate Security Giving the subordinates an opportunity to participate in the decision-making process must not bring with it any awareness on their part of unavoidable catastrophic events. For example, a subordinate who is made aware in the participation process that he will lose his job *regardless* of any decisions towards which he might contribute may experience a drop in motivation. Furthermore, to make it possible for the subordinate to be willing to participate, he must be given the feeling that no matter what he says or thinks his status or role in the plant setting will not be affected adversely. This point has been made effectively in the available literature.[28]

---

[26]For analytical purposes, this article differentiates between conditions regarding the dynamics of participation as a psychological process and all conditions outside this psychological participation-to-motivation link. The latter category of conditions is treated under the present heading.

[27]See Chester I. Barnard, *Organization and Management* (Cambridge, 1948), p. 48.

[28]See McGregor, "Conditions for Effective Leadership in the Industrial Situation," *passim.*

   b Manager-Subordinate Stability Giving subordinates an opportunity to participate in the decision-making process must not threaten seriously to undermine the formal authority of the managers of the enterprise. For example, in some cases managers may have good reasons to assume that participation may lead non-managers to doubt the competence of the formal leadership, or that serious crises would result were it to develop that the subordinates were right while the final managerial decision turned out to be in disagreement with them and incorrect.

4 Inter-plant Strategy Providing opportunities for participation must not open channels of communication to competing enterprises. "Leaks" of information to a competitor from subordinates who have participated in a given decision-making process must be avoided if participation is to be applicable.

5 Provision for Communication Channels For participation to be effective, channels must be provided through which the employee may take part in the decision-making process. These channels must be available continuously and their use must be convenient and practical.[29]

6 Education for Participation For participation to be effective, efforts must be made to educate subordinates regarding its function and purpose in the overall functioning of the enterprise.[30]
   It must be stressed that the conditions stipulated in this section are dynamic in their own right and may be affected by the very process of participation as well as by other factors.

VI Effects of Participation as a Function of Time

An area of research that still remains relatively unexplored is that relating to the variation of the effects of participation with time. Some experimental studies have examined these effects in terms of increased productivity over a period of several weeks or months and found no appreciable reductions in productivity with time; while other evidence indicates that in some cases participation may have a sort of "shock" effect, leading to a surge of interest and increased motivation, with a subsequent decline.[31] Inadequate attention seems to have been given to this rather crucial question, and the present writers know of no studies that have traced the effects of participation (or other motivational devices) over periods as long as a year. However, on a priori grounds, and on the basis of experimental evidence, it would seem that, after an initial spurt, a plateau of beneficial effects will be attained, which finally will dissolve into a decline, unless additional managerial devices are skilfully employed.

[29]For a rigorous mathematical treatment of channels of communication within groups see Alex Bavelas, "A Mathematical Model for Group Structures" (*Applied Anthropology,* Summer, 1948, pp. 16 ff.).
   [30]See French, Kornhauser, and Marrow, "Conflict and Co-operation in Industry," p. 30.
   [31]For evidence of no decline in the motivational effect of certain participational procedures in an industrial re-training situation after a relatively brief time period subsequent to initiation of participation had elapsed, see L. Coch and J. R. P. French, "Overcoming Resistance to Change" (*Human Relations,* vol. 1, no. 4, pp. 522–523).

The Contingency Model: New Directions For Leadership Utilization

Fred E. Fiedler

Leadership research has come a long way from the simple concepts of earlier years which centered on the search for the magic leadership trait. We have had to replace the old cherished notion that "leaders are born and not made." These increasingly complex formulations postulate that some types of leaders will behave and perform differently in a given situation than other types. The Contingency Model is one of the earliest and most articulated of these theories;[1] taking into account the personality of the leader as well as aspects of the situation which affect the leader's behavior and performance. This model has given rise to well over one-hundred empirical studies. This article briefly reviews the current status of the Contingency Model and then discusses several new developments which promise to have considerable impact on our thinking about leadership as well as on the management of executive manpower.

The Contingency Model

The theory holds that the effectiveness of a task group or of an organization depends on two main factors: the personality of the leader and the degree to which the situation gives the leader power, control and influence over the situation or, conversely, the degree to which the situation confronts the leader with uncertainty.[2]

Leader Personality   The first of these factors distinguishes leader personality in terms of two different motivational systems, i.e., the basic or primary goals as well as the secondary goals which people pursue once their more pressing needs are satisfied. One type of person, whom we shall call "relationship-motivated," primarily seeks to maintain good interpersonal relationships with coworkers. These basic goals become very apparent in uncertain and anxiety provoking situations in which we try to make sure that the important needs are secured. Under these conditions the relationship-motivated individual will seek out others and solicit their support; however, under conditions in which he or she feels quite secure and relaxed—because this individual has achieved the major goals of having close relations with subordinates—he or she will seek the esteem and admiration of others. In a leadership situation where task performance results in esteem and admiration from superiors, this leader will tend to concentrate on behaving in a task-relevant manner, sometimes to the detriment of relations with immediate subordinates.

The relationship-motivated leader's counterpart has as a major goal the accomplishment of some tangible evidence of his or her worth. This person gets

Reprinted by permission of the publisher from *Journal of Contemporary Business*, Autumn 1974, pp. 65–79.

satisfaction from the task itself and from knowing that he or she has done well. In a leadership situation which is uncertain and anxiety provoking, this person will, therefore, put primary emphasis on completing the task. However, when this individual has considerable control and influence and knows, therefore, the task will get done, he or she will relax and be concerned with subordinates' feelings and satisfactions. In other words, business before pleasure, but business *with* pleasure whenever possible.

Of course, these two thumbnail sketches are oversimplified, but they do give a picture which tells us, first, that we are dealing with different types of people and, second, that they differ in their primary and secondary goals and, consequently, in the way they behave under various conditions. Both the relationship-motivated and the task-motivated persons may be pleasant and considerate toward their members. However, the task-motivated leader will be considerate in situations in which he or she is secure, i.e., in which the individual's power and influence are high; the relationship-motivated leader will be considerate when his or her control and influence are less assured, when some uncertainty is present.

These motivational systems are measured by the Least Preferred Coworker score (LPC) which is obtained by first asking an individual to think of all people with whom he or she has ever worked, and then to describe the one person with whom this individual has been able to work least well. The description of the least preferred coworker is made on a short, bipolar, eight-point scale, from 16 to 22 item-scale of the semantic differential format. The LPC score is the sum of the item scores; e.g.:

Friendly	: __ : __ : __ : __ : __ : __ : __ :	Unfriendly
	1 2 3 4 5 6 7 8	
Cooperative	: __ : __ : __ : __ : __ : __ : __ :	Uncooperative
	1 2 3 4 5 6 7 8	

High-LPC persons, i.e., individuals who describe their LPC in relatively positive terms, seem primarily relationship-motivated. Low-LPC persons, those who describe their least preferred coworker in very unfavorable terms, are basically task-motivated. Therefore, as can be seen, the LPC score is not a description of leader behavior because the behavior of high- and low-LPC people changes with different situations.

Relationship-motivated people seem more open, more approachable and more like McGregor's "Theory Y" managers, while the task-motivated leaders tend to be more controlled and more controlling persons, even though they may be as likeable and pleasant as their relationship-motivated colleagues.[3]

Current evidence suggests that the LPC scores and the personality attributes they reflect are almost as stable as most other personality measures. (For example, test-retest reliabilities for military leaders have been .72 over an 8-month period[4] and .67 over a 2-year period for faculty members).[5] Changes do occur, but in the absence of major upsets in the individual's life, they tend to be gradual and relatively small.

The Leadership Situation   The second variable, "situational favorableness,"[6] indicates the degree to which the situation gives the leader control and influence and the ability to predict the consequences of his or her behavior.[7] A situation in which the leader cannot predict the consequences of the decision tends to be stressful and anxiety arousing.

One rough but useful method for defining situational favorableness is based on three subscales. These are the degree to which (a) the leader is, or feels, accepted and supported by his or her members (leader-member relations); (b) the task is clear-cut, programmed and structured as to goals, procedures and measurable progress and success (task structure); and (c) the leader's position provides power to reward and punish and, thus, to obtain compliance from subordinates (position power).

Groups then can be categorized as being high or low on each of these three dimensions by dividing them at the median or, on the basis of normative scores, into those with good and poor leader-member relations, task structure and position power. This leads to an eight-celled classification shown on the horizontal axis of Figure I. The eight cells or "octants" are scaled from "most favorable" (octant I) to the left of the graph to "least favorable" (octant VIII) to the right. A leader obviously will have the most control and influence in groups that fall into octant I; i.e., in which this leader is accepted, has high position power and a structured task. The leader will have somewhat less control and influence in octant II, where he or she is accepted and has a structured task, but little

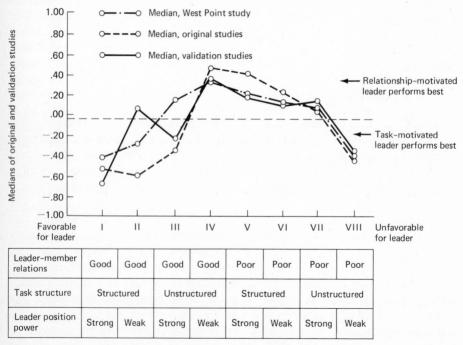

Figure I

position power, and so on to groups in octant VIII, where control and influence will be relatively small because the leader is not accepted by his or her group, has a vague, unstructured task and little position power. Situational favorableness and LPC are, of course, neither empirically nor logically related to each other.

The Personality-Situation Interaction   The basic findings of the Contingency Model are that task-motivated leaders perform generally best in very "favorable" situations, i.e., either under conditions in which their power, control and influence are very high (or, conversely, where uncertainty is very low) or where the situation is unfavorable, where they have low power, control and influence. Relationship-motivated leaders tend to perform best in situations in which they have moderate power, control and influence. The findings are summarized in Figure I. The horizontal axis indicates the eight cells of the situational favorableness dimension, with the most favorable end on the left side of the graph's axis. The vertical axis indicates the *correlation coefficients* between the leader's LPC score and the group's performance. A high correlation in the positive direction, indicated by a point above the midline of the graph, shows that the relationship-motivated leaders performed better than the task-motivated leaders. A negative correlation, shown by a point which falls below the midline of the graph, indicates that the task-motivated leaders performed better than relationship-motivated leaders, i.e., the higher the LPC score, the lower the group's performance.

The solid curve connects the median correlations within each of the octants obtained in the original studies (before 1963) on which the model was based. The broken line connects the median correlations obtained in various validation studies from 1964–1971.[8] As can be seen, the two curves are very similar, and the points on the curves correlate .76 ($p < .01$). Only in octant 2 is there a major discrepancy. However, it should be pointed out that there are very few groups in real life which have a highly structured task while the leader has low position power, e.g., in high school basketball teams and student surveying parties. Most of the validation evidence for octant 2 comes from laboratory studies in which this type of situation may be difficult to reproduce. However, the field study results for this octant are in the negative direction, just as the model predicts.

The most convincing validation evidence comes from a well-controlled experiment conducted by Chemers and Skrzypek at the U.S. Military Academy at West Point.[9] LPC scores as well as sociometric performance ratings to predict leader-member relations were obtained several weeks *prior* to the study, and groups then were assembled in advance, based on having the leader's LPC score and the expressed positive or negative feelings of group members about one another. The results of the Chemers and Skrzypek study are shown in the figure as a dotted line and give nearly a point-for-point replication of the original model with a correlation of .86 ($p < .01$). A subsequent reanalysis of the Chemers and Skrzypek data by Shiflett showed that the Contingency Model accounted for no less than 28 percent of the variance in group performance.[10] This is a very high degree of prediction, especially in a study in which variables such as the group

members' intelligence, the leader's ability, the motivational factors of participants and similar effects were uncontrolled. Of course, it is inconceivable that
data of this nature could be obtained by pure chance.

A different and somewhat clearer description of the Contingency Model is
presented schematically in Figure II. As before, the situational favorableness
dimension is indicated on the horizontal axis, extending from the most favorable
situation on the left to the relatively least favorable situation on the right.
However, here the vertical axis indicates the group or organizational performance; the solid line on the graph is the schematic performance curve of
relationship-motivated (high-LPC) leaders, while the dashed line indicates the
performance of task-motivated (low-LPC) leaders.

These curves show, first of all, that both the relationship- and the task-
motivated leaders perform well under some situations but not under others.
Therefore, it is not accurate to speak of a "good" or a "poor" leader, rather, a
leader may perform well in one type of situation but not in another. Outstanding
directors of research teams do not necessarily make good production foremen or
military leaders, and outstanding battle field commanders, like General Patton,
do not necessarily make good chiefs of staff or good chairmen of volunteer
school picnic committees.

The second major implication of Figure II is that leaders performance
depends as much on the situation to which the organization assigns him (her) as
on his or her own personality. Hence, organizational improvement can be

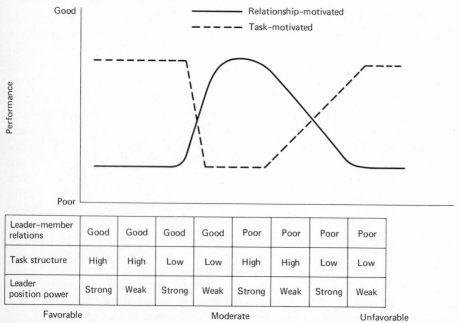

Figure II The Performance of Relationship- and Task-motivated Leaders in Different Situa-
tional-Favorableness Conditions.

achieved either by changing the leader's personality and motivational system—
which is at best a very difficult and uncertain process—or by modifying the
degree to which the situation provides the leader with power and influence. It
should be obvious from the graph that certain leaders perform better with less
rather than more power, i.e., some leaders let the power "go to their heads,"
they become cocky and arrogant, while others need security to function well.

Extensions of the Contingency Model   Two important tests of any theory are
the degree to which it allows us to understand phenomena which do not follow
common-sense expectations and, second, the extent to which it predicts non-
obvious findings. In both of these respects, the Contingency Model has demonstrated its usefulness. We present here several important findings from recent
studies, and then discuss some implications for management.

Effects of Experience and Training   One of the major research efforts in the
area of leadership and management has been the attempt to develop training
methods which will improve organizational performance. However, until now
the various training programs have failed to live up to their expectations.
Stogdill concluded that:

> The research on leadership training is generally inadequate in both design and
> execution. It has failed to address itself to the most crucial problem of leadership—
> . . . [the] effects of leadership on group performance and member satisfaction.[11]

The Contingency Model would predict that training should increase the
performance of some leaders and also decrease the performance of others.
However, it raises the question of whether any current method of training
logically can result in an across-the-board increase in organizational leadership
performance.[12]

As pointed out before, a group's performance depends on the leader's
personality as well as the degree to which the situation provides him or her with
control, power and influence. If the leader's power and influence are increased
by experience and training, the "match" between leader personality and situational favorableness would change. However, increasing the leader's power and
influence is exactly the goal of most leadership training. For example, technical
training increases the leader's expert power; coaching and orthodox training
programs which use the case study and lecture method are designed to increase
the structure of the task by providing the leader with methods for dealing with
problems which, otherwise, would require him or her to think of new solutions.
Human relations training is designed to develop better relations with group
members, thus enabling the leader to exert more personal influence or "referent
power."

For example, let us take a newly promoted supervisor of a production
department in which he has not worked before. As he begins his new job, some
of the tasks may seem unfamiliar and he will be unsure of his exact duties and

responsibilities. He also may be uncertain of the power his position provides—how, for example, will the group react if he tries to dock an old, experienced worker who had come in late? Is this type of disciplinary measure acceptable to the group even though it may be allowed by the union contract? He may wonder how he should handle a problem with a fellow supervisor in the plant on whom he has to depend for parts and supplies. Should he file a formal complaint or should he talk to him personally?

After several years on the job, our supervisor will have learned the ropes; he will know how far he can go in disciplining his workers, how to trouble-shoot various machines and how to deal with other managers in the organization. Thus, for the experienced supervisor the job is structured, his position power is high and his relations with his group are probably good. In other words, his leadership situation is very favorable.

When he first started on the job, his leadership situation probably was only moderately favorable. If you will recall, relationship-motivated leaders tend to perform best in moderately favorable situations, while task-motivated leaders perform better in very favorable situations. Therefore, a relationship-motivated leader will perform well at first before gaining experience (e.g., by using the resources of group members and inviting their participation); a task-motivated leader will perform well after becoming experienced. In other words, the relationship-motivated leader actually should perform less well after gaining experi-

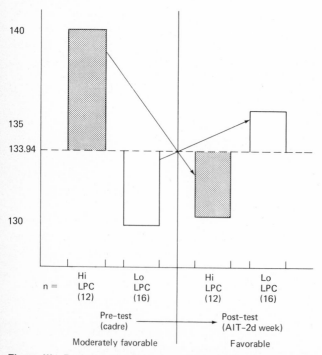

Figure III Performance of High- and Low-LPC Leaders as a Function of Increased Experience and More Structured Task Assignment over Five Months.

ence, while the task-motivated leader's performance should increase with greater experience.

A substantial number of studies now support this prediction.[13] A good example comes from a longitudinal study of infantry squad leaders who were assigned to newly organized units.[14] Their performance was evaluated by the same judges shortly after they joined their squads and, again, approximately 5 months later after their squads had passed the combat readiness test. As Figure III shows, the data are exactly as predicted by the Contingency Model. Similar results have been obtained in studies on the effects of training and experience of post office managers, managers of consumer cooperatives, police patrol supervisors and leaders of various military units.

The effect of leadership training on performance also was demonstrated by a very ingenious experiment conducted at the University of Utah.[15] ROTC cadets and students were assembled *a priori* into four-man teams with high- and low-LPC leaders. One-half of the team leaders were given training in decoding cryptographic messages, i.e., they were shown how to decode simple messages easily by first counting all the letters in the message and considering the most frequent letter an "e." A three-letter word, ending with the supposed "e" is then likely to be a "the," etc. The other half of the leaders were given no training of this type. All teams operated under a fairly high degree of tension, as indicated by subsequent ratings of the group atmosphere. Because the task is by definition unstructured, the situation was moderately favorable for the trained leaders but unfavorable for the untrained leaders. Therefore, we would expect that the relationship-motivated leaders would perform better with training, while the task-motivated leaders would perform more effectively in the unfavorable situation, i.e., without the benefit of training. As can be seen in Figure IV, the findings support the predictions of the model.

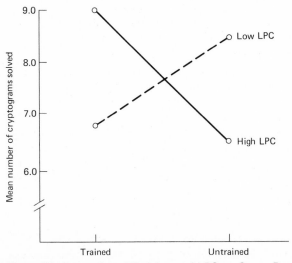

Figure IV   Interaction of Training and LPC on Group Productivity.

Further Implications

Selection   It seems highly likely from these and similar findings that we need to reconsider our management selection strategies. Obviously, the old adage calling for "the right man for the right job" is not as simple as it once appeared. The right person for a particular job today may be the wrong person in 6 months or in 1 or 2 years. As we have seen, the job which presents a very favorable leadership situation for the experienced leader presents a moderately favorable situation for the leader who is new and inexperienced or untrained. Hence, under these conditions a relationship-motivated leader should be chosen for the long run. The job which is moderately favorable for the experienced and trained leader is likely to represent an unfavorable leadership situation for the inexperienced leader. Hence, a task-motivated leader should be selected for the short run, and a relationship-motivated leader should be selected for the long run.

Rotation   Figure IV suggests that certain types of leaders will reach a "burn-out point" after they have stayed on the job for a given length of time. They will become bored, stale, disinterested and no longer challenged. A rational rotation policy obviously must be designed to rotate these leaders at the appropriate time to new and more challenging jobs. The other types of leaders, e.g., the task-motivated leaders represented in Figure IV, should be permitted to remain on the job so that they can become maximally efficient.

Most organizations and, in particular, the military services, have a rotation system which (at least in theory) moves all officers to new jobs after a specified period of time. Such a rigid system is likely to be dysfunctional because it does not properly allow for individual differences which determine the time required by different types of people to reach their best performance. Recent research by Bons also has shown that the behavior and performance of leaders is influenced by such other organizational changes as the transfer of a leader from one unit to a similar unit and by a reorganization which involves the reassignment of the leader's superiors.[16]

The Contingency Model clearly is a very complex formulation of the leadership problem. Whether it is more complex than is necessary, as some of its critics have claimed, or whether it is still not sufficiently complex, as others have averred, remains an open question. It is clear at this point that the theory not only predicts leadership performance in field studies and laboratory experiments, but also that it serves as a very important and fruitful source of new hypotheses in the area of leadership.

Notes

This paper is based on research performed under ARPA Order 454, Contract N00014-67-A-0103-0013 with the Advanced Research Projects Agency, United States Navy (Fred E. Fiedler, Principal Investigator) and Contract NR 177-472, N00014-67-A-0103-0012 with the Office of Naval Research, Department of the Navy (Fred E. Fiedler, Principal Investigator).

1   F. E. Fiedler, "A Contingency Model of Leadership Effectiveness," in L. Berkowitz, ed., *Advances in Experimental Social Psychology* (Academic Press, 1964); ———, *A Theory of Leadership Effectiveness* (New York: McGraw-Hill, 1967); ———and M. M. Chemers, *Leadership and Effective Management* (Glenview, Ill.: Scott, Foresman & Co., 1974).
2   D. Nebeker, "Situational Favorability and Environmental Uncertainty: An Integrative Study," *Administrative Science Quarterly* (1974, in press).
3   L. K. Michaelsen, "Leader Orientation, Leader Behavior, Group Effectiveness and Situational Favorability: An Empirical Extension of the Contingency Model," *Organizational Behavior and Human Performance*, 9(1973), pp. 226–245.
4   P. M. Bons, "The Effect of Changes in Leadership Environment on the Behavior of Relationship- and Task-Motivated Leaders" (Ph.D. diss., University of Washington, 1974).
5   Joyce Prothero, "Personality and Situational Effects on the Job-Related Behavior of Faculty Members" (Honors thesis, University of Washington, 1974).
6   F. E. Fiedler, *Leadership Effectiveness*.
7   D. Nebeker, "Situational Favorability."
8   F. E. Fiedler, "Validation and Extension of the Contingency Model of Leadership Effectiveness: A Review of Empirical Findings," *Psychological Bulletin*, 76(1971), pp. 128–148.
9   M. M. Chemers and G. J. Skrzypek, "Experimental Test of the Contingency Model of Leadership Effectiveness," *Journal of Personality and Social Psychology*, 24 (1972), pp. 172–177.
10 S. C. Shiflett, "The Contingency Model of Leadership Effectiveness: Some Implications of Its Statistical and Methodological Properties," *Behavioral Science*, 18 (1973), pp. 429–441.
11 R. M. Stogdill, *Handbook of Leadership: A Survey of Theory and Research* (New York: Free Press, 1974).
12 F. E. Fiedler, "The Effects of Leadership Training and Experience: A Contingency Model Interpretation," *Administrative Science Quarterly*, 17(1972), pp. 453–470.
13 *Ibid.*
14 F. E. Fiedler, P. M. Bons and L. L. Hastings, "New Strategies for Leadership Utilization," in W. T. Singleton and P. Spurgeon, eds., *Defense Psychology* [NATO, Division of Scientific Affairs (1974, in press)].
15 M. M. Chemers et al., "Leader LPC, Training and Effectiveness: An Experimental Examination," *Journal of Personality and Social Psychology* (1974, in press).
16 P. M. Bons, "Changes in Leadership."

The Search for a Theory of Leadership

Victor H. Vroom

The potential importance to society of an adequate understanding of the leadership process cannot be underestimated. Any knowledge that the behavioral sciences could contribute to the identification and enhancement of leadership in organized human endeavor could be of considerable value in increasing the effectiveness of the organizations in society.

For many years, the research that has been conducted on the topic of leadership was purely of academic interest and had little if any impact on the day-to-day workings of organizations. There are some recent indications that the situation is now changing. Contributions ranging from the new profession of organization development (Bennis, 1969) to the technology of assessment centers (Bray and Grant, 1966) show promise of contributing to the effectiveness of organizational leadership. More elusive, however, has been the formulation of a theory of leadership. Such a theory should be consistent not only with the vast amount of research that has been conducted on leadership but also with general knowledge of the processes that govern the behavior of individuals and of organizations. If a general theory of leadership could be developed, it could constitute a firm foundation for enhancing leadership in organizations.

Search for a theory of this kind within the behavioral sciences has been filled with false starts, based on erroneous and oversimplified conceptions. One of the false starts stemmed from a conception of leadership as a general personality trait—i.e., a single quality that people possess in different amounts. If reliable and valid measures of this trait could be developed, they could be used in selecting people for leadership positions. However, as Fiedler has correctly pointed out in his chapter, the search for traits that distinguish leaders from followers or effective leaders from ineffective ones has been unsuccessful. His conclusion and the conclusions of most other people who have examined the evidence is that the relationships between traits and leadership varies markedly with the situation. The question, Who will be the best leader? is akin to asking, What will be the best fishing bait?. Neither question can be adequately answered as stated.

In retrospect, this conclusion is not surprising. In fact, it would be surprising to find that the nature of the group or organization, its prevalent norms and values and the critical problems it faces in its relation to its own environment, have nothing to do with the kinds of people elevated to leadership status or with those who prove to be effective in carrying out their leadership roles.

If there are no stable or invariant personality characteristics that distinguish leaders from non-leaders or effective leaders from less effective ones, it is still possible that there are methods or styles of leadership that are more effective than others. A second approach, which also could be termed "a false start," involved looking not at the personality of the effective leader but at the way in which he behaves in carrying out his leadership role. It assumed that there were stable behavioral correlates of effective leadership. Research based on such an assumption was directed toward answering such questions as, How do leaders of effective groups behave in their leadership role that distinguishes them from leaders who are less effective?, Are they autocratic or democratic in their leadership style? Do they exhibit more initiative or more consideration than those who are less effective?

If simple answers to such questions could be obtained, they could point to ways to be an effective leader or, at least, provide a sound empirical foundation for leadership training. But once again answers were not simple. The Ohio State studies that Fiedler cites and another parallel set of studies conducted at the University of Michigan had limited success in identifying consistent correlations between patterns of leadership behavior and measures of group performance or effectiveness.

One conclusion that can be drawn from all this research is that the problems were more complicated than was originally expected. For example, it became clear that the situation was an overlooked source of influence. Initiative and other measures of leadership behavior were associated with group effectiveness in some situations but not in others. However, to conclude that "issues are complex" or that "it depends on the situation" is merely to indicate a further direction for research rather than a specific testable solution to society's need for effective leadership.

Fiedler and his Contingency Model represent one approach to this problem. In a sense, his theory is an outgrowth of the search for personality characteristics that are associated with leadership, since the measure that he employs, LPC, is a simple psychological test and its relationship to leadership behavior is a matter of some uncertainty (Graen, Orris, and Alvares, 1971). However, unlike the earlier work stemming from a conception of leadership as a personality variable, his work and that of his associates involves an attempt to classify situations and determine those in which there were positive and negative relationships between LPC and group performance.

The search process employed by Fiedler and his associates was inductive and empirical rather than theoretical and deductive. The system of octants was based on empirical results showing wide variance in the correlations that have been obtained between LPC and group performance. As the reader can see in Figure 36 in his paper, the ability of the octant system (which Fiedler terms the favorableness of the situation) to account for these differences is very high. There is, however, some controversy concerning the capacity of the theory to account for data collected subsequent to its formulation. (Graen, Alvares, Orris and Martella, 1970).

There are other empirical facts concerning leadership that are more difficult to integrate with the Contingency Model. Fiedler challenges the common notion that leaders change their behavior depending on the situation. In the view of this writer, his position stems more from the difficulty of incorporating such behavior changes within the basic framework he has adopted rather than consideration of the evidence. Lewin's classic dictum (1951) that behavior is a function of both personal and environmental properties appears no less applicable to leadership behavior than to behavior in other settings. The situation or environment not only influences the consequences of a given pattern of leadership behavior but also plays an important role in determining that behavior. A number of recent studies have shown that certain aspects of leadership behavior previously regarded as stable elements of leadership style vary markedly with the situation. Lowin and Craig (1968) have shown that leaders exhibit less consideration, more initiative, and much closer supervision toward subordinates who are low in performance than toward those who are high in performance. In a more recent study Heller (1971) has found that the extent to which leaders share power with their subordinates varies with the kind of decision being made. For example, managers are more likely to share power in decisions affecting a subordinate's employees than in decisions affecting the subordinate himself.

Vroom and Yetton have made what appears to be a different assumption from Fiedler's—that leaders can and do vary their behavior with the demands of the situation. They distinguish between normative models of leadership that purport to prescribe behavior for different classes of situations and descriptive models that attempt to predict how leaders will behave in different classes of situations. In one paper (Vroom and Yetton, 1971) they introduce a taxonomy of leadership styles varying in the extent to which the leader provides his subordinates with an opportunity to participate in making decisions. Five leadership styles are described, ranging from autocratic in which the leader makes the decision by himself and issues an order to his subordinates, to group decision-making, in which the leader serves as chairman of a meeting aimed at reaching consensus on the course of action to be taken. A normative model is presented that is purported to be consistent with research evidence concerning the consequences of participation. It represents a method for analyzing the properties of the problem to be solved to determine how involved subordinates should be in its solution, if at all.

A subsequent paper (Vroom and Yetton, 1972) deals with descriptive models of leadership behavior. The questions addressed concern the factors in the situation, in the personality of the leader, and in their interrelationship, which influence the extent to which leaders provide their subordinates with an opportunity to participate in decision-making. The evidence is overwhelming that leaders do vary their behavior with the situation, although the manner in which they do so varies from one leader to another.

This program of research suggests an alternative to Fiedler's conceptualization of leadership behavior. Instead of attempting to account for differences among leaders in terms of a single personality variable such as LPC, it relates these differences to programs or decision rules that leaders employ in attempting to fit their actions to the various situations that they encounter. Expressed in this way, a program for selecting and placing leaders requires matching the programs or decision rules employed by an individual to those required by his role.

Similarly, a program for leadership training would involve modifying or developing such programs to better fit the critical tasks that the leader's role entails.

The issue of leadership training is also difficult to handle with the Contingency Model. LPC and the behavior patterns that it is assumed to represent are assumed to be stable leadership characteristics and consequently unmodifiable by training. If training is to have any effects, a matter about which Fiedler expresses some doubt, it must be through modifying the favorableness of the situation. This formulation appears awkward and sidesteps such issues as differences in methods and objectives of training and their appropriateness to different leaders and situations.

Fiedler's Contingency Model represents an ambitious and interesting effort to go beyond the correct but vacuous statement that, "Leadership depends on the situation" and shows on what properties of situations and of persons the phenomenon of leadership depends. To be sure, the theory is crude in its present form and the practical implications are, at this point, matters of considerable uncertainty. Like most pioneering efforts, it will undoubtedly be shown to be incorrect in detail if not in substance. If it survives the test of future research, it could prove to be a valuable aid in placing leaders in situations that match their personal qualities and, in addition, provide some rough guidelines for engineering the job to fit the leader. If the Contingency Model does not pass that test, we will have but one more indication of the complexity of the processes on which a theory of leadership must ultimately be founded.

Suggestions for Future Reading

Bennis, W. G., *Organization Development: Its Nature, Origins and Prospects* (Reading, Massachusetts: Addison-Wesley, 1969).

Bray, D. W., and D. L. Grant, "The Assessment Center in the Measurement of Potential for Business Management," *Psychological Monographs,* Vol. 80, No. 625, entire (1966).

Graen, G., J. B. Orris, and K. M. Alvares, "The Contingency Model of Leadership Effectiveness: Some Experimental Results," *Journal of Applied Psychology,* Vol. 55 (1971), pp. 196–204.

Graen, G., K. Alvares, J. B. Orris, and J. A. Martella, "Contingency Model of Leadership Effectiveness: Antecedent and Evidential Results," *Psychological Bulletin,* Vol. 74 (1970), pp. 285–296.

Heller, F. A., *Managerial Decision-Making* (London: Tavistock Publishers, 1971).

Lewin, K., "Frontiers in Group Dynamics," in D. Cartwright (Ed.), *Field Theory in Social Science* (New York: Harper & Bros., 1951), pp. 188–237.

Lowin, A., and J. R. Craig, "The Influence of Level of Performance on Managerial Style: An Experimental Object-Lesson in the Ambiguity of Correlational Data," *Organizational Behavior and Human Performance,* Vol. 3 (1968), pp. 440–458.

Vroom, V. H., and P. W. Yetton, Leadership and Decision-Making. Unpublished Manuscript, W.P. 42-71-2. Carnegie-Mellon University Graduate School of Industrial Administration, November, 1971.

Vroom, V. H., and P. W. Yetton, Some Descriptive Studies of Participation in Decision-Making. Unpublished Manuscript, W.P. 75-72-1. Carnegie-Mellon University Graduate School of Industrial Administration, February 1972.

Reading Related to Chapter 16

An Integrating Principle and an Overview
Rensis Likert

The managers whose performance is impressive appear to be fashioning a better system of management. [Earlier] two generalizations were stated based on the available research findings:

> The supervisors and managers in American industry and government who are achieving the highest productivity, lowest costs, least turnover and absence, and the highest levels of employee motivation and satisfaction display, on the average, a different pattern of leadership from those managers who are achieving less impressive results. The principles and practices of these high-producing managers are deviating in important ways from those called for by present-day management theories.

> The high-producing managers whose deviations from existing theory and practice are creating improved procedures have not yet integrated their deviant principles into a theory of management. Individually, they are often clearly aware of how a particular practice of theirs differs from generally accepted methods, but the magnitude, importance, and systematic nature of the differences when the total pattern is examined do not appear to be recognized.

Based upon the principles and practices of the managers who are achieving the best results, a newer theory of organization and management can be stated. An attempt will be made in this chapter to present briefly some of the over-all characteristics of such a theory and to formulate a general integrating principle which can be useful in attempts to apply it.

There is no doubt that further research and experimental testing of the theory in pilot operations will yield evidence pointing to modifications of many aspects of the newer theory suggested in this volume. Consequently, in reading this and subsequent chapters it will be well not to quarrel with the specific aspects of the newer theory as presented. These specifics are intended as

From *New Patterns of Management,* McGraw-Hill Book Company, Inc., New York, 1961, chap. 8, pp. 97–106. Reprinted by permission of the publisher.

stimulants for discussion and as encouragement for experimental field tests of the theory. It will be more profitable to seek to understand the newer theory's general basic character and, whenever a specific aspect or derivation appears to be in error, to formulate more valid derivations and propositions.

Research findings indicate that the general pattern of operations of the highest-producing managers tends to differ from that of the managers of mediocre and low-producing units by more often showing the following characteristics:

A preponderance of favorable attitudes on the part of each member of the organization toward all the other members, toward superiors, toward the work, toward the organization—toward all aspects of the job. These favorable attitudes toward others reflect a high level of mutual confidence and trust throughout the organization. The favorable attitudes toward the organization and the work are not those of easy complacency, but are the attitudes of identification with the organization and its objectives and a high sense of involvement in achieving them. As a consequence, the performance goals are high and dissatisfaction may occur whenever achievement falls short of the goals set.

This highly motivated, cooperative orientation toward the organization and its objectives is achieved by harnessing effectively all the major motivational forces which can exercise significant influence in an organizational setting and which, potentially, can be accompanied by cooperative and favorable attitudes. Reliance is not placed solely or fundamentally on the economic motive of buying a man's time and using control and authority as the organizing and coordinating principle of the organization. On the contrary, the following motives are all used fully and in such a way that they function in a cumulative and reinforcing manner and yield favorable attitudes:

The ego motives. These are referred to throughout . . . as the desire to achieve and maintain a sense of personal worth and importance. This desire manifests itself in many forms, depending upon the norms and values of the persons and groups involved. Thus, it is responsible for such motivational forces as the desire for growth and significant achievement in terms of one's own values and goals, i.e., self-fulfillment, as well as the desire for status, recognition, approval, acceptance, and power and the desire to undertake significant and important tasks.

The security motives.

Curiosity, creativity, and the desire for new experiences.

The economic motives.

By tapping all the motives which yield favorable and cooperative attitudes, maximum motivation oriented toward realizing the organization's goals as well as the needs of each member of the organization is achieved. The substantial decrements in motivational forces which occur when powerful motives are pulling in opposite directions are thereby avoided. These conflicting forces exist, of course, when hostile and resentful attitudes are present.

The organization consists of a tightly knit, effectively functioning social system. This social system is made up of interlocking work groups with a high degree of group loyalty among the members and favorable attitudes and trust between superiors and subordinates. Sensitivity to others and relatively high levels of skill in personal interaction and the functioning of groups are also present. These skills permit effective participation in decisions on common problems. Participation is used, for example, to establish organizational objectives which are a satisfactory integration of the needs and desires of all members of the organization and of persons functionally related to it. High levels of reciprocal influence occur, and high levels of total coordinated influence are achieved in the organization. Communication is efficient and effective. There is a flow from one part of the organization to another of all the relevant information important for each decision and action. The leadership in the organization has developed what might well be called a highly effective social system for interaction and mutual influence.

Measurements of organizational performance are used primarily for self-guidance rather than for superimposed control. To tap the motives which bring cooperative and favorable rather than hostile attitudes, participation and involvement in decisions is a habitual part of the leadership processes. This kind of decision-making, of course, calls for the full sharing of available measurements and information. Moreover, as it becomes evident in the decision-making process that additional information or measurements are needed, steps are taken to obtain them.

In achieving operations which are more often characterized by the above pattern of highly cooperative, well-coordinated activity, the highest producing managers use all the technical resources of the classical theories of management, such as time-and-motion study, budgeting, and financial controls. They use these resources at least as completely as do the low-producing managers, but in quite different ways. This difference in use arises from the differences in the motives which the high-producing, in contrast to the low-producing, managers believe are important in influencing human behavior.

The low-producing managers, in keeping with traditional practice, feel that the way to motivate and direct behavior is to exercise control through authority. Jobs are organized, methods are prescribed, standards are set, performance goals and budgets are established. Compliance with them is sought through the use of hierarchical and economic pressures.

The highest-producing managers feel, generally, that this manner of functioning does not produce the best results, that the resentment created by direct exercise of authority tends to limit its effectiveness. They have learned that better results can be achieved when a different motivational process is employed. As suggested above, they strive to use all those major motives which have the potentiality of yielding favorable and cooperative attitudes in such a way that favorable attitudes are, in fact, elicited and the motivational forces are mutually reinforcing. Motivational forces stemming from the economic motive are not then blunted by such other motivations as group goals which restrict the quantity or quality of output. The full strength of all economic, ego, and other motives is generated and put to use.

Widespread use of participation is one of the more important approaches employed by the high-producing managers in their efforts to get full benefit from the technical resources of the classical theories of management coupled with high levels of reinforcing motivation. This use of participation applies to all aspects of the job and work, as, for example, in setting work goals and budgets, controlling costs, organizing the work, etc.

In these and comparable ways, the high-producing managers make full use of the technical resources of the classical theories of management. They use these resources in such a manner, however, that favorable and cooperative attitudes are created and all members of the organization endeavor to pull concertedly toward commonly accepted goals which they have helped to establish.

This brief description of the pattern of management which is more often characteristic of the high-producing than of the low-producing managers points to what appears to be a critical difference. The high-producing managers have developed their organizations into highly coordinated, highly motivated, cooperative social systems. Under their leadership, the different motivational forces in each member of the organization have coalesced into a strong force aimed at accomplishing the mutually established objectives of the organization. This general pattern of highly motivated, cooperative members seems to be a central characteristic of the newer management system being developed by the highest-producing managers.

How do these high-producing managers build organizations which display this central characteristic? Is there any general approach or underlying principle which they rely upon in building highly motivated organizations? There seems to be, and clues as to the nature of the principle can be obtained by reexamining some of the [previous] materials. . . . The research findings show, for example, that those supervisors and managers whose pattern of leadership yields consistently favorable attitudes more often think of employees as "human beings rather than just as persons to get the work done." Consistently, in study after study, the data show that treating people as "human beings" rather than as "cogs in a machine" is a variable highly related to the attitudes and motivation of the subordinate at every level in the organization. . . .

The superiors who have the most favorable and cooperative attitudes in their work groups display the following characteristics:

The attitude and behavior of the superior toward the subordinate as a person, *as perceived by the subordinate,* is as follows:

He is supportive, friendly, and helpful rather than hostile. He is kind but firm, never threatening, genuinely interested in the well-being of subordinates and endeavors to treat people in a sensitive, considerate way. He is just, if not generous. He endeavors to serve the best interests of his employees as well as of the company.

He shows confidence in the integrity, ability, and motivations of subordinates rather than suspicion and distrust.

His confidence in subordinates leads him to have high expectations as to their level of performance. With confidence that he will not be disappointed, he expects much, not little. (This, again, is fundamentally a supportive rather than a critical or hostile relationship.)

He sees that each subordinate is well trained for his particular job. He endeavors also to help subordinates be promoted by training them for jobs at the next level. This involves giving them relevant experience and coaching whenever the opportunity offers.

He coaches and assists employees whose performance is below standard. In the case of a subordinate who is clearly misplaced and unable to do his job satisfactorily, he endeavors to find a position well suited to that employee's abilities and arranges to have the employee transferred to it.

The behavior of the superior in directing the work is characterized by such activity as:

Planning and scheduling the work to be done, training subordinates, supplying them with material and tools, initiating work activity, etc.

Providing adequate technical competence, particularly in those situations where the work has not been highly standardized.

The leader develops his subordinates into a working team with high group loyalty by using participation and the other kinds of group-leadership practices summarized [earlier].

The Integrating Principle

These results and similar data from other studies (Argyris, 1957; March & Simon, 1958; Viteles, 1953) show that subordinates react favorably to experiences which they feel are supportive and contribute to their sense of importance and personal worth. Similarly, persons react unfavorably to experiences which are threatening and decrease or minimize their sense of dignity and personal worth. These findings are supported also by substantial research on personality development (Argyris, 1957; Rogers, 1942; Rogers, 1951) and group behavior (Cartwright & Zander, 1960). Each of us wants appreciation, recognition, influence, a feeling of accomplishment, and a feeling that people who are important to us believe in us and respect us. We want to feel that we have a place in the world.

This pattern of reaction appears to be universal and seems to be the basis for the general principle used by the high-producing managers in developing their highly motivated, cooperative organizations. These managers have discovered that the motivational forces acting in each member of an organization are most likely to be cumulative and reinforcing when the interactions between each individual and the others in the organization are of such a character that they convey to the individual a feeling of support and recognition for his importance and worth as a person. These managers, therefore, strive to have the interactions between the members of their organization of such a character that each member of the organization feels confident in his potentialities and believes that his abilities are being well used.

A second factor, however, is also important. As we have seen [previously], an individual's reaction to any situation is always a function not of the absolute character of the interaction, but of his perception of it. It is how he sees things that counts, not objective reality. Consequently, an individual member of an organization will always interpret an interaction between himself and the organization in terms of his background and culture, his experience and expectations. The pattern of supervision and the language used that might be effective with a railroad's maintenance-of-way crew, for example, would not be suitable in an office full of young women. A subordinate tends also to expect his superior to behave in ways consistent with the personality of the superior. All this means that each of us, as a subordinate or as a peer or as a superior, reacts in terms of his own particular background, experience, and expectations. In order, therefore, to have an interaction viewed as supportive, it is essential that it be of such a character that the individual himself, in the light of his experience and expectations, sees it as supportive. This provides the basis for stating the general principle which the high-producing managers seem to be using and which will be referred to as the *principle of supportive relationships*. This principle, which provides an invaluable guide in any attempt to apply the newer theory of management in a specific plant or organization, can be briefly stated: *The leadership and other processes of the organization must be such as to ensure a maximum probability that in all interactions and all relationships with the organization each member will, in the light of his background, values, and expectations, view the experience as supportive and one which builds and maintains his sense of personal worth and importance.*

The Principle of Supportive Relationships as an Organizing Concept

This general principle provides a fundamental formula for obtaining the full potential of every major motive which can be constructively harnessed in a working situation. There is impressive evidence, for example, that economic motivations will be tapped more effectively when the conditions specified by the principle of supportive relationships are met (Katz & Kahn, 1951; Krulee, 1955). In addition, as motives are used in the ways called for by this general principle, the attitudes accompanying the motives will be favorable and the different motivational forces will be cumulative and reinforcing. Under these circumstances, the full power from each of the available motives will be added to that from the others to yield a maximum of coordinated, enthusiastic effort.

The principle of supportive relationships points to a dimension essential for the success of every organization, namely, that the mission of the organization be seen by its members as genuinely important. To be highly motivated, each member of the organization must feel that the organization's objectives are of significance and that his own particular task contributes in an indispensable manner to the organization's achievement of its objectives. He should see his role as difficult, important, and meaningful. This is necessary if the individual is to achieve and maintain a sense of personal worth and importance. When jobs do not meet this specification they should be reorganized so that they do. This is likely to require the participation of those involved in the work in a manner suggested in subsequent chapters.

The term "supportive" is used frequently in subsequent chapters and also is a key word in the principle of supportive relationships. Experiences, relationships, etc., are considered to be supportive when the individual involved sees the experience (in terms of his values, goals, expectations, and aspirations) as contributing to or maintaining his sense of personal worth and importance.

The principle of supportive relationships contains within it an important clue to its effective use. To apply this general principle, a superior must take into consideration the experience and expectations of each of his subordinates. In determining what these expectations are, he cannot rely solely on his observations and impressions. It helps the superior to try to put himself in his subordinate's shoes and endeavor to see things as the subordinate sees them, but this is not enough. Too often, the superior's estimates are wrong. He needs direct evidence if he is to know how the subordinate views things and to estimate the kinds of behavior and interaction which will be seen by the subordinate as supportive. The superior needs accurate information as to how his behavior is actually seen by the subordinate. Does the subordinate, in fact, perceive the superior's behavior as supportive?

There are two major ways to obtain this evidence. In a complex organization it can be found by the use of measurements of the intervening variables. . . . It can also be obtained by the development of work-group relationships, which not only facilitate but actually require, as part of the group building and maintenance functions, candid expressions by group members of their perceptions and reactions to the behavior of others. . . .

The Central Role of the Work Group

An important theoretical derivation can be made from the principle of supportive relationships. This derivation is based directly on the desire to achieve and maintain a sense of personal worth, which is a central concept of the principle. The most important source of satisfaction for this desire is the response we get from the people we are close to, in whom we are interested, and whose approval and support we are eager to have. The face-to-face groups with whom we spend the bulk of our time are, consequently, the most important to us. Our work group is one in which we spend much of our time and one in which we are particularly eager to achieve and maintain a sense of personal worth. As a consequence, most persons are highly motivated to behave in ways consistent with the goals and values of their work group in order to obtain recognition, support, security, and favorable reactions from this group. It can be concluded, therefore, that *management will make full use of the potential capacities of its human resources only when each person in an organization is a member of one or more effectively functioning work groups that have a high degree of group loyalty, effective skills of interaction, and high performance goals.*

The full significance of this derivation becomes more evident when we examine the research findings that show how groups function when they are well knit and have effective interaction skills. Research shows, for example, that the greater the attraction and loyalty to the group, the more the individual is motivated (1) to accept the goals and decisions of the group; (2) to seek to influence the goals and decisions of the group so that they are consistent with his own experience and his own goals; (3) to communicate fully to the members of the group; (4) to welcome communication and influence attempts from the other members; (5) to behave so as to help implement the goals and decisions that are seen as most important to the group; and (6) to behave in ways calculated to

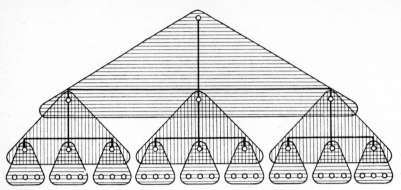

Figure 1 The Overlapping Group Form of Organization. Work groups vary in size as circumstances require although shown here as consisting of four persons.

receive support and favorable recognition from members of the group and especially from those who the individual feels are the more powerful and higher-status members (Cartwright & Zander, 1960). Groups which display a high level of member attraction to the group and high levels of the above characteristics will be referred to . . . as *highly effective groups*. These groups are described more fully [elsewhere].

As our theoretical derivation has indicated, an organization will function best when its personnel function not as individuals but as members of highly effective work groups with high performance goals. Consequently, management should deliberately endeavor to build these effective groups, linking them into an over-all organization by means of people who hold overlapping group membership (Figure 1). The superior in one group is a subordinate in the next group, and so on through the organization. If the work groups at each hierarchical level are well knit and effective, the linking process will be accomplished well. Staff as well as line should be characterized by this pattern of operation.

The dark lines in Figure 1 are intended to show that interaction occurs between individuals as well as in groups. The dark lines are omitted at the lowest level in the chart in order to avoid complexity. Interaction between individuals occurs there, of course, just as it does at higher levels in the organization.

In most organizations, there are also various continuing and *ad hoc* committees, committees related to staff functions, etc., which should also become highly effective groups and thereby help further to tie the many parts of the organization together. These links are in addition to the linking provided by the overlapping members in the line organization. Throughout the organization, the supervisory process should develop and strengthen group functioning. This theoretically ideal organizational structure provides the framework for the management system called for by the newer theory.

References

Argyris, C.: *Personality and Organization*. New York: Harper, 1957.
Cartwright, D., & Zander, A. (Eds.): *Group Dynamics: Research and Theory* (2d ed.). Evanston, Ill.: Row, Peterson, 1960.

Katz, D., & Kahn, R. L.: Human Organization and Worker Motivation. In L. Reed Tripp (Ed.), *Industrial Productivity*. Madison, Wis.: Industrial Relations Research Association, 1951, pp. 146–171.

Krulee, G. K.: The Scanlon Plan: Co-operation Through Participation. *J. Business, University of Chicago,* 1955, **28** (2), 100–113.

March, J. G., & Simon, H. A.: *Organizations*. New York: Wiley, 1958.

Rogers, C. R.: *Counseling and Psychotherapy*. Boston: Houghton Mifflin, 1942.

Rogers, C. R.: *Client-centered Therapy*. Boston: Houghton Mifflin, 1951.

Viteles, M. S.: *Motivation and Morale in Industry*. New York: Norton, 1953.

Readings Related to Chapter 17

Job Satisfaction:
Sorting Out the Nonsense

William Gomberg

Social scientists—alias behavioral scientists—have become preoccupied with the worker and his alleged unhappiness. Back in November 1970 the scientists on the staff of the Survey Research Center of the University of Michigan published a study based on interviews with a large number of workers.

Neil Herrick of the U.S. Department of Labor, closely associated with the project, noted 25 aspects of work into which inquiry was made. The eight aspects of work receiving top ranking in importance follow in the sequence in which the results were arranged: interesting work; enough equipment and help to get the job done; enough information; enough authority; good pay; opportunity to develop special abilities; job security; and seeing the result of one's work.

Implying that trade unions are wont to concentrate exclusively on pay and job security, Herrick suggests that "we take the worker at his word and seriously question traditional notions regarding his needs and priorities."

This summation has been used by a widely assorted collection of behavioral scientists to conclude that the worker is concerned beyond all else with the nature of his work, the actual job description, constrained by a technology that is assumed to be fixed and that this source of frustration has been completely neglected by the trade unions, which have confined themselves to the problems of job security and job pay.

In another lengthy document, Work in America, they offer their services to overcome these problems: they suggest the formation of a public corporation with the following kinds of functions:

1 To compile and certify a roster of qualified consultants to assist employers with the technical problems in altering work.

Reprinted by permission of the publisher from the *AFL-CIO American Federationist*, June 1973, pp. 14–19.

2   To provide a resource to which management and labor can turn for advice and assistance.

3   To provide an environment in which researchers from various disciplines who are working on job redesign can meet with employers, unions and workers to pool their experiences and findings.

Work in America was prepared by a 10-man task force, headed by James O'Toole, a social anthropologist, for the U.S. Department of Health, Education and Welfare.

A review of these documents, their analysis of what ails the American workers, their knowledge of the role of unions in responding to workers needs and their wants, their philosophy of past experimentation and present remedial prescriptions are long overdue.

Mitchell Fein, an industrial engineer, questions the findings of the Michigan Survey Group. He notes that they have used the term "worker" to encompass managers, professionals, and the like as well as the conventional blue-collar worker.

The Survey Research Center data was reworked by Fein to separate out the blue-collar data and he found that pay, which was fifth in the university analysis, jumped to first place. My own feeling is that these first eight work aspects may be listed in most any manner. Fein could have spared himself the effort. The number of measurement points separating these characteristics is so minute that any ranking is arbitrary—they are virtually all of equal weight. The important consideration is that Herrick's conclusion betrays a superficial knowledge of what collective bargaining is all about.

The general public, when it reads about collective bargaining, confines its attention to wages. The professional understands that the myriad of working conditions, out of which virtually all arguments arise during the course of the administration of the contract, are closely tied to the remaining seven aspects of work that head the Survey Research Center list. Grievances over promotions, lack of equipment to do the job right, lack of help and information to do the job right dominate the grievance procedure. They are the warp and woof of daily collective bargaining.

The scope of collective bargaining has been a constant tug-of-war with management. Back in 1946 President Truman called an industrial relations conference attended by the leading management and labor spokesmen. His hope was that they could come to an accommodation to avoid costly strikes. The late George W. Taylor analyzed the reasons for the foundering of the conference. One of the two principal reasons he listed for the failure of the meeting was the insistence of management that the labor movement pledge to confine itself to the immediate employer-employe relationship. Subjects like the technology of production, the methods of manufacture, the setting of production standards, the location of plants, the allocation of work all were to be respected as management prerogatives exclusively. The trade unions refused, arguing that the interests of labor were as broad as the entire production process.

When the automobile industry insisted that production standards were not a subject for bargaining, the union retained the right to strike over the question of production standards and has not hesitated to invoke this right when it felt that the workers' interests were threatened.

Back in the 1950s it took a long strike at the International Harvester Corporation before a system was devised between the company and the Auto Workers to make production standards a subject for grievances that could be resolved either by voluntary arbitration or a strike. Production standards had originally been excluded from the grievance procedure on management's insistence. But with strikes occurring repeatedly, it then became management's turn to want production standards disputes resolved by a grievance procedure. The conflict was resolved by permitting the parties to use the route of the strike or arbitration. For all practical purposes, the strike has been abandoned.

Now it is one thing for a Barbara Garson, a magazine publicist, to publish nonsense in the June 1972 Harpers that the Lordstown strike was a revolt of young workers against an older leadership who supinely accepted managerial tyranny over the speed of the assembly line. It is quite another to find this line of conventional nonsense in a scholarly report. Labor historian Tom Brooks has pointed out how an identical strike at the Norwood Plant of Chevrolet of much older workers at virtually the same time was ignored because it did not fit the counter culture image of the behaviorists that a new generation of youngsters were unique young rebels. A good case can be made for work improvement without involving the exaggerations of the marginal intellectual sensationalists at the fringe of every movement, thereby alienating the real rank and file.

The HEW document on work observes that all of the problems of modern job design are attributable to Frederick W. Taylor, who is accused of fractionating work and making the worker an extension of the machine with the implicit, supine consent of the labor movement.

This must be news to many unions, including the Machinists, which has had a long history of conflict in this area early in this century. And it perhaps explains the impatience of Machinists Vice President William W. Winpisinger, who has pointed out that just as job dissatisfaction in the workplace yielded to trade union solutions in the past, such dissatisfaction can be decreased to the extent that trade union solutions are applied today.

As a case in hand, Winpisinger says that "perhaps when workers first negotiated the right to bid on better shifts, overtime and promotions on the basis of length of service, they weren't thinking in terms of 'job enrichment,' but in actual practice that's what they got."

There are deep roots to Winpisinger's thinking. In 1912, a young professor, Robert Franklin Hoxie of the University of Chicago, was retained by John R. Commons of the University of Wisconsin, who had undertaken an investigation of the scientific management movement on behalf of Congress. In the manuscript published in 1915, Scientific Management and Labor, Hoxie listed the objections of the labor movement to scientific management. The Machinists union was then in the forefront of the federation's struggle with this innovation. With the machinists in the vanguard, the trade unionists indicted the new technique on the grounds that it:

- tends to deprive the worker of thought, initiative, achievement and joy in his work;
- tends to eliminate skilled crafts;
- is destructive of mechanical education and skill;
- tends to deprive the worker of the possibility of learning a trade;
- condemns the worker to a monotonous routine;
- dwarfs and represses the worker intellectually;
- tends to destroy the individuality and inventive genius of the worker;
- stimulates and drives the workers up to the limits of nervous and physical exhaustion and over fatigue and overstrains them;
- tends to reduce the workers to complete dependence on the employer — to the condition of industrial serfs.

"Most significant of all, scientific management puts into the hands of employers at large an immense mass of information and methods which may be used unscrupulously to the detriment of the workers and offers no guarantee against the abuse of its professed principles and practices. And most important of all, it forces the workers to depend upon the employers conception of fairness and limits the democratic safeguards of the workers!"

Now for a trade union group which was fighting back in 1915 to be told now that it is reactionary invokes some justifiable impatience with job enrichment experts who are now attempting to reverse the alleged handicaps of job fractionation.

For many years the labor movement was at complete loggerheads with the scientific management movement. No small part of the reason for that conflict was the personality of Frederick W. Taylor himself. His autocratic ways hardly endeared him to the members of the labor movement. However, in 1919 Samuel Gompers, meeting together with Morris L. Cook, an engineer who understood the principles of democracy, established a new relationship between the scientific management movement and the trade unionists.

Morris L. Cook co-authored a book with Philip Murray in 1940 called Organized Labor and Production in which were laid down the fundamental principles of the participative management movement that is now being rediscovered by the sociologists. This volume was founded upon a set of principles laid down by Robert G. Valentine, a Boston social worker turned management expert, in a famous paper in 1916, The Relationship Between Efficiency and Consent. This principle was stated as follows: "The organization of workers can be counted on to consent to all that makes for efficiency under constitutional industrial relations. They will contest the share in the management and share of the product between themselves and the consumer. For the most part, the labor agreements in operation today are looked upon by employers as a necessary evil and by the workers as steps in their reassertion of rights as consumers and having little detailed relation to production processes. The beginning of something far better than this is seen in the agreements in the garment trades wherein the manufacturers, the workers and the public are all represented as parties.''

Valentine later became consultant both to the Ladies' Garment Workers Union and their employers in an attempt to stabilize the setting of production rates. It was this pioneer experience that was drawn upon by the later leadership of the ILGWU when they created the first union-sponsored Industrial Engineering Department, converting industrial engineering and scientific management from a substitute and threat to collective bargaining to a tool of collective bargaining.

The division of labor does not date from Frederick W. Taylor—it goes back to Adam Smith, who wrote in the Wealth of Nations in 1776: "This great increase of the quantity of work which in consequence of the division of labor, the same number of people are capable of performing, is owing to three different circumstances; first, to the increase of dexterity in every particular workman; secondly, to the saving of the time which is commonly lost in passing from one species of work to another; and lastly, to the invention of a great number of machines which facilitate one man to do the work of many."

Adam Smith, when he wrote these lines, was as aware as the modern behavioralist that what specialization did to the worker as a human being exacted a social cost—the "externalities" as they are called by the modern economist. Those costs shifted by the management to others because the price does not appear in conventional accounting systems have been a subject over which trade unionists have mulled long before they were formalized by economists and ecologists.

The labor movement has spent no small part of its energy in reassigning the costs of externalities so that they no longer fall exclusively on the workers. They have pioneered sickness, health and pension programs to lighten his burden. Labor's lobby has put legislation on the books requiring the observance of a safety code in the 1970 Occupational Safety and Health Act that is unprecedented.

It, too, is aware that the division of labor, like many another phenomenon, can be carried so far that it reaches a point of diminishing returns. It is also aware that the reunification of work can be carried so far that we will have happy workers producing for customers who have been priced out of the market. Reaching an intelligent balance is an occasion for rational analysis rather than evangelistic preaching.

All workers are not the same. Many workers will take advantage of the undemanding nature of their market-oriented work to engage in reverie or in thinking about things of more importance to them than their work. The worker may find his or her primary source of satisfaction in the after hours living that his or her market-oriented work provides so that he or she is able to do what he or she is really interested in during leisure hours. When the jobs of these workers are enriched, very often the monotony of 15 repetitive jobs instead of the monotony of one job becomes a source of distraction rather than satisfaction.

The labor movement has endeavored in the past to provide opportunities to management who were seeking higher production and its members who were seeking more challenging work. Labor history is replete with labor-management experiments like the Baltimore and Ohio plan on the railroads from 1926 to the depression in which workers were able to show management aspects of management's task that the latter had overlooked.

This is only one of a long line of historic undertakings. As late as 1960 the Kaiser Steel Long Range Union-Management Plan displayed how creative workers could be who were technically oriented and were given a chance to participate jointly in the cost savings. The rediscovery of participative management by the behaviorists in the last few years is more an invention of vocabulary than occupational technique. The kind of material published by Professor Louis Davis on how different jobs will be in the post-industrial era and how they will be more demanding than our present tasks strikes me about as authentic as the observations of those seers who not long ago told us about all the upgraded jobs that were going to flow from automation. The jobs remain as trivialized as ever, and I suspect that the so-called post industrial era will carry more than its share of such trivialized work.

The trade unionists have probably done more to eliminate sub-human work by raising wages than all of the elaborate schemes of the scholars laid end to end. When employers find that they must pay high wages for what they consider sub-human, repetitive work they somehow manage to automate the job so that it is no longer performed by a human.

In fact, the higher the wage, the more likely the employer is to seek a capital substitute for the worker. For example, suppose an international road building contractor owns a trench digging machine that does the work of 100 men. He only owns one of these machines and he has contracts to dig ditches in Taiwan and in New York City. Where is he likely to use the machine? Obviously in New York City where the rate for common labor, protected by unions, is quite high rather than in Taiwan where a few cents an hour additional expended by employing more labor spares the employer the risk of investing in a machine.

All of the claims being made for the miraculous increases in productivity and worker satisfaction by the evangelistic behaviorists have been heard before.

Back in the 1930s a management consultant, Allan Mogensen, founded the work simplification movement. He was training workers and management in participative techniques. Workers were indoctrinated with a set of motion principles to apply to their various jobs. They took great joy in using their ingenuity to fractionate their jobs and other jobs with the same miraculous reports of increased productivity that we now get from the behaviorist for doing the opposite of the work simplification experts. This former enthusiasm ran its course.

In fact, behaviorists have invented a name for these spurts in productivity that seem to come with any kind of initial attention to long neglected workers. They call it "the Hawthorne effect" after the pioneering experiments at the Hawthorne plant of the Bell System in Chicago in the 1930s. A proper test calls for an extended longitudinal study of many of these modifications to see if they are real. Too often the initial spurt is followed by a return to "normal."

The behaviorists ask for the labor movement's commitment to a program for experimentation using their rediscovered techniques. It seems the labor movement has a right to look at past experimentation of the behaviorists and ask what kind·of commitment are the behaviorists ready to give the labor movement.

M. Scott Myers, the author of Overcoming Union Opposition to Job Enrichment, writes in the Harvard Business Review for May-June 1971 that "applications of the job enrichment concept, particularly in non-union work forces, have enabled managers to transform potentially hostile creativity into constructive outlets before it could be crystallized into anti-organization efforts. Moreover, job enrichment in the non-union organization is harnessing talent in a manner that gives a competitive advantage to the organization and also offers the only realistic strategy for preventing the unionization of its workforce."

The same Myers is then advertised for a seminar in Dallas in February 1973 in which he offers to give you a strategy and tactics to avoid a union and simultaneously to gain union-management cooperation if you have a union—a little something for everybody.

Another prize package of the behaviorists is the alleged miracle that took place in the Harwood Manufacturing Company when it merged with Weldon Pajama.

The Harwood "miracle" has been hailed as a unique experiment in employe participation which resulted in decisive increases in productivity and job satisfaction after the Harwood company absorbed Weldon Pajama.

We are indebted to Fein for the analysis that it was not participative management, but indeed quite authoritative management—albeit with due process, since it was a union plant.

Here is what Fein has said about Harwood:

"When Harwood purchased the Weldon Company in 1962, all sorts of traditional business problems were encountered and Harwood management moved into Weldon and restructured it in its own image. The complete case history of Weldon is described in 'Management by Participation.' The foreword of the book says that it '. . . reports an extraordinary successful improvement of a failing organization through introduction of a new management system. An unprofitable enterprise was made profitable, and a better place to work, in the short span of two years. Many managers and students will want to know how this was done. Harwood management made '. . . a business decision to undertake a participative approach to the salvaging of the Weldon enterprise.'

"Though Harwood's management stated they were devoted to the participative approach to managing, nowhere in the book is there any evidence that the changeover in management practices involved appreciable participation by the employes in formulating decisions or in making changes. There was no restructuring of jobs or job enrichment. Nor is there any mention that Weldon's workers participated to any appreciable extent in creating improvements, in work methods and systems. Management's efforts seemed to have been concentrated on revising the management organization and eliminating the former one-man rule of the company, and the raising of productivity.

"The major improvement in plant productivity was obtained from a straight-forward, conventional, industrial engineering program established by a firm of consulting engineers. A rise in productivity of 30 percentage points was obtained, measured by operator productivity, from 85 percent of standard to 115 percent. Management reports the improvements were created as follows:' . . . the earnings development program with individual operators was the most potent of the steps undertaken, contributing perhaps 11 percentage points of the total gain of 30 points. Next in influence were the weeding out of low earners . . . and the provision of training for supervisors and staff in interpersonal relations, each contributing about 5 percentage points to the total gain. The group consultation and problem resolution program with operators appears to have contributed about 3 percentage points. The balance of 6 percentage points can be viewed as arising from miscellaneous sources or from a combination of the several program elements.'

"The industrial engineers' section of the Weldon case history reports that the fundamental goal selected for concentration and agreed upon by all in management as the problem of first priority was raising employe earnings which were based on an incentive plan. The goal was reached in one year. This section reads just as would a typical case of resurrecting a disintegrated incentive plan. Some of the engineers' efforts were spent in ' . . . three- to four-hour production studies of the operator to estimate her performance potential.' The engineers encouraged the operator to change to more effective methods and to raise her skill. 'An operator was helped in this manner until an outcome was apparent, until her earnings increased or she was deemed unlikely to change.' During this period, ' . . . an effort was made to get rid of the remaining employes with chronically low production records and histories of frequent absence.' The success achieved in raising productivity at Weldon seems to have been obtained by using conventional practices on the plant floor. The approach followed was what any competent plant manager would have employed.

"Harwood-Weldon management may have designed its management organization on participative principles. But the managing style with respect to the production employes seemed to be quite firm; behaviorists might even label it authoritarian." I would add constrained by due process because it is unionized, albeit conventionally.

Of even more interest is Fein's analysis of the much publicized General Food-Pet Food case in Topeka, Kan., which is a non-union operation. Basically, what is claimed is that it was an innovative experiment in rescuing and revamping a low-morale workforce. But it really was a matter of running away from the original problems, in an Illinois plant, and building an ideal work environment through a careful selection of new personnel and the advantages of new physical facilities in Kansas.

"In discussing the General Food-Pet case, the HEW task force shows its myopia and bias toward the problems in plants which affect management and workers," Fein says. "Typical is their description of why General Foods management decided to build a new plant at Topeka: 'Management built this plant because the employes in an existing plant manifested many severe symptoms of alienation. Because of their indifference and inattention, the continuous process type of technology used in the plant was susceptible to frequent shutdowns, to product waste and to costly recycling. There were serious acts of sabotage and violence. Employes worked effectively for only a few hours a day and strongly resisted changes that would have resulted in a further utilization of manpower.'

"This statement sounds as if it were written by the PR department of a company which was preparing a public case for abandoning its old plant. Actually it was obtained from a paper prepared by Richard E. Walton of Harvard, one of the consultants to the HEW task force, specifically for the HEW project. Nowhere in the HEW report or Walton's paper is there any indication of the union's official attitude and position with regard to what occurred at the plant.

"In reporting the case of the GF-Topeka plant in Harvard Business Review and in his HEW paper, Walton omitted a most critical piece of information which greatly affects the interpretation of what occurred and why. Walton states that the key features of the new plant organization were: 'autonomous work groups . . . integrated support functions. . . challenging job assignments . . . job mobility and rewards for learning . . . facilitative leadership . . . managerial decision making for operators . . . self government for the plant community . . . congruent physical and social context . . . learning and evolution. The full report of what occurred over a two-year period is too long to be repeated here, but it is available for reference.

"What was not reported by Walton in either of his two papers was the strategy for hiring employes for the new plant. This is described by L. D. Ketchum, Manager of Organization Development Operations at G-F. An ad was run in the local press:

" 'General Foods—Topeka plant needs production people: Work in a new, modern Gaines Pet Food Plant with an exciting new organization concept which will allow you to participate in all phases of plant operations.

" 'Qualifications: mechanical aptitude: willing to accept greater responsibility; willing to work rotating shifts; desire to learn multiple jobs and new skills.

" 'If you would like to work with an organization that emphasizes individual potential, learning and responsibility, with excellent earnings and benefits, job interviews will be conducted. . . .' "

The hiring process proceeded as follows, according to Fein's description: 625 people applied. (Other reports say over 700 applied.) Screening by the State Employment Service and the team leaders eliminated 312. Many of these eliminated themselves. Testing eliminated 76, so 237 remained. The physical examination eliminated 18, and the balance went through an in-depth interview, an hour each, with three different team leaders and this eliminated 121. The team leaders then designed a selection weekend and began with 98, eliminated 35, leaving 63 who were offered jobs. King, a consultant to the program, adds that when the applicants were down to 98, they were invited to spend a Saturday at the plant for the final selections. After a one and a half hour tour of the plant, the applicants worked for two hours on a NASA problem exercise, to determine how they would react under different circumstances at work. The supervisors then selected 63 for jobs in the plant.

"Walton did not reveal that the new Topeka employes were screened for special skills and profiles to match the organization criteria that had been established for the new plant," Fein continues. "In a normal employe market, screening one out of four applicants is considered fairly tight. Here only one out 10 was selected. The new Topeka employes were a special breed; they were 'non-union achievers' who preferred working in autonomous situations. They were obviously not typical of a cross-section of the Kankakee employes.

"Nowhere does Walton mention that the problem-ridden plant is located at Kankakee, Ill., and employes 1,200. At a 10-1 ratio, in hiring for a 1,200 employe plant, they would have to screen over 12,000. Where would all the people come from?

"Walton says: 'Using standard principles industrial engineers originally estimated 110 employes should man the plant. Yet the team concept, coupled with the integration of support activites into team responsibilities, has resulted in a manpower level of slightly less than 70 people.'

"Attributing the superior performance of the Topeka employes to the organization development principles completely ignores that the Topeka employes were carefully selected for the plant and may have had very different skills and attitudes from the Kankakee employes. Walton cannot use industrial engineers to sanctify his comparison because the comparison is not valid. Work measurement principles in industrial engineering require that the measurement criteria must be developed separately for each plant, unless it is demonstrated that the plants are identical. Common sense reveals that these two plants are not comparable, especially in the workforce. It is like putting together a basketball team of 8-footers to play a normal height team.

"The results obtained at Topeka are valid only for Topeka. This was a stacked experiment in a small plant with conditions set up and controlled to achieve a desired result. These employes were not a cross-section of the population, or even of Topeka. The plant and its operations are not typical of those in industry today. What are the other managers to do? Screen one in 10 employes and only hire these? And what about the other nine?

"The GF-Topeka case proves nothing of value for operation managers. Had the behaviorists gone to work on the Kankakee plant and shown how they converted a rundown plant, bursting with labor problems, into a plant where management and employes told glowingly of their accomplishments, the behaviorists would have earned the gratitude of everyone. Instead, they turned their backs on a plant which typifies the problems of the big city plants. Worse, they tantalize management with the prospect that, in building a new plant, with new equipment, with carefully selected employes and no union, productivity will be higher. Many managers have dreamed of relocating their plants into the wheat fields or the hills to escape from the big city syndrome. Is this Walton's message to managers in his article, How to Counter Alienation in the Plants? And is this case the HEW task force's contribution to the solution of the problems of the big city plants?''

My object in citing these cases written up in the HEW report but analyzed by Fein is not to make the point that behaviorists are anti-union as a class. They are not. What is worse is that by and large, so many of them are indifferent. They are without conviction in the matter. Now such an attitude is understandable in value free engineers, but how are we to regard evangelistic behaviorial scientists converted to participative managerial democracy who have failed to understand democracy's most fundamental tenet? Democracy cannot exist where management is free to give and to take without any countervailing force. Such "democracy" makes as much sense as a U.S. government without any institutionalized checks and balances. The labor movement will expect more than is offered if it is to tie in with the behaviorists. The opportunity is theirs.

One possibility for a new era lies in legislation introduced in February by Sen. Edward M. Kennedy (D-Mass.) with the joint sponsorship of 13 senators, called the Worker Alienation Research and Technical Assistance Act of 1973.

The bill provides $10 million for research into the problem of worker alienation in all occupations and technical assistance to those unions, workers, companies, state and local governments seeking to find ways to relieve this problem.

This bill, if passed, could mean the beginning of a new era in which more and more workers actually participate in the decision-making of the enterprise. It can usher in a new era for cooperation between behaviorial scientists with a real democratic commitment, enlightened management and trade unionists. I am sure that is what the senators have in mind. Let us hope that Scott Myers' adventure in Orwellian Doublewrite becomes the exception rather than the rule when describing the behaviorist's future behavior.

The behaviorists have pointed up a problem. Their lack of knowledge of labor history may have led to an exaggeration of what they have come up with. Nevertheless, the problem is real. Its solution calls not only for technical competence, but moral commitment.

What's Wrong with Work in America?: A Review Essay

Harold Wool

The rash of rank-and-file union contract rejections and wildcat strikes during the late 1960's and early 1970's, particularly the well-publicized strike by workers at the General Motors facility in Lordstown, Ohio, highlight what some are interpreting as a sort of gut revolt against work as it is organized in the American economy.

Reports of apathy, absenteeism, and even industrial sabotage among blue-collar workers, of poor morale among some white-collar workers (particularly those in repetitive dead-end jobs), of college youths' disdain of bureaucratic jobs in government or industry, and even of executives forsaking promising careers to head out to fields unknown—all these have caused some observers, notably commentators from the print and broadcast media, to question the future of work in American society. Is our commitment to the work ethic fading?

Since all of these symptoms appeared to imply some weakening of this commitment, it is not surprising that the search for a culprit has turned its spotlight on the institution of work itself—the way it is organized, its adequacy in meeting human needs, and the effects of work upon other dimensions of human welfare. A special focus of concern has been the "blue-collar worker" with the automobile assembly-line worker as the inevitable archetype. The "blue-collar blues" has become part of the media lexicon, together with knowing references to more esoteric psychological terms such as "work satisfiers and dissatisfiers," "alienation," and "anomie."

The media, moreover, have simply reflected a growing concern on the part of key officials in industry, labor, and the Government—a concern that "all is not well" among important segments of our nation's work force. An initial official effort to place these concerns in broader perspective was contained in a paper on the "Problems of the Blue-Collar Worker," prepared in early 1970 by U.S. Department of Labor staff for an ad hoc White House Task Group.[1] The paper pointed to symptoms of growing disaffection among lower-middle-income workers (those in the $5,000–10,000 family income range), and suggested that this was due to a combination of pressures: an "economic squeeze," resulting from inflationary pressures and limited advancement opportunities; a "social squeeze," reflected especially in deterioration of their communities and in racial ethnic conflicts; and a "workplace squeeze" associated with a variety of depressing working conditions, ranging from grinding monotony to unpleasant or unsafe work environments.

Further evidence that job satisfaction had become a matter of top-policy interest was provided by this reference in President Nixon's 1971 Labor Day

From *Monthly Labor Review*, March 1973, pp. 38–44. Reprinted by permission.

Message: "In our quest for a better environment, we must always remember that the most important part of the quality of life is the quality of work, and the new need for job satisfaction is the key to the quality of work."

Against this backdrop, Elliot Richardson, then Secretary of Health, Education, and Welfare, approved initiation in December 1971 of a broadgaged study of the "institution of work" and of its implications for health, education, and welfare.

The study was conducted by a 10-member Task Force, chaired by James O'Toole, a social anthropologist serving as a staff assistant in Secretary Richardson's office. Patterned after an earlier HEW study group on higher education policies, the members of the task force were apparently given full rein to develop their own thinking on the issues, independent of the usual bureaucratic constraints. The resulting report, *Work in America,* was released in December 1971, together with a cautious foreword by Secretary Richardson, which praised the report for "the breadth of its perspective and its freshness of outlook," but clearly disassociated himself and the Administration from many of its recommendations.

The Task Force View

The study takes as its point of departure the premise that "work"—broadly defined as socially useful activity—is central to the lives of most adults. In addition to the obvious economic functions of work, work performs an essential psychological and social role in providing individuals with a status, a sense of identity, and an opportunity for social interaction. Referring to recent surveys as evidence, it concludes that individuals on welfare and the poor generally have the same needs and compulsions for work as do those in the economic mainstream.[2]

But, though the work ethic is still "alive" in America, the report finds that it is not "well"—and it ascribes this condition to the institution of work itself. Citing a variety of psychological studies and survey findings, the task force concludes that large numbers of American workers at all occupational levels are pervasively dissatisfied with the quality of their working lives. Significant numbers of employed workers are locked in to "dull, repetitive seemingly meaningless tasks, offering little challenge or autonomy." And many others, including large numbers of older workers, "suffer the ultimate in job dissatisfaction" in being completely deprived of an opportunity to work at "meaningful" jobs.

The principal sources of worker discontent as seen by the authors are to be found in the confines of the individual workplace itself. The central villains of the piece are (1) the process of work breakdown and specialization associated with the pernicious influence of Frederick W. Taylor and his industrial engineer disciples, and (2) the diminished opportunities for work autonomy, resulting from the shift in locus of jobs from self-employment or small scale enterprises to large impersonal corporate and government bureaucracies. Although these trends are recognized as having been underway for many decades, what is new in the current climate, the study contends, is a revolutionary change in attitudes and values among many members of the work force—youth, minority members, and

women. With higher expectations generated by increased educational achievement, these groups in particular are placing greater emphasis on the intrinsic
aspects of work, its inherent challenge and interest, and less on strictly material
rewards. In the case of minority workers, the study recognizes that large
numbers are still concerned with the elemental needs for a job—any job—that
pays a living wage, but it notes relatively high rates of discontent among black
workers in many better paying jobs as well. The relegation of women to poor
paying, low status jobs, and the plight of older workers, both in and out of the
labor force, are also discussed.

This complex of discontents is, in turn, identified as the root cause of
various ills besetting the American economy—"reduced productivity," "the
doubling of man-days per year lost through strikes," and increases in absenteeism, sabotage, and turnover rates. In addition, a variety of other ills are attributed to work-related problems, including problems of physical and mental health,
family instability, and drug and alcohol addiction.

Since the central diagnosis for this wide array of economic and social
problems is found in the faulty organization of work, the principal remedy
presented by the task force is the reorganization of work. Although "work
redesign" is never explicitly defined by the authors, a number of recent experiments are cited—both here and abroad—which have had in common an extensive restructuring of jobs designed to broaden and vary the scope of workers'
duties and to provide increased worker autonomy and participation in work-
related decision, often accompanied by some form of profit sharing. Collaborative efforts by labor, management and government in Norway and Sweden,
resulting in a number of pilot job redesign projects, are cited as a model for
emulation.[3]

Although work redesign is identified as the "keystone" of the report, the
authors concede that this is not a sufficient solution to the problems of work—
and of workers—in America. The final two chapters therefore address themselves, more generally, to a range of other work-related problems and possible
solutions. Since some jobs can "never be made satisfying," an alternative
approach is to facilitate movement of workers out of these jobs, through a
massive midcareer retraining option or "self-renewal program" for workers.

In a concluding chapter, the report addresses itself broadly to a variety of
other manpower and welfare policy issues. It endorses a "total employment"
strategy, designed to produce "reasonably satisfying" jobs not only for the 5
million workers currently reported as unemployed but for an estimated 10 to 30
million additional persons who are under-employed, on welfare, or out of the
labor market but who—the authors contend—would take meaningful jobs, if
available. This is to be accomplished through a combination of large-scale
manpower training and public employment programs and through appropriate
fiscal and monetary policies. With respect to welfare reform, it is strongly critical
of mandatory work provisions, as applied to welfare mothers, as reflecting a lack
of appreciation of the social value of the mother's role in housekeeping and
childrearing activites. The report suggests that policy emphasis be shifted to
obtaining suitable employment for the fathers, while upgrading the status of

housework—in part, by including housewives in the statistical count of the labor force.

Evaluating the Report

From this summary, the coolness of official response to this study will not be difficult to understand.

For somewhat different reasons, this reviewer also has mixed feelings about the value of this study as a basis for broad social policy. Its strength—and its weaknesses—lie in its advocacy of a humanistic approach to assessment of work as a social institution. Its perspective is primarily that of the behavioral scientist, who appraises the "value" of work in terms of its total impact upon the individual—in contradistinction to the market-oriented perspective of many economists, who view work primarily as another factor contributing to the GNP and measure its "value" solely in terms of financial rewards. The task force offers insightful—if still fragmentary—documentation concerning the ways in which many jobs (both blue collar and white collar) are proving "dissatisfying" particularly to some members of the new generation. And scattered through its chapters are a number of provocative recommendations which deserve further study and followthrough. However, in its zeal to advance the cause of "humanization of work" the report suffers from overgeneralization concerning the extent and nature of work dissatisfaction and from overstatement of the potentials of work redesign as a primary solution to work-related ills.

A central theme of this study is that "a general increase in their educational and economic status has placed many American workers in a position where having an interesting job is now as important as having a job that pays well" and that the organization of work "has not changed fast enough to keep up with rapid and widescale changes in worker attitudes, aspirations and values."[4] From this premise it is reasonable to infer that the level of worker discontent has significantly increased in recent years.

A Look at Available Data

Yet a review of available research and statistical evidence offers very limited support for this hypothesis. For this purpose we have explored two types of data: (1) job satisfaction survey findings, and (2) those statistical indicators which have frequently been cited as manifestations of worker discontent, such as quit rates, strikes, absenteeism, and productivity.

Job Satisfaction Surveys   In a recent review of the extensive literature on job satisfaction, Robert Kahn reports that some 2,000 surveys of "job satisfaction" were conducted in the United States over a period of several decades. These surveys have varied greatly in scope and design, from intensive studies of workers in a particular plant, occupation, or industry to much more general polls covering a national cross-section of the work force. In spite of these differences, Kahn—as well as earlier observers—has noted a certain consistency in the response patterns. "Few people call themselves extremely satisfied with their jobs, but still fewer report extreme dissatisfaction. The modal response is on the positive side of neutrality—'pretty satisfied.' The proportion dissatisfied ranges from 10 to 21 percent . . . Commercial polls, especially those of the Roper organization, asked direct questions about job satisfaction in hundreds of samples and seldom found the proportion of dissatisfied response exceeding 20 percent.''[5] Neither Kahn nor other scholars could detect a consistent trend in job satisfaction from the available data.

Statistical Indicators   It is not unreasonable to infer, as does the task force report, that job dissatisfaction will be reflected in a variety of cost-increasing worker behaviors, such as low productivity, high voluntary turnover, high absenteeism, and increased strike activity. Research evidence based mainly on specific plant or industry studies is available to support at least some of these direct relationships, notably in the case of turnover and absenteeism. If worker discontent has been significantly increasing, some indication of this might be reflected in the overall trends of the relevant statistical indicators. Yet the evidence in this respect is inconclusive:

1   Labor Turnover   A detailed multivariate analysis of quit rates of manu-facturing workers recently completed by the Bureau of Labor Statistics indicates that year-to-year fluctuations in these rates over a 20-year period are largely explained by cyclical variations in job opportunities, as measured by the rate of new hires, and that there has been *no* discernible trend in the quit rate over this period.[6]

2   Absenteeism   In the absence of any direct program for statistic reporting of absenteeism trends, the Bureau of Labor Statistics has analyzed data from the Current Population Survey on trends in the proportion of workers who have been absent from their jobs for all or part of a week due to illness or other personal reasons. This initial analysis does point to a small increase in worker absence rates since 1966. The average daily rate of unscheduled absences rose from 3.3 percent in 1967 to 3.6 percent in 1972, an increase of about 10 percent. The data are, however, far from conclusive, and do not provide a basis for generalization longer-term trends or their causes.[7]

3   Strikes   A sharp increase in a level of strike activity was recorded in the second half of the 1960's and in the early 1970's. Man-days of idleness due to strikes rose from 0.13 percent of estimated working time in 1961–65 to 0.26 percent in 1966–71. However, the incidence of strikes normally tends to increase during inflationary periods. Strike idleness, as a percentage of working time, was actually considerably higher during the years immediately following the end of World War II (1946–50) and following the outbreak of the Korean War (1952–53) than during the more recent period of rapid price increases. Moreover, "bread and butter" issues, such as pay, benefits, job security, and union organization or security issues, have continued to account for all but a modest percentage of all strikes. In 1971, only 5.5 percent of strike idleness was attributed to plant administration or other working condition issues.[8]

4   Productivity   Productivity growth, as measured by output per man-hour in the private economy, which had experienced a longer-term growth trend of about 3–3½ percent a year, slackened appreciably following the mid-1960's and dropped to less than 1 percent a year in 1969 and 1970. Declines in productivity growth have occurred in the past during or immediately after periods of high economic activity. The productivity growth rate rebounded sharply, moreover, in 1971–72, thus suggesting that cyclical factors, rather than any deep-seated worker unrest, were mainly responsible for the previous decline.[9]

5 *Labor Force Participation* Abstention from work or work-seeking activity is the ultimate form of rejection of work as an institution. Yet there has been no evidence of a downtrend in the overall proportion of the population, 16 years and over, reported as in the labor force. In fact, this percentage has increased over the past two decades, from 59.9 percent in 1950 to 61.3 percent in 1970.[10]

There have been some important divergent trends among different components of the working-age population. Thus, the labor force participation rate of men has declined from 86.8 percent in 1950 to 80.6 percent in 1970, mainly due to steady reductions in worker rates among school and college-age youth and among men 55 years and over. It is difficult, however, to interpret the decline in labor force rates for men as reflecting a rejection of work as an institution, in the face of the fact that their sisters and wives have flocked into the labor force in unprecedented numbers over this same time span, increasing their labor force participation rate from 33.9 percent in 1950 to 43.4 percent in 1970 with most of the increase occurring among married women. The desire to supplement family income was apparently a decisive factor inducing their entry into the labor force, even though these women have been disproportionately concentrated in low paying and often routine types of work.

From this necessarily brief review, it will be evident that there is little objective evidence to support an inference of a rising wave of discontent among workers, associated directly with the nature of their jobs. Fluctuations in some of the indicators, which appeared at first blush to support this hypothesis (such as labor turnover rates, strike activity and productivity growth rates) can, on closer inspection, be attributed to quite different causes, notably to the tight labor market and inflationary trends prevailing in the late 1960's and to associated labor market forces. The overall labor force participation trends—such as the sharp and sustained inflow of married women into gainful employment—simply cannot be reconciled with any hypothesis of an extensive rejection of "low quality" work. The available absenteeism data, which suggest some increase since the mid-1960's, are still too incomplete to support any broad generalizations—although they do tend to reinforce more specific reports concerning the special frustrations of the automobile industry assembly-line workers. Even the mass of survey data designed to elicit direct measures of job dissatisfaction have failed to show any consistent trend.

Why Are Supposed Trends Not Visible?

If this trend has not in fact developed in visible and measurable dimensions, we may well ask "Why not?" Is it because the statistical barometers for measuring emerging social trends are too incomplete, too gross, and too insensitive for this purpose? Or is it because the theoretical constructs which lead to certain expectations as to worker behaviors and attitudes simply do not conform to reality?

Most of the available statistical indicators are clearly much too aggregative to serve as reliable indexes of worker discontent. Statistical series such as productivity and labor turnover were designed for quite different purposes. Much more disaggregation of the data, and supplementary research, is needed before we can reliably isolate the influence of specific causal factors. And we are still in the early stages of development of meaningful indexes of job satisfaction and of absenteeism. It is quite possible, therefore, that the available measures— separately and in combination—are too crude and insensitive to detect any new emerging social force.

In part, however, the explanation lies in the model of worker aspirations and behavior postulated by the social psychologists. Their point of departure is a hierarchical ordering of human needs, which, as outlined by Abraham Maslow, begins with satisfaction of basic material wants, such as food and shelter, and ascends to higher order needs, such as "self esteem" and "self actualization." An alternative formulation by Herzberg is couched in terms of "extrinsic" and "intrinsic" job factors. Extrinsic factors, such as poor pay, inadequate benefits, or poor physical working conditions may lead to job dissatisfaction, while true satisfaction depends upon the intrinsic nature of the job, its work content, and its inherent challenge and interest. But both models lead to the inference that, as the general wage level increases and physical working conditions improve, the emphasis shifts from strictly economic issues to demands for improvement in the nature of work itself.

It is difficult to challenge this scale of aspirations in the abstract. In fact, numerous surveys indicate that when workers are asked what aspects of work are most important to them, "interesting work" often heads the list, particularly among the more educated or more affluent segments of the population. Given this apparent scale of values and the rising "affluence" of American workers, why—then—have most workers not overtly attempted to change the contents of their work? For example, has the continued concentration of organized labor on "bread and butter" issues, rather than "quality of work," simply reflected a lack of sensitivity on the part of union leaders to the real needs of their members—or has it in fact reflected the priorities of their rank-and-file members?

As a broad generalization, we believe that the latter assumption corresponds much closer to reality. One fallacy in the Maslow-Herzberg model of worker aspirations, as a guide to behavior, lies in its inherently static premises. Even though individual earnings and family incomes have increased steadily over the decades, the great majority of American workers certainly do not consider themselves as "affluent," when they relate their spendable income to their spending needs, for what they now consider an acceptable standard of living. As Christopher Jencks has recently pointed out, this escalation of living standards "is not just a matter of 'rising expectations' or of people's needing to 'keep up with the Joneses'" but is due in part to the fact that with changes in our mode of life, such goods as an automobile, a telephone, or packaged foods have become an integral part of our cost of living—of participating in our social system.[11] Thus, when hard choices have to be made between a monotonous job in a regimented environment, which pays relatively well and which offers job security, and a poorer paying, less secure but more "satisfying" job, most workers— particularly those with family commitments—are still not in a position to make the trade-off in favor of meeting their "intrinsic" needs.

Moreover, most workers and most union leaders tend to be highly skeptical of the real potential of "job enrichment" as a practicable means of improving their work environment. This skepticism results from earlier experiences when worker participation, profit sharing, and similar approaches were instituted by some firms as an alternative to pay increases or as a means of staving off unionization. This point of view has recently been colorfully expressed by William W. Winpisinger, general vice-president of the International Association of Machinists:

> If you want to enrich the job, enrich the pay check. The better the wage, the greater the job satisfaction. There is no better cure for the blue-collar blues.[12]

The Quest for Autonomy

One of the more questionable premises made by the authors concerning the nature and sources of worker discontent is the assumption that large numbers of workers have an urge for "autonomy" at the work place and are chafing at the disciplines and controls imposed by large bureaucratic organizations—whether big business or big government. Is this in fact a major preoccupation of most workers in our society today—or is it an image created by popular emphasis on extremes: the extreme of the real frustrations of the automobile assembly-line worker, on the one hand, and of the revolt of some (probably small) fraction of upper-middle-class youth, on the other?

Certainly, one of the most "bureaucratic" organizations in modern society today is the military; no other large organization imposes equal constraints upon both the working lives and the personal lives of its labor force. Yet in 1972, while the Vietnam war was still underway, over 330,000 young men, about one-fourth of the militarily eligible manpower pool, elected to voluntarily enlist in military service. This total excludes about 85,000 additional draft-motivated enlistees, as well as many thousands of others who offered to enlist, but failed to meet physical or mental test standards. Between 1970 and 1972, voluntary (not draft-motivated) enlistments into the Army had risen by fully 80 percent, largely in response to major increases in compensation and other special inducements offered as part of the effort to move to an all-volunteer military force.[13] Numerous surveys have shown that few young men have any great illusions about the "intrinsic" aspects of most enlisted jobs: by large majorities, young high school graduates (who account for a large majority of enlistees) have recognized that civilian jobs are far preferable to military service in terms of such criteria as "freedom," "interesting work," and "highly respected job."[14] Yet, when faced with the limited range of choices open to them, large numbers of young men have been willing to accept the constraints and risks of military service in exchange for some of its visible benefits—its training and educational opportunities, its opportunity for travel and new experiences, and its material rewards.

In similar vein, prestige rankings of various civilian occupations, based on a number of surveys, have failed to reveal any consistent preference for autonomous, self-directed employment, in comparison with more regimented, but better paying and more secure occupations. Office machine operators and bookkeepers rate higher than small independent farmers in these rankings. Assembly-line workers outrank taxi drivers, in popular esteem.[15] And as we have previously noted, many millions of married women have moved from household work, which—though unpaid—has the virtue of being self-directed, into the more regimented world of gainful employment.

The foregoing comments are clearly not designed to imply that "all is well" with the quality of work in America or that, as a nation, we can afford to be complacent about some of the danger signals which have been brought to our attention. The fact that over 10 percent of employed workers express general dissatisfaction with their jobs, that many more are dissatisfied with specific aspects of their work situation, and that these proportions are much higher for youth, for women, and for minorities, is a challenge to management, unions, and the government to pursue corrective actions.

However, if our interpretation of the recent labor market behavior and attitudes of American workers is valid, it does imply a different set of criteria for measuring quality of jobs and a different set of priorities for improvement of the quality of work. Our premise is that workers have no difficulty in distinguishing between the "good" and the "bad" jobs in our economy. The least desirable jobs, typically, are inferior *both* in terms of pay and related benefits and in terms of the intrinsic nature of the work itself. Included in this category are most domestic service and hired farm labor jobs and a large proportion of the 20 million jobs occupied by workers in the private nonfarm economy which, according to a recent BLS survey, paid less than $2.50 per hour in April 1970.[16] Numerous unskilled or semiskilled jobs paying somewhat higher wages can also be included in this category because of the oppressive nature of the work and lack of advancement opportunities.

It has been possible for employers to recruit an adequate supply of workers for most of these low-level jobs because of the continued existence of a large pool of workers who have had no effective labor market choices. Included in this pool are a disproportionate number of minority members, teenaged youth, women, and recent immigrants—who share common handicaps of limited skill, limited work experience, restricted mobility, and various forms of institutionalized discrimination. These categories of workers constitute a relatively large share of the 5 million "visibly" unemployed workers and probably represent an even larger proportion of the "invisible" unemployed not included in our statistics of active job-seekers. So long as this reservoir of low-wage labor is available, employers have little incentive to increase the pay or to enhance the quality of these jobs.

The most potent strategy for improving the quality of these jobs and/or reducing their relative numbers is by reducing the size of this reserve pool of workers. It is no coincidence that the most significant progress in improving the relative status of low-wage workers in this country has been made during periods of acute wartime labor shortage, such as during World War II. It is no coincidence, either, that employer initiatives for experimentation with work redesign abroad have been most evident in countries such as Sweden and West Germany, which have managed their economies with much lower ratios of peacetime unemployment than in the United States—and have been initiated in precisely those industries, such as the automobile industry, which have most acutely felt a labor shortage situation.

The most important single set of measures which can contribute to improvements of *quality* of work in America are, thus, those designed to increase the *quantity* of work in America. This requires a much more positive national commitment to a maximum employment policy—even, if need be, at the cost of a somewhat higher level of acceptable inflation. In turn, a climate of sustained high employment can make possible more effective implementation of specific manpower and labor market policies designed to upgrade the status of workers in low level jobs and to promote equality of employment opportunity. It may, in fact, bring us closer to the era of the "post-subsistence" economy when those jobs which do not meet minimum economic *and* psychological standards will be effectively ruled out from the labor market competition.

There should be no illusion that these goals are easily attainable—either through the recommendations scattered through *Work in America* or through those proposed in the numerous other recent studies concerned with national manpower and economic policies. We can only share Secretary Richardson's expressed sentiments that this report represents "a beginning and not a conclusion" and hope that its goal will be actively pursued by the Administration of which he is so prominent a member.

Notes

1　Report initially summarized in *The New York Times,* June 30, 1970, p. 1. See also Jerome M. Rosow, "The Problems of Lower-Middle-Income Workers," in Sar A. Levitan, ed., *Blue Collar Workers: A Symposium of Middle America,* (New York, McGraw-Hill, 1971), pp. 76–95.

2　For a report of one such survey, see Leonard Goodwin, "Welfare mothers and the work ethnic," *Monthly Labor Review,* August 1972, pp. 35–7.

3　Some of these efforts are described by Joseph Mire in "European workers' participation in management," *Monthly Labor Review,* February 1973, pp. 9–15.

4　*Work in America,* pp. x, xi.

5　Robert L. Kahn, "The Meaning of Work: Interpretation and Proposals for Measurement," in Angus Campbell and Phillip E. Converse, *The Human Meaning of Social Change* (New York, Russell Sage Foundation, 1972), pp. 173–4.

6 Paul A. Armknecht and John L. Early, "Quits in Manufacturing: A Study of Their Causes," *Monthly Labor Review,* November 1972, pp. 31–7.

7 Based on a forthcoming BLS study on absences from work.

8 *Work Stoppages in 1971,* Summary Report, U.S. Department of Labor, June 1972, table r. 4. In 1972, strike idleness declined to 1.4 working days per thousand from 2.6 in 1971. *Work Stoppages 1972,* U.S. Department of Labor, Press Release 73-865, January 9, 1973.

9 *Economic Report of the President,* January 1973, pp. 34, 231.

10 *Manpower Report of the President, 1972,* pp. 157, 192.

11 Christopher Jencks, *Inequality: A Reassessment of the Effect of and Schooling in America* (New York, Basic Books, Inc., 1972), p. 5.

12 Paper presented before the annual meeting of the Industrial Relations Research Association, December 1972, at Toronto, Canada.

13 Based on unpublished data, Office of Assistant Secretary of Defense, (M&RA).

14 Harold Wool, *The Military Specialist: Skilled Manpower for the Armed Forces* (Baltimore, Md., The Johns Hopkins University Press, 1969), p. 114.

15 Paul M. Siegal, *Prestige in the American Occupational Structure,* unpublished doctoral dissertation, University of Chicago, 1971, table 5.

16 Stevan Sternlieb and Alvin Bauman, "Employment characteristics of low-wage workers," *Monthly Labor Review,* July 1972, p.11.

Government Approaches to the Humanization of Work

Neal Q. Herrick

I Introduction

This paper will not propose new governmental approaches to the humanization of work nor will it evaluate present ones. It will simply report on certain activites which are being undertaken or contemplated in the United States. Most of these activities have only been initiated since the summer of 1972 and are in their very early stages of development. Accordingly, their status is changing day by day. In addition to reporting on events in the United States, this paper will make very brief and general reference to some recent activities and plans of international organizations.

First, I will define what is meant by the phrase "to humanize work." Then the particular focus of this paper will be described. To humanize work (See Herrick and Maccoby—Humanizing Work: A Priority Goal of the 1970's, 1972, unpublished) is to provide workers with conditions of security, equity, individuation and democracy. Security in one's job is a condition which fosters and allows

Reprinted by permission of Neal Q. Herrick and the Industrial Relations Research Association from *Industrial Relations Research Association, 25th Anniversary Proceedings,* 1972, pp. 160–165.

positive work involvement. The fear of working oneself out of a job is a reality to many workers. The condition of equity exists when the workers' share in the profits is commensurate with their contribution to value added, when a reasonable division of the profit between capital and labor occurs, and when compensation is both internally consistent and at least at the prevailing level. Individuation implies conditions allowing for autonomy, personal growth, craftsmanship and learning. This condition is best met by a combination of on-the-job and off-the-job opportunities. Democracy is perhaps the most difficult of the four conditions—both to define and to implement. Basically, it involves a situation where workers can collectively influence the conditions of their work and govern their actions, work methods, hours of work, work assignments etc. during the course of the work day.

It is clear that the total body of United States labor law addresses itself, in one way or another, to the attainment of these four basic conditions of work. For example, the Social Security Act of 1935 produced an unemployment insurance system, a retirement system and state aid to people in search of work. The Fair Labor Standards Act of 1938 sets minimum standards as to the equity of compensation and the Civil Rights Act of 1964 aims toward equity for minority groups. The Manpower Development and Training Act of 1972 provides opportunities for learning and growth particularly among the disadvantaged—and a series of industrial relations laws beginning with the Railway Labor Act in 1926 provided for a system of representative democracy and trade unionism.

In recent years, there have been signs that these past accomplishments in humanizing work have not been enough. Indications of worker alienation (e.g., rising absenteeism) suggest the need for new approaches. These new approaches may be characterized as addressing a different set of worker needs or—perhaps more accurately—the same needs viewed in a different light: the need for security in one's own workplace; the need for equity in terms of a fair share of any productivity increases due to greater worker skills and involvement; the need for learning, growth, and craftsmanship through freedom from restrictive procedures and close supervision—in short, autonomy; and the need for democracy—not the representative brand but the kind where small groups of workers have a say in deciding their day-to-day conditions and activities. Addressing these kinds of needs, which appear to be increasingly important to the present day workforce, is an extremely complex problem for the institutions of society. It is a problem which does not appear to lend itself to solution through mandatory legislation and is difficult—though not, I believe, impossible—to translate into collective bargaining demands. In general, the approach the government is presently taking toward meeting these newly surfaced needs may be said to consist of research activities which are beginning to evolve into experimentation and demonstration projects.

II International Activities

Before describing the United States situation, a few words about international interest. The North Atlantic Treaty Organization (NATO) through its Committee on the Challenge of Modern Society (CCMS), assigned the United Kingdom (UK) the task of looking into the matter of worker dissatisfaction. A paper was presented in 1971 which recommended increased experimental and demonstration projects and the UK is expected to make its concluding recommendations shortly. The Organization for Economic Cooperation and Development (OECD) held a conference on work motivation for businessmen from the developed countries in the spring of 1971 and plans to convene a working party in 1973 to consider how the OECD member nations might work together on problems of the "internal industrial environment" and related issues of worker dissatisfaction. OECD's Social Indicator Development Program is also considering the possibility of regular indicators of worker satisfaction/dissatisfaction. The Institute for Labor Studies of the International Labor Organization in Geneva is just completing a major international study of worker participation and is considering the establishment of an on-going program of research in work humanization.

III   United States Activities

A   Legislative   On August 14, 1972, Senators Kennedy, Javits, Nelson and Stevenson introduced the "Worker Alienation Research and Technical Assistance Act of 1972." This Act proposed an appropriation of $10 million to provide for research into the problem of alienation among American workers and to give technical assistance to companies, unions, and state and local governments seeking ways to deal with the problem. Under the Act, the Secretaries of Labor and Health, Education and Welfare would:

- Conduct research to determine the extent and severity of job discontent,
- Look into methods being used both here and abroad to decrease worker alienation,
- Disseminate the results of this research to unions, companies, schools of management and industrial engineering and the general public,
- Provide technical assistance to workers, unions, companies and state and local governments for experimental and demonstration projects in humanizing work,
- Support the Department of Labor's triennial nationwide survey of working conditions,
- Assist in developing curriculum and programs for training and retraining specialists in work humanization methods,
- Conduct pilot work humanization projects in Federal agencies, and
- Make recommendations on further legislation by December 31, 1973 and annually thereafter.

The Kennedy bill was introduced shortly after hearings on the subject were held by the Senate Subcommittee on Employment, Manpower and Poverty in early summer of 1972. Congresswoman Bella S. Abzug introduced a House version of the bill on August 17, 1972. No hearings have been held on this proposed legislation.

B   Executive   The executive arm of government, as authorized by the Congress, has been supporting research into the causes and nature of job satisfaction and dissatisfaction for some years. More recently, there have been plans to diffuse knowledge of job dissatisfaction causes and solutions through experimental and demonstration projects.

   1   The U.S. Department of Labor has funded a number of research projects in this area over the past several years. In 1969 a nationwide Working Conditions Survey was instituted which provides normative data on physical and economic conditions of work and on worker attitudes, behavior and job satisfaction. This survey will be done for the second time in January and February of 1973. In addition, the Department has funded many other research projects dealing either directly or tangentially, with worker attitudes. For example, the most recent issue of Manpower Research and Development Projects lists at least 12 such efforts. The most recent Department of Labor initiative is an extension of the Working Conditions Survey into a number of selected establishments in order to validate worker self-reports against employer data and to relate work structures and work attitudes to productivity. In addition, the Department of Labor held quarterly seminars on the humanization of work for small groups of trade union and industry officials in April, June, September and December 1972. These seminars brought experts in the field of restructuring work together with these key officials in order to provide them with information regarding possible solutions.

   2   The National Commission on Productivity (NCOP) plans to sponsor a Quality of Work Program consisting of work humanization efforts in a number of major corporations and—crossing corporation and company lines—in one city of the United States. It is planned to assess the extent to which the establishments involved provide the conditions of humanized work, to measure the human and economic outcomes of existing conditions, to set up worker-management councils which will consider ways to improve the quality of work, and to periodically measure human and economic outcomes as work becomes more humanized. The NCOP commissioned a study of worker attitudes toward productivity (now complete) and is planning future studies of (1) institutional (i.e., labor/management/government) relationships and their impact on programs to improve the quality of work and (2) the relationships among work structures, work attitudes and productivity.

   3   In the spring of 1971, the Secretary of Health, Education and Welfare brought together a small group of individuals to produce a report describing workplace problems and possible solutions. This report, titled "Work in America," was issued in late-December 1972 and is available through the MIT Press. In addition, the Secretary is charged under the Occupational Safety and Health Act of 1970 with doing research into the psychological factors involved in safety and health. Accordingly, the National Institute for Occupational Safety and Health (NIOSH) has launched a number of research projects in this area and is supporting and working with the U.S. Department of Labor in carrying out its

Triennial Working Conditions Survey. The National Institute for Mental Health (NIMH) is also interested in the psychological aspects of work and is currently studying work problems in specific blue-collar occupations (e.g., garbage collector).

IV Conclusions

The U.S. Government has enacted and is administering a large body of labor law. This body of labor law, combined with the efforts and activities of the trade union movement, has done much to humanize the American workplace. Now there appears to be a need for some new approaches to the humanization of work. This need is underlined by symptoms of dysfunction such as rising absenteeism rates and indications that other forms of worker withdrawal (e.g., alcoholism, drug use, tardiness, etc.) are also on the rise. So the new approaches to work humanization have a utilitarian as well as a humanistic goal. They strive to motivate employees and to involve them in the work process. In general terms, research has shed some light on the worker needs which must be met in order to reduce destructive behavior. Some indication of what workers consider dehumanizing can be found in studies such as the U.S. Department of Labor's Triennial Working Conditions Survey and Dr. Harold L. Sheppard's work at the W. E. Upjohn Institute. These studies indicate that workers are particularly dissatisfied when their work does not give them an opportunity to develop their special abilities, when it is boring, and when there is no chance for autonomy at work. Workers are concerned with the negative effects of boredom, lack of stimulation, overcontrol, and the waste of their abilities and potentialities.

Having defined the causes of the problem to this extent, it appears that government is beginning to consider the next step: encouraging the development of specific processes and programs designed to meet these needs, installing these processes and programs on an experimental and demonstration basis, and learning—through careful measurement of the human and economic results— exactly what programs and combinations of programs work best under different social, technological and industry situations. Until this process of experiment and demonstration has shed considerably more light on the problem, it is difficult to speculate on what—if any—will be the eventual involvement of government in new approaches to the humanization of work.

For a More Effective Organization: Match the Job to the Man

Edward E. Lawler III

Of all the ways society serves the individual, few are more meaningful than providing individuals with decent jobs. And it is not likely to be a decent society for any of us until it is for all of us.

John Gardner
1968

Work can be made a more rewarding place to be and organizations can be made more effective if approaches to organizational design treat employees as individuals. This important and optimistic statement is supported by a number of recent studies; however, it is often overlooked in the national debate over employee alienation and job satisfaction, a debate that has been preoccupied with what in many ways is the least important issue: whether job dissatisfaction and alienation are increasing.

Twenty, thirty, even forty years ago, social scientists were pointing out that the way organizations and jobs are designed frequently creates dissatisfying and alienating work experiences. They were also noting such serious social consequences of work alienation and job dissatisfaction as physical illness, mental illness, alcoholism, drug abuse, and shorter life spans. A more recent concern has been that when job dissatisfaction is high, individuals do not grow and develop. And there is no doubt that because work is still dissatisfying for many, everyone in our country is worse off. Thus, we need to concentrate our energies on searching for better ways to design work organizations, rather than on debating whether the situation is worsening.

The research that I have been involved in over the past ten years on organization and job design suggests a number of approaches that organizations can take to make work more satisfying, interesting, involving, and sometimes more motivating. All of these efforts have a common aspect: They all recognize that for the work-experience to be a positive, growth-producing one, the work situation must be designed to fit the differences that exist among people in their skills, needs, and abilities.

Unfortunately, many organization theorists have argued for the principle of standardization in the design of organizations. Inherent in the concept of standardization is the view that everyone should be treated the same, but treating everyone the same inevitably leads to treating some people in ways that are dissatisfying, dehumanizing, and ineffective. The reason for this is simple: Because of the differences among people, no single way of dealing with individu-

Reprinted by permission of the publisher from *Organizational Dynamics*, Summer 1974, pp. 19–29.

als is ever the best way to deal with all or even most individuals. Further, the whole concept of treating people in a standardized, homogeneous manner runs counter to the need of many people to be treated as individuals. We know from the research that one of the greatest contributors to alienation is the collective treatment of individuals without regard for their distinctiveness and sense of unique identity. Work organizations are given to this collective treatment because they mass-produce products and frequently handle their employees in a standardized, mass-production way designed to deal with the "average" person. Dissatisfaction is an inevitable result, since very few people are average.

What we need, then, are ways of running organizations that recognize the importance of treating people differently and placing them in environments and work situations that fit their unique needs, skills, and abilities. How can this be done? It isn't easy, because the more people are treated as individuals, the more complex organizations become. But according to the data I and others have collected, there are some approaches that have already been tried and that seem to work well. I should like to share the results of this research and give some examples of how an organization can structure its practices and policies to fit the important differences that exist among individuals.

In considering ways that make work more satisfying, we must not forget that society cannot tolerate approaches that will seriously undermine the economic effectiveness of organizations in order to increase employee satisfaction. Psychologists used to believe that job satisfaction was capable of causing employees to perform better. If this were true, there would be no problem finding new work designs that would increase job satisfaction without harming organizational effectiveness. Unfortunately, my own research and that of many other psychologists shows that satisfaction does not cause employees to work harder. In fact, it has a very low relationship to performance and is probably best thought of as a consequence of performance. Despite this, there is evidence that increasing the job satisfaction of employees can increase the effectiveness of organizations. Why is this so? Satisfied employees are absent less, late less, and less likely to quit. Absenteeism, turnover, and tardiness are very expensive—more costly than most realize. Recent research, for example, shows that the loss of an employee usually costs an organization ten times his or her monthly salary. Thus, because increases in employee satisfaction result in decreases in turnover, absenteeism, and tardiness, organization changes that increase job satisfaction can increase the economic effectiveness of organizations even though they do not increase motivation.

Job Design

One of the most commonly suggested cures for worker alienation and job dissatisfaction is job enrichment. It has been suggested that if we enrich people's jobs, the results will be lower absenteeism, lower turnover, less tardiness, higher productivity, higher job satisfaction, and less alienation. We now have a considerable amount of research data on the effect of job enrichment. It does, indeed, show that the average person is both happier and more effective working on an enriched job than he or she is working on the traditional, standardized, specialized, repetitive, routine job. However, as I remarked before, not everyone is average.

There are many people (at this point, we are not sure how many) who are happier working on repetitive, monotonous, boring jobs. In a recent study, for example, I found a number of telephone operators who did not react favorably to enriched jobs. The older employees, in particular, tended to prefer the more repetitive jobs because they had adjusted to them and knew how to do them well. In addition, the new design threatened to disrupt some of the comfortable interpersonal relationships they had established. Thus, any job enrichment effort that enriches the jobs of everyone in a work area or of everyone doing a particular type of work is bound to make some people less happy and less productive. Admittedly, as a rule, performance and satisfaction go up, but can we afford to engage in work redesign practices that make the work experiences of some people more negative? I don't think we can, when there is an alternative available, and in this case there often is an alternative.

The idea of an alternative is nicely illustrated by the job design approach taken in a Motorola plant where the same product is produced in two different ways—on an assembly line and on a bench where one worker puts the entire product together. This particular version of job design allows people to work on the kind of job that they are most comfortable with. Those people who prefer routine, repetitive jobs have them; those people who prefer enriched jobs have them. Originally, only a few employees chose to work on the enriched jobs; eventually, about half of the 60 workers decided to work on them. Individualizing jobs to meet the needs and abilities of the employees seemed to result in both the individual's and the organization's being better off, for absenteeism and turnover went down, while product quality went up.

A similar approach has been tried out at Non-Linear Systems with good results. There, however, the employees were allowed to share the work among the members of their teams. Some teams chose to have each member produce the whole product, while others decided to have different people work on different parts of the assembly process. The result was a high degree of individualization.

My own research suggests that the kind of a solution arrived at in Motorola and Non-Linear Systems can be applied in many other situations. Job enrichment can be selectively done and can be limited to only those people who will respond positively to an enriched job. There are, however, many practical problems involved in giving individuals jobs that involve the optimal degree of enrichment for them. For example, there is the problem of who is to decide how much a given job should be enriched. Many social scientists suggest that these decisions should not be made by the individual workers and go on to suggest that individuals should be "coerced" to experience situations where higher-order needs can be satisfied (for example, enriched jobs), because unless they experience them, they won't know what they are missing. I don't think, however, that this position is correct. Our responsibility as social scientists is to provide valid data to individuals about the results of doing certain things. It is not to coerce people into certain actions that we feel are "good" for them. Forcing someone to try an enriched job is somewhat akin to arguing that a virgin should be raped because otherwise he or she cannot know what is being missed. Thus, I don't think that organizations should be defined as providing a high quality of working life only if everyone has his higher-order needs satisfied. Instead, they should be defined as providing a high quality of working life if everyone has a realistic opportunity to satisfy his higher-order needs if he wants to.

The use of work modules represents one approach to giving individuals a greater opportunity to determine the nature of their jobs. As proposed, it would divide up tasks into modules of work, each of which would last for several hours. Employees would then ask to work on a set of modules that together would constitute a day's work. So far this approach has not been tried anywhere, so it is difficult to spell out the details of how it would work. Probably the closest approximation of it that is presently operational is in the airline industry, where pilots and stewardesses request different flights and thus have some control over when and on what they work. To be effective, the use of a work module approach would have to take place in conjunction with some job enrichment activities. Otherwise, employees might be faced with choosing among modules that were all made up of simple, repetitive tasks, so that they would have no real choice. Using work modules has the very distinct advantage of letting individuals pick their work settings, thus taking into account individual needs and preferences. It also recognizes that different individuals prefer different tasks and facilitates the matching of individuals with tasks.

Fringe Benefits and Pay Systems

A clear example of where research suggests organizations can and should treat everyone in a different manner is in the area of fringe benefits. At the present time, regardless of their marital status, age, education, and so on, employees receive the same fringe benefits package—one that is designed for the hypothetical average employee. A considerable amount of research shows that the fringe benefits packages offered by most organizations are favored by only 10 percent of their employees, because, again, there are few "average" employees. To put it in a different way, given the opportunity, 90 percent of the employees would choose different fringe benefits. Despite this, most organizations continue giving everyone the same benefits. Thus, inevitably some employees receive unwanted and inadequate fringe packages, and further, they are denied the opportunity to improve them. Can this situation be changed?

Yes. People can be given the opportunity to choose fringe benefits that fit their own set of needs. Employees can be given the amount of money the organization is presently spending on their pay (salary plus fringes) and they can divide it up themselves among cash and a large number of fringe benefits. This "cafeteria" kind of plan allows the organization to control its costs, so that it ultimately spends the same amount of money as it would in the standardized fringe benefits plan. Both the organization and its employees stand to benefit if the employees receive only those fringe benefits that they desire.

First, the employees will feel that they are being paid more, because they will realize for the first time the value of the benefits they receive and will receive only those that they value. Second, working for the organization should become more attractive, because the employees will be receiving a more highly valued reward package, and this should reduce turnover and make recruiting easier. The systems division of TRW and the Educational Testing Service are among the companies that are experimenting with these flexible benefits.

It would be foolish, however, to overlook the technical problems that are involved in implementing a cafeteria plan. It is not simple to work out a choice system; there are various tax and insurance problems involved. But the experience so far of organizations that have tried it shows that these problems are solvable and worth solving. They are worth solving because this is an area where an organization can design its policies to fit the needs and desires of its employees.

It is also interesting to note that when given the chance, employees do seem to make responsible choices. Older people invest more in retirement, younger people with families get good medical protection, and so on. This finding is in notable contrast to the common but fallacious notion that if employees are given the opportunity for decision making in this area, they will make unwise choices, and therefore, organizations need to protect their employees by choosing the fringe benefits packages that are best for them.

There is another way in which pay systems can be individualized. Most organizations pay people according to the jobs they perform; thus, all people who do the same job receive the same basic pay, regardless of their skills and abilities. In short, the job is paid, rather than the person. On the other hand, several plants, including the General Foods plant at Topeka, Kansas, have successfully experimented with a way of paying people that recognizes difference among individuals in terms of their skills and abilities, that pays the person, not the job. It recognizes that the kind of work an individual may be doing at the moment does not necessarily reflect his abilities and knowledge. Thus, these companies pay people in terms of the number of jobs they are capable of doing, rather than in terms of the job they may be doing at the time. In this system, employees can increase their pay as they become able to do other jobs. An active training and job rotation plan is offered to help individuals learn new jobs and thereby increase their pay.

Although the results are just coming in, they are encouraging. First, it seems that individuals feel more fairly treated because now their individual skills and abilities are recognized and rewarded. Second, the organizations gain emplòyees who are more versatile. The capacity to transfer employees easily allows the organization unprecedented flexibility in adjusting to market demands and to problems of absenteeism, tardiness, and turnover. It also solves some of the difficult problems that are involved when an employee must be shifted from a higher paying job to a lower paying job or the reverse.

Even if an organization does not go to a skill based pay plan, it can depart from the established practice of paying all employees on the basis of the same job evaluation system. As part of a recent study of mine, employees in four work groups were given the opportunity to design their own pay plans. The result: Each group designed slightly different plans, because each had somewhat different needs. All groups decided to operate with a three-pay-grade system, but since the groups differed in the skill levels their jobs needed, they set different minimum time periods for reaching the higher pay grades. The impact of this process on the employees was very positive. Satisfaction went up because the employees had a chance to design a plan that fitted their individual needs. Incidentally, the employees behaved very responsibly when given the opportunity to design their pay system. They set pay rates for themselves that were in line with the market and that management felt were fair.

Selection

There is one area in which organizations make a conscious, research-based, and often effective attempt to assure that individuals fit into the jobs and job situations where they are placed: Most organizations conduct lengthy and often well-researched selection and placement programs. They typically measure the employee's ability, background, and so on and then decide whether or not the individual can handle a particular job. This is an important process and one that often does ensure that individuals will fit and perform well in the jobs that they take. Two practices are noticeably missing, however, in the selection programs of most organizations, and as a result, misplacement and/or unsatisfying job placement frequently occurs.

First, most selection procedures ignore the issue of whether the individual will be satisfied in the job. Instead, they emphasize ability assessment in an attempt to determine whether the person can do the job. This is a serious omission in most selection programs and often leads to unsatisfying job placement and high turnover, and it subverts both organizational effectiveness and the quality of individual life.

Second, most selection programs leave out information designed to help the job applicant decide whether he can perform the job and will find it satisfying. Organizations typically place great emphasis on attracting people to apply for job openings, because they realize that only if a large number of applicants appear for a job can their selection program operate effectively. However, in their attempt to attract many applicants, they often fail to give a realistic picture of what the jobs will be like. Because the individuals do not have a good picture of what their jobs are like, they start work with unrealistic expectations and are often quickly disillusioned. The result is rapid turnover.

Several research studies have shown that this is a problem that can be solved to the benefit of all by giving individuals accurate information about the nature of the jobs. For example, one study with life insurance salesmen showed that when the applicants were given an accurate picture of all aspects of prospective jobs, they seemed to make good choices about whether to go to work for the company. They were less likely to quit and more effective than were employees who decided to come to work as life insurance agents without accurate pictures of their jobs. Another study has shown that telephone operators who were given accurate pictures of their prospective jobs were less prone to quit than those who were not and also tended to be more satisfied once they began work.

What kind of information should individuals receive? In addition to simple descriptive information about the nature of the prospective jobs and job situations, my research suggests that applicants should be supplied with: the results of job satisfaction surveys, employee descriptions of prospective supervisors, and data on turnover and grievance problems associated with a particular work setting. In addition, employers could aid the individual's decision process by feeding back the results of any psychological tests that were administered. The results of such tests are typically retained for company use to aid the organization in the selection process, but there is no reason why the results of these tests and an explanation of their implications cannot be shown to the applicant, to give him individualized information about the nature of his fit with the job environment.

Why does a realistic job preview tend to produce more satisfaction and lower turnover? The answer seems quite simple. Given accurate information, people are able to determine with some precision whether particular job situations will fit their needs and abilities. Further, they develop realistic expectations about the nature of the job and disappointment is minimized. This helps both the individual and the organization, since it reduces turnover and increases satisfaction.

Leadership

Most organizations spend considerable amounts of money training managers to use particular leadership styles. Psychologists have been active in this kind of training and have argued that more democratic and participative leadership will increase employee satisfaction and performance. This view has been accepted by many organizations, and they have invested considerable amounts of money in training supervisors to be more democratic in their leadership styles.

The issue of how democratic management affects employees is not a new one, and there is a great deal of data about it. As a rule, participative management is more likely to produce high levels of satisfaction and motivation than is authoritarian management. Thus, when organizations change the leadership styles of their managers from highly authoritarian to more democratic, they often improve the performance and motivation of their employees. However, they do not improve the satisfaction and motivation of all their employees. Again, the problem is that not everyone is average.

To put the issue quite simply, our research at Michigan shows clearly that some people prefer to be directed and ordered, while others prefer self-direction and self-control. Young, well-educated employees who work on technical and high-level jobs are particularly likely to want to exercise self-control. The desire of employees to participate in decision making varies according to the type of decision. For example, most employees simply are not interested in participating in decisions that involve corporate finance, such as what kinds of bonds to issue.

Individuals also differ in their abilities to participate in decision making. Some lack the mental abilities and education required to understand certain types of problems. Frequently, organizations fail to recognize these facts, and in their leadership training programs and their leadership practices an inordinately high value is placed on leaders who consistently "treat everyone the same." The concept of equal treatment is usually equated with fair and good supervision, but the research evidence suggests just the opposite. It shows that effective leadership involves individual treatment, in which the supervisor recognizes individual differences and alters his behavior accordingly. For this to be done well, supervisors must be able to diagnose situations and individuals and use the resulting information in selecting their leadership styles. Admittedly, it is not easy to do this kind of diagnosis, but it is a skill that can be developed and one that must be developed if leaders are to become more effective.

Hours of Work

One of the traditional assumptions about how organizations are best run is that everyone should come to work at the same time and leave at the same time. This assumption is congruent with the idea that standardization is important and that everyone should be treated in the same way. It is inconsistent, however, with the fact that people have different preferences about when they want to come to work and when they want to leave work. It also ignores the fact that people find themselves in different family situations, that transportation is not equally available for everyone, and that there are a number of disadvantages in having everyone arrive simultaneously, namely, overcrowding, transportation problems, and so on.

Some have suggested the four-day, 40-hour workweek as a way of improving the quality of life in organizations, but in terms of treating people as individuals, it is equally as bad as the five-day, 40-hour workweek. It, too, ignores the differences among individuals. Some people prefer the four-day, 40-hour week to the five-day, 40-hour week, but many do not. Thus, a change from the five-day, 40-hour workweek to the four-day, 40-hour workweek helps some and harms others. Again, we have the fact that many people are not average.

There is now an encouraging trend with respect to hours of work. More and more organizations are adopting flexible work hours that allow some people to come to work early and leave early and others to come late and leave late. Admittedly, there are a number of complexities in getting the approach operational. By and large, however, the companies that have tried it have found that the problems are soluble and have developed practical mechanisms for resolving them.

For example, a number of companies work with a set of core hours, perhaps four a day, when everyone is present, so that necessary meetings, communications, and so on can take place. Others have developed log books in order to tell when people will be at work so that events can be scheduled accordingly. The idea of flexible work hours can also be extended to include having individuals work weeks of different lengths. For example, some employees could work 40-

hour weeks while others worked 20- or even 10-hour weeks. This would make it possible for husbands and wives to share a job, and it would recognize that while the 40-hour week is accepted by most, it certainly doesn't fit everyone's needs. Installation of the module concept, incidentally, could make it much easier to vary working hours, since individuals could sign up for as many modules as they wanted.

Flexible work hours and similar experiments will undoubtedly spread, because not only do they cater to individual preferences with regard to hours of work, but they also do much to eliminate tardiness—a continual headache in most organizations. In short, many organizations can individualize their employees' work hours. This is not a panacea for all the problems of job satisfaction and alienation, but it is one more way that organizations can adapt themselves to the needs and desires of individuals.

Summary and Conclusions

Organizations can change their job designs, selection, evaluation, pay, work hours, and leadership styles in order to adapt to the needs of individuals and thereby create working environments that will be more effective, satisfying, motivating, and less alienating. Of course, not all organizations can change all of these aspects in order to create better individual-organization fits. It is also clear that not one of these practices in and of itself is going to solve the problems of alienation, dissatisfaction, and low motivation. Taken together, though, and combined with a real concern for the individuality of each employee, they can make a contribution.

It is to be hoped that the practices suggested here are just the forerunners of other, soon to be articulated, practices that will allow further individualization. In my view, it is crucial that we develop more ways for organizations to adapt to the unique needs of each employee, to provide more acceptable job situations and thereby reduce organizational ineffectiveness. It should also help make work a place where people can grow and develop. If our sense of social responsibility is not sufficient to prompt us to action, simple self-interest should be, for making work better for some can make society better for all.

Selected Bibliography

A new book of mine, *Behavior in Organizations* (McGraw-Hill, 1975), with L. W. Porter and J. R. Hackman, extensively considers the role of individual differences in determining behavior in organizations. It is a general text that is written for beginning students and managers.

The best summary of the work on job design that is available is a book by Louis Davis and James Taylor, *The Design of Jobs* (Penguin, 1972). It contains most of the important articles that have been written on job design. Robert Kahn described the work module approach in a recent *Psychology Today* article ("The Work Module—A Tonic for Lunchpail Lassitude," 1973, Vol. 6, No. 44).

Most of the behavioral research on pay is reviewed in my book *Pay and Organizational Effectiveness* (McGraw-Hill, 1971). This book considers the relevant theory research and practice and can be read by a manager who has a background in either pay administration or behavioral science. A classic book in this area is W. F. Whyte's *Money and Motivation* (Harper, 1955). It does a nice job of highlighting how individuals differ in their reactions to pay.

Marvin Dunnette's book *Personnel Selection and Placement* (Wadsworth, 1966) presents a good discussion of the issues involved in dealing with individual differences in the selection process. An article by J. Wanous, "Effects of a Realistic Job Preview on Job Acceptance, Job Attitudes, and Job Survival" (*Journal of Applied Psychology*, Vol. 58, No. 3), provides a good discussion of the use of realistic job previews.

A recent book by Victor Vroom and P. Yetton, *Leadership and Decision Making* (University of Pittsburgh Press, 1973), deals with how and why leadership styles should be varied according to situations. It is research-oriented but can be read by the nonprofessional.

Readings Related to Chapter 18

Interpersonal Relationships: U.S.A. 2000[1]

Carl R. Rogers

* * *

In view of my past prejudices I find it somewhat difficult but necessary to say that of all of the institutions of present-day American life, industry is perhaps best prepared to meet the year 2000. I am not speaking of its technical ability. I am speaking of the vision it is acquiring in regard to the importance of persons, of interpersonal relationships, and of open communication. That vision, to be sure, is often unrealized but it does exist.

Let me speculate briefly on the interpersonal aspect of industrial functioning. It is becoming increasingly clear to the leaders of any complex modern industry that the old hierarchical system of boss and employees is obsolete. If a factory is turning out one simple product, such a system may still work. But if it is in the business of producing vehicles for space or elaborate electronic devices, it is definitely inadequate. What takes its place? The only road to true efficiency seems to be that of persons communicating freely with persons—from below to above, from peer to peer, from above to below, from a member of one division to a member of another division. It is only through this elaborate, individually initiated network of open human communication that the essential information and know-how can pervade the organization. No one individual can possibly "direct" such complexity.

Thus if I were to hazard a guess in regard to industry in the year 2000 it would be something different from the predictions about increasing technical skill, increasing automation, increasing management by computers, and the like.

Reprinted by special permission from *Applied Behavioral Science,* July–August–September 1968, pp. 275–276. © 1968 by NTL Institute.

[1]This paper was part of a symposium entitled "USA 2000," sponsored by the Esalen Institute and held in San Francisco, California, January 10, 1968.

All of those predictions will doubtless come true but the interpersonal aspect is less often discussed. I see many industries, by the year 2000, giving as much attention to the quality of interpersonal relationships and the quality of communication as they currently do to the technological aspects of their business. They will come to value persons as persons, and to recognize that only out of the *communicated* knowledge of all members of the organization can innovation and progress come. They will pay more attention to breakdowns in personal communication than to breakdowns of the circuitry in their computers. They will be forced to recognize that only as they are promoting the growth and fulfillment of the individuals on the payroll will they be promoting the growth and development of the organization.

* * *

Organizations of the Future*
Warren Bennis

Recently, I predicted that in the next 25 to 50 years we will participate in the end of bureaucracy as we know it and the rise of new social systems better suited to 20th Century demands of industrialization.[1] This forecast was based on the evolutionary principle that every age develops an organizational form appropriate to its genius and that the prevailing form of pyramidal-hierarchical organization, known by sociologists as "bureaucracy" and most businessmen as "that damn bureaucracy," was out of joint with contemporary realities.

I realize now that my prediction is already a distinct reality so that prediction is foreshadowed by practice.

I should like to make clear that by "bureaucracy" I mean the typical organizational structure that coordinates the business of most every human organization we know of: industry, government, university, R & D labs, military, religious, voluntary, and so forth.

Bureaucracy, as I refer to it here, is a useful social invention, perfected during the Industrial Revolution to organize and direct the activities of the business firm. Max Weber, the German sociologist who developed the theory of

From *Personnel Administration*, September–October 1967, pp. 6–19. Reprinted by permission of the International Personnel Management Association, 1313 East 60th St., Chicago, Ill. 60637.

Author's note: This article is adapted from a talk presented at the 22nd National Conference, American Society for Training and Development, May 2–6, 1966, Pittsburgh, Pa. Subsequently, several colleagues helped me edit the manuscript to avoid some possible traps and misstatements, and I am grateful to them: Charles Myers, Donald Marquis, Bill Humes, Ted Alfred, Dave Sirota, Charles Savage, Robert Kahn, Bill McKelvey, and Dave Kolb. They do not necessarily endorse the ideas expressed, of course.

bureaucracy around the turn of the century, once described bureaucracy as a social machine.

The bureaucratic "machine model" was developed as a reaction against the personal subjugation, nepotism, cruelty, and capricious and subjective judgments that often passed for managerial practices during the early days of the Industrial Revolution. Bureaucracy emerged out of the need for more predictability, order, and precision. It was an organization ideally suited to the values and the demands of Victorian Empire. And just as bureaucracy emerged as a creative response to a radically new age, so today new organizational shapes and forms are surfacing before our eyes.

* * *

I shall try first to show why the conditions of our modern industrialized world will bring about the decline of bureaucracy and force a reconsideration of new organizational structures. Then, I will suggest a rough model of the organization of the future. Finally, I shall set forth the new tasks and challenges for the training and development manager.

Why Is Bureaucracy Vulnerable?

There are at least four relevant threats to bureaucracy. The first is a human, basically psychological one, which I shall return to later on, while the other three spring from extraordinary changes in our environment. The latter three are (1) rapid and unexpected change, (2) growth in size where volume of organization's traditional activities is not enough to sustain growth, and (3) complexity of modern technology where integration of activities and persons of very diverse, highly specialized competence is required.[2]

It might be useful to examine the extent to which these conditions exist *right now*.

Rapid and Unexpected Change   It may be enough simply to cite the knowledge and population explosion. More revealing, however, are the statistics that demonstrate these events:

- Our productivity per man hour now doubles almost every 20 years rather than every 40 years, which was true before World War II.
- The federal government alone spent 16 billion in R&D activities in 1965 and will spend 35 billion by 1980.
- The time lag between a technical discovery and recognition of its commercial uses was 30 years before World War I, 16 years between the wars, and only 9 years since World War II.
- In 1946 only 30 cities in the world had populations of more than one million. Today there are 80. In 1930 there were 40 people for each square mile of the earth's land surface. Today, there are 63. By the year 2,000, there are expected to be 142.

Growth in Size   Not only have more organizations grown larger, but they have become more complex and more international. Firms like Standard Oil of New Jersey (with 57 foreign affiliates), Socony Mobil, National Cash Register, Singer, Burroughs, and Colgate-Palmolive derive more than half their income or earnings from foreign sales. A long list of others, such as Eastman Kodak, Pfizer, Caterpillar Tractor, International Harvester, Corn Products, and Minnesota Mining and Manufacturing make from 30 to 50 percent of their sales abroad.[3] General Motors' sales are not only nine times those of Volkswagen, they are also bigger than the gross national product of The Netherlands and well over those of a hundred other countries. If we have seen the sun set on the British Empire, it will be a long time before it sets on the empires of General Motors, ITT, Royal Dutch/Shell and Unilever.

Today's Activities Require Persons of Very Diverse, Highly Specialized Competence   Numerous dramatic examples can be drawn from studies of labor markets and job mobility. At some point during the past decade, the U.S. became the first nation in the world ever to employ more people in *service occupations* than in the production of tangible goods. Examples of this trend are:

- In the field of education, the *increase* in employment between 1950 and 1960 was greater than the total number employed in the steel, copper, and aluminum industries.
- In the field of health, the *increase* in employment between 1950 and 1960 was greater than the total number employed in automobile manufacturing in either year.
- In financial firms, the *increase* in employment between 1950 and 1960 was greater than total employment in mining in 1960.[4]

Rapid change, hurried growth, and increase in specialists: with these three logistical conditions we should expect bureaucracy to decline.

Change in Managerial Behavior

Earlier I mentioned a fourth factor which seemed to follow along with the others, though its exact magnitude, nature, and antecedents appear more obscure and shadowy due to the relative difficulty of assigning numbers to it. This factor stems from the personal observation that over the past decade there has been a fundamental change in the basic philosophy that underlies managerial behavior. The change in philosophy is reflected most of all in:

- A new concept of *Man,* based on increased knowledge of his complex and shifting needs, which replaces an oversimplified, innocent push-button idea of man.
- A new concept of *power,* based on collaboration and reason, which replaces a model of power based on coercion and threat.

- A new concept of *organization values,* based on humanistic-democratic ideals, which replaces the depersonalized mechanistic value system of bureaucracy.

These transformations of Man, power, and values have gained wide intellectual acceptance in management quarters. They have caused a terrific amount of rethinking on the part of many organizations. They have been used as a basis for policy formulation by many large-scale organizations. This philosophy is clearly not compatible with bureaucratic practices.

The primary cause of this shift in management philosophy stems not from the bookshelf but from the manager himself. Many of the behavioral scientists, like McGregor or Likert, have clarified and articulated—even legitimized—what managers have only half registered to themselves. I am convinced that the success of McGregor's *The Human Side of Enterprise* was based on a rare empathy for a vast audience of managers who were wistful for an alternative to a mechanistic conception of authority. It foresaw a vivid utopia of more authentic human relationships than most organizational practices allow. Furthermore, I suspect that the desire for relationships has little to do with a profit motive *per se,* though it is often rationalized as doing so.[5] The real push for these changes stems from some powerful needs, not only to humanize the organization, but to use the organization as a crucible of personal growth and development, for self-realization.[6]

Core Organization Problems

As a result of these changes affecting organizations of the future, new problems and tasks are emerging. They fall, I believe, into five major categories, which I visualize as the core tasks confronting organizations of the future.

1 *Integration* encompasses the entire range of issues having to do with the incentives, rewards, and motivation of the individual and how the organization succeeds or fails in adjusting to these needs. In other words, it is the ratio between individual needs and organizational demands that creates the transaction most satisfactory to both. The problem of *integration* grows out of our "consensual society," where personal attachments play a great part, where the individual is appreciated, in which there is concern for his well-being, not just in a veterinary-hygiene sense, but as a moral, integrated personality.

2 The problem of *social influence* is essentially the problem of power and how power is distributed. It is a complex issue and alive with controversy, partly because of an ethical component and partly because studies of leadership and power distribution can be interpreted in many ways, and almost always in ways which coincide with one's biases (including a cultural leaning toward democracy).

The problem of power has to be seriously reconsidered because of dramatic situational changes that make the possibility of one-man rule or the "Great Man" not necessarily "bad" but impractical. I am referring to changes in the role of top management. Peter Drucker, over 12 years ago, listed 41 major responsibilities of the chief executive and declared that "90 percent of the trouble we are having with the chief executive's job is rooted in our superstition of the one-man chief."[7] The broadening product base of industry, impact of new technology, the scope of international operations, make one-man control quaint, if not obsolete.

Managing Conflict

3 The problem of *collaboration* grows out of the very same social processes of conflict and sterotyping, and centrifugal forces that divide nations and communities. They also employ furtive, often fruitless, always crippling mechanisms of conflict resolution: avoidance or suppression, annihilation of the weaker party by the stronger, sterile compromises, and unstable collusions and coalitions. Particularly as organizations become more complex they fragment and divide, building tribal patterns and symbolic codes which often work to exclude others (secrets and noxious jargon, for example) and on occasion to exploit differences for inward (and always fragile) harmony. Some large organizations, in fact, can be understood only through an analysis of their cabals, cliques, and satellites, where a venture into adjacent spheres of interest is taken under cover of darkness and fear of ambush. Dysfunctional intergroup conflict is so easily stimulated, that one wonders if it is rooted in our archaic heritage when man struggled, with an imperfect symbolic code and early consciousness, for his territory. Robert R. Blake in his experiments has shown how simple it is to induce conflict, how difficult to arrest it.[8] Take two groups of people who have never been together before, and give them a task that will be judged by an impartial jury. In less than one hour, each group devolves into a tightly-knit band with all the symptoms of an "in-group." They regard their product as a "masterwork" and the other group's as "commonplace," at best. "Other" becomes "enemy;" "We are good; they are bad. We are right; they are wrong."[9]

Jaap Rabbie, conducting experiments on the antecedents of intergroup conflict at the University of Utrecht, has been amazed by the ease with which conflict and stereotype develop.[10] He brings into the experimental room two groups and distributes green name tags and green pens to one group and refers to it as the "green group." He distributes red pens and red name tags to the other group and refers to it as the "red group." The groups do not compete; they do not even interact. They are in sight of each other for only minutes while they silently complete a questionnaire. Only 10 minutes is needed to activate defensiveness and fear.

In a recent essay on animal behavior, Erikson develops the idea of "pseudo-species."[11] Pseudo-species act as if they were separate species created at the beginning of time by supernatural intent. He argues:

Man has evolved (by whatever kind of evolution and for whatever adaptive reasons) in pseudo-species, i.e., tribes, clans, classes, etc. Thus, each develops not only a *distinct sense of identity* but also a conviction of harboring *the* human identity, fortified against other pseudo-species by prejudices which mark them as extraspecific and inimical to 'genuine' human endeavor. Paradoxically, however, newly born man is (to use Ernst Mayr's term) a generalist creature who could be made to fit into any

number of pseudo-species and must, therefore, become 'specialized' during a prolonged childhood. . . .

Modern organizations abound with pseudo-species, bands of specialists held
together by the illusion of a unique identity and with a tendency to view other
pseudo-species with suspicion and mistrust. Ways must be discovered to produce generalists and diplomats, and we must find more effective means of
managing inevitable conflict and minimizing the pseudo-conflict. This is not to
say that conflict is always avoidable and dysfunctional. Some types of conflict
may lead to productive and creative ends.

    4 The problem of *adaptation* is caused by our turbulent environment. The
pyramidal structure of bureaucracy, where power was concentrated at the top,
seemed perfect to "run a railroad." And undoubtedly for the routinized tasks of
the nineteenth and early twentieth centuries, bureaucracy was and still is an
eminently suitable social arrangement. However, rather than a placid and predictable environment, what predominates today is a dynamic and uncertain one
in which there is a deepening interdependence among the economic and other
facets of society.

    5 Finally, the problem of *revitalization*. As Alfred North Whitehead says:

> The art of free society consists first in the maintenance of the symbolic code, and
> secondly, in the fearlessness of revision. . . . Those societies which cannot combine
> reverence to their symbols with freedom of revision must ultimately decay . . .

Growth and decay emerge as the penultimate conditions of contemporary society. Organizations, as well as societies, must be concerned with those social
structures that engender bouyancy, resilience, and a "fearlessness of revision."

    I introduce the term "revitalization" to embrace all the social mechanisms
that stagnate and regenerate and with the process of this cycle. The elements of
revitalization are:

- An ability to learn from experience and to codify, store, and retrieve the
relevant knowledge.
- An ability to "learn how to learn," that is, to develop methodologies for
improving the learning process.
- An ability to acquire and use feedback mechanisms on performance, to
develop a "process orientation," in short, to be self-analytical.
- An ability to direct one's own destiny.

These qualities have a good deal in common with what John Gardner calls "self-
renewal." For the organization, it means conscious attention to its own evolution. Without a planned methodology and explicit direction, the enterprise will
not realize its potential.

    *Integration, Distribution of Power, Collaboration, Adaptation, and Revital-
ization are the major human problems of the next 25 years. How Organizations
cope with and manage these tasks will undoubtedly determine the viability and
growth of the enterprise.*

ORGANIZATIONS OF THE FUTURE[12]

Against this background I should like to set forth some of the conditions that will determine organizational life in the next two or three decades:

1 The Environment Rapid technological change and diversification will lead to interpenetration of the government with business.

Partnerships between government and business will be typical. It will be a truly mixed economy. Because of the immensity and expense of the projects, there will be fewer identical units competing for the same buyers and sellers. Organizations will become more interdependent.

The four main features of the environment are:

- Interdependence rather than competition.
- Turbulence and uncertainty rather than readiness and certainty.
- Large scale rather than small scale enterprises.
- Complex and multi-national rather than simple national enterprises.

2 Population Characteristics The most distinctive characteristic of our society is, and will become even more so, education. Within 15 years, two-thirds of our population living in metropolitan areas will have attended college. Adult education is growing even faster, probably because of the rate of professional obsolescence. The Killian report showed that the average engineer required further education only 10 years after gaining his degree. It will become almost routine for the experienced physician, engineer, and executive to go back to school for advanced training every two or three years. Some 50 universities, in addition to a dozen large corporations, offer advanced management courses to successful men in the middle and upper ranks of business. Before World War II, only two such programs existed, both new, both struggling to get students.

All of this education is not just "nice," it is necessary. As Secretary of Labor Wirtz recently pointed out, computers can do the work of most high school graduates—cheaper and more effectively. Fifty years ago education was regarded as "nonwork" and intellectuals on the payroll were considered "overhead." Today the survival of the firm depends on the effective exploitation of brain power.

One other characteristic of the population which will aid our understanding of organizations of the future is increasing job mobility. The ease of transportation, coupled with the needs of a dynamic environment, change drastically the idea of "owning" a job—or "having roots." Already 20 percent of our population change their mailing address at least once a year.

3 Work Values The increased level of education and mobility will change the values we hold about work. People will be more intellectually committed to their *professional* careers and will probably require more involvement, participation, and autonomy.

Also, people will be more "other-directed," taking cues for their norms and values from their immediate environment rather than tradition. We will tend to rely more heavily on temporary social arrangements.[13] We will tend to have relationships rather than relatives.

4 Tasks and Goals The tasks of the organization will be more technical, complicated, and unprogrammed. They will rely on intellect instead of muscle. And they will be too complicated for one person to comprehend, to say nothing of control. Essentially, they will call for the collaboration of specialists in a project or a team-form of organization.

There will be a complication of goals. Business will increasingly concern itself with its adaptive or innovative-creative capacity. In addition, meta-goals will have to be articulated; that is, supra-goals which shape and provide the foundation for the goal structure. For example, one meta-goal might be a system for detecting new and changing goals; another could be a system for deciding priorities among goals.

Finally, more conflict and contradiction can be expected from diverse standards of organizational effectiveness. One reason for this is that professionals tend to identify more with the goals of their profession than with those of their immediate employer. University professors can be used as a case in point. Within the University, there may be a conflict between teaching and research. Often, more of a professor's income derives from outside sources, such as foundations and consultant work. They tend not to be good "company men" because they divide their loyalty between their professional values and organizational goals.

Organic-Adaptive Structure

5 Organization The social structure of organizations of the future will have some unique characteristics. The key word will be "temporary"; there will be adaptive, rapidly changing *temporary systems*. These will be "task forces" organized around problems-to-be-solved by groups of relative strangers who represent a diverse set of professional skills. The groups will be arranged on an organic rather than mechanical model; they will evolve in response to a problem rather than to programmed role expectations. The "executive" thus becomes a coordinator or "linking pin" between various task forces. He must be a man who can speak the diverse languages of research, with skills to relay information and to mediate between groups. People will be evaluated not vertically according to rank and status, but flexibly and functionally according to skill and professional training. Organizational charts will consist of project groups rather than functional groups. This trend is already visible today in the aerospace and construction industries, as well as many professional and consulting firms.

Adaptive, problem-solving, temporary systems of diverse specialists, linked together by coordinating and task evaluating specialists in an organic flux—this is the organizational form that will gradually replace bureaucracy as we know it. As no catchy phrase comes to mind, I call this an organic-adaptive structure.

6 Motivation The organic-adaptive structure should increase motivation, and thereby effectiveness, because it enhances satisfactions intrinsic to the task. There is a harmony between the educated individual's need for meaningful, satisfactory, and creative tasks and a flexible organizational structure.

There will, however, also be reduced commitment to work groups, for these groups, as I have already mentioned, will be transient structures. I would predict that in the organic-adaptive system, people will learn to develop quick and intense relationships on the job, and learn to bear the loss of more enduring work relationships. Because of the added ambiguity of roles, time will have to be spent on continual rediscovery of the appropriate organizational mix.

Americans Prepared

The American experience of frontier neighbors, after all, prepares us for this, so I don't view "temporary systems" as such a grand departure. These "brief encounters" need not be more superficial than long and chronic ones. I have seen too many people, some occupying adjacent offices for many years, who have never really experienced or encountered each other. They look at each other with the same vacant stares as people do on buses and subways, and perhaps they are passengers waiting for their exit.

Europeans typically find this aspect of American life frustrating. One German expatriate told me of his disenchantment with "friendly Americans." At his first party in this country, he met a particularly sympathetic fellow and the two of them fell into a warm conversation which went on for several hours. Finally, they had to leave to return to their homes, but like soul-mates, they couldn't part. They went down into the city street and walked round and round on this cold winter night, teeth chattering and arms bound. Finally, both stiff with cold, the American hailed a cab and went off with a wave. The European was stunned. He didn't know his new "friend's" name. He never saw or heard from him again. "That's your American friendship," he told me.

That *is* American friendship: intense, spontaneous, total involvement, unpredictable in length, impossible to control. They are happenings, simultaneously "on" and transitory and then "off" and then new lights and new happenings.

A Swiss woman in Max Frisch's *I'm Not Stiller* sums it up this way: "Apparently all these frank and easy-going people did not expect anything else from a human relationship. There was no need for this friendly relationship to go on growing."[14]

TRAINING REQUIREMENTS FOR ORGANIZATIONS OF THE FUTURE

How can we best plan for the organizational developments I forecast? And how can training and development directors influence and direct this destiny? One thing is clear: There will be a dramatically new role for the manager of training and development. Let us look at some of the new requirements.

1   Training for Change   The remarkable aspect of our generation is its commitment to change, in thought and action. Can training and development managers develop an educational process which:

- Helps us to identify with the adaptive process without fear of losing our identity?
- Increases our tolerance for ambiguity without fear of losing intellectual mastery?
- Increases our ability to collaborate without fear of losing individuality?
- Develops a willingness to participate in our own social evolution while recognizing implacable forces?

Putting it differently, it seems to me that *we should be trained in an attitude toward inquiry and novelty rather than the particular content of a job;* training for change means developing "learning men."

2   Systems Counseling   It seems to me that management (and personnel departments) have failed to come to grips with the reality of *social systems.* It is embarrassing to state this after decades of research have been making the same point. We have proved that productivity can be modified by group norms, that training effects fade out and deteriorate if training goals are not compatible with the goals of the social system, that group cohesiveness is a powerful motivator, that intergroup conflict is a major problem facing modern organization, that individuals take many of their cues from their primary work group, that identification with the work group turns out to be the only stable predictor of productivity, and so on. Yet this evidence is so frequently ignored that I can only infer that there is something naturally preferable (almost an involuntary reflex) in locating the sources of all problems in the individual and diagnosing situations as functions of faulty individuals rather than as symptoms of malfunctioning social systems.

If this reflex is not arrested, it can have serious repercussions. In these new organizations, where roles will be constantly changing and certainly ambiguous, where changes in one sub-system will clearly affect other sub-systems, where diverse and multinational activities have to be coordinated and integrated, where individuals engage simultaneously in multiple roles and group memberships (and role conflict is endemic), a systems viewpoint must be developed. Just as it is no longer possible to make any enduring change in a "problem child" without treating the entire family, it will not be possible to influence individual behavior without working with his particular sub-system. This means that our training and development managers of the future must perform the functions of *systems counselors.*

3   Changing Motivation   The rate at which professional-technical-managerial types join organizations is higher than any other employment category. While it isn't fully clear what motivates them, two important factors emerge.

The first is a strong urge to "make it" professionally, to be respected by professional colleagues. Loyalty to an organization may increase if it encourages professional growth. Thus, the "good place to work" will resemble a super-graduate school, abounding with mature, senior colleagues, where the employee will work not only to satisfy organizational demands but, perhaps primarily, those of his profession.

The other factor involves the quest for self-realization, for personal growth which may not be task-related. That remark, I am well aware, questions four centuries of encrusted Protestant Ethic. And I feel uncertain as to how (or even *if*) these needs can be met by an organization. However, we must hope for social inventions to satisfy these new desires. Training needs to take more responsibility for attitudes about continuing education so that it is not considered a "retread" or a "repair factory" but a natural and inescapable aspect of work. The idea that education has a terminal point and that adults have somehow "finished" is old-fashioned. A "drop-out" should be redefined to mean anyone who *hasn't returned* to school.

However the problem of professional and personal growth is resolved, it is clear that many of our older forms of incentive, based on lower echelons of the need hierarchy, will have to be reconstituted.

4 Socialization for Adults   In addition to continuing education, we have to face the problem of continuing socialization, or the institutional influences which society provides to create good citizens. Put simply, it means training in values, attitudes, ethics, and morals. We allot these responsibilities typically to the family, to church, to schools. We incorrectly assume that socialization stops when the individual comes of age. Most certainly, we are afraid of socialization for adults, as if it implies the dangers of a delayed childhood disease, like whooping cough.

Or to be more precise, we frown not on socialization, but on conscious and responsible control of it. In fact, our organizations are magnificent, if undeliberate, vehicles of socialization. They teach values, inculcate ethics, create norms, dictate right and wrong, influence attitudes necessary for success and all the rest. The men who succeed tend to be well socialized and the men who don't, are not: "Yeah, Jones was a marvelous worker, but he never fit in around here." And most universities grant tenure where their norms and values are most accepted, although this is rarely stated.

Taking conscious responsibility for the socialization process will become imperative in tomorrow's organization. And finding men with the right technical capability will not be nearly as difficult as finding men with the right set of values and attitudes. Of course, consciously guiding this process is a trying business, alive with problems, not the least being the ethical one: Do we have the right to shape attitudes and values? We really do not have a choice. Can we avoid it? How bosses lead and train subordinates, how individuals are treated, what and who gets rewarded, the subtle cues transmitted and learned without seeming recognition, occur spontaneously. What we can choose are the mechanisms of socialization—how coercive we are, how much individual freedom we give, how we transmit values. What will be impermissible is a denial to recognize that we find some values more desirable and to accept responsibility for consciously and openly communicating them.

5 Developing Problem-solving Teams One of the most difficult and important challenges for the training and development manager will be the task of promoting conditions for effective collaboration or building synergetic teams. Synergy is where individuals actually contribute more and perform better as a result of a collaborative and supportive environment. They play "over their heads," so to speak. The challenge I am referring to is the building of synergetic teams.

Of course, the job isn't an easy one. An easy way out is to adopt the "zero synergy" strategy. This means that the organization attempts to hire the best individuals it can and then permits them to "cultivate their own gardens." This is a strategy of isolation that can be observed in almost every university organization.

[Until universities take a serious look at their strategy of zero synergy, there is little hope that they will solve their vexing problems. The Berkeley protests were symptomatic of at least four self-contained, uncommunicating social systems (students, faculty, administration, trustees) without the trust, empathy, interaction (to say nothing of a tradition) to develop meaningful collaboration. To make matters even more difficult, if possible, academic types may, by nature (and endorsed by tradition) see themselves as "loners" and divergent to the majority. They all want to be independent together, so to speak. Academic narcissism goes a long way on the lecture platform but may be positively disruptive for developing a community.]

Another approach has the same effect but appears different. It is the pseudo-democratic style, in which a phony harmony and conflict-avoidance persists.

In addition to our lack of background and experience in building synergy (and our strong cultural biases against group efforts), teams take time to develop. They are like other highly complicated organisms and, just as we wouldn't expect a newborn to talk, we shouldn't expect a new team to work effectively from the start. Teams require trust and commitment and these ingredients require a period of gestation.

Expensive and time-consuming as it is, building synergetic and collaborative frameworks will become essential. The problems that confront us are too complex and diversified for one man or one discipline. They require a blending of skills, slants, and disciplines for their solution and only effective problem-solving *teams* will be able to get on with the job.

6 Developing Supra-organizational Goals and Commitments The President of ABC (the fictitious name of a manufacturing company) was often quoted as saying:

> The trouble with ABC is that nobody aside from me ever gives one damn about the overall goals of this place. They're all seeing the world through the lenses of their departmental biases. What we need around here are people who wear the ABC hat, not the engineering hat or the sales hat or the production hat.

After he was heard muttering this rather typical president's dirge, a small group of individuals, who thought they could wear the ABC hat, formed a group they called the ABC HATS. They came from *various* departments and hierarchical levels and represented a microcosm of the entire organization. The ABC HATS group has continued to meet over the past few years and has played a central role in influencing top policy.

It seems to me that training and development managers could affect the development of their organizations if they would encourage the formation of HATS groups. What worries me about the organization of the future, of specialized professionals and an international executive staff, is that their professional and regional outlook brings along with it only a relative truth and a distortion of reality. This type of organization is extremely vulnerable to the hardening of pseudo-species and a compartmentalized approach to problems.

Training and development can be helpful in a number of ways:

- They can identify and support those individuals who are "linking pins" individuals who have a facility for psychological and intellectual affinity with a number of diverse languages and cultures. These individuals will become the developers of problem-solving teams.
- They can perform the HATS function, which is another way of saying that training and development managers should be managers who keep over-all goals in mind and modulate the professional biases which are intrinsic to the specialists' work.
- They can work at the interfaces of the pseudo-species in order to create more inter-group understanding and interface articulation.

Today, we see each of the intellectual disciplines burrowing deeper into its own narrow sphere of interest. (Specialism, by definition, implies a peculiar slant, a segmented vision. A cloak and suit manufacturer went to Rome and managed to get an audience with His Holiness. Upon his return a friend asked him, "What did the Pope look like?" The tailor answered, "A 41 Regular.") Yet, the most interesting problems turn up at the intersection between disciplines and it may take an outsider to identify these. Even more often, the separate disciplines go their crazy-quilt way and rely more and more on internal standards of evidence and competence. They dismiss the outsider as an amateur with a contemptuous shrug. The problem with intellectual effort today (and I include my own field of organizational psychology) is that no one is developing the grand synthesis.

Organizations, too, require "philosophers," individuals who provide articulation between seemingly inimical interests, who break down the pseudo-species, and who transcend vested interests, regional ties, and professional biases in arriving at the solution to problems.

To summarize, I have suggested that the training and development director of the future has in store at least six new and different functions: (1) training for change, (2) systems counseling; (3) developing new incentives, (4) socializing adults, (5) building collaborative, problem-solving teams, and (6) developing supra-organizational goals and commitments. Undoubtedly there are others and some that cannot be anticipated. It is clear that they signify a fundamentally different role for personnel management from "putting out fires" and narrow maintenance functions. If training and development is to realize its true promise, its role and its image must change from maintenance to innovation.

I have seen this new role develop in a number of organizations, not easily or overnight, but pretty much in the way I have described it here. It might be useful to review briefly the conditions present in the cases I know about:

The personnel manager or some sub-system within personnel (it might be called "employee relations" or "industrial relations" or "career development") took an *active, innovative* role with respect to organizational goals and forcibly took responsibility for organizational growth and development.

Secondly, this group shifted its emphasis away from personnel functions *per se* (like compensation and selection) and toward organizational problems, like developing effective patterns of collaboration, or fostering an innovative atmosphere or reducing inter-group conflict, or organizational goal-setting and long-run planning.

Thirdly, this group developed a close working relationship to various subsystems in the organization, an organic, task-oriented relationship, not the frequently observed mechanical "line-staff" relationship.

Fourthly, they were viewed as full-fledged members of the management team, instead of the "head-shrinkers" or the "headquarters group." This was the hardest to establish in all cases, but turned out to be the most important. In fact, in one case, the man responsible for spearheading the organizational development effort has recently taken an important line job. The reverse happens too. Line management participates in so-called personnel activities, almost as if they are an adjunct to staff. Distinctions between line and staff blur in this context and an organic linkage develops, often serving as a prototype of a collaborative, problem-solving team.

One single factor stands out in retrospect over all others. There was always the conviction and the ability to make the training and development department the leading edge, the catalyst for organizational change and adaptability. Rather than performing the more traditional role, these groups became centers for innovation and organizational revitalization, and their leaders emerged as change-agents, the new managers of tomorrow's organizations.

I should now add another point in conclusion. It emerges from the previous points. They describe a far more autonomous, organizationally influential, self-directed role than trainers have been given or have asked for in the past.

Human Problems Confronting Contemporary Organizations

Problem	Bureaucratic solutions	New 20th century conditions
	Integration	
The problem of how to integrate individual needs and organizational goals.	No solution because of no problem. Individual vastly over-simplified, regarded as passive instrument. Tension between "personality" and role disregarded.	Emergence of human sciences and understanding of man's complexity. Rising aspirations. Humanistic-democratic ethos.
	Social influence	
The problem of the distribution of power and sources of power and authority.	An explicit reliance on legal-rational power, but an implicit usage of coercive power. In any case, a confused, ambiguous shifting complex of competence, coercion, and legal code.	Separation of management from ownership. Rise of trade unions and general education. Negative and unintended effects of authoritarian rule.
	Collaboration	
The problem of producing mechanisms for the control of conflict.	The "rule of hierarchy" to resolve conflicts between ranks and the "rule of coordination" to resolve conflict between horizontal groups. "Loyalty."	Specialization and professionalization and increased need for interdependence. Leadership too complex for one-man rule or omniscience.
	Adaptation	
The problem of responding appropriately to changes induced by the environment.	Environment stable, simple, and predictable; tasks routine. Adapting to change occurs in haphazard and adventitious ways. Unanticipated consequences abound.	External environment of firm more "turbulent," less predictable. Unprecedented rate of technological change.
	"Revitalization"	
The problem of growth and decay.	Underlying assumption that the future will be certain and basically similar, if not more so, to the past.	Rapid changes in technologies, tasks, manpower, raw materials, norms and values of society, goals of enterprise and society all make constant attention to the process of revision imperative.

If the training group is to be concerned with adult socialization, for example, it would be myopically irresponsible if not worse for them to define socialization in terms of momentary needs of the organization. Rather, they must take at least some of the responsibility for enunciating the goals and conditions of the enterprise. In a way, their systems counseling function is "organizational socialization." If they take responsibility for socializing both the members as people and the organization as a human system, then they must have values and standards which are somehow prior and outside both.

In fact, the emerging role I outline implies that the roles of the top management and training director become more interchangeable than ever before.

References

1 "The Decline of Bureaucracy and Organizations of the Future." Invited address presented to the Division of Industrial and Business Psychology at the American Psychological Association meeting, Los Angeles, Calif., Sept. 5, 1964.

2 A. H. Rubenstein and C. Haberstroh, *Some Theories of Organization,* (Revised Edition). Irwin-Dorsey, Homewood, Ill., 1966.

3 Richard J. Barber, "American Business Goes Global." *The New Republic.* April 30, 1966, 14–18.

4 Victor R. Fuchs, "The First Service Economy." *The Public Interest.* Winter 1966, 7–17.

5 Chris Argyris, *Interpersonal Competence and Organizational Effectiveness.* Homewood, Ill.: Irwin-Dorsey, 1962.

6 *The Varieties of Religious Experience.* The Modern Library, Random House, N.Y., 1902, 475–476.

7 D. Ron Daniel, "Team at the Top." *Harvard Business Review,* March–April 1965, 74–82.

8 Robert R. Blake, Herbert A Shepard and Jane S. Mouton, *Managing Intergroup Conflict in Industry,* Gulf Publishing, Houston, Texas, 1964.

9 Carl Rogers, "Dealing with Psychological Tensions," *Journal of Applied Behavioral Sciences,* Jan.–Feb.–March 1965, 6–24.

10 Personal communication, Jan. 1966.

11 Erik Erikson, "Ontogeny of Ritualization." Paper presented to the Royal Society in June 1965.

12 Adapted from my earlier paper, "Beyond Bureaucracy," *Trans-action,* July–August 1965.

13 "On Temporary Systems." In M. B. Miles (ed.), *Innovation in Education,* Bureau of Publications, Teachers College, Columbia University, N.Y., 1964, 437–490.

14 Penguin Books, Harmondsworth Middlesex. 1961, p. 244.

The Yesterday, Today, and Tomorrow of Organizations

Harold J. Leavitt

*   *   *

The New Nomads of Organization

Way back at the beginning, before Taylor, in the virgin world, organizations were nomadic. They were wandering, entrepreneurial bands of men. They were companies, in the original sense of the word, companies of men. With Taylorism and Henry Ford, this nomadic form gave way to a more static life style. Organizations became farmers, tough, independent farmers, staking their claims, carving out their plots of land and exploiting their soil, routinely but also autonomously. Then the knowledge explosion provided a kind of rebirth of nomadism. Organizations no longer had to be anchored to their traditional tasks and to their traditional structures. The new, highly flexible technology and the new, high-powered technologists could provide a different sort of anchor. The organization could become mobile again, searching for tasks unlike anything it had undertaken before. It could become nomadic again, not in a geographic sense but creatively, searching for new applications for its new, expensive and perpetually hungry technology. But the nomadic organizations of the seventies will be nomads in a crowded and independent world. Now the environment is more differentiated, more populous. It provides more opportunities, but it also makes for harder going. In the new environment, the traditional free-moving, autonomous business organization must begin to give way. So must the tough-thinking, rapid-fire decision-making, crisis-eating company president. So, too, must the kindly morale builder. The appropriate new company president begins to look much more like—heaven help us—a politician who must juggle both the conflicting forces rising from within his organizations, and those pressing in from outside groups. He needs wit and he needs sensitivity. Such an image of a company president may seem almost 180 degrees from the current beliefs of many businessmen. Many of them feel, for example, that current businessman types, tough and decisive, should be running universities. Then the current student disturbances would cease forthwith. However, the converse is the more likely future: not that businessmen will run universities like businesses, *but that university-type men will be running businesses like universities.*

For the university in an odd way presents an interesting parallel to the business organization of the future. Internally it is made up of many diverse groups over whom the administration can exert little direct authority. The faculty is a collection of prima donnas who may have some departmental loyalty, but are most loyal only to their professions. The students are a kind of transient body, vocally self-interested, but neither clearly consumers nor employees, not well

Excerpts reprinted from *European Business,* vol. 29, pp. 28–33, 1971, by permission of the publisher.

organized and not always rational. And then there are the Board of Trustees, and the community groups, and all the other factions of society who feel it appropriate to exert pressure on the university. In that kind of setting the university president does not sit in his command post, punching out action decisions and ordering people about. On the contrary, he arbitrates, he confronts, he debates, he negotiates. And out of the negotiation process he tries to build not only viability and innovativeness, but adaptiveness.

Many company presidents of the 1970s will have to do just such political and diplomatic juggling, inside the organization and outside too.

All this projects an organizational world which is very different and yet in many ways very much the same. It is not a question of the new replacing the old, but of the new added on to the old. Certain tasks, for example, and certain kinds of industries are likely to remain highly routinized. The changes they will be experiencing are perhaps of only two kinds: they will be automating, and they will also be involved in a new blue-collar participative revolution. Perhaps economics and sociology will force them to make the life of the production worker a more challenging one.

At the middle levels of line management, which had become slowly more participative in the 50s, the two quite polar trends should continue and remain somewhat in conflict. One is an accelerating trend toward a higher degree of programming and control, emerging from Management Science. We are already seeing some of the oddities generated by those counterforces. I recently asked a large company president whether or not his company had been centralizing or decentralizing. He answered, "We're decentralizing, of course. It's easy to decentralize now, because the computer has given us much better central control over our people. Now we can let them do as they please, today; but we can slap them down tomorrow if our control reports show that they have failed." In one sense, there is greater autonomy, in another sense, much tighter control.

But moving upward and outward in the organization, in amongst the planners, the staff people and top management itself, there will be a desperate race for the better utilization of human resources. It is with staff managers and our higher levels of executives, with technologists and professionals and researchers that we shall continue to search for the conditions that fertilize creativity and imagination.

Learning to Like Irregularity

If, finally, we examine the total package that we are facing—the shrinking world, the explosion of knowledge, the organizational population explosion, our massive social and economic tasks, emerging new value systems—at least one thing seems clear: rigid old authoritarian mechanisms will slowly fall to lower and lower positions, for they were designed for an orderly, slow-to-change, almost static world. And organizational ambiguity, uncertainty, irregularity will become the normal state. We shall have to build new tools and new organizational structures to deal with that sort of continuously exploding world. Another thing is also certain, surely: management will never be simple again.

Human Asset Accounting

Rensis Likert

Evidence was presented [in earlier chapters] for the necessity of including estimates of the current value of the human organization and of customer goodwill in all financial reports of a firm.

The absence of these estimates for each profit center and for the entire corporation is not due to a lack of interest on the part of the accounting profession (Hermanson, 1964). Cultural lag and the usual gaps in communication among the relevant sciences are the culprits. To create human asset accounting and to make reasonably accurate estimates of its two dimensions—the current value of the human organization and customer goodwill—require close cooperation between accountants and social scientists highly competent in the measurement of the causal and intervening variables.

Such cooperation is now starting. It will require from five to ten years and many million dollars' worth of work to collect the data and to make the computations required before human asset accounting can become fully operational. Sophisticated measurement and accounting procedures should emerge from this work, enabling firms to incorporate in their financial reports reasonably accurate estimates of the current value of the human assets of an enterprise. These procedures will enable a firm not only to know the current value of these resources, but also what changes or trends are occurring from time to time in the magnitudes of these assets. In addition, it will be possible to prepare these estimates for each profit center of the firm and, where appropriate and useful, for any smaller unit within a firm.

Computing a firm's original investment in its human organization is a much simpler problem than estimating the current value of that investment. This is true for the company as a whole and for such units as profit centers, departments, and other subunits. There are several alternate methods for obtaining estimates of the original investment in the human side of an enterprise.

One way is to base these estimates on start-up costs. The problem in many ways is comparable to estimating a firm's current investment in machinery which it has built itself and continues to use for a period of time. The actual cost of building a machine can readily be computed. The human start-up costs of a new plant, unit, or department can be computed similarly, although the task of doing so is more complex and difficult. These start-up costs should include what it has cost to hire and train the personnel and to develop them into a coordinated organization operating in a reasonbly satisfactory manner.

Start-up costs can be computed for various kinds of operations and for various-size units. As these human investment costs become available for the widely different kinds of operations performed by a particular enterprise, they

From *The Human Organization: Its Management and Value*, McGraw-Hill Book Company, New York, 1967, chap. 9, pp. 146–155. Reprinted by permission of the publisher.

can be used as a basis for estimating the magnitude of the investment a firm has in its human organization—for the entire corporation or for any of its units.

A second way of estimating the magnitude of the investment in the human organization is to obtain data on the costs of hiring and training personnel for each of the many different kinds of positions in the company. The sum of these costs for every person in the firm usually will be substantial. It underestimates, however, the true investment in the human side of the enterprise, since it does not reflect the additional investment made during the period when the members of the firm were establishing effective cooperative working relationships[1] with one another. These cooperative working relationships might appropriately be called the synergistic component. To establish them takes an appreciable period of time and involves substantial costs.

This approach will require a tremendous amount of work if it is done for every kind of position and every member of the organization. The cost and effort of making these estimates can be reduced substantially by probability sampling. Efficient designs will yield estimates closely approximating those which would be obtained were all the jobs and all the positions examined.

Estimating the Current Value of the Human Organization

Although computing a firm's investment in building its human organization or its customer goodwill may be difficult, obtaining reasonably accurate estimates of the *current* value of the human organization is a much more difficult and complex task. It is, moreover, much more important. For the reasons discussed at length in [other chapters], it is essential that reasonably accurate information be currently available to all levels of management as to changes and trends in the present value of its human organization. Managers and all other members of the organization and shareholders need to be kept correctly informed on these matters, since the health, profitability, and long-range survival of the enterprise depend upon sound decisions guided by measurements which reflect the current value of its human organization.

Human Asset Accounting

Human assets, as used in this volume, refer both to the value of the productive capacity of a firm's human organization and to the value of its customer goodwill.

The productive capability of its human organization can be illustrated by thinking of two firms in the same business. Both are of the same size and have identical equipment and technology. One, however, produces more and earns more than the other, because its personnel is superior to the other's with regard to such variables as the following:

1 Level of intelligence and aptitudes
2 Level of training

---

[1]The nature of these relationships is described on pp. 183–185 of [Likert's] *New Patterns of Management* [McGraw-Hill Book Company, New York, 1961].

3 Level of performance goals and motivation to achieve organizational success

4 Quality of leadership

5 Capacity to use differences for purposes of innovation and improvement, rather than allowing differences to develop into bitter, irreconcilable, interpersonal conflict

6 Quality of communication upward, downward, and laterally

7 Quality of decision making

8 Capacity to achieve cooperative teamwork versus competitive striving for personal success at the expense of organization

9 Quality of the control processes of organization and the levels of felt responsibility which exist

10 Capacity to achieve effective coordination

11 Capacity to use experience and measurements to guide decisions, improve operations, and introduce innovations

The difference in the economic value of the human organizations of these two firms would be reflected by the differences between them in present and future earnings, attributable to the differences in their human organizations. Similarly, differences in the value of customer goodwill would be reflected in the differences between them in the ease and costs of making sales, i.e., in the difference in the motivation among customers to buy the product of one firm, rather than that of the other.

Human asset accounting refers to activity devoted to attaching dollar estimates to the value of a firm's human organization and its customer goodwill. If able, well-trained personnel leave the firm, the human organization is worth less; if they join it, the firm's human assets are increased. If bickering, distrust, and irreconcilable conflict become greater, the human enterprise is worth less; if the capacity to use differences constructively and engage in cooperative teamwork improves, the human organization is a more valuable asset.

Since estimates of the current value of a firm's human organization are both necessary and difficult to obtain, it is highly desirable to use several alternate approaches in developing methods for making these estimates. The results from one approach can serve as a check on those obtained from the others. The initial estimates from any procedure, of course, are likely to have relatively large errors of estimate. As the methodology improves, two important developments will occur. The size of the errors will decrease, and the accuracy of estimating the magnitude of these errors will increase. The accuracy of human asset accounting will increase correspondingly.

The essential first step in developing procedures for applying human asset accounting to a firm's human organization is to undertake periodic measurements of the key causal and intervening variables. These measurements must be available over several years' time to provide the data for the needed computations. The data required for the initial computations should be collected at quite frequent intervals, quarterly or even more often.

The optimum frequency for the measurements will vary with the kind of work involved. The more nearly the work involves the total man, such as research and development (R&D) tasks, the shorter should be the intervals between successive measurements, for, as was mentioned in Chapter 5, the time lag between changes in the causal, intervening, and end-result variables is much less for such work than for work which is machine-paced. The sequence of developments . . . requires a shorter time interval for R&D and other complex tasks than for machine-paced or simple, repetitive tasks. Unfavorable attitudes lead much more rapidly to decreased productivity. A scientist who feels resentful toward his organization or manager rapidly becomes unproductive. With machine-paced and similar work, which usually employs only a part of the capabilities of the total man (e.g., hands), a longer period of time is required before the adverse effects of unfavorable reactions and attitudes manifest themselves in the forms of norms to restrict production, of increased grievances and similar developments, and, finally, in lower performance. For this kind of work, consequently, the intervals between periodic measurements can be longer than for professional and other complex work.

The total period of time required for the cycles . . . to reach reasonable equilibrium, of course, will vary also with the kind of work. The cycle reaches a stable relationship much more quickly with complex tasks than with machine-paced and simple, repetitive tasks. Complex tasks require less time to reach stable relationships; machine-paced and similar work require more time.[2]

The measurements of the causal and intervening variables should be obtained for the corporation as a whole and for each profit center or unit in the company for which productivity, costs, waste, and earnings can be computed. After these measurements have been made over a sufficient period of time for relatively stable relationships to develop or for the sequence of relationships to complete their full cycle, the necessary data will be available to relate the causal and intervening measurements to the earnings record. By using appropriate statistical procedures, relationships can be computed among the causal, intervening, and such end-result variables as costs and earnings. The resulting mathematical relationships will enable one to estimate the productive and earnings capability of any profit center, or smaller unit, based upon its present scores on the causal and intervening variables. These estimates of probable subsequent productivity, costs, and earnings will reveal the earning power of the human organization *at the time* the causal and intervening variables were measured, even though the level of estimated subsequent earnings may not be achieved until much later. These estimates of probable subsequent productivity, costs, and earnings provide the basis for attaching to any profit center, unit, or total corporation a statement of the present value of its human organization.

Corporations which have a number of relatively comparable units, such as chain stores, will have a distinct advantage in using the method just suggested.

---

[2]The influence of different kinds of work upon the cycle of relationships among the causal, intervening, and end-result variables is discussed more fully in Chapter 6, *New Patterns of Management*.

The data from several comparable units will yield more reliable estimates by providing far more observations upon which to base calculations. Moreover, differences among the units can be used as well as changes for any particular unit over time. Based on these differences, computations can be made of the relation of earnings to each pattern of causal and intervening variables using, of course, optimum time intervals. By capitalizing the greater earnings of the better units, estimates of the present value of the human organization can be obtained.

It is probable that after sufficient research has been done and sufficient data and experience obtained, it will be feasible to do human asset accounting in much the same way that standard costs are now used to estimate the manufacturing costs of new products. Another use of standard estimates is the MTM (Methods-Time Measurement) process of setting a standard time for the performance of a particular task. Experience has shown that standard estimates can be used successfully in accounting and in industrial engineering. A comparable process should be equally successful in human asset accounting.

Present Earnings May Yield Incorrect Estimate

Many corporations at present are making estimates of the current value of the human organization and of customer goodwill. This is done whenever a new firm or division is acquired. Every year there are a substantial number of acquisitions. In each instance, an appropriate value has to be placed on the acquired firm. The purchase price generally is substantially larger than the current value of the physical and financial assets and reflects allowances for both customer and employee goodwill. Both the firm which is acquired and the corporation acquiring it make these estimates in arriving at a fair price. An important factor in arriving at these estimates usually is the current and recent earnings of the acquired firm. This approach has to be used cautiously, however, since it contains a source of error which at times can be sizable. If the acquired firm has been using the approach to cost reduction based on personnel limitations, tightened budgets, and tighter standards and is at a point of high earnings but decreasing value of the human organization . . . , then an estimate of the value of the human assets based on current earnings is likely to be appreciably inflated.

Estimating the Value of Customer Goodwill

Customer goodwill, like the value of the human organization, is an asset of substantial magnitude in most companies. The sizable costs in opening new markets or marketing new products demonstrate the magnitude of the current value of this asset in most companies.

This asset can vary appreciably from time to time, depending upon the behavior of the firm's management (a causal variable), the resulting motivation and behavior of the firm's personnel (intervening variables), and the corresponding price and quality of product and service provided to customers (end-result variables).

Cash income can be increased for a period of time by selling shoddy products and rendering poor service while charging the usual prices. This income should not be reported and treated as earnings in financial statements, however, since it is actually achieved by cashing in on the firm's customer loyalty. It represents a liquidation, often at a fraction of its value, of customer goodwill. Such "earnings" are as spurious and misleading as those derived from liquidating part of the firm's investment in its human organization.

Customer goodwill, as well as the value of the human organization, should be reflected at its present value in every financial statement. This can be done by drawing upon the methodological resources created by social-psychological research. The same basic concepts and methodology employed in estimating the current value of the human organization can be used to attach dollar amounts to the current value of customer goodwill. Favorable customer attitudes create motivational forces to buy a firm's products. One set of estimates of the current value of these motivational forces can be obtained by methods available for measuring the sales influence of advertising and marketing efforts. A method for obtaining the relevant measurements was published several years ago (Likert, 1936).

Imbalance in Fiscal Management

In considering the desirability and expense of undertaking the work required for human asset accounting, it should be recognized that the present practice of treating, with great precision, a fraction of the firm's assets and completely ignoring assets of roughly the same or greater magnitude represents a serious imbalance. A firm's financial reports would be much more useful and appreciably more accurate if approximately the same level of accuracy were maintained in dealing with *all* of the firm's assets. The equity of the shareholders would be protected far better than at present if there were more balance in the accounting effort.

It is perfectly feasible for a company to establish a balanced effort in their accounting activities without an appreciable increase in their total accounting costs. This can be done by placing all accounting on a sample basis and using sample designs which yield estimates of acceptable accuracy. There would be a substantial reduction in the costs of the usual physical asset and financial asset accounting, and this saving could be used for human asset accounting, i.e., for obtaining estimates of the current value of the human organization and of customer goodwill.

This use of sampling methods in the accounting work would result in small sampling errors in the reports dealing with the physical and financial assets. At present, these reports usually contain no errors due to sampling, since a 100 percent sample is generally used. With sophisticated, weighted sampling designs, however, the sampling errors would be smaller than the other errors which arise from various assumptions, such as those used in handling depreciation and comparable problems.

The facts are clear. If sophisticated sampling methods were applied to physical and financial accounting, the maximum probable error would be so small as to be unimportant in its consequences. If sound sampling methods were used in conducting human asset accounting, physical asset accounting, and financial asset accounting, the errors due to sampling would be negligible, and a firm would have appreciably more accurate fiscal reports than at present. The sampling errors in such financial reports, on the average, would be only a fraction of the size of the errors which now occur in financial reports which are based on 100 percent sampling of the physical and financial assets and no sampling of the human assets.

Interim Steps to Increase the Accuracy of Financial Reports

There is, of course, an interim problem to be dealt with. Even though a firm started tomorrow to do the research required to develop the necessary procedures for human asset accounting, several years would be required before it could be put into effect. In the meantime, however, corporate officers can take an important step which will enable them to safeguard company assets more completely and to improve appreciably the accuracy and adequacy of the information provided them.

The proposed step is to introduce the periodic measurement of the causal and intervening variables and *to have a record of these measurements made a part of every production and financial report.* This should be done for all fiscal and production reports, both those for profit centers and those for the entire corporation.

These measurements would help the board and the other managers of the firm to interpret more correctly the production and financial reports they receive. If there were no changes from one period to the next in the scores on the causal and intervening variables, the financial report could be considered essentially correct, insofar as any changes in the current value of the human organization are concerned. If, however, these measurements of the causal and intervening variables showed an unfavorable shift, then the financial report should be viewed as overstating the actual situation. Under such circumstances the report would reflect a more favorable picture than the actual facts and would include as earnings funds which were really derived from the liquidation of human assets. Conversely, if the measurements of the causal and intervening variables were to reflect a favorable shift, then the financial report would understate the real situation, since management actually would be doing a better job than the report revealed. The true earnings and changes in assets would be more favorable than the financial report showed.

The measurements of the causal and intervening variables can be used in this manner to assure that there are no serious mistakes in the interpretation of the financial and production reports for any unit, profit center, or the entire company. Managers of units which achieved part of their earnings or productivity by liquidating human assets would have their financial and production reports correspondingly discounted. On the other hand, managers who added to company assets by improving their human organization would have their performance records viewed as understating their total managerial performance.

Changes in the size and composition of the labor force should be taken into consideration also.

Bankers making loans, investment houses, and others who are interested in the earnings and success of an enterprise should be just as interested as boards and senior officers in having these periodic measurements of the causal and intervening variables available. These data, as we have seen, are essential for the correct interpretation of production and fiscal data.

It is equally important to have similar periodic measurements of customer goodwill accompany financial reports and for the same reasons. These data should be interpreted and used in essentially the same way as the measurements of the causal and intervening variables.

As soon as corporate officers arrange to have the measurements of the causal and intervening variables and of customer goodwill as part of production and financial reports, enterprises will be managed more successfully. Better decisions will be made at all management levels, because these decisions will be based on more accurate facts. Senior officers and boards will not be misinformed, as they may be at present, concerning the management systems used by the managers who achieve the highest earnings year in and year out. With accurate information to guide its decisions, top management would not superimpose a System 2 manager on a System 4 operation and thereby destroy one of their most valuable assets.* The present management of large corporations whose previous managements have built great loyalty and high motivation committed to corporate success at all levels in the organization will not be able to show impressive but fictitious earnings over many years' time by progressively increasing the pressure and tightening the controls on their subordinate managers, supervisors, and nonsupervisory employees, i.e., shifting toward System 2 from System 3 or 4.

Probably the most important improvement in fiscal management will be the profound changes which measurements of the human dimensions of an enterprise will bring in the generally accepted concepts of how a corporation or department should be managed to be financially most successful. The cold hard facts of accurate measurements will wipe out many of the erroneous concepts which are widely held today but which are based on incomplete accounting and short-run financial analyses of only a portion of a firm's total assets.

The Opportunity Is Limited

The opportunity to use measurements of the causal and intervening variables during the interim period in the manner suggested will be affected by the management system of the firm and trends in this system. As was pointed out [earlier] cooperative motivation is necessary to obtain the most accurate measurements of the causal, intervening, and end-result variables over any period of

---

*Editor's Note: Likert's explanation of his Systems 1, 2, 3, and 4 appears in his "Table of Organizational and Performance Characteristics of Different Management Systems," pp. 14–24 in *The Human Organization,* chap. 2, "A Look at Management Systems."

time. A firm's capacity to use the interim steps suggested, therefore, will be influenced by its management system and the trends in this system. Companies which are using System 4 or are shifting toward it will have the cooperative motivation required for measurements to be accurate. Firms shifting toward System 1 or using System 1 or 2 will be unlikely to have such cooperative motivation.

Firms striving to use a science-based management system will have a distinct advantage over other companies in the adequacy and accuracy of the information made available to them to guide decisions and to evaluate results.

Index

Index